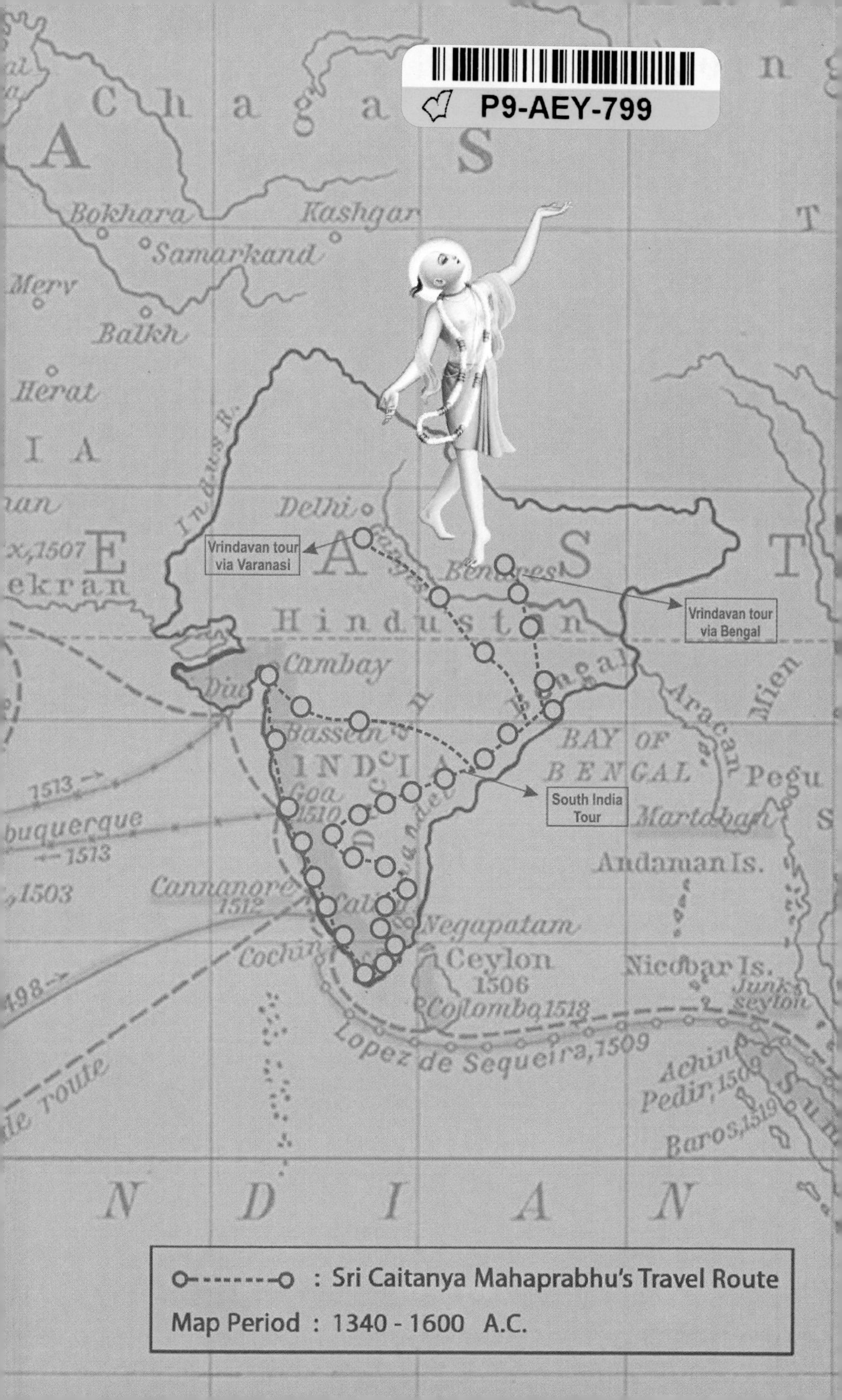
Bokhara
Kashgar
Samarkand
Merv
Balkh
Herat
Indus R.
Delhi
Vrindavan tour
via Varanasi
Vrindavan tour
via Bengal
Hindustan
Bengal
Cambay
Diu
Bassein
INDIA
Goa
1510
Cannanore
1512
Cochin
Negapatam
Ceylon
1506
Colombo 1518
Lopez de Sequeira, 1509
BAY OF
BENGAL
South India
Tour
Aracan
Pegu
Martaban
Andaman Is.
Nicobar Is.
1513
1503
N D I A N
: Sri Caitanya Mahaprabhu's Travel Route
Map Period : 1340 - 1600 A.C.

শ্রীচৈতন্যচরিতামৃত

ŚRĪ CAITANYA-CARITĀMṚTA

Books by His Divine Grace
A. C. Bhaktivedanta Swami Prabhupāda:

- Bhagavad-gītā As It Is
- Śrīmad-Bhāgavatam (1st to 12th Cantos)
- Śrī Caitanya-Caritāmṛta (9 vols.)
- Kṛṣṇa, The Supreme Personality of Godhead
- Teachings of Lord Caitanya
- The Nectar of Devotion
- The Nectar of Instruction
- Śrī Īśopaniṣad
- Light of the Bhāgavata
- Easy Journey to Other Planets
- The Science of Self-Realization
- Kṛṣṇa Consciousness: The Topmost Yoga System
- Perfect Questions, Perfect Answers
- Teachings of Lord Kapila, the Son of Devahuti
- Transcendental Teachings of Prahlāda Mahārāja
- Teachings of Queen Kuntī
- Kṛṣṇa, the Reservoir of Pleasure
- The Path of Perfection
- Life Comes from Life
- Message of Godhead
- The Perfection of Yoga
- Beyond Birth and Death
- On the Way to Kṛṣṇa
- Rāja-vidyā: The King of Knowledge
- Elevation to Kṛṣṇa Consciousness
- Kṛṣṇa Consciousness: The Matchless Gift
- Selected Verses from the Vedic Scriptures
- Back to Godhead magazine (founder).

A complete catalogue is available upon request.
Bhaktivedanta Book Trust, ISKCON Temple, Hare Krishna Land, Juhu, Mumbai 400 049. India. The above books are also available at ISKCON centres. Please contact a centre near to your place.

All Glories to Śrī Guru and Gaurāṅga

Śrī Caitanya-caritāmṛta

of Kṛṣṇadāsa Kavirāja Gosvāmī

Madhya-līlā, Volume Two
Chapters 7–11

with the original Bengali text, roman transliteration, English equivalents, translation and elaborate purports

by

HIS DIVINE GRACE

A. C. Bhaktivedanta Swami Prabhupāda

Founder-Ācārya of the International Society for Krishna Consciousness

BHAKTIVEDANTA BOOK TRUST

Śrī Caitanya-Caritāmṛta Madhya-Līlā, Vol.2

1st printing in India: 2,000 Sets
2nd to 8th printings: 21,500 Sets
9th printing, September 2023: 4,000 Sets

ISBN 978-81-89574-67-3
ISBN 978-81-89574-63-5 (9-volume set)

Published and Printed by
Bhaktivedanta Book Trust
Hare Krishna Land
Juhu, Mumbai 400 049, India

E-mail : admin@indiabbt.com

C8AB

Contents

Introduction

Śrī Caitanya-caritāmṛta, by Śrīla Kṛṣṇadāsa Kavirāja Gosvāmī, is the principal work on the life and teachings of Śrī Kṛṣṇa Caitanya Mahāprabhu. Caitanya Mahāprabhu is the pioneer of a great social and religious movement that began in India about five hundred years ago and that has directly and indirectly influenced the subsequent course of religious and philosophical thinking not only in India but throughout the world. That Śrī Kṛṣṇa Caitanya's influence has spread so far is due in large part to the efforts of His Divine Grace A. C. Bhaktivedanta Swami Prabhupāda, the present work's translator and commentator and the founder and *ācārya* (spiritual guide) of the International Society for Krishna Consciousness.

Caitanya Mahāprabhu is thus a figure of great historical significance. However, our conventional method of historical analysis—that of seeing a man as a product of his times—fails here, for Śrī Kṛṣṇa Caitanya is a personality who transcends the limited scope of historical settings.

At a time when, in the West, man was directing his explorative spirit toward studying the structure of the physical universe and circumnavigating the world in search of new oceans and continents, Śrī Kṛṣṇa Caitanya, in the East, was inaugurating and masterminding a revolution directed inward, toward a scientific understanding of the highest knowledge of man's spiritual nature.

The chief historical sources for the life of Śrī Kṛṣṇa Caitanya are the *kadacas* (diaries) kept by Murāri Gupta and Svarūpa Dāmodara Gosvāmī. Murāri Gupta, a physician and close associate of Śrī Kṛṣṇa Caitanya's, recorded extensive notes on the first twenty-four years of His life, culminating in His initiation into the renounced order, *sannyāsa.* The events of the rest of Caitanya Mahāprabhu's forty-eight years were recorded in the diary of Svarūpa Dāmodara Gosvāmī, another of His intimate associates.

Śrī Caitanya-caritāmṛta is divided into three sections, called *līlās,* a word that literally means "pastimes"—*Ādi-līlā* (the early period), *Madhya-līlā* (the middle period) and *Antya-līlā* (the final period). The notes of Murāri Gupta form the basis of the *Ādi-līlā,* and Svarūpa Dāmodara's diary provides the details for the *Madhya-* and *Antya-līlās.*

The first twelve chapters of the *Ādi-līlā* constitute the preface for the entire work. By referring to Vedic scriptural evidence, Kṛṣṇadāsa Kavirāja establishes that Caitanya Mahāprabhu is the *avatāra* (incarnation) of God for the Age of Kali—the current epoch, which began five thousand years ago and is characterized by materialism, hypocrisy and dissension. The author also proves that Caitanya Mahāprabhu is identical to Lord Kṛṣṇa and explains that He descends to liberally grant the fallen souls of this degraded age pure love of God by propagating *saṅkīrtana*—literally, "congregational glorification of God"—especially by organizing massive public chanting of the *mahā-mantra* (Great Chant for Deliverance). In addition, in the twelve-chapter preface Kṛṣṇadāsa Kavirāja reveals the esoteric purpose of Lord Caitanya's appearance in the world, describes His co-*avatāras* and principal devotees, and summarizes His teachings. In the remaining portion of the *Ādi-līlā,* chapters thirteen through seventeen, the author briefly recounts Lord Caitanya's divine birth and His life until He accepted the renounced order. This account includes His childhood miracles, schooling, marriage and early philosophical confrontations, as well as His organization of a widespread *saṅkīrtana* movement and His civil disobedience against the repression of the Muslim government.

The *Madhya-līlā,* the longest of the three divisions, narrates in detail Lord Caitanya's extensive and eventful travels throughout India as a renounced mendicant, teacher, philosopher, spiritual preceptor and mystic. During this period of six years, Śrī Caitanya Mahāprabhu transmits His teachings to His principal disciples. He debates and converts many of the renowned philosophers and theologians of His time, including Śaṅkarites, Buddhists and Muslims, and incorporates their many thousands of followers and disciples into His own burgeoning numbers. The author also includes in this section a dramatic account of Caitanya Mahāprabhu's miraculous activities at the giant Ratha-yātrā (Car Festival) in Jagannātha Purī, Orissa.

The *Antya-līlā* concerns the last eighteen years of Śrī Caitanya's manifest presence, spent in semiseclusion near the famous Jagannātha temple at Purī. During these final years, Śrī Kṛṣṇa Caitanya drifted deeper and deeper into trances of spiritual ecstasy unparalleled in all of religious and literary history, Eastern or Western. His perpetual and ever-increasing religious beatitude, graphically described in the eye-witness accounts of Svarūpa Dāmodara Gosvāmī, His constant companion during this period, clearly defy the investigative and descriptive abilities of modern psychologists and phenomenologists of religious experience.

The author of this great classic, Kṛṣṇadāsa Kavirāja Gosvāmī, born around the beginning of the sixteenth century, was a disciple of Raghunātha dāsa Gosvāmī, a confidential follower of Caitanya Mahāprabhu's. Raghunātha dāsa, a renowned ascetic saint, heard and memorized all the activities of Caitanya Mahāprabhu told to him by Svarūpa Dāmodara Gosvāmī. After the passing away of Śrī Caitanya Mahāprabhu and Svarūpa Dāmodara, Raghunātha dāsa, unable to bear the pain of separation from these objects of his complete devotion, traveled to Vṛndāvana, intending to commit suicide by jumping from Govardhana Hill. In Vṛndāvana, however, he encountered Śrīla Rūpa Gosvāmī and Śrīla Sanātana Gosvāmī, two of the most confidential disciples of Caitanya Mahāprabhu. They convinced him to give up his planned suicide and impelled him to reveal to them the spiritually inspiring events of Lord Caitanya's later life. Kṛṣṇadāsa Kavirāja Gosvāmī was also residing in Vṛndāvana at this time, and Raghunātha dāsa Gosvāmī endowed him with a full comprehension of the transcendental life of Śrī Caitanya Mahāprabhu.

By this time, contemporary and near-contemporary scholars and devotees had already written several biographical works on the life of Śrī Kṛṣṇa Caitanya. These included *Śrī Caitanya-carita,* by Murāri Gupta, *Caitanya-maṅgala,* by Locana dāsa Ṭhākura, and *Caitanya-bhāgavata.* This latter work, by Vṛndāvana dāsa Ṭhākura, who was then considered the principal authority on Śrī Caitanya's life, was highly revered. While composing his important work, Vṛndāvana dāsa, fearing that it would become too voluminous, avoided elaborately describing many of the events of Caitanya Mahāprabhu's life, particularly the later ones. Anxious to hear of these later pastimes, the devotees in Vṛndāvana requested Kṛṣṇadāsa Kavirāja Gosvāmī, whom they respected as a great saint and scholar, to compose a book narrating these episodes in detail. Upon this request, and with the permission and blessings of the Madana-mohana Deity of Vṛndāvana, he began compiling *Śrī Caitanya-caritāmṛta,* which, due to its literary excellence and philosophical thoroughness, is today universally regarded as the foremost work on the life and profound teachings of Śrī Caitanya Mahāprabhu.

Kṛṣṇadāsa Kavirāja Gosvāmī commenced work on the text at a very advanced age and in failing health, as he vividly describes in the text itself: "I have now become too old and disturbed by invalidity. While writing, my hands tremble. I cannot remember anything, nor can I see or hear properly. Still I write, and this is a great wonder." That he completed the greatest literary gem of medieval India under such debilitating conditions is surely one of the wonders of literary history.

As mentioned above, this English translation and commentary is the work of His Divine Grace A. C. Bhaktivedanta Swami Prabhupāda, the world's most distinguished teacher of Indian religious and philosophical thought. Śrīla Prabhupāda's commentary is based upon two Bengali commentaries, one by his *guru,* Śrīla Bhaktisiddhānta Sarasvatī Gosvāmī, the eminent Vedic scholar, teacher and saint who predicted, "The time will come when the people of the world will learn Bengali to read *Śrī Caitanya-caritāmṛta,*" and the other by Śrīla Bhaktisiddhānta Sarasvatī's father, Śrīla Bhaktivinoda Ṭhākura, who pioneered the propagation of Śrī Caitanya Mahāprabhu's teachings in the modern era.

Śrīla Prabhupāda is himself a disciplic descendant of Śrī Caitanya Mahāprabhu, and he is the first scholar to execute systematic English translations of the major works of Śrī Kṛṣṇa Caitanya's followers. His consummate Bengali and Sanskrit scholarship and intimate familiarity with the precepts of Śrī Kṛṣṇa Caitanya are a fitting combination that eminently qualifies him to present this important classic to the English-speaking world. The ease and clarity with which he expounds upon difficult philosophical concepts enable even a reader totally unfamiliar with Indian religious tradition to understand and appreciate this profound and monumental work.

The entire text, with commentary, presented in nine lavishly illustrated volumes by the Bhaktivedanta Book Trust, represents a contribution of major importance to the intellectual, cultural and spiritual life of contemporary man.

—The Publishers

Editor's note: Revisions in this edition are based on the transcripts of His Divine Grace A. C. Bhaktivedanta Swami Prabhupāda's original dictation of the translations, word meanings and purports of *Śrī Caitanya-caritāmṛta.*

CHAPTER SEVEN

The Lord Begins His Tour of South India

In his *Amṛta-pravāha-bhāṣya,* Śrīla Bhaktivinoda Ṭhākura summarizes the Seventh Chapter as follows. Śrī Caitanya Mahāprabhu accepted the renounced order of life in the month of Māgha (January–February) and went to Jagannātha Purī in the month of Phālguna (February–March). He saw the Dola-yātrā festival during the month of Phālguna, and in the month of Caitra He liberated Sārvabhauma Bhaṭṭācārya. During the month of Vaiśākha, He began to tour South India. When He proposed to travel to South India alone, Śrī Nityānanda Prabhu gave Him a *brāhmaṇa* assistant named Kṛṣṇadāsa. When Śrī Caitanya Mahāprabhu was beginning His tour, Sārvabhauma Bhaṭṭācārya gave Him four sets of clothes and requested Him to see Rāmānanda Rāya, who was residing at that time on the bank of the river Godāvarī. Along with other devotees, Nityānanda Prabhu accompanied the Lord to Ālālanātha, but there Lord Caitanya left them all behind and went ahead with the *brāhmaṇa* Kṛṣṇadāsa. The Lord began chanting the *mantra* "*kṛṣṇa kṛṣṇa kṛṣṇa kṛṣṇa kṛṣṇa kṛṣṇa kṛṣṇa he.*" In whatever village He spent the night, whenever a person came to see Him in His shelter, the Lord implored him to preach the Kṛṣṇa consciousness movement. After teaching the people of one village, the Lord proceeded to other villages to increase devotees. In this way He finally reached Kūrma-sthāna. While there, He bestowed His causeless mercy upon a *brāhmaṇa* called Kūrma and cured another *brāhmaṇa,* named Vāsudeva, who was suffering from leprosy. After curing this *brāhmaṇa* leper, Śrī Caitanya Mahāprabhu received the title Vāsudevāmṛta-prada, meaning "one who delivered nectar to the leper Vāsudeva."

TEXT 1

ধন্যং তং নৌমি চৈতন্যং বাসুদেবং দয়ার্দ্রধী ।
নষ্টকুষ্ঠং রূপপুষ্টং ভক্তিতুষ্টং চকার যঃ ॥ ১ ॥

dhanyaṁ taṁ naumi caitanyaṁ
vāsudevaṁ dayārdra-dhī
naṣṭa-kuṣṭhaṁ rūpa-puṣṭaṁ
bhakti-tuṣṭaṁ cakāra yaḥ

dhanyam—auspicious; *tam*—unto Him; *naumi*—I offer obeisances; *caitanyam*—Śrī Caitanya Mahāprabhu; *vāsudevam*—unto the *brāhmaṇa* Vāsudeva; *dayā-ārdra-dhī*—being compassionate; *naṣṭa-kuṣṭham*—cured the leprosy; *rūpa-puṣṭam*—beautiful; *bhakti-tuṣṭam*—satisfied in devotional service; *cakāra*—made; *yaḥ*—the Supreme Personality of Godhead.

TRANSLATION

Lord Caitanya Mahāprabhu, being very compassionate toward a brāhmaṇa named Vāsudeva, cured him of leprosy. He transformed him into a beautiful man satisfied with devotional service. I offer my respectful obeisances unto the glorious Lord Śrī Caitanya Mahāprabhu.

TEXT 2

জয় জয় শ্রীচৈতন্য জয় নিত্যানন্দ ।
জয়াদ্বৈতচন্দ্র জয় গৌরভক্তবৃন্দ ॥ ২ ॥

jaya jaya śrī-caitanya jaya nityānanda
jayādvaita-candra jaya gaura-bhakta-vṛnda

jaya jaya—all glories; *śrī-caitanya*—to Lord Caitanya Mahāprabhu; *jaya*—all glories; *nityānanda*—to Lord Nityānanda Prabhu; *jaya advaita-candra*—all glories to Advaita Ācārya; *jaya gaura-bhakta-vṛnda*—all glories to the devotees of Lord Caitanya.

TRANSLATION

All glories to Lord Caitanya Mahāprabhu! All glories to Lord Nityānanda Prabhu! All glories to Advaita Ācārya! And all glories to all the devotees of Lord Caitanya!

TEXT 3

এই মতে সার্বভৌমের নিস্তার করিল ।
দক্ষিণ-গমনে প্রভুর ইচ্ছা উপজিল ॥ ৩ ॥

ei-mate sārvabhaumera nistāra karila
dakṣiṇa-gamane prabhura icchā upajila

ei-mate—in this way; *sārvabhaumera*—of Sārvabhauma Bhaṭṭācārya; *nistāra*—the liberation; *karila*—was executed; *dakṣiṇa-gamane*—in going to South India; *prabhura*—of the Lord; *icchā*—a desire; *upajila*—arose.

TRANSLATION

After delivering Sārvabhauma Bhaṭṭācārya, the Lord desired to go to South India to preach.

TEXT 4

মাঘ-শুক্লপক্ষে প্রভু করিল সন্ন্যাস ।
ফাল্গুনে আসিয়া কৈল নীলাচলে বাস ॥ ৪ ॥

māgha-śukla-pakṣe prabhu karila sannyāsa
phālgune āsiyā kaila nīlācale vāsa

māgha-śukla-pakṣe—in the waxing fortnight of the month of Māgha; *prabhu*—the Lord; *karila*—accepted; *sannyāsa*—the renounced order of life; *phālgune*—in the next month, Phālguna; *āsiyā*—coming; *kaila*—did; *nīlācale*—at Jagannātha Purī; *vāsa*—residence.

TRANSLATION

Śrī Caitanya Mahāprabhu accepted the renounced order during the waxing fortnight of the month of Māgha. During the following month, Phālguna, He went to Jagannātha Purī and resided there.

TEXT 5

ফাল্গুনের শেষে দোলযাত্রা সে দেখিল ।
প্রেমাবেশে তাঁহা বহু নৃত্যগীত কৈল ॥ ৫ ॥

phālgunera śeṣe dola-yātrā se dekhila
premāveśe tāṅhā bahu nṛtya-gīta kaila

phālgunera—of the month of Phālguna; *śeṣe*—at the end; *dola-yātrā*—the Dola-yātrā festival; *se*—that; *dekhila*—saw; *prema-āveśe*—in the ecstasy of love of Godhead; *tāṅhā*—there; *bahu*—much; *nṛtya-gīta*—chanting and dancing; *kaila*—performed.

TRANSLATION

At the end of the month of Phālguna, He witnessed the Dola-yātrā ceremony, and in His usual ecstatic love of God, He chanted and danced in various ways on the occasion.

TEXT 6

চৈত্রে রহি' কৈল সার্বভৌম-বিমোচন ।
বৈশাখের প্রথমে দক্ষিণ যাইতে হৈল মন ॥ ৬ ॥

caitre rahi' kaila sārvabhauma-vimocana
vaiśākhera prathame dakṣiṇa yāite haila mana

caitre—in the month of Caitra (March–April); *rahi'*—residing there; *kaila*—did; *sārvabhauma-vimocana*—liberation of Sārvabhauma Bhaṭṭācārya; *vaiśākhera*—of the month of Vaiśākha; *prathame*—at the beginning; *dakṣiṇa*—to South India; *yāite*—to go; *haila*—it was; *mana*—the mind.

TRANSLATION

During the month of Caitra, while living at Jagannātha Purī, the Lord delivered Sārvabhauma Bhaṭṭācārya, and at the beginning of the next month (Vaiśākha), He decided to go to South India.

TEXTS 7–8

নিজগণ আনি' কহে বিনয় করিয়া ।
আলিঙ্গন করি' সবায় শ্রীহস্তে ধরিয়া ॥ ৭ ॥
তোমা-সবা জানি আমি প্রাণাধিক করি' ।
প্রাণ ছাড়া যায়, তোমা-সবা ছাড়িতে না পারি ॥ ৮ ॥

nija-gaṇa āni' kahe vinaya kariyā
āliṅgana kari' sabāya śrī-haste dhariyā

tomā-sabā jāni āmi prāṇādhika kari'
prāṇa chāḍā yāya, tomā-sabā chāḍite nā pāri

nija-gaṇa āni'—calling all the devotees; *kahe*—said; *vinaya*—humbleness; *kariyā*—showing; *āliṅgana kari'*—embracing; *sabāya*—all of them; *śrī-haste*—with His hands; *dhariyā*—catching them; *tomā-sabā*—all of you; *jāni*—I know; *āmi*—I; *prāṇa-adhika*—more than My life; *kari'*—taking; *prāṇa chāḍā*—giving up life; *yāya*—is possible; *tomā-sabā*—all of you; *chāḍite*—to give up; *nā pāri*—I am not able.

TRANSLATION

Śrī Caitanya Mahāprabhu called all His devotees together and, holding them by the hand, humbly informed them, "You are all more dear to Me than My life. I can give up My life, but to give you up is difficult for Me.

TEXT 9

তুমি-সব বন্ধু মোর বন্ধুকৃত্য কৈলে ।
ইহাঁ আনি' মোরে জগন্নাথ দেখাইলে ॥ ৯ ॥

tumi-saba bandhu mora bandhu-kṛtya kaile
ihāṅ āni' more jagannātha dekhāile

tumi-saba—all of you; *bandhu*—friends; *mora*—My; *bandhu-kṛtya*—duties of a friend; *kaile*—you have executed; *ihāṅ*—here; *āni'*—bringing; *more*—to Me; *jagannātha*—Lord Jagannātha; *dekhāile*—you have shown.

TRANSLATION

"You are all My friends, and you have properly executed the duties of friends by bringing Me here to Jagannātha Purī and giving Me the chance to see Lord Jagannātha in the temple.

TEXT 10

এবে সবা-স্থানে মুঞি মাগোঁ এক দানে ।
সবে মেলি' আজ্ঞা দেহ, যাইব দক্ষিণে ॥ ১০ ॥

ebe sabā-sthāne muñi māgoṅ eka dāne
sabe meli' ājñā deha, yāiba dakṣiṇe

ebe—now; *sabā-sthāne*—from all of you; *muñi*—I; *māgoṅ*—beg; *eka dāne*—one gift; *sabe meli'*—all combining together; *ājñā deha*—give permission; *yāiba*—I shall go; *dakṣiṇe*—to South India.

TRANSLATION

"I now beg all of you for one bit of charity. Please give Me permission to leave for a tour of South India.

TEXT 11

বিশ্বরূপ-উদ্দেশে অবশ্য আমি যাব ।
একাকী যাইব, কাহো সঙ্গে না লইব ॥ ১১ ॥

viśvarūpa-uddeśe avaśya āmi yāba
ekākī yāiba, kāho saṅge nā la-iba

viśvarūpa-uddeśe—to find Viśvarūpa; *avaśya*—certainly; *āmi*—I; *yāba*—shall go; *ekākī*—alone; *yāiba*—I shall go; *kāho*—someone; *saṅge*—in association; *nā*—not; *la-iba*—I shall take.

TRANSLATION

"I shall go to search out Viśvarūpa. Please forgive Me, but I want to go alone; I do not wish to take anyone with Me.

TEXT 12

সেতুবন্ধ হৈতে আমি না আসি যাবৎ ।
নীলাচলে তুমি সব রহিবে তাবৎ ॥ ১২ ॥

setubandha haite āmi nā āsi yāvat
nīlācale tumi saba rahibe tāvat

setubandha—the extreme southern point of India; *haite*—from; *āmi*—I; *nā*—not; *āsi*—returning; *yāvat*—as long as; *nīlācale*—in Jagannātha Purī; *tumi*—you; *saba*—all; *rahibe*—should stay; *tāvat*—that long.

TRANSLATION

"Until I return from Setubandha, all of you dear friends should remain at Jagannātha Purī."

TEXT 13

বিশ্বরূপ-সিদ্ধি-প্রাপ্তি জানেন সকল ।
দক্ষিণ-দেশ উদ্ধারিতে করেন এই ছল ॥ ১৩ ॥

viśvarūpa-siddhi-prāpti jānena sakala
dakṣiṇa-deśa uddhārite karena ei chala

viśvarūpa—of Viśvarūpa; *siddhi*—of perfection; *prāpti*—achievement; *jānena*—the Lord knows; *sakala*—everything; *dakṣiṇa-deśa*—South India; *uddhārite*—just to liberate; *karena*—makes; *ei*—this; *chala*—pretense.

TRANSLATION

Knowing everything, Śrī Caitanya Mahāprabhu was aware that Viśvarūpa had already passed away. A pretense of ignorance was necessary, however, so that He could go to South India and liberate the people there.

TEXT 14

শুনিয়া সবার মনে হৈল মহাদুঃখ ।
নিঃশব্দ হইলা, সবার শুকাইল মুখ ॥ ১৪ ॥

śuniyā sabāra mane haila mahā-duḥkha
niḥśabda ha-ilā, sabāra śukāila mukha

śuniyā—hearing this; *sabāra*—of all the devotees; *mane*—in the minds; *haila*—there was; *mahā-duḥkha*—great unhappiness; *niḥśabda*—silent; *ha-ilā*—became; *sabāra*—of everyone; *śukāila*—dried up; *mukha*—the faces.

TRANSLATION

Upon hearing this message from Śrī Caitanya Mahāprabhu, all the devotees became very unhappy and remained silent with sullen faces.

TEXT 15

নিত্যানন্দপ্রভু কহে, — "ঐছে কৈছে হয়।
একাকী যাইবে তুমি, কে ইহা সহয় ॥ ১৫ ॥

nityānanda-prabhu kahe,—"aiche kaiche haya
ekākī yāibe tumi, ke ihā sahaya

nityānanda-prabhu kahe—Lord Nityānanda Prabhu replied; *aiche kaiche haya*—how is this possible; *ekākī*—alone; *yāibe*—shall go; *tumi*—You; *ke*—who; *ihā*—this; *sahaya*—can tolerate.

TRANSLATION

Nityānanda Prabhu then said, "How is it possible for You to go alone? Who can tolerate this?

TEXT 16

দুই-এক সঙ্গে চলুক, না পড় হঠ-রঙ্গে।
যারে কহ সেই দুই চলুক্ তোমার সঙ্গে ॥ ১৬ ॥

dui-eka saṅge caluka, nā paḍa haṭha-raṅge
yāre kaha sei dui caluk tomāra saṅge

dui—two; *eka*—or one; *saṅge*—with You; *caluka*—let go; *nā*—do not; *paḍa*—fall; *haṭha-raṅge*—in the clutches of thieves and rogues;

yāre—whoever; *kaha*—You say; *sei*—those; *dui*—two; *caluk*—let go; *tomāra*—You; *saṅge*—along with.

TRANSLATION

"Let one or two of us go with You; otherwise You may fall into the clutches of thieves and rogues along the way. They may be whomever You like, but two persons should go with You.

TEXT 17

দক্ষিণের তীর্থপথ আমি সব জানি।
আমি সঙ্গে যাই, প্রভু, আজ্ঞা দেহ তুমি ॥" ১৭ ॥

dakṣiṇera tīrtha-patha āmi saba jāni
āmi saṅge yāi, prabhu, ājñā deha tumi"

dakṣiṇera—of South India; *tīrtha-patha*—the ways to different places of pilgrimage; *āmi*—I; *saba*—all; *jāni*—know; *āmi*—I; *saṅge*—with You; *yāi*—go; *prabhu*—O My Lord; *ājñā*—order; *deha*—give; *tumi*—You.

TRANSLATION

"Indeed, I know all the paths to the different places of pilgrimage in South India. Just order Me, and I shall go with You."

TEXT 18

প্রভু কহে, "আমি —নর্তক, তুমি —সূত্রধার।
তুমি যৈছে নাচাও, তৈছে নর্তন আমার ॥ ১৮ ॥

prabhu kahe, "āmi—nartaka, tumi—sūtra-dhāra
tumi yaiche nācāo, taiche nartana āmāra

prabhu kahe—the Lord replied; *āmi*—I; *nartaka*—a dancer; *tumi*—You; *sūtra-dhāra*—wire-puller; *tumi*—You; *yaiche*—just as; *nācāo*—make dance; *taiche*—in that way; *nartana*—dancing; *āmāra*—My.

TRANSLATION

The Lord replied, "I am simply a dancer, and You are the wire-puller. However You pull the wires to make Me dance, I shall dance in that way.

TEXT 19

সন্ন্যাস করিয়া আমি চলিলাঙ বৃন্দাবন ।
তুমি আমা লঞা আইলে অদ্বৈত-ভবন ॥ ১৯ ॥

sannyāsa kariyā āmi calilāṅ vṛndāvana
tumi āmā lañā āile advaita-bhavana

sannyāsa kariyā—after accepting the renounced order; *āmi*—I; *calilāṅ*—went; *vṛndāvana*—toward Vṛndāvana; *tumi*—You; *āmā*—Me; *lañā*—taking; *āile*—went; *advaita-bhavana*—to the house of Advaita Prabhu.

TRANSLATION

"After accepting the sannyāsa order, I decided to go to Vṛndāvana, but You took Me instead to the house of Advaita Prabhu.

TEXT 20

নীলাচল আসিতে পথে ভাঙ্গিলা মোর দণ্ড ।
তোমা-সবার গাঢ়-স্নেহে আমার কার্য-ভঙ্গ ॥ ২০ ॥

nīlācala āsite pathe bhāṅgilā mora daṇḍa
tomā-sabāra gāḍha-snehe āmāra kārya-bhaṅga

nīlācala—to Jagannātha Purī; *āsite*—going there; *pathe*—on the road; *bhāṅgilā*—You broke; *mora*—My; *daṇḍa*—*sannyāsa* staff; *tomā-sabāra*—of all of you; *gāḍha-snehe*—on account of the deep affection; *āmāra*—My; *kārya-bhaṅga*—disturbance of activities.

TRANSLATION

"While on the way to Jagannātha Purī, You broke My sannyāsa staff. I know that all of you have great affection for Me, but such things disturb My activities.

TEXT 21

জগদানন্দ চাহে আমা বিষয় ভুঞ্জাইতে।
যেই কহে সেই ভয়ে চাহিয়ে করিতে॥ ২১ ॥

jagadānanda cāhe āmā viṣaya bhuñjāite
yei kahe sei bhaye cāhiye karite

jagadānanda—Jagadānanda; *cāhe*—wants; *āmā*—Me; *viṣaya*—sense gratification; *bhuñjāite*—to cause to enjoy; *yei kahe*—whatever he says; *sei*—that; *bhaye*—out of fear; *cāhiye*—I want; *karite*—to do.

TRANSLATION

"Jagadānanda wants Me to enjoy bodily sense gratification, and out of fear I do whatever he tells Me.

TEXT 22

কভু যদি ইঁহার বাক্য করিয়ে অন্যথা।
ক্রোধে তিন দিন মোরে নাহি কহে কথা॥ ২২ ॥

kabhu yadi iṅhāra vākya kariye anyathā
krodhe tina dina more nāhi kahe kathā

kabhu—sometimes; *yadi*—if; *iṅhāra*—of Jagadānanda; *vākya*—the words; *kariye*—I do; *anyathā*—other than; *krodhe*—in anger; *tina dina*—for three days; *more*—to Me; *nāhi*—not; *kahe*—speaks; *kathā*—words.

TRANSLATION

"If I sometimes do something against his desire, out of anger he will not talk to Me for three days.

TEXT 23

মুকুন্দ হয়েন দুঃখী দেখি' সন্ন্যাস-ধর্ম।
তিনবারে শীতে স্নান, ভূমিতে শয়ন॥ ২৩ ॥

mukunda hayena duḥkhī dekhi' sannyāsa-dharma
tinabāre śīte snāna, bhūmite śayana

mukunda—Mukunda; *hayena*—becomes; *duḥkhī*—unhappy; *dekhi'*—seeing; *sannyāsa-dharma*—My regulative principles in the renounced order; *tina-bāre*—three times; *śīte*—in the winter; *snāna*—bath; *bhūmite*—on the ground; *śayana*—lying down.

TRANSLATION

"Being a sannyāsī, I have a duty to lie down on the ground and to take a bath three times a day, even during the winter. But Mukunda becomes very unhappy when he sees My severe austerities.

TEXT 24

অন্তরে দুঃখী মুকুন্দ, নাহি কহে মুখে।
ইহার দুঃখ দেখি' মোর দ্বিগুণ হয়ে দুঃখে ॥ ২৪ ॥

antare duḥkhī mukunda, nāhi kahe mukhe
ihāra duḥkha dekhi' mora dvi-guṇa haye duḥkhe

antare—within himself; *duḥkhī*—unhappy; *mukunda*—Mukunda; *nāhi*—not; *kahe*—says; *mukhe*—in the mouth; *ihāra*—of him; *duḥkha*—the unhappiness; *dekhi'*—seeing; *mora*—My; *dvi-guṇa*—twice; *haye*—there is; *duḥkhe*—the unhappiness.

TRANSLATION

"Of course, Mukunda does not say anything, but I know that he is very unhappy within, and upon seeing him unhappy, I become twice as unhappy.

TEXT 25

আমি ত' — সন্ন্যাসী, দামোদর — ব্রহ্মচারী।
সদা রহে আমার উপর শিক্ষা-দণ্ড ধরি' ॥ ২৫ ॥

āmi ta'—sannyāsī, dāmodara—brahmacārī
sadā rahe āmāra upara śikṣā-daṇḍa dhari'

āmi ta'—I indeed; *sannyāsī*—in the renounced order of life; *dāmodara*—Dāmodara; *brahmacārī*—in a stage of complete celibacy; *sadā*—always; *rahe*—remains; *āmāra upara*—on Me; *śikṣā-daṇḍa*—a stick for My education; *dhari'*—keeping.

TRANSLATION

"Although I am in the renounced order of life and Dāmodara is a brahmacārī, he still keeps a stick in his hand just to educate Me.

TEXT 26

ইঁহার আগে আমি না জানি ব্যবহার।
ইঁহারে না ভায় স্বতন্ত্র চরিত্র আমার ॥ ২৬ ॥

iṅhāra āge āmi nā jāni vyavahāra
iṅhāre nā bhāya svatantra caritra āmāra

iṅhāra āge—in front of him; *āmi*—I; *nā*—not; *jāni*—know; *vyavahāra*—social etiquette; *iṅhāre*—for him; *nā*—not; *bhāya*—exists; *svatantra*—independent; *caritra*—character; *āmāra*—My.

TRANSLATION

"According to Dāmodara, I am still a neophyte as far as social etiquette is concerned; therefore he does not like My independent nature.

TEXT 27

লোকাপেক্ষা নাহি ইঁহার কৃষ্ণকৃপা হৈতে।
আমি লোকাপেক্ষা কভু না পারি ছাড়িতে ॥ ২৭ ॥

lokāpekṣā nāhi iṅhāra kṛṣṇa-kṛpā haite
āmi lokāpekṣā kabhu nā pāri chāḍite

loka-apekṣā—care for society; *nāhi*—there is none; *iṅhāra*—of Dāmodara; *kṛṣṇa-kṛpā*—the mercy of the Lord; *haite*—from; *āmi*—I; *loka-apekṣā*—dependence on public opinion; *kabhu*—at any time; *nā*—not; *pāri*—able; *chāḍite*—to give up.

TRANSLATION

"Dāmodara Paṇḍita and others are more advanced in receiving the mercy of Lord Kṛṣṇa; therefore they are independent of public opinion. As such, they want Me to enjoy sense gratification, even though it be unethical. But since I am a poor sannyāsī, I cannot abandon the duties of the renounced order, and therefore I follow them strictly.

PURPORT

A *brahmacārī* is supposed to assist a *sannyāsī;* therefore a *brahmacārī* should not try to instruct a *sannyāsī.* That is the etiquette. Consequently Dāmodara should not have advised Śrī Caitanya Mahāprabhu of His duty.

TEXT 28

অতএব তুমি সব রহ নীলাচলে ।
দিন কত আমি তীর্থ ভ্রমিব একলে ॥" ২৮ ॥

ataeva tumi saba raha nīlācale
dina kata āmi tīrtha bhramiba ekale"

ataeva—therefore; *tumi*—you; *saba*—all; *raha*—remain; *nīlācale*—at Jagannātha Purī; *dina*—days; *kata*—some; *āmi*—I; *tīrtha*—the sacred places of pilgrimage; *bhramiba*—I shall tour; *ekale*—alone.

TRANSLATION

"You should all therefore remain here in Nīlācala for some days while I tour the sacred places of pilgrimage alone."

TEXT 29

ইঁহা-সবার বশ প্রভু হয়ে যে যে গুণে ।
দোষারোপ-চ্ছলে করে গুণ আস্বাদনে ॥ ২৯ ॥

iṅhā-sabāra vaśa prabhu haye ye ye guṇe
doṣāropa-cchale kare guṇa āsvādane

iṅhā-sabāra—of all the devotees; *vaśa*—controlled; *prabhu*—the Lord; *haye*—is; *ye ye*—whatever; *guṇe*—by the qualities; *doṣa-āropa-chale*—on the plea of attributing faults; *kare*—does; *guṇa*—high qualities; *āsvādane*—tasting.

TRANSLATION

Actually the Lord was controlled by the good qualities of all His devotees. On the pretense of attributing faults, He tasted all these qualities.

PURPORT

All the accusations made by Śrī Caitanya Mahāprabhu against His beloved devotees actually showed His great appreciation of their intense love for Him. Yet He mentioned these faults one after another as if He were offended by their intense affection. The personal associates of Śrī Caitanya Mahāprabhu sometimes behaved contrary to regulative principles out of intense love for the Lord, and because of their love Śrī Caitanya Mahāprabhu Himself sometimes violated the regulative principles of a *sannyāsī*. In the eyes of the public, such violations are not good, but Śrī Caitanya Mahāprabhu was so controlled by His devotees' love that He was obliged to break some of the rules. Although accusing them, Śrī Caitanya Mahāprabhu was indirectly indicating that He was very satisfied with their behavior in pure love of Godhead. Therefore in verse 27 He mentions that His devotees and associates place more importance on love of Kṛṣṇa than on social etiquette. There are many instances of devotional service rendered by previous *ācāryas* who did not care about social behavior when intensely absorbed in love for Kṛṣṇa. Unfortunately, as long as we are within this material world, we must observe social customs to avoid criticism by the general populace. This is Śrī Caitanya Mahāprabhu's desire.

TEXT 30

চৈতন্যের ভক্ত-বাৎসল্য — অকথ্য-কথন ।
আপনে বৈরাগ্য-দুঃখ করেন সহন ॥ ৩০ ॥

caitanyera bhakta-vātsalya — akathya-kathana
āpane vairāgya-duḥkha karena sahana

caitanyera—of Lord Śrī Caitanya Mahāprabhu; *bhakta-vātsalya*—the love for His devotees; *akathya-kathana*—indescribable by words; *āpane*—personally; *vairāgya*—of the renounced order; *duḥkha*—unhappiness; *karena*—does; *sahana*—toleration.

TRANSLATION

No one can properly describe Lord Śrī Caitanya Mahāprabhu's affection for His devotees. He always tolerated all kinds of personal unhappiness resulting from His acceptance of the renounced order of life.

TEXT 31

সেই দুঃখ দেখি' যেই ভক্ত দুঃখ পায়।
সেই দুঃখ তাঁর শক্ত্যে সহন না যায় ॥ ৩১ ॥

sei duḥkha dekhi' yei bhakta duḥkha pāya
sei duḥkha tāṅra śaktye sahana nā yāya

sei duḥkha—that unhappiness; *dekhi'*—seeing; *yei*—whatever; *bhakta*—the devotees; *duḥkha*—unhappiness; *pāya*—get; *sei duḥkha*—that unhappiness; *tāṅra*—His; *śaktye*—by the power; *sahana*—toleration; *nā*—not; *yāya*—possible.

TRANSLATION

The regulative principles observed by Caitanya Mahāprabhu were sometimes intolerable, and all the devotees became greatly affected by them. Although strictly observing the regulative principles, Caitanya Mahāprabhu could not tolerate the unhappiness felt by His devotees.

TEXT 32

গুণে দোষোদগার-চ্ছলে সবা নিষেধিয়া।
একাকী ভ্রমিবেন তীর্থ বৈরাগ্য করিয়া ॥ ৩২ ॥

guṇe doṣodgāra-cchale sabā niṣedhiyā
ekākī bhramibena tīrtha vairāgya kariyā

guṇe—in the good qualities; *doṣa-udgāra-chale*—on the plea of attributing faults; *sabā*—all of them; *niṣedhiyā*—forbidding; *ekākī*—alone; *bhramibena*—will tour; *tīrtha*—the sacred places of pilgrimage; *vairāgya*—regulative principles of the renounced order of life; *kariyā*—observing.

TRANSLATION

Therefore, to prevent them from accompanying Him and becoming unhappy, Śrī Caitanya Mahāprabhu declared their good qualities to be faults.

PURPORT

The Lord wanted to tour all the places of pilgrimage alone and strictly observe the duties of the renounced order.

TEXT 33

তবে চারিজন বহু মিনতি করিল।
স্বতন্ত্র ঈশ্বর প্রভু কভু না মানিল ॥ ৩৩ ॥

tabe cāri-jana bahu minati karila
svatantra īśvara prabhu kabhu nā mānila

tabe—thereafter; *cāri-jana*—four men; *bahu*—many; *minati*—petitions; *karila*—submitted; *svatantra*—independent; *īśvara*—the Supreme Personality of Godhead; *prabhu*—Śrī Caitanya Mahāprabhu; *kabhu*—at any time; *nā*—not; *mānila*—accepted.

TRANSLATION

Four devotees then humbly insisted that they go with the Lord, but Śrī Caitanya Mahāprabhu, being the independent Supreme Personality of Godhead, did not accept their request.

TEXT 34

তবে নিত্যানন্দ কহে, — যে আজ্ঞা তোমার।
দুঃখ সুখ যে হউক্ কর্তব্য আমার ॥ ৩৪ ॥

tabe nityānanda kahe,—ye ājñā tomāra
duḥkha sukha ye ha-uk kartavya āmāra

tabe—thereupon; *nityānanda*—Lord Nityānanda Prabhu; *kahe*—says; *ye ājñā*—whatever order; *tomāra*—Your; *duḥkha sukha*—distress or happiness; *ye*—whatever; *ha-uk*—let there be; *kartavya*—the duty; *āmāra*—My.

TRANSLATION

Thereupon Lord Nityānanda said, "Whatever You order is My duty, regardless of whether it results in happiness or unhappiness.

TEXT 35

কিন্তু এক নিবেদন করোঁ আর বার।
বিচার করিয়া তাহা কর অঙ্গীকার ॥ ৩৫ ॥

kintu eka nivedana karoṅ āra bāra
vicāra kariyā tāhā kara aṅgīkāra

kintu—but; *eka*—one; *nivedana*—petition; *karoṅ*—I do; *āra bāra*—again; *vicāra*—consideration; *kariyā*—giving; *tāhā*—that; *kara*—do; *aṅgīkāra*—acceptance.

TRANSLATION

"Yet I still submit one petition to You. Please consider it, and if You think it proper, please accept it.

TEXT 36

কৌপীন, বহির্বাস আর জলপাত্র।
আর কিছু নাহি যাবে, সবে এই মাত্র ॥ ৩৬ ॥

kaupīna, bahir-vāsa āra jala-pātra
āra kichu nāhi yābe, sabe ei mātra

kaupīna—loincloth; *bahir-vāsa*—outer garments; *āra*—and; *jala-pātra*—waterpot; *āra kichu*—anything else; *nāhi*—not; *yābe*—will go; *sabe*—all; *ei*—this; *mātra*—only.

TRANSLATION

"You must take with You a loincloth, external clothes and a waterpot. You should take nothing more than this.

TEXT 37

তোমার দুই হস্ত বদ্ধ নাম-গণনে ।
জলপাত্র-বহির্বাস বহিবে কেমনে ॥ ৩৭ ॥

tomāra dui hasta baddha nāma-gaṇane
jala-pātra-bahirvāsa vahibe kemane

tomāra—Your; *dui*—two; *hasta*—hands; *baddha*—engaged; *nāma*—the holy name; *gaṇane*—in counting; *jala-pātra*—waterpot; *bahir-vāsa*—external garments; *vahibe*—will carry; *kemane*—how.

TRANSLATION

"Since Your two hands will always be engaged in chanting and counting the holy names, how will You be able to carry the waterpot and external garments?

PURPORT

From this verse it is clear that Caitanya Mahāprabhu was chanting the holy names a fixed number of times daily. The Gosvāmīs used to follow in the footsteps of Śrī Caitanya Mahāprabhu, and Haridāsa Ṭhākura also followed this principle. Concerning the Gosvāmīs—Śrīla Rūpa Gosvāmī, Śrīla Sanātana Gosvāmī, Śrīla Raghunātha Bhaṭṭa Gosvāmī, Śrīla Jīva Gosvāmī, Śrīla Gopāla Bhaṭṭa Gosvāmī and Śrīla Raghunātha dāsa Gosvāmī—Śrīnivāsa Ācārya confirms, *saṅkhyā-pūrvaka-nāma-gāna-natibhiḥ.* (*Ṣaḍ-gosvāmy-aṣṭaka* 6) In addition to other duties, Śrī Caitanya Mahāprabhu introduced the system of chanting the holy name of the Lord a fixed number of times daily, as confirmed in this verse (*tomāra dui hasta baddha nāma-gaṇane*). Caitanya Mahāprabhu used to count on His fingers. While one hand was engaged in chanting, the other hand kept the number of rounds. This is corroborated in the *Caitanya-candrāmṛta* and also in Śrīla Rūpa Gosvāmī's *Stava-mālā:*

badhnan prema-bhara-prakampita-karo granthīn kaṭī-dorakaiḥ
saṅkhyātuṁ nija-loka-maṅgala-hare-kṛṣṇeti nāmnāṁ japan
(*Caitanya-candrāmṛta* 16)

hare kṛṣṇety uccaiḥ sphurita-rasano nāma-gaṇanā-
kṛta-granthi-śreṇī-subhaga-kaṭi-sūtrojjvala-karaḥ
(*Prathama-caitanyāṣṭaka* 5)

Therefore devotees in the line of Śrī Caitanya Mahāprabhu must chant at least sixteen rounds daily, and this is the number prescribed by the International Society for Krishna Consciousness. Haridāsa Ṭhākura daily chanted 300,000 names. Sixteen rounds is about 28,000 names. There is no need to imitate Haridāsa Ṭhākura or the other Gosvāmīs, but chanting the holy name a fixed number of times daily is essential for every devotee.

TEXT 38

প্রেমাবেশে পথে তুমি হবে অচেতন।
এ-সব সামগ্রী তোমার কে করে রক্ষণ ॥ ৩৮ ॥

premāveśe pathe tumi habe acetana
e-saba sāmagrī tomāra ke kare rakṣaṇa

prema-āveśe—in ecstatic love of God; *pathe*—on the way; *tumi*—You; *habe*—will be; *acetana*—unconscious; *e-saba*—all this; *sāmagrī*—paraphernalia; *tomāra*—Your; *ke*—who; *kare*—does; *rakṣaṇa*—protection.

TRANSLATION

"When, along the way, You fall unconscious in ecstatic love of Godhead, who will protect Your belongings—the waterpot, garments and so forth?"

TEXT 39

'কৃষ্ণদাস'-নামে এই সরল ব্রাহ্মণ।
ইঁহো সঙ্গে করি' লহ, ধর নিবেদন ॥ ৩৯ ॥

His Divine Grace
A. C. Bhaktivedanta Swami Prabhupāda
Founder-Ācārya of the International Society for Krishna Consciousness

PLATES ONE AND TWO: Above, Śrī Raṅga-kṣetra (9.79), the largest temple in India, where Lord Caitanya Mahāprabhu chanted and danced in ecstatic love of Godhead. Below, the temple of Cidāmbaram, which was visited by Śrī Caitanya Mahāprabhu in His tour of South India. (9.73)

PLATES THREE AND FOUR: Left, in Māyāpur, a reconstruction of the house of Advaita Ācārya, the incarnation of Lord Caitanya as a devotee. Right, the Tirupati temple, a famous holy place of pilgrimage in South India. (9.64)

PLATE FIVE: "Accompanied by His personal associates and Sārvabhauma Bhaṭṭācārya, Śrī Caitanya Mahāprabhu circumambulated the altar of Jagannātha. The Lord then departed on His South Indian tour." (7.58)

PLATE SIX: When Śrī Caitanya Mahāprabhu touched the leper Vāsudeva, both his leprosy and his distress went far away. Indeed, his body became very beautiful, to his great happiness.(7.141)

PLATE SEVEN: Śrī Caitanya Mahāprabhu embraced Śrī Rāmānanda Rāya very firmly, and they both almost lost consciousness out of ecstatic love. (8.22)

PLATE EIGHT: "Then Gāyatrī, mother of the Vedas, having been manifested by the divine sound of Śrī Kṛṣṇa's flute, entered the lotus mouth of Brahmā through his eight earholes." (8.138)

PLATE NINE: Śrī Ṣaḍbhuja, the six-armed form revealed by Lord Caitanya, indicates that He is Lord Rāmacandra (symbolized by the bow and arrow) and Lord Kṛṣṇa (symbolized by the flute), as well as Lord Caitanya Himself (symbolized by the staff and waterpot).

PLATE TEN: The happiness of the *gopīs* increases ten million times when they serve to engage Śrī Śrī Rādhā and Kṛṣṇa in Their transcendental pastimes. (8.208)

PLATE ELEVEN: When Śrī Caitanya Mahāprabhu revealed to Rāmānanda Rāya His real form as Śrī Śrī Rādhā and Kṛṣṇa combined, Rāmānanda fainted in transcendental bliss. (8.282)

PLATE TWELVE: As the big bird flew away with the large plate in its beak, the untouchable food was strewn all over the Buddhists. Then the plate itself fell on the head of the chief Buddhist, knocking him unconscious. (9.54-55)

PLATE THIRTEEN: In Śrī Śaila, Caitanya Mahāprabhu visited Lord Śiva and his wife Durgā, who were dressed as *brāhmaṇas*. (9.175)

PLATE FOURTEEN: After Lord Rāmacandra had killed Rāvaṇa, the fire-god (Agni) delivered the real Sītā to the Lord. (9.206)

PLATE FIFTEEN: Śrīpāda Madhvācārya (11th century A.D.) is known throughout India for his erudite scholarship and devotion to the Lord. Śrī Caitanya Mahāprabhu chose to take intiation in his sampradāya, or disciplic line. (9.245)

PLATE SIXTEEN: Lord Caitanya embraced the seven palm trees and sent them all back to Vaikuṇṭha. (9.313)

PLATE SEVENTEEN: Upon returning from His South Indian tour, Lord Caitanya met all His devotees and took them into His private quarters, where He showed great love and affection for each of them. (11.130)

'kṛṣṇadāsa'-nāme ei sarala brāhmaṇa
iṅho saṅge kari' laha, dhara nivedana

kṛṣṇa-dāsa-nāme—named Kṛṣṇadāsa; *ei*—this; *sarala*—simple; *brāhmaṇa*—*brāhmaṇa; iṅho*—he; *saṅge*—with You; *kari'*—accepting; *laha*—take; *dhara*—just catch; *nivedana*—the petition.

TRANSLATION

Śrī Nityānanda Prabhu continued, "Here is a simple brāhmaṇa named Kṛṣṇadāsa. Please accept him and take him with You. That is My request.

PURPORT

This Kṛṣṇadāsa, known as Kālā Kṛṣṇadāsa, is not the Kālā Kṛṣṇadāsa mentioned in the Eleventh Chapter, verse 37, of the *Ādi-līlā.* The Kālā Kṛṣṇadāsa mentioned in the Eleventh Chapter is one of the twelve *gopālas* (cowherd boys) who appeared to substantiate the pastimes of Lord Caitanya Mahāprabhu. He is known as a great devotee of Lord Nityānanda Prabhu. The *brāhmaṇa* named Kālā Kṛṣṇadāsa who went with Śrī Caitanya to South India and later to Bengal is mentioned in the *Madhya-līlā,* Tenth Chapter, verses 62–79. One should not take these two to be the same person.

TEXT 40

জলপাত্র-বস্ত্র বহি' তোমা-সঙ্গে যাবে ।
যে তোমার ইচ্ছা, কর, কিছু না বলিবে ॥ ৪০ ॥

jala-pātra-vastra vahi' tomā-saṅge yābe
ye tomāra icchā, kara, kichu nā balibe

jala-pātra—waterpot; *vastra*—and garments; *vahi'*—carrying; *tomā-saṅge*—with You; *yābe*—will go; *ye*—whatever; *tomāra icchā*—Your desire; *kara*—You do; *kichu nā balibe*—he will not say anything.

TRANSLATION

"He will carry Your waterpot and garments. You may do whatever You like; he will not say a word."

TEXT 41

তবে তাঁর বাক্য প্রভু করি' অঙ্গীকারে।
তাহা-সবা লঞা গেলা সার্বভৌম ঘরে ॥ ৪১ ॥

tabe tāṅra vākya prabhu kari' aṅgīkāre
tāhā-sabā lañā gelā sārvabhauma-ghare

tabe—thereupon; *tāṅra*—of Lord Nityānanda Prabhu; *vākya*—the words; *prabhu*—Lord Caitanya Mahāprabhu; *kari'*—doing; *aṅgīkāre*—acceptance; *tāhā-sabā*—all of them; *lañā*—taking; *gelā*—went; *sārvabhauma-ghare*—to the house of Sārvabhauma Bhaṭṭācārya.

TRANSLATION

Accepting the request of Lord Nityānanda Prabhu, Lord Caitanya took all His devotees and went to the house of Sārvabhauma Bhaṭṭācārya.

TEXT 42

নমস্করি' সার্বভৌম আসন নিবেদিল।
সবাকারে মিলি' তবে আসনে বসিল ॥ ৪২ ॥

namaskari' sārvabhauma āsana nivedila
sabākāre mili' tabe āsane vasila

namaskari'—offering obeisances; *sārvabhauma*—Sārvabhauma Bhaṭṭācārya; *āsana*—sitting places; *nivedila*—offered; *sabākāre*—all of them; *mili'*—meeting; *tabe*—after that; *āsane vasila*—he took his seat.

TRANSLATION

As soon as they entered his house, Sārvabhauma Bhaṭṭācārya offered the Lord obeisances and a place to sit. After seating all the others, the Bhaṭṭācārya took his seat.

TEXT 43

নানা কৃষ্ণবার্তা কহি' কহিল তাঁহারে।
'তোমার ঠাঞি আইলাঙ আজ্ঞা মাগিবারে ॥ ৪৩ ॥

nānā kṛṣṇa-vārtā kahi' kahila tāṅhāre
'tomāra ṭhāñi āilāṅ ājñā māgibāre

nānā—various; *kṛṣṇa-vārtā*—topics on Lord Kṛṣṇa; *kahi'*—discussing; *kahila*—He informed; *tāṅhāre*—Sārvabhauma Bhaṭṭācārya; *tomāra ṭhāñi*—to your place; *āilāṅ*—I have come; *ājñā*—order; *māgibāre*—to beg.

TRANSLATION

After they had discussed various topics about Lord Kṛṣṇa, Śrī Caitanya Mahāprabhu informed Sārvabhauma Bhaṭṭācārya, "I have come to your place just to receive your order.

TEXT 44

সন্ন্যাস করি' বিশ্বরূপ গিয়াছে দক্ষিণে।
অবশ্য করিব আমি তাঁর অন্বেষণে ॥ ৪৪ ॥

sannyāsa kari' viśvarūpa giyāche dakṣiṇe
avaśya kariba āmi tāṅra anveṣaṇe

sannyāsa kari'—after accepting the *sannyāsa* order; *viśvarūpa*—Viśvarūpa (the elder brother of Śrī Caitanya Mahāprabhu); *giyāche*—has gone; *dakṣiṇe*—to South India; *avaśya*—certainly; *kariba*—shall do; *āmi*—I; *tāṅra*—of Him; *anveṣaṇe*—searching for.

TRANSLATION

"My elder brother, Viśvarūpa, has taken sannyāsa and gone to South India. Now I must go search for Him.

TEXT 45

আজ্ঞা দেহ, অবশ্য আমি দক্ষিণে চলিব।
তোমার আজ্ঞাতে সুখে লেউটি' আসিব' ॥ ৪৫ ॥

ājñā deha, avaśya āmi dakṣiṇe caliba
tomāra ājñāte sukhe leuṭi' āsiba'

ājñā deha—please give permission; *avaśya*—certainly; *āmi*—I; *dakṣiṇe*—in South India; *caliba*—shall go; *tomāra*—your; *ājñāte*—by the order; *sukhe*—in happiness; *leuṭi'*—returning; *āsiba*—I shall come.

TRANSLATION

"Please permit Me to go, for I must tour South India. With your permission, I shall soon return very happily."

TEXT 46

শুনি' সার্বভৌম হৈলা অত্যন্ত কাতর ।
চরণে ধরিয়া কহে বিষাদ-উত্তর ॥ ৪৬ ॥

śuni' sārvabhauma hailā atyanta kātara
caraṇe dhariyā kahe viṣāda-uttara

śuni'—hearing this; *sārvabhauma*—Sārvabhauma Bhaṭṭācārya; *hailā*—became; *atyanta*—greatly; *kātara*—agitated; *caraṇe*—the lotus feet; *dhariyā*—taking; *kahe*—says; *viṣāda*—of lamentation; *uttara*—a reply.

TRANSLATION

Upon hearing this, Sārvabhauma Bhaṭṭācārya became very much agitated. Catching hold of the lotus feet of Caitanya Mahāprabhu, he gave this sorrowful reply.

TEXT 47

'বহুজন্মের পুণ্যফলে পাইনু তোমার সঙ্গ ।
হেন-সঙ্গ বিধি মোর করিলেক ভঙ্গ ॥ ৪৭ ॥

'bahu-janmera puṇya-phale pāinu tomāra saṅga
hena-saṅga vidhi mora karileka bhaṅga

bahu-janmera—of many births; *puṇya-phale*—as the fruit of pious activities; *pāinu*—I got; *tomāra*—Your; *saṅga*—association; *hena-saṅga*—such association; *vidhi*—providence; *mora*—my; *karileka*—has done; *bhaṅga*—breaking.

TRANSLATION

"After many births, due to some pious activity I got Your association. Now providence is breaking this invaluable association.

TEXT 48

শিরে বজ্র পড়ে যদি, পুত্র মরি' যায়।
তাহা সহি, তোমার বিচ্ছেদ সহন না যায় ॥ ৪৮ ॥

śire vajra paḍe yadi, putra mari' yāya
tāhā sahi, tomāra viccheda sahana nā yāya

śire—on the head; *vajra*—a thunderbolt; *paḍe*—falls; *yadi*—if; *putra*—son; *mari'*—dying; *yāya*—goes; *tāhā*—that; *sahi*—I can tolerate; *tomāra*—Your; *viccheda*—separation; *sahana*—enduring; *nā yāya*—cannot be done.

TRANSLATION

"If a thunderbolt falls on my head or if my son dies, I can tolerate it. But I cannot endure the unhappiness of separation from You.

TEXT 49

স্বতন্ত্র-ঈশ্বর তুমি করিবে গমন।
দিন কথো রহ, দেখি তোমার চরণ' ॥ ৪৯ ॥

svatantra-īśvara tumi karibe gamana
dina katho raha, dekhi tomāra caraṇa'

svatantra-īśvara—the independent Supreme Personality of Godhead; *tumi*—You; *karibe*—will make; *gamana*—departure; *dina*—days; *katho*—some; *raha*—please stay; *dekhi*—I may see; *tomāra caraṇa*—Your lotus feet.

TRANSLATION

"My dear Lord, You are the independent Supreme Personality of Godhead. Certainly You will depart. I know that. Still, I ask You to stay here a few days more so that I can see Your lotus feet."

TEXT 50

তাহার বিনয়ে প্রভুর শিথিল হৈল মন।
রহিল দিবস কথো, না কৈল গমন ॥ ৫০ ॥

tāhāra vinaye prabhura śithila haila mana
rahila divasa katho, nā kaila gamana

tāhāra—of Sārvabhauma Bhaṭṭācārya; *vinaye*—on the request; *prabhura*—of Lord Śrī Caitanya Mahāprabhu; *śithila*—slackened; *haila*—became; *mana*—the mind; *rahila*—stayed; *divasa*—days; *katho*—a few; *nā*—not; *kaila*—did; *gamana*—departure.

TRANSLATION

Upon hearing Sārvabhauma Bhaṭṭācārya's request, Caitanya Mahāprabhu relented. He stayed a few days longer and did not depart.

TEXT 51

ভট্টাচার্য আগ্রহ করি' করেন নিমন্ত্রণ।
গৃহে পাক করি' প্রভুকে করা'ন ভোজন ॥ ৫১ ॥

bhaṭṭācārya āgraha kari' karena nimantraṇa
gṛhe pāka kari' prabhuke karā'na bhojana

bhaṭṭācārya—Sārvabhauma Bhaṭṭācārya; *āgraha*—eagerness; *kari'*—showing; *karena*—did; *nimantraṇa*—invitation; *gṛhe*—at home; *pāka*—cooking; *kari'*—doing; *prabhuke*—Lord Śrī Caitanya Mahāprabhu; *karā'na*—made; *bhojana*—eating.

TRANSLATION

The Bhaṭṭācārya eagerly invited Lord Caitanya Mahāprabhu to his home and fed Him very nicely.

TEXT 52

তাঁহার ব্রাহ্মণী, তাঁর নাম — 'ষাঠীর মাতা'।
রান্ধি' ভিক্ষা দেন তেঁহো, আশ্চর্য তাঁর কথা ॥ ৫২ ॥

tāṅhāra brāhmaṇī, tāṅra nāma — 'ṣāṭhīra mātā'
rāndhi' bhikṣā dena teṅho, āścarya tāṅra kathā

tāṅhāra brāhmaṇī — his wife; *tāṅra nāma* — her name; *ṣāṭhīra mātā* — the mother of Ṣāṭhī; *rāndhi'* — cooking; *bhikṣā dena* — offers food; *teṅho* — she; *āścarya* — wonderful; *tāṅra* — her; *kathā* — narration.

TRANSLATION

The Bhaṭṭācārya's wife, whose name was Ṣāṭhīmātā ["the mother of Ṣāṭhī"], did the cooking. The narrations of these pastimes are very wonderful.

TEXT 53

আগে ত' কহিব তাহা করিয়া বিস্তার।
এবে কহি প্রভুর দক্ষিণ-যাত্রা-সমাচার ॥ ৫৩ ॥

āge ta' kahiba tāhā kariyā vistāra
ebe kahi prabhura dakṣiṇa-yātrā-samācāra

āge — later; *ta'* — indeed; *kahiba* — I shall speak; *tāhā* — all those incidents; *kariyā* — doing; *vistāra* — elaboration; *ebe* — now; *kahi* — let me describe; *prabhura* — of Lord Caitanya Mahāprabhu; *dakṣiṇa* — in South India; *yātrā* — of the touring; *samācāra* — the narration.

TRANSLATION

Later I shall tell about this in elaborate detail, but at present I wish to describe Śrī Caitanya Mahāprabhu's South Indian tour.

TEXT 54

দিন পাঁচ রহি' প্রভু ভট্টাচার্য-স্থানে।
চলিবার লাগি' আজ্ঞা মাগিলা আপনে ॥ ৫৪ ॥

dina pāṅca rahi' prabhu bhaṭṭācārya-sthāne
calibāra lāgi' ājñā māgilā āpane

dina pāṅca—five days; *rahi'*—staying; *prabhu*—Lord Śrī Caitanya Mahāprabhu; *bhaṭṭācārya-sthāne*—at Sārvabhauma Bhaṭṭācārya's place; *calibāra lāgi'*—for starting; *ājñā*—order; *māgilā*—begged; *āpane*—personally.

TRANSLATION

After staying five days at the home of Sārvabhauma Bhaṭṭācārya, Śrī Caitanya Mahāprabhu personally asked his permission to depart for South India.

TEXT 55

প্রভুর আগ্রহে ভট্টাচার্য সম্মত হইলা।
প্রভু তাঁরে লঞা জগন্নাথ-মন্দিরে গেলা ॥ ৫৫ ॥

prabhura āgrahe bhaṭṭācārya sammata ha-ilā
prabhu tāṅre lañā jagannātha-mandire gelā

prabhura āgrahe—by the eagerness of Śrī Caitanya Mahāprabhu; *bhaṭṭācārya*—Sārvabhauma Bhaṭṭācārya; *sammata ha-ilā*—became agreeable; *prabhu*—Lord Śrī Caitanya Mahāprabhu; *tāṅre*—him (Sārvabhauma Bhaṭṭācārya); *lañā*—taking; *jagannātha-mandire*—to the temple of Lord Jagannātha; *gelā*—went.

TRANSLATION

After receiving the Bhaṭṭācārya's permission, Lord Caitanya Mahāprabhu went to see Lord Jagannātha in the temple. He took the Bhaṭṭācārya with Him.

TEXT 56

দর্শন করি' ঠাকুর-পাশ আজ্ঞা মাগিলা।
পূজারী প্রভুরে মালা-প্রসাদ আনি' দিলা ॥ ৫৬ ॥

darśana kari' ṭhākura-pāśa ājñā māgilā
pūjārī prabhure mālā-prasāda āni' dilā

darśana kari'—visiting the Lord; *ṭhākura-pāśa*—from the Lord; *ājñā māgilā*—begged permission; *pūjārī*—the priest; *prabhure*—unto

Lord Śrī Caitanya Mahāprabhu; *mālā* — garland; *prasāda* — remnants of food; *āni'* — bringing; *dilā* — delivered.

TRANSLATION

Seeing Lord Jagannātha, Śrī Caitanya Mahāprabhu also begged His permission. The priest then immediately delivered prasādam and a garland to Lord Caitanya.

TEXT 57

আজ্ঞা-মালা পাঞা হর্ষে নমস্কার করি' ।
আনন্দে দক্ষিণ-দেশে চলে গৌরহরি ॥ ৫৭ ॥

ājñā-mālā pāñā harṣe namaskāra kari'
ānande dakṣiṇa-deśe cale gaurahari

ājñā-mālā — the garland of permission; *pāñā* — getting; *harṣe* — in great jubilation; *namaskāra* — obeisances; *kari'* — offering; *ānande* — with great pleasure; *dakṣiṇa-deśe* — to South India; *cale* — goes; *gaurahari* — Lord Śrī Caitanya Mahāprabhu.

TRANSLATION

Thus receiving Lord Jagannātha's permission in the form of a garland, Śrī Caitanya Mahāprabhu offered obeisances, and then in great jubilation He prepared to depart for South India.

TEXT 58

ভট্টাচার্য-সঙ্গে আর যত নিজগণ ।
জগন্নাথ প্রদক্ষিণ করি' করিলা গমন ॥ ৫৮ ॥

bhaṭṭācārya-saṅge āra yata nija-gaṇa
jagannātha pradakṣiṇa kari' karilā gamana

bhaṭṭācārya-saṅge — with Sārvabhauma Bhaṭṭācārya; *āra* — and; *yata* — all; *nija-gaṇa* — personal devotees; *jagannātha* — Lord Jagannātha; *pradakṣiṇa* — circumambulation; *kari'* — finishing; *karilā* — made; *gamana* — departure.

TRANSLATION

Accompanied by His personal associates and Sārvabhauma Bhaṭṭācārya, Śrī Caitanya Mahāprabhu circumambulated the altar of Jagannātha. The Lord then departed on His South Indian tour.

TEXT 59

সমুদ্র-তীরে তীরে আলালনাথ-পথে ।
সার্বভৌম কহিলেন আচার্য-গোপীনাথে ॥ ৫৯ ॥

samudra-tīre tīre ālālanātha-pathe
sārvabhauma kahilena ācārya-gopīnāthe

samudra-tīre—on the shore of the sea; *tīre*—on the shore; *ālālanātha-pathe*—on the path to the temple of Ālālanātha; *sārvabhauma*—Sārvabhauma Bhaṭṭācārya; *kahilena*—said; *ācārya-gopīnāthe*—to Gopīnātha Ācārya.

TRANSLATION

While the Lord was going along the path to Ālālanātha, which was located on the seashore, Sārvabhauma Bhaṭṭācārya gave the following orders to Gopīnātha Ācārya.

TEXT 60

চারি কৌপীন-বহির্বাস রাখিয়াছি ঘরে ।
তাহা, প্রসাদান্ন, লঞা আইস বিপ্রদ্বারে ॥ ৬০ ॥

cāri kopīna-bahirvāsa rākhiyāchi ghare
tāhā, prasādānna, lañā āisa vipra-dvāre

cāri kopīna-bahirvāsa—four sets of loincloths and external clothing; *rākhiyāchi*—I have kept; *ghare*—at home; *tāhā*—that; *prasāda-anna*—remnants of food of Lord Jagannātha; *lañā*—taking; *āisa*—come here; *vipra-dvāre*—by means of some *brāhmaṇa.*

TRANSLATION

"Bring the four sets of loincloths and outer garments I keep at home, and also some prasādam of Lord Jagannātha. You may carry these things with the help of some brāhmaṇa."

TEXT 61

তবে সার্বভৌম কহে প্রভুর চরণে।
অবশ্য পালিবে, প্রভু, মোর নিবেদনে ॥ ৬১ ॥

tabe sārvabhauma kahe prabhura caraṇe
avaśya pālibe, prabhu, mora nivedane

tabe—thereafter; *sārvabhauma*—Sārvabhauma Bhaṭṭācārya; *kahe*—said; *prabhura caraṇe*—unto the lotus feet of the Lord; *avaśya*—certainly; *pālibe*—You will keep; *prabhu*—my Lord; *mora*—my; *nivedane*—request.

TRANSLATION

While Śrī Caitanya Mahāprabhu was departing, Sārvabhauma Bhaṭṭācārya submitted the following at His lotus feet, "My Lord, I have one final request that I hope You will kindly fulfill.

TEXT 62

'রামানন্দ রায়' আছে গোদাবরী-তীরে।
অধিকারী হয়েন তেঁহো বিদ্যানগরে ॥ ৬২ ॥

'rāmānanda rāya' āche godāvarī-tīre
adhikārī hayena teṅho vidyānagare

rāmānanda rāya—Rāmānanda Rāya; *āche*—there is; *godāvarī-tīre*—on the bank of river Godāvarī; *adhikārī*—a responsible officer; *hayena*—is; *teṅho*—he; *vidyānagare*—in the town known as Vidyānagara.

TRANSLATION

"In the town of Vidyānagara, on the bank of the Godāvarī, there is a responsible government officer named Rāmānanda Rāya.

PURPORT

In the *Amṛta-pravāha-bhāṣya,* Śrīla Bhaktivinoda Ṭhākura states that Vidyānagara is today known as Porbandar. There is another Porbandar in western India, in the province of Gujarat.

TEXT 63

শূদ্র বিষয়ি-জ্ঞানে উপেক্ষা না করিবে।
আমার বচনে তাঁরে অবশ্য মিলিবে ॥ ৬৩ ॥

śūdra viṣayi-jñāne upekṣā nā karibe
āmāra vacane tāṅre avaśya milibe

śūdra—the fourth social division; *viṣayi-jñāne*—by the impression of being a worldly man; *upekṣā*—negligence; *nā karibe*—should not do; *āmāra*—my; *vacane*—on the request; *tāṅre*—him; *avaśya*—certainly; *milibe*—You should meet.

TRANSLATION

"Please do not neglect him, thinking he belongs to a śūdra family engaged in material activities. It is my request that You meet him without fail."

PURPORT

In the *varṇāśrama-dharma,* the *śūdra* is the fourth division in the social status. *Paricaryātmakaṁ karma śūdrasyāpi svabhāva-jam* (Bg. 18.44). *Śūdras* are meant to engage in the service of the three higher classes—*brāhmaṇas, kṣatriyas* and *vaiśyas.* Śrī Rāmānanda Rāya belonged to the *karaṇa* class, which is the equivalent of the *kāyastha* class in Bengal. This class is regarded all over India as *śūdra.* It is said that the Bengali *kāyasthas* were originally engaged as servants of *brāhmaṇas* who came from North India to Bengal. Later, the clerical class became the *kāyasthas* in Bengal. Now there are many mixed classes known as *kāyastha.* Sometimes it is said in Bengal that those who cannot claim any particular class belong to the *kāyastha* class. Although these *kāyasthas* or *karaṇas* are considered *śūdras,* they are very intelligent and highly educated. Most of them are professionals such as lawyers or politicians. Thus in Bengal the *kāyasthas* are sometimes considered *kṣatriyas.* In Orissa, however, the *kāyastha* class, which includes the *karaṇas,* is considered in the *śūdra* category. Śrīla Rāmānanda Rāya belonged to this *karaṇa* class; therefore he was considered a *śūdra.* He was also the governor of South India under the regime of Mahārāja Pratāparudra of Orissa.

In other words, Sārvabhauma Bhaṭṭācārya informed Lord Caitanya Mahāprabhu that Rāmānanda Rāya, although belonging to the *śūdra* class, was a highly responsible government officer. As far as spiritual advancement is concerned, materialists, politicians and *śūdras* are generally disqualified. Sārvabhauma Bhaṭṭācārya therefore requested that Lord Caitanya Mahāprabhu not neglect Rāmānanda Rāya, who was highly advanced spiritually although he was born a *śūdra* and a materialist.

A *viṣayī* is one who is attached to family life and is interested only in wife, children and worldly sense gratification. The senses can be engaged either in worldly enjoyment or in the service of the Lord. Those who are not engaged in the service of the Lord and are interested only in material sense gratification are called *viṣayī.* Śrīla Rāmānanda Rāya was engaged in government service, and he belonged to the *karaṇa* class. He was certainly not a *sannyāsī* in saffron cloth, yet he was in the transcendental position of a *paramahaṁsa* householder. Before becoming Caitanya Mahāprabhu's disciple, Sārvabhauma Bhaṭṭācārya considered Rāmānanda Rāya an ordinary *viṣayī* because he was a householder engaged in government service. However, when the Bhaṭṭācārya was actually enlightened in Vaiṣṇava philosophy, he could understand the exalted transcendental position of Śrī Rāmānanda Rāya; therefore he referred to him as *adhikārī.* An *adhikārī* is one who knows the transcendental science of Kṛṣṇa and is engaged in His service; therefore all *gṛhastha* devotees are designated as *dāsa adhikārī.*

TEXT 64

তোমার সঙ্গের যোগ্য তেঁহো এক জন ।
পৃথিবীতে রসিক ভক্ত নাহি তাঁর সম ॥ ৬৪ ॥

tomāra saṅgera yogya teṅho eka jana
pṛthivīte rasika bhakta nāhi tāṅra sama

tomāra—Your; *saṅgera*—of association; *yogya*—fit; *teṅho*—he (Rāmānanda Rāya); *eka*—one; *jana*—person; *pṛthivīte*—in the world; *rasika*—expert in transcendental mellows; *bhakta*—devotee; *nāhi*—there is none; *tāṅra sama*—like him.

TRANSLATION

Sārvabhauma Bhaṭṭācārya continued, "Rāmānanda Rāya is a fit person to associate with You; no other devotee can compare with him in knowledge of the transcendental mellows.

TEXT 65

পাণ্ডিত্য আর ভক্তিরস, — দুঁহের তেঁহো সীমা।
সম্ভাষিলে জানিবে তুমি তাঁহার মহিমা ॥ ৬৫ ॥

pāṇḍitya āra bhakti-rasa, — duṅhera teṅho sīmā
sambhāṣile jānibe tumi tāṅhāra mahimā

pāṇḍitya — learning; *āra* — and; *bhakti-rasa* — the mellows of devotional service; *duṅhera* — of these two; *teṅho* — he; *sīmā* — the limit; *sambhāṣile* — when You talk with him; *jānibe* — will know; *tumi* — You; *tāṅhāra* — his; *mahimā* — glories.

TRANSLATION

"He is a most learned scholar as well as an expert in devotional mellows. Actually he is most exalted, and if You talk with him, You will see how glorious he is.

TEXT 66

অলৌকিক বাক্য চেষ্টা তাঁর না বুঝিয়া।
পরিহাস করিয়াছি তাঁরে 'বৈষ্ণব' বলিয়া ॥ ৬৬ ॥

alaukika vākya ceṣṭā tāṅra nā bujhiyā
parihāsa kariyāchi tāṅre 'vaiṣṇava' baliyā

alaukika — uncommon; *vākya* — words; *ceṣṭā* — endeavor; *tāṅra* — his; *nā* — without; *bujhiyā* — understanding; *parihāsa* — joking; *kariyāchi* — I have done; *tāṅre* — unto him; *vaiṣṇava* — a devotee of the Lord; *baliyā* — as.

TRANSLATION

"I could not realize when I first spoke with Rāmānanda Rāya that his topics and endeavors were all transcendentally uncommon. I made fun of him simply because he was a Vaiṣṇava."

PURPORT

Anyone who is a not a Vaiṣṇava, or an unalloyed devotee of the Supreme Lord, must be a materialist. A Vaiṣṇava living according to Śrī Caitanya Mahāprabhu's injunctions is certainly not on the materialistic platform. Caitanya means "spiritual force." All of Śrī Caitanya Mahāprabhu's activities were carried out on the platform of spiritual understanding; therefore only those who are on the spiritual platform are able to understand the activities of Śrī Caitanya Mahāprabhu. Materialistic persons cannot understand these activities and are generally known as *karmīs* or *jñānīs.* The *jñānīs* are mental speculators who simply try to understand what is spirit and what is matter. Their process is *neti neti:* "This is not spirit, this is not Brahman." The *jñānīs* are a little more advanced than the dull-headed *karmīs,* who are simply interested in sense gratification. Before becoming a Vaiṣṇava, Sārvabhauma Bhaṭṭācārya was a mental speculator (*jñānī*), and being such, he always cut jokes with Vaiṣṇavas. A Vaiṣṇava never agrees with the speculative system of the *jñānīs.* Both the *jñānīs* and *karmīs* depend on direct sense perception for their imperfect knowledge. The *karmīs* never agree to accept anything not directly perceived, and the *jñānīs* put forth only hypotheses. However, the Vaiṣṇavas, the unalloyed devotees of the Lord, do not follow the process of acquiring knowledge by direct sense perception or mental speculation. Because they are servants of the Supreme Lord, devotees receive knowledge directly from the Supreme Personality of Godhead as He speaks it in the *Bhagavad-gītā,* or sometimes as He imparts it from within as the *caittya-guru.* As Lord Kṛṣṇa states in the *Bhagavad-gītā* (10.10):

teṣāṁ satata-yuktānāṁ bhajatāṁ prīti-pūrvakam
dadāmi buddhi-yogaṁ taṁ yena mām upayānti te

"To those who are constantly devoted to serving Me with love, I give the understanding by which they can come to Me."

The *Vedas* are considered to have been spoken by the Supreme Lord. They were first realized by Brahmā, who is the first created being within the universe (*tene brahma hṛdā ya ādi-kavaye*). Our process is to receive knowledge through the *paramparā* system, from Kṛṣṇa to Brahmā, to Nārada, Vyāsa, Śrī Caitanya Mahāprabhu and the six

Gosvāmīs. By disciplic succession, Lord Brahmā was enlightened from within by the original person, Kṛṣṇa. Our knowledge is fully perfect due to being handed from master to disciple. A Vaiṣṇava is always engaged in the transcendental loving service of the Lord, and thus neither *karmīs* nor *jñānīs* can understand the activities of a Vaiṣṇava. It is said, *vaiṣṇavera kriyā-mudrā vijñeha nā bujhaya:* even the most learned man depending on direct perception of knowledge cannot understand the activities of a Vaiṣṇava. After being initiated into Vaiṣṇavism by Śrī Caitanya Mahāprabhu, Sārvabhauma Bhaṭṭācārya realized what a mistake he had made in trying to understand Rāmānanda Rāya, who was very learned and whose endeavors were all directed to rendering transcendental loving service to the Lord.

TEXT 67

তোমার প্রসাদে এবে জানিনু তাঁর তত্ত্ব।
সম্ভাষিলে জানিবে তাঁর যেমন মহত্ত্ব ॥ ৬৭ ॥

tomāra prasāde ebe jāninu tāṅra tattva
sambhāṣile jānibe tāṅra yemana mahattva

tomāra prasāde—by Your mercy; *ebe*—now; *jāninu*—I have understood; *tāṅra*—of him (Rāmānanda Rāya); *tattva*—the truth; *sambhāṣile*—in talking together; *jānibe*—You will know; *tāṅra*—his; *yemana*—such; *mahattva*—greatness.

TRANSLATION

The Bhaṭṭācārya said, "By Your mercy I can now understand the truth about Rāmānanda Rāya. In talking with him, You also will acknowledge his greatness."

TEXT 68

অঙ্গীকার করি' প্রভু তাঁহার বচন।
তাঁরে বিদায় দিতে তাঁরে কৈল আলিঙ্গন ॥ ৬৮ ॥

aṅgīkāra kari' prabhu tāṅhāra vacana
tāṅre vidāya dite tāṅre kaila āliṅgana

aṅgīkāra kari'—accepting this proposal; *prabhu*—Lord Caitanya Mahāprabhu; *tāṅhāra*—of him (Sārvabhauma Bhaṭṭācārya); *vacana*—the request; *tāṅre*—unto him; *vidāya dite*—to offer farewell; *tāṅre*—him; *kaila*—did; *āliṅgana*—embracing.

TRANSLATION

Lord Śrī Caitanya Mahāprabhu accepted Sārvabhauma Bhaṭṭācārya's request that He meet Rāmānanda Rāya. Bidding Sārvabhauma farewell, the Lord embraced him.

TEXT 69

"ঘরে কৃষ্ণ ভজি' মোরে করিহ আশীর্বাদে।
নীলাচলে আসি' যেন তোমার প্রসাদে॥" ৬৯॥

"ghare kṛṣṇa bhaji' more kariha āśīrvāde
nīlācale āsi' yena tomāra prasāde"

ghare—at home; *kṛṣṇa*—Lord Kṛṣṇa; *bhaji'*—worshiping; *more*—unto Me; *kariha*—do; *āśīrvāde*—blessing; *nīlācale*—at Jagannātha Purī; *āsi'*—returning; *yena*—so that; *tomāra*—your; *prasāde*—by the mercy.

TRANSLATION

Śrī Caitanya Mahāprabhu asked the Bhaṭṭācārya to bless Him while he engaged in the devotional service of Lord Kṛṣṇa at home, so that by Sārvabhauma's mercy the Lord could return to Jagannātha Purī.

PURPORT

The word *kariha āśīrvāde* means "continue to bestow your blessings upon Me." Being a *sannyāsī,* Caitanya Mahāprabhu was in the fourth order of life and was thus due all respect and adoration, whereas Sārvabhauma Bhaṭṭācārya, as a householder, was in the second order. A *sannyāsī* is supposed to offer blessings to a *gṛhastha,* yet now, by His practical behavior, Śrī Caitanya Mahāprabhu requested the blessings of a *gṛhastha.* This incident shows the special significance of Śrī Caitanya Mahāprabhu's preaching. He gave equal status to everyone, regardless of material considerations. His movement is thoroughly spiritual. Although apparently a *gṛhastha* (householder), Sārvabhauma Bhaṭṭācārya was unlike the so-called *karmīs* interested in sense gratification. After being initiated by Śrī Caitanya Mahāprabhu, the Bhaṭṭācārya was perfectly situated in the spiritual order; therefore it was quite possible for him to offer blessings even to a *sannyāsī.* He was always engaged in the service of the Lord, even at home. In our disciplic line we have the example of a perfect householder *paramahaṁsa*—Śrīla Bhaktivinoda Ṭhākura. In his book *Śaraṇāgati,* Bhaktivinoda Ṭhākura states, *ye-dina gṛhe, bhajana dekhi', gṛhete goloka bhāya* (*Śaraṇāgati* 31.6). Whenever a householder glorifies the Supreme Lord in his home, his activities are immediately transformed into the activities of Goloka Vṛndāvana, spiritual activities taking place in the Goloka Vṛndāvana planet of Kṛṣṇa. Activities exhibited by Kṛṣṇa Himself at Bhauma Vṛndāvana, the Vṛndāvana-dhāma existing on this planet, are not different from His activities on the planet Goloka Vṛndāvana. This is proper realization of Vṛndāvana anywhere. In our Kṛṣṇa consciousness movement we inaugurated the New Vṛndāvana activities, wherein devotees are always engaged in the transcendental loving service of the Lord, and this is not different from Goloka Vṛndāvana. The conclusion is that one who acts strictly in the line of Śrī Caitanya Mahāprabhu is competent to offer blessings to *sannyāsīs,* even though he be a *gṛhastha* householder. Although he is in an exalted position, a *sannyāsī* still must elevate himself to the transcendental platform by rendering service to the Lord. By His actual behavior, Caitanya Mahāprabhu begged the blessings of Sārvabhauma Bhaṭṭācārya. In this way He set the example of how one should expect blessings from a Vaiṣṇava regardless of his social position.

TEXT 70

এত বলি' মহাপ্রভু করিলা গমন।
মূর্চ্ছিত হঞা তাহাঁ পড়িলা সার্বভৌম ॥ ৭০ ॥

eta bali' mahāprabhu karilā gamana
mūrcchita hañā tāhāṅ paḍilā sārvabhauma

eta bali'—saying this; *mahāprabhu*—Śrī Caitanya Mahāprabhu; *karilā*—made; *gamana*—departure; *mūrcchita*—fainted; *hañā*—becoming; *tāhāṅ*—there; *paḍilā*—fell down; *sārvabhauma*—Sārvabhauma Bhaṭṭācārya.

TRANSLATION

Saying this, Śrī Caitanya Mahāprabhu departed on His tour, and Sārvabhauma Bhaṭṭācārya immediately fainted and fell to the ground.

TEXT 71

তাঁরে উপেক্ষিয়া কৈল শীঘ্র গমন ।
কে বুঝিতে পারে মহাপ্রভুর চিত্ত-মন ॥ ৭১ ॥

tāṅre upekṣiyā kaila śīghra gamana
ke bujhite pāre mahāprabhura citta-mana

tāṅre—unto Sārvabhauma Bhaṭṭācārya; *upekṣiyā*—not paying serious attention; *kaila*—did; *śīghra*—very fast; *gamana*—walking; *ke*—who; *bujhite*—to understand; *pāre*—is able; *mahāprabhura*—of Śrī Caitanya Mahāprabhu; *citta-mana*—the mind and intention.

TRANSLATION

Although Sārvabhauma Bhaṭṭācārya fainted, Śrī Caitanya Mahāprabhu did not take notice of him. Rather, He left quickly. Who can understand the mind and intention of Śrī Caitanya Mahāprabhu?

PURPORT

It was naturally expected that when Sārvabhauma Bhaṭṭācārya fainted and fell to the ground Śrī Caitanya Mahāprabhu would have taken care of him and waited for him to regain consciousness, but He did not do so. Rather, Śrī Caitanya Mahāprabhu immediately started on His tour. It is therefore very difficult to understand the activities of a transcendental person. Sometimes they may seem rather odd, but a transcendental personality remains in his position, unaffected by material considerations.

TEXT 72

মহানুভাবের চিত্তের স্বভাব এই হয়।
পুষ্প-সম কোমল, কঠিন বজ্রময় ॥ ৭২ ॥

mahānubhāvera cittera svabhāva ei haya
puṣpa-sama komala, kaṭhina vajra-maya

mahā-anubhāvera—of a great personality; *cittera*—of the mind; *svabhāva*—the nature; *ei haya*—this is; *puṣpa-sama*—like a flower; *komala*—soft; *kaṭhina*—hard; *vajra-maya*—like a thunderbolt.

TRANSLATION

This is the nature of the mind of an uncommon personality. Sometimes it is soft like a flower, but sometimes it is as hard as a thunderbolt.

PURPORT

The softness of a flower and the hardness of a thunderbolt are reconciled in the behavior of a great personality. The following quotation from *Uttara-rāma-carita* (2.7) explains this behavior. One may also consult the *Madhya-līlā,* Third Chapter, verse 212.

TEXT 73

বজ্রাদপি কঠোরাণি মৃদূনি কুসুমাদপি।
লোকোত্তরাণাং চেতাংসি কো নু বিজ্ঞাতুমীশ্বরঃ ॥ ৭৩ ॥

vajrād api kaṭhorāṇi
mṛdūni kusumād api
lokottarāṇāṁ cetāṁsi
ko nu vijñātum īśvaraḥ

vajrāt api—than a thunderbolt; *kaṭhorāṇi*—harder; *mṛdūni*—softer; *kusumāt api*—than a flower; *loka-uttarāṇām*—persons above the human platform of behavior; *cetāṁsi*—the hearts; *kaḥ*—who; *nu*—but; *vijñātum*—to understand; *īśvaraḥ*—able.

TRANSLATION

"The hearts of those who are above common behavior are sometimes harder than a thunderbolt and sometimes softer than a flower. How can one accommodate such contradictions in great personalities?"

TEXT 74

নিত্যানন্দপ্রভু ভট্টাচার্যে উঠাইল ।
তাঁর লোকসঙ্গে তাঁরে ঘরে পাঠাইল ॥ ৭৪ ॥

nityānanda prabhu bhaṭṭācārye uṭhāila
tāṅra loka-saṅge tāṅre ghare pāṭhāila

nityānanda prabhu—Lord Śrī Nityānanda Prabhu; *bhaṭṭācārye*—Sārvabhauma Bhaṭṭācārya; *uṭhāila*—raised; *tāṅra*—His; *loka-saṅge*—along with associates; *tāṅre*—him (the Bhaṭṭācārya); *ghare*—to his home; *pāṭhāila*—sent.

TRANSLATION

Lord Nityānanda Prabhu raised Sārvabhauma Bhaṭṭācārya and with the help of His men saw him to his home.

TEXT 75

ভক্তগণ শীঘ্র আসি' লৈল প্রভুর সাথ ।
বস্ত্র-প্রসাদ লঞা তবে আইলা গোপীনাথ ॥ ৭৫ ॥

bhakta-gaṇa śīghra āsi' laila prabhura sātha
vastra-prasāda lañā tabe āilā gopīnātha

bhakta-gaṇa—devotees; *śīghra*—very swiftly; *āsi'*—coming; *laila*—took; *prabhura*—of the Lord; *sātha*—the company; *vastra*—the garments; *prasāda*—and Lord Jagannātha's *prasādam; lañā*—with; *tabe*—thereafter; *āilā*—came; *gopīnātha*—Gopīnātha Ācārya.

TRANSLATION

Immediately all the devotees came and partook of Śrī Caitanya Mahāprabhu's company. Afterwards, Gopīnātha Ācārya came with the garments and prasādam.

TEXT 76

সবা-সঙ্গে প্রভু তবে আলালনাথ আইলা ।
নমস্কার করি' তারে বহুস্তুতি কৈলা ॥ ৭৬ ॥

sabā-saṅge prabhu tabe ālālanātha āilā
namaskāra kari' tāre bahu-stuti kailā

sabā-saṅge—with all of them; *prabhu*—Lord Śrī Caitanya Mahāprabhu; *tabe*—then; *ālālanātha*—the place named Ālālanātha; *āilā*—reached; *namaskāra kari'*—offering obeisances; *tāre*—Lord Śrī Caitanya Mahāprabhu; *bahu-stuti*—many prayers; *kailā*—offered.

TRANSLATION

All the devotees followed Śrī Caitanya Mahāprabhu to a place known as Ālālanātha. There they all offered respects and various prayers.

TEXT 77

প্রেমাবেশে নৃত্যগীত কৈল কতক্ষণ ।
দেখিতে আইলা তাহাঁ বৈসে যত জন ॥ ৭৭ ॥

premāveśe nṛtya-gīta kaila kata-kṣaṇa
dekhite āilā tāhāṅ vaise yata jana

prema-āveśe—in the great ecstasy of love of Godhead; *nṛtya-gīta*—dancing and chanting; *kaila*—performed; *kata-kṣaṇa*—for some time; *dekhite*—to see; *āilā*—came; *tāhāṅ*—there; *vaise*—who live; *yata jana*—all the men.

TRANSLATION

In great ecstasy, Śrī Caitanya Mahāprabhu danced and chanted for some time. Indeed, all the neighbors came to see Him.

TEXT 78

চৌদিকেতে সব লোক বলে 'হরি' 'হরি'।
প্রেমাবেশে মধ্যে নৃত্য করে গৌরহরি ॥ ৭৮ ॥

caudikete saba loka bale 'hari' 'hari'
premāveśe madhye nṛtya kare gaurahari

caudikete—all around; *saba loka*—all persons; *bale*—shout; *hari hari*—the holy name of the Lord; *prema-āveśe*—in ecstatic love; *madhye*—in the middle; *nṛtya kare*—dances; *gaurahari*—Śrī Caitanya Mahāprabhu.

TRANSLATION

All around Śrī Caitanya Mahāprabhu, who is also known as Gaurahari, people began to shout the holy name of Hari. Lord Caitanya, immersed in His usual ecstasy of love, danced in the midst of them.

TEXT 79

কাঞ্চন-সদৃশ দেহ, অরুণ বসন।
পুলকাশ্রু-কম্প-স্বেদ তাহাতে ভূষণ ॥ ৭৯ ॥

kāñcana-sadṛśa deha, aruṇa vasana
pulakāśru-kampa-sveda tāhāte bhūṣaṇa

kāñcana-sadṛśa—like molten gold; *deha*—a body; *aruṇa*—saffron; *vasana*—garments; *pulaka-aśru*—standing up of bodily hair and crying; *kampa*—trembling; *sveda*—perspiration; *tāhāte*—therein; *bhūṣaṇa*—the ornaments.

TRANSLATION

The body of Śrī Caitanya Mahāprabhu was naturally very beautiful. It was like molten gold dressed in saffron cloth. Indeed, He was most beautiful for being ornamented with the ecstatic symptoms, which caused His bodily hair to stand on end, tears to well up in His eyes, and His body to tremble and perspire all over.

TEXT 80

দেখিয়া লোকের মনে হৈল চমৎকার ।
যত লোক আইসে, কেহ নাহি যায় ঘর ॥ ৮০ ॥

dekhiyā lokera mane haila camatkāra
yata loka āise, keha nāhi yāya ghara

dekhiyā—seeing all this; *lokera*—of the people; *mane*—in the minds; *haila*—there was; *camatkāra*—astonishment; *yata*—all; *loka*—people; *āise*—came there; *keha*—anyone; *nāhi*—not; *yāya*—goes; *ghara*—home.

TRANSLATION

Everyone present was astonished to see Śrī Caitanya Mahāprabhu's dancing and His bodily transformations. Whoever came did not want to return home.

TEXT 81

কেহ নাচে, কেহ গায়, 'শ্রীকৃষ্ণ' 'গোপাল' ।
প্রেমেতে ভাসিল লোক,—স্ত্রী-বৃদ্ধ-আবাল ॥ ৮১ ॥

keha nāce, keha gāya, 'śrī-kṛṣṇa' 'gopāla'
premete bhāsila loka,—strī-vṛddha-ābāla

keha nāce—someone dances; *keha gāya*—someone chants; *śrī-kṛṣṇa*—Lord Śrī Kṛṣṇa's name; *gopāla*—Gopāla's name; *premete*—in love of Godhead; *bhāsila*—floated; *loka*—all the people; *strī*—women; *vṛddha*—old men; *ā-bāla*—from the children.

TRANSLATION

Everyone—including children, old men and women—began to dance and to chant the holy names of Śrī Kṛṣṇa and Gopāla. In this way they all floated in the ocean of love of Godhead.

TEXT 82

দেখি' নিত্যানন্দ প্রভু কহে ভক্তগণে ।
এইরূপে নৃত্য আগে হবে গ্রামে-গ্রামে ॥ ৮২ ॥

dekhi' nityānanda prabhu kahe bhakta-gaṇe
ei-rūpe nṛtya āge habe grāme-grāme

dekhi'—seeing this; *nityānanda*—Lord Nityānanda Prabhu; *prabhu*—the Lord; *kahe*—says; *bhakta-gaṇe*—unto the devotees; *ei-rūpe*—in this way; *nṛtya*—dancing; *āge*—ahead; *habe*—there will be; *grāme-grāme*—in every village.

TRANSLATION

Upon seeing the chanting and dancing of Lord Śrī Caitanya Mahāprabhu, Lord Nityānanda predicted that later there would be dancing and chanting in every village.

PURPORT

This prediction of Śrī Nityānanda Prabhu's is applicable not only in India but also all over the world. That is now happening by His grace. The members of the International Society for Krishna Consciousness are now traveling from one village to another in the Western countries and are even carrying the Deity with them. These devotees distribute various literatures all over the world. We hope that these devotees who are preaching the message of Śrī Caitanya Mahāprabhu will very seriously follow strictly in His footsteps. If they follow the rules and regulations and chant sixteen rounds daily, their endeavor to preach the cult of Śrī Caitanya Mahāprabhu will certainly be successful.

TEXT 83

অতিকাল হৈল, লোক ছাড়িয়া না যায়।
তবে নিত্যানন্দ-গোসাঞি সৃজিলা উপায় ॥ ৮৩ ॥

atikāla haila, loka chāḍiyā nā yāya
tabe nityānanda-gosāñi sṛjilā upāya

atikāla—very late; *haila*—it was; *loka*—the people in general; *chāḍiyā*—giving up; *nā yāya*—do not go; *tabe*—at that time; *nityānanda*—Śrīla Nityānanda Prabhu; *gosāñi*—the spiritual master; *sṛjilā*—invented; *upāya*—a means.

TRANSLATION

Seeing that it was already getting late, Lord Nityānanda Prabhu, the spiritual master, invented a means to disperse the crowd.

TEXT 84

মধ্যাহ্ন করিতে গেলা প্রভুকে লঞা।
তাহা দেখি' লোক আইসে চৌদিকে ধাঞা ॥ ৮৪ ॥

madhyāhna karite gelā prabhuke lañā
tāhā dekhi' loka āise caudike dhāñā

madhyāhna karite—to take lunch at noon; *gelā*—went; *prabhuke*—Lord Śrī Caitanya Mahāprabhu; *lañā*—taking; *tāhā dekhi'*—seeing that; *loka*—the people in general; *āise*—came; *caudike*—all around; *dhāñā*—running.

TRANSLATION

When Lord Nityānanda Prabhu took Śrī Caitanya Mahāprabhu for lunch at noon, everyone came running around Them.

TEXT 85

মধ্যাহ্ন করিয়া আইলা দেবতা-মন্দিরে।
নিজগণ প্রবেশি' কপাট দিল বহির্দ্বারে ॥ ৮৫ ॥

madhyāhna kariyā āilā devatā-mandire
nija-gaṇa praveśi' kapāṭa dila bahir-dvāre

madhyāhna kariyā—performing bathing, etc.; *āilā*—came back; *devatā-mandire*—to the temple of the Lord; *nija-gaṇa praveśi'*—allowing His own men; *kapāṭa dila*—shut; *bahir-dvāre*—the outside door.

TRANSLATION

After finishing Their baths, They returned at noon to the temple. Admitting His own men, Śrī Nityānanda Prabhu closed the outside door.

TEXT 86

তবে গোপীনাথ দুইপ্রভুরে ভিক্ষা করাইল।
প্রভুর শেষ প্রসাদান্ন সবে বাঁটি' খাইল ॥ ৮৬ ॥

tabe gopīnātha dui-prabhure bhikṣā karāila
prabhura śeṣa prasādānna sabe bāṅṭi' khāila

tabe—thereupon; *gopīnātha*—Gopīnātha Ācārya; *dui-prabhure*—unto the two Lords Caitanya Mahāprabhu and Nityānanda Prabhu; *bhikṣā karāila*—gave *prasādam* to eat; *prabhura*—of the Lord; *śeṣa*—the remnants; *prasāda-anna*—food; *sabe*—all of them; *bāṅṭi'*—sharing; *khāila*—ate.

TRANSLATION

Gopīnātha Ācārya then brought prasādam for the two Lords to eat, and after They had eaten, the remnants of the food were distributed to all the devotees.

TEXT 87

শুনি' শুনি' লোক-সব আসি' বহির্দ্বারে।
'হরি' 'হরি' বলি' লোক কোলাহল করে ॥ ৮৭ ॥

śuni' śuni' loka-saba āsi' bahir-dvāre
'hari' 'hari' bali' loka kolāhala kare

śuni' śuni'—hearing this; *loka-saba*—all the people; *āsi'*—coming there; *bahir-dvāre*—to the outside door; *hari hari*—the holy name of the Lord; *bali'*—chanting; *loka*—all the people; *kolāhala*—tumultuous sound; *kare*—made.

TRANSLATION

Hearing about this, everyone there came to the outside door and began chanting the holy name, "Hari! Hari!" Thus there was a tumultuous sound.

TEXT 88

তবে মহাপ্রভু দ্বার করাইল মোচন।
আনন্দে আসিয়া লোক পাইল দরশন ॥ ৮৮ ॥

tabe mahāprabhu dvāra karāila mocana
ānande āsiyā loka pāila daraśana

tabe—thereupon; *mahāprabhu*—Śrī Caitanya Mahāprabhu; *dvāra*—the door; *karāila*—made; *mocana*—opening; *ānande*—in great pleasure; *āsiyā*—coming; *loka*—all the people; *pāila*—got; *daraśana*—sight.

TRANSLATION

After lunch, Śrī Caitanya Mahāprabhu made them open the door. In this way everyone received His audience with great pleasure.

TEXT 89

এইমত সন্ধ্যা পর্যন্ত লোক আসে, যায়।
'বৈষ্ণব' হইল লোক, সবে নাচে, গায় ॥ ৮৯ ॥

ei-mata sandhyā paryanta loka āse, yāya
'vaiṣṇava' ha-ila loka, sabe nāce, gāya

ei-mata—in this way; *sandhyā paryanta*—until evening; *loka*—people; *āse yāya*—come and go; *vaiṣṇava*—devotees; *ha-ila*—became; *loka*—all the people; *sabe*—all of them; *nāce*—dance; *gāya*—and chant.

TRANSLATION

The people came and went until evening, and all of them became Vaiṣṇava devotees and began to chant and dance.

TEXT 90

এইরূপে সেই ঠাঞি ভক্তগণ-সঙ্গে।
সেই রাত্রি গোঙাইলা কৃষ্ণকথা-রঙ্গে ॥ ৯০ ॥

ei-rūpe sei ṭhāñi bhakta-gaṇa-saṅge
sei rātri goṅāilā kṛṣṇa-kathā-raṅge

ei-rūpe—in this way; *sei ṭhāñi*—in that place; *bhakta-gaṇa-saṅge*—with the devotees; *sei rātri*—that night; *goṅāilā*—passed; *kṛṣṇa-kathā-raṅge*—in great pleasure discussing Lord Kṛṣṇa.

TRANSLATION

Śrī Caitanya Mahāprabhu then passed the night there and discussed the pastimes of Lord Kṛṣṇa with His devotees with great pleasure.

TEXT 91

প্রাতঃকালে স্নান করি' করিলা গমন ।
ভক্তগণে বিদায় দিলা করি' আলিঙ্গন ॥ ৯১ ॥

prātaḥ-kāle snāna kari' karilā gamana
bhakta-gaṇe vidāya dilā kari' āliṅgana

prātaḥ-kāle—in the morning; *snāna*—bath; *kari'*—after taking; *karilā*—started; *gamana*—tour; *bhakta-gaṇe*—to all the devotees; *vidāya*—farewell; *dilā*—gave; *kari'*—doing; *āliṅgana*—embracing.

TRANSLATION

The next morning, after taking His bath, Śrī Caitanya Mahāprabhu started on His South Indian tour. He bade farewell to the devotees by embracing them.

TEXT 92

মূর্চ্ছিত হঞা সবে ভূমিতে পড়িলা ।
তাঁহা-সবা পানে প্রভু ফিরি' না চাহিলা ॥ ৯২ ॥

mūrcchita hañā sabe bhūmite paḍilā
tāṅhā-sabā pāne prabhu phiri' nā cāhilā

mūrcchita hañā—becoming unconscious; *sabe*—all; *bhūmite*—to the ground; *paḍilā*—fell down; *tāṅhā-sabā*—all of them;

pāne—toward; *prabhu*—Lord Śrī Caitanya Mahāprabhu; *phiri'*—turning; *nā*—not; *cāhilā*—saw.

TRANSLATION

Although they all fell to the ground unconscious, the Lord did not turn to see them but proceeded onward.

TEXT 93

বিচ্ছেদে ব্যাকুল প্রভু চলিলা দুঃখী হঞা ।
পাছে কৃষ্ণদাস যায় জলপাত্র লঞা ॥ ৯৩ ॥

vicchede vyākula prabhu calilā duḥkhī hañā
pāche kṛṣṇadāsa yāya jala-pātra lañā

vicchede—in separation; *vyākula*—perturbed; *prabhu*—Lord Śrī Caitanya Mahāprabhu; *calilā*—went on; *duḥkhī*—unhappy; *hañā*—becoming; *pāche*—just behind; *kṛṣṇadāsa*—His servant Kṛṣṇadāsa; *yāya*—went; *jala-pātra*—the waterpot; *lañā*—taking.

TRANSLATION

In separation, the Lord became very much perturbed and walked on unhappily. His servant, Kṛṣṇadāsa, who was carrying His waterpot, followed behind.

TEXT 94

ভক্তগণ উপবাসী তাহাঁই রহিলা ।
আর দিনে দুঃখী হঞা নীলাচলে আইলা ॥ ৯৪ ॥

bhakta-gaṇa upavāsī tāhāṅi rahilā
āra dine duḥkhī hañā nīlācale āilā

bhakta-gaṇa—the devotees; *upavāsī*—fasting; *tāhāṅi*—there; *rahilā*—remained; *āra dine*—on the next day; *duḥkhī*—unhappy; *hañā*—becoming; *nīlācale*—to Jagannātha Purī; *āilā*—returned.

TRANSLATION

All the devotees remained there and fasted, and the next day they all unhappily returned to Jagannātha Purī.

TEXT 95

মত্তসিংহ-প্রায় প্রভু করিলা গমন।
প্রেমাবেশে যায় করি' নাম-সংকীর্তন ॥ ৯৫ ॥

matta-siṁha-prāya prabhu karilā gamana
premāveśe yāya kari' nāma-saṅkīrtana

matta-siṁha—a mad lion; *prāya*—almost like; *prabhu*—Lord Śrī Caitanya Mahāprabhu; *karilā*—did; *gamana*—touring; *prema-āveśe*—in ecstatic love; *yāya*—goes; *kari'*—performing; *nāma-saṅkīrtana*—chanting Kṛṣṇa's name.

TRANSLATION

Almost like a mad lion, Lord Śrī Caitanya Mahāprabhu went on His tour filled with ecstatic love and performing saṅkīrtana, chanting Kṛṣṇa's names as follows.

TEXT 96

কৃষ্ণ! কৃষ্ণ! কৃষ্ণ! কৃষ্ণ! কৃষ্ণ! কৃষ্ণ! কৃষ্ণ! হে।
কৃষ্ণ! কৃষ্ণ! কৃষ্ণ! কৃষ্ণ! কৃষ্ণ! কৃষ্ণ! কৃষ্ণ! হে ॥
কৃষ্ণ! কৃষ্ণ! কৃষ্ণ! কৃষ্ণ! কৃষ্ণ! কৃষ্ণ! রক্ষ মাম্।
কৃষ্ণ! কৃষ্ণ! কৃষ্ণ! কৃষ্ণ! কৃষ্ণ! কৃষ্ণ! পাহি মাম্ ॥
রাম! রাঘব! রাম! রাঘব! রাম! রাঘব! রক্ষ মাম্।
কৃষ্ণ! কেশব! কৃষ্ণ! কেশব! কৃষ্ণ! কেশব! পাহি মাম্ ॥ ৯৬ ॥

kṛṣṇa! kṛṣṇa! kṛṣṇa! kṛṣṇa! kṛṣṇa! kṛṣṇa! kṛṣṇa! he
kṛṣṇa! kṛṣṇa! kṛṣṇa! kṛṣṇa! kṛṣṇa! kṛṣṇa! kṛṣṇa! he
kṛṣṇa! kṛṣṇa! kṛṣṇa! kṛṣṇa! kṛṣṇa! kṛṣṇa! rakṣa mām
kṛṣṇa! kṛṣṇa! kṛṣṇa! kṛṣṇa! kṛṣṇa! kṛṣṇa! pāhi mām
rāma! rāghava! rāma! rāghava! rāma! rāghava! rakṣa mām
kṛṣṇa! keśava! kṛṣṇa! keśava! kṛṣṇa! keśava! pāhi mām

kṛṣṇa—Lord Kṛṣṇa; *he*—O; *rakṣa*—please protect; *mām*—Me; *pāhi*—please maintain; *rāma*—Lord Rāma; *rāghava*—descendant of King Raghu; *keśava*—killer of the Keśī demon.

TRANSLATION

The Lord chanted:

Kṛṣṇa! Kṛṣṇa! Kṛṣṇa! Kṛṣṇa! Kṛṣṇa! Kṛṣṇa! Kṛṣṇa! he
Kṛṣṇa! Kṛṣṇa! Kṛṣṇa! Kṛṣṇa! Kṛṣṇa! Kṛṣṇa! Kṛṣṇa! he
Kṛṣṇa! Kṛṣṇa! Kṛṣṇa! Kṛṣṇa! Kṛṣṇa! Kṛṣṇa! rakṣa mām
Kṛṣṇa! Kṛṣṇa! Kṛṣṇa! Kṛṣṇa! Kṛṣṇa! Kṛṣṇa! pāhi mām

That is, "O Lord Kṛṣṇa, please protect Me and maintain Me." He also chanted:

Rāma! Rāghava! Rāma! Rāghava! Rāma! Rāghava! rakṣa mām
Kṛṣṇa! Keśava! Kṛṣṇa! Keśava! Kṛṣṇa! Keśava! pāhi mām

That is, "O Lord Rāma, descendant of King Raghu, please protect Me. O Kṛṣṇa, O Keśava, killer of the Keśī demon, please maintain Me."

TEXT 97

এই শ্লোক পড়ি' পথে চলিলা গৌরহরি ।
লোক দেখি' পথে কহে, —বল 'হরি' 'হরি' ॥ ৯৭ ॥

ei śloka paḍi' pathe calilā gaurahari
loka dekhi' pathe kahe, —bala 'hari' 'hari'

ei śloka paḍi'—reciting this verse *kṛṣṇa! kṛṣṇa!; pathe*—on the way; *calilā*—went; *gaurahari*—Lord Śrī Caitanya Mahāprabhu; *loka dekhi'*—seeing other people; *pathe*—on the way; *kahe*—He says; *bala*—say; *hari hari*—the holy name of Lord Hari.

TRANSLATION

Chanting this verse, Lord Śrī Caitanya Mahāprabhu, known as Gaurahari, went on His way. As soon as He saw someone, He would request him to chant "Hari! Hari!"

TEXT 98

সেই লোক প্রেমমত্ত হঞা বলে 'হরি' 'কৃষ্ণ' ।
প্রভুর পাছে সঙ্গে যায় দর্শন-সতৃষ্ণ ॥ ৯৮ ॥

sei loka prema-matta hañā bale 'hari' 'kṛṣṇa'
prabhura pāche saṅge yāya darśana-satṛṣṇa

sei loka—that person; *prema-matta*—maddened in love of Godhead; *hañā*—becoming; *bale*—says; *hari kṛṣṇa*—the holy name of Lord Hari and Lord Kṛṣṇa; *prabhura pāche*—behind the Lord; *saṅge*—with Him; *yāya*—goes; *darśana-satṛṣṇa*—being very eager to see Him.

TRANSLATION

Whoever heard Lord Caitanya Mahāprabhu chant "Hari! Hari!" also chanted the holy name of Lord Hari and Kṛṣṇa. In this way they all followed the Lord, very eager to see Him.

TEXT 99

কতক্ষণে রহি' প্রভু তারে আলিঙ্গিয়া ।
বিদায় করিল তারে শক্তি সঞ্চারিয়া ॥ ৯৯ ॥

kata-kṣaṇe rahi' prabhu tāre āliṅgiyā
vidāya karila tāre śakti sañcāriyā

kata-kṣaṇe rahi'—after remaining for some time; *prabhu*—Lord Śrī Caitanya Mahāprabhu; *tāre*—each of them; *āliṅgiyā*—embracing; *vidāya karila*—bade farewell; *tāre*—in each of them; *śakti*—spiritual potency; *sañcāriyā*—investing.

TRANSLATION

After some time the Lord would embrace these people and bid them return home, having invested each of them with spiritual potency.

PURPORT

In his *Amṛta-pravāha-bhāṣya,* Śrīla Bhaktivinoda Ṭhākura explains that this spiritual potency is the essence of the pleasure potency and the knowledge potency. By these two potencies, one is empowered with devotional service. Lord Kṛṣṇa Himself or His representative, the unalloyed devotee, can mercifully bestow these combined potencies upon any man. Being thus endowed with such potencies, one can become an unalloyed devotee of the Lord. Anyone favored by Lord Śrī Caitanya Mahāprabhu was empowered with this *bhakti-śakti.*

Thus the Lord's followers were able to preach Kṛṣṇa consciousness by divine grace.

TEXT 100

সেইজন নিজ-গ্রামে করিয়া গমন ।
'কৃষ্ণ' বলি' হাসে, কান্দে, নাচে অনুক্ষণ ॥ ১০০ ॥

sei-jana nija-grāme kariyā gamana
'kṛṣṇa' bali' hāse, kānde, nāce anukṣaṇa

sei-jana—that person; *nija-grāme*—to his own village; *kariyā gamana*—returning there; *kṛṣṇa bali'*—saying the holy name of Lord Kṛṣṇa; *hāse*—laughs; *kānde*—cries; *nāce*—dances; *anukṣaṇa*—always.

TRANSLATION

Each of these empowered persons would return to his own village, always chanting the holy name of Kṛṣṇa and sometimes laughing, crying and dancing.

TEXT 101

যারে দেখে, তারে কহে, —কহ কৃষ্ণনাম ।
এইমত 'বৈষ্ণব' কৈল সব নিজ-গ্রাম ॥ ১০১ ॥

yāre dekhe, tāre kahe,—kaha kṛṣṇa-nāma
ei-mata 'vaiṣṇava' kaila saba nija-grāma

yāre dekhe—whomever he meets; *tāre*—to him; *kahe*—he says; *kaha kṛṣṇa-nāma*—kindly chant the Hare Kṛṣṇa *mantra; ei-mata*—in this way; *vaiṣṇava*—devotees of the Supreme Personality of Godhead; *kaila*—made; *saba*—all; *nija-grāma*—his own village.

TRANSLATION

Such an empowered person would request everyone and anyone—whomever he saw—to chant the holy name of Kṛṣṇa. In this way all the villagers would also become devotees of the Supreme Personality of Godhead.

PURPORT

In order to become an empowered preacher, one must be favored by Lord Śrī Caitanya Mahāprabhu or His devotee, the spiritual master. One must also request everyone to chant the *mahā-mantra.* In this way, such a person can convert others to Vaiṣṇavism, showing them how to become pure devotees of the Supreme Personality of Godhead.

TEXT 102

গ্রামান্তর হৈতে দেখিতে আইল যত জন।
তাঁর দর্শন-কৃপায় হয় তাঁর সম ॥ ১০২ ॥

grāmāntara haite dekhite āila yata jana
tāṅra darśana-kṛpāya haya tāṅra sama

grāma-antara haite—from different villages; *dekhite*—to see; *āila*—came; *yata jana*—all the persons; *tāṅra*—his; *darśana-kṛpāya*—by the mercy of seeing him; *haya*—become; *tāṅra sama*—similar Vaiṣṇavas.

TRANSLATION

People from different villages who came to see such an empowered individual would become like him simply by seeing him and receiving the mercy of his glance.

TEXT 103

সেই যাই' গ্রামের লোক বৈষ্ণব করয়।
অন্যগ্রামী আসি' তাঁরে দেখি' বৈষ্ণব হয় ॥ ১০৩ ॥

sei yāi' grāmera loka vaiṣṇava karaya
anya-grāmī āsi' tāṅre dekhi' vaiṣṇava haya

sei—that Vaiṣṇava; *yāi'*—going to his own village; *grāmera loka*—all the people of the village; *vaiṣṇava*—devotees; *karaya*—makes; *anya-grāmī*—inhabitants from different villages; *āsi'*—coming there; *tāṅre dekhi'*—by seeing him; *vaiṣṇava haya*—become devotees.

TRANSLATION

When each of these newly empowered individuals returned to his own village, he also converted the villagers into devotees. And when others came from different villages to see him, they were also converted.

TEXT 104

সেই যাই' আর গ্রামে করে উপদেশ।
এইমত 'বৈষ্ণব' হৈল সব দক্ষিণ-দেশ॥ ১০৪॥

sei yāi' āra grāme kare upadeśa
ei-mata 'vaiṣṇava' haila saba dakṣiṇa-deśa

sei—that man; *yāi'*—going; *āra*—different; *grāme*—to the villages; *kare*—gives; *upadeśa*—instruction; *ei-mata*—in this way; *vaiṣṇava*—devotees; *haila*—became; *saba*—all; *dakṣiṇa-deśa*—the people of South India.

TRANSLATION

In this way, as empowered men went from one village to another, all the people of South India became devotees.

TEXT 105

এইমত পথে যাইতে শত শত জন।
'বৈষ্ণব' করেন তাঁরে করি' আলিঙ্গন॥ ১০৫॥

ei-mata pathe yāite śata śata jana
'vaiṣṇava' karena tāṅre kari' āliṅgana

ei-mata—in this way; *pathe*—on the way; *yāite*—while passing; *śata śata*—hundreds and hundreds; *jana*—persons; *vaiṣṇava*—devotees; *karena*—makes; *tāṅre*—Him; *kari'*—doing; *āliṅgana*—embracing.

TRANSLATION

Thus many hundreds of people became Vaiṣṇavas when they passed the Lord on the way and were embraced by Him.

TEXT 106

যেই গ্রামে রহি' ভিক্ষা করেন যাঁর ঘরে ।
সেই গ্রামের যত লোক আইসে দেখিবারে ॥ ১০৬ ॥

yei grāme rahi' bhikṣā karena yāṅra ghare
sei grāmera yata loka āise dekhibāre

yei grāme—in whatever village; *rahi'*—staying; *bhikṣā*—alms; *karena*—accepts; *yāṅra*—whose; *ghare*—at home; *sei*—that; *grāmera*—of the village; *yata loka*—all the persons; *āise*—come; *dekhibāre*—to see.

TRANSLATION

In whatever village Śrī Caitanya Mahāprabhu stayed to accept alms, many people came to see Him.

TEXT 107

প্রভুর কৃপায় হয় মহাভাগবত ।
সেই সব আচার্য হঞা তারিল জগৎ ॥ ১০৭ ॥

prabhura kṛpāya haya mahābhāgavata
sei saba ācārya hañā tārila jagat

prabhura kṛpāya—by the mercy of the Lord; *haya*—become; *mahā-bhāgavata*—first-class devotees; *sei saba*—all such persons; *ācārya*—teachers; *hañā*—becoming; *tārila*—liberated; *jagat*—the whole world.

TRANSLATION

By the mercy of the Supreme Lord, Śrī Caitanya Mahāprabhu, all these persons became first-class devotees. Later they became teachers or spiritual masters and liberated the entire world.

TEXT 108

এইমত কৈলা যাবৎ গেলা সেতুবন্ধে ।
সর্বদেশ 'বৈষ্ণব' হৈল প্রভুর সম্বন্ধে ॥ ১০৮ ॥

ei-mata kailā yāvat gelā setubandhe
sarva-deśa 'vaiṣṇava' haila prabhura sambandhe

ei-mata—in this way; *kailā*—performed; *yāvat*—until; *gelā*—went; *setubandhe*—to the southernmost part of India; *sarva-deśa*—all the countries; *vaiṣṇava*—devotees; *haila*—became; *prabhura*—Lord Śrī Caitanya Mahāprabhu; *sambandhe*—in connection with.

TRANSLATION

In this way the Lord went to the extreme southern part of India, and He converted all the provinces to Vaiṣṇavism.

TEXT 109

নবদ্বীপে যেই শক্তি না কৈলা প্রকাশে ।
সে শক্তি প্রকাশি' নিস্তারিল দক্ষিণদেশে ॥ ১০৯ ॥

navadvīpe yei śakti nā kailā prakāśe
se śakti prakāśi' nistārila dakṣiṇa-deśe

navadvīpe—at Navadvīpa; *yei*—that which; *śakti*—the potency; *nā*—not; *kailā*—did; *prakāśe*—manifestation; *se*—that; *śakti*—potency; *prakāśi'*—manifesting; *nistārila*—delivered; *dakṣiṇa-deśe*—South India.

TRANSLATION

Lord Śrī Caitanya Mahāprabhu did not manifest His spiritual potencies at Navadvīpa, but He did manifest them in South India and liberated all the people there.

PURPORT

At that time there were many *smārtas* (nondevotee followers of Vedic rituals) at the holy place of Navadvīpa, which was also the birthplace of Lord Śrī Caitanya Mahāprabhu. Followers of the *smṛti-śāstra* are called *smārtas.* Most of them are nondevotees, and their main business is following the brahminical principles strictly. However, they are not enlightened in devotional service. In Navadvīpa all the learned scholars are followers of the *smṛti-śāstra,* and Lord Caitanya Mahāprabhu did not attempt to convert them.

Therefore the author has remarked that the spiritual potency Lord Śrī Caitanya Mahāprabhu did not manifest at Navadvīpa was by His grace manifested in South India. Thus everyone there became a Vaiṣṇava. By this it is to be understood that people are really interested in preaching in a favorable situation. If the candidates for conversion are too disturbing, a preacher may not attempt to spread Kṛṣṇa consciousness amongst them. It is better to go where the situation is more favorable. This Kṛṣṇa consciousness movement was first attempted in India, but the people of India, being absorbed in political thoughts, did not take to it. They were entranced by the political leaders. We preferred, therefore, to come to the West, following the order of our spiritual master, and by the grace of Lord Caitanya Mahāprabhu this movement is becoming successful.

TEXT 110

প্রভুকে যে ভজে, তারে তাঁর কৃপা হয়।
সেই সে এ-সব লীলা সত্য করি' লয় ॥ ১১০ ॥

prabhuke ye bhaje, tāre tāṅra kṛpā haya
sei se e-saba līlā satya kari' laya

prabhuke—Lord Śrī Caitanya Mahāprabhu; *ye*—anyone who; *bhaje*—worships; *tāre*—unto him; *tāṅra*—of Lord Caitanya Mahāprabhu; *kṛpā*—the mercy; *haya*—there is; *sei se*—such person; *e-saba*—all these; *līlā*—pastimes; *satya*—truth; *kari'*—accepting as; *laya*—takes.

TRANSLATION

Lord Śrī Caitanya Mahāprabhu's empowering of others can be understood by one who is actually a devotee of the Lord and who has received His mercy.

TEXT 111

অলৌকিক-লীলায় যার না হয় বিশ্বাস।
ইহলোক, পরলোক তার হয় নাশ ॥ ১১১ ॥

alaukika-līlāya yāra nā haya viśvāsa
iha-loka, para-loka tāra haya nāśa

alaukika—uncommon; *līlāya*—in the pastimes; *yāra*—of someone; *nā*—not; *haya*—there is; *viśvāsa*—faith; *iha-loka*—in this world; *para-loka*—in the next world; *tāra*—of him; *haya*—there is; *nāśa*—destruction.

TRANSLATION

If one does not believe in the uncommon transcendental pastimes of the Lord, he is vanquished both in this world and in the next.

TEXT 112

প্রথমেই কহিল প্রভুর যেরূপে গমন ।
এইমত জানিহ যাবৎ দক্ষিণ-ভ্রমণ ॥ ১১২ ॥

prathamei kahila prabhura ye-rūpe gamana
ei-mata jāniha yāvat dakṣiṇa-bhramaṇa

prathamei—at the beginning; *kahila*—I have explained; *prabhura*—of Lord Śrī Caitanya Mahāprabhu; *ye-rūpe*—as; *gamana*—the touring; *ei-mata*—in this way; *jāniha*—you should know; *yāvat*—as long as; *dakṣiṇa-bhramaṇa*—touring in South India.

TRANSLATION

Whatever I have stated about the beginning of the Lord's tour should also be understood to hold for as long as the Lord toured South India.

TEXT 113

এইমত যাইতে যাইতে গেলা কূর্মস্থানে ।
কূর্ম দেখি' কৈল তাঁরে স্তবন-প্রণামে ॥ ১১৩ ॥

ei-mata yāite yāite gelā kūrma-sthāne
kūrma dekhi' kaila tāṅre stavana-praṇāme

ei-mata—in this way; *yāite yāite*—while passing; *gelā*—He went; *kūrma-sthāne*—to the place of pilgrimage known as Kūrma-kṣetra; *kūrma dekhi'*—seeing Lord Kūrma; *kaila*—offered; *tāṅre*—unto Him; *stavana*—prayers; *praṇāme*—and obeisances.

TRANSLATION

When Lord Śrī Caitanya Mahāprabhu came to the holy place known as Kūrma-kṣetra, He saw the Deity and offered prayers and obeisances.

PURPORT

Kūrma-sthāna is a well-known place of pilgrimage. There is a temple there of Kūrmadeva. In the *Prapannāmṛta* it is said that Lord Jagannātha took Śrī Rāmānujācārya from Jagannātha Purī and one night threw him to Kūrma-kṣetra. Kūrma-kṣetra is situated on the line of the Southern Railway in India. One has to go to the railway station known as Cikā Kola Road. From this station one goes eight miles to the east to reach the holy place known as Kūrmācala. Those who speak the Telugu language consider this holy place very important. This statement is reported in the government gazette known as *Gañjāma Manual.* There is the Deity of Kūrma there, and, as mentioned above, Śrīla Rāmānujācārya was thrown from Jagannātha Purī to this place. At that time he thought that the Deity of Kūrma was Lord Śiva's deity; therefore he was fasting there. Later, when he understood that the *kūrma-mūrti* was another form of Lord Viṣṇu, he instituted very gorgeous worship of Lord Kūrma. This statement is found in the *Prapannāmṛta* (Chapter Thirty-six). The holy place of Kūrma-kṣetra, or Kūrma-sthāna, was actually reestablished by Śrīpāda Rāmānujācārya under the influence of Lord Jagannātha-deva at Jagannātha Purī. Later the temple came under the jurisdiction of the king of Vijaya-nagara. The Deity was worshiped by the Vaiṣṇavas of the Madhvācārya-sampradāya. In the temple there are some inscriptions said to be written by Śrī Narahari Tīrtha, who was in the disciplic succession of Madhvācārya. Śrīla Bhaktisiddhānta Sarasvatī Ṭhākura explains those inscriptions as follows: (1) Śrī Puruṣottama Yati appeared as the instructor of many learned men. He was a very favorite devotee of Lord Viṣṇu. (2) His preaching was accepted throughout the world with great respect, and by his power he liberated many nondevotees with strong reason and logic. (3) He initiated Ānanda Tīrtha and converted many foolish men to accept *sannyāsa* and punished them with his rod. (4) All his writings and words are very potent. He gave people devotional service to Lord

Viṣṇu so they could be elevated to liberation in the spiritual world. (5) His instructions in devotional service were able to elevate any man to the lotus feet of the Lord. (6) Narahari Tīrtha was also initiated by him and became the ruler of Kaliṅga Province. (7) Narahari Tīrtha fought with the Śabaras, who were *caṇḍālas,* or hunters, and thus saved the temple of Kūrma. (8) Narahari Tīrtha was a very religious and powerful king. (9) He died in the Śaka Era 1203, in the month of Vaiśākha, in the fortnight of the moon's waxing period, on the day of Ekādaśī, after the temple was constructed and dedicated to the holy name of Yogānanda Nṛsiṁhadeva. The tablet is dated 1281 A.D., 29 March, Saturday.

TEXT 114

প্রেমাবেশে হাসি' কান্দি' নৃত্য-গীত কৈল ।
দেখি' সর্ব লোকের চিত্তে চমৎকার হৈল ॥ ১১৪ ॥

premāveśe hāsi' kāndi' nṛtya-gīta kaila
dekhi' sarva lokera citte camatkāra haila

prema-āveśe—in great ecstasy of love of Godhead; *hāsi'*—laughing; *kāndi'*—crying; *nṛtya-gīta*—dancing and chanting; *kaila*—performed; *dekhi'*—seeing; *sarva lokera*—of all the people there; *citte*—within the hearts; *camatkāra*—astonishment; *haila*—there was.

TRANSLATION

While at this place, Lord Śrī Caitanya Mahāprabhu was in His usual ecstasy of love of Godhead and was laughing, crying, dancing and chanting. Everyone who saw Him was astonished.

TEXT 115

আশ্চর্য শুনিয়া লোক আইল দেখিবারে ।
প্রভুর রূপ-প্রেম দেখি' হৈলা চমৎকারে ॥ ১১৫ ॥

āścarya śuniyā loka āila dekhibāre
prabhura rūpa-prema dekhi' hailā camatkāre

āścarya—wonderful occurrence; *śuniyā*—hearing; *loka*—people; *āila*—came; *dekhibāre*—to see; *prabhura*—of Lord Śrī Caitanya

Mahāprabhu; *rūpa*—beauty; *prema*—and love of Godhead; *dekhi'*—seeing; *hailā*—there was; *camatkāre*—astonishment.

TRANSLATION

After hearing of these wonderful occurrences, everyone came to see Him there. When they saw the beauty of the Lord and His ecstatic condition, they were all struck with wonder.

TEXT 116

দর্শনে 'বৈষ্ণব' হৈল, বলে 'কৃষ্ণ' 'হরি'।
প্রেমাবেশে নাচে লোক ঊর্ধ্ববাহু করি' ॥ ১১৬ ॥

darśane 'vaiṣṇava' haila, bale 'kṛṣṇa' 'hari'
premāveśe nāce loka ūrdhva bāhu kari'

darśane—in seeing; *vaiṣṇava haila*—they became devotees; *bale*—started to say; *kṛṣṇa*—Lord Kṛṣṇa; *hari*—Lord Hari; *prema-āveśe*—in the great ecstasy of love of Godhead; *nāce*—dance; *loka*—all the people; *ūrdhva bāhu kari'*—raising the arms.

TRANSLATION

Just by seeing Lord Caitanya Mahāprabhu, everyone became a devotee. They began to chant "Kṛṣṇa" and "Hari" and all the holy names. They all were merged in a great ecstasy of love, and they began to dance, raising their arms.

TEXT 117

কৃষ্ণনাম লোকমুখে শুনি' অবিরাম।
সেই লোক 'বৈষ্ণব' কৈল অন্য সব গ্রাম ॥ ১১৭ ॥

kṛṣṇa-nāma loka-mukhe śuni' avirāma
sei loka 'vaiṣṇava' kaila anya saba grāma

kṛṣṇa-nāma—the holy name of Lord Kṛṣṇa; *loka-mukhe*—from the mouth of those people; *śuni'*—hearing; *avirāma*—always; *sei loka*—those persons; *vaiṣṇava*—devotees; *kaila*—made; *anya*—other; *saba*—all; *grāma*—villages.

TRANSLATION

Always hearing them chant the holy names of Lord Kṛṣṇa, the residents of all the other villages also became Vaiṣṇavas.

TEXT 118

এইমত পরম্পরায় দেশ 'বৈষ্ণব' হৈল ।
কৃষ্ণনামামৃত-বন্যায় দেশ ভাসাইল ॥ ১১৮ ॥

ei-mata paramparāya deśa 'vaiṣṇava' haila
kṛṣṇa-nāmāmṛta-vanyāya deśa bhāsāila

ei-mata—in this way; *paramparāya*—by disciplic succession; *deśa*—the country; *vaiṣṇava haila*—became devotees; *kṛṣṇa-nāma-amṛta*—of the nectar of the holy name of Kṛṣṇa; *vanyāya*—in the inundation; *deśa*—the whole country; *bhāsāila*—overflooded.

TRANSLATION

By hearing the holy name of Kṛṣṇa, the entire country became Vaiṣṇava. It was as if the nectar of the holy name of Kṛṣṇa overflooded the entire country.

TEXT 119

কতক্ষণে প্রভু যদি বাহ্য প্রকাশিলা ।
কূর্মের সেবক বহু সম্মান করিলা ॥ ১১৯ ॥

kata-kṣaṇe prabhu yadi bāhya prakāśilā
kūrmera sevaka bahu sammāna karilā

kata-kṣaṇe—after some time; *prabhu*—Lord Caitanya Mahāprabhu; *yadi*—when; *bāhya*—external consciousness; *prakāśilā*—manifested; *kūrmera*—of the Lord Kūrma Deity; *sevaka*—a servant; *bahu*—much; *sammāna*—respect; *karilā*—showed.

TRANSLATION

After some time, when Lord Śrī Caitanya Mahāprabhu manifested His external consciousness, a priest of the Lord Kūrma Deity gave Him various offerings.

TEXT 120

যেই গ্রামে যায় তাহাঁ এই ব্যবহার।
এক ঠাঞি কহিল, না কহিব আর বার ॥ ১২০ ॥

yei grāme yāya tāhāṅ ei vyavahāra
eka ṭhāñi kahila, nā kahiba āra bāra

yei grāme—to whichever village; *yāya*—He goes; *tāhāṅ*—there; *ei*—this; *vyavahāra*—behavior; *eka ṭhāñi*—one place; *kahila*—described; *nā*—not; *kahiba*—shall describe; *āra*—another; *bāra*—time.

TRANSLATION

Śrī Caitanya Mahāprabhu's mode of preaching has already been explained, and I shall not repeat the explanation. In whichever village the Lord entered, His behavior was the same.

TEXT 121

'কূর্ম'-নামে সেই গ্রামে বৈদিক ব্রাহ্মণ।
বহু শ্রদ্ধা-ভক্ত্যে কৈল প্রভুর নিমন্ত্রণ ॥ ১২১ ॥

'kūrma'-nāme sei grāme vaidika brāhmaṇa
bahu śraddhā-bhaktye kaila prabhura nimantraṇa

kūrma-nāme—of the name Kūrma; *sei*—that; *grāme*—in the village; *vaidika brāhmaṇa*—a Vedic *brāhmaṇa; bahu*—much; *śraddhā-bhaktye*—with faith and devotion; *kaila*—made; *prabhura*—of Śrī Caitanya Mahāprabhu; *nimantraṇa*—invitation.

TRANSLATION

In one village there was a Vedic brāhmaṇa named Kūrma. He invited Lord Caitanya Mahāprabhu to his home with great respect and devotion.

TEXT 122

ঘরে আনি' প্রভুর কৈল পাদ প্রক্ষালন।
সেই জল বংশ-সহিত করিল ভক্ষণ ॥ ১২২ ॥

ghare āni' prabhura kaila pāda prakṣālana
sei jala vaṁśa-sahita karila bhakṣaṇa

ghare āni'—after bringing Him home; *prabhura*—of Lord Śrī Caitanya Mahāprabhu; *kaila*—did; *pāda prakṣālana*—washing of the lotus feet; *sei jala*—that water; *vaṁśa-sahita*—with all the family members; *karila bhakṣaṇa*—drank.

TRANSLATION

This brāhmaṇa brought Lord Caitanya Mahāprabhu to his home, washed His lotus feet and, with his family members, drank that water.

TEXT 123

অনেকপ্রকার স্নেহে ভিক্ষা করাইল।
গোসাঞিির শেষান্ন সবংশে খাইল ॥ ১২৩ ॥

aneka-prakāra snehe bhikṣā karāila
gosāñira śeṣānna sa-vaṁśe khāila

aneka-prakāra—various kinds; *snehe*—in affection; *bhikṣā*—food; *karāila*—made Him eat; *gosāñira*—of Lord Caitanya Mahāprabhu; *śeṣa-anna*—remnants of food; *sa-vaṁśe*—with all the members of the family; *khāila*—ate.

TRANSLATION

With great affection and respect, that Kūrma brāhmaṇa made Śrī Caitanya Mahāprabhu eat all kinds of food. After that, the remnants were shared by all the members of the family.

TEXT 124

'যেই পাদপদ্ম তোমার ব্রহ্মা ধ্যান করে।
সেই পাদপদ্ম সাক্ষাৎ আইল মোর ঘরে ॥ ১২৪ ॥

'yei pāda-padma tomāra brahmā dhyāna kare
sei pāda-padma sākṣāt āila mora ghare

yei—those; *pāda-padma*—lotus feet; *tomāra*—Your; *brahmā*—Lord Brahmā; *dhyāna kare*—meditates on; *sei pāda-padma*—those lotus feet; *sākṣāt*—directly; *āila*—have come; *mora*—my; *ghare*—to the home.

TRANSLATION

The brāhmaṇa then began to pray, "O my Lord, Your lotus feet are meditated upon by Lord Brahmā, and these very lotus feet have come into my home.

TEXT 125

মোর ভাগ্যের সীমা না যায় কহন ।
আজি মোর শ্লাঘ্য হৈল জন্ম-কুল-ধন ॥ ১২৫ ॥

mora bhāgyera sīmā nā yāya kahana
āji mora ślāghya haila janma-kula-dhana

mora—my; *bhāgyera*—of the fortune; *sīmā*—the limit; *nā*—not; *yāya*—possible; *kahana*—describing; *āji*—today; *mora*—my; *ślāghya*—glorious; *haila*—became; *janma*—birth; *kula*—family; *dhana*—and wealth.

TRANSLATION

"My dear Lord, there is no limit to my great fortune. It cannot be described. Today my family, birth and riches have all been glorified."

TEXT 126

কৃপা কর, প্রভু, মোরে, যাঙ তোমা-সঙ্গে ।
সহিতে না পারি দুঃখ বিষয়-তরঙ্গে ॥' ১২৬ ॥

kṛpā kara, prabhu, more, yāṅ tomā-saṅge
sahite nā pāri duḥkha viṣaya-taraṅge'

kṛpā kara—kindly show favor; *prabhu*—O my Lord; *more*—unto me; *yāṅ*—I go; *tomā-saṅge*—with You; *sahite nā pāri*—I cannot tolerate; *duḥkha*—the troubles; *viṣaya-taraṅge*—in the waves of materialistic life.

TRANSLATION

The brāhmaṇa begged Lord Caitanya Mahāprabhu, "My dear Lord, kindly show me favor and let me go with You. I can no longer tolerate the waves of misery caused by materialistic life."

PURPORT

This statement is applicable for everyone, regardless of how rich or prosperous one may be. Narottama dāsa Ṭhākura has confirmed this statement: *saṁsāra-viṣānale, divā-niśi hiyā jvale.* He states that the materialistic way of life causes a burning in the heart. One cannot make any provisions for the troublesome life of the material world. It is a fact that one may be very happy as far as riches are concerned and one may be very opulent in every respect, yet one has to manage the *viṣayas* to meet the demands of the body and of so many family members and subordinates. One has to take so much trouble to minister to others. Narottama dāsa Ṭhākura therefore prays: *viṣaya chāḍiyā kabe śuddha ha'be mana.* Thus one must become freed from the materialistic way of life. One has to merge himself in the ocean of transcendental bliss. In other words, one cannot relish transcendental bliss without being freed from the materialistic way of life. It appears that the *brāhmaṇa* named Kūrma was materially very happy, for he expressed his family tradition as *janma-kula-dhana.* Now, being glorious, he wanted to leave all these material opulences. He wanted to travel with Śrī Caitanya Mahāprabhu. According to the Vedic way of civilization, one should leave his family after attaining fifty years of age and go to the forest of Vṛndāvana to devote the rest of his life to the service of the Lord.

TEXT 127

প্রভু কহে, — "ঐছে বাৎ কভু না কহিবা ।
গৃহে রহি' কৃষ্ণ-নাম নিরন্তর লৈবা ॥ ১২৭ ॥

prabhu kahe, — "aiche bāt kabhu nā kahibā
gṛhe rahi' kṛṣṇa-nāma nirantara laibā

prabhu kahe—Śrī Caitanya Mahāprabhu said; *aiche bāt*—such words; *kabhu*—at any time; *nā kahibā*—you should not speak; *gṛhe rahi'*—staying at home; *kṛṣṇa-nāma*—the holy name of the Lord; *nirantara*—always; *laibā*—you should chant.

TRANSLATION

Śrī Caitanya Mahāprabhu replied, "Don't speak like that again. Better to remain at home and chant the holy name of Kṛṣṇa always.

PURPORT

It is not advisable in this Age of Kali to leave one's family suddenly, for people are not trained as proper *brahmacārīs* and *gṛhasthas.* Therefore Śrī Caitanya Mahāprabhu advised the *brāhmaṇa* not to be too eager to give up family life. It would be better to remain with his family and try to become purified by chanting the Hare Kṛṣṇa *mahā-mantra* regularly under the direction of a spiritual master. This is the instruction of Śrī Caitanya Mahāprabhu. If this principle is followed by everyone, there is no need to accept *sannyāsa.* In the next verse Śrī Caitanya Mahāprabhu advises everyone to become an ideal householder by offenselessly chanting the Hare Kṛṣṇa *mantra* and teaching the same principle to everyone he meets.

TEXT 128

যারে দেখ, তারে কহ 'কৃষ্ণ' উপদেশ।
আমার আজ্ঞায় গুরু হঞা তার' এই দেশ॥ ১২৮॥

yāre dekha, tāre kaha 'kṛṣṇa'-upadeśa
āmāra ājñāya guru hañā tāra' ei deśa

yāre—whomever; *dekha*—you meet; *tāre*—him; *kaha*—tell; *kṛṣṇa-upadeśa*—the instruction of the *Bhagavad-gītā* as it is spoken by the Lord or of *Śrīmad-Bhāgavatam,* which advises one to worship Śrī Kṛṣṇa; *āmāra ājñāya*—under My order; *guru hañā*—becoming a spiritual master; *tāra'*—deliver; *ei deśa*—this country.

TRANSLATION

"Instruct everyone to follow the orders of Lord Śrī Kṛṣṇa as they are given in the Bhagavad-gītā and Śrīmad-Bhāgavatam. In this way become a spiritual master and try to liberate everyone in this land."

PURPORT

This is the sublime mission of the International Society for Krishna Consciousness. Many people come and inquire whether they have to give up family life to join the Society, but that is not our mission. One can remain comfortably in his residence. We simply request everyone to chant the *mahā-mantra:* Hare Kṛṣṇa, Hare Kṛṣṇa, Kṛṣṇa Kṛṣṇa, Hare Hare/ Hare Rāma, Hare Rāma, Rāma Rāma, Hare Hare. If one is a little literate and can read *Bhagavad-gītā As It Is* and *Śrīmad-Bhāgavatam,* that is so much the better. These works are now available in an English translation and are done very authoritatively to appeal to all classes of men. Instead of living engrossed in material activities, people throughout the world should take advantage of this movement and chant the Hare Kṛṣṇa *mahā-mantra* at home with their families. One should also refrain from sinful activities—illicit sex, meat-eating, gambling and intoxication. Out of these four items, illicit sex is very sinful. Every person must get married. Every woman especially must get married. If the women outnumber the men, some men can accept more than one wife. In that way there will be no prostitution in society. If men can marry more than one wife, illicit sex life will be stopped. One can also produce many nice preparations to offer Kṛṣṇa—grain, fruit, flowers and milk. Why should one indulge in unnecessary meat-eating and maintain horrible slaughterhouses? What is the use of smoking and drinking tea and coffee? People are already intoxicated by material enjoyment, and if they indulge in further intoxication, what chance is there for self-realization? Similarly, one should not partake in gambling and unnecessarily agitate the mind. The real purpose of human life is to attain the spiritual platform and return to Godhead. That is the *summum bonum* of spiritual realization. The Kṛṣṇa consciousness movement is trying to elevate human society to the perfection of life by pursuing the method described by Śrī Caitanya Mahāprabhu in His advice to the *brāhmaṇa* Kūrma. That is, one should stay at home, chant the Hare Kṛṣṇa *mantra* and preach the instructions of Kṛṣṇa as they are given in the *Bhagavad-gītā* and *Śrīmad-Bhāgavatam.*

TEXT 129

কভু না বাধিবে তোমার বিষয়-তরঙ্গ।
পুনরপি এই ঠাঞি পাবে মোর সঙ্গ॥" ১২৯॥

kabhu nā bādhibe tomāra viṣaya-taraṅga
punarapi ei ṭhāñi pābe mora saṅga"

kabhu—at any time; *nā*—not; *bādhibe*—will obstruct; *tomāra*—your; *viṣaya-taraṅga*—materialistic way of life; *punarapi*—again; *ei ṭhāñi*—at this place; *pābe*—you will get; *mora*—My; *saṅga*—association.

TRANSLATION

Śrī Caitanya Mahāprabhu further advised the brāhmaṇa Kūrma, "If you follow this instruction, your materialistic life at home will not obstruct your spiritual advancement. Indeed, if you follow these regulative principles, we will again meet here, or, rather, you will never lose My company."

PURPORT

This is an opportunity for everyone. If one simply follows the instructions of Śrī Caitanya Mahāprabhu, under the guidance of His representative, and chants the Hare Kṛṣṇa *mantra,* teaching everyone as far as possible the same principle, the contamination of the materialistic way of life will not even touch him. It does not matter whether one lives in a holy place like Vṛndāvana, Navadvīpa or Jagannātha Purī or in the midst of European cities, where the materialistic way of life is very prominent. If a devotee follows the instructions of Śrī Caitanya Mahāprabhu, he lives in the company of the Lord. Wherever he lives, he converts that place into Vṛndāvana and Navadvīpa. This means that materialism cannot touch him. This is the secret of success for one advancing in Kṛṣṇa consciousness.

TEXT 130

এই মত যাঁর ঘরে করে প্রভু ভিক্ষা ।
সেই ঐছে কহে, তাঁরে করায় এই শিক্ষা ॥ ১৩০ ॥

ei mata yāṅra ghare kare prabhu bhikṣā
sei aiche kahe, tāṅre karāya ei śikṣā

ei mata—in this way; *yāṅra*—of whom; *ghare*—at the home; *kare*—does; *prabhu*—Lord Śrī Caitanya Mahāprabhu; *bhikṣā*—accepting *prasādam; sei*—that man; *aiche*—similarly; *kahe*—says; *tāṅre*—unto him; *karāya*—does; *ei*—this; *śikṣā*—enlightenment.

TRANSLATION

At whosever house Śrī Caitanya accepted His alms by taking prasādam, He would convert the dwellers to His saṅkīrtana movement and advise them just as He advised the brāhmaṇa named Kūrma.

PURPORT

The cult of Śrī Caitanya Mahāprabhu is explained here very nicely. One who surrenders to Him and is ready to follow Him with heart and soul does not need to change his location. Nor is it necessary for one to change his status. One may remain a householder, a medical practitioner, an engineer or whatever. It doesn't matter. One only has to follow the instruction of Śrī Caitanya Mahāprabhu, chant the Hare Kṛṣṇa *mahā-mantra* and instruct relatives and friends in the teachings of the *Bhagavad-gītā* and *Śrīmad-Bhāgavatam.* One has to learn humility and meekness at home, following the instructions of Śrī Caitanya Mahāprabhu, and in that way one's life will be spiritually successful. One should not try to be an artificially advanced devotee, thinking, "I am a first-class devotee." Such thinking should be avoided. It is best not to accept any disciples. One has to become purified at home by chanting the Hare Kṛṣṇa *mahā-mantra* and preaching the principles enunciated by Śrī Caitanya Mahāprabhu. Thus one can become a spiritual master and be freed from the contamination of material life.

There are many *sahajiyās* who decry the activities of the six Gosvāmīs—Śrīla Rūpa, Sanātana, Raghunātha dāsa, Bhaṭṭa Raghunātha, Jīva and Gopāla Bhaṭṭa Gosvāmīs—who are the personal associates of Śrī Caitanya Mahāprabhu and who enlightened society by writing books on devotional service. Similarly, Narottama dāsa Ṭhākura and other great *ācāryas* like Madhvācārya, Rāmānujācārya and others accepted many thousands of disciples to induce them to render devotional service. However, there is a class of *sahajiyās* who think that these activities are opposed to the principles of devotional service. Indeed, they consider such activities simply another phase of materialism. Thus opposing the principles of Śrī Caitanya Mahāprabhu, they commit offenses at His lotus feet. They should better consider His instructions and, instead of seeking to be considered humble and meek, should refrain from criticizing the followers of Śrī Caitanya Mahāprabhu who engage in preaching. To protect His preachers, Śrī Caitanya Mahāprabhu has given much clear advice in these verses of *Śrī Caitanya-caritāmṛta.*

TEXTS 131–132

পথে যাইতে দেবালয়ে রহে যেই গ্রামে।
যাঁর ঘরে ভিক্ষা করে, সেই মহাজনে ॥ ১৩১ ॥
কূর্মে যৈছে রীতি, তৈছে কৈল সর্ব ঠাঞি।
নীলাচলে পুনঃ যাবৎ না আইলা গোসাঞি ॥ ১৩২ ॥

pathe yāite devālaye rahe yei grāme
yāṅra ghare bhikṣā kare, sei mahā-jane

kūrme yaiche rīti, taiche kaila sarva-ṭhāñi
nīlācale punaḥ yāvat nā āilā gosāñi

pathe yāite—while passing on the road; *devālaye*—in a temple; *rahe*—He stays; *yei grāme*—in any village; *yāṅra ghare*—at whose place; *bhikṣā kare*—takes alms or eats; *sei mahā-jane*—to such a great personality; *kūrme*—unto the *brāhmaṇa* Kūrma; *yaiche*—just as; *rīti*—the process; *taiche*—in the same way; *kaila*—did; *sarva-ṭhāñi*—in all places; *nīlācale*—to Jagannātha Purī; *punaḥ*—again; *yāvat*—until; *nā*—not; *āilā*—returned; *gosāñi*—the Lord.

TRANSLATION

While on His tour, Śrī Caitanya Mahāprabhu would spend the night at a temple or on the roadside. Whenever He accepted food from a person, He would give him the same advice He gave the brāhmaṇa named Kūrma. He adopted this process until He returned to Jagannātha Purī from His South Indian tour.

TEXT 133

অতএব ইহাঁ কহিলাঙ করিয়া বিস্তার।
এইমত জানিবে প্রভুর সর্বত্র ব্যবহার ॥ ১৩৩ ॥

ataeva ihāṅ kahilāṅ kariyā vistāra
ei-mata jānibe prabhura sarvatra vyavahāra

ataeva—therefore; *ihāṅ*—here; *kahilāṅ*—I have described; *kariyā vistāra*—elaborately; *ei-mata*—in this way; *jānibe*—you will know; *prabhura*—of Śrī Caitanya Mahāprabhu; *sarvatra*—everywhere; *vyavahāra*—the behavior.

TRANSLATION

Thus I have described the Lord's behavior elaborately in the case of Kūrma. In this way, you will know Śrī Caitanya Mahāprabhu's dealings throughout South India.

TEXT 134

এইমত সেই রাত্রি তাহাঁই রহিলা ।
প্রাতঃকালে প্রভু স্নান করিয়া চলিলা ॥ ১৩৪ ॥

ei-mata sei rātri tāhāṅi rahilā
prātaḥ-kāle prabhu snāna kariyā calilā

ei-mata—in this way; *sei rātri*—that night; *tāhāṅi*—there; *rahilā*—stayed; *prātaḥ-kāle*—in the morning; *prabhu*—Śrī Caitanya Mahāprabhu; *snāna*—bath; *kariyā*—taking; *calilā*—again started.

TRANSLATION

Thus Lord Śrī Caitanya Mahāprabhu would remain at night in one place, and the next morning, after bathing, He would start again.

TEXT 135

প্রভুর অনুব্রজি' কূর্ম বহু দূর আইলা ।
প্রভু তাঁরে যত্ন করি' ঘরে পাঠাইলা ॥ ১৩৫ ॥

prabhura anuvraji' kūrma bahu dūra āilā
prabhu tāṅre yatna kari' ghare pāṭhāilā

prabhura—Lord Śrī Caitanya Mahāprabhu; *anuvraji'*—following behind; *kūrma*—the *brāhmaṇa* named Kūrma; *bahu*—much; *dūra*—distance; *āilā*—came; *prabhu*—Lord Śrī Caitanya Mahāprabhu; *tāṅre*—him; *yatna kari'*—taking much care; *ghare*—to his home; *pāṭhāilā*—sent.

TRANSLATION

When Śrī Caitanya Mahāprabhu left, the brāhmaṇa Kūrma followed Him a great distance, but eventually Lord Caitanya took care to send him back home.

TEXT 136

'বাসুদেব'-নাম এক দ্বিজ মহাশয়।
সর্বাঙ্গে গলিত কুষ্ঠ, তাতে কীড়াময় ॥ ১৩৬ ॥

'vāsudeva'-nāma eka dvija mahāśaya
sarvāṅge galita kuṣṭha, tāte kīḍā-maya

vāsudeva-nāma—of the name Vāsudeva; *eka dvija*—one *brāhmaṇa; mahāśaya*—a great person; *sarva-aṅge*—all over his body; *galita*—acute; *kuṣṭha*—leprosy; *tāte*—in that; *kīḍā-maya*—full of living worms.

TRANSLATION

There was also a brāhmaṇa named Vāsudeva, who was a great person but was suffering from leprosy. Indeed, his body was filled with living worms.

TEXT 137

অঙ্গ হৈতে যেই কীড়া খসিয়া পড়য়।
উঠাঞা সেই কীড়া রাখে সেই ঠাঞ ॥ ১৩৭ ॥

aṅga haite yei kīḍā khasiyā paḍaya
uṭhāñā sei kīḍā rākhe sei ṭhāña

aṅga haite—from his body; *yei*—which; *kīḍā*—a worm; *khasiyā*—drops; *paḍaya*—falling off; *uṭhāñā*—picking up; *sei*—that; *kīḍā*—worm; *rākhe*—places; *sei ṭhāña*—in the same place.

TRANSLATION

Although suffering from leprosy, the brāhmaṇa Vāsudeva was enlightened. As soon as one worm fell from his body, he would pick it up and place it back again in the same location.

TEXT 138

রাত্রিতে শুনিলা তেঁহো গোসাঞির আগমন।
দেখিবারে আইলা প্রভাতে কূর্মের ভবন ॥ ১৩৮ ॥

rātrite śunilā teṅho gosāñira āgamana
dekhibāre āilā prabhāte kūrmera bhavana

rātrite—at night; *śunilā*—heard; *teṅho*—he; *gosāñira*—of Lord Śrī Caitanya Mahāprabhu; *āgamana*—the arrival; *dekhibāre*—to see Him; *āilā*—he came; *prabhāte*—in the morning; *kūrmera*—of the *brāhmaṇa* named Kūrma; *bhavana*—to the house.

TRANSLATION

Then one night Vāsudeva heard of Lord Caitanya Mahāprabhu's arrival, and in the morning he came to see the Lord at the house of Kūrma.

TEXT 139

প্রভুর গমন কূর্ম-মুখেতে শুনিঞা ।
ভূমিতে পড়িলা দুঃখে মূর্চ্ছিত হঞা ॥ ১৩৯ ॥

prabhura gamana kūrma-mukhete śuniñā
bhūmite paḍilā duḥkhe mūrcchita hañā

prabhura—of Lord Śrī Caitanya Mahāprabhu; *gamana*—the going; *kūrma-mukhete*—from the mouth of the *brāhmaṇa* Kūrma; *śuniñā*—hearing; *bhūmite*—on the ground; *paḍilā*—fell down; *duḥkhe*—in great distress; *mūrcchita*—unconsciousness; *hañā*—becoming.

TRANSLATION

When the leper Vāsudeva came to Kūrma's house to see Caitanya Mahāprabhu, he was informed that the Lord had already left. The leper then fell to the ground unconscious.

TEXT 140

অনেক প্রকার বিলাপ করিতে লাগিলা ।
সেইক্ষণে আসি' প্রভু তাঁরে আলিঙ্গিলা ॥ ১৪০ ॥

aneka prakāra vilāpa karite lāgilā
sei-kṣaṇe āsi' prabhu tāṅre āliṅgilā

aneka prakāra—various kinds; *vilāpa*—lamentation; *karite*—to do; *lāgilā*—began; *sei-kṣaṇe*—immediately; *āsi'*—coming back; *prabhu*—Śrī Caitanya Mahāprabhu; *tāṅre*—him; *āliṅgilā*—embraced.

TRANSLATION

When Vāsudeva, the leper brāhmaṇa, was lamenting due to not being able to see Caitanya Mahāprabhu, the Lord immediately returned to that spot and embraced him.

TEXT 141

প্রভু-স্পর্শে দুঃখ-সঙ্গে কুষ্ঠ দূরে গেল।
আনন্দ সহিতে অঙ্গ সুন্দর হইল ॥ ১৪১ ॥

prabhu-sparśe duḥkha-saṅge kuṣṭha dūre gela
ānanda sahite aṅga sundara ha-ila

prabhu-sparśe—by the touch of Śrī Caitanya Mahāprabhu; *duḥkha-saṅge*—along with his unhappiness; *kuṣṭha*—the infection of leprosy; *dūre*—to a distant place; *gela*—went; *ānanda sahite*—with great pleasure; *aṅga*—whole body; *sundara*—beautiful; *ha-ila*—became.

TRANSLATION

When Śrī Caitanya Mahāprabhu touched him, both the leprosy and his distress went to a distant place. Indeed, Vāsudeva's body became very beautiful, to his great happiness.

TEXT 142

প্রভুর কৃপা দেখি' তাঁর বিস্ময় হৈল মন।
শ্লোক পড়ি' পায়ে ধরি, করয়ে স্তবন ॥ ১৪২ ॥

prabhura kṛpā dekhi' tāṅra vismaya haila mana
śloka paḍi' pāye dhari, karaye stavana

prabhura—of Lord Śrī Caitanya Mahāprabhu; *kṛpā*—the mercy; *dekhi'*—seeing; *tāṅra*—of the *brāhmaṇa* Vāsudeva; *vismaya haila mana*—there was astonishment in his mind; *śloka paḍi'*—reciting a verse; *pāye dhari*—touching His lotus feet; *karaye stavana*—offers prayers.

TRANSLATION

The brāhmaṇa Vāsudeva was astonished to behold the wonderful mercy of Śrī Caitanya Mahāprabhu, and he began to recite a verse from Śrīmad-Bhāgavatam, touching the Lord's lotus feet.

TEXT 143

ক্বাহং দরিদ্রঃ পাপীয়ান্ ক্ব কৃষ্ণঃ শ্রীনিকেতনঃ ।
ব্রহ্মবন্ধুরিতি স্মাহং বাহুভ্যাং পরিরম্ভিতঃ ॥ ১৪৩ ॥

kvāhaṁ daridraḥ pāpīyān
kva kṛṣṇaḥ śrī-niketanaḥ
brahma-bandhur iti smāhaṁ
bāhubhyāṁ parirambhitaḥ

kva—who; *aham*—I; *daridraḥ*—poor; *pāpīyān*—sinful; *kva*—who; *kṛṣṇaḥ*—the Supreme Personality of Godhead; *śrī-niketanaḥ*—the transcendental form of all opulence; *brahma-bandhuḥ*—the friend of a *brāhmaṇa,* not fit even to be called a *brāhmaṇa; iti*—thus; *sma*—certainly; *aham*—I; *bāhubhyām*—by the arms; *parirambhitaḥ*—embraced.

TRANSLATION

He said, "'Who am I? A sinful, poor friend of a brāhmaṇa. And who is Kṛṣṇa? The Supreme Personality of Godhead, full in six opulences. Nonetheless, He has embraced me with His two arms.'"

PURPORT

This verse was spoken by Sudāmā Brāhmaṇa in *Śrīmad-Bhāgavatam* (10.81.16), in connection with his meeting Lord Kṛṣṇa.

TEXTS 144–145

বহু স্তুতি করি' কহে, —শুন, দয়াময় ।
জীবে এই গুণ নাহি, তোমাতে এই হয় ॥ ১৪৪ ॥
মোরে দেখি' মোর গন্ধে পলায় পামর ।
হেন-মোরে স্পর্শ' তুমি, —স্বতন্ত্র ঈশ্বর ॥ ১৪৫ ॥

bahu stuti kari' kahe, — śuna, dayā-maya
jīve ei guṇa nāhi, tomāte ei haya

more dekhi' mora gandhe palāya pāmara
hena-more sparśa' tumi, — svatantra īśvara

bahu — many; *stuti* — prayers; *kari'* — presenting; *kahe* — says; *śuna* — kindly hear; *dayā-maya* — O greatly merciful Lord; *jīve* — in the living entity; *ei* — this; *guṇa* — quality; *nāhi* — there is not; *tomāte* — in You; *ei* — this; *haya* — is; *more dekhi'* — by seeing me; *mora gandhe* — from smelling my body; *palāya* — runs away; *pāmara* — even a sinful man; *hena-more* — such a person as me; *sparśa'* — touch; *tumi* — You; *svatantra* — fully independent; *īśvara* — the Supreme Personality of Godhead.

TRANSLATION

The brāhmaṇa Vāsudeva continued, "O my merciful Lord, such mercy is not possible for ordinary living entities. Such mercy can be found only in You. Upon seeing me, even a sinful person goes away due to my bad bodily odor. Yet You have touched me. Such is the independent behavior of the Supreme Personality of Godhead."

TEXT 146

কিন্তু আছিলাঙ ভাল অধম হঞা ।
এবে অহঙ্কার মোর জন্মিবে আসিয়া ॥ ১৪৬ ॥

kintu āchilāṅ bhāla adhama hañā
ebe ahaṅkāra mora janmibe āsiyā

kintu — but; *āchilāṅ* — I was; *bhāla* — all right; *adhama* — the lowest of mankind; *hañā* — being; *ebe* — now; *ahaṅkāra* — pride; *mora* — my; *janmibe* — will appear; *āsiyā* — coming.

TRANSLATION

Being meek and humble, the brāhmaṇa Vāsudeva worried that he would become proud after being cured by the grace of Śrī Caitanya Mahāprabhu.

TEXT 147

প্রভু কহে, — "কভু তোমার না হবে অভিমান।
নিরন্তর কহ তুমি 'কৃষ্ণ' 'কৃষ্ণ' নাম ॥ ১৪৭ ॥

prabhu kahe, — "kabhu tomāra nā habe abhimāna
nirantara kaha tumi 'kṛṣṇa' 'kṛṣṇa' nāma

prabhu kahe—the Lord said; *kabhu*—at any time; *tomāra*—your; *nā*—not; *habe*—there will be; *abhimāna*—pride; *nirantara*—incessantly; *kaha*—chant; *tumi*—you; *kṛṣṇa kṛṣṇa nāma*—the holy name of Lord Kṛṣṇa.

TRANSLATION

To protect the brāhmaṇa, Śrī Caitanya Mahāprabhu advised him to chant the Hare Kṛṣṇa mantra incessantly. By doing so, he would never become unnecessarily proud.

TEXT 148

কৃষ্ণ উপদেশি' কর জীবের নিস্তার।
অচিরাতে কৃষ্ণ তোমা করিবেন অঙ্গীকার ॥" ১৪৮ ॥

kṛṣṇa upadeśi' kara jīvera nistāra
acirāte kṛṣṇa tomā karibena aṅgīkāra"

kṛṣṇa upadeśi'—instructing about Kṛṣṇa; *kara*—just do; *jīvera*—of all living entities; *nistāra*—the liberation; *acirāte*—very soon; *kṛṣṇa*—Lord Kṛṣṇa; *tomā*—you; *karibena*—will make; *aṅgīkāra*—acceptance.

TRANSLATION

Śrī Caitanya Mahāprabhu also advised Vāsudeva to preach about Kṛṣṇa and thus liberate living entities. As a result, Kṛṣṇa would very soon accept him as His devotee.

PURPORT

Although Vāsudeva Vipra was a leper and had suffered greatly, still, after Śrī Caitanya Mahāprabhu cured him He instructed him to preach Kṛṣṇa consciousness. Indeed, the only return the Lord wanted was that Vāsudeva preach the instructions of Kṛṣṇa and liberate all human beings. That is the process of the International Society for Krishna Consciousness. Each and every member of this Society was rescued from a very abominable condition, but now they are engaged in preaching the cult of Kṛṣṇa consciousness. They are not only cured of the disease called materialism but are also living a very happy life. Everyone accepts them as great devotees of Kṛṣṇa, and their qualities are manifest in their very faces. If one wants to be recognized as a devotee by Kṛṣṇa, he should take to preaching work, following the advice of Śrī Caitanya Mahāprabhu. Then one will undoubtedly attain the lotus feet of Śrī Kṛṣṇa Caitanya, Lord Kṛṣṇa Himself, without delay.

TEXT 149

এতেক কহিয়া প্রভু কৈল অন্তর্ধানে ।
দুই বিপ্র গলাগলি কান্দে প্রভুর গুণে ॥ ১৪৯ ॥

eteka kahiyā prabhu kaila antardhāne
dui vipra galāgali kānde prabhura guṇe

eteka—so much; *kahiyā*—speaking; *prabhu*—Lord Śrī Caitanya Mahāprabhu; *kaila*—made; *antardhāne*—disappearance; *dui vipra*—the two *brāhmaṇas,* Kūrma and Vāsudeva; *galāgali*—embracing one another; *kānde*—cry; *prabhura guṇe*—due to the mercy of Śrī Caitanya Mahāprabhu.

TRANSLATION

After instructing the brāhmaṇa Vāsudeva in that way, Śrī Caitanya Mahāprabhu disappeared from that place. Then the two brāhmaṇas, Kūrma and Vāsudeva, embraced each other and began to cry, remembering the transcendental qualities of Śrī Caitanya Mahāprabhu.

TEXT 150

'বাসুদেবোদ্ধার' এই কহিল আখ্যান ।
'বাসুদেবামৃতপ্রদ' হৈল প্রভুর নাম ॥ ১৫০ ॥

'vāsudevoddhāra' ei kahila ākhyāna
'vāsudevāmṛta-prada' haila prabhura nāma

vāsudeva-uddhāra—giving liberation to Vāsudeva; *ei*—this; *kahila*—is described; *ākhyāna*—narration; *vāsudeva-amṛta-prada*—the giver of nectar to Vāsudeva; *haila*—became; *prabhura nāma*—Lord Śrī Caitanya Mahāprabhu's holy name.

TRANSLATION

Thus I have described how Śrī Caitanya Mahāprabhu reclaimed the leper Vāsudeva and so received the name Vāsudevāmṛta-prada.

PURPORT

The name Vāsudevāmṛta-prada is mentioned in the verses composed by Sārvabhauma Bhaṭṭācārya.

TEXT 151

এত ত' কহিল প্রভুর প্রথম গমন।
কূর্ম-দরশন, বাসুদেব-বিমোচন ॥ ১৫১ ॥

ei ta' kahila prabhura prathama gamana
kūrma-daraśana, vāsudeva-vimocana

ei ta' kahila—thus I have described; *prabhura*—of Lord Śrī Caitanya Mahāprabhu; *prathama gamana*—the beginning of the tour; *kūrma-daraśana*—visiting the temple of Kūrma; *vāsudeva-vimocana*—and liberating the leper *brāhmaṇa* of the name Vāsudeva.

TRANSLATION

Thus I end my description of the beginning of the tour of Śrī Caitanya Mahāprabhu, His visiting the temple of Kūrma and His liberating the leper brāhmaṇa Vāsudeva.

TEXT 152

শ্রদ্ধা করি' এই লীলা যে করে শ্রবণ।
অচিরাতে মিলয়ে তারে চৈতন্য-চরণ ॥ ১৫২ ॥

śraddhā kari' ei līlā ye kare śravaṇa
acirāte milaye tāre caitanya-caraṇa

śraddhā kari'—with great faith; *ei līlā*—this pastime; *ye*—anyone; *kare*—does; *śravaṇa*—hearing; *acirāte*—very soon; *milaye*—meets; *tāre*—him; *caitanya-caraṇa*—the lotus feet of Śrī Caitanya Mahāprabhu.

TRANSLATION

One who hears these pastimes of Śrī Caitanya Mahāprabhu with great faith will surely very soon attain the lotus feet of Lord Śrī Caitanya Mahāprabhu.

PURPORT

When a person actually revives his consciousness with thoughts of Kṛṣṇa by the mercy of Śrī Caitanya Mahāprabhu, he revives his spiritual life and becomes addicted to the service of the Lord. Only then can he act as an *ācārya.* In other words, everyone should engage in preaching, following in the footsteps of Śrī Caitanya Mahāprabhu. In this way one will be very much appreciated by Lord Kṛṣṇa and will quickly be recognized by Him. Actually a devotee of Śrī Caitanya Mahāprabhu must engage in preaching in order to increase the followers of the Lord. By thus preaching actual Vedic knowledge all over the world, one will benefit all mankind.

TEXT 153

চৈতন্যলীলার আদি-অন্ত নাহি জানি ।
সেই লিখি, যেই মহান্তের মুখে শুনি ॥ ১৫৩ ॥

caitanya-līlāra ādi-anta nāhi jāni
sei likhi, yei mahāntera mukhe śuni

caitanya-līlāra—of the pastimes of Śrī Caitanya Mahāprabhu; *ādi*—beginning; *anta*—and end; *nāhi*—not; *jāni*—I know; *sei*—that; *likhi*—I write; *yei*—which; *mahāntera*—of the great personalities; *mukhe*—from the mouths; *śuni*—I hear.

TRANSLATION

I admit that I do not know the beginning or the end of Śrī Caitanya Mahāprabhu's pastimes. However, whatever I have written I have heard from the mouths of great personalities.

TEXT 154

ইথে অপরাধ মোর না লইও, ভক্তগণ।
তোমা-সবার চরণ — মোর একান্ত শরণ ॥ ১৫৪ ॥

ithe aparādha mora nā la-io, bhakta-gaṇa
tomā-sabāra caraṇa — mora ekānta śaraṇa

ithe — in this; *aparādha* — offenses; *mora* — my; *nā la-io* — do not take; *bhakta-gaṇa* — O devotees; *tomā* — of your; *sabāra* — of all; *caraṇa* — the lotus feet; *mora* — my; *ekānta* — only; *śaraṇa* — shelter.

TRANSLATION

O devotees, please do not consider my offenses in this regard. Your lotus feet are my only shelter.

TEXT 155

শ্রীরূপ-রঘুনাথ-পদে যার আশ।
চৈতন্য-চরিতামৃত কহে কৃষ্ণদাস ॥ ১৫৫ ॥

śrī-rūpa-raghunātha-pade yāra āśa
caitanya-caritāmṛta kahe kṛṣṇadāsa

śrī-rūpa — Śrīla Rūpa Gosvāmī; *raghunātha* — Śrīla Raghunātha dāsa Gosvāmī; *pade* — at the lotus feet; *yāra* — whose; *āśa* — expectation; *caitanya-caritāmṛta* — the book named *Caitanya-caritāmṛta;* *kahe* — describes; *kṛṣṇa-dāsa* — Śrīla Kṛṣṇadāsa Kavirāja Gosvāmī.

TRANSLATION

Praying at the lotus feet of Śrī Rūpa and Śrī Raghunātha, always desiring their mercy, I, Kṛṣṇadāsa, narrate Śrī Caitanya-caritāmṛta, following in their footsteps.

Thus end the Bhaktivedanta purports to Śrī Caitanya-caritāmṛta, Madhya-līlā, *Seventh Chapter, describing the start of the Lord's tour of South India and the liberation of the* brāhmaṇa *Vāsudeva.*

CHAPTER EIGHT

Talks Between Śrī Caitanya Mahāprabhu and Rāmānanda Rāya

The summary of the Eighth Chapter is given by Śrīla Bhaktivinoda Ṭhākura in his *Amṛta-pravāha-bhāṣya.* After visiting the temple of Jiyaḍa-nṛsiṁha, Śrī Caitanya Mahāprabhu went to the banks of the river Godāvarī, to a place known as Vidyānagara. When Śrīla Rāmānanda Rāya went there to take his bath, they met. After introducing himself, Śrī Rāmānanda Rāya requested Śrī Caitanya Mahāprabhu to remain in the village for some days. Honoring his request, Caitanya Mahāprabhu stayed there in the home of some Vedic *brāhmaṇas.* In the evening, Śrīla Rāmānanda Rāya used to come to see Śrī Caitanya Mahāprabhu. Rāmānanda Rāya, who was clothed in ordinary dress, offered the Lord respectful obeisances. Śrī Caitanya Mahāprabhu questioned him on the object and process of worship and also asked him to recite verses from the Vedic literature.

First of all, Śrīla Rāmānanda Rāya enunciated the system of the *varṇāśrama* institution. He recited various verses about *karmārpaṇa,* stating that everything should be dedicated to the Lord. He then spoke of detached action, knowledge mixed with devotional service, and finally the spontaneous loving service of the Lord. After hearing Śrīla Rāmānanda Rāya recite some verses, Śrī Caitanya Mahāprabhu accepted the principle of pure devotional service devoid of all kinds of speculation. After this, Śrī Caitanya Mahāprabhu asked Rāmānanda Rāya to explain the higher platform of devotional service. Then Śrīla

Rāmānanda Rāya explained unalloyed devotional service, love of Godhead, and serving the Lord in the moods of pure servitude, fraternity and parental love. Finally he spoke of serving the Lord in conjugal love. He then spoke of how conjugal love can be developed in various ways. This conjugal love attains its highest perfection in Śrīmatī Rādhārāṇī's love for Kṛṣṇa. He next described the position of Śrīmatī Rādhārāṇī and the transcendental mellows of love of God. Śrīla Rāmānanda Rāya then recited a verse of his own concerning the platform of ecstatic vision, technically called *prema-vilāsa-vivarta.* Śrīla Rāmānanda Rāya also explained that all stages of conjugal love can be attained through the mercy of the residents of Vṛndāvana, especially by the mercy of the *gopīs.* All these subject matters were thus vividly described. Gradually Rāmānanda Rāya could understand the position of Śrī Caitanya Mahāprabhu, and when Śrī Caitanya Mahāprabhu exhibited His real form, Rāmānanda Rāya fell unconscious. After some days, Śrī Caitanya Mahāprabhu asked Rāmānanda Rāya to retire from government service and come to Jagannātha Purī. These descriptions of the meetings between Rāmānanda Rāya and Śrī Caitanya Mahāprabhu are taken from the notebook of Svarūpa Dāmodara Gosvāmī.

TEXT 1

সঞ্চার্য রামাভিধ-ভক্তমেঘে
স্বভক্তিসিদ্ধান্তচয়ামৃতানি ।
গৌরাব্ধিরেতৈরমুনা বিতীর্ণৈ-
স্তজ্জ্ঞত্ব-রত্নালয়তাং প্রযাতি ॥ ১ ॥

sañcārya rāmābhidha-bhakta-meghe
sva-bhakti-siddhānta-cayāmṛtāni
gaurābdhir etair amunā vitīrṇais
taj-jñatva-ratnālayatāṁ prayāti

sañcārya—by empowering; *rāma-abhidha*—of the name Rāma; *bhakta-meghe*—in the cloudlike devotee; *sva-bhakti*—of His own devotional service; *siddhānta*—of conclusions; *caya*—all collections; *amṛtāni*—nectar; *gaura-abdhiḥ*—the ocean known as Śrī Caitanya Mahāprabhu; *etaiḥ*—by these; *amunā*—by the cloud known as Rāmānanda Rāya; *vitīrṇaiḥ*—distributed; *tat-jñatva*—of knowledge of devotional service; *ratna-ālayatām*—the quality of being an ocean containing valuable jewels; *prayāti*—achieved.

TRANSLATION

Śrī Caitanya Mahāprabhu, who is known as Gaurāṅga, is the ocean of all conclusive knowledge in devotional service. He empowered Śrī Rāmānanda Rāya, who may be likened to a cloud of devotional service. This cloud was filled with the water of all the conclusive purports of devotional service and was empowered by the ocean to spread this water over the sea of Śrī Caitanya Mahāprabhu Himself. Thus the ocean of Caitanya Mahāprabhu became filled with the jewels of the knowledge of pure devotional service.

TEXT 2

জয় জয় শ্রীচৈতন্য জয় নিত্যানন্দ ।
জয়াদ্বৈতচন্দ্র জয় গৌরভক্তবৃন্দ ॥ ২ ॥

jaya jaya śrī-caitanya jaya nityānanda
jayādvaita-candra jaya gaura-bhakta-vṛnda

jaya jaya—all glories; *śrī-caitanya*—Lord Śrī Caitanya Mahāprabhu; *jaya*—all glories; *nityānanda*—to Lord Nityānanda; *jaya advaita-candra*—all glories to Advaita Ācārya; *jaya gaura-bhakta-vṛnda*—all glories to the devotees of Śrī Caitanya Mahāprabhu.

TRANSLATION

All glories to Lord Śrī Caitanya Mahāprabhu! All glories to Lord Nityānanda! All glories to Advaita Ācārya! And all glories to all the devotees of Lord Śrī Caitanya Mahāprabhu!

TEXT 3

পূর্ব-রীতে প্রভু আগে গমন করিলা ।
'জিয়ড়নৃসিংহ'-ক্ষেত্রে কতদিনে গেলা ॥ ৩ ॥

pūrva-rīte prabhu āge gamana karilā
'jiyaḍa-nṛsiṁha'-kṣetre kata-dine gelā

pūrva-rīte—according to His previous program; *prabhu*—Lord Śrī Caitanya Mahāprabhu; *āge*—ahead; *gamana*—going; *karilā*—did; *jiyaḍa-nṛsiṁha*—of the name Jiyaḍa-nṛsiṁha; *kṣetre*—at the place of pilgrimage; *kata-dine*—after some days; *gelā*—arrived.

TRANSLATION

According to His previous program, Lord Śrī Caitanya Mahāprabhu went forward on His tour and after some days arrived at the place of pilgrimage known as Jiyaḍa-nṛsiṁha.

PURPORT

The Jiyaḍa-nṛsiṁha temple is situated on the top of a hill about five miles away from Visakhapatnam. There is a railway station on the South Indian Railway known as Siṁhācala. The temple known as Siṁhācala is the best temple in the vicinity of Visakhapatnam. This temple is very affluent and is a typical example of the architecture of the area. On one stone tablet it is mentioned that formerly a queen covered the Deity with gold plate. This is mentioned in the *Visakhapatnam Gazetteer*. About the temple, there are residential quarters for the priests and devotees. Indeed, at the present moment there are many residential quarters to accommodate visiting devotees. The original Deity is situated within the depths of the temple, but there is another Deity, a duplicate, known as the *vijaya-mūrti*. This smaller Deity can be moved from the temple and taken on public processions. Priests who generally belong to the Rāmānuja-sampradāya are in charge of the Deity worship.

TEXT 4

নৃসিংহ দেখিয়া কৈল দণ্ডবৎপ্রণতি ।
প্রেমাবেশে কৈল বহু নৃত্য-গীত-স্তুতি ॥ ৪ ॥

nṛsiṁha dekhiyā kaila daṇḍavat-praṇati
premāveśe kaila bahu nṛtya-gīta-stuti

nṛsiṁha dekhiyā—upon seeing Lord Nṛsiṁha in the temple; *kaila*—did; *daṇḍavat-praṇati*—offering of obeisances, falling flat before the Deity; *premāveśe*—in ecstatic love; *kaila*—did; *bahu*—all kinds of; *nṛtya*—dancing; *gīta*—chanting; *stuti*—and offering of prayers.

TRANSLATION

Upon seeing the Deity of Lord Nṛsiṁha in the temple, Śrī Caitanya Mahāprabhu offered His respectful obeisances by falling flat. Then, in ecstatic love, He performed various dances, chanted, and offered prayers.

TEXT 5

"শ্রীনৃসিংহ, জয় নৃসিংহ, জয় জয় নৃসিংহ।
প্রহ্লাদেশ জয় পদ্মামুখপদ্মভৃঙ্গ ॥" ৫ ॥

"śrī-nṛsiṁha, jaya nṛsiṁha, jaya jaya nṛsiṁha
prahlādeśa jaya padmā-mukha-padma-bhṛṅga"

śrī-nṛsiṁha—Lord Nṛsiṁha with Lakṣmī; *jaya nṛsiṁha*—all glories to Lord Nṛsiṁha; *jaya jaya*—again and again glories; *nṛsiṁha*—to Nṛsiṁhadeva; *prahlāda-īśa*—to the Lord of Prahlāda Mahārāja; *jaya*—all glories; *padmā*—of the goddess of fortune; *mukha-padma*—of the lotuslike face; *bhṛṅga*—the bee.

TRANSLATION

"'All glories to Nṛsiṁhadeva! All glories to Nṛsiṁhadeva, who is the Lord of Prahlāda Mahārāja and, like a honeybee, is always engaged in beholding the lotuslike face of the goddess of fortune.'

PURPORT

The goddess of fortune is always embraced by Lord Nṛsiṁhadeva. This is mentioned in the commentary on *Śrīmad-Bhāgavatam* written by the great commentator Śrīla Śrīdhara Svāmī. The following verse was composed by Śrīdhara Svāmī in his commentary on the Tenth Canto of *Śrīmad-Bhāgavatam* (10.87.1):

vāg-īśā yasya vadane lakṣmīr yasya ca vakṣasi
yasyāste hṛdaye samvit taṁ nṛsiṁham ahaṁ bhaje

"Lord Nṛsiṁhadeva is always assisted by Sarasvatī, the goddess of learning, and He is always embracing the goddess of fortune to His chest. The Lord is always complete in knowledge within Himself. Let us offer obeisances unto Nṛsiṁhadeva."

Similarly, in his commentary on the First Canto of *Śrīmad-Bhāgavatam* (1.1.1), Śrīdhara Svāmī describes Lord Nṛsiṁhadeva in this way:

prahlāda-hṛdayāhlādaṁ bhaktāvidyā-vidāraṇam
śarad-indu-ruciṁ vande pārīndra-vadanaṁ harim

"Let me offer my obeisances unto Lord Nṛsiṁhadeva, who is always enlightening Prahlāda Mahārāja within his heart and who always kills the nescience that attacks the devotees. His mercy is distributed like moonshine, and His face is like that of a lion. Let me offer my obeisances unto Him again and again."

TEXT 6

উগ্রোঽপ্যনুগ্র এবায়ং স্বভক্তানাং নৃকেশরী ।
কেশরীব স্বপোতানামন্যেষামুগ্রবিক্রমঃ ॥ ৬ ॥

ugro 'py anugra evāyaṁ
sva-bhaktānāṁ nṛ-keśarī
keśarīva sva-potānām
anyeṣāṁ ugra-vikramaḥ

ugraḥ—ferocious; *api*—although; *anugraḥ*—not ferocious; *eva*—certainly; *ayam*—this; *sva-bhaktānām*—to His pure devotees; *nṛ-keśarī*—having the body of a human being and a lion; *keśarī iva*—like a lioness; *sva-potānām*—to her young cubs; *anyeṣām*—to others; *ugra*—ferocious; *vikramaḥ*—whose strength.

TRANSLATION

"'Although very ferocious, the lioness is very kind to her cubs. Similarly, although very ferocious to nondevotees like Hiraṇyakaśipu,

Lord Nṛsiṁhadeva is very, very soft and kind to devotees like Prahlāda Mahārāja.'"

PURPORT

This verse was composed by Śrīdhara Svāmī in his commentary on the Seventh Canto of *Śrīmad-Bhāgavatam* (7.9.1).

TEXT 7

এইমত নানা শ্লোক পড়ি' স্তুতি কৈল ।
নৃসিংহ-সেবক মালা-প্রসাদ আনি' দিল ॥ ৭ ॥

ei-mata nānā śloka paḍi' stuti kaila
nṛsiṁha-sevaka mālā-prasāda āni' dila

ei-mata—in this way; *nānā*—various; *śloka*—verses; *paḍi'*—reciting; *stuti*—prayers; *kaila*—offered; *nṛsiṁha-sevaka*—the priest of Lord Nṛsiṁhadeva in the temple; *mālā*—garlands; *prasāda*—and remnants of the food of Lord Nṛsiṁhadeva; *āni'*—bringing; *dila*—offered.

TRANSLATION

In this way Lord Śrī Caitanya Mahāprabhu recited different verses from the śāstra. The priest of Lord Nṛsiṁhadeva then brought garlands and the remnants of the Lord's food and offered them to Śrī Caitanya Mahāprabhu.

TEXT 8

পূর্ববৎ কোন বিপ্রে কৈল নিমন্ত্রণ ।
সেই রাত্রি তাহাঁ রহি' করিলা গমন ॥ ৮ ॥

pūrvavat kona vipre kaila nimantraṇa
sei rātri tāhāṅ rahi' karilā gamana

pūrva-vat—as previously; *kona*—some; *vipre*—*brāhmaṇa; kaila*—made; *nimantraṇa*—invitation; *sei rātri*—that night; *tāhāṅ*—there; *rahi'*—staying; *karilā*—did; *gamana*—touring.

TRANSLATION

As usual, a brāhmaṇa offered Śrī Caitanya Mahāprabhu an invitation. The Lord passed the night in the temple and then commenced His tour again.

TEXT 9

প্রভাতে উঠিয়া প্রভু চলিলা প্রেমাবেশে ।
দিগ্‌বিদিক্ নাহি জ্ঞান রাত্রি-দিবসে ॥ ৯ ॥

prabhāte uṭhiyā prabhu calilā premāveśe
dig-vidik nāhi jñāna rātri-divase

prabhāte—in the morning; *uṭhiyā*—rising; *prabhu*—Lord Śrī Caitanya Mahāprabhu; *calilā*—went; *prema-āveśe*—in great ecstatic love; *dik-vidik*—the right or wrong direction; *nāhi*—there was not; *jñāna*—knowledge; *rātri-divase*—day and night.

TRANSLATION

The next morning, in the great ecstasy of love, Lord Śrī Caitanya Mahāprabhu started on His tour with no knowledge of the proper direction, and He continued the whole day and night.

TEXT 10

পূর্ব্ববৎ 'বৈষ্ণব' করি' সর্ব লোকগণে ।
গোদাবরী-তীরে প্রভু আইলা কতদিনে ॥ ১০ ॥

pūrvavat 'vaiṣṇava' kari' sarva loka-gaṇe
godāvarī-tīre prabhu āilā kata-dine

pūrva-vat—as previously; *vaiṣṇava*—devotees; *kari'*—making; *sarva*—all; *loka-gaṇe*—the people; *godāvarī-tīre*—on the bank of the river Godāvarī; *prabhu*—the Lord; *āilā*—arrived; *kata-dine*—after some days.

TRANSLATION

As previously, Śrī Caitanya Mahāprabhu converted to Vaiṣṇavism many people He met on the road. After some days, the Lord reached the banks of the river Godāvarī.

TEXT 11

গোদাবরী দেখি' হইল 'যমুনা'-স্মরণ।
তীরে বন দেখি' স্মৃতি হৈল বৃন্দাবন ॥ ১১ ॥

godāvarī dekhi' ha-ila 'yamunā'-smaraṇa
tīre vana dekhi' smṛti haila vṛndāvana

godāvarī—the river Godāvarī; *dekhi'*—seeing; *ha-ila*—there was; *yamunā smaraṇa*—remembrance of the river Yamunā; *tīre*—on the banks; *vana*—the forests; *dekhi'*—seeing; *smṛti*—remembrance; *haila*—there was; *vṛndāvana*—Śrī Vṛndāvana.

TRANSLATION

When He saw the river Godāvarī, the Lord remembered the river Yamunā, and when He saw the forest on the banks of the river, He remembered Śrī Vṛndāvana-dhāma.

TEXT 12

সেই বনে কতক্ষণ করি' নৃত্য-গান।
গোদাবরী পার হঞা তাহাঁ কৈল স্নান ॥ ১২ ॥

sei vane kata-kṣaṇa kari' nṛtya-gāna
godāvarī pāra hañā tāhāṅ kaila snāna

sei vane—in that forest; *kata-kṣaṇa*—for some time; *kari'*—performing; *nṛtya-gāna*—dancing and chanting; *godāvarī*—the river; *pāra hañā*—crossing; *tāhāṅ*—there; *kaila*—took; *snāna*—bath.

TRANSLATION

After performing His usual chanting and dancing for some time in this forest, the Lord crossed the river and took His bath on the other bank.

TEXT 13

ঘাট ছাড়ি' কতদূরে জল-সন্নিধানে।
বসি' প্রভু করে কৃষ্ণনাম-সংকীর্তনে ॥ ১৩ ॥

ghāṭa chāḍi' kata-dūre jala-sannidhāne
vasi' prabhu kare kṛṣṇa-nāma-saṅkīrtane

ghāṭa chāḍi'—leaving the bathing place; *kata-dūre*—a short distance away; *jala-sannidhāne*—near the water; *vasi'*—sitting; *prabhu*—the Lord; *kare*—does; *kṛṣṇa-nāma-saṅkīrtane*—chanting of the holy name of Lord Kṛṣṇa.

TRANSLATION

After bathing in the river, the Lord walked a little distance from the bathing place and engaged in chanting the holy name of Kṛṣṇa.

TEXT 14

হেনকালে দোলায় চড়ি' রামানন্দ রায় ।
স্নান করিবারে আইলা, বাজনা বাজায় ॥ ১৪ ॥

hena-kāle dolāya caḍi' rāmānanda rāya
snāna karibāre āilā, bājanā bājāya

hena-kāle—at this time; *dolāya caḍi'*—riding on a palanquin; *rāmānanda rāya*—Śrīla Rāmānanda Rāya; *snāna*—bath; *karibāre*—to take; *āilā*—came there; *bājanā bājāya*—accompanied by a musical band.

TRANSLATION

At that time, accompanied by the sounds of music, Rāmānanda Rāya came there on a palanquin to take his bath.

TEXT 15

তাঁর সঙ্গে বহু আইলা বৈদিক ব্রাহ্মণ ।
বিধিমতে কৈল তেঁহো স্নানাদি-তর্পণ ॥ ১৫ ॥

tāṅra saṅge bahu āilā vaidika brāhmaṇa
vidhi-mate kaila teṅho snānādi-tarpaṇa

tāṅra saṅge—with him; *bahu*—many; *āilā*—came; *vaidika*—following the Vedic principles; *brāhmaṇa*—*brāhmaṇas; vidhi-*

mate—according to ritualistic ceremonies; *kaila*—did; *teṅho*—he, Śrīla Rāmānanda Rāya; *snāna-ādi-tarpaṇa*—bathing and offering oblations, etc.

TRANSLATION

Many brāhmaṇas following the Vedic principles accompanied Rāmānanda Rāya. According to the Vedic rituals, Rāmānanda Rāya took his bath and offered oblations to his forefathers.

TEXT 16

প্রভু তাঁরে দেখি' জানিল — এই রামরায়।
তাঁহারে মিলিতে প্রভুর মন উঠি' ধায় ॥ ১৬ ॥

prabhu tāṅre dekhi' jānila — ei rāma-rāya
tāṅhāre milite prabhura mana uṭhi' dhāya

prabhu—Śrī Caitanya Mahāprabhu; *tāṅre*—him; *dekhi'*—seeing; *jānila*—could understand; *ei*—this; *rāma-rāya*—Śrīla Rāmānanda Rāya; *tāṅhāre*—him; *milite*—to meet; *prabhura*—of Lord Caitanya Mahāprabhu; *mana*—mind; *uṭhi'*—rising; *dhāya*—runs after.

TRANSLATION

Śrī Caitanya Mahāprabhu could understand that the person who had come to bathe in the river was Rāmānanda Rāya. The Lord wanted so much to meet him that His mind immediately began running after him.

TEXT 17

তথাপি ধৈর্য ধরি' প্রভু রহিলা বসিয়া।
রামানন্দ আইলা অপূর্ব সন্ন্যাসী দেখিয়া ॥ ১৭ ॥

tathāpi dhairya dhari' prabhu rahilā vasiyā
rāmānanda āilā apūrva sannyāsī dekhiyā

tathāpi—still; *dhariya dhari'*—keeping patient; *prabhu*—Lord Śrī Caitanya Mahāprabhu; *rahilā*—remained; *vasiyā*—sitting;

rāmānanda—Śrīla Rāmānanda Rāya; *āilā*—arrived; *apūrva*—wonderful; *sannyāsī*—renunciant; *dekhiyā*—seeing.

TRANSLATION

Although Śrī Caitanya Mahāprabhu was running after him mentally, He patiently remained sitting. Rāmānanda Rāya, seeing the wonderful sannyāsī, then came to see Him.

TEXT 18

সূর্যশত-সম কান্তি, অরুণ বসন।
সুবলিত প্রকাণ্ড দেহ, কমল-লোচন ॥ ১৮ ॥

sūrya-śata-sama kānti, aruṇa vasana
subalita prakāṇḍa deha, kamala-locana

sūrya-śata—hundreds of suns; *sama*—like; *kānti*—luster; *aruṇa*—saffron; *vasana*—garments; *subalita*—very strongly built; *prakāṇḍa*—big; *deha*—body; *kamala-locana*—eyes like lotus petals.

TRANSLATION

Śrīla Rāmānanda Rāya then saw Śrī Caitanya Mahāprabhu to be as brilliant as a hundred suns. The Lord was covered by a saffron garment. He was large in body and very strongly built, and His eyes were like lotus petals.

TEXT 19

দেখিয়া তাঁহার মনে হৈল চমৎকার।
আসিয়া করিল দণ্ডবৎ নমস্কার ॥ ১৯ ॥

dekhiyā tāṅhāra mane haila camatkāra
āsiyā karila daṇḍavat namaskāra

dekhiyā—seeing; *tāṅhāra*—his; *mane*—in the mind; *haila*—there was; *camatkāra*—wonder; *āsiyā*—coming there; *karila*—did; *daṇḍa-vat*—like a rod; *namaskāra*—obeisances.

TRANSLATION

When Rāmānanda Rāya saw the wonderful sannyāsī, he was struck with wonder. He went to Him and immediately offered his respectful obeisances, falling down flat like a rod.

TEXT 20

উঠি' প্রভু কহে, — উঠ, কহ 'কৃষ্ণ' 'কৃষ্ণ'।
তারে আলিঙ্গিতে প্রভুর হৃদয় সতৃষ্ণ ॥ ২০ ॥

uṭhi' prabhu kahe, — ūṭha, kaha 'kṛṣṇa' 'kṛṣṇa'
tāre āliṅgite prabhura hṛdaya satṛṣṇa

uṭhi' — rising; *prabhu* — the Lord; *kahe* — said; *uṭha* — get up; *kaha* — chant; *kṛṣṇa kṛṣṇa* — the holy name of Lord Kṛṣṇa; *tāre* — him; *āliṅgite* — to embrace; *prabhura* — of Lord Śrī Caitanya Mahāprabhu; *hṛdaya* — the heart; *sa-tṛṣṇa* — very eager.

TRANSLATION

The Lord stood up and asked Rāmānanda Rāya to arise and chant the holy name of Kṛṣṇa. Indeed, Śrī Caitanya Mahāprabhu was very eager to embrace him.

TEXT 21

তথাপি পুছিল, — তুমি রায় রামানন্দ ?
তেঁহো কহে, — সেই হঙ দাস শূদ্র মন্দ ॥ ২১ ॥

tathāpi puchila, — tumi rāya rāmānanda?
teṅho kahe, — sei haṅa dāsa śūdra manda

tathāpi — still; *puchila* — He inquired; *tumi* — you; *rāya rāmānanda* — Rāmānanda Rāya; *teṅho kahe* — he replied; *sei haṅa* — I am that; *dāsa* — servant; *śūdra* — belonging to the *śūdra* community; *manda* — very low.

TRANSLATION

Śrī Caitanya Mahāprabhu then inquired whether he was Rāmānanda Rāya, and he replied, "Yes, I am Your very low servant, and I belong to the śūdra community."

TEXT 22

তবে তারে কৈল প্রভু দৃঢ় আলিঙ্গন ।
প্রেমাবেশে প্রভু-ভৃত্য দোঁহে অচেতন ॥ ২২ ॥

tabe tāre kaila prabhu dṛḍha āliṅgana
premāveśe prabhu-bhṛtya doṅhe acetana

tabe—thereafter; *tāre*—him; *kaila*—did; *prabhu*—Lord Śrī Caitanya Mahāprabhu; *dṛḍha*—firm; *āliṅgana*—embracing; *prema-āveśe*—in ecstatic love; *prabhu-bhṛtya*—the servant and the master; *doṅhe*—both; *acetana*—unconscious.

TRANSLATION

Śrī Caitanya Mahāprabhu then embraced Śrī Rāmānanda Rāya very firmly. Indeed, both the master and the servant almost lost consciousness due to ecstatic love.

TEXT 23

স্বাভাবিক প্রেম দোঁহার উদয় করিলা ।
দুঁহা আলিঙ্গিয়া দুঁহে ভূমিতে পড়িলা ॥ ২৩ ॥

svābhāvika prema doṅhāra udaya karilā
duṅhā āliṅgiyā duṅhe bhūmite paḍilā

svābhāvika—natural; *prema*—love; *doṅhāra*—of both of them; *udaya*—awakening; *karilā*—there was; *duṅhā*—both; *āliṅgiyā*—embracing; *duṅhe*—both of them; *bhūmite*—to the ground; *paḍilā*—fell down.

TRANSLATION

Their natural love for each other was awakened in them both, and they embraced and fell to the ground.

PURPORT

Śrīla Rāmānanda Rāya was an incarnation of the *gopī* Viśākhā. Since Śrī Caitanya Mahāprabhu was Lord Kṛṣṇa Himself, there was naturally an awakening of love between Viśākhā and Kṛṣṇa. Śrī Kṛṣṇa Caitanya Mahāprabhu is the combination of Śrīmatī Rādhārāṇī and Kṛṣṇa, and the *gopī* Viśākhā is a principal *gopī* assisting Śrīmatī Rādhārāṇī. Thus the natural love between Rāmānanda Rāya and Śrī Caitanya Mahāprabhu awakened and they embraced.

TEXT 24

স্তম্ভ, স্বেদ, অশ্রু, কম্প, পুলক, বৈবর্ণ্য।
দুঁহার মুখেতে শুনি' গদ্গদ 'কৃষ্ণ'বর্ণ ॥ ২৪ ॥

stambha, sveda, aśru, kampa, pulaka, vaivarṇya
duṅhāra mukhete śuni' gadgada 'kṛṣṇa' varṇa

stambha—paralysis; *sveda*—perspiration; *aśru*—tears; *kampa*—shivering; *pulaka*—horripilation; *vaivarṇya*—paleness; *duṅhāra*—of both of them; *mukhete*—in the mouth; *śuni'*—hearing; *gadgada*—faltering; *kṛṣṇa varṇa*—Kṛṣṇa's name.

TRANSLATION

When they embraced each other, ecstatic symptoms—paralysis, perspiration, tears, shivering, paleness and standing up of the bodily hairs—appeared. The word "Kṛṣṇa" came from their mouths falteringly.

TEXT 25

দেখিয়া ব্রাহ্মণগণের হৈল চমৎকার।
বৈদিক ব্রাহ্মণ সব করেন বিচার ॥ ২৫ ॥

dekhiyā brāhmaṇa-gaṇera haila camatkāra
vaidika brāhmaṇa saba karena vicāra

dekhiyā—seeing this; *brāhmaṇa-gaṇera*—of the ritualistic *brāhmaṇas; haila*—there was; *camatkāra*—wonder; *vaidika*—followers of Vedic ritualistic ceremonies; *brāhmaṇa*—the *brāhmaṇas; saba*—all; *karena*—did; *vicāra*—consideration.

TRANSLATION

When the stereotyped, ritualistic brāhmaṇas who were following the Vedic principles saw this ecstatic manifestation of love, they were struck with wonder. All these brāhmaṇas began to reflect as follows.

TEXT 26

এই ত' সন্ন্যাসীর তেজ দেখি ব্রহ্মসম ।
শূদ্রে আলিঙ্গিয়া কেনে করেন ক্রন্দন ॥ ২৬ ॥

ei ta' sannyāsīra teja dekhi brahma-sama
śūdre āliṅgiyā kene karena krandana

ei ta'—this indeed; *sannyāsīra*—of the *sannyāsī,* Śrī Caitanya Mahāprabhu; *teja*—bodily effulgence; *dekhi*—we see; *brahma-sama*—exactly like Brahman; *śūdre*—a *śūdra,* or worker; *āliṅgiyā*—embracing; *kene*—why; *karena*—does; *krandana*—crying.

TRANSLATION

The brāhmaṇas thought, "We can see that this sannyāsī has a luster like the effulgence of Brahman, but how is it He is crying upon embracing a śūdra, a member of the fourth caste in the social order?"

TEXT 27

এই মহারাজ — মহাপণ্ডিত, গম্ভীর ।
সন্ন্যাসীর স্পর্শে মত্ত হইলা অস্থির ॥ ২৭ ॥

ei mahārāja — mahā-paṇḍita, gambhīra
sannyāsīra sparśe matta ha-ilā asthira

ei mahārāja—this Rāmānanda Rāya, who is the Governor; *mahā-paṇḍita*—a very learned person; *gambhīra*—grave; *sannyāsīra sparśe*—by touching a *sannyāsī; matta*—mad; *ha-ilā*—became; *asthira*—restless.

TRANSLATION

They thought, "This Rāmānanda Rāya is the Governor of Madras, a highly learned and grave person, a mahā-paṇḍita, but upon touching this sannyāsī he has become restless like a madman."

TEXT 28

এইমত বিপ্রগণ ভাবে মনে মন।
বিজাতীয় লোক দেখি, প্রভু কৈল সম্বরণ ॥ ২৮ ॥

ei-mata vipra-gaṇa bhāve mane mana
vijātīya loka dekhi, prabhu kaila samvaraṇa

ei-mata—in this way; *vipra-gaṇa*—all the *brāhmaṇas; bhāve*—think; *mane mana*—within their minds; *vijātīya loka*—outside people; *dekhi*—seeing; *prabhu*—Lord Caitanya Mahāprabhu; *kaila*—did; *samvaraṇa*—restraining.

TRANSLATION

While the brāhmaṇas were thinking in this way about the activities of Śrī Caitanya Mahāprabhu and Rāmānanda Rāya, Śrī Caitanya Mahāprabhu saw those outsiders and restrained His transcendental emotions.

PURPORT

Rāmānanda Rāya was intimately related to Śrī Caitanya Mahāprabhu; therefore he can be accepted as a *sajātīya,* a person within the intimate circle of the Lord. The *brāhmaṇas,* however, were followers of the Vedic rituals and were not able to have an intimate connection with Śrī Caitanya Mahāprabhu. Consequently they are called *vijātīya-loka.* In other words, they were not pure devotees. One may be a highly learned *brāhmaṇa,* but if he is not a pure devotee he is a *vijātīya,* an outcaste, one outside devotional service—in other words, a nondevotee. Although Śrī Caitanya Mahāprabhu and Rāmānanda Rāya were embracing in ecstasy, the Lord restrained His transcendental emotions upon seeing the outsider *brāhmaṇas.*

TEXT 29

সুস্থ হঞা দুঁহে সেই স্থানেতে বসিলা ।
তবে হাসি' মহাপ্রভু কহিতে লাগিলা ॥ ২৯ ॥

sustha hañā duṅhe sei sthānete vasilā
tabe hāsi' mahāprabhu kahite lāgilā

su-stha hañā—becoming steady; *duṅhe*—both of them; *sei*—that; *sthānete*—in the place; *vasilā*—sat down; *tabe*—then; *hāsi'*—smiling; *mahāprabhu*—Caitanya Mahāprabhu; *kahite*—to speak; *lāgilā*—began.

TRANSLATION

When they regained their sanity, they both sat down, and Śrī Caitanya Mahāprabhu smiled and began to speak as follows.

TEXT 30

'সার্বভৌম ভট্টাচার্য কহিল তোমার গুণে ।
তোমারে মিলিতে মোরে করিল যতনে ॥ ৩০ ॥

'sārvabhauma bhaṭṭācārya kahila tomāra guṇe
tomāre milite more karila yatane

sārvabhauma bhaṭṭācārya—Sārvabhauma Bhaṭṭācārya; *kahila*—has spoken; *tomāra*—your; *guṇe*—good qualities; *tomāre*—you; *milite*—to meet; *more*—Me; *karila*—made; *yatane*—endeavor.

TRANSLATION

"Sārvabhauma Bhaṭṭācārya spoke of your good qualities, and he made a great endeavor to convince Me to meet you.

TEXT 31

তোমা মিলিবারে মোর এথা আগমন ।
ভাল হৈল, অনায়াসে পাইলুঁ দরশন ॥ ৩১ ॥

tomā milibāre mora ethā āgamana
bhāla haila, anāyāse pāiluṅ daraśana'

tomā—you; *milibāre*—to meet; *mora*—My; *ethā*—here; *āgamana*—coming; *bhāla haila*—it was very good; *anāyāse*—without difficulty; *pāiluṅ*—I have gotten; *daraśana*—interview.

TRANSLATION

"Indeed, I have come here just to meet you. It is very good that even without making an effort I have gotten your interview here."

TEXT 32

রায় কহে — সার্বভৌম করে ভৃত্যজ্ঞান ।
পরোক্ষেহ মোর হিতে হয় সাবধান ॥ ৩২ ॥

rāya kahe,—sārvabhauma kare bhṛtya-jñāna
parokṣeha mora hite haya sāvadhāna

rāya kahe—Rāmānanda Rāya replied; *sārvabhauma*—Sārvabhauma Bhaṭṭācārya; *kare*—does; *bhṛtya-jñāna*—thinks of me as his servant; *parokṣeha*—in my absence; *mora*—of me; *hite*—for the benefit; *haya*—is; *sāvadhāna*—always careful.

TRANSLATION

Rāmānanda Rāya replied, "Sārvabhauma Bhaṭṭācārya thinks of me as his servant. Even in my absence he is very careful to do me good.

TEXT 33

তাঁর কৃপায় পাইনু তোমার দরশন ।
আজি সফল হৈল মোর মনুষ্যজনম ॥ ৩৩ ॥

tāṅra kṛpāya pāinu tomāra daraśana
āji saphala haila mora manuṣya-janama

tāṅra kṛpāya—by his mercy; *pāinu*—I have gotten; *tomāra*—Your; *daraśana*—interview; *āji*—today; *sa-phala*—successful; *haila*—has become; *mora*—my; *manuṣya-janama*—birth as a human being.

TRANSLATION

"By his mercy I have received Your interview here. Consequently I consider that today I have become a successful human being.

TEXT 34

সার্বভৌমে তোমার কৃপা, —তার এই চিহ্ন।
অস্পৃশ্য স্পর্শিলে হঞা তাঁর প্রেমাধীন ॥ ৩৪ ॥

sārvabhaume tomāra kṛpā,—tāra ei cihna
aspṛśya sparśile hañā tāṅra premādhīna

sārvabhaume—unto Sārvabhauma Bhaṭṭācārya; *tomāra*—Your; *kṛpā*—mercy; *tāra*—of such mercy; *ei*—this; *cihna*—the symptom; *aspṛśya*—untouchable; *sparśile*—You have touched; *hañā*—becoming; *tāṅra*—his; *prema-adhīna*—influenced by love.

TRANSLATION

"I can see that You have bestowed special mercy upon Sārvabhauma Bhaṭṭācārya. Therefore You have touched me, although I am untouchable. This is due only to his love for You.

TEXT 35

কাহাঁ তুমি —সাক্ষাৎ ঈশ্বর নারায়ণ।
কাহাঁ মুঞি —রাজসেবী বিষয়ী শূদ্রাধম ॥ ৩৫ ॥

kāhāṅ tumi—sākṣāt īśvara nārāyaṇa
kāhāṅ muñi—rāja-sevī viṣayī śūdrādhama

kāhāṅ—whereas; *tumi*—You; *sākṣāt*—directly; *īśvara nārāyaṇa*—the Supreme Personality of Godhead; *kāhāṅ*—whereas; *muñi*—I; *rāja-sevī*—government servant; *viṣayī*—materialist; *śūdra-adhama*—worse than a *śūdra,* or fourth-class man.

TRANSLATION

"You are the Supreme Personality of Godhead, Nārāyaṇa Himself, and I am only a government servant interested in materialistic activities. Indeed, I am the lowest among men of the fourth caste.

TEXT 36

মোর স্পর্শে না করিলে ঘৃণা, বেদভয়।
মোর দর্শন তোমা বেদে নিষেধয় ॥ ৩৬ ॥

mora sparśe nā karile ghṛṇā, veda-bhaya
mora darśana tomā vede niṣedhaya

mora—of me; *sparśe*—by the touch; *nā*—not; *karile*—You did; *ghṛṇā*—hatred; *veda-bhaya*—afraid of the injunctions of the *Vedas;* *mora*—of me; *darśana*—seeing; *tomā*—You; *vede*—the Vedic injunctions; *niṣedhaya*—forbid.

TRANSLATION

"You do not fear the Vedic injunctions stating that You should not associate with a śūdra. You were not contemptuous of my touch, although in the Vedas You are forbidden to associate with śūdras.

PURPORT

In the *Bhagavad-gītā* (9.32) the Lord says:

māṁ hi pārtha vyapāśritya ye 'pi syuḥ pāpa-yonayaḥ
striyo vaiśyās tathā śūdrās te 'pi yānti parāṁ gatim

"O son of Pṛthā, those who take shelter in Me, though they be of lower birth—women, *vaiśyas* [merchants], as well as *śūdras* [workers]—can attain the supreme destination."

The word *pāpa-yonayaḥ* means "born of lower-caste women." The *vaiśyas* are merchants, and the *śūdras* or workers are servents. According to Vedic classifications, they belong to a lower social order. A low life means a life without Kṛṣṇa consciousness. High and low positions in society were calculated by considering a person's Kṛṣṇa consciousness. A *brāhmaṇa* is considered to be on the highest platform because he knows Brahman, the Absolute Truth. The second caste, the *kṣatriya* caste, also know Brahman, but not as well as the *brāhmaṇas.* The *vaiśyas* and *śūdras* do not clearly understand God consciousness, but if they take to Kṛṣṇa consciousness by the mercy of Kṛṣṇa and the spiritual master, they do not remain in the lower castes (*pāpa-yonayaḥ*). It is clearly stated: *te 'pi yānti paraṁ gatim.*

Unless one has attained the highest standard of life, one cannot return home, back to Godhead. One may be a *śūdra, vaiśya* or woman, but if one is situated in the service of the Lord in Kṛṣṇa consciousness, one should not be considered *strī, śūdra, vaiśya* or lower than *śūdra.* Though a person may be from a lowborn family, if he is engaged in the Lord's service he should never be considered to belong to a lowborn family. The *Padma Purāṇa* forbids, *vīkṣate jāti-sāmānyāt sa yāti narakaṁ-dhruvam.* A person goes to hell quickly when he considers a devotee of the Lord in terms of birth. Although Śrī Rāmānanda Rāya supposedly took birth in a *śūdra* family, he is not to be considered a *śūdra,* for he was a great advanced devotee. Indeed, he was on the transcendental platform. Śrī Caitanya Mahāprabhu therefore embraced him. Out of spiritual humility, Śrī Rāmānanda Rāya presented himself as a *śūdra* (*rāja-sevī viṣayī śūdrādhama*). Even though one may engage in government service or in any other pounds-shillings-pence business—in short, in materialistic life—he need only take to Kṛṣṇa consciousness. Kṛṣṇa consciousness is a very simple process. One need only chant the holy names of the Lord and strictly follow the principles forbidding sinful activity. In this way one can no longer be considered an untouchable, a *viṣayī* or a *śūdra.* One who is advanced in spiritual life should not associate with nondevotees—namely men in government service and men engaged in materialistic activity for sense gratification or in the service of others. Such men are considered *viṣayī,* materialistic. It is said:

niṣkiñcanasya bhagavad-bhajanonmukhasya
pāraṁ paraṁ jigamiṣor bhava-sāgarasya
sandarśanaṁ viṣayiṇām atha yoṣitāṁ ca
hā hanta hanta viṣa-bhakṣaṇato 'py asādhu

"A person who is very seriously engaged in cultivating devotional service with a view to crossing the ocean of nescience and who has completely abandoned all material activities should never see a *śūdra,* a *vaiśya* or a woman." (*Śrī Caitanya-candrodaya-nāṭaka* 8.23)

TEXT 37

তোমার কৃপায় তোমায় করায় নিন্দ্যকর্ম।
সাক্ষাৎ ঈশ্বর তুমি, কে জানে তোমার মর্ম ॥ ৩৭ ॥

tomāra kṛpāya tomāya karāya nindya-karma
sākṣāt īśvara tumi, ke jāne tomāra marma

tomāra kṛpāya—Your mercy; *tomāya*—unto You; *karāya*—induces; *nindya-karma*—forbidden actions; *sākṣāt īśvara*—directly the Supreme Personality of Godhead; *tumi*—You; *ke jāne*—who can know; *tomāra*—Your; *marma*—purpose.

TRANSLATION

"You are the Supreme Personality of Godhead Himself; therefore no one can understand Your purpose. By Your mercy You are touching me, although this is not sanctioned by the Vedas.

PURPORT

A *sannyāsī* is strictly forbidden to see the *viṣayīs,* the materialistic people. But Śrī Caitanya Mahāprabhu, out of His boundless and causeless mercy, could show favor to anyone, regardless of birth and position.

TEXT 38

আমা নিস্তারিতে তোমার ইহাঁ আগমন।
পরম-দয়ালু তুমি পতিত-পাবন ॥ ৩৮ ॥

āmā nistārite tomāra ihāṅ āgamana
parama-dayālu tumi patita-pāvana

āmā nistārite—to deliver me; *tomāra*—Your; *ihāṅ*—here; *āgamana*—appearance; *parama-dayālu*—greatly merciful; *tumi*—You; *patita-pāvana*—the deliverer of all fallen souls.

TRANSLATION

"You have come here specifically to deliver me. You are so merciful that You alone can deliver all fallen souls.

PURPORT

Śrīla Narottama dāsa Ṭhākura sings in his *Prārthanā* (39):

śrī-kṛṣṇa-caitanya-prabhu dayā kara more,
tomā vinā ke dayālu jagat-saṁsāre

patita-pāvana-hetu tava avatāra,
mo sama patita prabhu nā pāibe āra

"My dear Lord, please be merciful to me. Who can be more merciful than Your Lordship within these three worlds? You appear as an incarnation just to reclaim the conditioned, fallen souls, but I assure You that You will not find a soul more fallen than me."

Śrī Caitanya Mahāprabhu's specific mission is to deliver fallen souls. Of course, in this Age of Kali there is hardly anyone who is not fallen according to the calculations of Vedic behavior. In His instructions to Rūpa Gosvāmī, Śrī Caitanya Mahāprabhu described the so-called followers of Vedic religion in this way (*Madhya* 19.146):

veda-niṣṭha-madhye ardheka veda 'mukhe' māne
veda-niṣiddha pāpa kare, dharma nāhi gaṇe

So-called followers of Vedic principles simply accept the *Vedas* formally, but they act against Vedic principles. This is symptomatic of this Age of Kali. People claim to follow a certain type of religion, saying formally, "I am Hindu," "I am Muslim," "I am Christian," "I am this or that," but actually no one follows the principles enunciated in religious scriptures. This is the disease of this age. Therefore the merciful Śrī Caitanya Mahāprabhu has simply advised us to chant the Hare Kṛṣṇa *mahā-mantra: harer nāma harer nāma harer nāmaiva kevalam.* The Lord can deliver anyone and everyone, even though one may have fallen from the injunctions of revealed scriptures. This is Śrī Caitanya Mahāprabhu's special mercy. Consequently He is known as *patita-pāvana,* the deliverer of all fallen souls.

TEXT 39

মহান্ত-স্বভাব এই তারিতে পামর ।
নিজ কার্য নাহি তবু যান তার ঘর ॥ ৩৯ ॥

mahānta-svabhāva ei tārite pāmara
nija kārya nāhi tabu yāna tāra ghara

mahānta-svabhāva—the nature of saintly persons; *ei*—this; *tārite*—to deliver; *pāmara*—fallen souls; *nija*—own; *kārya*—business; *nāhi*—there is not; *tabu*—still; *yāna*—goes; *tāra*—his; *ghara*—house.

TRANSLATION

"It is the general practice of all saintly people to deliver the fallen. Therefore they go to people's houses, although they have no personal business there.

PURPORT

A *sannyāsī* is supposed to beg from door to door. He does not beg simply because he is hungry. His real purpose is to enlighten the occupant of every house by preaching Kṛṣṇa consciousness. A *sannyāsī* does not abandon his superior position and become a beggar just for the sake of begging. Similarly, a person in householder life may be very important, but he may also voluntarily take to the mendicant way of life. Rūpa Gosvāmī and Sanātana Gosvāmī were ministers, but they voluntarily accepted the mendicant's life in order to humbly preach Śrī Caitanya Mahāprabhu's message. It is said about them: *tyaktvā tūrṇam aśeṣa-maṇḍala-pati-śreṇīṁ sadā tuccha-vat bhūtvā dīna-gaṇeśakau karuṇayā kaupīna-kanthāśritau.* Although the Gosvāmīs were very aristocratic, on the order of Śrī Caitanya Mahāprabhu they became mendicants just to deliver the fallen souls. One should also consider that those who engage in the missionary activities of the Kṛṣṇa consciousness movement are under the guidance of Śrī Caitanya Mahāprabhu. They are not actually beggars; their real business is to deliver fallen souls. Therefore they may go from door to door just to introduce a book about Kṛṣṇa consciousness so that people can become enlightened by reading. Formerly *brahmacārīs* and *sannyāsīs* used to beg from door to door. At the present moment, especially in the Western countries, a person may be handed over to the police if he begs from door to door. In Western countries, begging is considered criminal. Members of the Kṛṣṇa consciousness movement have no business begging. Instead, they work very hard to introduce some literatures about Kṛṣṇa consciousness so that people can read them and be benefited. But if one gives some contribution to a Kṛṣṇa conscious man, he never refuses it.

TEXT 40

মহদ্বিচলনং নৃণাং গৃহিণাং দীনচেতসাম্ ।
নিঃশ্রেয়সায় ভগবন্নান্যথা কল্পতে ক্বচিৎ ॥ ৪০ ॥

mahad-vicalanaṁ nṝṇāṁ
gṛhiṇāṁ dīna-cetasām
niḥśreyasāya bhagavan
nānyathā kalpate kvacit

mahat-vicalanam—the wandering of saintly persons; *nṝṇām*—of human beings; *gṛhiṇām*—who are householders; *dīna-cetasām*—low-minded; *niḥśreyasāya*—for the ultimate benefit; *bhagavan*—O my Lord; *na anyathā*—not any other purpose; *kalpate*—one imagines; *kvacit*—at any time.

TRANSLATION

"'My dear Lord, sometimes great saintly persons go to the homes of householders, although these householders are generally low-minded. When a saintly person visits their homes, one can understand that it is for no other purpose than to benefit the householders.'

PURPORT

This verse is from *Śrīmad-Bhāgavatam* (10.8.4).

TEXT 41

আমার সঙ্গে ব্রাহ্মণাদি সহস্রেক জন ।
তোমার দর্শনে সবার দ্রবীভূত মন ॥ ৪১ ॥

āmāra saṅge brāhmaṇādi sahasreka jana
tomāra darśane sabāra dravī-bhūta mana

āmāra saṅge—with me; *brāhmaṇa-ādi*—*brāhmaṇas* and others; *sahasreka*—more than one thousand; *jana*—persons; *tomāra*—of You; *darśane*—in seeing; *sabāra*—of all of them; *dravī-bhūta*—became melted; *mana*—the hearts.

TRANSLATION

"Along with me there are about a thousand men—including the brāhmaṇas—and all of them appear to have had their hearts melted simply by seeing You.

TEXT 42

'কৃষ্ণ' 'কৃষ্ণ' নাম শুনি সবার বদনে ।
সবার অঙ্গ — পুলকিত, অশ্রু — নয়নে ॥ ৪২ ॥

'kṛṣṇa' 'kṛṣṇa' nāma śuni sabāra vadane
sabāra aṅga—pulakita, aśru—nayane

kṛṣṇa kṛṣṇa—"Kṛṣṇa," "Kṛṣṇa"; *nāma*—the holy name; *śuni*—I hear; *sabāra*—of everyone; *vadane*—in the mouths; *sabāra*—of all; *aṅga*—the bodies; *pulakita*—gladdened; *aśru*—tears; *nayane*—in the eyes.

TRANSLATION

"I hear everyone chanting the holy name of Kṛṣṇa. Everyone's body is thrilled with ecstasy, and there are tears in everyone's eyes.

TEXT 43

আকৃত্যে-প্রকৃত্যে তোমার ঈশ্বর-লক্ষণ ।
জীবে না সম্ভবে এই অপ্রাকৃত গুণ ॥ ৪৩ ॥

ākṛtye-prakṛtye tomāra īśvara-lakṣaṇa
jīve nā sambhave ei aprākṛta guṇa

ākṛtye—in bodily features; *prakṛtye*—in behavior; *tomāra*—of You; *īśvara*—of the Supreme Personality of Godhead; *lakṣaṇa*—the symptoms; *jīve*—in an ordinary living being; *nā*—not; *sambhave*—possible; *ei*—these; *aprākṛta*—transcendental; *guṇa*—qualities.

TRANSLATION

"My dear Sir, according to Your behavior and bodily features, You are the Supreme Personality of Godhead. It is impossible for ordinary living beings to possess such transcendental qualities."

PURPORT

Śrī Caitanya Mahāprabhu's bodily features were uncommon. Indeed, His body was extraordinary in its measurements. The measurement of His chest and the measurement of His forearms were the same. This is called *nyagrodha-parimaṇḍala.* As far as His nature is concerned, He was kind to everyone. No one but the Supreme Personality of Godhead can be kind to everyone. Therefore the Lord's name is Kṛṣṇa, "all-attractive." As stated in the *Bhagavad-gītā* (14.4), Kṛṣṇa is the kind father of everyone. In every species of life (*sarva-yoniṣu*), He is the original father, the seed-giver (*bīja-pradaḥ pitā*). How, then, can He be unkind to any living entity? One may be a man, an animal or even a tree, but the Lord is kind to everyone. That is God's qualification. He also says in the *Bhagavad-gītā* (9.29), *samo 'haṁ sarva-bhūteṣu:* "I am equally kind to everyone." And He advises, *sarva-dharmān parityajya mām ekaṁ śaraṇaṁ vraja:* "Give up all other engagements and simply surrender unto Me." This instruction is meant not only for Arjuna but for all living entities. Whoever takes advantage of this offer is immediately immune to all sinful activity and returns home, back to Godhead. While present on this planet, Śrī Caitanya Mahāprabhu made the same offer.

TEXT 44

প্রভু কহে, — তুমি মহা-ভাগবতোত্তম।
তোমার দর্শনে সবার দ্রব হৈল মন ॥ ৪৪ ॥

prabhu kahe, — tumi mahā-bhāgavatottama
tomāra darśane sabāra drava haila mana

prabhu kahe — the Lord replied; *tumi* — you; *mahā-bhāgavata-uttama* — the best of the topmost devotees; *tomāra darśane* — by seeing you; *sabāra* — of everyone; *drava* — melted; *haila* — became; *mana* — the heart.

TRANSLATION

The Lord replied to Rāmānanda Rāya, "Sir, you are the best of the topmost devotees; therefore simply the sight of you has melted everyone's heart.

PURPORT

Unless one is a first-class devotee, he cannot be a preacher. A preacher is generally a topmost devotee, but in order to meet the general populace, he has to come to distinguish between devotees and nondevotees. Otherwise, an advanced devotee makes no such distinctions. Indeed, he always sees that everyone is engaged in the service of the Lord. When one engages in preaching work, he must distinguish between people and understand that some people are not engaged in the devotional service of the Lord. The preacher then has to take compassion upon such innocent people who do not know how to worship the Lord. In *Śrīmad-Bhāgavatam* (11.2.45), the symptoms of a topmost devotee are described as follows:

sarva-bhūteṣu yaḥ paśyed bhagavad-bhāvam ātmanaḥ
bhūtāni bhagavaty ātmany eṣa bhāgavatottamaḥ

"The advanced devotee sees that all living entities are part and parcel of the Supreme Personality of Godhead. Everyone is in Kṛṣṇa, and Kṛṣṇa is also within everyone. Such a vision is possible only for a person who is very advanced in devotional service."

TEXT 45

অন্যের কি কথা, আমি — 'মায়াবাদী সন্ন্যাসী' ।
আমিহ তোমার স্পর্শে কৃষ্ণ-প্রেমে ভাসি ॥ ৪৫ ॥

anyera ki kathā, āmi — 'māyāvādī sannyāsī'
āmiha tomāra sparśe kṛṣṇa-preme bhāsi

anyera — of others; *ki kathā* — what to speak; *āmi* — I; *māyāvādī sannyāsī* — a *sannyāsī* of the Māyāvādī sect; *āmiha* — I; *tomāra* — of you; *sparśe* — by the touch; *kṛṣṇa* — of Kṛṣṇa; *preme* — in love; *bhāsi* — float.

TRANSLATION

"Although I am a Māyāvādī sannyāsī, a nondevotee, I am also floating in the ocean of love of Kṛṣṇa simply by touching you. And what to speak of others?

TEXT 46

এই জানি' কঠিন মোর হৃদয় শোধিতে ।
সার্বভৌম কহিলেন তোমারে মিলিতে ॥ ৪৬ ॥

ei jāni' kaṭhina mora hṛdaya śodhite
sārvabhauma kahilena tomāre milite

ei jāni'—knowing this; *kaṭhina*—very hard; *mora*—My; *hṛdaya*—heart; *śodhite*—to rectify; *sārvabhauma*—Sārvabhauma Bhaṭṭācārya; *kahilena*—asked; *tomāre*—you; *milite*—to meet.

TRANSLATION

"Sārvabhauma Bhaṭṭācārya knew this would happen, and thus to rectify My heart, which is very hard, he asked Me to meet you."

TEXT 47

এইমত দুঁহে স্তুতি করে দুঁহার গুণ ।
দুঁহে দুঁহার দরশনে আনন্দিত মন ॥ ৪৭ ॥

ei-mata duṅhe stuti kare duṅhāra guṇa
duṅhe duṅhāra daraśane ānandita mana

ei-mata—in this way; *duṅhe*—both of them; *stuti*—praise; *kare*—offer; *duṅhāra*—of both of them; *guṇa*—qualities; *duṅhe*—both of them; *duṅhāra*—of both of them; *daraśane*—by the seeing; *ānandita*—pleased; *mana*—the minds.

TRANSLATION

In this way each of them praised the qualities of the other, and both of them were pleased to see each other.

TEXT 48

হেনকালে বৈদিক এক বৈষ্ণব ব্রাহ্মণ ।
দণ্ডবৎ করি' কৈল প্রভুরে নিমন্ত্রণ ॥ ৪৮ ॥

hena-kāle vaidika eka vaiṣṇava brāhmaṇa
daṇḍavat kari' kaila prabhure nimantraṇa

hena-kāle—at this time; *vaidika*—a follower of the Vedic ritualistic ceremonies; *eka*—one; *vaiṣṇava brāhmaṇa*—a *brāhmaṇa* following Vaiṣṇava principles; *daṇḍavat*—obeisances offered by falling flat; *kari'*—offering; *kaila*—made; *prabhure*—unto Lord Śrī Caitanya Mahāprabhu; *nimantraṇa*—invitation.

TRANSLATION

At this time a brāhmaṇa Vaiṣṇava following the Vedic principles came and offered obeisances. He fell flat before Śrī Caitanya Mahāprabhu and invited Him for lunch.

TEXT 49

নিমন্ত্রণ মানিল তাঁরে বৈষ্ণব জানিয়া ।
রামানন্দে কহে প্রভু ঈষৎ হাসিয়া ॥ ৪৯ ॥

nimantraṇa mānila tāṅre vaiṣṇava jāniyā
rāmānande kahe prabhu īṣat hāsiyā

nimantraṇa—the invitation; *mānila*—accepted; *tāṅre*—him (the *brāhmaṇa*); *vaiṣṇava*—a devotee; *jāniyā*—understanding; *rāmānande*—unto Rāmānanda; *kahe*—said; *prabhu*—Śrī Caitanya Mahāprabhu; *īṣat*—a little; *hāsiyā*—smiling.

TRANSLATION

Lord Śrī Caitanya Mahāprabhu accepted the invitation, knowing the brāhmaṇa to be a devotee, and slightly smiling, He spoke as follows to Rāmānanda Rāya.

PURPORT

Śrī Caitanya Mahāprabhu accepted the invitation of the Vaiṣṇava *brāhmaṇa.* Even though one is a *brāhmaṇa* strictly following all the rules and regulations of brahminical culture, if he is not a devotee, a follower of Śrī Caitanya Mahāprabhu, one should not accept his invitation. At the present moment people have become so degraded that they do not even follow the Vedic principles, to say nothing of Vaiṣṇava principles. They eat anything and everything—whatever they like—and therefore the members of the Kṛṣṇa consciousness movement should be very cautious about accepting invitations.

TEXT 50

তোমার মুখে কৃষ্ণকথা শুনিতে হয় মন।
পুনরপি পাই যেন তোমার দরশন ॥ ৫০ ॥

tomāra mukhe kṛṣṇa-kathā śunite haya mana
punarapi pāi yena tomāra daraśana

tomāra mukhe—in your mouth; *kṛṣṇa-kathā*—talks on Kṛṣṇa; *śunite*—to hear; *haya*—there is; *mana*—My mind; *punarapi*—again; *pāi*—I may get; *yena*—if possible; *tomāra*—your; *daraśana*—interview.

TRANSLATION

"I wish to hear from you about Lord Kṛṣṇa. Indeed, My mind is inclined to desire this; therefore I wish to see you again."

TEXTS 51–52

রায় কহে,—আইলা যদি পামর শোধিতে।
দর্শনমাত্রে শুদ্ধ নহে মোর দুষ্ট চিত্তে ॥ ৫১ ॥
দিন পাঁচ-সাত রহি' করহ মার্জন।
তবে শুদ্ধ হয় মোর এই দুষ্ট মন ॥ ৫২ ॥

rāya kahe, āilā yadi pāmara śodhite
darśana-mātre śuddha nahe mora duṣṭa citte

dina pāṅca-sāta rahi' karaha mārjana
tabe śuddha haya mora ei duṣṭa mana

rāya kahe—Rāmānanda Rāya replied; *āilā*—You have come; *yadi*—although; *pāmara*—a fallen soul; *śodhite*—to rectify; *darśana-mātre*—simply seeing You; *śuddha nahe*—not purified; *mora*—my; *duṣṭa*—polluted; *citte*—consciousness; *dina*—days; *pāṅca-sāta*—five or seven; *rahi'*—staying; *karaha*—kindly do; *mārjana*—cleansing; *tabe*—then; *śuddha*—pure; *haya*—it is; *mora*—my; *ei*—this; *duṣṭa*—polluted; *mana*—mind.

TRANSLATION

Rāmānanda Rāya replied, "My Lord, although You have come to correct me, a fallen soul, my mind is not yet purified simply by seeing You. Please stay for five or seven days and kindly cleanse my polluted mind. After that much time, my mind will certainly be pure."

TEXT 53

যদ্যপি বিচ্ছেদ দোঁহার সহন না যায়।
তথাপি দণ্ডবৎ করি' চলিলা রামরায় ॥ ৫৩ ॥

yadyapi viccheda doṅhāra sahana nā yāya
tathāpi daṇḍavat kari' calilā rāma-rāya

yadyapi—although; *viccheda*—separation; *doṅhāra*—of both of them; *sahana*—toleration; *nā*—not; *yāya*—possible; *tathāpi*—still; *daṇḍavat*—obeisances; *kari'*—offering; *calilā*—departed; *rāma-rāya*—Rāmānanda Rāya.

TRANSLATION

Although neither could tolerate separation from the other, Rāmānanda Rāya nonetheless offered his obeisances to Lord Śrī Caitanya Mahāprabhu and departed.

TEXT 54

প্রভু যাই' সেই বিপ্রঘরে ভিক্ষা কৈল।
দুই জনার উৎকণ্ঠায় আসি' সন্ধ্যা হৈল ॥ ৫৪ ॥

prabhu yāi' sei vipra-ghare bhikṣā kaila
dui janāra utkaṇṭhāya āsi' sandhyā haila

prabhu—Lord Śrī Caitanya Mahāprabhu; *yāi'*—going; *sei*—that; *vipra-ghare*—to the house of the *brāhmaṇa; bhikṣā*—lunch; *kaila*—accepted; *dui*—two; *janāra*—of the persons; *utkaṇṭhāya*—in the impatience; *āsi'*—coming; *sandhyā*—evening; *haila*—appeared.

TRANSLATION

Lord Śrī Caitanya Mahāprabhu then went to the house of the brāhmaṇa who had invited Him and took His lunch there. When the evening of that day arrived, both Rāmānanda Rāya and the Lord were eager to meet each other again.

TEXT 55

প্রভু স্নান-কৃত্য করি' আছেন বসিয়া ।
একভৃত্য-সঙ্গে রায় মিলিলা আসিয়া ॥ ৫৫ ॥

prabhu snāna-kṛtya kari' āchena vasiyā
eka-bhṛtya-saṅge rāya mililā āsiyā

prabhu—the Lord; *snāna-kṛtya*—the daily duty of bathing; *kari'*—finishing; *āchena*—was; *vasiyā*—sitting; *eka*—one; *bhṛtya*—servant; *saṅge*—with; *rāya*—Rāya Rāmānanda; *mililā*—met; *āsiyā*—coming.

TRANSLATION

After finishing His evening bath, Śrī Caitanya Mahāprabhu sat down and waited for Rāmānanda Rāya to come. Then Rāmānanda Rāya, accompanied by one servant, came to meet Him.

PURPORT

A Vaiṣṇava who is supposed to be advanced in spiritual understanding—be he a householder or a *sannyāsī*—must bathe three times a day: morning, noon and evening. When one is engaged in the service of the Deity, he must especially follow the principles of the

Padma Purāṇa and take regular baths. He should also, after bathing, decorate his body with the twelve *tilakas.*

TEXT 56

নমস্কার কৈল রায়, প্রভু কৈল আলিঙ্গনে ।
দুই জনে কৃষ্ণ-কথা কয় রহঃস্থানে ॥ ৫৬ ॥

namaskāra kaila rāya, prabhu kaila āliṅgane
dui jane kṛṣṇa-kathā kaya rahaḥ-sthāne

namaskāra—obeisances; *kaila*—offered; *rāya*—Rāmānanda Rāya; *prabhu*—Lord Śrī Caitanya Mahāprabhu; *kaila*—did; *āliṅgane*—embracing; *dui*—two; *jane*—the persons; *kṛṣṇa-kathā*—talks about Kṛṣṇa; *kaya*—discussed; *rahaḥ-sthāne*—in a secluded place.

TRANSLATION

Rāmānanda Rāya approached Lord Śrī Caitanya and offered his respectful obeisances, and the Lord embraced him. Then they began to discuss Kṛṣṇa in a secluded place.

PURPORT

The word *rahaḥ-sthāne,* "in a secluded place," is very significant. Talks about Kṛṣṇa and His pastimes—especially His pastimes in Vṛndāvana and His dealings with the *gopīs*—are all very confidential. They are not subject matter for public discussion because those who have no understanding of the transcendental nature of Kṛṣṇa's pastimes always commit great offenses, thinking Kṛṣṇa to be an ordinary human being and the *gopīs* ordinary girls. Following the principle of Lord Śrī Caitanya Mahāprabhu, who never discussed the dealings between Kṛṣṇa and the *gopīs* publicly, devotees in the Kṛṣṇa consciousness movement are enjoined not to discuss the pastimes of Lord Kṛṣṇa in Vṛndāvana in public. For the general public, *saṅkīrtana* is the most effective method to awaken Kṛṣṇa consciousness. If possible, one should discuss the principles enunciated in the *Bhagavad-gītā.* Śrī Caitanya Mahāprabhu followed this principle very strictly and discussed the philosophy of the *Bhagavad-gītā* with learned scholars like Sārvabhauma Bhaṭṭācārya and Prakāśānanda Sarasvatī. However,

He taught the principles of the *bhakti* cult to students like Sanātana Gosvāmī and Rūpa Gosvāmī, and He discussed with Śrī Rāmānanda Rāya the topmost devotional dealings between Kṛṣṇa and the *gopīs.* For the general populace, He performed *saṅkīrtana* very vigorously. We must also follow these principles in preaching Kṛṣṇa consciousness all over the world.

TEXT 57

প্রভু কহে, — "পড় শ্লোক সাধ্যের নির্ণয়।"
রায় কহে, — "স্বধর্মাচরণে বিষ্ণুভক্তি হয় ॥" ৫৭ ॥

prabhu kahe, — "paḍa śloka sādhyera nirṇaya"
rāya kahe, — "sva-dharmācaraṇe viṣṇu-bhakti haya"

prabhu kahe — Lord Śrī Caitanya Mahāprabhu said; *paḍa* — just recite; *śloka* — a verse from the revealed scriptures; *sādhyera* — of the aim of life; *nirṇaya* — an ascertainment; *rāya kahe* — Rāmānanda Rāya replied; *sva-dharma-ācaraṇe* — by executing one's occupational duty; *viṣṇu-bhakti* — devotional service to Lord Viṣṇu; *haya* — there is.

TRANSLATION

Śrī Caitanya Mahāprabhu ordered Rāmānanda Rāya, "Recite a verse from the revealed scriptures concerning the ultimate goal of life."

Rāmānanda replied, "If one executes the prescribed duties of his social position, he awakens his original Kṛṣṇa consciousness.

PURPORT

In this connection, Śrī Rāmānujācārya states in the *Vedārtha-saṅgraha* that devotional service is naturally very dear to the living entity. Indeed, it is life's goal. This devotional service is supreme knowledge, or Kṛṣṇa consciousness, and it brings detachment from all material activity. In the transcendental position, a living being can perfectly acknowledge the superiority of serving the Supreme Lord. The devotees attain the Supreme Lord only by devotional service. Having such knowledge, one engages in his occupational duty, and that is called *bhakti-yoga.* By performing *bhakti-yoga,* one can rise to the platform of pure devotional service.

A great saint, the father of Śrīla Vyāsadeva, Parāśara Muni, has specifically mentioned that devotional service to the Lord can ultimately be awakened in human society by the discharge of duties in accordance with the *varṇāśrama* system. The Supreme Personality of Godhead instituted *varṇāśrama-dharma* to give human beings a chance to return home, back to Godhead. The Supreme Personality of Godhead, Lord Śrī Kṛṣṇa, who is known in the *Bhagavad-gītā* as Puruṣottama—the greatest of all personalities—personally came and declared that the institution of *varṇāśrama-dharma* was founded by Him. As stated in the *Bhagavad-gītā* (4.13):

cātur-varṇyaṁ mayā sṛṣṭaṁ guṇa-karma-vibhāgaśaḥ
tasya kartāram api māṁ viddhy akartāram avyayam

Elsewhere in the *Bhagavad-gītā* (18.45–46) the Lord says:

sve sve karmaṇy abhirataḥ saṁsiddhiṁ labhate naraḥ
sva-karma-nirataḥ siddhiṁ yathā vindati tac chṛṇu

yataḥ pravṛttir bhūtānāṁ yena sarvam idaṁ tatam
sva-karmaṇā tam abhyarcya siddhiṁ vindati mānavaḥ

Human society should be divided into four divisions—*brāhmaṇa, kṣatriya, vaiśya* and *śūdra*—and everyone should always engage in his occupational duty. The Lord says that those engaged in their occupational duty can attain perfection simply by rendering loving devotional service to the Lord while executing their particular duty. Actually the modern ideal of a classless society can be introduced only by Kṛṣṇa consciousness. Let men perform their occupational duty, and let them give their profits to the service of the Lord. In other words, one can attain the perfection of life by discharging one's occupational duty and employing the results in the service of the Lord. This method is confirmed by great personalities like Bodhāyana, Taṅka, Dramiḍa, Guhadeva, Kapardi and Bhāruci. It is also confirmed by the *Vedānta-sūtra.*

TEXT 58

বর্ণাশ্রমাচারবতা পুরুষেণ পরঃ পুমান্ ।
বিষ্ণুরারাধ্যতে পন্থা নান্যত্তত্তোষকারণম্ ॥ ৫৮ ॥

varṇāśramācāra-vatā
puruṣeṇa paraḥ pumān
viṣṇur ārādhyate panthā
nānyat tat-toṣa-kāraṇam

varṇa-āśrama-ācāra-vatā—who behaves according to the system of four divisions of social order and four divisions of spiritual life; *puruṣeṇa*—by a man; *paraḥ*—the supreme; *pumān*—person; *viṣṇuḥ*—Lord Viṣṇu; *ārādhyate*—is worshiped; *panthā*—way; *na*—not; *anyat*—another; *tat-toṣa-kāraṇam*—cause of satisfying the Lord.

TRANSLATION

"'The Supreme Personality of Godhead, Lord Viṣṇu, is worshiped by the proper execution of prescribed duties in the system of varṇa and āśrama. There is no other way to satisfy the Supreme Personality of Godhead. One must be situated in the institution of the four varṇas and āśramas.'"

PURPORT

This is a quotation from the *Viṣṇu Purāṇa* (3.8.9). As stated by Śrīla Bhaktivinoda Ṭhākura in his *Amṛta-pravāha-bhāṣya,* "The purport is that one can realize life's perfection simply by satisfying the Supreme Personality of Godhead." This is also confirmed in *Śrīmad-Bhāgavatam* (1.2.13):

ataḥ pumbhir dvija-śreṣṭhā varṇāśrama-vibhāgaśaḥ
sv-anuṣṭhitasya dharmasya saṁsiddhir hari-toṣaṇam

"O best among the twice-born, it is therefore concluded that the highest perfection one can achieve by discharging the duties prescribed for one's own occupation according to caste divisions and orders of life is to please the Personality of Godhead."

Every man should perform his occupational duty in the light of his particular tendency. According to his abilities, one should accept a position in the *varṇāśrama* institution. The divisions of *brāhmaṇa, kṣatriya, vaiśya* and *śūdra* are natural divisions within society. Indeed, everyone has a prescribed duty according to the *varṇāśrama-dharma.* Those who properly execute their prescribed duties live peacefully and are not disturbed by material conditions. The spiritual orders—*brahmacarya, gṛhastha, vānaprastha* and *sannyāsa*—are called *āśramas.* If one executes his prescribed duty in both the social and spiritual orders, the Supreme Personality of Godhead is satisfied. If one neglects his duties, however, he becomes a transgressor and a candidate for a hellish condition. Actually we see that different people are engaged in different ways; therefore there must be divisions according to work. To attain perfection, one must make devotional service the center of life. In this way one can awaken his natural instincts by work, association and education. One should accept the *varṇāśrama* divisions by qualification, not by birth. Unless this system is introduced, human activities cannot be systematically executed.

The *brāhmaṇas* are the intellectuals who can understand the Supreme Personality of Godhead. They are always engaged in the cultivation of knowledge. It does not matter whether one is born in India or outside India. Those who are naturally very heroic and who tend to rule over others are called *kṣatriyas.* Those who tend to produce food by agricultural methods, protect cows and other animals and engage in trade are called *vaiśyas,* or merchants. Those who are not sufficiently intelligent to be *brāhmaṇas, kṣatriyas* or *vaiśyas* are required to serve a master and are called *śūdras.* Thus everyone can engage in the service of the Lord and awaken his natural Kṛṣṇa consciousness. If a society does not function according to such natural divisions, the social orders become degraded. The conclusion is that the scientific method of *varṇāśrama-dharma* should be adopted by society.

TEXT 59

প্রভু কহে,—“এহো বাহ্য, আগে কহ আর।”
রায় কহে, “কৃষ্ণে কর্মার্পণ—সর্বসাধ্য-সার ॥” ৫৯ ॥

prabhu kahe,—"eho bāhya, āge kaha āra"
rāya kahe, "kṛṣṇe karmārpaṇa—sarva-sādhya-sāra"

prabhu kahe—the Lord said; *eho*—this; *bāhya*—external; *āge*—ahead; *kaha*—say; *āra*—more; *rāya kahe*—Śrī Rāmānanda

Rāya said; *kṛṣṇe*—unto Kṛṣṇa; *karma-arpaṇa*—offering the results of activities; *sarva-sādhya-sāra*—the essence of all means of perfection.

TRANSLATION

The Lord replied, "This is external. You had better tell Me of some other means."

Rāmānanda replied, "To offer the results of one's activities to Kṛṣṇa is the essence of all perfection."

TEXT 60

যৎ করোষি যদশ্নাসি যজ্জুহোষি দদাসি যৎ ।
যত্তপস্যসি কৌন্তেয় তৎ কুরুষ্ব মদর্পণম্ ॥ ৬০ ॥

yat karoṣi yad aśnāsi
yaj juhoṣi dadāsi yat
yat tapasyasi kaunteya
tat kuruṣva mad-arpaṇam

yat—whatever; *karoṣi*—you do; *yat*—whatever; *aśnāsi*—you eat; *yat*—whatever; *juhoṣi*—you offer in sacrifice; *dadāsi*—you give in charity; *yat*—whatever; *yat*—whatever; *tapasyasi*—you perform as austerity; *kaunteya*—O son of Kuntī; *tat*—that; *kuruṣva*—just do; *mat*—unto Me; *arpaṇam*—offering.

TRANSLATION

Rāmānanda Rāya continued, "'My dear son of Kuntī, whatever you do, whatever you eat, whatever you offer in sacrifice, whatever you give in charity, and whatever austerities you perform, all the results of such activities should be offered to Me, Kṛṣṇa, the Supreme Personality of Godhead.'"

PURPORT

The Lord has said that the *varṇāśrama-dharma* is not properly executed in this Age of Kali; therefore He ordered Rāmānanda Rāya to go further into the matter. Rāmānanda replied with this verse from the *Bhagavad-gītā* (9.27), which instructs that while remaining in the system of *varṇāśrama-dharma* one may offer the results of his activities to Lord Śrī Kṛṣṇa in loving service. Naturally Lord Śrī Caitanya Mahāprabhu was asking Rāmānanda Rāya about the execution of devotional service. Rāmānanda Rāya first enunciated the principle of *varṇāśrama-dharma* in consideration of materialistic people. However, this conception is not transcendental. As long as one is in the material world, he must follow the principles of *varṇāśrama-dharma,* but devotional service is transcendental. The system of *varṇāśrama-dharma* refers to the three modes of material nature, but transcendental devotional service is on the absolute platform.

Śrī Caitanya Mahāprabhu belongs to the spiritual world, and His methods for propagating the *saṅkīrtana* movement are also imported from the spiritual world. Śrīla Narottama dāsa Ṭhākura has sung: *golokera prema-dhana, hari-nāma-saṅkīrtana, rati na janmila kene tāya.* This states that the *saṅkīrtana* movement has nothing to do with this material world. It is imported from the spiritual world, Goloka Vṛndāvana. Narottama dāsa Ṭhākura laments that mundane people do not take this *saṅkīrtana* movement seriously. Considering the position of devotional service and the *saṅkīrtana* movement, Śrī Caitanya Mahāprabhu deemed the system of *varṇāśrama-dharma* to be material, although it aims at elevation to the spiritual platform. However, the *saṅkīrtana* movement can raise one immediately to the spiritual platform. Consequently it is said that *varṇāśrama-dharma* is external, and Caitanya Mahāprabhu requested Rāmānanda Rāya to proceed deeper into the matter and uncover the spiritual platform.

Sometimes materialists consider Lord Viṣṇu a material conception. Impersonalists think that above Lord Viṣṇu is the impersonal Brahman. The impersonalists misunderstand the worship of Lord Viṣṇu. They worship Lord Viṣṇu to merge into His body. In order that *viṣṇu-ārādhana* not be misunderstood, Śrī Caitanya Mahāprabhu requested that Śrī Rāmānanda Rāya proceed further and clear up the issue. Rāmānanda Rāya quoted the verse from the *Bhagavad-gītā* stating that the results of one's occupational duty may be offered to Lord Viṣṇu or Kṛṣṇa. In *Śrīmad-Bhāgavatam* (1.2.8) it is also said:

dharmaḥ sv-anuṣṭhitaḥ puṁsāṁ viṣvaksena-kathāsu yaḥ
notpādayed yadi ratiṁ śrama eva hi kevalam

"If one executes the occupational duties of *varṇāśrama-dharma* but does not cultivate his dormant Kṛṣṇa consciousness, his activities are futile. His occupation simply becomes unnecessary labor."

TEXT 61

প্রভু কহে, — "এহো বাহ্য, আগে কহ আর।"
রায় কহে, "স্বধর্ম-ত্যাগ, — এই সাধ্য-সার॥" ৬১॥

prabhu kahe, — "eho bāhya, āge kaha āra"
rāya kahe, — "svadharma-tyāga, ei sādhya-sāra"

prabhu kahe — the Lord replied; *eho* — this; *bāhya* — external; *āge* — ahead; *kaha* — speak; *āra* — more; *rāya kahe* — Rāmānanda Rāya replied; *sva-dharma-tyāga* — relinquishing one's occupational duties; *ei* — this; *sādhya-sāra* — the essence of all perfection.

TRANSLATION

"This is also external," Śrī Caitanya Mahāprabhu said. "Please proceed and speak further on this matter."

Rāmānanda Rāya replied, "To give up one's occupational duties in the varṇāśrama system is the essence of perfection."

PURPORT

A *brāhmaṇa* may renounce his family and accept *sannyāsa.* Others — *kṣatriyas* and *vaiśyas* — may also give up their families and take to Kṛṣṇa consciousness. Such renunciation is called *karma-tyāga.* By such renunciation, the Supreme Personality of Godhead is satisfied.

In contrast, the process of renouncing the results of one's activities by offering these results to Kṛṣṇa is not considered uncontaminated, because, although such a process implies that one recognizes Kṛṣṇa as the Supreme Person, it still involves one in activities on the material platform. Since such activities are within the material universe, Śrī Caitanya Mahāprabhu considered them external. To correct this, Rāmānanda Rāya recommended that one take to the renounced order of life in order to transcend material activities. This is supported by the following verse from *Śrīmad-Bhāgavatam* (11.11.32).

TEXT 62

আজ্ঞায়ৈবং গুণান্ দোষান্ময়াদিষ্টানপি স্বকান্।
ধর্মান্ সংত্যজ্য যঃ সর্বান্ মাং ভজেৎ স চ সত্তমঃ ॥ ৬২ ॥

ājñāyaivaṁ guṇān doṣān
mayādiṣṭān api svakān
dharmān santyajya yaḥ sarvān
māṁ bhajet sa ca sattamaḥ

ājñāya—knowing perfectly; *evam*—thus; *guṇān*—qualities; *doṣān*—faults; *mayā*—by Me; *ādiṣṭān*—instructed; *api*—although; *svakān*—own; *dharmān*—occupational duties; *santyajya*—giving up; *yaḥ*—anyone who; *sarvān*—all; *mām*—unto Me; *bhajet*—may render service; *saḥ*—he; *ca*—and; *sat-tamaḥ*—a first-class person.

TRANSLATION

Rāmānanda Rāya continued, "'Occupational duties are described in the religious scriptures. If one analyzes them, he can fully understand their qualities and faults and then give them up completely to render service unto the Supreme Personality of Godhead. Such a person is considered a first-class man.'

TEXT 63

সর্বধর্মান্ পরিত্যজ্য মামেকং শরণং ব্রজ।
অহং ত্বাং সর্বপাপেভ্যো মোক্ষয়িষ্যামি মা শুচঃ ॥ ৬৩ ॥

sarva-dharmān parityajya
mām ekaṁ śaraṇaṁ vraja
ahaṁ tvāṁ sarva-pāpebhyo
mokṣayiṣyāmi mā śucaḥ

sarva-dharmān—all kinds of occupational duties; *parityajya*—giving up; *mām ekam*—unto Me only; *śaraṇam*—as shelter; *vraja*—go; *aham*—I; *tvām*—unto you; *sarva-pāpebhyaḥ*—from all the reactions of sinful life; *mokṣayiṣyāmi*—will give liberation; *mā*—don't; *śucaḥ*—worry.

TRANSLATION

"As stated in scripture [Bg. 18.66], 'After giving up all kinds of religious and occupational duties, if you come to Me, the Supreme Personality of Godhead, and take shelter, I will give you protection from all of life's sinful reactions. Do not worry.'"

PURPORT

In this connection, Śrīla Raghunātha dāsa Gosvāmī instructs in his book *Manaḥ-śikṣā* (2):

na dharmaṁ nādharmaṁ śruti-gaṇa-niruktaṁ kila kuru
vraje rādhā-kṛṣṇa-pracura-paricaryām iha tanu

He has thus enjoined that we should not perform religious or irreligious activities as prescribed in the *Vedas.* The best course is to engage always in the service of Lord Kṛṣṇa and Rādhārāṇī. That is the perfection of everything in this life. Similarly, in *Śrīmad-Bhāgavatam* (4.29.46) it is said by Nārada Muni:

yadā yasyānugṛhṇāti bhagavān ātma-bhāvitaḥ
sa jahāti matiṁ loke vede ca pariniṣṭhitām

"When one actually takes to the loving service of the Supreme Personality of Godhead, he gives up all duties in the material world, as well as all duties prescribed by the Vedic literatures. In this way one is fixed in the service of the Lord."

TEXT 64

প্রভু কহে, — "এহো বাহ্য, আগে কহ আর।"
রায় কহে, — "জ্ঞানমিশ্রা ভক্তি — সাধ্যসার ॥" ৬৪ ॥

prabhu kahe, — "eho bāhya, āge kaha āra"
rāya kahe, "jñāna-miśrā bhakti — sādhya-sāra"

prabhu kahe — the Lord said; *eho* — this; *bāhya* — external; *āge* — ahead; *kaha* — say; *āra* — more; *rāya kahe* — Rāya replied; *jñāna-miśrā bhakti* — devotional service mixed with empiric knowledge; *sādhya-sāra* — is the essence of perfection.

TRANSLATION

After hearing Rāmānanda Rāya speak in this way, Lord Śrī Caitanya Mahāprabhu again rejected his statement and said, "Go ahead and say something more."

Rāmānanda Rāya then replied, "Devotional service mixed with empiric knowledge is the essence of perfection."

PURPORT

Devotional service mixed with non-Vedic speculative knowledge is certainly not pure devotional service. Therefore Śrīla Bhaktisiddhānta Sarasvatī in his *Anubhāṣya* preaches that self-realization following the execution of ritualistic ceremonies is in the neutral stage between liberation and conditioned life. It is a place beyond this material world, in the river Virajā, where the three modes of material nature are subdued or neutralized in the unmanifest stage. However, the spiritual world is a manifestation of spiritual energy and is known as Vaikuṇṭhaloka, "the place where there is no anxiety." The material world, known as *brahmāṇḍa,* is the creation of the external energy. Between the two creations—the material creation and the spiritual creation—is a river known as Virajā, as well as a place known as Brahmaloka. Virajā-nadī and Brahmaloka are shelters for living entities disgusted with material life and inclined to impersonal existence by way of denying material variegatedness. Since these places are not situated in the Vaikuṇṭhalokas, or the spiritual world, Śrī Caitanya Mahāprabhu proclaims them to be external. In the Brahmaloka and Virajā-nadī, one cannot conceive of the Vaikuṇṭhalokas. Brahmaloka and Virajā-nadī are also attained after difficult austerities, but in these realms there is no understanding of the Supreme Personality of Godhead and His transcendental loving service. Without such spiritual knowledge, simple detachment from material conditions is but another side of material existence. From the spiritual point of view, it is all external. When Śrī Caitanya Mahāprabhu rejected this proposal, Rāmānanda Rāya suggested that devotional service based on philosophy and logic is a more advanced position. He therefore quoted the following verse from the *Bhagavad-gītā* (18.54).

TEXT 65

ব্রহ্মভূতঃ প্রসন্নাত্মা ন শোচতি ন কাঙ্ক্ষতি ।
সমঃ সর্বেষু ভূতেষু মদ্ভক্তিং লভতে পরাম্ ॥ ৬৫ ॥

brahma-bhūtaḥ prasannātmā
na śocati na kāṅkṣati
samaḥ sarveṣu bhūteṣu
mad-bhaktiṁ labhate parām

brahma-bhūtaḥ—freed from material conceptions of life but attached to an impersonal situation; *prasanna-ātmā*—fully joyful; *na śocati*—he does not lament; *na kāṅkṣati*—he does not hanker; *samaḥ*—equally disposed; *sarveṣu*—all; *bhūteṣu*—to the living entities; *mat-bhaktim*—My devotional service; *labhate*—achieves; *parām*—transcendental.

TRANSLATION

Rāmānanda Rāya continued, "According to the Bhagavad-gītā, 'One who is thus transcendentally situated at once realizes the Supreme Brahman and becomes fully joyful. He never laments or desires to have anything. He is equally disposed toward every living entity. In that state he attains pure devotional service unto Me.'"

PURPORT

In this verse from the *Bhagavad-gītā* it is said that a person who accepts the theory of monism—being always engaged in empiric philosophical discussions about spiritual life—becomes joyful and is relieved from all material lamentation and hankering. At that stage, one is equipoised. He sees all living entities as spiritual beings. After attaining this elevated stage, one can attain pure devotional service. The conclusion is that devotional service mixed with ritualistic fruitive activity is inferior to spiritual service based on empiric philosophic discussion.

TEXT 66

প্রভু কহে,—"এহো বাহ্য, আগে কহ আর ।"
রায় কহে, "জ্ঞানশূন্যা ভক্তি—সাধ্যসার ॥" ৬৬ ॥

prabhu kahe, "eho bāhya, āge kaha āra"
rāya kahe, — "jñāna-śūnyā bhakti — sādhya-sāra"

prabhu kahe — the Lord said; *eho* — this; *bāhya* — external; *āge* — ahead; *kaha* — speak; *āra* — further; *rāya kahe* — Rāmānanda Rāya replied; *jñāna-śūnyā bhakti* — devotional service independent of logic and empiric philosophy; *sādhya-sāra* — the essence of the perfection of life.

TRANSLATION

After hearing this, the Lord, as usual, rejected it, considering it to be external devotional service. He again asked Rāmānanda Rāya to speak further, and Rāmānanda Rāya replied, "Pure devotional service without any touch of speculative knowledge is the essence of perfection."

PURPORT

In his *Anubhāṣya* commentary, Śrīla Bhaktisiddhānta Sarasvatī Ṭhākura says that this stage — devotional service mixed with speculative knowledge — is also external and not within the jurisdiction of pure devotional service as practiced in Vaikuṇṭhaloka. As soon as there is some conception of materialistic thought — be it positive or negative — the service is not spiritual. It may be free from material contamination, but because there is mental speculation the devotional service is not pure and freed from the contamination of material life. A living entity who wants to be completely pure must be above this material conception. The negation of material existence does not necessarily mean spiritual existence. After material existence is negated, spiritual existence — namely *sac-cid-ānanda* — still may not be manifested. Until one comes to the stage of actually understanding one's eternal relationship with the Supreme Lord, he cannot enter into spiritual life. Spiritual life means becoming detached from material life and engaging in the loving service of the Lord. Śrī Caitanya Mahāprabhu therefore asked Rāmānanda Rāya to explain something transcendental to devotional service mixed with speculative knowledge. A pure devotee is completely surrendered to the lotus feet of the Lord, and only by his love does he conquer Kṛṣṇa, who cannot be conquered by anyone. Kṛṣṇa always stands victorious over everything. No one can conquer Him. One can attain the stage of pure devotion simply by fully surrendering. This is next corroborated by *Śrīmad-Bhāgavatam* (10.14.3), wherein Lord Brahmā, defeated by the potency of Śrī Kṛṣṇa, fully surrendered unto the Lord.

TEXT 67

জ্ঞানে প্রয়াসমুদপাস্য নমন্ত এব।
জীবন্তি সন্মুখরিতাং ভবদীয়বার্তাম্।
স্থানে স্থিতাঃ শ্রুতিগতাং তনুবাঙ্মনোভি-
র্যে প্রায়শোঽজিত জিতোঽপ্যসি তৈস্ত্রিলোক্যাম্॥ ৬৭॥

jñāne prayāsam udapāsya namanta eva
jīvanti san-mukharitāṁ bhavadīya-vārtām
sthāne sthitāḥ śruti-gatāṁ tanu-vāṅ-manobhir
ye prāyaśo 'jita jito 'py asi tais tri-lokyām

jñāne—in gaining knowledge; *prayāsam*—unnecessary endeavor; *udapāsya*—setting far aside; *namantaḥ*—completely surrendering; *eva*—certainly; *jīvanti*—live; *sat-mukharitām*—declared by great realized devotees; *bhavadīya-vārtām*—discussions about You, the Supreme Personality of Godhead; *sthāne sthitāḥ*—situated in their own positions; *śruti-gatām*—received aurally; *tanu-vāk-manobhiḥ*—by the body, words and mind; *ye*—those who; *prāyaśaḥ*—almost always; *ajita*—O my unconquerable Lord (beyond perception and unlimitedly independent); *jitaḥ*—conquered; *api*—indeed; *asi*—You are; *taiḥ*—by such pure devotees; *tri-lokyām*—within the three worlds.

TRANSLATION

Rāmānanda Rāya continued, "[Lord Brahmā said:] 'My dear Lord, those devotees who have thrown away the impersonal conception of the Absolute Truth and have therefore abandoned discussing empiric philosophical truths should hear from self-realized devotees about Your holy name, form, pastimes and qualities. They should completely follow the principles of devotional service and remain free from illicit sex, gambling, intoxication and animal slaughter. Surrendering themselves fully with body, words and mind, they can

live in any āśrama or social status. Indeed, You are conquered by such persons, although You are always unconquerable.'"

TEXT 68

প্রভু কহে, — "এহো হয়, আগে কহ আর।"
রায় কহে, — "প্রেমভক্তি — সর্বসাধ্যসার ॥" ৬৮ ॥

prabhu kahe, "eho haya, āge kaha āra"
rāya kahe, "prema-bhakti — sarva-sādhya-sāra"

prabhu kahe — the Lord said; *eho haya* — this is all right; *āge kaha āra* — speak something more; *rāya kahe* — Rāya replied; *prema-bhakti* — ecstatic love in devotional service to the Lord; *sarva-sādhya-sāra* — the essence of all perfection.

TRANSLATION

At this point, Śrī Caitanya Mahāprabhu replied, "This is all right, but still you can speak more on the subject."

Rāmānanda Rāya then replied, "Ecstatic love for the Supreme Personality of Godhead is the essence of all perfection."

PURPORT

In his *Amṛta-pravāha-bhāṣya,* Śrīla Bhaktivinoda Ṭhākura summarizes the conversation up to this point, where Lord Caitanya Mahāprabhu says to Rāmānanda Rāya, *eho haya, āge kaha āra:* "This is the process accepted in devotional service, but there is something more than this. Therefore please explain what is beyond." Simply executing the duties of all *varṇas* and *āśramas* is not as good as offering all the results of one's activities to the Lord. When one gives up all fruitive activity and fully surrenders to the Lord, he attains *sva-dharma-tyāga,* wherein he abandons the social order and takes to the renounced order. That is certainly better. However, better than the renounced order is cultivation of knowledge mixed with devotional service. Yet all these activities are external to the activities of the spiritual world. There is no touch of pure devotional service in them. Pure devotional service cannot be attained by empiric philosophy, nor can perfection be attained simply by good association. Devotional service by self-realization is a different subject matter. It is untouched by fruitive activity, for one surrenders the results of activities to the Lord, abandons prescribed duties and accepts the renounced order of life. Such devotional service is situated on a higher platform than that of empiric philosophical speculation with a mixture of *bhakti.* This is verified by Śrīla Rūpa Gosvāmī in his *Bhakti-rasāmṛta-sindhu* (1.1.11):

anyābhilāṣitā-śūnyaṁ jñāna-karmādy-anāvṛtam
ānukūlyena kṛṣṇānu-śīlanaṁ bhaktir uttamā

"One should render transcendental loving service to the Supreme Lord Kṛṣṇa favorably and without desire for material profit or gain through fruitive activities or philosophical speculation. That is called pure devotional service."

Devotional activities, however, sometimes appear to be impure in the neophyte stage, but in the mature stage they are completely pure, or free from material activity. Therefore Rāmānanda Rāya replied after hearing the last statement of Śrī Caitanya Mahāprabhu: *prema-bhakti — sarva-sādhya-sāra.* Śrī Caitanya Mahāprabhu actually accepted this verse (*jñāne prayāsam*) as the basic principle of perfection. One has to practice this principle in order to make further progress. When further progress is actually made, one comes to the platform of ecstatic loving service to the Lord. This first stage is technically called *sādhana-bhakti,* or devotional service in practice. The result of *sādhana-bhakti* must be ecstatic love, attachment for the Supreme Personality of Godhead, which is also called *prema-bhakti.* In the neophyte stage, *sādhana-bhakti* includes faith, association with devotees, and practicing devotional service. Thus one is freed from all unwanted things. One then becomes fixed in devotional service and increases his desire to act in devotional service. Thus one becomes attached to the Lord and His devotional service.

TEXT 69

নানোপচার-কৃতপূজনমার্তবন্ধোঃ ।
প্রেম্ণৈব ভক্তহৃদয়ং সুখবিদ্রুতং স্যাৎ ।

যাবৎ ক্ষুদস্তি জঠরে জরঠা পিপাসা
তাবৎ সুখায় ভবতো ননু ভক্ষ্য-পেয়ে ॥ ৬৯ ॥

nānopacāra-kṛta-pūjanam ārta-bandhoḥ
premṇaiva bhakta-hṛdayaṁ sukha-vidrutaṁ syāt
yāvat kṣud asti jaṭhare jaraṭhā pipāsā
tāvat sukhāya bhavato nanu bhakṣya-peye

nānā-upacāra—by varieties of offerings; *kṛta*—performed; *pūjanam*—worshiping; *ārta-bandhoḥ*—of the Supreme Personality of Godhead, who is the friend of all distressed persons; *premṇā*—by ecstatic love; *eva*—indeed; *bhakta-hṛdayam*—the heart of a devotee; *sukha-vidrutam*—melted in transcendental bliss; *syāt*—becomes; *yāvat*—as long as; *kṣut*—appetite; *asti*—there is; *jaṭhare*—in the stomach; *jaraṭhā*—strong; *pipāsā*—thirst; *tāvat*—so long; *sukhāya*—for happiness; *bhavataḥ*—are; *nanu*—indeed; *bhakṣya*—eatables; *peye*—and drinkables.

TRANSLATION

Rāmānanda Rāya continued, "'As long as there is hunger and thirst within the stomach, varieties of food and drink make one feel very happy. Similarly, when the Lord is worshiped with pure love, the various activities performed in the course of that worship awaken transcendental bliss in the heart of the devotee.'

TEXT 70

কৃষ্ণভক্তিরসভাবিতা মতিঃ
ক্রীয়তাং যদি কুতোঽপি লভ্যতে।
তত্র লৌল্যমপি মূল্যমেকলং
জন্মকোটিসুকৃতৈর্ন লভ্যতে ॥ ৭০ ॥

kṛṣṇa-bhakti-rasa-bhāvitā matiḥ
krīyatāṁ yadi kuto 'pi labhyate
tatra laulyam api mūlyam ekalaṁ
janma-koṭi-sukṛtair na labhyate

kṛṣṇa-bhakti-rasa-bhāvitā—absorbed in the mellows of executing devotional service to Kṛṣṇa; *matiḥ*—intelligence; *krīyatām*—let it be purchased; *yadi*—if; *kutaḥ api*—somewhere; *labhyate*—is available; *tatra*—there; *laulyam*—greed; *api*—indeed; *mūlyam*—price; *ekalam*—only; *janma-koṭi*—of millions of births; *sukṛtaiḥ*—by pious activities; *na*—not; *labhyate*—is obtained.

TRANSLATION

"'Pure devotional service in Kṛṣṇa consciousness cannot be had even by pious activity in hundreds and thousands of lives. It can be attained only by paying one price—that is, intense greed to obtain it. If it is available somewhere, one must purchase it without delay.'"

PURPORT

The previous two verses are included in the *Padyāvalī* (13, 14), an anthology compiled by Śrīla Rūpa Gosvāmī. Verse 69 refers to devotional service in faith, and verse 70 refers to devotional service rendered out of intense greed. The first is devotional service rendered in accordance with the regulative principles, and the second refers to spontaneous loving service of the Lord without extraneous endeavor. Henceforward the basic principle underlying the talks between Śrī Caitanya Mahāprabhu and Rāmānanda Rāya will be spontaneous loving service to the Lord. The regulative principles according to the injunctions of the *śāstras* are necessary insofar as one's original dormant Kṛṣṇa consciousness is not spontaneously awakened. An example of spontaneous action is the flowing of rivers into the ocean. Nothing can stop this flow of water. Similarly, when one's dormant Kṛṣṇa consciousness is awakened, it spontaneously flows to the lotus feet of Kṛṣṇa without impediment. Whatever will be spoken henceforth by Rāmānanda Rāya based on spontaneous love will be agreeable to Śrī Caitanya Mahāprabhu, and the Lord will ask him more and more about this subject.

TEXT 71

প্রভু কহে,—"এহো হয়, আগে কহ আর।"
রায় কহে, "দাস্য-প্রেম—সর্বসাধ্যসার॥" ৭১॥

prabhu kahe, "eho haya, āge kaha āra"
rāya kahe, "dāsya-prema — sarva-sādhya-sāra"

prabhu kahe — the Lord said; *eho haya* — this is all right; *āge kaha āra* — please speak more; *rāya kahe* — Rāmānanda Rāya replied; *dāsya-prema* — spontaneous love in the humor of servitude; *sarva-sādhya-sāra* — the essence of perfection.

TRANSLATION

Hearing up to the point of spontaneous love, the Lord said, "This is all right, but if you know more, please tell Me."

In reply, Rāmānanda Rāya said, "Spontaneous loving service in servitude — as exchanged by master and servant — is the highest perfection.

PURPORT

Spontaneous loving service to the Lord is called devotional service with an intimate attachment between the servitor and the served. This intimacy is called *mamatā.* Between the servitor and the served there is a feeling of oneness. This *mamatā* begins with *dāsya-prema,* service rendered to the master by the servant. Unless there is such a relationship, the loving affairs between the Lord and His devotee are not actually fixed. When the devotee feels "The Lord is my master" and renders service unto Him, Kṛṣṇa consciousness is awakened. This fixed consciousness is on a higher platform than simple cognizance of love of Godhead.

TEXT 72

যন্নামশ্রুতিমাত্রেণ পুমান্ ভবতি নির্মলঃ ।
তস্য তীর্থপদঃ কিংবা দাসানামবশিষ্যতে ॥ ৭২ ॥

yan-nāma-śruti-mātreṇa
pumān bhavati nirmalaḥ
tasya tīrtha-padaḥ kiṁ vā
dāsānām avaśiṣyate

yat — of whom; *nāma* — of the name; *śruti-mātreṇa* — simply by hearing; *pumān* — a person; *bhavati* — becomes; *nirmalaḥ* — pure;

tasya—of Him; *tīrtha-padaḥ*—of the Supreme Personality of Godhead, at whose lotus feet are all places of pilgrimage; *kim*—what; *vā*—more; *dāsānām*—of the servants; *avaśiṣyate*—is remaining.

TRANSLATION

"'A man becomes purified simply by hearing the holy name of the Supreme Personality of Godhead, whose lotus feet create the holy places of pilgrimage. Therefore what remains to be attained by those who have become His servants?'

PURPORT

This is a quotation from *Śrīmad-Bhāgavatam* (9.5.16) and is an admission by the great sage Durvāsā Muni. Durvāsā Muni, a caste *brāhmaṇa* and great *yogī*, used to hate Mahārāja Ambarīṣa. When he decided to chastise Mahārāja Ambarīṣa through his yogic powers, he was chased by the Sudarśana *cakra* of the Supreme Personality of Godhead. When things were settled, he said, "When the holy name of the Supreme Personality of Godhead is heard by any person, that person is immediately sanctified. The Supreme Lord is master of the devotees, and the devotees, under His shelter, naturally come to own His opulences."

TEXT 73

ভবন্তমেবানুচরন্নিরন্তরঃ
প্রসান্তনিঃশেষমনোরথান্তরঃ ।
কদাহমৈকান্তিকনিত্যকিঙ্করঃ
প্রহর্ষয়িষ্যামি স-নাথ-জীবিতম্ ॥ ৭৩ ॥

bhavantam evānucaran nirantaraḥ
praśānta-niḥśeṣa-mano-rathāntaraḥ
kadāham aikāntika-nitya-kiṅkaraḥ
praharṣayiṣyāmi sa-nātha-jīvitam

bhavantam—You; *eva*—certainly; *anucaran*—serving; *nirantaraḥ*—always; *praśānta*—pacified; *niḥśeṣa*—all; *manaḥ-ratha*—desires; *antaraḥ*—other; *kadā*—when; *aham*—I; *aikāntika*—exclusive;

nitya—eternal; *kiṅkaraḥ*—servant; *praharṣayiṣyāmi*—I shall become joyful; *sa-nātha*—with a fitting master; *jīvitam*—living.

TRANSLATION

"'By serving You constantly, one is freed from all material desires and is completely pacified. When shall I engage as Your permanent eternal servant and always feel joyful to have such a perfect master?'"

PURPORT

This is a statement made by the great saintly devotee Yāmunācārya in his *Stotra-ratna* (43).

TEXT 74

প্রভু কহে, — "এহো হয়, কিছু আগে আর ।"
রায় কহে, — "সখ্য-প্রেম — সর্বসাধ্যসার ॥" ৭৪ ॥

prabhu kahe, "eho haya, kichu āge āra"
rāya kahe, "sakhya-prema—sarva-sādhya-sāra"

prabhu kahe—the Lord said; *eho haya*—this is also right; *kichu*—something; *āge*—ahead; *āra*—more; *rāya kahe*—Rāmānanda Rāya replied; *sakhya-prema*—transcendental loving service in fraternity; *sarva-sādhya-sāra*—the highest perfectional stage.

TRANSLATION

Hearing this from Rāmānanda Rāya, the Lord again requested him to go a step further. In reply, Rāmānanda Rāya said, "Loving service to Kṛṣṇa rendered in fraternity is the highest perfection.

PURPORT

As long as loving service is rendered to the Lord in the master-servant relationship, there is some fear, for the servant is always afraid of the master, despite the intimacy of self-interest. In this stage the servant is always afraid of the master and respectful of Him. When the devotee is further advanced, he has nothing to fear. He considers the Lord and himself on an equal level. At such a time, the devotee is fully convinced that Lord Kṛṣṇa is a friend and cannot at all be dissatisfied if the devotee lives with Him on an equal level. This understanding is called *viśrambha,* that is, devoid of a respectful attitude. When this attitude is chosen, it becomes *sakhya-prema,* or love of Godhead in friendship. On this stage there is developed consciousness of equality between the Lord and the devotee.

TEXT 75

ইত্থং সতাং ব্রহ্মসুখানুভূত্যা দাস্যং গতানাং পরদৈবতেন।
মায়াশ্রিতানাং নরদারকেণ সার্দ্ধং বিজহ্রুঃ কৃতপুণ্যপুঞ্জাঃ ॥ ৭৫ ॥

itthaṁ satāṁ brahma-sukhānubhūtyā
dāsyaṁ gatānāṁ para-daivatena
māyāśritānāṁ nara-dārakeṇa
sārdhaṁ vijahruḥ kṛta-puṇya-puñjāḥ

ittham—in this way; *satām*—of persons who prefer the impersonal feature of the Lord; *brahma*—of the impersonal effulgence; *sukha*—by the happiness; *anubhūtyā*—who is realized; *dāsyam*—the mode of servitude; *gatānām*—of those who have accepted; *para-daivatena*—who is the supreme worshipable Deity; *māyā-āśritānām*—for ordinary persons under the clutches of the external energy; *nara-dārakeṇa*—with Him, who is like a boy of this material world; *sārdham*—in friendship; *vijahruḥ*—played; *kṛta-puṇya-puñjāḥ*—those who have accumulated volumes of pious activities.

TRANSLATION

"'Neither those engaged in the self-realization of appreciating the Brahman effulgence of the Lord, nor those engaged in devotional service while accepting the Supreme Personality of Godhead as master, nor those under the clutches of Māyā, thinking the Lord an ordinary person, can understand that certain exalted personalities, after accumulating volumes of pious activities, are now playing with the Lord in friendship as cowherd boys.'"

PURPORT

This is a statement made by Śukadeva Gosvāmī (*Bhāg.* 10.12.11), who appreciated the good fortune of the cowherd boys who played with Kṛṣṇa and ate with Him on the banks of the Yamunā.

TEXT 76

প্রভু কহে, — "এহো উত্তম, আগে কহ আর।"
রায় কহে, "বাৎসল্য-প্রেম — সর্বসাধ্যসার ॥" ৭৬ ॥

prabhu kahe, — "eho uttama, āge kaha āra"
rāya kahe, "vātsalya-prema — sarva-sādhya-sāra"

prabhu kahe — the Lord said; *eho uttama* — it is very good; *āge* — still further; *kaha* — speak; *āra* — more; *rāya kahe* — Rāya replied; *vātsalya-prema* — loving service to the Lord in the stage of parental love; *sarva-sādhya-sāra* — the highest perfectional stage.

TRANSLATION

The Lord said, "This statement is very good, but please proceed even further."

Rāmānanda Rāya then replied, "Loving service to the Lord in the parental relationship is the highest perfectional stage."

PURPORT

The stage of loving service to the Lord in parental affection is an advanced stage of love in fraternity. In the fraternal relationship there is a sense of equality, but when that sense of equality is advanced in affection, one attains the platform of parental love. In this connection, the following verse is cited from *Śrīmad-Bhāgavatam* (10.8.46), wherein Śukadeva Gosvāmī voices his appreciation of Nanda Mahārāja's and mother Yaśodā's intense love for Kṛṣṇa.

TEXT 77

নন্দঃ কিমকরোদ্‌ব্রহ্মন্ শ্রেয় এবং মহোদয়ম্।
যশোদা বা মহাভাগা পপৌ যস্যাঃ স্তনং হরিঃ ॥ ৭৭ ॥

nandaḥ kim akarod brahman
śreya evaṁ mahodayam
yaśodā vā mahā-bhāgā
papau yasyāḥ stanaṁ hariḥ

nandaḥ—Nanda Mahārāja; *kim*—what; *akarot*—has performed; *brahman*—O *brāhmaṇa; śreyaḥ*—auspicious activities; *evam*—thus; *mahā-udayam*—rising to such an exalted position as the father of Kṛṣṇa; *yaśodā*—mother Yaśodā; *vā*—or; *mahā-bhāgā*—most fortunate; *papau*—drank; *yasyāḥ*—of whom; *stanam*—by the breasts; *hariḥ*—the Supreme Personality of Godhead.

TRANSLATION

Rāmānanda Rāya continued, "'O brāhmaṇa, what pious activities did Nanda Mahārāja perform by which he received the Supreme Personality of Godhead Kṛṣṇa as his son? And what pious activities did mother Yaśodā perform that made the Absolute Supreme Personality of Godhead Kṛṣṇa call her "Mother" and suck her breasts?'

TEXT 78

নেমং বিরিঞ্চো ন ভবো ন শ্রীরপ্যঙ্গসংশ্রয়া ।
প্রসাদং লেভিরে গোপী যত্তৎ প্রাপ বিমুক্তিদাৎ ॥ ৭৮ ॥

nemaṁ viriñco na bhavo
na śrīr apy aṅga-saṁśrayā
prasādaṁ lebhire gopī
yat tat prāpa vimukti-dāt

na—not; *imam*—this (love of Godhead); *viriñcaḥ*—Lord Brahmā; *na*—not; *bhavaḥ*—Lord Śiva; *na*—nor; *śrīḥ*—the goddess of fortune; *api*—even; *aṅga*—on the chest of Viṣṇu; *saṁśrayā*—who is sheltered; *prasādam*—favor; *lebhire*—have obtained; *gopī*—mother Yaśodā; *yat*—which; *tat*—that; *prāpa*—obtained; *vimukti-dāt*—from the person who gives liberation.

TRANSLATION

"'The favor mother Yaśodā obtained from Śrī Kṛṣṇa, the bestower of liberation, was never obtained even by Lord Brahmā or Lord Śiva, nor

even by the goddess of fortune, who always remains on the chest of the Supreme Personality of Godhead Viṣṇu.'"

PURPORT

This is a statement from *Śrīmad-Bhāgavatam* (10.9.20). Kṛṣṇa agreed to be bound by mother Yaśodā after she had given up trying to bind Kṛṣṇa with ropes. This is another appreciation made by Śukadeva Gosvāmī in his narration of the pastimes of Kṛṣṇa before Mahārāja Parīkṣit.

TEXT 79

প্রভু কহে, — "এহো উত্তম, আগে কহ আর।"
রায় কহে, "কান্তাপ্রেম সর্বসাধ্যসার ॥" ৭৯ ॥

prabhu kahe, "eho uttama, āge kaha āra"
rāya kahe, "kāntā-prema sarva-sādhya-sāra"

prabhu kahe—the Lord replied; *eho uttama*—this is very good; *āge*—ahead; *kaha*—speak; *āra*—more; *rāya kahe*—Rāmānanda Rāya replied; *kāntā-prema*—loving service between husband and wife; *sarva-sādhya-sāra*—the highest perfectional stage.

TRANSLATION

The Lord said, "Your statements are certainly getting better and better one after the other, but surpassing all of them is another transcendental mellow, and you can speak of that as the most sublime."

Rāmānanda Rāya then replied, "Conjugal attachment for Kṛṣṇa is the topmost position in love of Godhead.

PURPORT

In general, love of Godhead is devoid of the intimacy of ownership. In the case of love in servitude, there is a want of confidence. There is a want of increased affection in the fraternal relationship, and even when this affection increases in the parental relationship, there is nonetheless a want of complete freedom. However, when one becomes a conjugal lover of Kṛṣṇa, everything lacking in the other relationships is completely manifest. Love of Godhead lacks nothing in the conjugal stage. The summary of this verse is that parental love of Godhead is certainly higher than fraternal love and that conjugal love is higher yet. It was when Śrī Caitanya Mahāprabhu requested Rāmānanda Rāya to go further that he came to the point of the conjugal relationship, which is the highest perfectional stage of transcendental love.

TEXT 80

নায়ং শ্রিয়োহঙ্গ উ নিতান্তরতেঃ প্রসাদঃ
স্বর্যোষিতাং নলিনগন্ধরুচাং কুতোহন্যাঃ ।
রাসোৎসবেহস্য ভুজদণ্ডগৃহীতকণ্ঠ-
লব্ধাশিষাং য উদগাদ্‌ব্রজসুন্দরীণাম্ ॥ ৮০ ॥

nāyaṁ śriyo 'ṅga u nitānta-rateḥ prasādaḥ
svar-yoṣitāṁ nalina-gandha-rucāṁ kuto 'nyāḥ
rāsotsave 'sya bhuja-daṇḍa-gṛhīta-kaṇṭha-
labdhāśiṣāṁ ya udagād vraja-sundarīṇām

na—not; *ayam*—this; *śriyaḥ*—of the goddess of fortune; *aṅge*—on the chest; *u*—alas; *nitānta-rateḥ*—who is very intimately related; *prasādaḥ*—the favor; *svaḥ*—of the heavenly planets; *yoṣitām*—of women; *nalina*—of the lotus flower; *gandha*—having the aroma; *rucām*—and bodily luster; *kutaḥ*—much less; *anyāḥ*—others; *rāsa-utsave*—in the festival of the *rāsa* dance; *asya*—of Lord Śrī Kṛṣṇa; *bhuja-daṇḍa*—by the arms; *gṛhīta*—embraced; *kaṇṭha*—their necks; *labdha-āśiṣām*—who achieved such a blessing; *yaḥ*—which; *udagāt*—became manifest; *vraja-sundarīṇām*—of the beautiful *gopīs,* the transcendental girls of Vrajabhūmi

TRANSLATION

"'When Lord Śrī Kṛṣṇa was dancing with the gopīs in the rāsa-līlā, the gopīs were embraced around the neck by the Lord's arms. This transcendental favor was never bestowed upon the goddess of fortune or the other consorts in the spiritual world. Nor was such a thing ever imagined by the most beautiful girls in the heavenly planets, girls whose bodily luster and aroma resemble the beauty and fragrance of

lotus flowers. And what to speak of worldly women, who may be very, very beautiful according to material estimation?'

PURPORT

This verse (*Bhāg.* 10.47.60) was spoken by Uddhava when he visited Śrī Vṛndāvana to deliver a message from Kṛṣṇa to the *gopīs.* Uddhava remained in Vṛndāvana to observe the activities of the *gopīs* there. When he saw the ecstatic love for Kṛṣṇa in separation manifested by the *gopīs,* he appreciated their supreme love and therefore expressed his feelings in this verse. He admitted that the fortune of the *gopīs* could not be compared even to the fortune of the goddess of fortune, to say nothing of the beautiful girls in the heavenly planets.

TEXT 81

তাসামাবিরভূচ্ছৌরিঃ স্ময়মানমুখাম্বুজঃ ।
পীতাম্বরধরঃ স্রগ্বী সাক্ষান্মন্মথমন্মথঃ ॥ ৮১ ॥

tāsām āvirabhūc chauriḥ
smayamāna-mukhāmbujaḥ
pītāmbara-dharaḥ sragvī
sākṣān manmatha-manmathaḥ

tāsām—among them; *āvirabhūt*—appeared; *śauriḥ*—Lord Kṛṣṇa; *smayamāna*—smiling; *mukha-ambujaḥ*—with a face like a lotus flower; *pīta-ambara-dharaḥ*—wearing yellow garments; *sragvī*—garlanded with flowers; *sākṣāt*—directly; *manmatha*—of Cupid; *manmathaḥ*—the bewilderer.

TRANSLATION

"'Suddenly, due to their feelings of separation, Lord Kṛṣṇa appeared among the gopīs dressed in yellow garments and wearing a flower garland. His lotus face was smiling, and He was directly attracting the mind of Cupid.'

PURPORT

This verse is from *Śrīmad-Bhāgavatam* (10.32.2). When the *rāsa* dance was going on, Kṛṣṇa suddenly disappeared, and the *gopīs* became so overwhelmed, due to His separation and their intense love for Him, that Kṛṣṇa was obliged to appear again.

TEXT 82

কৃষ্ণ-প্রাপ্তির উপায় বহুবিধ হয়।
কৃষ্ণপ্রাপ্তি-তারতম্য বহুত আছয় ॥ ৮২ ॥

kṛṣṇa-prāptira upāya bahu-vidha haya
kṛṣṇa-prāpti-tāratamya bahuta āchaya

kṛṣṇa-prāptira—of achieving the lotus feet of Kṛṣṇa; *upāya*—means; *bahu-vidha*—various; *haya*—there are; *kṛṣṇa-prāpti*—of achieving the favor of Lord Kṛṣṇa; *tāratamya*—comparisons; *bahuta*—various; *āchaya*—there are.

TRANSLATION

"There are various means and processes by which one may attain the favor of Lord Kṛṣṇa. All those transcendental processes will be studied from the viewpoint of comparative importance.

TEXT 83

কিন্তু যাঁর যেই রস, সেই সর্বোত্তম।
তটস্থ হঞা বিচারিলে, আছে তর-তম ॥ ৮৩ ॥

kintu yāṅra yei rasa, sei sarvottama
taṭa-stha hañā vicārile, āche tara-tama

kintu—nevertheless; *yāṅra*—of some devotees; *yei rasa*—whatever the mellow of exchanges of love; *sei*—that; *sarva-uttama*—the best; *taṭa-stha*—neutral; *hañā*—being; *vicārile*—if considering; *āche*—there is; *tara-tama*—lower and higher levels.

TRANSLATION

"It is true that whatever relationship a particular devotee has with the Lord is the best for him; still, when we study all the different methods from a neutral position, we can understand that there are higher and lower degrees of love.

PURPORT

In this regard, Śrīla Bhaktisiddhānta Sarasvatī Ṭhākura explains that this verse does not advocate the whimsical invention of some methods of love of Godhead. Such inventions cannot be accepted as topmost. Indeed, such concoctions are not recommended in these verses. Śrīla Rūpa Gosvāmī has said in the *Bhakti-rasāmṛta-sindhu* (1.2.101):

śruti-smṛti-purāṇādi-pañcarātra-vidhiṁ vinā
aikāntikī harer bhaktir utpātāyaiva kalpate

He clearly mentions in this verse that one must refer to the Vedic literatures and other, supplementary literatures and follow the conclusion of the *Vedas.* An invented devotional attitude simply creates disturbances in the transcendental realm. If a person overly addicted to family life takes to *Śrīmad-Bhāgavatam* or Kṛṣṇa consciousness to earn a livelihood, his activity is certainly offensive. One should not become a caste *guru* and sell *mantras* for the benefit of mundane customers, nor should one make disciples for a livelihood. All these activities are offensive. One should not make a livelihood by forming a professional band to carry out congregational chanting, nor should one perform devotional service when one is attached to mundane society, friendship and love. Nor should one be dependent on so-called social etiquette. All of this is mental speculation. None of these things can be compared to unalloyed devotional service. No one can compare unalloyed devotional service, Kṛṣṇa consciousness, to mundane activities. There are many unauthorized parties pretending to belong to the Śrī Caitanya cult, and some are known as *āula, bāula, karttābhajā, neḍā, daraveśa, sāṅi, sakhībhekī, smārta, jāta-gosāñi, ativāḍī, cūḍādhārī* and *gaurāṅga-nāgari.*

Moreover, there are those who take the caste *gosvāmīs'* opinions of such parties as bona fide, comparing these opinions to those of the six Gosvāmīs, headed by Śrī Rūpa and Śrī Sanātana. This is simply another cheating process. There are also nondevotees who compose un-authorized songs, who establish different temples for money, who worship the Deity as priests for salaries, who accept caste brahmanism as all in all, and who do not know the value of a pure Vaiṣṇava. Actually the caste *brāhmaṇas* of the *smārta* community are opposed to the principles of the *Sātvata-pañcarātra.* Furthermore, there are many

Māyāvādīs and those overly addicted to material sense enjoyment. None of these can be compared to a person who is purely engaged in preaching Kṛṣṇa consciousness. Every Kṛṣṇa conscious person is constantly endeavoring to utilize different transcendental devices in the service of the Lord. Such a devotee renounces all material enjoyment and completely dedicates himself to the service of his spiritual master and Lord Śrī Caitanya Mahāprabhu. He may be a perfect celibate, a restrained householder, a regulated *vānaprastha* or a *tridaṇḍi-sannyāsī* in the renounced order. It doesn't matter. The pseudo transcendentalists and the pure devotees cannot be compared, nor can one argue that a person can invent his own way of worship.

The purport in presenting this verse necessitates explaining the comparative positions of the transcendental mellows known as *śānta, dāsya, sakhya, vātsalya* and *mādhurya.* All these *rasas,* or mellows, are situated on the transcendental platform. Pure devotees take shelter of one of them and thus progress in spiritual life. Actually one can take shelter of such spiritual mellows only when one is completely uncontaminated by material attachment. When one is completely free from material attachment, the feelings of the transcendental mellows are awakened in the heart of the devotee. That is *svarūpa-siddhi,* the perfection of one's eternal relationship with the Supreme Lord. *Svarūpa-siddhi,* the eternal relationship with the Supreme Lord, may be situated in any one of the transcendental mellows. Each and every one of them is as perfect as the others. But by comparative study an unbiased person can realize that the mellow of servitorship is better than the mellow of neutrality, that the mellow of fraternity is better than the mellow of servitorship, that the parental mellow is better than that of fraternity, and that above all other mellows is the mellow of conjugal love. However, these are all spiritually situated on the same platform because all these relationships of perfection in love are based on a central point—Kṛṣṇa.

These mellows cannot be compared to the feelings one derives from demigod worship. Kṛṣṇa is one, but the demigods are different. They are material. Love for Kṛṣṇa cannot be compared to material love for different demigods. Because Māyāvādīs are on the material platform, they recommend the worship of Śiva or Durgā and say that worship of Kālī and Kṛṣṇa are the same. However, on the spiritual platform there is no demigod worship. The only worshipable object is Kṛṣṇa.

Therefore although there is no difference between a devotee in *śānta-rasa* or *dāsya-rasa, vātsalya-rasa* or *mādhurya-rasa,* one can still make a comparative study of the intensity of love in these different transcendental positions. For example, it may be said that *dāsya-rasa* is better than *śānta-rasa,* yet transcendental love of God is there in both of them. Similarly, we can judge that love of Godhead in fraternity is better than love of Godhead in neutrality and servitorship. Similarly, love of Godhead in parental affection is better than love in fraternity. And, as stated before, love of God in the conjugal *rasa* is superior to that in the parental *rasa.*

The analysis of different types of love of Godhead has been made by expert *ācāryas* who know all about devotional service on the transcendental platform. Unfortunately, inexperienced and unauthorized persons in the mundane world, not understanding the transcendental position of pure love, try to find some material fault in the transcendental process. This is simply impudence on the part of spiritually inexperienced people. Such faultfinding is symptomatic of unfortunate mundane wranglers.

TEXT 84

যথোত্তরমসৌ স্বাদবিশেষোল্লাসময্যপি ।
রতির্বাসনয়া স্বাদ্বী ভাসতে কাপি কস্যচিৎ ॥ ৮৪ ॥

yathottaram asau svāda-
viśeṣollāsa-mayy api
ratir vāsanayā svādvī
bhāsate kāpi kasyacit

yathā uttaram—one after another; *asau*—that; *svāda-viśeṣa*—of particular tastes; *ullāsa*—pleasing; *mayī*—empowered with; *api*—although; *ratiḥ*—love; *vāsanayā*—by desire; *svādvī*—sweet; *bhāsate*—appears; *kā api*—someone; *kasyacit*—one of them.

TRANSLATION

"'Increasing love is experienced in various tastes, one above another. But that love which has the highest taste in the gradual succession of desires manifests itself in the form of conjugal love.'

PURPORT

This verse is from Śrīla Rūpa Gosvāmī's *Bhakti-rasāmṛta-sindhu* (2.5.38), and it also appears in *Ādi-līlā,* Chapter Four, verse 45.

TEXT 85

পূর্ব-পূর্ব-রসের গুণ — পরে পরে হয় ।
দুই-তিন গণনে পঞ্চ পর্যন্ত বাড়য় ॥ ৮৫ ॥

pūrva-pūrva-rasera guṇa — pare pare haya
dui-tina gaṇane pañca paryanta bāḍaya

pūrva-pūrva — of each previous; *rasera* — of the mellow; *guṇa* — the qualities; *pare pare* — in each subsequent; *haya* — there are; *dui-tina* — two and then three; *gaṇane* — in counting; *pañca* — five; *paryanta* — up to; *bāḍaya* — increases.

TRANSLATION

"There is a gradual order of improvement in transcendental mellows from the initial ones to the later ones. In each subsequent mellow the qualities of the previous mellows are manifested, counting from two, then three, and up to the point of five complete qualities.

TEXT 86

গুণাধিক্যে স্বাদাধিক্য বাড়ে প্রতি-রসে ।
শান্ত-দাস্য-সখ্য-বাৎসল্যের গুণ মধুরেতে বৈসে ॥ ৮৬ ॥

guṇādhikye svādādhikya bāḍe prati-rase
śānta-dāsya-sakhya-vātsalyera guṇa madhurete vaise

guṇa-ādhikye — by the increase of transcendental qualities; *svāda-ādhikya* — increase of taste; *bāḍe* — increases; *prati-rase* — in each mellow; *śānta* — of neutrality; *dāsya* — of servitude; *sakhya* — of fraternity; *vātsalyera* — and of parental affection; *guṇa* — the qualities; *madhurete* — in the conjugal mellow; *vaise* — appear.

TRANSLATION

"As the qualities increase, so the taste also increases in each and every mellow. Therefore the qualities found in śānta-rasa, dāsya-rasa, sakhya-rasa and vātsalya-rasa are all manifested in conjugal love [mādhurya-rasa].

TEXT 87

আকাশাদির গুণ যেন পর-পর ভূতে।
দুই-তিন ক্রমে বাড়ে পঞ্চ পৃথিবীতে ॥ ৮৭ ॥

ākāśādira guṇa yena para-para bhūte
dui-tina krame bāḍe pañca pṛthivīte

ākāśa-ādira—of the sky, air and so on; *guṇa*—the qualities; *yena*—just as; *para-para*—one after another; *bhūte*—in the material elements; *dui-tina*—two and then three; *krame*—by gradations; *bāḍe*—increase; *pañca*—all five; *pṛthivīte*—in earth.

TRANSLATION

"The qualities in the material elements—sky, air, fire, water and earth—increase one after another by a gradual process of one, two and three, and at the last stage, in the element earth, all five qualities are completely visible.

TEXT 88

পরিপূর্ণ-কৃষ্ণপ্রাপ্তি এই 'প্রেমা' হৈতে।
এই প্রেমার বশ কৃষ্ণ — কহে ভাগবতে ॥ ৮৮ ॥

paripūrṇa-kṛṣṇa-prāpti ei 'premā' haite
ei premāra vaśa kṛṣṇa — kahe bhāgavate

paripūrṇa—completely full; *kṛṣṇa-prāpti*—achievement of the lotus feet of Lord Kṛṣṇa; *ei*—this; *premā*—love of Godhead; *haite*—from; *ei premāra*—of this type of love of Godhead; *vaśa*—under the control; *kṛṣṇa*—Lord Kṛṣṇa; *kahe*—it is said; *bhāgavate*—in *Śrīmad-Bhāgavatam.*

TRANSLATION

"Complete attainment of the lotus feet of Lord Kṛṣṇa is made possible by love of Godhead, specifically mādhurya-rasa, or conjugal love. Lord Kṛṣṇa is indeed captivated by this standard of love. This is stated in Śrīmad-Bhāgavatam.

PURPORT

To explain the topmost quality of conjugal love, Śrīla Kṛṣṇadāsa Kavirāja Gosvāmī gives the example of the material elements—sky, air, fire, water and earth. In the sky (space) there is the quality of sound. Similarly, in air there are the qualities of sound and touch. In fire, there are three qualities—sound, touch and form. In water there are four qualities—sound, touch, form and taste. Finally, in earth there are all five qualities—sound, touch, form, taste and also smell. Now, one can see that the quality of the sky is in all—namely in air, fire, water and earth. In earth we can find all the qualities of material nature. The same can be applied to the *rasa* known as *mādhurya-rasa,* or conjugal love. In conjugal love there are the qualities of neutrality, servitorship, fraternity and parental affection, as well as those of conjugal love itself. The conclusion is that through conjugal love the Lord is completely satisfied.

Conjugal love (*mādhurya-rasa*) is also known as *śṛṅgāra-rasa.* It is the conclusion of *Śrīmad-Bhāgavatam* that in the complete combination of loving service to the Lord—namely in conjugal love—the Supreme Lord fully agrees to be under the control of the devotee. The highest form of conjugal love is represented by Śrīmatī Rādhārāṇī; therefore in the pastimes of Rādhā and Kṛṣṇa we can see that Kṛṣṇa is always subjugated by Śrīmatī Rādhārāṇī's influence.

TEXT 89

ময়ি ভক্তির্হি ভূতানামমৃতত্বায় কল্পতে।
দিষ্ট্যা যদাসীন্মৎস্নেহো ভবতীনাং মদাপনঃ ॥ ৮৯ ॥

mayi bhaktir hi bhūtānām
amṛtatvāya kalpate
diṣṭyā yad āsīn mat-sneho
bhavatīnāṁ mad-āpanaḥ

mayi—unto Me; *bhaktiḥ*—devotional service; *hi*—certainly; *bhūtānām*—of all living entities; *amṛtatvāya*—for becoming eternal; *kalpate*—is meant; *diṣṭyā*—fortunately; *yat*—what; *āsīt*—there is; *mat-snehaḥ*—affection for Me; *bhavatīnām*—of all of you; *mat-āpanaḥ*—the means of getting My favor.

TRANSLATION

"Lord Kṛṣṇa told the gopīs, 'The means of attaining My favor is loving service unto Me, and fortunately you are all thus engaged. Those living beings who render service unto Me are eligible to be transferred to the spiritual world and attain eternal life with knowledge and bliss.'

PURPORT

The fulfillment of human life is summarized in this verse from *Śrīmad-Bhāgavatam* (10.82.44). There are two important words in this verse: *bhakti* (devotional service) and *amṛtatva* (eternal life). The aim of human life is to attain the natural position of eternal life. This eternal life can be achieved only by devotional service.

TEXT 90

কৃষ্ণের প্রতিজ্ঞা দৃঢ় সর্বকালে আছে।
যে যৈছে ভজে, কৃষ্ণ তারে ভজে তৈছে ॥ ৯০ ॥

kṛṣṇera pratijñā dṛḍha sarva-kāle āche
ye yaiche bhaje, kṛṣṇa tāre bhaje taiche

kṛṣṇera—of Lord Kṛṣṇa; *pratijñā*—the promise; *dṛḍha*—firm; *sarva-kāle*—in all times; *āche*—there is; *ye*—anyone; *yaiche*—just as; *bhaje*—renders service; *kṛṣṇa*—Lord Kṛṣṇa; *tāre*—him; *bhaje*—reciprocates with; *taiche*—so for all time.

TRANSLATION

"Lord Kṛṣṇa has made a firm promise for all time. If one renders service unto Him, Kṛṣṇa correspondingly gives him an equal amount of success in devotional service to the Lord.

PURPORT

It is a completely mistaken idea that one can worship Kṛṣṇa in any form or in any way and still attain the ultimate result of receiving the favor of the Lord. This is a decision made by gross materialists. Generally such men say that you can manufacture your own way of worshiping the Supreme Lord and that any type of worship is sufficient to approach the Supreme Personality of Godhead. Certainly there are different means for attaining different results in fruitive activity, speculative knowledge, mystic *yoga* and austerity. Crude men therefore say that one who adopts any of these methods achieves the Supreme Personality of Godhead's favor. They claim that it doesn't matter what kind of method one adopts. A general analogy is given: If one wishes to arrive at a certain place, there are many roads leading there, and one can go to that place by any one of these roads. Similarly, these gross materialists say, there are different ways to attain the favor of the Supreme Personality of Godhead. They claim that one can conceive of the Supreme Personality of Godhead as goddess Durgā, goddess Kālī, Lord Śiva, demigod Gaṇeśa, Lord Rāmacandra, Kṛṣṇa, the impersonal Brahman or whatever, and one can chant the Lord's name in any way and in any form. Such materialists claim that since ultimately all these names and forms are one, the result is the same. They also give the analogy that a man who has different names will answer if called by any one of them. Therefore, they claim, there is no need to chant the Hare Kṛṣṇa *mantra.* If one chants the name of Kālī, Durgā, Śiva, Gaṇeśa or anyone else, the result will be the same.

Such claims made by mental speculators are no doubt very pleasing to mental speculators, but those who are actually in knowledge do not admit such conclusions, which are against the authority of the *śāstras.* A bona fide *ācārya* will certainly not accept such a conclusion. As Kṛṣṇa clearly states in the *Bhagavad-gītā* (9.25):

yānti deva-vratā devān pitṝn yānti pitṛ-vratāḥ
bhūtāni yānti bhūtejyā yānti mad-yājino 'pi mām

"Those who worship the demigods will take birth among the demigods, those who worship the ancestors go to the ancestors, those who worship ghosts and spirits will take birth among such beings, and those who worship Me will live with Me."

Only the devotees of the Lord can be admitted to His kingdom—not the demigod worshipers, *karmīs, yogīs* or anyone else. A person who desires elevation to the heavenly planets worships various demigods, and material nature may be pleased to offer such devotees their desired positions. The material nature gives a person his own nature, by which he increases affection for different types of demigods. However, the *Bhagavad-gītā* (7.20) says that demigod worship is meant for men who have lost all their intelligence:

kāmais tais tair hṛta-jñānāḥ prapadyante 'nya-devatāḥ
taṁ taṁ niyamam āsthāya prakṛtyā niyatāḥ svayā

"Those whose intelligence has been stolen by material desires surrender unto demigods and follow the particular rules and regulations of worship according to their own natures."

Although one may be elevated to the heavenly planets, the results of such a benediction are limited:

anta-vat tu phalaṁ teṣāṁ tad bhavaty alpa-medhasām
devān deva-yajo yānti mad-bhaktā yānti mām api

"Men of small intelligence worship the demigods, and their fruits are limited and temporary. Those who worship the demigods go to the planets of the demigods, but My devotees ultimately reach My supreme planet." (Bg. 7.23)

Being elevated to the heavenly planets or other material planets does not mean attaining an eternal life of knowledge and bliss. At the end of the material world, all attainments of material elevation will also end. Again, according to Kṛṣṇa in the *Bhagavad-gītā* (18.55), only those who engage in His loving devotional service will be admitted to the spiritual world and return to Godhead, not others:

bhaktyā mām abhijānāti yāvān yaś cāsmi tattvataḥ
tato māṁ tattvato jñātvā viśate tad-anantaram

"One can understand Me as I am, as the Supreme Personality of Godhead, only by devotional service. And when one is in full consciousness of Me by such devotion, he can enter into the kingdom of God."

Impersonalists cannot understand the Supreme Personality of Godhead; therefore it is not possible for them to enter into the spiritual kingdom of God and return home, back to Godhead. Actually one attains different results by different means. It is not that all achievements are one and the same. Those interested in the four principles of *dharma, artha, kāma* and *mokṣa* cannot be compared to those interested in the unalloyed devotional service of the Lord. *Śrīmad-Bhāgavatam* (1.1.2) therefore says:

dharmaḥ projjhita-kaitavo 'tra paramo nirmatsarāṇāṁ satāṁ
vedyaṁ vāstavam atra vastu śiva-daṁ tāpa-trayonmūlanam
śrīmad-bhāgavate mahā-muni-kṛte kiṁ vā parair īśvaraḥ
sadyo hṛdy avarudhyate 'tra kṛtibhiḥ śuśrūṣubhis tat-kṣaṇāt

"Completely rejecting all religious activities which are materially motivated, this *Bhāgavata Purāṇa* propounds the highest truth, which is understandable by those devotees who are pure in heart. The highest truth is reality distinguished from illusion for the welfare of all. Such truth uproots the threefold miseries. This beautiful *Bhāgavatam,* compiled by the great sage Śrī Vyāsadeva, is sufficient in itself for God realization. As soon as one attentively and submissively hears the message of *Bhāgavatam,* he becomes attached to the Supreme Lord."

Those who aspire after liberation attempt to merge into the impersonal Brahman. To this end they execute ritualistic religious ceremonies, but *Śrīmad-Bhāgavatam* considers this a cheating process. Indeed, such people can never dream of returning home, back to Godhead. There is a gulf of difference between the goal of *dharma, artha, kāma* and *mokṣa* and the goal of devotional service.

The goddess Durgā is the superintending deity of this material world, which is made of material elements. The demigods are simply different directors engaged in operating the departments of material activities, and they are under the influence of the same material energy. Kṛṣṇa's internal potencies, however, have nothing to do with the creation of this cosmic material world. The spiritual world and all spiritual activities are under the direction of the internal, spiritual energy, and such activities are performed by Yogamāyā, the spiritual energy. Yogamāyā is the spiritual or internal energy of the Supreme Personality of Godhead. Those who are interested in being promoted to the spiritualworld and engaging in the service of the Lord attain spiritual perfection under the control of Yogamāyā. Those who are interested in material promotion engage in ritualistic religious ceremonies and economic development to develop sense gratification. They ultimately attempt to merge into the impersonal existence of the Lord. Such people generally become impersonalists. They are interested in worshiping Lord Śiva or goddess Durgā, but their return is one hundred percent materialistic.

Following the example of the *gopīs,* the devotees sometimes worship the goddess Kātyāyanī, but they understand that Kātyāyanī is an incarnation of Yogamāyā. The *gopīs* worshiped Kātyāyanī, Yogamāyā, to attain Kṛṣṇa as their husband. On the other hand, it is stated in the *Sapta-śatī* scripture that a *kṣatriya* king named Suratha and a rich *vaiśya* named Samādhi worshiped material nature in the form of goddess Durgā to attain material perfection. If one tries to mingle the worship of Yogamāyā with that of Mahāmāyā, considering them one and the same, he does not really show very high intelligence. The idea that everything is one is a kind of foolishness indulged in by those with less brain substance. Fools and rascals say that the worship of Yogamāyā and the worship of Mahāmāyā are the same. This conclusion is simply the result of mental speculation, and it has no practical effect. In the material world, sometimes one gives an exalted title to an utterly worthless thing; in Bengal this is known as giving a blind child a name like Padmalocana, which means "lotus-eyed." One may foolishly call a blind child Padmalocana, but such an appellation does not bear any meaning.

In the spiritual world the Absolute Lord is always identical with His name, fame, form, qualities and pastimes. Such identity is impossible in the material world, where the name of a person is different from the person himself. The Supreme Lord has many holy names like Paramātmā, Brahman and "the creator," but one who worships the Lord as the creator cannot understand the relationship between a devotee and the Lord in the five types of transcendental mellows, nor can he understand the conception of Kṛṣṇa. One cannot understand the six transcendental opulences of the Lord simply by understanding the Supreme Personality of Godhead as impersonal Brahman.

Impersonal realization of the Absolute Truth is certainly transcendental, but this does not mean that one who has attained this realization can understand the *sac-cid-ānanda* form of the

Lord. Similarly, Paramātmā realization—realization of the plenary expansion of the Absolute Truth within everyone's heart—is also an incomplete understanding of the Absolute Truth. Even a devotee of the Personality of Godhead Nārāyaṇa cannot actually understand the transcendental attractive features of Kṛṣṇa. Indeed, a devotee of Kṛṣṇa who is attached to the sublime attractive features of the Lord does not consider Nārāyaṇa very important. When the *gopīs* sometimes saw Kṛṣṇa in the form of Nārāyaṇa, they were not very much attracted to Him. The *gopīs* never addressed Kṛṣṇa as Rukmiṇī-ramaṇa. Kṛṣṇa's devotees in Vṛndāvana address Him as Rādhāramaṇa, Nandanandana and Yaśodānandana, but not as Vasudeva-nandana or Devakī-nandana. Although according to the material conception Nārāyaṇa, Rukmiṇī-ramaṇa and Kṛṣṇa are one and the same, in the spiritual world one cannot use the name Rukmiṇī-ramaṇa or Nārāyaṇa in place of the name Kṛṣṇa. If one does so out of a poor fund of knowledge, his mellow with the Lord becomes spiritually faulty and is called *rasābhāsa,* an overlapping of transcendental mellows. The advanced devotee who has actually realized the transcendental features of the Lord will not commit the mistake of creating a *rasā-bhāsa* situation by using one name for another. Because of the influence of Kali-yuga, there is much *rasābhāsa* in the name of extravagance and liberal-mindedness. Such fanaticism is not very much appreciated by pure devotees.

TEXT 91

যে যথা মাং প্রপদ্যন্তে তাংস্তথৈব ভজাম্যহম্ ।
মম বর্ত্মানুবর্তন্তে মনুষ্যাঃ পার্থ সর্বশঃ ॥ ৯১ ॥

ye yathā māṁ prapadyante
tāṁs tathaiva bhajāmy aham
mama vartmānuvartante
manuṣyāḥ pārtha sarvaśaḥ

ye—they; *yathā*—as; *mām*—unto Me; *prapadyante*—surrender; *tān*—unto them; *tathā eva*—in the same proportion; *bhajāmi*—bestow My favor; *aham*—I; *mama*—My; *vartma*—way; *anuvartante*—follow; *manuṣyāḥ*—men; *pārtha*—My dear Arjuna; *sarvaśaḥ*—in all respects.

TRANSLATION

"[According to Lord Kṛṣṇa in the Bhagavad-gītā (4.11):] 'As all surrender unto Me, I reward them accordingly. Everyone follows My path in all respects, O son of Pṛthā.'

TEXT 92

এই 'প্রেমে'র অনুরূপ না পারে ভজিতে।
অতএব 'ঋণী' হয় — কহে ভাগবতে ॥ ৯২ ॥

ei 'preme'ra anurūpa nā pāre bhajite
ataeva 'ṛṇī' haya —kahe bhāgavate

ei—this; *premera*—of love of God; *anurūpa*—exactly to the proportion; *nā*—not; *pāre*—is able; *bhajite*—to reciprocate; *ataeva*—therefore; *ṛṇī*—debtor; *haya*—becomes; *kahe*—is stated; *bhāgavate*—in *Śrīmad-Bhāgavatam.*

TRANSLATION

"In Śrīmad-Bhāgavatam [10.32.22] it is said that Lord Kṛṣṇa cannot proportionately reciprocate devotional service in the mādhurya-rasa; therefore He always remains a debtor to such devotees.

TEXT 93

ন পারয়েঽহং নিরবদ্যসংযুজাং
স্বসাধুকৃত্যং বিবুধায়ুষাপি বঃ।
যা মাভজন্ দুর্জয়-গেহশৃঙ্খলাঃ
সংবৃশ্চ্য তদ্বঃ প্রতিযাতু সাধুনা ॥ ৯৩ ॥

na pāraye 'haṁ niravadya-saṁyujām
sva-sādhu-kṛtyaṁ vibudhāyuṣāpi vaḥ
yā mābhajan durjaya-geha-śṛṅkhalāḥ
saṁvṛścya tad vaḥ pratiyātu sādhunā

na—not; *pāraye*—am able; *aham*—I; *niravadya*—without duplicity; *saṁyujām*—meeting; *sva-sādhu-kṛtyam*—your own honest activities; *vibudha-āyuṣā api*—even with a duration of life like that of the demigods; *vaḥ*—you; *yā*—who; *mā*—Me; *abhajan*—have worshiped; *durjaya*—difficult to surmount; *geha*—of household life; *śṛṅkhalāḥ*—the chains; *saṁvṛścya*—cutting off; *tat*—that; *vaḥ*—your; *pratiyātu*—let there be a return; *sādhunā*—by pious activities.

TRANSLATION

"When the gopīs were overwhelmed with dissatisfaction due to Lord Kṛṣṇa's absence from the rāsa-līlā, Kṛṣṇa returned to them and told them, 'My dear gopīs, our meeting is certainly free of all material contamination. I must admit that in many lives it would be impossible for Me to repay My debt to you because you have cut off the bondage of family life just to search for Me. Consequently I am unable to repay you. Therefore please be satisfied with your honest activities in this regard.'

TEXT 94

যদ্যপি কৃষ্ণ-সৌন্দর্য — মাধুর্যের ধুর্য ।
ব্রজদেবীর সঙ্গে তাঁর বাড়য়ে মাধুর্য ॥ ৯৪ ॥

yadyapi kṛṣṇa-saundarya—mādhuryera dhurya
vraja-devīra saṅge tāṅra bāḍaye mādhurya

yadyapi—although; *kṛṣṇa-saundarya*—the beauty of Lord Kṛṣṇa; *mādhuryera*—of sweetness; *dhurya*—the supermost; *vraja-devīra*—the *gopīs; saṅge*—in company with; *tāṅra*—His; *bāḍaye*—increases; *mādhurya*—the sweetness.

TRANSLATION

"Although Kṛṣṇa's unparalleled beauty is the topmost sweetness of love of Godhead, His sweetness increases unlimitedly when He is in the company of the gopīs. Consequently Kṛṣṇa's exchange of love with the gopīs is the topmost perfection of love of Godhead.

PURPORT

Kṛṣṇa and His devotees become perfectly intimate in conjugal love of Godhead. In other mellows, the Lord and the devotees do not enjoy transcendental bliss as perfectly. The next verse (*Śrīmad-Bhāgavatam* 10.33.6) will illustrate this point.

TEXT 95

তত্রাতিশুশুভে তাভির্ভগবান্ দেবকীসুতঃ।
মধ্যে মণীনাং হৈমানাং মহামরকতো যথা ॥ ৯৫ ॥

tatrātiśuśubhe tābhir
bhagavān devakī-sutaḥ
madhye maṇīnāṁ haimānāṁ
mahā-marakato yathā

tatra—there; *ati-śuśubhe*—was very beautiful; *tābhiḥ*—by them; *bhagavān*—the Supreme Personality of Godhead; *devakī-sutaḥ*—son of Devakī; *madhye*—in the midst; *maṇīnām*—of valuable jewels; *haimānām*—lined with gold; *mahā-marakataḥ*—the jewel of the name *marakata; yathā*—as.

TRANSLATION

"'Although the son of Devakī, the Supreme Personality of Godhead, is the reservoir of all kinds of beauty, when He is among the gopīs He nonetheless becomes more beautiful, for He resembles a marakata jewel surrounded by gold and other jewels.'"

TEXT 96

প্রভু কহে, এই — 'সাধ্যাবধি' সুনিশ্চয়।
কৃপা করি' কহ, যদি আগে কিছু হয় ॥ ৯৬ ॥

prabhu kahe,—ei 'sādhyāvadhi' suniścaya
kṛpā kari' kaha, yadi āge kichu haya

prabhu kahe—Lord Śrī Caitanya Mahāprabhu replied; *ei*—this; *sādhya-avadhi*—the highest limit of perfection; *su-niścaya*—certainly; *kṛpā kari'*—being merciful to Me; *kaha*—please speak; *yadi*—if; *āge*—further; *kichu haya*—there is something.

TRANSLATION

Lord Caitanya Mahāprabhu replied, "This is certainly the limit of perfection, but please be merciful to Me and speak more if there is more."

TEXT 97

রায় কহে, — ইহার আগে পুছে হেন জনে ।
এতদিন নাহি জানি, আছয়ে ভুবনে ॥ ৯৭ ॥

rāya kahe, — ihāra āge puche hena jane
eta-dina nāhi jāni, āchaye bhuvane

rāya kahe — Rāmānanda Rāya replied; *ihāra āge* — beyond this point; *puche* — inquires; *hena* — such; *jane* — a person; *eta-dina* — until this day; *nāhi jāni* — I did not know; *āchaye* — there is; *bhuvane* — within this material world.

TRANSLATION

Rāya Rāmānanda replied, "Until this day I did not know anyone within this material world who could inquire beyond this perfectional stage of devotional service.

TEXT 98

ইঁহার মধ্যে রাধার প্রেম — 'সাধ্যশিরোমণি' ।
যাঁহার মহিমা সর্বশাস্ত্রেতে বাখানি ॥ ৯৮ ॥

iṅhāra madhye rādhāra prema — 'sādhya-śiromaṇi'
yāṅhāra mahimā sarva-śāstrete vākhāni

iṅhāra madhye — among the loving affairs of the *gopīs; rādhāra prema* — the love of Godhead of Śrīmatī Rādhārāṇī; *sādhya-śiromaṇi* — the topmost perfection; *yāṅhāra* — of which; *mahimā* — the glorification; *sarva-śāstrete* — in every scripture; *vākhāni* — description.

TRANSLATION

"Among the loving affairs of the gopīs," Rāmānanda Rāya continued, "Śrīmatī Rādhārāṇī's love for Śrī Kṛṣṇa is topmost. Indeed, the glories of Śrīmatī Rādhārāṇī are highly esteemed in all revealed scriptures.

TEXT 99

যথা রাধা প্রিয়া বিষ্ণোস্তস্যাঃ কুণ্ডং প্রিয়ং তথা ।
সর্বগোপীষু সৈবৈকা বিষ্ণোরত্যন্তবল্লভা ॥ ৯৯ ॥

yathā rādhā priyā viṣṇos
tasyāḥ kuṇḍaṁ priyaṁ tathā
sarva-gopīṣu saivaikā
viṣṇor atyanta-vallabhā

yathā—just as; *rādhā*—Śrīmatī Rādhārāṇī; *priyā*—very dear; *viṣṇoḥ*—to Lord Kṛṣṇa; *tasyāḥ*—Her; *kuṇḍam*—bathing place; *priyam*—very dear; *tathā*—so also; *sarva-gopīṣu*—among all the *gopīs; sā*—She; *eva*—certainly; *ekā*—alone; *viṣṇoḥ*—of Lord Kṛṣṇa; *atyanta-vallabhā*—very dear.

TRANSLATION

"'Just as Śrīmatī Rādhārāṇī is most dear to Śrī Kṛṣṇa, Her bathing place [Rādhā-kuṇḍa] is also dear to Him. Among all the gopīs, Śrīmatī Rādhārāṇī is supermost and very dear to Lord Kṛṣṇa.'

PURPORT

This verse is from the *Padma Purāṇa* and is included in the *Laghu-bhāgavatāmṛta* (2.1.45), by Śrīla Rūpa Gosvāmī. It also appears in the *Ādi-līlā,* Chapter Four, verse 215, and again in the *Madhya-līlā,* Chapter Eighteen, verse 8.

TEXT 100

অনয়ারাধিতো নূনং ভগবান্ হরিরীশ্বরঃ ।
যন্নো বিহায় গোবিন্দঃ প্রীতো যামনয়দ্রহঃ ॥ ১০০ ॥

anayārādhito nūnaṁ
bhagavān harir īśvaraḥ
yan no vihāya govindaḥ
prīto yām anayad rahaḥ

anayā—by Her; *ārādhitaḥ*—worshiped; *nūnam*—indeed; *bhagavān*—the Supreme Personality of Godhead; *hariḥ*—Kṛṣṇa; *īśvaraḥ*—the Lord; *yat*—from which; *naḥ*—us; *vihāya*—rejecting; *govindaḥ*—Lord Śrī Kṛṣṇa; *prītaḥ*—satisfied; *yām*—whom; *anayat*—brought; *rahaḥ*—a secluded place.

TRANSLATION

"[When the gopīs began to talk among themselves, they said:] 'Dear friends, the gopī who has been taken away by Kṛṣṇa to a secluded place must have worshiped the Lord more than anyone else.'"

PURPORT

The name Rādhā is derived from this verse (*Bhāg.* 10.30.28), from the words *anayārādhitaḥ,* meaning "by Her the Lord is worshiped." Sometimes the critics of *Śrīmad-Bhāgavatam* find it difficult to find Rādhārāṇī's holy name in that book, but the secret is disclosed here in the word *ārādhita,* from which the name Rādhā has come. Of course, the name of Rādhārāṇī is directly mentioned in other *Purāṇas.* This *gopī's* worship of Kṛṣṇa is topmost, and therefore Her name is Rādhā, or "the topmost worshiper."

TEXT 101

প্রভু কহে,—আগে কহ, শুনিতে পাই সুখে।
অপূর্বামৃত-নদী বহে তোমার মুখে ॥ ১০১ ॥

prabhu kahe—āge kaha, śunite pāi sukhe
apūrvāmṛta-nadī vahe tomāra mukhe

prabhu kahe—the Lord said; *āge*—ahead; *kaha*—please speak; *śunite*—to hear; *pāi*—I get; *sukhe*—happiness; *apūrva-amṛta*—of unprecedented nectar; *nadī*—a river; *vahe*—flows; *tomāra mukhe*—from your mouth.

TRANSLATION

Lord Śrī Caitanya Mahāprabhu said, "Please speak on. I am very happy to hear you because a river of unprecedented nectar is flowing from your mouth.

TEXT 102

চুরি করি' রাধাকে নিল গোপীগণের ডরে ।
অন্যাপেক্ষা হৈলে প্রেমের গাঢ়তা না স্ফুরে ॥ ১০২ ॥

curi kari' rādhāke nila gopī-gaṇera ḍare
anyāpekṣā haile premera gāḍhatā nā sphure

curi kari'—stealing; *rādhāke*—Śrīmatī Rādhārāṇī; *nila*—took away; *gopī-gaṇera*—of the *gopīs; ḍare*—out of fear; *anya-apekṣā*—dependence on others; *haile*—if there is; *premera*—of love; *gāḍhatā*—the intensity; *nā*—not; *sphure*—manifests.

TRANSLATION

"During the rāsa dance Śrī Kṛṣṇa did not exchange loving affairs with Śrīmatī Rādhārāṇī due to the presence of the other gopīs. Because of the dependence of the others, the intensity of love between Rādhā and Kṛṣṇa was not manifested. Therefore He stole Her away.

PURPORT

Out of fear of the other *gopīs,* Lord Śrī Kṛṣṇa took Śrīmatī Rādhārāṇī to a secluded place. In this regard, the verse *kaṁsārir api* (verse 106 in this chapter) will be quoted from the *Gīta-govinda* of Jayadeva Gosvāmī.

TEXT 103

রাধা লাগি' গোপীরে যদি সাক্ষাৎ করে ত্যাগ ।
তবে জানি, —রাধায় কৃষ্ণের গাঢ়-অনুরাগ ॥ ১০৩ ॥

rādhā lāgi' gopīre yadi sākṣāt kare tyāga
tabe jāni,—rādhāya kṛṣṇera gāḍha-anurāga

rādhā lāgi'—for the sake of Śrīmatī Rādhārāṇī; *gopīre*—the *gopīs; yadi*—if; *sākṣāt*—directly; *kare*—does; *tyāga*—rejection; *tabe*—then; *jāni*—we can understand; *rādhāya*—in Śrīmatī Rādhārāṇī; *kṛṣṇera*—of Lord Kṛṣṇa; *gāḍha*—intense; *anurāga*—affection.

TRANSLATION

"If Lord Kṛṣṇa rejected the company of the other gopīs for Śrīmatī Rādhārāṇī, we can understand that Lord Śrī Kṛṣṇa has intense affection for Her."

TEXT 104

রায় কহে, —তবে শুন প্রেমের মহিমা ।
ত্রিজগতে রাধা-প্রেমের নাহিক উপমা ॥ ১০৪ ॥

rāya kahe,—tabe śuna premera mahimā
tri-jagate rādhā-premera nāhika upamā

rāya kahe—Rāmānanda Rāya replied; *tabe*—then; *śuna*—please hear; *premera*—of that love; *mahimā*—the glories; *tri-jagate*—within the three worlds; *rādhā-premera*—of the loving affairs of Śrīmatī Rādhārāṇī; *nāhika*—there is not; *upamā*—comparison.

TRANSLATION

Rāmānanda Rāya continued, "Please therefore hear from me about the glories of Śrīmatī Rādhārāṇī's loving affairs. They are beyond compare within these three worlds.

TEXT 105

গোপীগণের রাস-নৃত্য-মণ্ডলী ছাড়িয়া ।
রাধা চাহি' বনে ফিরে বিলাপ করিয়া ॥ ১০৫ ॥

gopī-gaṇera rāsa-nṛtya-maṇḍalī chāḍiyā
rādhā cāhi' vane phire vilāpa kariyā

gopī-gaṇera—of the *gopīs; rāsa-nṛtya*—of *rāsa* dancing; *maṇḍalī*—the circle; *chāḍiyā*—rejecting; *rādhā*—Śrīmatī

Rādhārāṇī; *cāhi'*—desiring; *vane*—in the forest; *phire*—wanders; *vilāpa*—lamentation; *kariyā*—doing.

TRANSLATION

"Finding Herself treated equally with all the other gopīs, Śrīmatī Rādhārāṇī displayed Her tricky behavior and left the circle of the rāsa dance. Missing Śrīmatī Rādhārāṇī's presence, Kṛṣṇa became very unhappy and began to lament and wander throughout the forest to search Her out.

TEXT 106

কংসারিরপি সংসারবাসনাবদ্ধশৃঙ্খলাম্ ।
রাধামাধায় হৃদয়ে তত্যাজ ব্রজসুন্দরীঃ ॥ ১০৬ ॥

kaṁsārir api saṁsāra-
vāsanā-baddha-śṛṅkhalām
rādhām ādhāya hṛdaye
tatyāja vraja-sundarīḥ

kaṁsa-ariḥ—the enemy of Kaṁsa; *api*—moreover; *saṁsāra-vāsanā*—desirous of the essence of enjoyment (*rāsa-līlā*); *baddha-śṛṅkhalām*—being perfectly attracted to such activities; *rādhām*—Śrīmatī Rādhārāṇī; *ādhāya*—taking; *hṛdaye*—within the heart; *tatyāja*—left aside; *vraja-sundarīḥ*—the other beautiful *gopīs.*

TRANSLATION

"'Lord Kṛṣṇa, the enemy of Kaṁsa, took Śrīmatī Rādhārāṇī within His heart, for He desired to dance with Her. Thus He left the arena of the rāsa dance and the company of all the other beautiful damsels of Vraja.

TEXT 107

ইতস্ততস্তামনুসৃত্য রাধিকা-
মনঙ্গবাণব্রণখিন্নমানসঃ ।
কৃতানুতাপঃ স কলিন্দনন্দিনী
তটান্তকুঞ্জে বিষসাদ মাধবঃ ॥ ১০৭ ॥

itas tatas tām anusṛtya rādhikām
anaṅga-bāṇa-vraṇa-khinna-mānasaḥ
kṛtānutāpaḥ sa kalinda-nandinī
taṭānta-kuñje viṣasāda mādhavaḥ

itaḥ tataḥ—hither and thither; *tām*—Her; *anusṛtya*—searching out; *rādhikām*—Śrīmatī Rādhārāṇī; *anaṅga*—of Cupid; *bāṇa-vraṇa*—by a wound from the arrow; *khinna-mānasaḥ*—whose heart is injured; *kṛta-anutāpaḥ*—repentant for misbehavior; *saḥ*—He (Lord Kṛṣṇa); *kalinda-nandinī*—of the river Yamunā; *taṭa-anta*—on the edge of the bank; *kuñje*—in the bushes; *viṣasāda*—lamented; *mādhavaḥ*—Lord Kṛṣṇa.

TRANSLATION

"'Being afflicted by the arrow of Cupid and unhappily regretting His mistreating Śrīmatī Rādhārāṇī, Mādhava, Lord Kṛṣṇa, began to search for Her along the banks of the Yamunā River. When He failed to find Her, He entered the bushes of Vṛndāvana and began to lament.'

PURPORT

These two verses are from the *Gīta-govinda* (3.1–2), written by Jayadeva Gosvāmī.

TEXT 108

এই দুই-শ্লোকের অর্থ বিচারিলে জানি ।
বিচারিতে উঠে যেন অমৃতের খনি ॥ ১০৮ ॥

ei dui-ślokera artha vicārile jāni
vicārite uṭhe yena amṛtera khani

ei—these; *dui*—two; *ślokera*—of the verses; *artha*—the meanings; *vicārile*—if considering; *jāni*—I can understand; *vicārite*—while considering; *uṭhe*—arises; *yena*—like; *amṛtera*—of nectar; *khani*—a mine.

TRANSLATION

"Simply by considering these two verses one can understand what nectar there is in such dealings. It is exactly like freeing a mine of nectar.

TEXT 109

শতকোটি গোপী-সঙ্গে রাস-বিলাস।
তার মধ্যে এক-মূর্ত্যে রহে রাধা-পাশ॥ ১০৯॥

śata-koṭi gopī-saṅge rāsa-vilāsa
tāra madhye eka-mūrtye rahe rādhā-pāśa

śata-koṭi—hundreds of thousands; *gopī-saṅge*—with the *gopīs; rāsa-vilāsa*—dancing in the *rāsa* dance; *tāra madhye*—among them; *eka-mūrtye*—by one of His transcendental forms; *rahe*—remains; *rādhā-pāśa*—by the side of Śrīmatī Rādhārāṇī.

TRANSLATION

"Although Kṛṣṇa was in the midst of hundreds of thousands of gopīs during the rāsa dance, He still kept Himself in one of His transcendental forms by the side of Śrīmatī Rādhārāṇī.

TEXT 110

সাধারণ-প্রেমে দেখি সর্বত্র 'সমতা'।
রাধার কুটিল-প্রেমে হইল 'বামতা'॥ ১১০॥

sādhāraṇa-preme dekhi sarvatra 'samatā'
rādhāra kuṭila-preme ha-ila 'vāmatā'

sādhāraṇa-preme—in general love of Godhead; *dekhi*—we see; *sarvatra*—everywhere; *samatā*—equality; *rādhāra*—of Śrīmatī Rādhārāṇī; *kuṭila-preme*—in the crooked love of Godhead; *ha-ila*—there was; *vāmatā*—opposition.

TRANSLATION

"Lord Kṛṣṇa is equal to everyone in His general dealings, but due to the conflicting ecstatic love of Śrīmatī Rādhārāṇī, there were opposing elements.

TEXT 111

অহেরিব গতিঃ প্রেম্ণঃ স্বভাবকুটিলা ভবেৎ।
অতো হেতোরহেতোশ্চ যূনোর্মান উদঞ্চতি॥ ১১১॥

aher iva gatiḥ premṇaḥ
svabhāva-kuṭilā bhavet
ato hetor ahetoś ca
yūnor māna udañcati

aheḥ—of the snake; *iva*—like; *gatiḥ*—the movement; *premṇaḥ*—of the loving affairs; *svabhāva*—by nature; *kuṭilā*—crooked; *bhavet*—is; *ataḥ*—therefore; *hetoḥ*—from some cause; *ahetoḥ*—from the absence of a cause; *ca*—and; *yūnoḥ*—of the young couple; *mānaḥ*—anger; *udañcati*—appears.

TRANSLATION

"'The progress of loving affairs between a young boy and a young girl is like the movement of a snake. On account of this, two types of anger arise between a young boy and girl—anger with cause and anger without cause.'

PURPORT

During the *rāsa* dance, one form of Kṛṣṇa was between every two *gopīs.* But by the side of Śrīmatī Rādhārāṇī there was only one Kṛṣṇa. Although this was the case, Śrīmatī Rādhārāṇī still manifested disagreement with Kṛṣṇa. This verse is from the *Ujjvala-nīlamaṇi* (*Śṛṅgāra-bheda-kathana* 102), written by Śrīla Rūpa Gosvāmī.

TEXT 112

ক্রোধ করি' রাস ছাড়ি' গেলা মান করি' ।
তাঁরে না দেখিয়া ব্যাকুল হৈল শ্রীহরি ॥ ১১২ ॥

krodha kari' rāsa chāḍi' gelā māna kari'
tāṅre nā dekhiyā vyākula haila śrī-hari

krodha kari'—becoming angry; *rāsa chāḍi'*—leaving the *rāsa* dance; *gelā*—went; *māna kari'*—being resentful; *tāṅre*—Śrīmatī Rādhārāṇī; *nā dekhiyā*—not seeing; *vyākula*—very anxious; *haila*—became; *śrī-hari*—Lord Kṛṣṇa.

TRANSLATION

"When Rādhārāṇī left the rāsa dance out of anger and resentment, Lord Śrī Kṛṣṇa became very anxious because He could not see Her.

TEXT 113

সম্যক্সার বাসনা কৃষ্ণের রাসলীলা ।
রাসলীলা-বাসনাতে রাধিকা শৃঙ্খলা ॥ ১১৩ ॥

samyak-sāra vāsanā kṛṣṇera rāsa-līlā
rāsa-līlā-vāsanāte rādhikā śṛṅkhalā

samyak-sāra—the complete and essential; *vāsanā*—desire; *kṛṣṇera*—of Lord Kṛṣṇa; *rāsa-līlā*—the dancing in the *rāsa-līlā; rāsa-līlā-vāsanāte*—in the desire to dance the *rāsa* dance; *rādhikā*—Śrīmatī Rādhārāṇī; *śṛṅkhalā*—the medium of bondage.

TRANSLATION

"Lord Kṛṣṇa's desire in the rāsa-līlā circle is perfectly complete, but Śrīmatī Rādhārāṇī is the binding link in that desire.

TEXT 114

তাঁহা বিনু রাসলীলা নাহি ভায় চিত্তে ।
মণ্ডলী ছাড়িয়া গেলা রাধা অন্বেষিতে ॥ ১১৪ ॥

tāṅhā vinu rāsa-līlā nāhi bhāya citte
maṇḍalī chāḍiyā gelā rādhā anveṣite

tāṅhā vinu—without Her; *rāsa-līlā*—the *rāsa* dance; *nāhi*—not; *bhāya*—illuminates; *citte*—within the heart; *maṇḍalī chāḍiyā*—leaving the circle of the *rāsa* dance; *gelā*—went; *rādhā*—Śrīmatī Rādhārāṇī; *anveṣite*—to search for.

TRANSLATION

"The rāsa dance does not shine in the heart of Kṛṣṇa without Śrīmatī Rādhārāṇī. Therefore, He also gave up the circle of the rāsa dance and went out to search for Her.

TEXT 115

ইতস্ততঃ ভ্রমি' কাহাঁ রাধা না পাঞা ।
বিষাদ করেন কামবাণে খিন্ন হঞা ॥ ১১৫ ॥

itas-tataḥ bhrami' kāhāṅ rādhā nā pāñā
viṣāda karena kāma-bāṇe khinna hañā

itaḥ-tataḥ—here and there; *bhrami'*—wandering; *kāhāṅ*—anywhere; *rādhā*—Śrīmatī Rādhārāṇī; *nā*—not; *pāñā*—finding; *viṣāda*—lamentation; *karena*—does; *kāma-bāṇe*—by the arrow of Cupid; *khinna*—hurt; *hañā*—becoming.

TRANSLATION

"When Kṛṣṇa went out to search for Śrīmatī Rādhārāṇī, He wandered here and there. Not finding Her, He became afflicted by the arrow of Cupid and began to lament.

TEXT 116

শতকোটি-গোপীতে নহে কাম-নির্বাপণ ।
তাহাতেই অনুমানি শ্রীরাধিকার গুণ ॥ ১১৬ ॥

śata-koṭi-gopīte nahe kāma-nirvāpaṇa
tāhātei anumāni śrī-rādhikāra guṇa

śata-koṭi—hundreds of thousands; *gopīte*—in the midst of *gopīs; nahe*—there is not; *kāma-nirvāpaṇa*—satisfaction of lust; *tāhātei*—by that way; *anumāni*—we can imagine; *śrī-rādhikāra guṇa*—the transcendental quality of Śrīmatī Rādhārāṇī.

TRANSLATION

"Since Kṛṣṇa's lusty desires were not satisfied even in the midst of hundreds of thousands of gopīs and He was thus searching after Śrīmatī Rādhārāṇī, we can easily imagine how transcendentally qualified She is."

TEXT 117

প্রভু কহে — যে লাগি' আইলাম তোমা-স্থানে ।
সেই সব তত্ত্ববস্তু হৈল মোর জ্ঞানে ॥ ১১৭ ॥

prabhu kahe — ye lāgi' āilāma tomā-sthāne
sei saba tattva-vastu haila mora jñāne

prabhu kahe — the Lord said; *ye lāgi'* — for the matter of which; *āilāma* — I have come; *tomā-sthāne* — to your place; *sei saba* — all those; *tattva-vastu* — objects of truth; *haila* — were; *mora* — My; *jñāne* — in knowledge.

TRANSLATION

After hearing this, Lord Caitanya Mahāprabhu said to Rāmānanda Rāya, "That for which I have come to your residence has now become an object of truth in My knowledge.

TEXT 118

এবে সে জানিলুঁ সাধ্য-সাধন-নির্ণয় ।
আগে আর আছে কিছু, শুনিতে মন হয় ॥ ১১৮ ॥

ebe se jāniluṅ sādhya-sādhana-nirṇaya
āge āra āche kichu, śunite mana haya

ebe — now; *se* — that; *jāniluṅ* — I have understood; *sādhya* — of the ultimate goal; *sādhana* — and of the process; *nirṇaya* — the ascertainment; *āge* — ahead; *āra* — more; *āche* — there is; *kichu* — something; *śunite* — to hear; *mana* — the mind; *haya* — it is.

TRANSLATION

"Now I have come to understand the sublime goal of life and the process of achieving it. Nevertheless, I think that there is something more ahead, and My mind is desiring to have it.

TEXT 119

'কৃষ্ণের স্বরূপ' কহ 'রাধার স্বরূপ' ।
'রস' কোন্ তত্ত্ব, 'প্রেম' — কোন্ তত্ত্বরূপ ॥ ১১৯ ॥

'kṛṣṇera svarūpa' kaha 'rādhāra svarūpa'
'rasa' kon tattva, 'prema'—kon tattva-rūpa

kṛṣṇera—of Lord Kṛṣṇa; *svarūpa*—the transcendental features; *kaha*—speak; *rādhāra*—of Śrīmatī Rādhārāṇī; *svarūpa*—the transcendental features; *rasa*—mellows; *kon*—what; *tattva*—that truth; *prema*—love of Godhead; *kon*—what; *tattva-rūpa*—actual form.

TRANSLATION

"Kindly explain the transcendental features of Kṛṣṇa and Śrīmatī Rādhārāṇī. Also explain the truth of transcendental mellows and the transcendental form of love of Godhead.

TEXT 120

কৃপা করি' এই তত্ত্ব কহ ত' আমারে।
তোমা-বিনা কেহ ইহা নিরূপিতে নারে ॥ ১২০ ॥

kṛpā kari' ei tattva kaha ta' āmāre
tomā-vinā keha ihā nirūpite nāre

kṛpā kari'—showing your mercy; *ei tattva*—all these truths; *kaha*—explain; *ta'*—certainly; *āmāre*—unto Me; *tomā-vinā*—except for you; *keha*—someone; *ihā*—this; *nirūpite*—to ascertain; *nāre*—not able.

TRANSLATION

"Kindly explain all these truths to Me. But for yourself, no one can ascertain them."

TEXT 121

রায় কহে,—ইহা আমি কিছুই না জানি।
তুমি যেই কহাও, সেই কহি আমি বাণী ॥ ১২১ ॥

rāya kahe,—ihā āmi kichui nā jāni
tumi yei kahāo, sei kahi āmi vāṇī

rāya kahe—Rāmānanda Rāya said; *ihā*—this; *āmi*—I; *kichui*—something; *nā*—not; *jāni*—know; *tumi*—You; *yei*—whatever; *kahāo*—make me say; *sei*—those; *kahi*—speak; *āmi*—I; *vāṇī*—words.

TRANSLATION

Śrī Rāmānanda Rāya replied, "I do not know anything about this. I simply vibrate the sound You make me speak.

TEXT 122

তোমার শিক্ষায় পড়ি যেন শুক-পাঠ।
সাক্ষাৎ ঈশ্বর তুমি, কে বুঝে তোমার নাট ॥ ১২২ ॥

tomāra śikṣāya paḍi yena śuka-pāṭha
sākṣāt īśvara tumi, ke bujhe tomāra nāṭa

tomāra śikṣāya—by Your instruction; *paḍi*—I recite; *yena*—like; *śuka-pāṭha*—the reciting of a parrot; *sākṣāt*—directly; *īśvara*—the Supreme Personality of Godhead; *tumi*—You; *ke*—who; *bujhe*—can understand; *tomāra*—Your; *nāṭa*—dramatic performance.

TRANSLATION

"I simply repeat like a parrot whatever instructions You have given me. You are the Supreme Personality of Godhead Himself. Who can understand Your dramatic performances?

TEXT 123

হৃদয়ে প্রেরণ কর, জিহ্বায় কহাও বাণী।
কি কহিয়ে ভাল-মন্দ, কিছুই না জানি ॥ ১২৩ ॥

hṛdaye preraṇa kara, jihvāya kahāo vāṇī
ki kahiye bhāla-manda, kichui nā jāni

hṛdaye—within the heart; *preraṇa*—direction; *kara*—You give; *jihvāya*—on the tongue; *kahāo*—You make me speak; *vāṇī*—words; *ki*—what; *kahiye*—I am speaking; *bhāla-manda*—good or bad; *kichui*—something; *nā*—not; *jāni*—I know.

TRANSLATION

"You inspire me within the heart and make me speak with the tongue. I do not know whether I am speaking well or badly."

TEXT 124

প্রভু কহে, —মায়াবাদী আমি ত' সন্ন্যাসী।
ভক্তিতত্ত্ব নাহি জানি, মায়াবাদে ভাসি॥ ১২৪॥

prabhu kahe, — māyāvādī āmi ta' sannyāsī
bhakti-tattva nāhi jāni, māyāvāde bhāsi

prabhu kahe—the Lord said; *māyāvādī*—a follower of the Māyāvāda philosophy; *āmi*—I; *ta'*—certainly; *sannyāsī*—one in the renounced order of life; *bhakti-tattva*—the truths of transcendental loving service; *nāhi*—not; *jāni*—I know; *māyāvāde*—in the philosophy of impersonalism; *bhāsi*—I float.

TRANSLATION

Lord Caitanya Mahāprabhu said, "I am a Māyāvādī in the renounced order of life, and I do not even know what transcendental loving service to the Lord is. I simply float in the ocean of Māyāvāda philosophy.

TEXT 125

সার্বভৌম-সঙ্গে মোর মন নির্মল হইল।
'কৃষ্ণভক্তি-তত্ত্ব কহ', তাঁহারে পুছিল॥ ১২৫॥

sārvabhauma-saṅge mora mana nirmala ha-ila
'kṛṣṇa-bhakti-tattva kaha,' tāṅhāre puchila

sārvabhauma-saṅge—in the company of Sārvabhauma Bhaṭṭācārya; *mora*—My; *mana*—mind; *nirmala*—clarified; *ha-ila*—became; *kṛṣṇa-bhakti-tattva*—the truths of transcendental loving service to Kṛṣṇa; *kaha*—please explain; *tāṅhāre*—to him; *puchila*—I inquired.

TRANSLATION

"Due to the association of Sārvabhauma Bhaṭṭācārya, My mind became enlightened. Therefore I asked him about the truths of transcendental loving service to Kṛṣṇa.

TEXT 126

তেঁহো কহে — আমি নাহি জানি কৃষ্ণকথা ।
সবে রামানন্দ জানে, তেঁহো নাহি এথা ॥ ১২৬ ॥

teṅho kahe — āmi nāhi jāni kṛṣṇa-kathā
sabe rāmānanda jāne, teṅho nāhi ethā

teṅho kahe — he replied; *āmi* — I; *nāhi* — not; *jāni* — know; *kṛṣṇa-kathā* — topics of Lord Kṛṣṇa; *sabe* — all; *rāmānanda* — Rāmānanda Rāya; *jāne* — knows; *teṅho* — he; *nāhi* — not; *ethā* — here.

TRANSLATION

"Sārvabhauma Bhaṭṭācārya told me, 'I do not actually know about the topics of Lord Kṛṣṇa. They are all known only to Rāmānanda Rāya, but he is not present here.'"

TEXT 127

তোমার ঠাঞি আইলাঙ তোমার মহিমা শুনিয়া ।
তুমি মোরে স্তুতি কর 'সন্ন্যাসী' জানিয়া ॥ ১২৭ ॥

tomāra ṭhāñi āilāṅa tomāra mahimā śuniyā
tumi more stuti kara 'sannyāsī' jāniyā

tomāra ṭhāñi — to your presence; *āilāṅa* — I have come; *tomāra* — your; *mahimā* — glories; *śuniyā* — hearing; *tumi* — you; *more* — Me; *stuti* — praising; *kara* — do; *sannyāsī* — a person in the renounced order of life; *jāniyā* — knowing as.

TRANSLATION

Lord Śrī Caitanya Mahāprabhu continued, "After hearing about your glories, I have come to your place. But you are offering Me words of praise out of respect for a sannyāsī, one in the renounced order of life.

PURPORT

Śrīla Bhaktisiddhānta Sarasvatī Ṭhākura explains that a mundane person, being enriched by mundane opulences, must always know that the transcendental opulences of the advanced devotees are far more important than the materialistic opulences of a person like himself. A materialistic person with material opulences should not be very proud or puffed up before a transcendental devotee. If one approaches a transcendental devotee on the strength of one's material heritage, opulence, education and beauty and does not offer respect to the advanced devotee of the Lord, the Vaiṣṇava devotee may offer formal respects to such a materially puffed-up person, but he may not deliver transcendental knowledge to him. Indeed, the devotee sees him as a non-*brāhmaṇa* or *śūdra.* Such a puffed-up person cannot understand the science of Kṛṣṇa. A proud person is deceived in transcendental life and, despite having attained a human form, will again glide into hellish conditions. By His personal example, Śrī Caitanya Mahāprabhu explains how one should be submissive and humble before a Vaiṣṇava, even though one may be situated on a high platform. Such is the teaching of Śrī Caitanya Mahāprabhu as the *ācārya* of the world, the supreme spiritual master and teacher.

TEXT 128

কিবা বিপ্র, কিবা ন্যাসী, শূদ্র কেনে নয়।
যেই কৃষ্ণতত্ত্ববেত্তা, সেই 'গুরু' হয় ॥ ১২৮ ॥

kibā vipra, kibā nyāsī, śūdra kene naya
yei kṛṣṇa-tattva-vettā, sei 'guru' haya

kibā—whether; *vipra*—a *brāhmaṇa; kibā*—whether; *nyāsī*—a *sannyāsī; śūdra*—a *śūdra; kene*—why; *naya*—not; *yei*—anyone who; *kṛṣṇa-tattva-vettā*—a knower of the science of Kṛṣṇa; *sei*—that person; *guru*—the spiritual master; *haya*—is.

TRANSLATION

"Whether one is a brāhmaṇa, a sannyāsī or a śūdra—regardless of what he is—he can become a spiritual master if he knows the science of Kṛṣṇa."

PURPORT

This verse is very important to the Kṛṣṇa consciousness movement. In his *Amṛta-pravāha-bhāṣya,* Śrīla Bhaktivinoda Ṭhākura explains that one should not think that because Śrī Caitanya Mahāprabhu was born a *brāhmaṇa* and was situated in the topmost spiritual order as a *sannyāsī*, it was improper for Him to receive instructions from Śrīla Rāmānanda Rāya, who belonged to the *śūdra* caste. To clarify this matter, Śrī Caitanya Mahāprabhu informed Rāmānanda Rāya that knowledge of Kṛṣṇa consciousness is more important than caste. In the system of *varṇāśrama-dharma* there are various duties for the *brāhmaṇas, kṣatriyas, vaiśyas* and *śūdras.* Actually the *brāhmaṇa* is supposed to be the spiritual master of all other *varṇas*, or classes, but as far as Kṛṣṇa consciousness is concerned, everyone is capable of becoming a spiritual master because knowledge in Kṛṣṇa consciousness is on the platform of the spirit soul. To spread Kṛṣṇa consciousness, one need only be cognizant of the science of the spirit soul. It does not matter whether one is a *brāhmaṇa, kṣatriya, vaiśya, śūdra, sannyāsī, gṛhastha* or whatever. If one simply understands this science, he can become a spiritual master.

It is stated in the *Hari-bhakti-vilāsa* that one should not accept initiation from a person who is not in the brahminical order if there is a fit person in the brahminical order present. This instruction is meant for those who are overly dependent on the mundane social order and is suitable for those who want to remain in mundane life. If one understands the truth of Kṛṣṇa consciousness and seriously desires to attain transcendental knowledge for the perfection of life, he can accept a spiritual master from any social status, provided the spiritual master is fully conversant with the science of Kṛṣṇa. Śrīla Bhaktisiddhānta Sarasvatī Ṭhākura also states that although one is situated as a *brāhmaṇa, kṣatriya, vaiśya, śūdra, brahmacārī, vānaprastha, gṛhastha* or *sannyāsī*, if he is conversant in the science of Kṛṣṇa he can become a spiritual master as *vartma-pradarśaka-guru, dīkṣā-guru* or *śikṣā-guru.* The spiritual master who first gives information about spiritual life is called the *vartma-pradarśaka-guru*, the spiritual master who initiates according to the regulations of the *śāstras* is called the *dīkṣā-guru*, and the spiritual master who gives instructions for elevation is called the *śikṣā-guru.* Factually the qualifications of a spiritual master depend on his knowledge of the science of Kṛṣṇa. It does not matter whether he is a *brāhmaṇa, kṣatriya, sannyāsī* or *śūdra.* This injunction given by Śrī Caitanya

Mahāprabhu is not at all against the injunctions of the *śāstras.* In the *Padma Purāṇa* it is said:

> *na śūdrā bhagavad-bhaktās te 'pi bhāgavatottamāḥ*
> *sarva-varṇeṣu te śūdrā ye na bhaktā janārdane*

One who is actually advanced in spiritual knowledge of Kṛṣṇa is never a *śūdra,* even though he may have been born in a *śūdra* family. However, even if a *vipra,* or *brāhmaṇa,* is very expert in the six brahminical activities (*paṭhana, pāṭhana, yajana, yājana, dāna, pratigraha*) and is also well versed in the Vedic hymns, he cannot become a spiritual master unless he is a Vaiṣṇava. But if one is born in the family of *caṇḍālas* yet is well versed in Kṛṣṇa consciousness, he can become a *guru.* These are the śāstric injunctions, and strictly following these injunctions, Śrī Caitanya Mahāprabhu, as a *gṛhastha* named Śrī Viśvambhara, was initiated by a *sannyāsī-guru* named Īśvara Purī. Similarly, Śrī Nityānanda Prabhu was initiated by Mādhavendra Purī, a *sannyāsī.* According to others, however, He was initiated by Lakṣmīpati Tīrtha. Advaita Ācārya, although a *gṛhastha,* was initiated by Mādhavendra Purī, and Śrī Rasikānanda, although born in a *brāhmaṇa* family, was initiated by Śrī Śyāmānanda Prabhu, who was not born in a caste *brāhmaṇa* family. There are many instances in which a born *brāhmaṇa* took initiation from a person who was not born in a *brāhmaṇa* family. The brahminical symptoms are explained in *Śrīmad-Bhāgavatam* (7.11.35), wherein it is stated:

> *yasya yal-lakṣaṇaṁ proktaṁ puṁso varṇābhivyañjakam*
> *yad anyatrāpi dṛśyeta tat tenaiva vinirdiśet*

If a person is born in a *śūdra* family but has all the qualities of a spiritual master, he should be accepted not only as a *brāhmaṇa* but as a qualified spiritual master also. This is also the instruction of Śrī Caitanya Mahāprabhu. Śrīla Bhaktisiddhānta Sarasvatī Ṭhākura therefore introduced the sacred thread ceremony for all Vaiṣṇavas according to the rules and regulations.

Sometimes a Vaiṣṇava who is a *bhajanānandī* does not take the *sāvitra-saṁskāra* (sacred thread initiation), but this does not mean that this system should be used for preaching work. There are two kinds of Vaiṣṇavas—*bhajanānandī* and *goṣṭhy-ānandī.* A *bhajanānandī* is not interested in preaching work, but a *goṣṭhy-*

ānandī is interested in spreading Kṛṣṇa consciousness to benefit the people and increase the number of Vaiṣṇavas. A Vaiṣṇava is understood to be above the position of a *brāhmaṇa.* As a preacher, he should be recognized as a *brāhmaṇa;* otherwise there may be a misunderstanding of his position as a Vaiṣṇava. However, a Vaiṣṇava *brāhmaṇa* is not selected on the basis of his birth but according to his qualities. Unfortunately, those who are unintelligent do not know the difference between a *brāhmaṇa* and a Vaiṣṇava. They are under the impression that unless one is a *brāhmaṇa* he cannot be a spiritual master. For this reason only, Śrī Caitanya Mahāprabhu makes the statement in this verse:

kibā vipra, kibā nyāsī, śūdra kene naya
yei kṛṣṇa-tattva-vettā, sei 'guru' haya

If one becomes a *guru,* he is automatically a *brāhmaṇa.* Sometimes a caste *guru* says that *ye kṛṣṇa-tattva-vettā, sei guru haya* means that one who is not a *brāhmaṇa* may become a *śikṣā-guru* or a *vartma-pradarśaka-guru* but not an initiator *guru.* According to such caste *gurus,* birth and family ties are considered foremost. However, the hereditary consideration is not acceptable to Vaiṣṇavas. The word *guru* is equally applicable to the *vartma-pradarśaka-guru, śikṣā-guru* and *dīkṣā-guru.* Unless we accept the principle enunciated by Śrī Caitanya Mahāprabhu, this Kṛṣṇa consciousness movement cannot spread all over the world. According to Śrī Caitanya Mahāprabhu's intentions, *pṛthivīte āche yata nagarādi-grāma sarvatra pracāra haibe mora nāma.* Śrī Caitanya Mahāprabhu's cult must be preached all over the world. This does not mean that people should take to His teachings and remain *śūdras* or *caṇḍālas.* As soon as one is trained as a pure Vaiṣṇava, he must be accepted as a bona fide *brāhmaṇa.* This is the essence of Śrī Caitanya Mahāprabhu's instructions in this verse.

TEXT 129

'সন্ন্যাসী' বলিয়া মোরে না করিহ বঞ্চন ।
কৃষ্ণ-রাধা-তত্ত্ব কহি' পূর্ণ কর মন ॥ ১২৯ ॥

'sannyāsī' baliyā more nā kariha vañcana
kṛṣṇa-rādhā-tattva kahi' pūrṇa kara mana

sannyāsī—a person in the renounced order of life; *baliyā*—taking as; *more*—Me; *nā kariha*—do not do; *vañcana*—cheating; *kṛṣṇa-rādhā-tattva*—the truth about Rādhā-Kṛṣṇa; *kahi'*—describing; *pūrṇa*—complete; *kara*—make; *mana*—My mind.

TRANSLATION

Śrī Caitanya Mahāprabhu continued, "Please do not try to cheat Me, thinking of Me as a learned sannyāsī. Please satisfy My mind by just describing the truth of Rādhā and Kṛṣṇa."

TEXTS 130–131

যদ্যপি রায় — প্রেমী, মহাভাগবতে ।
তাঁর মন কৃষ্ণমায়া নারে আচ্ছাদিতে ॥ ১৩০ ॥
তথাপি প্রভুর ইচ্ছা — পরম প্রবল ।
জানিলেহ রায়ের মন হৈল টলমল ॥ ১৩১ ॥

yadyapi rāya—premī, mahā-bhāgavate
tāṅra mana kṛṣṇa-māyā nāre ācchādite

tathāpi prabhura icchā—parama prabala
jānileha rāyera mana haila ṭalamala

yadyapi—although; *rāya*—Rāmānanda Rāya; *premī*—a great lover of Kṛṣṇa; *mahā-bhāgavate*—a topmost devotee; *tāṅra*—his; *mana*—mind; *kṛṣṇa-māyā*—the illusory energy of Kṛṣṇa; *nāre*—not able; *ācchādite*—to cover; *tathāpi*—still; *prabhura icchā*—the Lord's desire; *parama prabala*—very intense; *jānileha*—even though it was known; *rāyera mana*—the mind of Rāmānanda Rāya; *haila*—there was; *ṭalamala*—agitation.

TRANSLATION

Śrī Rāmānanda Rāya was a great devotee of the Lord and a lover of God, and although his mind could not be covered by Kṛṣṇa's illusory energy, and although he could understand the mind of the Lord, which was very strong and intense, Rāmānanda's mind became a little agitated.

PURPORT

The perfect devotee always acts according to the desires of the Supreme Personality of Godhead. But a materialistic man is carried away by the waves of the material energy. Śrīla Bhaktivinoda Ṭhākura has said, *māyāra vaśe, yāccha bhese, khāccha hābuḍubu, bhāi.* A person under the grip of the material energy is carried away by the waves of that illusory energy. In other words, a person in the material world is a servant of *māyā.* However, a person in the spiritual energy is a servant of the Supreme Personality of Godhead. Although Rāmānanda Rāya knew that nothing was unknown to Śrī Caitanya Mahāprabhu, he nonetheless began to speak further on the subject because the Lord desired it.

TEXT 132

রায় কহে, — "আমি — নট, তুমি — সূত্রধার ।
যেই মত নাচাও, তৈছে চাহি নাচিবার ॥ ১৩২ ॥

rāya kahe, — "āmi — naṭa, tumi — sūtra-dhāra
yei mata nācāo, taiche cāhi nācibāra

rāya kahe — Rāmānanda Rāya replied; *āmi* — I; *naṭa* — dancer; *tumi* — You; *sūtra-dhāra* — the puller of the strings; *yei* — whatever; *mata* — way; *nācāo* — You make me dance; *taiche* — in that way; *cāhi* — I want; *nācibāra* — to dance.

TRANSLATION

Śrī Rāmānanda Rāya said, "I am just a dancing puppet, and You pull the strings. Whichever way You make me dance, I will dance.

TEXT 133

মোর জিহ্বা — বীণাযন্ত্র, তুমি — বীণা-ধারী ।
তোমার মনে যেই উঠে, তাহাই উচ্চারি ॥ ১৩৩ ॥

mora jihvā — vīṇā-yantra, tumi — vīṇā-dhārī
tomāra mane yei uṭhe, tāhāi uccāri

mora jihvā—my tongue; *vīṇā-yantra*—a stringed instrument; *tumi*—You; *vīṇā-dhārī*—the player of the stringed instrument; *tomāra mane*—in Your mind; *yei uṭhe*—whatever arises; *tāhāi*—that; *uccāri*—I vibrate.

TRANSLATION

"My dear Lord, my tongue is just like a stringed instrument, and You are its player. Therefore I simply vibrate whatever arises in Your mind."

TEXT 134

পরম ঈশ্বর কৃষ্ণ — স্বয়ং ভগবান্ ।
সর্ব-অবতারী, সর্বকারণ-প্রধান ॥ ১৩৪ ॥

parama īśvara kṛṣṇa—svayaṁ bhagavān
sarva-avatārī, sarva-kāraṇa-pradhāna

parama—supreme; *īśvara*—controller; *kṛṣṇa*—Lord Kṛṣṇa; *svayam*—personally; *bhagavān*—the Supreme Personality of Godhead; *sarva-avatārī*—the source of all incarnations; *sarva-kāraṇa-pradhāna*—the supreme cause of all causes.

TRANSLATION

Rāmānanda Rāya then began to speak on kṛṣṇa-tattva. "Kṛṣṇa is the Supreme Personality of Godhead," he said. "He is personally the original Godhead, the source of all incarnations and the cause of all causes.

TEXT 135

অনন্ত বৈকুণ্ঠ, আর অনন্ত অবতার ।
অনন্ত ব্রহ্মাণ্ড ইহাঁ, — সবার আধার ॥ ১৩৫ ॥

ananta vaikuṇṭha, āra ananta avatāra
ananta brahmāṇḍa ihāṅ,—sabāra ādhāra

ananta vaikuṇṭha—innumerable Vaikuṇṭha planets; *āra*—and; *ananta avatāra*—innumerable incarnations; *ananta brahmāṇḍa*

—innumerable universes; *ihāṅ*—in this material world; *sabāra*—of all of them; *ādhāra*—the resting place.

TRANSLATION

"There are innumerable Vaikuṇṭha planets, as well as innumerable incarnations. In the material world also there are innumerable universes, and Kṛṣṇa is the supreme resting place for all of them.

TEXT 136

সচ্চিদানন্দ-তনু, ব্রজেন্দ্রনন্দন ।
সর্বৈশ্বর্য-সর্বশক্তি-সর্বরস-পূর্ণ ॥ ১৩৬ ॥

sac-cid-ānanda-tanu, vrajendra-nandana
sarvaiśvarya-sarvaśakti-sarvarasa-pūrṇa

sat-cit-ānanda-tanu—Kṛṣṇa's body is transcendental, full of knowledge, bliss and eternity; *vrajendra-nandana*—the son of Mahārāja Nanda; *sarva-aiśvarya*—all opulences; *sarva-śakti*—all potencies; *sarva-rasa-pūrṇa*—the reservoir of all transcendental mellows.

TRANSLATION

"The transcendental body of Śrī Kṛṣṇa is eternal and full of bliss and knowledge. He is the son of Nanda Mahārāja. He is full of all opulences and potencies, as well as all spiritual mellows.

TEXT 137

ঈশ্বরঃ পরমঃ কৃষ্ণঃ সচ্চিদানন্দবিগ্রহ ।
অনাদিরাদির্গোবিন্দঃ সর্বকারণকারণম্ ॥ ১৩৭ ॥

īśvaraḥ paramaḥ kṛṣṇaḥ
sac-cid-ānanda-vigrahaḥ
anādir ādir govindaḥ
sarva-kāraṇa-kāraṇam

īśvaraḥ—the controller; *paramaḥ*—supreme; *kṛṣṇaḥ*—Lord Kṛṣṇa; *sat*—eternal existence; *cit*—absolute knowledge; *ānanda*—absolute bliss; *vigrahaḥ*—whose form; *anādiḥ*—without beginning; *ādiḥ*—the origin of everything; *govindaḥ*—a name of Lord Kṛṣṇa; *sarva*—all; *kāraṇa*—of causes; *kāraṇam*—He is the original cause.

TRANSLATION

"'Kṛṣṇa, who is known as Govinda, is the supreme controller. He has an eternal, blissful, spiritual body. He is the origin of all. He has no other origin, for He is the prime cause of all causes.'

PURPORT

This verse is from the *Brahma-saṁhitā* (5.1).

TEXT 138

বৃন্দাবনে 'অপ্রাকৃত নবীন মদন' ।
কামগায়ত্রী কামবীজে যাঁর উপাসন ॥ ১৩৮ ॥

vṛndāvane 'aprākṛta navīna madana'
kāma-gāyatrī kāma-bīje yāṅra upāsana

vṛndāvane—in Vṛndāvana; *aprākṛta*—spiritual; *navīna*—new; *madana*—Cupid; *kāma-gāyatrī*—hymns of desire; *kāma-bīje*—by the spiritual seed of desire called *klīm; yāṅra*—of whom; *upāsana*—the worship.

TRANSLATION

"In the spiritual realm of Vṛndāvana, Kṛṣṇa is the spiritual, ever-fresh Cupid. He is worshiped by the chanting of the Kāma-gāyatrī mantra, with the spiritual seed klīm.

PURPORT

Vṛndāvana is described in the *Brahma-saṁhitā* (5.56) in this way:

śriyaḥ kāntāḥ kāntaḥ parama-puruṣaḥ kalpa-taravo
drumā bhūmiś cintāmaṇi-gaṇa-mayī toyam amṛtam
kathā gānaṁ nāṭyaṁ gamanam api vaṁśī priya-sakhī
cid-ānandaṁ jyotiḥ param api tad āsvādyam api ca

sa yatra kṣīrābdhiḥ sravati surabhībhyaś ca su-mahān
nimeṣārdhākhyo vā vrajati na hi yatrāpi samayaḥ
bhaje śvetadvīpaṁ tam aham iha golokam iti yaṁ
vidantas te santaḥ kṣiti-virala-cārāḥ katipaye

The spiritual realm of Vṛndāvana is always spiritual. The goddess of fortune and the *gopīs* are always present there. They are Kṛṣṇa's beloveds, and all of them are as spiritual as Kṛṣṇa. In Vṛndāvana, Kṛṣṇa is the Supreme Person and is the husband of all the *gopīs* and the goddess of fortune. The trees in Vṛndāvana are wish-fulfilling trees. The land is made of touchstone, and the water is nectar. Words are musical vibrations, and all movements are dancing. The flute is the Lord's constant companion. The planet Goloka Vṛndāvana is self-luminous like the sun and is full of spiritual bliss. The perfection of life lies in tasting that spiritual existence; therefore everyone should cultivate its knowledge. In Vṛndāvana, spiritual cows are always supplying spiritual milk. Not a single moment is wasted there—in other words, there is no past, present or future. Not a single particle of time is wasted. Within this material universe, the devotees worship that transcendental abode as Goloka Vṛndāvana. Lord Brahmā himself said, "Let me worship that spiritual land where Kṛṣṇa is present." This transcendental Vṛndāvana is not appreciated by those who are not devotees or self-realized souls because this Vṛndāvana-dhāma is all spiritual. The pastimes of the Lord there are also spiritual. None are material. According to a prayer by Śrīla Narottama dāsa Ṭhākura (*Prārthanā* 1):

āra kabe nitāi-cāṅdera karuṇā karibe
saṁsāra-vāsanā mora kabe tuccha ha'be

"When will Lord Nityānanda have mercy upon me so that I can realize the uselessness of material pleasure?"

viṣaya chāḍiyā kabe śuddha ha'be mana
kabe hāma heraba śrī-vṛndāvana

"When will my mind be cleansed of all material dirt so that I will be able to feel the presence of spiritual Vṛndāvana?"

rūpa-raghunātha-pade haibe ākuti
kabe hāma bujhaba se yugala-pirīti

"When will I be attracted to the instructions of the Gosvāmīs so that I will be able to understand what is Rādhā and Kṛṣṇa and what is Vṛndāvana?"

These verses indicate that one first has to be purified of all material desires and all attraction for fruitive activity and speculative knowledge if one wishes to understand Vṛndāvana.

In reference to the words *aprākṛta navīna madana, aprākṛta* refers to that which is the very opposite of the material conception. The Māyāvādīs consider this to be zero or impersonal, but that is not the case. Everything in the material world is dull, but in the spiritual world everything is alive. The desire for enjoyment is present both in Kṛṣṇa and in His parts and parcels, the living entities. In the spiritual world, such desires are also spiritual. No one should mistakenly consider such desires to be material. In the material world, if one is sexually inclined and enjoys sex life, he enjoys something temporary. His enjoyment vanishes after a few minutes. However, in the spiritual world the same enjoyment may be there, but it never vanishes. It is continuously enjoyed. In the spiritual world such sex pleasure appears to the enjoyer to be more and more relishable with each new feature. In the material world, however, sex enjoyment becomes distasteful after a few minutes only, and it is never permanent. Because Kṛṣṇa appears very much sexually inclined, He is called the new Cupid in the spiritual world. There is no material inebriety in such desire, however.

Gāyantaṁ trāyate yasmād gāyatrī tvaṁ tataḥ smṛtā: one who chants the Gāyatrī *mantra* is gradually delivered from the material clutches. In other words, that which delivers one from material entanglement is called Gāyatrī. An explanation of the Gāyatrī *mantra* can be found in the *Madhya-līlā,* Chapter Twenty-one, text 125:

kāma-gāyatrī-mantra-rūpa, haya kṛṣṇera svarūpa,
sārdha-cabbiśa akṣara tāra haya
se akṣara 'candra' haya, kṛṣṇe kari' udaya,
trijagat kailā kāmamaya

The Kāma-gāyatrī *mantra* is just like a Vedic hymn, but it is the Supreme Personality of Godhead Himself. There is no difference between the Kāma-gāyatrī and Kṛṣṇa. Both are composed of twenty-four and a half transcendental syllables (see *Madhya* 21.125–29). The *mantra* depicted in letters is also Kṛṣṇa, and the *mantra* rises just like the moon. Due to this, there is a perverted reflection of desire in human society and among all kinds of living entities. In the *mantra klīṁ kāma-devāya vidmahe puṣpa-bāṇāya dhīmahi tan no 'naṅgaḥ pracodayāt,* Kṛṣṇa is called Kāma-deva, Puṣpa-bāṇa and Anaṅga. Kāma-deva is Madana-mohana, the Deity who establishes our relationship with Kṛṣṇa; Puṣpa-bāṇa ("He who carries an arrow made of flowers") is Govinda, the Personality of Godhead who accepts our devotional service; and Anaṅga is Gopījana-vallabha, who satisfies all the *gopīs* and is the ultimate goal of life. This Kāma-gāyatrī (*klīṁ kāma-devāya vidmahe puṣpa-bāṇāya dhīmahi tan no 'naṅgaḥ pracodayāt*) simply does not belong to this material world. When one is advanced in spiritual understanding, he can worship the Supreme Personality of Godhead with his spiritually purified senses and fulfill the desires of the Lord.

man-manā bhava mad-bhakto mad-yājī māṁ namaskuru
mām evaiṣyasi satyaṁ te pratijāne priyo 'si me

"Always think of Me and become My devotee. Worship Me and offer your homage unto Me. Thus you will come to Me without fail. I promise you this because you are My very dear friend." (Bg. 18.65)

In the *Brahma-saṁhitā* (5.27–28) it is stated:

atha veṇu-ninādasya trayī-mūrti-mayī gatiḥ
sphurantī praviveśāśu mukhābjāni svayambhuvaḥ

gāyatrīṁ gāyatas tasmād adhigatya saroja-jaḥ
saṁskṛtaś cādi-guruṇā dvijatām agamat tataḥ

trayyā prabuddho 'tha vidhir vijñāta-tattva-sāgaraḥ
tuṣṭāva veda-sāreṇa stotreṇānena keśavam

"Then Gāyatrī, mother of the *Vedas,* having been manifested by the divine sound of Śrī Kṛṣṇa's flute, entered the lotus mouth of Brahmā, the self-born, through his eight earholes. Thus the lotus-born Brahmā received the Gāyatrī *mantra,* which had sprung from the song of Śrī Kṛṣṇa's flute. In this way he attained twice-born status, having been initiated by the supreme, primal preceptor, Godhead Himself. Enlightened by the recollection of that Gāyatrī, which embodies the three *Vedas,* Brahmā became acquainted with the expanse of the ocean of truth. Then he worshiped Śrī Kṛṣṇa, the essence of all the *Vedas,* with a hymn."

The vibration of Kṛṣṇa's flute is the origin of the Vedic hymns. Lord Brahmā, who is seated on a lotus flower, heard the sound vibration of Kṛṣṇa's flute and was thereby initiated by the Gāyatrī *mantra.*

TEXT 139

পুরুষ, যোষিৎ, কিবা স্থাবর-জঙ্গম।
সর্ব-চিত্তাকর্ষক, সাক্ষাৎ মন্মথ-মদন ॥ ১৩৯ ॥

puruṣa, yoṣit, kibā sthāvara-jaṅgama
sarva-cittākarṣaka, sākṣāt manmatha-madana

puruṣa—a male; *yoṣit*—a female; *kibā*—all; *sthāvara-jaṅgama*—living entities who cannot move and living entities who can move; *sarva*—of everyone; *citta-ākarṣaka*—the attractor of the minds; *sākṣāt*—directly; *manmatha-madana*—captivator of Cupid himself.

TRANSLATION

"The very name Kṛṣṇa means that He attracts even Cupid. He is therefore attractive to everyone—male and female, moving and inert living entities. Indeed, Kṛṣṇa is known as the all-attractive one.

PURPORT

Just as there are many orbs in the material world called stars or planets, in the spiritual world there are many spiritual planets called Vaikuṇṭhalokas. The spiritual universe, however, is situated far, far away from the cluster of material universes. Material scientists cannot even estimate the number of planets and stars within this universe. They are also incapable of traveling to other stars by spaceship. According to the *Bhagavad-gītā* (8.20), there is also a spiritual world:

paras tasmāt tu bhāvo 'nyo 'vyakto 'vyaktāt sanātanaḥ
yaḥ sa sarveṣu bhūteṣu naśyatsu na vinaśyati

"Yet there is another unmanifested nature, which is eternal and is transcendental to this manifested and unmanifested matter. It is supreme and is never annihilated. When all in this world is annihilated, that part remains as it is."

Thus there is another nature, which is superior to material nature. The word *bhāva* or *svabhāva* refers to nature. The spiritual nature is eternal, and even when all the material universes are destroyed, the planets in the spiritual world abide. They remain exactly as the spirit soul remains even after the annihilation of the material body. That spiritual world is called the *aprākṛta* (antimaterial) world. In this transcendental, spiritual world or universe, the highest planetary system is known as Goloka Vṛndāvana. That is the abode of Lord Kṛṣṇa Himself, who is also all-spiritual. Kṛṣṇa is known there as Aprākṛta-madana. The name Madana refers to Cupid, but Kṛṣṇa is the spiritual Madana. His body is not material like the body of Cupid in this material universe. Kṛṣṇa's body is all-spiritual—*sac-cid-ānanda-vigraha*. Therefore He is called Aprākṛta-madana. He is also known as Manmatha-madana, which means that He is attractive even to Cupid. Sometimes Kṛṣṇa's activities and attractive features are misinterpreted by gross materialists who accuse Him of being immoral because He danced with the *gopīs*, but such an accusation results from not knowing that Kṛṣṇa is beyond this material world. His body is *sac-cid-ānanda-vigraha*, completely spiritual. There is no material contamination in His body, and one should not consider His body a lump of flesh and bones. The Māyāvādī philosophers conceive of Kṛṣṇa's body as material, and this is an abominable, grossly materialistic conception. Just as Kṛṣṇa is completely spiritual, the *gopīs* are also spiritual, and this is confirmed in the *Brahma-saṁhitā* (5.37):

ānanda-cin-maya-rasa-pratibhāvitābhis
tābhir ya eva nija-rūpatayā kalābhiḥ
goloka eva nivasaty akhilātma-bhūto
govindam ādi-puruṣaṁ tam ahaṁ bhajāmi

"I worship Govinda, the primeval Lord. He resides in His own realm, Goloka, with Rādhā, who resembles His own spiritual figure and who embodies the ecstatic potency (*hlādinī*). Their companions are Her confidantes, who embody extensions of Her bodily form and who are imbued and permeated with ever-blissful spiritual *rasa*."

The *gopīs* are also of the same spiritual quality (*nija-rūpatayā*) because they are expansions of Kṛṣṇa's pleasure potency. Neither Kṛṣṇa nor the *gopīs* have anything to do with lumps of matter or the material conception. In the material world the living entity is encaged within a material body, and due to ignorance he thinks that he is the body. Therefore here the enjoyment of lusty desires between male and female is all material. One cannot compare the lusty desires of a materialistic man to the transcendental lusty desires of Kṛṣṇa. Unless one is advanced in spiritual science, he cannot understand the lusty desires between Kṛṣṇa and the *gopīs.* In the *Caitanya-caritāmṛta* the lusty desire of the *gopīs* is compared to gold. The lusty desires of a materialistic man, on the other hand, are compared to iron. At no stage can iron and gold be equated. The living entities—moving and nonmoving—are part and parcel of Kṛṣṇa; therefore they originally have the same kind of lusty desire as His. But when this lusty desire is expressed through matter, it is abominable. When a living entity is spiritually advanced and liberated from material bondage, he can understand Kṛṣṇa in truth. As stated in the *Bhagavad-gītā* (4.9):

janma karma ca me divyam evaṁ yo vetti tattvataḥ
tyaktvā dehaṁ punar janma naiti mām eti so 'rjuna

"One who knows the transcendental nature of My appearance and activities does not, upon leaving the body, take his birth again in this material world but attains My eternal abode, O Arjuna."

When one can understand the body of Kṛṣṇa as well as the Lord's lusty desires, one is immediately liberated. A conditioned soul encaged within the material body cannot understand Kṛṣṇa. As stated in the *Bhagavad-gītā* (7.3):

manuṣyāṇāṁ sahasreṣu kaścid yatati siddhaye
yatatām api siddhānāṁ kaścin māṁ vetti tattvataḥ

"Out of many thousands among men, one may endeavor for perfection, and of those who have achieved perfection, hardly one knows Me in truth."

The word *siddhaye* indicates liberation. Only after being liberated from material conditioning can one understand Kṛṣṇa. When one can understand Kṛṣṇa as He is (*tattvataḥ*), one actually lives in the spiritual world, although apparently living within the material body. This technical science can be understood when one is actually spiritually advanced.

In his *Bhakti-rasāmṛta-sindhu* (1.2.187), Śrīla Rūpa Gosvāmī says:

īhā yasya harer dāsye karmaṇā manasā girā
nikhilāsv apy avasthāsu jīvan-muktaḥ sa ucyate

When a person in this material world desires only to serve Kṛṣṇa with love and devotion, he is liberated, even though functioning within this material world. As the *Bhagavad-gītā* (14.26) confirms:

māṁ ca yo 'vyabhicāreṇa bhakti-yogena sevate
sa guṇān samatītyaitān brahma-bhūyāya kalpate

"One who engages in full devotional service, unfailing in all circumstances, at once transcends the modes of material nature and thus comes to the level of Brahman."

Simply by engaging in the loving service of the Lord one can attain liberation. As stated in the *Bhagavad-gītā* (18.54), *brahma-bhūtaḥ prasannātmā na śocati na kāṅkṣati.* A person who is highly advanced in spiritual knowledge and who has attained the *brahma-bhūta* stage neither laments nor hankers for anything material. That is the stage of spiritual realization.

Śrīla Bhaktivinoda Ṭhākura considers the *brahma-bhūta* stage in two divisions — *svarūpa-gata* and *vastu-gata.* One who has understood Kṛṣṇa in truth but is still maintaining some material connection is known to be situated in his *svarūpa,* his original consciousness. When that original consciousness is completely spiritual, it is called Kṛṣṇa consciousness. One who lives in such consciousness is actually living in Vṛndāvana. He may live anywhere; material location doesn't matter. When by the grace of Kṛṣṇa one thus advances, he becomes completely uncontaminated by the material body and mind and at that time factually lives in Vṛndāvana. That stage is called *vastu-gata.*

One should execute his spiritual activities in the *svarūpa-gata* stage of consciousness. He should also chant the *cin-mayī* Gāyatrī, the spiritual *mantras oṁ namo bhagavate vāsudevāya, klīṁ kṛṣṇāya govindāya gopījana-vallabhāya svāhā* and *klīṁ kāma-devāya vidmahe puṣpa-bāṇāya dhīmahi tan no 'naṅgaḥ pracodayāt.* These are the Kāma-gāyatrī or *kāma-bīja mantras.* One should be initiated by a bona fide spiritual master and worship Kṛṣṇa with these transcendental *mantras.*

As explained by Kṛṣṇadāsa Kavirāja Gosvāmī in the previous verse and the current verse:

vṛndāvane 'aprākṛta navīna madana'
kāma-gāyatrī kāma-bīje yāṅra upāsana

puruṣa, yoṣit, kibā sthāvara-jaṅgama
sarva-cittākarṣaka, sākṣāt manmatha-madana

A person who is properly purified and initiated by the spiritual master worships the Supreme Personality of Godhead, Kṛṣṇa, by chanting this *mantra,* the Kāma-gāyatrī with the *kāma-bīja.* As the *Bhagavad-gītā* (18.65) confirms, one should engage in transcendental worship in order to be fit for being attracted by Kṛṣṇa, the all-attractive:

man-manā bhava mad-bhakto mad-yājī māṁ namaskuru
mām evaiṣyasi satyaṁ te pratijāne priyo 'si me

"Always think of Me and become My devotee. Worship Me and offer your homage unto Me. Thus you will come to Me without fail. I promise you this because you are My very dear friend."

Since every living entity is part and parcel of Kṛṣṇa, Kṛṣṇa is naturally attractive. Due to the material covering, one's attraction for Kṛṣṇa is checked. One is not usually attracted by Kṛṣṇa in the material world, but as soon as one is liberated from material conditioning, he is naturally attracted. Therefore it is said in this verse, *sarva-cittākarṣaka:* "Everyone is naturally attracted by Kṛṣṇa." This attraction is within everyone's heart, and when the heart is cleansed, that attraction is manifested (*ceto-darpaṇa-mārjanaṁ bhava-mahā-dāvāgni-nirvāpaṇam*).

TEXT 140

তাসামাবিরভূচ্ছৌরিঃ স্ময়মানমুখাম্বুজঃ ।
পীতাম্বরধরঃ স্রগ্বী সাক্ষান্মন্মথ-মন্মথঃ ॥ ১৪০ ॥

tāsām āvirabhūc chauriḥ
smayamāna-mukhāmbujaḥ
pītāmbara-dharaḥ sragvī
sākṣān manmatha-manmathaḥ

tāsām—among them; *āvirabhūt*—appeared; *śauriḥ*—Lord Kṛṣṇa; *smayamāna*—smiling; *mukha-ambujaḥ*—lotus face; *pīta-*

ambara-dharaḥ—dressed with yellow garments; *sragvī*—decorated with a flower garland; *sākṣāt*—directly; *manmatha*—of Cupid; *manmathaḥ*—Cupid.

TRANSLATION

"'When Kṛṣṇa left the rāsa-līlā dance, the gopīs became very morose, and when they were grieving, Kṛṣṇa reappeared dressed in yellow garments. Wearing a flower garland and smiling, He was attractive even to Cupid. In this way Kṛṣṇa appeared among the gopīs.'

PURPORT

This verse is from *Śrīmad-Bhāgavatam* (10.32.2).

TEXT 141

নানা-ভক্তের রসামৃত নানাবিধ হয় ।
সেই সব রসামৃতের 'বিষয়' 'আশ্রয়' ॥ ১৪১ ॥

nānā-bhaktera rasāmṛta nānā-vidha haya
sei saba rasāmṛtera 'viṣaya' 'āśraya'

nānā-bhaktera—of various types of devotees; *rasa-amṛta*—the nectar of devotion or transcendental mellows; *nānā-vidha*—different varieties; *haya*—there are; *sei saba*—all these; *rasa-amṛtera*—of the nectar of devotion; *viṣaya*—subject; *āśraya*—object.

TRANSLATION

"Each and every devotee has a certain type of transcendental mellow in relation to Kṛṣṇa. But in all transcendental relationships the devotee is the worshiper [āśraya] and Kṛṣṇa is the object of worship [viṣaya].

TEXT 142

অখিলরসামৃতমূর্তিঃ
প্রসৃমর-রুচিরুদ্ধ-তারকা-পালিঃ ।
কলিত-শ্যামা-ললিতো
রাধাপ্রেয়ান্ বিধুর্জয়তি ॥ ১৪২ ॥

akhila-rasāmṛta-mūrtiḥ
prasṛmara-ruci-ruddha-tārakā-pāliḥ
kalita-śyāmā-lalito
rādhā-preyān vidhur jayati

akhila-rasa-amṛta-mūrtiḥ—the reservoir of all pleasure, in which exist all the mellows of devotional service, namely *śānta, dāsya, sakhya, vātsalya* and *mādhurya; prasṛmara*—spreading forth; *ruci*—by His bodily luster; *ruddha*—who has subjugated; *tārakā*—the *gopī* named Tārakā; *pāliḥ*—the *gopī* named Pāli; *kalita*—who has absorbed the minds of; *śyāmā*—the *gopī* named Śyāmā; *lalitaḥ*—and the *gopī* named Lalitā; *rādhā-preyān*—dearmost to Śrīmatī Rādhārāṇī; *vidhuḥ*—Kṛṣṇa, the Supreme Personality of Godhead; *jayati*—all glories to.

TRANSLATION

"'Let Kṛṣṇa, the Supreme Personality of Godhead, be glorified! By virtue of His expanding attractive features, He subjugated the gopīs named Tārakā and Pāli and absorbed the minds of Śyāmā and Lalitā. He is the most attractive lover of Śrīmatī Rādhārāṇī and is the reservoir of pleasure for devotees in all transcendental mellows.'

PURPORT

Everyone has a particular transcendental mellow by which he loves and serves Kṛṣṇa. Kṛṣṇa is the most attractive feature for every kind of devotee. He is therefore called *akhila-rasāmṛta-mūrti,* the transcendental form of attraction for all kinds of devotees, whether the devotee be in the *śānta-rasa, dāsya-rasa, sakhya-rasa, vātsalya-rasa* or *mādhurya-rasa.*

This is the opening verse of the *Bhakti-rasāmṛta-sindhu,* by Śrīla Rūpa Gosvāmī.

TEXT 143

শৃঙ্গার-রসরাজময়-মূর্তিধর ।
অতএব আত্মপর্যন্ত-সর্ব-চিত্ত-হর ॥ ১৪৩ ॥

śṛṅgāra-rasarāja-maya-mūrti-dhara
ataeva ātma-paryanta-sarva-citta-hara

śṛṅgāra-rasa-rāja-maya—consisting of the mellow of conjugal love, which is the king of mellows; *mūrti-dhara*—Kṛṣṇa, the personified reservoir of all pleasure; *ataeva*—therefore; *ātma-paryanta*—even up to His own self; *sarva*—all; *citta*—of hearts; *hara*—the attractor.

TRANSLATION

"Kṛṣṇa is all-attractive for devotees in all mellows because He is the personification of the conjugal mellow. Kṛṣṇa is attractive not only to all the devotees, but to Himself as well.

TEXT 144

বিশ্বেষামনুরঞ্জনেন জনয়ন্নানন্দমিন্দীবর-
শ্রেণীশ্যামলকোমলৈরুপনয়ন্নঙ্গৈরনঙ্গোৎসবম্ ।
স্বচ্ছন্দং ব্রজসুন্দরীভিরভিতঃ প্রত্যঙ্গমালিঙ্গিতঃ
শৃঙ্গারঃ সখি মূর্তিমানিব মধৌ মুগ্ধো হরিঃ ক্রীড়তি ॥ ১৪৪ ॥

viśveṣām anurañjanena janayann ānandam indīvara-
śreṇī-śyāmala-komalair upanayann aṅgair anaṅgotsavam
svacchandaṁ vraja-sundarībhir abhitaḥ praty-aṅgam āliṅgitaḥ
śṛṅgāraḥ sakhi mūrtimān iva madhau mugdho hariḥ krīḍati

viśveṣām—of all the *gopīs; anurañjanena*—by the act of pleasing; *janayan*—producing; *ānandam*—the bliss; *indīvara-śreṇī*—like a row of blue lotuses; *śyāmala*—bluish black; *komalaiḥ*—and soft; *upanayan*—bringing; *aṅgaiḥ*—with His limbs; *anaṅga-utsavam*—a festival for Cupid; *svacchandam*—without restriction; *vraja-sundarībhiḥ*—by the young women of Vraja; *abhitaḥ*—on both sides; *prati-aṅgam*—each limb; *āliṅgitaḥ*—embraced; *śṛṅgāraḥ*—amorous love; *sakhi*—O friend; *mūrti-mān*—embodied; *iva*—like; *madhau*—in the springtime; *mugdhaḥ*—perplexed; *hariḥ*—Lord Hari; *krīḍati*—plays.

TRANSLATION

"'My dear friends, just see how Śrī Kṛṣṇa is enjoying the season of spring! With the gopīs embracing each of His limbs, He is like amorous love personified. With His transcendental pastimes, He enlivens all

the gopīs and the entire creation. With His soft bluish black arms and legs, which resemble blue lotus flowers, He has created a festival for Cupid.'

PURPORT

This is a verse from the *Gīta-govinda* (1.11).

TEXT 145

লক্ষ্মীকান্তাদি অবতারের হরে মন।
লক্ষ্মী-আদি নারীগণের করে আকর্ষণ ॥ ১৪৫ ॥

lakṣmī-kāntādi avatārera hare mana
lakṣmī-ādi nārī-gaṇera kare ākarṣaṇa

lakṣmī-kānta-ādi—of the goddess of fortune's husband (Nārāyaṇa); *avatārera*—of the incarnation; *hare*—He enchants; *mana*—the mind; *lakṣmī*—the goddess of fortune; *ādi*—headed by; *nārī-gaṇera*—of all women; *kare*—does; *ākarṣaṇa*—attraction.

TRANSLATION

"He also attracts Nārāyaṇa, who is the incarnation of Saṅkarṣaṇa and the husband of the goddess of fortune. He attracts not only Nārāyaṇa but also all women, headed by the goddess of fortune, the consort of Nārāyaṇa.

TEXT 146

দ্বিজাত্মজা মে যুবয়োর্দিদৃক্ষুণা, ময়োপনীতা ভুবি ধর্মগুপ্তয়ে।
কলাবতীর্ণাববনের্ভরাসুরান্, হত্বেহ ভূয়স্ত্বরয়েতমন্তি মে ॥ ১৪৬ ॥

dvijātmajā me yuvayor didṛkṣuṇā
mayopanītā bhuvi dharma-guptaye
kalāvatīrṇāv avaner bharāsurān
hatveha bhūyas tvarayetam anti me

dvija-ātma-jāḥ—the sons of the *brāhmaṇa; me*—by Me; *yuvayoḥ*—of both of you; *didṛkṣuṇā*—desiring the sight; *mayā*—by Me; *upanītāḥ*—brought; *bhuvi*—in the world; *dharma-guptaye*—for the protection of religious principles; *kalā*—with all potencies; *avatīrṇau*—who descended; *avaneḥ*—of the world; *bhara-asurān*—the heavy load of demons; *hatvā*—having killed; *iha*—here in the spiritual world; *bhūyaḥ*—again; *tvarayā*—very soon; *itam*—please come back; *anti*—near; *me*—Me.

TRANSLATION

"[Addressing Kṛṣṇa and Arjuna, Lord Mahā-Viṣṇu (the Mahāpuruṣa) said:] 'I wanted to see both of you, and therefore I have brought the sons of the brāhmaṇa here. Both of you have appeared in the material world to reestablish religious principles, and you have both appeared here with all your potencies. After killing all the demons, please quickly return to the spiritual world.'

PURPORT

This is a quotation from *Śrīmad-Bhāgavatam* (10.89.58) concerning Kṛṣṇa's endeavor to take Arjuna beyond the material universe when Arjuna was searching for the sons of a *brāhmaṇa.*

Lord Mahā-Viṣṇu, who is situated beyond this material world, was also attracted by the bodily features of Kṛṣṇa. Mahā-Viṣṇu had actually stolen the sons of the *brāhmaṇa* in Dvārakā so that Kṛṣṇa and Arjuna would come visit Him. This verse is quoted to show that Kṛṣṇa is so attractive that He attracts Mahā-Viṣṇu.

TEXT 147

কস্যানুভাবোঽস্য ন দেব বিদ্মহে
তবাঙ্ঘ্রিরেণুস্পরশাধিকারঃ।
যদ্বাঞ্ছয়া শ্রীর্ললনাচরত্তপো
বিহায় কামান্ সুচিরং ধৃতব্রতা ॥ ১৪৭ ॥

kasyānubhāvo 'sya na deva vidmahe
tavāṅghri-reṇu-sparaśādhikāraḥ
yad-vāñchayā śrīr lalanācarat tapo
vihāya kāmān su-ciraṁ dhṛta-vratā

kasya—of what; *anubhāvaḥ*—a result; *asya*—of the serpent (Kāliya); *na*—not; *deva*—my Lord; *vidmahe*—we know; *tava aṅghri*—of Your lotus feet; *reṇu*—of the dust; *sparaśa*—for touching; *adhikāraḥ*—qualification; *yat*—which; *vāñchayā*—by desiring; *śrīḥ*—the goddess of fortune; *lalanā*—the topmost woman; *acarat*—performed; *tapaḥ*—austerity; *vihāya*—giving up; *kāmān*—all desires; *su-ciram*—for a long time; *dhṛta*—a law upheld; *vratā*—as a vow.

TRANSLATION

"'O Lord, we do not know how the serpent Kāliya attained such an opportunity to be touched by the dust of Your lotus feet. For this end, the goddess of fortune performed austerities for centuries, giving up all other desires and observing austere vows. Indeed, we do not know how this serpent Kāliya got such an opportunity.'

PURPORT

This verse from *Śrīmad-Bhāgavatam* (10.16.36) was spoken by the wives of the Kāliya serpent.

TEXT 148

আপন-মাধুর্যে হরে আপনার মন।
আপনা আপনি চাহে করিতে আলিঙ্গন ॥ ১৪৮ ॥

āpana-mādhurye hare āpanāra mana
āpanā āpani cāhe karite āliṅgana

āpana—own; *mādhurye*—by sweetness; *hare*—steals; *āpanāra*—His own; *mana*—mind; *āpanā*—Himself; *āpani*—He; *cāhe*—wants; *karite*—to do; *āliṅgana*—embracing.

TRANSLATION

"Lord Kṛṣṇa's sweetness is so attractive that it steals away His own mind. Thus even He wants to embrace Himself.

TEXT 149

অপরিকলিতপূর্বঃ কশ্চমৎকারকারী
স্ফুরতি মম গরীয়ানেষ মাধুর্যপূরঃ।

অয়মহমপি হন্ত প্রেক্ষ্য যং লুব্ধচেতাঃ
সরভসমুপভোক্তুং কাময়ে রাধিকেব ॥ ১৪৯ ॥

aparikalita-pūrvaḥ kaś camatkāra-kārī
sphurati mama garīyān eṣa mādhurya-pūraḥ
ayam aham api hanta prekṣya yaṁ lubdha-cetāḥ
sa-rabhasam upabhoktuṁ kāmaye rādhikeva

aparikalita-pūrvaḥ—not previously experienced; *kaḥ*—who; *camatkāra-kārī*—causing wonder; *sphurati*—manifests; *mama*—My; *garīyān*—more great; *eṣaḥ*—this; *mādhurya-pūraḥ*—abundance of sweetness; *ayam*—this; *aham*—I; *api*—even; *hanta*—alas; *prekṣya*—seeing; *yam*—which; *lubdha-cetāḥ*—My mind being bewildered; *sa-rabhasam*—impetuously; *upabhoktum*—to enjoy; *kāmaye*—desire; *rādhikā iva*—like Śrīmatī Rādhārāṇī.

TRANSLATION

"'Upon seeing His own reflection in a bejeweled pillar of His Dvārakā palace, Kṛṣṇa desired to embrace it, saying, "Alas, I have never seen such a person before. Who is He? Just by seeing Him I have become eager to embrace Him, exactly like Śrīmatī Rādhārāṇī."'"

PURPORT

This is a verse from Śrīla Rūpa Gosvāmī's *Lalita-mādhava* (8.34).

TEXT 150

এই ত' সংক্ষেপে কহিল কৃষ্ণের স্বরূপ।
এবে সংক্ষেপে কহি শুন রাধা-তত্ত্বরূপ ॥ ১৫০ ॥

ei ta' saṅkṣepe kahila kṛṣṇera svarūpa
ebe saṅkṣepe kahi śuna rādhā-tattva-rūpa

ei ta'—thus; *saṅkṣepe*—in brief; *kahila*—I have said; *kṛṣṇera*—of Lord Kṛṣṇa; *svarūpa*—the original form; *ebe*—now; *saṅkṣepe*—in summary; *kahi*—I shall speak; *śuna*—please hear; *rādhā*—of Śrīmatī Rādhārāṇī; *tattva-rūpa*—the actual position.

TRANSLATION

Śrī Rāmānanda Rāya then said, "I have thus briefly explained the original form of the Supreme Personality of Godhead. Now let me describe the position of Śrīmatī Rādhārāṇī.

TEXT 151

কৃষ্ণের অনন্ত-শক্তি, তাতে তিন — প্রধান।
'চিচ্ছক্তি', 'মায়াশক্তি', 'জীবশক্তি'-নাম ॥ ১৫১ ॥

kṛṣṇera ananta-śakti, tāte tina — pradhāna
'cic-chakti', 'māyā-śakti', 'jīva-śakti'-nāma

kṛṣṇera — of Lord Kṛṣṇa; *ananta-śakti* — unlimited potencies; *tāte* — in that; *tina* — three; *pradhāna* — chief; *cit-śakti* — spiritual potency; *māyā-śakti* — material potency; *jīva-śakti* — marginal potency, or living entities; *nāma* — named.

TRANSLATION

"Kṛṣṇa has unlimited potencies, which can be divided into three main parts. These are the spiritual potency, the material potency and the marginal potency, which is known as the living entities.

TEXT 152

'অন্তরঙ্গা', 'বহিরঙ্গা', 'তটস্থা' কহি যারে।
অন্তরঙ্গা 'স্বরূপ-শক্তি' — সবার উপরে ॥ ১৫২ ॥

'antaraṅgā', 'bahiraṅgā', 'taṭasthā' kahi yāre
antaraṅgā 'svarūpa-śakti' — sabāra upare

antaraṅgā — internal; *bahiraṅgā* — external; *taṭa-sthā* — marginal; *kahi* — we say; *yāre* — to whom; *antaraṅgā* — the internal potency; *svarūpa-śakti* — the personal energy; *sabāra upare* — above all.

TRANSLATION

"In other words, these are all potencies of God — internal, external and marginal. But the internal potency is the Lord's personal energy and stands over the other two.

TEXT 153

বিষ্ণুশক্তিঃ পরা প্রোক্তা ক্ষেত্রজ্ঞাখ্যা তথাপরা ।
অবিদ্যা-কর্মসংজ্ঞান্যা তৃতীয়া শক্তিরিষ্যতে ॥ ১৫৩ ॥

viṣṇu-śaktiḥ parā proktā
kṣetrajñākhyā tathā parā
avidyā-karma-saṁjñānyā
tṛtīyā śaktir iṣyate

viṣṇu-śaktiḥ—the potency of Lord Viṣṇu; *parā*—spiritual; *proktā*—it is said; *kṣetrajña-ākhyā*—the potency known as *kṣetra-jña; tathā*—as well as; *parā*—spiritual; *avidyā*—ignorance; *karma*—fruitive activities; *saṁjñā*—known as; *anyā*—other; *tṛtīyā*—third; *śaktiḥ*—potency; *iṣyate*—known thus.

TRANSLATION

"'The original potency of Lord Viṣṇu is superior, or spiritual, and the living entity actually belongs to that superior energy. But there is another energy, called the material energy, and this third energy is full of ignorance.'

PURPORT

This is a quotation from the *Viṣṇu Purāṇa* (6.7.61).

TEXT 154

সচ্চিদানন্দময় কৃষ্ণের স্বরূপ ।
অতএব স্বরূপ-শক্তি হয় তিন রূপ ॥ ১৫৪ ॥

sac-cid-ānanda-maya kṛṣṇera svarūpa
ataeva svarūpa-śakti haya tina rūpa

sat-cit-ānanda-maya—eternal bliss and knowledge; *kṛṣṇera*—of Lord Kṛṣṇa; *svarūpa*—the real transcendental form; *ataeva*—therefore; *svarūpa-śakti*—His spiritual personal potency; *haya*—is; *tina rūpa*—three forms.

TRANSLATION

"Originally Lord Kṛṣṇa is sac-cid-ānanda-vigraha, the transcendental form of eternity, bliss and knowledge; therefore His personal potency, the internal potency, has three different forms.

TEXT 155

আনন্দাংশে 'হ্লাদিনী', সদংশে 'সন্ধিনী'।
চিদংশে 'সম্বিৎ', যারে জ্ঞান করি' মানি ॥ ১৫৫ ॥

ānandāṁśe 'hlādinī', sad-aṁśe 'sandhinī'
cid-aṁśe 'samvit', yāre jñāna kari' māni

ānanda-aṁśe—in bliss; *hlādinī*—the pleasure-giving potency; *sat-aṁśe*—in eternity; *sandhinī*—the creative potency; *cit-aṁśe*—in knowledge; *samvit*—the knowledge potency; *yāre*—which; *jñāna*—knowledge; *kari'*—taking as; *māni*—I accept.

TRANSLATION

"Hlādinī is His aspect of bliss; sandhinī, of eternal existence; and samvit, of cognizance, which is also accepted as knowledge.

TEXT 156

হ্লাদিনী সন্ধিনী সম্বিৎ ত্বয্যেকা সর্বসংশ্রয়ে।
হ্লাদতাপকরী মিশ্রা ত্বয়ি নো গুণবর্জিতে ॥ ১৫৬ ॥

hlādinī sandhinī samvit
tvayy ekā sarva-saṁśraye
hlāda-tāpa-karī miśrā
tvayi no guṇa-varjite

hlādinī—that which generates pleasure; *sandhinī*—the potency of existence; *samvit*—the potency of knowledge; *tvayi*—unto You; *ekā*—principal internal potency; *sarva-saṁśraye*—You are the reservoir of all potencies; *hlāda*—pleasure; *tāpa-karī*—generator of pains; *miśrā*—mixed; *tvayi*—unto You; *na u*—never; *guṇa-varjite*—You, the transcendence, the Supreme Personality of Godhead.

TRANSLATION

"'My dear Lord, You are the transcendental reservoir of all transcendental qualities. Your pleasure potency, existence potency and knowledge potency are actually all one internal spiritual potency. The conditioned soul, although actually spiritual, sometimes experiences pleasure, sometimes pain and sometimes a mixture of pain and pleasure. This is due to his being touched by matter. But because You are above all material qualities, these are not found in You. Your superior spiritual potency is completely transcendental, and for You there is no such thing as relative pleasure, pleasure mixed with pain, or pain itself.'

PURPORT

This is a quotation from the *Viṣṇu Purāṇa* (1.12.69).

TEXT 157

কৃষ্ণকে আহ্লাদে, তা'তে নাম — 'হ্লাদিনী'।
সেই শক্তি-দ্বারে সুখ আস্বাদে আপনি ॥ ১৫৭ ॥

kṛṣṇake āhlāde, tā'te nāma — 'hlādinī'
sei śakti-dvāre sukha āsvāde āpani

kṛṣṇake — unto Kṛṣṇa; *āhlāde* — gives pleasure; *tā'te* — therefore; *nāma* — the name; *hlādinī* — pleasure-giving potency; *sei śakti* — that potency; *dvāre* — by means of; *sukha* — happiness; *āsvāde* — tastes; *āpani* — Lord Kṛṣṇa personally.

TRANSLATION

"The potency called hlādinī gives Kṛṣṇa transcendental pleasure. Through this pleasure potency, Kṛṣṇa personally tastes all spiritual pleasure.

TEXT 158

সুখরূপ কৃষ্ণ করে সুখ আস্বাদন।
ভক্তগণে সুখ দিতে 'হ্লাদিনী' — কারণ ॥ ১৫৮ ॥

sukha-rūpa kṛṣṇa kare sukha āsvādana
bhakta-gaṇe sukha dite 'hlādinī'—kāraṇa

sukha-rūpa—embodiment of pleasure; *kṛṣṇa*—Lord Kṛṣṇa; *kare*—does; *sukha*—happiness; *āsvādana*—tasting; *bhakta-gaṇe*—unto the devotees; *sukha*—happiness; *dite*—to give; *hlādinī*—the pleasure potency; *kāraṇa*—the cause.

TRANSLATION

"Lord Kṛṣṇa tastes all kinds of transcendental happiness, although He Himself is happiness personified. The pleasure relished by His pure devotees is also manifested by His pleasure potency.

TEXT 159

হ্লাদিনীর সার অংশ, তার 'প্রেম' নাম।
আনন্দচিন্ময়রস প্রেমের আখ্যান ॥ ১৫৯ ॥

hlādinīra sāra aṁśa, tāra 'prema' nāma
ānanda-cinmaya-rasa premera ākhyāna

hlādinīra—of this pleasure potency; *sāra*—the essential; *aṁśa*—part; *tāra*—its; *prema*—love of God; *nāma*—name; *ānanda*—full of pleasure; *cit-maya-rasa*—the platform of spiritual mellows; *premera*—of love of Godhead; *ākhyāna*—the explanation.

TRANSLATION

"The most essential part of this pleasure potency is love of Godhead [prema]. Consequently, the explanation of love of Godhead is also a transcendental mellow full of pleasure.

TEXT 160

প্রেমের পরম-সার 'মহাভাব' জানি।
সেই মহাভাবরূপা রাধা-ঠাকুরাণী ॥ ১৬০ ॥

premera parama-sāra 'mahābhāva' jāni
sei mahābhāva-rūpā rādhā-ṭhākurāṇī

premera—of love of Godhead; *parama-sāra*—the essential part; *mahā-bhāva*—the transcendental ecstasy of the name *mahābhāva; jāni*—we know; *sei*—that; *mahā-bhāva-rūpā*—the personification of the *mahābhāva* transcendental ecstasy; *rādhā-ṭhākurāṇī*—Śrīmatī Rādhārāṇī.

TRANSLATION

"The essential part of love of Godhead is called mahābhāva, transcendental ecstasy, and that ecstasy is represented by Śrīmatī Rādhārāṇī.

TEXT 161

তয়োরপ্যুভয়োর্মধ্যে রাধিকা সর্বথাধিকা।
মহাভাবস্বরূপেয়ং গুণৈরতিবরীয়সী ॥ ১৬১ ॥

tayor apy ubhayor madhye
rādhikā sarvathādhikā
mahābhāva-svarūpeyaṁ
guṇair ativarīyasī

tayoḥ—of them; *api*—even; *ubhayoḥ*—of both (Candrāvalī and Rādhārāṇī); *madhye*—in the middle; *rādhikā*—Śrīmatī Rādhārāṇī; *sarvathā*—in every way; *adhikā*—greater; *mahā-bhāva-svarūpā*—the form of *mahābhāva; iyam*—this one; *guṇaiḥ*—with good qualities; *ativarīyasī*—the best of all.

TRANSLATION

"'Among the gopīs of Vṛndāvana, Śrīmatī Rādhārāṇī and another gopī are considered chief. But when we compare the gopīs, it appears that Śrīmatī Rādhārāṇī is most important because Her real feature expresses the highest ecstasy of love. The ecstasy of love experienced by the other gopīs cannot be compared to that of Śrīmatī Rādhārāṇī.'

PURPORT

This is a quotation from Śrīla Rūpa Gosvāmī's *Ujjvala-nīlamaṇi* (4.3).

TEXT 162

প্রেমের 'স্বরূপ-দেহ' — প্রেম-বিভাবিত।
কৃষ্ণের প্রেয়সী-শ্রেষ্ঠা জগতে বিদিত ॥ ১৬২ ॥

premera 'svarūpa-deha' — prema-vibhāvita
kṛṣṇera preyasī-śreṣṭhā jagate vidita

premera — love of Godhead; *svarūpa-deha* — actual body; *prema* — by love of Godhead; *vibhāvita* — influence; *kṛṣṇera* — of Lord Kṛṣṇa; *preyasī* — of the dear friends; *śreṣṭhā* — topmost; *jagate* — throughout the whole world; *vidita* — known.

TRANSLATION

"The body of Śrīmatī Rādhārāṇī is a veritable transformation of love of Godhead; She is the dearmost friend of Kṛṣṇa, and this is known throughout the world.

TEXT 163

আনন্দচিন্ময়রস-প্রতিভাবিতাভি-
স্তাভির্য এব নিজরূপতয়া কলাভিঃ।
গোলোক এব নিবসত্যখিলাত্মভূতো
গোবিন্দমাদিপুরুষং তমহং ভজামি ॥ ১৬৩ ॥

ānanda-cinmaya-rasa-pratibhāvitābhis
tābhir ya eva nija-rūpatayā kalābhiḥ
goloka eva nivasaty akhilātma-bhūto
govindam ādi-puruṣaṁ tam ahaṁ bhajāmi

ānanda — bliss; *cit* — knowledge; *maya* — consisting of; *rasa* — mellows; *prati* — every second; *bhāvitābhiḥ* — who are engrossed with; *tābhiḥ* — with those; *yaḥ* — who; *eva* — certainly; *nija-rūpatayā* — with His own form; *kalābhiḥ* — who are parts of portions of His pleasure potency; *goloke* — in Goloka Vṛndāvana; *eva* — certainly; *nivasati* — resides; *akhila-ātma* — as the soul of all; *bhūtaḥ* — who exists; *govindam* — Lord Govinda; *ādi-puruṣam* — the original personality; *tam* — Him; *aham* — I; *bhajāmi* — worship.

TRANSLATION

"'I worship Govinda, the primeval Lord, who resides in His own realm, Goloka, with Rādhā, who resembles His own spiritual figure and who embodies the ecstatic potency [hlādinī]. Their companions are Her confidantes, who embody extensions of Her bodily form and who are imbued and permeated with ever-blissful spiritual rasa.'

PURPORT

This is a quotation from the *Brahma-saṁhitā* (5.37).

TEXT 164

সেই মহাভাব হয় 'চিন্তামণি-সার'।
কৃষ্ণ-বাঞ্ছা পূর্ণ করে এই কার্য তাঁর ॥ ১৬৪ ॥

sei mahābhāva haya 'cintāmaṇi-sāra'
kṛṣṇa-vāñchā pūrṇa kare ei kārya tāṅra

sei—that; *mahā-bhāva*—supreme ecstasy; *haya*—is; *cintāmaṇi-sāra*—the essence of spiritual life; *kṛṣṇa-vāñchā*—all the desires of Lord Kṛṣṇa; *pūrṇa kare*—fulfills; *ei*—this; *kārya*—business; *tāṅra*—Her.

TRANSLATION

"That supreme ecstasy of Śrīmatī Rādhārāṇī is the essence of spiritual life. Her only business is to fulfill all the desires of Kṛṣṇa.

TEXT 165

'মহাভাব-চিন্তামণি' রাধার স্বরূপ।
ললিতাদি সখী — তাঁর কায়ব্যূহরূপ ॥ ১৬৫ ॥

'mahābhāva-cintāmaṇi' rādhāra svarūpa
lalitādi sakhī—tāṅra kāya-vyūha-rūpa

mahā-bhāva—of the topmost spiritual ecstasy; *cintā-maṇi*—the touchstone; *rādhāra svarūpa*—the transcendental form of Śrīmatī

Rādhārāṇī; *lalitā-ādi sakhī*—the *gopī* associates of Śrīmatī Rādhārāṇī; *tāṅra kāya-vyūha-rūpa*—expansions of Her spiritual body.

TRANSLATION

"Śrīmatī Rādhārāṇī is the topmost spiritual gem, and the other gopīs—Lalitā, Viśākhā and so on—are expansions of Her spiritual body.

TEXT 166

রাধা-প্রতি কৃষ্ণ-স্নেহ—সুগন্ধি উদ্বর্তন।
তা'তে অতি সুগন্ধি দেহ—উজ্জ্বল-বরণ ॥ ১৬৬ ॥

rādhā-prati kṛṣṇa-sneha—sugandhi udvartana
tā'te ati sugandhi deha—ujjvala-varaṇa

rādhā-prati—toward Śrīmatī Rādhārāṇī; *kṛṣṇa-sneha*—the affection of Lord Kṛṣṇa; *su-gandhi udvartana*—perfumed massage; *tā'te*—in that; *ati*—very; *su-gandhi*—perfumed; *deha*—the body; *ujjvala*—brilliant; *varaṇa*—luster.

TRANSLATION

"Śrīmatī Rādhārāṇī's transcendental body is brilliant in luster and full of all transcendental fragrances. Lord Kṛṣṇa's affection for Her is like a perfumed massage.

PURPORT

Sugandhi udvartana refers to a paste made of several perfumes and fragrant oils. This paste is massaged all over the body, and in this way the body's dirt and perspiration are removed. Śrīmatī Rādhārāṇī's body is automatically perfumed, but when Her body is massaged with the scented paste of Lord Kṛṣṇa's affection, Her entire body is doubly perfumed and made brilliant and lustrous. This is the beginning of Kṛṣṇadāsa Kavirāja Gosvāmī's description of Śrīmatī Rādhārāṇī's transcendental body. This description (found in verses 165–181) is based on a book by Śrīla Raghunātha dāsa Gosvāmī known as *Premāmbhoja-maranda*. Śrīla Bhaktivinoda Ṭhākura's translation of the original Sanskrit reads as follows:

"The love of the *gopīs* for Kṛṣṇa is full of transcendental ecstasy. It appears to be a brilliant jewel, and enlightened by such a transcendental jewel, Rādhārāṇī's body is further perfumed and decorated with *kuṅkuma*. In the morning Her body is bathed in the nectar of compassion, in the afternoon in the nectar of youth, and in the evening in the nectar of luster itself. In this way the bathing is performed, and Her body becomes as brilliant as the *cintāmaṇi* jewel. She is dressed in various kinds of silken garments, one of which is Her natural shyness.

"Her beauty is more and more enhanced, being decorated with the red *kuṅkuma* of beauty itself and the blackish musk of conjugal love. Thus Her body is decorated with different colors. Her ornaments embody the natural symptoms of ecstasy—trembling, tears, jubilation, stunning, perspiration, faltering of the voice, bodily redness, madness and dullness. In this way Her entire body is bedecked with these nine different jewels. Over and above this, the beauty of Her body is enhanced by Her transcendental qualities, which constitute the flower garland hanging on Her body. The ecstasy of love for Kṛṣṇa is known as *dhīrā* and *adhīrā*, sober and restless. Such ecstasy constitutes the covering of Śrīmatī Rādhārāṇī's body, and it is adorned by camphor. Her transcendental anger toward Kṛṣṇa is embodied as the arrangement of the hair on Her head, and the *tilaka* of Her great fortune shines on Her beautiful forehead. Śrīmatī Rādhārāṇī's earrings are the holy names of Kṛṣṇa, as well as the hearing of His name and fame. Her lips are always reddish due to the betel nut of ecstatic affection for Kṛṣṇa. The black ointment around Her eyes is Her tricky behavior with Kṛṣṇa brought about by love. Her joking with Kṛṣṇa and gentle smiling constitute the camphor with which She is perfumed. She sleeps in Her room with the aroma of pride, and when She lies down in Her bed, the transcendental variety of Her loving ecstasies is like a jeweled locket in the midst of Her necklace of separation. Her transcendental breasts are covered by Her sari in the form of affection and anger toward Kṛṣṇa. She has a stringed instrument known as a *kacchapī-vīṇā*, which is the fame and fortune that actually dries up the faces and breasts of the other *gopīs*. She always keeps Her hands on the shoulder of Her *gopī* friend, who represents Her youthful beauty, and although She is highly qualified with so many spiritual assets, She is nonetheless affected by the Cupid known as Kṛṣṇa. Thus She is defeated. Śrīla Raghunātha dāsa Gosvāmī offers his respectful obeisances to Śrīmatī Rādhārāṇī, taking a straw in his mouth. Indeed, he prays, 'O Gāndharvikā, Śrīmatī Rādhārāṇī, just as Lord Kṛṣṇa never rejects a surrendered soul, please don't reject me.'" This is a summary translation of the *Premāmbhoja-maranda,* which Kavirāja Gosvāmī quotes.

TEXT 167

কারুণ্যামৃত-ধারায় স্নান প্রথম।
তারুণ্যামৃত-ধারায় স্নান মধ্যম ॥ ১৬৭ ॥

kāruṇyāmṛta-dhārāya snāna prathama
tāruṇyāmṛta-dhārāya snāna madhyama

kāruṇya-amṛta—of the nectar of mercy; *dhārāya*—in the shower; *snāna*—bath; *prathama*—first; *tāruṇya-amṛta*—of the nectar of youth; *dhārāya*—in the shower; *snāna*—bath; *madhyama*—in the middle.

TRANSLATION

"Śrīmatī Rādhārāṇī takes Her first bath in the shower of the nectar of compassion, and She takes Her second bath in the nectar of youth.

PURPORT

Śrīmatī Rādhārāṇī first smears Her body with the paste of affection for kṛṣṇa. She then takes Her bath in the water of mercy. After passing the *paugaṇḍa* age (from five to ten years), Śrīmatī Rādhārāṇī first appears as mercy. The second bath is taken at noon in the water of *tāruṇyāmṛta,* or the nectar of youth. This is the actual expression of Her new youthfulness.

TEXT 168

লাবণ্যামৃত-ধারায় তদুপরি স্নান।
নিজ-লজ্জা-শ্যাম-পট্টসাটি-পরিধান ॥ ১৬৮ ॥

lāvaṇyāmṛta-dhārāya tad-upari snāna
nija-lajjā-śyāma-paṭṭasāṭi-paridhāna

lāvaṇya-amṛta-dhārāya—in the shower of the nectar of bodily luster; *tat-upari*—over and above that; *snāna*—the bath; *nija*—own; *lajjā*—shyness; *śyāma*—blackish; *paṭṭa*—silk; *sāṭi*—garments; *paridhāna*—wearing.

TRANSLATION

"After Her midday bath, Rādhārāṇī takes another bath in the nectar of bodily luster, and She puts on the garment of shyness, which is Her black silk sari.

PURPORT

Over and above the other baths, the bath taken in the afternoon is taken in the nectar of full beauty. This nectar represents the personal qualities of beauty and luster. Thus there are three baths in different kinds of water. Rādhārāṇī then puts on two garments—a lower and an upper garment. The upper garment is pinkish and is Her affection and attraction for Kṛṣṇa, and the lower garment, a blackish silk sari, is Her shyness.

TEXT 169

কৃষ্ণ-অনুরাগ দ্বিতীয় অরুণ-বসন ।
প্রণয়-মান-কঞ্চুলিকায় বক্ষ আচ্ছাদন ॥ ১৬৯ ॥

kṛṣṇa-anurāga dvitīya aruṇa-vasana
praṇaya-māna-kañculikāya vakṣa ācchādana

kṛṣṇa-anurāga—attraction for Kṛṣṇa; *dvitīya*—second; *aruṇa-vasana*—pinkish garment; *praṇaya*—of love; *māna*—and anger; *kañculikāya*—by a short blouse; *vakṣa*—breasts; *ācchādana*—covering.

TRANSLATION

"Śrīmatī Rādhārāṇī's affection for Kṛṣṇa is Her upper garment, which is pinkish in color. She then covers Her breasts with another garment, composed of affection and anger toward Kṛṣṇa.

TEXT 170

সৌন্দর্য — কুঙ্কুম, সখী-প্রণয় চন্দন।
স্মিতকান্তি — কর্পূর, তিনে — অঙ্গে বিলেপন ॥ ১৭০ ॥

saundarya — kuṅkuma, sakhī-praṇaya — candana
smita-kānti — karpūra, tine — aṅge vilepana

saundarya — Her personal beauty; *kuṅkuma* — a red powder known as *kuṅkuma; sakhī-praṇaya* — Her love for Her associates; *candana* — the sandalwood pulp; *smita-kānti* — the sweetness of Her smile; *karpūra* — camphor; *tine* — by these three things; *aṅge* — on the body; *vilepana* — smearing.

TRANSLATION

"Śrīmatī Rādhārāṇī's personal beauty is the reddish powder known as kuṅkuma, Her affection for Her associates is sandalwood pulp, and the sweetness of Her smile is camphor. All these, combined together, are smeared over Her body.

TEXT 171

কৃষ্ণের-উজ্জ্বল রস — মৃগমদ-ভর।
সেই মৃগমদে বিচিত্রিত কলেবর ॥ ১৭১ ॥

kṛṣṇera ujjvala-rasa — mṛgamada-bhara
sei mṛgamade vicitrita kalevara

kṛṣṇera — of Lord Kṛṣṇa; *ujjvala-rasa* — the conjugal mellow; *mṛga-mada* — of musk; *bhara* — an abundance; *sei* — that; *mṛga-made* — made by the aroma of the musk; *vicitrita* — decorated; *kalevara* — Her whole body.

TRANSLATION

"Conjugal love for Kṛṣṇa is an abundance of musk, and with that musk Her whole body is decorated.

TEXT 172

প্রচ্ছন্ন-মান বাম্য — ধম্মিল্ল-বিন্যাস।
'ধীরাধীরাত্মক' গুণ — অঙ্গে পটবাস ॥ ১৭২ ॥

pracchanna-māna vāmya — dhammilla-vinyāsa
'dhīrādhīrātmaka' guṇa — aṅge paṭa-vāsa

pracchanna — covered; *māna* — anger; *vāmya* — craftiness; *dhammilla* — of the bunches of hair; *vinyāsa* — arrangement; *dhīra-adhīra-ātmaka* — consisting of jealous anger, which is sometimes expressed and sometimes suppressed; *guṇa* — the quality; *aṅge* — on the body; *paṭa-vāsa* — silk covering.

TRANSLATION

"Craftiness and covered anger constitute the arrangement of Her hair. The quality of anger due to jealousy is the silk garment covering Her body.

TEXT 173

রাগ-তাম্বূলরাগে অধর উজ্জ্বল ।
প্রেমকৌটিল্য — নেত্রযুগলে কজ্জল ॥ ১৭৩ ॥

rāga-tāmbūla-rāge adhara ujjvala
prema-kauṭilya — netra-yugale kajjala

rāga — of love; *tāmbūla* — of the betel nut; *rāge* — by the reddish color; *adhara* — lips; *ujjvala* — brilliant; *prema-kauṭilya* — the double dealings in loving affairs; *netra-yugale* — on the two eyes; *kajjala* — the ointment.

TRANSLATION

"Her attachment for Kṛṣṇa is the reddish color of betel nuts on Her brilliant lips. Her double-dealings in loving affairs constitute the black ointment around Her eyes.

TEXT 174

'সূদ্দীপ্ত-সাত্ত্বিক' ভাব, হর্ষাদি 'সঞ্চারী' ।
এই সব ভাব-ভূষণ সব-অঙ্গে ভরি' ॥ ১৭৪ ॥

'sūddīpta-sāttvika' bhāva, harṣādi 'sañcārī'
ei saba bhāva-bhūṣaṇa saba-aṅge bhari'

su-uddīpta-sāttvika bhāva—blazing ecstasies of goodness; *harṣa-ādi*—like jubilation; *sañcārī*—the continuously existing ecstasies; *ei saba*—all these; *bhāva*—ecstasies; *bhūṣaṇa*—ornaments; *saba*—all; *aṅge*—body; *bhari'*—filling.

TRANSLATION

"The ornaments decorating Her body are the blazing ecstasies of goodness and the constantly existing ecstasies, headed by jubilation. All these ecstasies are the ornaments all over Her body.

TEXT 175

'কিলকিঞ্চিতাদি'-ভাব-বিংশতি-ভূষিত।
গুণশ্রেণী-পুষ্পমালা সর্বাঙ্গে পূরিত ॥ ১৭৫ ॥

'kila-kiñcitādi'-bhāva-viṁśati-bhūṣita
guṇa-śreṇī-puṣpamālā sarvāṅge pūrita

kila-kiñcita-ādi—headed by *kila-kiñcita; bhāva*—with the ecstasies; *viṁśati*—twenty; *bhūṣita*—decorated; *guṇa-śreṇī*—of Her attractive qualities; *puṣpa-mālā*—as a garland of flowers; *sarva-aṅge*—all over the body; *pūrita*—filled.

TRANSLATION

"Also ornamenting Her body are the twenty kinds of ecstatic symptoms beginning with kila-kiñcita. Her transcendental qualities constitute the flower garland hanging in fullness over Her body.

PURPORT

The twenty different moods headed by *kila-kiñcita* are described as follows. First, in connection with the body, there are *bhāva* (ecstasy), *hāva* (gestures) and *helā* (negligence); in relation to the self there are *śobhā* (beauty), *kānti* (luster), *dīpti* (brilliance), *mādhurya* (sweetness), *pragalbhatā* (impudence), *audārya* (magnanimity) and *dhairya* (patience); and in relation to nature there are *līlā* (pastimes), *vilāsa* (enjoyment), *vicchitti* (breaking off) and *vibhrama* (puzzlement). There are no English equivalents for the words *kila-kiñcita, moṭṭāyita* and *kuṭṭamita.*

Śrīmatī Rādhārāṇī's flower garland consists of Her qualities and is divided into mental, verbal and bodily parts. Her attitude of forgiveness and mercy is all mental. Her talks, which are very pleasing to the ear, are verbal. The bodily qualities are age, beauty, luster and grace.

TEXT 176

সৌভাগ্য-তিলক চারু-ললাটে উজ্জ্বল।
প্রেম-বৈচিত্ত্য — রত্ন, হৃদয় — তরল ॥ ১৭৬ ॥

saubhāgya-tilaka cāru-lalāṭe ujjvala
prema-vaicittya — ratna, hṛdaya — tarala

saubhāgya-tilaka — the *tilaka* of good fortune; *cāru* — beautiful; *lalāṭe* — on the forehead; *ujjvala* — brilliant; *prema* — of love of Godhead; *vaicittya* — diversity; *ratna* — the jewel; *hṛdaya* — the heart; *tarala* — the locket.

TRANSLATION

"The tilaka of good fortune is on Her beautiful broad forehead. Her various loving affairs are a gem, and Her heart is the locket.

TEXT 177

মধ্য-বয়স, সখী-স্কন্ধে কর-ন্যাস।
কৃষ্ণলীলা-মনোবৃত্তি-সখী আশপাশ ॥ ১৭৭ ॥

madhya-vayasa, sakhī-skandhe kara-nyāsa
kṛṣṇalīlā-manovṛtti-sakhī āśa-pāśa

madhya-vayasa — adolescence; *sakhī* — of a friend; *skandhe* — on the shoulder; *kara* — hand; *nyāsa* — keeping; *kṛṣṇa* — of Lord Kṛṣṇa; *līlā* — the pastimes; *manaḥ* — of the mind; *vṛtti* — activities; *sakhī* — *gopīs; āśa-pāśa* — here and there.

TRANSLATION

"Śrīmatī Rādhārāṇī's gopī friends are Her mental activities, which are concentrated on the pastimes of Śrī Kṛṣṇa. She keeps Her hand on the shoulder of a friend, who represents youth.

PURPORT

Rādhārāṇī's eight companions (*aṣṭa-sakhī*) are different varieties of pleasure connected with the pastimes of Kṛṣṇa. Following those pastimes of Śrī Kṛṣṇa are other activities, which are represented by the assistants of the *gopīs.*

TEXT 178

নিজাঙ্গ-সৌরভালয়ে গর্ব-পর্যঙ্ক।
তা'তে বসি' আছে, সদা চিন্তে কৃষ্ণসঙ্গ ॥ ১৭৮ ॥

nijāṅga-saurabhālaye garva-paryaṅka
tā'te vasi' āche, sadā cinte kṛṣṇa-saṅga

nija-aṅga—Her personal body; *saurabha-ālaye*—in the abode of aroma; *garva*—pride; *paryaṅka*—bedstead; *tā'te*—on that; *vasi'*—lying; *āche*—there is; *sadā*—always; *cinte*—thinks; *kṛṣṇa-saṅga*—the association of Kṛṣṇa.

TRANSLATION

"Śrīmatī Rādhārāṇī's bedstead is pride itself, and it is situated in the abode of Her bodily aroma. She is always seated there thinking of Kṛṣṇa's association.

TEXT 179

কৃষ্ণ-নাম-গুণ-যশ — অবতংস কাণে।
কৃষ্ণ-নাম-গুণ-যশ-প্রবাহ-বচনে ॥ ১৭৯ ॥

kṛṣṇa-nāma-guṇa-yaśa—avataṁsa kāṇe
kṛṣṇa-nāma-guṇa-yaśa-pravāha-vacane

kṛṣṇa—of Lord Kṛṣṇa; *nāma*—the holy name; *guṇa*—the qualities; *yaśa*—the fame; *avataṁsa*—ornaments; *kāṇe*—on the ear; *kṛṣṇa*—of Lord Kṛṣṇa; *nāma*—of the holy name; *guṇa*—of the qualities; *yaśa*—of the fame; *pravāha*—waves; *vacane*—in Her talking.

TRANSLATION

"Śrīmatī Rādhārāṇī's earrings are the name, fame and qualities of Lord Kṛṣṇa. The glories of Lord Kṛṣṇa's name, fame and qualities are always inundating Her speech.

TEXT 180

কৃষ্ণকে করায় শ্যামরস-মধু পান ।
নিরন্তর পূর্ণ করে কৃষ্ণের সর্বকাম ॥ ১৮০ ॥

kṛṣṇake karāya śyāma-rasa-madhu pāna
nirantara pūrṇa kare kṛṣṇera sarva-kāma

kṛṣṇake—unto Kṛṣṇa; *karāya*—She induces; *śyāma-rasa*—of the mellow of conjugal love; *madhu*—the honey; *pāna*—drinking; *nirantara*—constantly; *pūrṇa*—complete; *kare*—makes; *kṛṣṇera*—of Lord Kṛṣṇa; *sarva-kāma*—all kinds of lusty desires.

TRANSLATION

"Śrīmatī Rādhārāṇī induces Kṛṣṇa to drink the honey of the conjugal relationship. She is therefore engaged in satisfying all the lusty desires of Kṛṣṇa.

TEXT 181

কৃষ্ণের বিশুদ্ধপ্রেম-রত্নের আকর ।
অনুপম-গুণগণ-পূর্ণ কলেবর ॥ ১৮১ ॥

kṛṣṇera viśuddha-prema-ratnera ākara
anupama-guṇagaṇa-pūrṇa kalevara

kṛṣṇera—of Lord Kṛṣṇa; *viśuddha-prema*—of pure transcendental love; *ratnera*—of the valuable jewel; *ākara*—a mine;

anupama—unparalleled; *guṇa-gaṇa*—of groups of qualities; *pūrṇa*—full; *kalevara*—transcendental body.

TRANSLATION

"Śrīmatī Rādhārāṇī is a mine filled with valuable jewels of love for Kṛṣṇa. Her transcendental body is complete with unparalleled spiritual qualities.

TEXT 182

কা কৃষ্ণস্য প্রণয়জনিভূঃ শ্রীমতী রাধিকৈকা
কাস্য প্রেয়স্যনুপমগুণা রাধিকৈকা ন চান্যা।
জৈহ্ম্যং কেশে দৃশি তরলতা নিষ্ঠুরত্বং কুচেঽস্যা
বাঞ্ছাপূর্ত্যৈ প্রভবতি হরে রাধিকৈকা ন চান্যা ॥ ১৮২ ॥

kā kṛṣṇasya praṇaya-jani-bhūḥ śrīmatī rādhikaikā
kāsya preyasy anupama-guṇā rādhikaikā na cānyā
jaihmyaṁ keśe dṛśi taralatā niṣṭhuratvaṁ kuce 'syā
vāñchā-pūrtyai prabhavati hare rādhikaikā na cānyā

kā—who; *kṛṣṇasya*—of Lord Kṛṣṇa; *praṇaya-jani-bhūḥ*—the birthplace of love of Kṛṣṇa; *śrīmatī*—all-beautiful; *rādhikā*—Śrīmatī Rādhārāṇī; *ekā*—alone; *kā*—who; *asya*—His; *preyasī*—most dear friend; *anupama-guṇā*—having unparalleled qualities; *rādhikā*—Śrīmatī Rādhārāṇī; *ekā*—alone; *na*—not; *ca*—also; *anyā*—anyone else; *jaihmyam*—crookedness; *keśe*—in the hair; *dṛśi*—in the eyes; *taralatā*—unsteadiness; *niṣṭhuratvam*—firmness; *kuce*—in the breasts; *asyāḥ*—Her; *vāñchā*—of the desires; *pūrtyai*—to fulfill; *prabhavati*—manifests; *hareḥ*—of Lord Kṛṣṇa; *rādhikā*—Śrīmatī Rādhārāṇī; *ekā*—alone; *na*—not; *ca anyā*—anyone else.

TRANSLATION

"'If one asks about the origin of love of Kṛṣṇa, the answer is that the origin is in Śrīmatī Rādhārāṇī alone. Who is the most dear friend of Kṛṣṇa? The answer again is Śrīmatī Rādhārāṇī alone. No one else. Śrīmatī Rādhārāṇī's hair is very curly, Her two eyes are always moving

to and fro, and Her breasts are firm. Since all transcendental qualities are manifested in Śrīmatī Rādhārāṇī, She alone is able to fulfill all the desires of Kṛṣṇa. No one else.'

PURPORT

This is a quotation from *Śrī Govinda-līlāmṛta* (11.122) by Kṛṣṇadāsa Kavirāja Gosvāmī. It is a verse in the form of questions and answers describing the glories of Śrīmatī Rādhārāṇī.

TEXTS 183–184

যাঁর সৌভাগ্য-গুণ বাঞ্ছে সত্যভামা ।
যাঁর ঠাঞি কলাবিলাস শিখে ব্রজ-রামা ॥ ১৮৩ ॥
যাঁর সৌন্দর্যাদি-গুণ বাঞ্ছে লক্ষ্মী-পার্বতী ।
যাঁর পতিব্রতা-ধর্ম বাঞ্ছে অরুন্ধতী ॥ ১৮৪ ॥

yāṅra saubhāgya-guṇa vāñche satyabhāmā
yāṅra ṭhāñi kalā-vilāsa śikhe vraja-rāmā

yāṅra saundaryādi-guṇa vāñche lakṣmī-pārvatī
yāṅra pativratā-dharma vāñche arundhatī

yāṅra—whose; *saubhāgya*—of good fortune; *guṇa*—quality; *vāñche*—desires; *satyabhāmā*—Satyabhāmā, one of the queens of Kṛṣṇa; *yāṅra ṭhāñi*—from whom; *kalā-vilāsa*—the sixty-four arts; *śikhe*—learn; *vraja-rāmā*—all the *gopīs* in Vṛndāvana; *yāṅra*—whose; *saundarya-ādi*—such as beauty; *guṇa*—qualities; *vāñche*—desires; *lakṣmī*—the goddess of fortune; *pārvatī*—the wife of Lord Śiva; *yāṅra*—whose; *pati-vratā*—of chastity; *dharma*—principle; *vāñche*—desires; *arundhatī*—the wife of Vasiṣṭha Muni.

TRANSLATION

"Even Satyabhāmā, one of the queens of Śrī Kṛṣṇa, desires the fortunate position and excellent qualities of Śrīmatī Rādhārāṇī. All the gopīs learn the art of dressing from Śrīmatī Rādhārāṇī, and even the goddess of fortune, Lakṣmī, and the wife of Lord Śiva, Pārvatī, desire Her

beauty and qualities. Indeed, Arundhatī, the celebrated chaste wife of Vasiṣṭha, also wants to imitate the chastity and religious principles of Śrīmatī Rādhārāṇī.

TEXT 185

যাঁর সদ্‌গুণ-গণনে কৃষ্ণ না পায় পার।
তাঁর গুণ গণিবে কেমনে জীব ছার॥ ১৮৫॥

yāṅra sadguṇa-gaṇane kṛṣṇa nā pāya pāra
tāṅra guṇa gaṇibe kemane jīva chāra

yāṅra—whose; *sat-guṇa*—good qualities; *gaṇane*—in counting; *kṛṣṇa*—Lord Kṛṣṇa; *nā*—not; *pāya*—obtains; *pāra*—the limit; *tāṅra*—Her; *guṇa*—qualities; *gaṇibe*—can count; *kemane*—how; *jīva*—a living entity; *chāra*—most insignificant.

TRANSLATION

"Even Lord Kṛṣṇa Himself cannot reach the limit of the transcendental qualities of Śrīmatī Rādhārāṇī. How, then, can an insignificant living entity count them?"

TEXT 186

প্রভু কহে,—জানিলুঁ কৃষ্ণ-রাধা-প্রেম-তত্ত্ব।
শুনিতে চাহিয়ে দুঁহার বিলাস-মহত্ত্ব॥ ১৮৬॥

prabhu kahe,—jāniluṅ kṛṣṇa-rādhā-prema-tattva
śunite cāhiye duṅhāra vilāsa-mahattva

prabhu kahe—Lord Śrī Caitanya replied; *jāniluṅ*—now I have understood; *kṛṣṇa*—of Lord Kṛṣṇa; *rādhā*—of Śrīmatī Rādhārāṇī; *prema*—of the loving affairs; *tattva*—the truth; *śunite*—to hear; *cāhiye*—I desire; *duṅhāra*—of both of Them; *vilāsa-mahattva*—the greatness of the enjoyment.

TRANSLATION

Lord Śrī Caitanya Mahāprabhu replied, "Now I have come to understand the truth of the loving affairs between Rādhā and Kṛṣṇa.

Nonetheless, I still want to hear how both of Them gloriously enjoy such love."

TEXT 187

রায় কহে, — কৃষ্ণ হয় 'ধীর-ললিত' ।
নিরন্তর কামক্রীড়া — যাঁহার চরিত ॥ ১৮৭ ॥

rāya kahe, — kṛṣṇa haya 'dhīra-lalita'
nirantara kāma-krīḍā — yāṅhāra carita

rāya kahe — Rāmānanda Rāya replied; *kṛṣṇa* — Lord Kṛṣṇa; *haya* — is; *dhīra-lalita* — a person who can keep his girlfriend always in subjugation by different qualities; *nirantara* — constantly; *kāma-krīḍā* — pastimes of sexual enjoyment; *yāṅhāra* — of whom; *carita* — the character.

TRANSLATION

Rāya Rāmānanda replied, "Lord Kṛṣṇa is dhīra-lalita, for He can always keep His girlfriends in a subjugated state. Thus His only business is enjoying sense gratification.

PURPORT

We should always remember that Kṛṣṇa's sense gratification is never to be compared to the sense gratification of the material world. As we have already explained, Kṛṣṇa's sense gratification is just like gold. The perverted reflection of that sense gratification found in the material world is just like iron. The purport is that Kṛṣṇa is not impersonal. He has all the desires that are manifest in the perverted reflection within this material world. However, the qualities are different — one is spiritual, and the other is material. Just as there is a difference between life and death, there is a difference between spiritual sense gratification and material sense gratification.

TEXT 188

বিদগ্ধো নবতারুণ্যঃ পরিহাস-বিশারদঃ ।
নিশ্চিন্তো ধীরললিতঃ স্যাৎ প্রায়ঃ প্রেয়সীবশঃ ॥ ১৮৮ ॥

vidagdho nava-tāruṇyaḥ
parihāsa-viśāradaḥ
niścinto dhīra-lalitaḥ
syāt prāyaḥ preyasī-vaśaḥ

vidagdhaḥ—clever; *nava-tāruṇyaḥ*—always freshly youthful; *parihāsa*—in joking; *viśāradaḥ*—expert; *niścintaḥ*—without anxiety; *dhīra-lalitaḥ*—a hero in loving affairs; *syāt*—is; *prāyaḥ*—almost always; *preyasī-vaśaḥ*—one who keeps His girlfriends subjugated.

TRANSLATION

"'A person who is very cunning and always youthful, expert in joking and without anxiety, and who can keep his girlfriends always subjugated, is called dhīra-lalita.'

PURPORT

This verse is from the *Bhakti-rasāmṛta-sindhu* (2.1.230).

TEXT 189

রাত্রি-দিন কুঞ্জে ক্রীড়া করে রাধা-সঙ্গে ।
কৈশোর বয়স সফল কৈল ক্রীড়া-রঙ্গে ॥ ১৮৯ ॥

rātri-dina kuñje krīḍā kare rādhā-saṅge
kaiśora vayasa saphala kaila krīḍā-raṅge

rātri-dina—day and night; *kuñje*—in the gardens or bushes of Vṛndāvana; *krīḍā*—pastimes; *kare*—performs; *rādhā-saṅge*—with Rādhārāṇī; *kaiśora*—the pre-youthful; *vayasa*—age; *sa-phala*—fruitful; *kaila*—made; *krīḍā-raṅge*—taking pleasure in different pastimes.

TRANSLATION

"Day and night Lord Śrī Kṛṣṇa enjoys the company of Śrīmatī Rādhārāṇī in the bushes of Vṛndāvana. Thus His pre-youthful age is fulfilled through His affairs with Śrīmatī Rādhārāṇī.

TEXT 190

বাচা সূচিতশর্বরীরতিকলা-প্রাগল্‌ভ্যয়া রাধিকাং
ব্রীড়াকুঞ্চিত-লোচনাং বিরচয়ন্নগ্রে সখীনামসৌ।
তদ্বক্ষোরুহচিত্রকেলিমকরীপাণ্ডিত্যপারং গতঃ
কৈশোরং সফলীকরোতি কলয়ন্ কুঞ্জে বিহারং হরিঃ ॥ ১৯০॥

vācā sūcita-śarvarī-rati-kalā-prāgalbhyayā rādhikāṁ
vrīḍā-kuñcita-locanāṁ viracayann agre sakhīnām asau
tad-vakṣoruha-citra-keli-makarī-pāṇḍitya-pāraṁ gataḥ
kaiśoraṁ saphalī-karoti kalayan kuñje vihāraṁ hariḥ

vācā—by speech; *sūcita*—revealing; *śarvarī*—of the night; *rati*—in amorous pastimes; *kalā*—of the portion; *prāgalbhyayā*—the importance; *rādhikām*—Śrīmatī Rādhārāṇī; *vrīḍā*—from shame; *kuñcita-locanām*—having Her eyes closed; *viracayan*—making; *agre*—before; *sakhīnām*—Her friends; *asau*—that one; *tat*—of Her; *vakṣaḥ-ruha*—on the breasts; *citra-keli*—with variegated pastimes; *makarī*—in drawing dolphins; *pāṇḍitya*—of cleverness; *pāram*—the limit; *gataḥ*—who reached; *kaiśoram*—adolescence; *sa-phalī-karoti*—makes successful; *kalayan*—performing; *kuñje*—in the bushes; *vihāram*—pastimes; *hariḥ*—the Supreme Personality of Godhead.

TRANSLATION

"'Thus Lord Śrī Kṛṣṇa spoke of the sexual activities of the previous night. In this way He made Śrīmatī Rādhārāṇī close Her eyes out of shyness. Taking this opportunity, Śrī Kṛṣṇa painted various types of dolphins on Her breasts. Thus He became a very expert artist for all the gopīs. During such pastimes, the Lord enjoyed the fulfillment of His youth.'"

PURPORT

This quotation is also found in the *Bhakti-rasāmṛta-sindhu* (2.1.119).

TEXT 191

প্রভু কহে,—এহো হয়, আগে কহ আর।
রায় কহে,—ইহা বই বুদ্ধি-গতি নাহি আর ॥ ১৯১ ॥

prabhu kahe,—eho haya, āge kaha āra
rāya kahe,—īhā va-i buddhi-gati nāhi āra

prabhu kahe—Lord Caitanya Mahāprabhu said; *eho haya*—this is all right; *āge kaha āra*—please go forward and say more; *rāya kahe*—Rāmānanda Rāya replied; *ihā va-i*—except this; *buddhi-gati*—movement of my intelligence; *nāhi*—there is not; *āra*—any more.

TRANSLATION

Śrī Caitanya Mahāprabhu said, "This is all right, but please continue."

At that time Rāya Rāmānanda replied, "I don't think my intelligence goes beyond this."

TEXT 192

যেবা 'প্রেমবিলাস-বিবর্ত' এক হয়।
তাহা শুনি' তোমার সুখ হয়, কি না হয় ॥ ১৯২ ॥

yebā 'prema-vilāsa-vivarta' eka haya
tāhā śuni' tomāra sukha haya, ki nā haya

yebā—whatever; *prema-vilāsa-vivarta*—the resultant bewilderment or revolution in the ecstasy of loving affairs; *eka haya*—there is one topic; *tāhā*—that; *śuni'*—hearing; *tomāra*—Your; *sukha*—happiness; *haya*—is; *ki*—or; *nā*—not; *haya*—is.

TRANSLATION

Rāya Rāmānanda then informed Śrī Caitanya Mahāprabhu that there was another topic, known as prema-vilāsa-vivarta. "You may hear of this from me," Rāmānanda Rāya said, "but I do not know whether You will be happy with it or not."

PURPORT

These statements are set forth for our understanding, according to Śrīla Bhaktivinoda Ṭhākura in his *Amṛta-pravāha-bhāṣya.* In essence, Śrī Caitanya Mahāprabhu told Rāmānanda Rāya, "My dear Rāmānanda, the

the explanation you have given about the goal of life and the pastimes of Śrīmatī Rādhārāṇī and Kṛṣṇa is certainly the truth. Although this is factual, you can continue telling Me more if there is anything more to say." In reply, Rāmānanda Rāya said, "I do not think I have anything to say beyond this, but there is a topic known as *prema-vilāsa-vivarta,* which I may explain to You. I do not know whether it will bring You happiness or not."

TEXT 193

এত বলি' আপন-কৃত গীত এক গাহিল ।
প্রেমে প্রভু স্বহস্তে তাঁর মুখ আচ্ছাদিল ॥ ১৯৩ ॥

eta bali' āpana-kṛta gīta eka gāhila
preme prabhu sva-haste tāṅra mukha ācchādila

eta bali'—saying this; *āpana-kṛta*—composed by himself; *gīta*—song; *eka*—one; *gāhila*—sang; *preme*—in love of Godhead; *prabhu*—Śrī Caitanya Mahāprabhu; *sva-haste*—by His own hand; *tāṅra*—his (Rāmānanda Rāya's); *mukha*—mouth; *ācchādila*—covered.

TRANSLATION

Saying this, Rāmānanda Rāya began to sing a song he had composed, but Śrī Caitanya Mahāprabhu, out of the ecstasy of love of Godhead, immediately covered Rāmānanda's mouth with His own hand.

PURPORT

The topics that are about to be discussed between Lord Śrī Caitanya Mahāprabhu and Rāmānanda Rāya cannot be understood by a materialistic poet, nor by intelligence or material perception. Śrīla Bhaktisiddhānta Sarasvatī Ṭhākura states that the spiritual mellow can be realized only when one is situated on the transcendental platform beyond the material stage of goodness. That platform is called *viśuddha-sattva* (*sattvaṁ viśuddhaṁ vasudeva-śabditam*). Realization of the *viśuddha-sattva* platform is beyond the pale of the material world and is not perceived by bodily senses or mental speculation. Our identification with the gross body and subtle mind is different from spiritual understanding. Since the intelligence and mind are material, the loving affairs of Śrī Rādhā and Kṛṣṇa are beyond their perception. *Sarvopādhi-vinirmuktaṁ tat-paratvena nirmalam:* when we are free from all material designations and our senses are completely purified by the *bhakti* process, we can understand the sense activities of the Absolute Truth (*hṛṣīkeṇa hṛṣīkeśa-sevanaṁ bhaktir ucyate*).

The spiritual senses are beyond the material senses. A materialist can think only of the negation of material variety; he cannot understand spiritual variety. He thinks that spiritual variety simply contradicts material variety and is a negation or void, but such conceptions cannot even reach the precincts of spiritual realization. The wonderful activities of the gross body and subtle mind are always imperfect. They are below the degree of spiritual understanding and are ephemeral. The spiritual mellow is eternally wonderful and is described as *pūrṇa, śuddha, nitya-mukta*—that is, complete, perfectly pure and eternally liberated from all material conceptions. When we are unable to fulfill our material desires, there is certainly sorrow and confusion. This may be described as *vivarta.* But in spiritual life there is no sorrow, inebriety or imperfection. Śrīla Rāmānanda Rāya was expert in realizing the spiritual activities of Śrīmatī Rādhārāṇī and Kṛṣṇa, and Rāmānanda's spiritual experience was placed before Śrī Caitanya Mahāprabhu as he inquired whether the Lord approved his realization of spiritual truth.

There are three books prominent in this connection. One was written by Bhakta dāsa Bāula and is called *Vivarta-vilāsa.* Another was compiled by Jagadānanda Paṇḍita and is called *Prema-vivarta.* Śrī Rāmānanda Rāya's book is called *Prema-vilāsa-vivarta.* The *Vivarta-vilāsa* by Bhakta dāsa Bāula is completely different from the other two books. Sometimes a university student or professor tries to study these transcendental literatures and attempts to put forth a critical analysis from the mundane view, with an end to receiving degrees like a Ph.D. Such realization is certainly different from that of Rāmānanda Rāya. If one actually wants to take a Ph.D. degree from Śrī Caitanya Mahāprabhu and be approved by Rāmānanda Rāya, he must first become free from all material designations (*sarvopādhi-vinirmuktaṁ tat-paratvena nirmalam*). A person who identifies with his material body cannot understand these talks between Śrī Rāmānanda Rāya and Śrī Caitanya Mahāprabhu. Man-made religious scriptures and transcendental philosophical talks are quite different. Indeed, there is a gulf of difference between the two. This subject matter has been very diligently described by Śrīman Madhvācārya. Since material philosophers are situated in the material conception of life, they are unable to realize the spiritual *prema-vilāsa-vivarta.* They cannot accommodate an elephant upon a dish. Similarly, mundane speculators cannot capture the spiritual elephant within their limited conception. It is just like a frog's trying to measure the Atlantic Ocean by imagining it so many times larger than his well. Materialistic philosophers and *sahajiyās* cannot understand the talks between Rāmānanda Rāya and Śrī Caitanya Mahāprabhu concerning the pastimes of Śrī Rādhā and Kṛṣṇa. The only tendency of the impersonalists or the *prākṛta-sahajiyās* is to face the platform of impersonalism. They cannot understand spiritual variegatedness. Consequently, when Rāmānanda Rāya attempted to sing his own verses, Śrī Caitanya Mahāprabhu stopped him by covering his mouth with His own hand.

TEXT 194

পহিলেহি রাগ নয়নভঙ্গে ভেল ।
অনুদিন বাঢ়ল, অবধি না গেল ॥
না সো রমণ, না হাম রমণী ।
দুঁহু-মন মনোভব পেষল জানি' ॥
এ সখি, সে-সব প্রেমকাহিনী ।
কানুঠামে কহবি বিছুরল জানি' ॥
না খোঁজলুঁ দূতী, না খোঁজলুঁ আন্ ।
দুঁহুকেরি মিলনে মধ্য ত পাঁচবাণ ॥
অব্ সোহি বিরাগ, তুঁহু ভেলি দূতী ।
সু-পুরুখ-প্রেমকি ঐছন রীতি ॥ ১৯৪ ॥

pahilehi rāga nayana-bhaṅge bhela
anudina bāḍhala, avadhi nā gela

nā so ramaṇa, nā hāma ramaṇī
duṅhu-mana manobhava peṣala jāni'

e sakhi, se-saba prema-kāhinī
kānu-ṭhāme kahabi vichurala jāni'

nā khoṅjaluṅ dūtī, nā khoṅjaluṅ ān
duṅhukeri milane madhya ta pāṅca-bāṇa

ab sohi virāga, tuṅhu bheli dūtī
su-purukha-premaki aichana rīti

pahilehi—in the beginning; *rāga*—attraction; *nayana-bhaṅge*—by activities of the eyes; *bhela*—there was; *anu-dina*—gradually, day after day; *bāḍhala*—increased; *avadhi*—limit; *nā*—not; *gela*—reached; *nā*—not; *so*—He; *ramaṇa*—the enjoyer; *nā*—not; *hāma*—I; *ramaṇī*—the enjoyed; *duṅhu-mana*—both the minds; *manaḥ-bhava*—the mental situation; *peṣala*—pressed together; *jāni'*—knowing; *e*—this; *sakhi*—My dear friend; *se-saba*—all those; *prema-kāhinī*—affairs of love; *kānu-ṭhāme*—before Kṛṣṇa; *kahabi*—you will say; *vichurala*—He has forgotten; *jāni'*—knowing; *nā*—not; *khoṅjaluṅ*—searched out; *dūtī*—a messenger; *nā*—not; *khoṅjaluṅ*—searched out; *ān*—anyone else; *duṅhukeri*—of both of Us; *milane*—by the meeting; *madhya*—in the middle; *ta*—indeed; *pāṅca-bāṇa*—five arrows of Cupid; *ab*—now; *sohi*—that; *virāga*—separation; *tuṅhu*—you; *bheli*—became; *dūtī*—the messenger; *su-purukha*—of a beautiful person; *premaki*—of loving affairs; *aichana*—such; *rīti*—the consequence.

TRANSLATION

"'Alas, before We met there was an initial attachment between Us brought about by an exchange of glances. In this way attachment evolved. That attachment has gradually grown, and there is no limit to it. Now that attachment has become a natural sequence between Ourselves. It is not that it is due to Kṛṣṇa, the enjoyer, nor is it due to Me, for I am the enjoyed. It is not like that. This attachment was made possible by mutual meeting. This mutual exchange of attraction is known as manobhava, or Cupid. Kṛṣṇa's mind and My mind have merged together. Now, during this time of separation, it is very difficult to explain these loving affairs. My dear friend, though Kṛṣṇa might have forgotten all these things, you can understand and bring this message to Him. But during Our first meeting there was no messenger between Us, nor did I request anyone to see Him. Indeed, Cupid's five arrows were Our via media. Now, during this separation, that attraction

has increased to another ecstatic state. My dear friend, please act as a messenger on My behalf, because if one is in love with a beautiful person, this is the consequence.'

PURPORT

These verses were originally composed and sung by Rāmānanda Rāya himself. Śrīla Bhaktivinoda Ṭhākura suggests that during the time of conjugal enjoyment, the attachment might be compared to Cupid himself. However, during the period of separation, Cupid becomes a messenger of highly elevated love. This is called *prema-vilāsa-vivarta.* When there is separation, conjugal enjoyment itself acts like a messenger, and that messenger was addressed by Śrīmatī Rādhārāṇī as a friend. The essence of this transaction is that transcendental loving affairs are as relishable during separation as during conjugal enjoyment. When Śrīmatī Rādhārāṇī was fully absorbed in love of Kṛṣṇa, She mistook a black *tamāla* tree for Kṛṣṇa and embraced it. Such a mistake is called *prema-vilāsa-vivarta.*

TEXT 195

রাধায়া ভবতশ্চ চিত্তজতুনী স্বেদৈর্বিলাপ্য ক্রমাদ্
যুঞ্জন্নদ্রি-নিকুঞ্জ-কুঞ্জরপতে নির্ধূত-ভেদভ্রমম্ ।
চিত্রায় স্বয়মন্বরঞ্জয়দিহ ব্রহ্মাণ্ডহর্ম্যোদরে
ভূয়োভির্নব-রাগ-হিঙ্গুলভরৈঃ শৃঙ্গার-কারুঃ কৃতী ॥ ১৯৫ ॥

rādhāyā bhavataś ca citta-jatunī svedair vilāpya kramād
yuñjann adri-nikuñja-kuñjara-pate nirdhūta-bheda-bhramam
citrāya svayam anvarañjayad iha brahmāṇḍa-harmyodare
bhūyobhir nava-rāga-hiṅgula-bharaiḥ śṛṅgāra-kāruḥ kṛtī

rādhāyāḥ—of Śrīmatī Rādhārāṇī; *bhavataḥ ca*—and of You; *citta-jatunī*—the two minds like shellac; *svedaiḥ*—by perspiration; *vilāpya*—melting; *kramāt*—gradually; *yuñjan*—making; *adri*—of Govardhana Hill; *nikuñja*—in a solitary place for enjoyment; *kuñjara-pate*—O king of the elephants; *nirdhūta*—completely taken away; *bheda-bhramam*—the misunderstanding of differentiation; *citrāya*—for increasing the wonder; *svayam*—personally; *anvarañjayat*—colored; *iha*—in this world; *brahmāṇḍa*—of the universe; *harmya-udare*—within the palace; *bhūyobhiḥ*—by varieties of means; *nava-rāga*—of new attraction; *hiṅgula-bharaiḥ*—by the vermilion; *śṛṅgāra*—of loving affairs; *kāruḥ*—the craftsman; *kṛtī*—very expert.

TRANSLATION

"'O my Lord, You live in the forest of Govardhana Hill, and, like the king of elephants, You are expert in the art of conjugal love. O master of the universe, Your heart and Śrīmatī Rādhārāṇī's heart are just like shellac and are now melted in Your spiritual perspiration. Therefore one can no longer distinguish between You and Śrīmatī Rādhārāṇī. Now You have mixed Your newly invoked affection, which is like vermilion, with Your melted hearts, and for the benefit of the whole world You have painted both Your hearts red within this great palace of the universe.'"

PURPORT

This verse quoted by Rāmānanda Rāya is included in Śrīla Rūpa Gosvāmī's *Ujjvala-nīlamaṇi* (14.155).

TEXT 196

প্রভু কহে, — 'সাধ্যবস্তুর অবধি' এই হয়।
তোমার প্রসাদে ইহা জানিলুঁ নিশ্চয় ॥ ১৯৬ ॥

prabhu kahe,—'sādhya-vastura avadhi' ei haya
tomāra prasāde ihā jāniluṅ niścaya

prabhu kahe—Śrī Caitanya Mahāprabhu confirmed; *sādhya-vastura*—of the object of life; *avadhi'*—the limit; *ei*—this; *haya*—is; *tomāra*—of you; *prasāde*—by the mercy; *ihā*—this; *jāniluṅ*—I have understood; *niścaya*—conclusively.

TRANSLATION

Śrī Caitanya Mahāprabhu confirmed these verses recited by Śrī Rāmānanda Rāya, saying, "This is the limit of the goal of human life. Only by your mercy have I come to understand it conclusively.

TEXT 197

'সাধ্যবস্তু' 'সাধন' বিনু কেহ নাহি পায়।
কৃপা করি' কহ, রায়, পাবার উপায় ॥ ১৯৭ ॥

'sādhya-vastu' 'sādhana' vinu keha nāhi pāya
kṛpā kari' kaha, rāya, pābāra upāya

sādhya-vastu—the goal of life; *sādhana vinu*—without practicing the process; *keha nāhi pāya*—no one achieves; *kṛpā kari'*—very mercifully; *kaha*—please explain; *rāya*—My dear Rāmānanda Rāya; *pābāra upāya*—the means of achieving.

TRANSLATION

"The goal of life cannot be achieved unless one practices the process. Now, being merciful upon Me, please explain that means by which this goal can be attained."

TEXT 198

রায় কহে, — যেই কহাও, সেই কহি বাণী।
কি কহিয়ে ভাল-মন্দ, কিছুই না জানি ॥ ১৯৮ ॥

rāya kahe,—yei kahāo, sei kahi vāṇī
ki kahiye bhāla-manda, kichui nā jāni

rāya kahe—Rāmānanda Rāya replied; *yei*—whatever; *kahāo*—You make me speak; *sei*—that; *kahi*—I speak; *vāṇī*—message; *ki*—what; *kahiye*—I am speaking; *bhāla-manda*—good or bad; *kichui nā jāni*—I do not know anything.

TRANSLATION

Śrī Rāmānanda Rāya replied, "I do not know what I am saying, but You have made me speak what I have spoken, be it good or bad. I am simply repeating that message.

TEXT 199

ত্রিভুবন-মধ্যে ঐছে হয় কোন্ ধীর।
যে তোমার মায়া-নাটে হইবেক স্থির ॥ ১৯৯ ॥

tribhuvana-madhye aiche haya kon dhīra
ye tomāra māyā-nāṭe ha-ibeka sthira

tri-bhuvana-madhye—within the three worlds; *aiche*—so much; *haya*—there is; *kon*—who; *dhīra*—patient; *ye*—who; *tomāra*—Your; *māyā-nāṭe*—in the manipulation of different energies; *ha-ibeka*—will be; *sthira*—steady.

TRANSLATION

"Within these three worlds, who is so undisturbed that he can remain steady as You manipulate Your different energies?

TEXT 200

মোর মুখে বক্তা তুমি, তুমি হও শ্রোতা।
অত্যন্ত রহস্য, শুন, সাধনের কথা ॥ ২০০ ॥

mora mukhe vaktā tumi, tumi hao śrotā
atyanta rahasya, śuna, sādhanera kathā

mora mukhe—in my mouth; *vaktā*—speaker; *tumi*—You are; *tumi*—You; *hao*—are; *śrotā*—the hearer; *atyanta rahasya*—extremely mysterious; *śuna*—now please hear; *sādhanera kathā*—the discussion of the process.

TRANSLATION

"Actually You are speaking through my mouth, and at the same time You are listening. This is very mysterious. Anyway, kindly hear the explanation of the process by which the goal can be attained.

PURPORT

Śrīla Sanātana Gosvāmī has advised us to hear about Kṛṣṇa from a Vaiṣṇava. He has explicitly forbidden us to hear from an *avaiṣṇava.*

avaiṣṇava-mukhodgīrṇaṁ pūtaṁ hari-kathāmṛtam
śravaṇaṁ naiva kartavyaṁ sarpocchiṣṭaṁ yathā payaḥ

Thus quoting from *Padma Purāṇa,* Śrīla Sanātana Gosvāmī warns that one should not hear anything about Kṛṣṇa from an *avaiṣṇava,* however great a mundane scholar he may be. Milk touched by the lips of a serpent has poisonous effects; similarly, talks about Kṛṣṇa given by an *avaiṣṇava* are also poisonous. However, because a Vaiṣṇava is surrendered to the Supreme Personality of Godhead, his talks are spiritually potent. In the *Bhagavad-gītā* (10.10) the Supreme Lord says:

teṣāṁ satata-yuktānāṁ bhajatāṁ prīti-pūrvakam
dadāmi buddhi-yogaṁ taṁ yena mām upayānti te

"To those who are constantly devoted to worshiping Me with love, I give the understanding by which they can come to Me." When a pure Vaiṣṇava speaks, he speaks perfectly. How is this? His speech is managed by Kṛṣṇa Himself from within the heart. Śrīla Rāmānanda Rāya accepts this benediction from Śrī Caitanya Mahāprabhu; therefore he admits that whatever he was speaking was not derived from his own intelligence. Rather, everything was coming from Śrī Caitanya Mahāprabhu. According to the *Bhagavad-gītā* (15.15):

sarvasya cāhaṁ hṛdi sanniviṣṭo
mattaḥ smṛtir jñānam apohanaṁ ca
vedaiś ca sarvair aham eva vedyo
vedānta-kṛd veda-vid eva cāham

"I am seated in everyone's heart, and from Me come remembrance, knowledge and forgetfulness. By all the *Vedas,* I am to be known. Indeed I am the compiler of the *Vedānta,* and I am the knower of the *Vedas.*

All intelligence emanates from the Supreme Personality of Godhead, the Supersoul within the heart of everyone. Nondevotees want to ask the Supreme Lord for sense gratification; therefore nondevotees come under the influence of *māyā,* the illusory energy. A devotee, however, is directed by the Supreme Personality of Godhead and comes under the influence of *yogamāyā.* Consequently there is a gulf of difference between statements made by a devotee and those made by a nondevotee.

TEXT 201

রাধাকৃষ্ণের লীলা এই অতি গূঢ়তর ।
দাস্য-বাৎসল্যাদি-ভাবে না হয় গোচর ॥ ২০১ ॥

rādhā-kṛṣṇera līlā ei ati gūḍhatara
dāsya-vātsalyādi-bhāve nā haya gocara

rādhā-kṛṣṇera līlā—the pastimes of Rādhā and Kṛṣṇa; *ei*—this is; *ati*—very much; *gūḍhatara*—more confidential; *dāsya*—of servitude; *vātsalya-ādi*—and of parental love, etc.; *bhāve*—in the moods; *nā haya*—is not; *gocara*—appreciated.

TRANSLATION

"The pastimes of Rādhā and Kṛṣṇa are very confidential. They cannot be understood through the mellows of servitude, fraternity or parental affection.

TEXT 202

সবে এক সখীগণের ইহাঁ অধিকার ।
সখী হৈতে হয় এই লীলার বিস্তার ॥ ২০২ ॥

sabe eka sakhī-gaṇera ihāṅ adhikāra
sakhī haite haya ei līlāra vistāra

sabe—only; *eka*—one; *sakhī-gaṇera*—of the *gopīs; ihāṅ*—in this; *adhikāra*—qualification; *sakhī*—the *gopīs; haite*—from; *haya*—is; *ei līlāra*—of these pastimes; *vistāra*—the expansion.

TRANSLATION

"Actually, only the gopīs have the right to appreciate these transcendental pastimes, and only from them can these pastimes be expanded.

TEXT 203

সখী বিনা এই লীলা পুষ্ট নাহি হয় ।
সখী লীলা বিস্তারিয়া, সখী আস্বাদয় ॥ ২০৩ ॥

sakhī vinā ei līlā puṣṭa nāhi haya
sakhī līlā vistāriyā, sakhī āsvādaya

sakhī vinā—without the *gopīs; ei līlā*—these pastimes; *puṣṭa*—nourished; *nāhi haya*—are never; *sakhī*—the *gopīs;*

līlā—the pastimes; *vistāriyā*—expanding; *sakhī*—the *gopīs;* *āsvādaya*—taste this mellow.

TRANSLATION

"Without the gopīs, these pastimes between Rādhā and Kṛṣṇa cannot be nourished. Only by their cooperation are such pastimes broadcast. It is their business to taste the mellows.

TEXTS 204–205

সখী বিনা এই লীলায় অন্যের নাহি গতি ।
সখীভাবে যে তাঁরে করে অনুগতি ॥ ২০৪ ॥
রাধাকৃষ্ণ-কুঞ্জসেবা-সাধ্য সেই পায় ।
সেই সাধ্য পাইতে আর নাহিক উপায় ॥ ২০৫ ॥

sakhī vinā ei līlāya anyera nāhi gati
sakhī-bhāve ye tāṅre kare anugati

rādhā-kṛṣṇa-kuñjasevā-sādhya sei pāya
sei sādhya pāite āra nāhika upāya

sakhī vinā—without the *gopīs; ei līlāya*—in these pastimes; *anyera*—of others; *nāhi*—there is not; *gati*—entrance; *sakhī-bhāve*—in the mood of the *gopīs; ye*—anyone who; *tāṅre*—Lord Kṛṣṇa; *kare*—does; *anugati*—following; *rādhā-kṛṣṇa*—of Rādhā and Kṛṣṇa; *kuñja-sevā*—of service in the *kuñjas,* or gardens, of Vṛndāvana; *sādhya*—the goal; *sei pāya*—he gets; *sei*—that; *sādhya*—achievement; *pāite*—to receive; *āra*—other; *nāhika*—there is not; *upāya*—means.

TRANSLATION

"Without the help of the gopīs, one cannot enter into these pastimes. Only one who worships the Lord in the ecstasy of the gopīs, following in their footsteps, can engage in the service of Śrī Śrī Rādhā-Kṛṣṇa in the bushes of Vṛndāvana. Only then can one understand the conjugal love between Rādhā and Kṛṣṇa. There is no other procedure for understanding.

PURPORT

The means for returning home, for going back to Godhead, is devotional service, but everyone has a different taste in the Lord's service. One may be inclined to serve the Lord in servitude (*dāsya-rasa*), fraternity (*sakhya-rasa*) or parental love (*vātsalya-rasa*), but none of these can enable one to enter into the service of the Lord in conjugal love. To attain such service, one has to follow in the footsteps of the *gopīs* in the ecstasy of *sakhī-bhāva.* Then only can one understand the transcendental mellow of conjugal love.

In the *Ujjvala-nīlamaṇi,* Śrīla Rūpa Gosvāmī advises:

prema-līlā-vihārāṇāṁ
samyag vistārikā sakhī
viśrambha-ratna-peṭī ca

One who expands the conjugal love of Kṛṣṇa and His enjoyment among the *gopīs* is called a *sakhī.* Such a person is a confidential *gopī* in the conjugal affairs. Such assistants are like jewels in the form of Kṛṣṇa's confidantes. The actual business of the *sakhīs* is described thus in *Ujjvala-nīlamaṇi:*

mithaḥ prema-guṇotkīrtis tayor āsakti-kāritā
abhisāro dvayor eva sakhyāḥ kṛṣṇe samarpaṇam

narmāśvāsana-nepathyaṁ hṛdayodghāṭa-pāṭavam
chidra-saṁvṛtir etasyāḥ paty-ādeḥ parivañcanā

śikṣā saṅgamanaṁ kāle sevanaṁ vyajanādibhiḥ
tayor dvayor upālambhaḥ sandeśa-preṣaṇaṁ tathā

nāyikā-prāṇa-saṁrakṣā prayatnādyāḥ sakhī-kriyāḥ

In the conjugal pastimes of Kṛṣṇa, Kṛṣṇa is the hero (*nāyaka*), and Rādhikā is the heroine (*nāyikā*). The first business of the *gopīs* is to chant the glories of both the hero and the heroine. Their second business is to gradually create a situation in which the hero may be attracted to the heroine and vice versa. Their third business is to induce both of Them to approach each other. Their fourth business is to surrender unto Kṛṣṇa, the fifth is to create a jovial atmosphere, the sixth to give Them assurance to enjoy Their pastimes, the seventh to dress and decorate both hero and heroine, the eighth to show expertise in expressing Their desires, the ninth to conceal the faults of the heroine, the tenth to cheat their respective husbands and relatives, the eleventh to educate, the twelfth to enable both the hero and heroine to meet at the proper time, the thirteenth to fan the hero and heroine, the fourteenth to sometimes reproach the hero and heroine, the fifteenth to set conversations in motion, and the sixteenth to protect the heroine by various means.

Some materialistic *sahajiyās* who cannot actually understand the pastimes of Rādhā and Kṛṣṇa manufacture their own life-styles without referring to authority. Such *sahajiyās* are called *sakhī-bhekī,* and sometimes they are called *gaura-nāgarī.* They believe that the material body, which is fit to be eaten by jackals and dogs, is enjoyable for Kṛṣṇa. Consequently they artificially decorate the material body to attract Kṛṣṇa, thinking themselves *sakhīs.* But Kṛṣṇa is never attracted by the artificial grooming of the material body. As far as Śrīmatī Rādhārāṇī and Her *gopīs* are concerned, their bodies, homes, dresses, ornaments, endeavors and activities are all spiritual. All of these are meant to satisfy the spiritual senses of Kṛṣṇa. Indeed, they are so pleasing and endearing to Kṛṣṇa that He is subjugated by the influence of Śrīmatī Rādhārāṇī and Her friends. They have nothing to do with anything mundane within the fourteen planetary systems of the universe. Although Kṛṣṇa is attractive to everyone, He is nonetheless attracted by the *gopīs* and Śrīmatī Rādhārāṇī.

One should not be misled by mental concoctions, supposing his material body to be perfect and deeming oneself a *sakhī.* This is something like *ahaṅgrahopāsanā,* that is, a Māyāvādī's worship of his own body as the Supreme. Śrīla Jīva Gosvāmī has cautioned mundaners to abstain from such conceptions. He also warns that thinking oneself one of the associates of the Supreme without following in the footsteps of the *gopīs* is as offensive as thinking oneself the Supreme. Such thinking is an *aparādha.* One has to practice living in Vṛndāvana by hearing about the talks of the *gopīs* with Kṛṣṇa. However, one should not consider himself a *gopī,* for this is offensive.

TEXT 206

বিভুরপি সুখরূপঃ স্বপ্রকাশোঽপি ভাবঃ
ক্ষণমপি ন হি রাধাকৃষ্ণয়োর্যা ঋতে স্বাঃ ।

প্রবহতি রসপুষ্টিং চিদ্বিভূতীরিবেশঃ
শ্রয়তি ন পদমাসাং কঃ সখীনাং রসজ্ঞঃ ॥ ২০৬ ॥

vibhur api sukha-rūpaḥ sva-prakāśo 'pi bhāvaḥ
kṣaṇam api na hi rādhā-kṛṣṇayor yā ṛte svāḥ
pravahati rasa-puṣṭiṁ cid-vibhūtīr iveśaḥ
śrayati na padam āsāṁ kaḥ sakhīnāṁ rasa-jñaḥ

vibhuḥ—all-powerful; *api*—although; *sukha-rūpaḥ*—happiness personified; *sva-prakāśaḥ*—self-effulgent; *api*—although; *bhāvaḥ*—the completely spiritual activities; *kṣaṇam api*—even for a moment; *na*—never; *hi*—certainly; *rādhā-kṛṣṇayoḥ*—of Śrī Rādhā and Kṛṣṇa; *yāḥ*—whom; *ṛte*—without; *svāḥ*—His own entourage (the *gopīs*); *pravahati*—leads to; *rasa-puṣṭim*—completion of the highest humor; *cit-vibhūtīḥ*—spiritual potencies; *iva*—like; *īśaḥ*—the Supreme Personality of Godhead; *śrayati*—takes shelter of; *na*—not; *padam*—the position; *āsām*—of them; *kaḥ*—who; *sakhīnām*—of the personal associates; *rasa-jñaḥ*—one who is conversant with the science of mellows.

TRANSLATION

"'The pastimes of Śrī Rādhā and Kṛṣṇa are self-effulgent. They are happiness personified, unlimited and all-powerful. Even so, the spiritual humors of such pastimes are never complete without the gopīs, the Lord's personal friends. The Supreme Personality of Godhead is never complete without His spiritual potencies; therefore unless one takes shelter of the gopīs, one cannot enter into the company of Rādhā and Kṛṣṇa. Who can be interested in Their spiritual pastimes without taking their shelter?'

PURPORT

This is a quotation from the *Govinda-līlāmṛta* (10.17).

TEXT 207

সখীর স্বভাব এক অকথ্য-কথন ।
কৃষ্ণ-সহ নিজলীলায় নাহি সখীর মন ॥ ২০৭ ॥

sakhīra svabhāva eka akathya-kathana
kṛṣṇa-saha nija-līlāya nāhi sakhīra mana

sakhīra—of the *gopīs; svabhāva*—natural inclination; *eka*—one; *akathya*—inexplicable; *kathana*—narration; *kṛṣṇa-saha*—with Kṛṣṇa; *nija-līlāya*—in His personal pastimes; *nāhi*—not; *sakhīra*—of the *gopīs; mana*—the mind.

TRANSLATION

"There is an inexplicable fact about the natural inclinations of the gopīs. The gopīs never want to enjoy themselves with Kṛṣṇa personally.

TEXT 208

কৃষ্ণসহ রাধিকার লীলা যে করায়।
নিজ-সুখ হৈতে তাতে কোটি সুখ পায় ॥ ২০৮ ॥

kṛṣṇa saha rādhikāra līlā ye karāya
nija-sukha haite tāte koṭi sukha pāya

kṛṣṇa saha—with Kṛṣṇa; *rādhikāra*—of Śrīmatī Rādhārāṇī; *līlā*—the pastimes; *ye*—which; *karāya*—they bring about; *nija-sukha*—personal happiness; *haite*—than; *tāte*—in that; *koṭi*—ten million times; *sukha*—the happiness; *pāya*—they derive.

TRANSLATION

"The happiness of the gopīs increases ten million times when they serve to engage Śrī Śrī Rādhā and Kṛṣṇa in Their transcendental pastimes.

TEXT 209

রাধার স্বরূপ — কৃষ্ণপ্রেম-কল্পলতা।
সখীগণ হয় তার পল্লব-পুষ্প-পাতা ॥ ২০৯ ॥

rādhāra svarūpa—kṛṣṇa-prema-kalpalatā
sakhī-gaṇa haya tāra pallava-puṣpa-pātā

rādhāra svarūpa—the spiritual nature of Śrīmatī Rādhārāṇī; *kṛṣṇa-prema*—of love of Kṛṣṇa; *kalpa-latā*—a creeper; *sakhī-gaṇa*—the *gopīs*; *haya*—are; *tāra*—of that creeper; *pallava*—the twigs; *puṣpa*—flowers; *pātā*—and leaves.

TRANSLATION

"By nature, Śrīmatī Rādhārāṇī is just like a creeper of love of Godhead, and the gopīs are the twigs, flowers and leaves of that creeper.

TEXT 210

কৃষ্ণলীলামৃত যদি লতাকে সিঞ্চয় ।
নিজ-সুখ হৈতে পল্লবাদ্যের কোটি-সুখ হয় ॥ ২১০ ॥

kṛṣṇa-līlāmṛta yadi latāke siñcaya
nija-sukha haite pallavādyera koṭi-sukha haya

kṛṣṇa-līlāmṛta—the nectar of Kṛṣṇa's pastimes; *yadi*—if; *latāke*—the creeper; *siñcaya*—sprinkles; *nija-sukha haite*—than personal happiness; *pallava-ādyera*—of the twigs, flowers and leaves; *koṭi*—ten million times; *sukha*—the happiness; *haya*—there is.

TRANSLATION

"When the nectar of Kṛṣṇa's pastimes is sprinkled on that creeper, the happiness derived by the twigs, flowers and leaves is ten million times greater than that derived by the creeper itself.

PURPORT

In his *Amṛta-pravāha-bhāṣya,* Śrīla Bhaktivinoda Ṭhākura states, "Śrīmatī Rādhārāṇī is the creeper of love of Godhead, and the *gopīs* are exactly like twigs, flowers and leaves. When water is sprinkled on the creeper, the twigs, flowers and leaves indirectly receive all the benefits of the creeper itself. But water sprinkled directly on the twigs, leaves and flowers is not as effective as water sprinkled on the creeper's root. The *gopīs* are not as pleased when they directly mix with Kṛṣṇa as when they serve to unite Śrīmatī Rādhārāṇī with Kṛṣṇa. Their transcendental pleasure lies in uniting Them."

TEXT 211

সখ্যঃ শ্রীরাধিকায়া ব্রজকুমুদবিধোর্হ্লাদিনী-নামশক্তেঃ
সারাংশ-প্রেমবল্ল্যাঃ কিসলয়দলপুষ্পাদিতুল্যাঃ স্বতুল্যাঃ।
সিক্তায়াং কৃষ্ণলীলামৃতরসনিচয়ৈরুল্লসন্ত্যামমুষ্যাং
জাতোল্লাসাঃ স্বসেকাচ্ছতগুণমধিকং সন্তি যত্তন্ন চিত্রম্ ॥ ২১১ ॥

sakhyaḥ śrī-rādhikāyā vraja-kumuda-vidhor hlādinī-nāma-śakteḥ
sārāṁśa-prema-vallyāḥ kisalaya-dala-puṣpādi-tulyāḥ sva-tulyāḥ
siktāyāṁ kṛṣṇa-līlāmṛta-rasa-nicayair ullasantyām amuṣyāṁ
jātollāsāḥ sva-sekāc chata-guṇam adhikaṁ santi yat tan na citram

sakhyaḥ—friends like Lalitā and Viśākhā; *śrī-rādhikāyāḥ*—of Śrīmatī Rādhārāṇī; *vraja-kumuda*—of the lotuslike inhabitants of Vrajabhūmi; *vidhoḥ*—of the moon (Kṛṣṇa); *hlādinī*—pleasure-giving; *nāma*—of the name; *śakteḥ*—of the potency; *sāra-aṁśa*—the active principle; *prema-vallyāḥ*—of the creeper of love of Godhead; *kisalaya*—newly grown; *dala*—leaves; *puṣpa*—flowers; *ādi*—and so on; *tulyāḥ*—equal to; *sva-tulyāḥ*—equal to Herself; *siktāyām*—when sprinkled; *kṛṣṇa-līlā*—of the pastimes of Kṛṣṇa; *amṛta*—of the nectar; *rasa-nicayaiḥ*—by drops of the juice; *ullasantyām*—shining; *amuṣyām*—of Her, Śrīmatī Rādhārāṇī; *jāta-ullāsāḥ*—having awakened pleasure; *sva-sekāt*—than their own sprinkling; *śata-guṇam*—a hundred times; *adhikam*—more; *santi*—are; *yat*—which; *tat*—that; *na*—not; *citram*—wonderful.

TRANSLATION

"'All the gopīs, the personal friends of Śrīmatī Rādhārāṇī, are equal to Her. Kṛṣṇa is pleasing to the inhabitants of Vrajabhūmi, just as the moon is pleasing to the lotus flower. His pleasure-giving potency is known as āhlādinī, of which the active principle is Śrīmatī Rādhārāṇī. She is compared to a creeper with newly grown flowers and leaves. When the nectar of Kṛṣṇa's pastimes is sprinkled on Śrīmatī Rādhārāṇī, all Her friends, the gopīs, immediately appreciate the pleasure a hundred times more than if they were sprinkled themselves. Actually this is not at all wonderful.'

PURPORT

This verse is also from the *Govinda-līlāmṛta* (10.16).

TEXT 212

যদ্যপি সখীর কৃষ্ণ-সঙ্গমে নাহি মন ।
তথাপি রাধিকা যত্নে করান সঙ্গম ॥ ২১২ ॥

yadyapi sakhīra kṛṣṇa-saṅgame nāhi mana
tathāpi rādhikā yatne karāna saṅgama

yadyapi—although; *sakhīra*—of the *gopīs; kṛṣṇa-saṅgame*—directly enjoying with Kṛṣṇa; *nāhi*—not; *mana*—the mind; *tathāpi*—still; *rādhikā*—Śrīmatī Rādhārāṇī; *yatne*—with great endeavor; *karāna*—causes; *saṅgama*—association with Kṛṣṇa.

TRANSLATION

"Although the gopīs, Śrīmatī Rādhārāṇī's friends, do not desire to enjoy themselves directly with Kṛṣṇa, Śrīmatī Rādhārāṇī makes a great endeavor to induce Kṛṣṇa to enjoy Himself with the gopīs.

TEXT 213

নানা-চ্ছলে কৃষ্ণে প্রেরি' সঙ্গম করায় ।
আত্মকৃষ্ণ-সঙ্গ হৈতে কোটি-সুখ পায় ॥ ২১৩ ॥

nānā-cchale kṛṣṇe preri' saṅgama karāya
ātma-kṛṣṇa-saṅga haite koṭi-sukha pāya

nānā-chale—under different pleas; *kṛṣṇe*—unto Kṛṣṇa; *preri'*—sending; *saṅgama*—direct association; *karāya*—induces; *ātma-kṛṣṇa-saṅga*—personal association with Kṛṣṇa; *haite*—than; *koṭi-sukha*—ten million times more happiness; *pāya*—She gets.

TRANSLATION

"Presenting various pleas for the gopīs, Śrīmatī Rādhārāṇī sometimes sends the gopīs to Kṛṣṇa just to enable them to associate with Him directly. At such times, She enjoys a happiness ten million times greater than that enjoyed through direct association.

TEXT 214

অন্যোন্যে বিশুদ্ধ প্রেমে করে রস পুষ্ট।
তাঁ-সবার প্রেম দেখি' কৃষ্ণ হয় তুষ্ট॥ ২১৪॥

anyonye viśuddha preme kare rasa puṣṭa
tāṅ-sabāra prema dekhi' kṛṣṇa haya tuṣṭa

anyonye—by one another; *viśuddha*—transcendental; *preme*—in love of Godhead; *kare*—makes; *rasa*—the mellow; *puṣṭa*—nourished; *tāṅ-sabāra*—of all of them; *prema*—the love of Godhead; *dekhi'*—seeing; *kṛṣṇa*—Lord Kṛṣṇa; *haya*—becomes; *tuṣṭa*—satisfied.

TRANSLATION

"The transcendental mellow is nourished by that mutual behavior in transcendental love of Godhead. When Lord Kṛṣṇa sees how the gopīs have developed pure love for Him, He becomes very satisfied.

PURPORT

Śrīmatī Rādhārāṇī and the *gopīs* are not interested in their personal happiness derived from association with Kṛṣṇa. Rather, they become happy by seeing one another associate with Kṛṣṇa. In this way their dealings are further nourished by love of Godhead, and seeing this, Kṛṣṇa is very pleased.

TEXT 215

সহজ গোপীর প্রেম,—নহে প্রাকৃত কাম।
কামক্রীড়া-সাম্যে তার কহি 'কাম'-নাম॥ ২১৫॥

sahaja gopīra prema,—nahe prākṛta kāma
kāma-krīḍā-sāmye tāra kahi 'kāma'-nāma

sahaja—natural; *gopīra*—of the *gopīs; prema*—love of Godhead; *nahe*—is not; *prākṛta*—material; *kāma*—lust; *kāma-krīḍā*—lusty affairs; *sāmye*—in appearing equal to; *tāra*—of such activities; *kahi*—I speak; *kāma-nāma*—the name "lust."

TRANSLATION

"It is to be noted that the natural characteristic of the gopīs is to love the Supreme Lord. Their lusty desire is not to be compared to material lust. Nonetheless, because their desire sometimes appears to resemble material lust, their transcendental love for Kṛṣṇa is sometimes described as lust.

PURPORT

Śrīla Bhaktisiddhānta Sarasvatī Ṭhākura says that material lust should never be attributed to Kṛṣṇa, who is full of transcendental knowledge. Material lust cannot be engaged in the service of the Lord, for it is applicable to materialists, not to Kṛṣṇa. Only *prema,* or love of Godhead, is applicable for the satisfaction of Kṛṣṇa. *Prema* is full service rendered unto the Lord. The lusty affairs of the *gopīs* actually constitute the topmost love of Godhead because the *gopīs* never act for their own personal satisfaction. They are simply pleased by engaging other *gopīs* in the service of the Lord. The *gopīs* derive more transcendental pleasure from indirectly engaging other *gopīs* in the service of Kṛṣṇa than from engaging in His service themselves. That is the difference between material lust and love of Godhead. Lust applies to the material world, and love of Godhead applies only to Kṛṣṇa.

TEXT 216

প্রেমৈব গোপরামাণাং কাম ইত্যগমৎ প্রথাম্ ।
ইত্যুদ্ধবাদয়োঽপ্যেতং বাঞ্ছন্তি ভগবৎপ্রিয়াঃ ॥ ২১৬ ॥

premaiva gopa-rāmāṇāṁ
kāma ity agamat prathām
ity uddhavādayo 'py etaṁ
vāñchanti bhagavat-priyāḥ

premā—love of Godhead; *eva*—certainly; *gopa-rāmāṇām*—of all the *gopīs; kāmaḥ*—lust; *iti*—thus; *agamat*—became current; *prathām*—the process; *iti*—thus; *uddhava-ādayaḥ*—all devotees, headed by Uddhava; *api*—certainly; *etam*—this type of behavior; *vāñchanti*—desire; *bhagavat-priyāḥ*—those who are very, very dear to the Supreme Personality of Godhead.

TRANSLATION

"'Although the dealings of the gopīs with Kṛṣṇa are on the platform of pure love of Godhead, such dealings are sometimes considered to be lusty. But because they are completely spiritual, Uddhava and all the other dearmost devotees of the Lord desire to participate in them.'

PURPORT

This is a quotation from the *Bhakti-rasāmṛta-sindhu* (1.2.285).

TEXT 217

নিজেন্দ্রিয়সুখহেতু কামের তাৎপর্য ।
কৃষ্ণসুখ-তাৎপর্য গোপীভাব-বর্য ॥ ২১৭ ॥

nijendriya-sukha-hetu kāmera tātparya
kṛṣṇa-sukha-tātparya gopī-bhāva-varya

nija-indriya—of one's own senses; *sukha*—of the happiness; *hetu*—for the reason; *kāmera*—of lusty desire; *tātparya*—intention; *kṛṣṇa*—of Kṛṣṇa; *sukha*—the happiness; *tātparya*—intention; *gopī-bhāva-varya*—the foremost mood of the *gopīs.*

TRANSLATION

"Lusty desires are experienced when one is concerned with his own personal sense gratification. The mood of the gopīs is not like that. Their only desire is to satisfy the senses of Kṛṣṇa.

TEXT 218

নিজেন্দ্রিয়সুখবাঞ্ছা নাহি গোপিকার ।
কৃষ্ণে সুখ দিতে করে সঙ্গম-বিহার ॥ ২১৮ ॥

nijendriya-sukha-vāñchā nāhi gopikāra
kṛṣṇe sukha dite kare saṅgama-vihāra

nija-indriya-sukha—for personal sense gratification; *vāñchā*—the desire; *nāhi*—there is not; *gopikāra*—of the *gopīs; kṛṣṇe*—unto Kṛṣṇa; *sukha*—happiness; *dite*—to give; *kare*—do; *saṅgama-vihāra*—mingling and enjoying with Kṛṣṇa.

TRANSLATION

"Among the gopīs, there is not a pinch of desire for sense gratification. Their only desire is to give pleasure to Kṛṣṇa, and this is why they mingle with Him and enjoy with Him.

TEXT 219

যত্তে সুজাতচরণাম্বুরুহং স্তনেষু
ভীতাঃ শনৈঃ প্রিয় দধীমহি কর্কশেষু ।
তেনাটবীমটসি তদ্ব্যথতে ন কিংস্বিৎ
কূর্পাদিভির্ভ্রমতি ধীর্ভবদায়ুষাং নঃ ॥ ২১৯ ॥

yat te sujāta-caraṇāmburuhaṁ staneṣu
bhītāḥ śanaiḥ priya dadhīmahi karkaśeṣu
tenāṭavīm aṭasi tad vyathate na kiṁ svit
kūrpādibhir bhramati dhīr bhavad-āyuṣāṁ naḥ

yat—because; *te*—Your; *sujāta*—delicate; *caraṇa-ambu-ruham*—lotus feet; *staneṣu*—on the breasts; *bhītāḥ*—being afraid of; *śanaiḥ*—very carefully; *priya*—O dear one; *dadhīmahi*—we place; *karkaśeṣu*—very rough and hard; *tena*—by such lotus feet; *aṭavīm*—the forest; *aṭasi*—You wander; *tat vyathate*—that are pained; *na*—not; *kim svit*—whether; *kūrpa-ādibhiḥ*—by the small particles of stone; *bhramati*—bewilders; *dhīḥ*—intelligence; *bhavat-āyuṣām*—of persons who consider You as the duration of life; *naḥ*—of us.

TRANSLATION

"[All the gopīs said:] 'Dear Kṛṣṇa, we carefully hold Your delicate lotus feet upon our hard breasts. When You walk in the forest, Your soft lotus feet are pricked by small bits of stone. We fear that this is paining You. Since You are our life and soul, our minds are very much disturbed when Your lotus feet are pained.'

PURPORT

This is a quotation from *Śrīmad-Bhāgavatam* (10.31.19).

TEXT 220

সেই গোপীভাবামৃতে যাঁর লোভ হয়।
বেদধর্মলোক ত্যজি' সে কৃষ্ণে ভজয় ॥ ২২০ ॥

sei gopī-bhāvāmṛte yāṅra lobha haya
veda-dharma-loka tyaji' se kṛṣṇe bhajaya

sei—that; *gopī*—of the *gopīs; bhāva-amṛte*—in the nectar of the ecstasy; *yāṅra*—whose; *lobha*—attachment; *haya*—is; *veda-dharma*—religious principles of the Vedas; *loka*—popular opinion; *tyaji'*—giving up; *se*—he; *kṛṣṇe*—unto Kṛṣṇa; *bhajaya*—renders loving service.

TRANSLATION

"One who is attracted by that ecstatic love of the gopīs does not care about popular opinion or the regulative principles of Vedic life. Rather, he completely surrenders unto Kṛṣṇa and renders service unto Him.

TEXT 221

রাগানুগ-মার্গে তাঁরে ভজে যেই জন।
সেইজন পায় ব্রজে ব্রজেন্দ্রনন্দন ॥ ২২১ ॥

rāgānuga-mārge tāṅre bhaje yei jana
sei-jana pāya vraje vrajendra-nandana

rāga-anuga—of spontaneous attachment; *mārge*—on the path; *tāṅre*—Kṛṣṇa; *bhaje*—worships; *yei*—who; *jana*—a person; *sei-jana*—that person; *pāya*—gets; *vraje*—in Vṛndāvana; *vrajendra-nandana*—the son of Mahārāja Nanda.

TRANSLATION

"If one worships the Lord on the path of spontaneous love and goes to Vṛndāvana, he receives the shelter of Vrajendra-nandana, the son of Nanda Mahārāja.

PURPORT

In all, there are sixty-four items listed for the rendering of service unto Kṛṣṇa, and these are the regulative principles enjoined in the *śāstras* and given by the spiritual master. One has to serve Kṛṣṇa according to these regulative principles, but if one develops spontaneous love for Kṛṣṇa as exhibited in the activities of those who live in Vrajabhūmi, one attains the platform of *rāgānuga-bhakti.* One who has developed this spontaneous love is eligible for elevation to the platform enjoyed by the inhabitants of Vrajabhūmi. In Vrajabhūmi, there are no regulative principles set forth for Kṛṣṇa's service. Rather, everything is carried out in spontaneous, natural love for Kṛṣṇa. There is no question of following the principles of the Vedic system. Such principles are followed within this material world, and as long as one is on the material platform, he has to execute them. However, spontaneous love of Kṛṣṇa is transcendental. It may seem that the regulative principles are being violated, but the devotee is on the transcendental platform. Such service is called *guṇātīta,* or *nirguṇa,* for it is not contaminated by the three modes of material nature.

TEXT 222

ব্রজলোকের কোন ভাব লঞা যেই ভজে।
ভাবযোগ্য দেহ পাঞা কৃষ্ণ পায় ব্রজে॥ ২২২॥

vraja-lokera kona bhāva lañā yei bhaje
bhāva-yogya deha pāñā kṛṣṇa pāya vraje

vraja-lokera—of the planet known as Goloka Vṛndāvana; *kona*—some; *bhāva*—mood; *lañā*—accepting; *yei*—anyone who; *bhaje*—executes devotional service; *bhāva-yogya*—suitable for that spiritual attraction; *deha*—a body; *pāñā*—getting; *kṛṣṇa*—Lord Kṛṣṇa; *pāya*—gets; *vraje*—in Vṛndāvana.

TRANSLATION

"In his liberated stage the devotee is attracted by one of the five humors in the transcendental loving service of the Lord. As he continues to serve the Lord in that transcendental mood, he attains a spiritual body to serve Kṛṣṇa in Goloka Vṛndāvana.

TEXT 223

তাহাতে দৃষ্টান্ত — উপনিষদ্ শ্রুতিগণ ।
রাগমার্গে ভজি' পাইল ব্রজেন্দ্রনন্দন ॥ ২২৩ ॥

tāhāte dṛṣṭānta — upaniṣad śruti-gaṇa
rāga-mārge bhaji' pāila vrajendra-nandana

tāhāte — in this matter; *dṛṣṭānta* — the example; *upaniṣad śruti-gaṇa* — the great sages known as the personified *Upaniṣads* or *śrutis;* *rāga-mārge* — on the path of spontaneous love; *bhaji'* — worshiping; *pāila* — obtained; *vrajendra-nandana* — the lotus feet of Lord Kṛṣṇa.

TRANSLATION

"Those saintly persons who represent the Upaniṣads are vivid examples of this. By worshiping the Lord on the path of spontaneous love, they attained the lotus feet of Vrajendra-nandana, the son of Nanda Mahārāja.

PURPORT

In the Goloka Vṛndāvana planet, Kṛṣṇa's servants are headed by Raktaka and Patraka. Kṛṣṇa's friends are headed by Śrīdāmā, Subala and others. There are also elderly *gopīs* and the cowherd men, headed by Nanda Mahārāja, mother Yaśodā and others. All of these personalities are eternally engaged in the loving service of the Lord in accordance with their specific attachments for Kṛṣṇa. One who wants to return home to serve the Lord directly may be attracted to Kṛṣṇa as a servant, friend, father or mother. If a person continuously serves Kṛṣṇa during this life in a particular ecstasy, upon giving up the material body he attains a suitable spiritual body to serve Kṛṣṇa in terms of his particular attachment. One may serve as a servant, friend, father or mother. In the same way, one who wants to serve Kṛṣṇa in conjugal love can attain a body under the guidance of the *gopīs.* In this connection, the most vivid example is provided by those saintly personalities known as the *śrutis,* who represent the *Upaniṣads.* The *śrutis* understood that without serving Kṛṣṇa and following in the footsteps of the *gopīs* there would be no possibility of their entering the kingdom of God and serving Kṛṣṇa in the mood of conjugal love. Therefore they engaged in spontaneous loving service unto Kṛṣṇa and followed in the footsteps of the *gopīs.*

TEXT 224

নিভৃতমরুন্মনোঽক্ষদৃঢ়যোগযুজো হৃদি য-
ন্মুনয় উপাসতে তদরয়োঽপি যযুঃ স্মরণাৎ ।
স্ত্রিয় উরগেন্দ্রভোগভুজদণ্ডবিষক্ত-ধিয়ো
বয়মপি তে সমাঃ সমদৃশোঽঙ্ঘ্রিসরোজসুধাঃ ॥ ২২৪ ॥

nibhṛta-marun-mano 'kṣa-dṛḍha-yoga-yujo hṛdi yan
munaya upāsate tad arayo 'pi yayuḥ smaraṇāt
striya uragendra-bhoga-bhuja-daṇḍa-viṣakta-dhiyo
vayam api te samāḥ sama-dṛśo 'ṅghri-saroja-sudhāḥ

nibhṛta—controlled; *marut*—the life air; *manaḥ*—the mind; *akṣa*—senses; *dṛḍha*—strong; *yoga*—in the mystic *yoga* process; *yujaḥ*—who are engaged; *hṛdi*—within the heart; *yat*—who; *munayaḥ*—the great sages; *upāsate*—worship; *tat*—that; *arayaḥ*—the enemies; *api*—also; *yayuḥ*—obtain; *smaraṇāt*—from remembering; *striyaḥ*—the *gopīs; uraga-indra*—of serpents; *bhoga*—like the bodies; *bhuja*—the arms; *daṇḍa*—like rods; *viṣakta*—fastened to; *dhiyaḥ*—whose minds; *vayam api*—we also; *te*—Your; *samāḥ*—equal to them; *sama-dṛśaḥ*—having the same ecstatic emotions; *aṅghri-saroja*—of the lotus feet; *sudhāḥ*—the nectar.

TRANSLATION

"'Great sages conquer the mind and senses by practicing the mystic yoga system and controlling the breath. Thus engaging in mystic yoga, they see the Supersoul within their hearts and ultimately enter into impersonal Brahman. But even the enemies of the Supreme Personality of Godhead attain that position simply by thinking of the Supreme Lord. However, the damsels of Vraja, the gopīs, being attracted by the beauty of Kṛṣṇa, simply wanted to embrace Him and His arms, which are like serpents. Thus the gopīs ultimately tasted the

nectar of the lotus feet of the Lord. Similarly, we Upaniṣads can also taste the nectar of His lotus feet by following in the footsteps of the gopīs.'"

PURPORT

This is a quotation from *Śrīmad-Bhāgavatam* (10.87.23) spoken by the *śrutis,* the personified *Vedas.*

TEXT 225

'সমদৃশঃ'-শব্দে কহে 'সেই ভাবে অনুগতি'।
'সমাঃ'-শব্দে কহে শ্রুতির গোপীদেহ-প্রাপ্তি ॥ ২২৫ ॥

'sama-dṛśaḥ'-śabde kahe 'sei bhāve anugati'
'samāḥ'-śabde kahe śrutira gopī-deha-prāpti

sama-dṛśaḥ śabde—by the word *sama-dṛśaḥ; kahe*—it says; *sei*—that; *bhāve*—in the emotion; *anugati*—following; *samāḥ śabde*—by the word *samāḥ; kahe*—it says; *śrutira*—of the persons known as the *śrutis; gopī-deha*—the bodies of *gopīs; prāpti*—attainment.

TRANSLATION

"The word 'sama-dṛśaḥ,' mentioned in the fourth line of the previous verse, means 'following the mood of the gopīs.' The word 'samāḥ' means 'the śrutis' attaining a body like those of the gopīs.'

TEXT 226

'অঙ্ঘ্রি পদ্মসুধা'য় কহে 'কৃষ্ণসঙ্গানন্দ'।
বিধিমার্গে না পাইয়ে ব্রজে কৃষ্ণচন্দ্র ॥ ২২৬ ॥

'aṅghri-padma-sudhā'ya kahe 'kṛṣṇa-saṅgānanda'
vidhi-mārge nā pāiye vraje kṛṣṇa-candra

aṅghri-padma-sudhāya—by the nectar derived from the lotus feet of Kṛṣṇa; *kahe*—it says; *kṛṣṇa-saṅga-ānanda*—transcendental bliss by the association of Kṛṣṇa; *vidhi-mārge*—on the path of regulative principles; *nā pāiye*—one does not get; *vraje*—in Goloka Vṛndāvana; *kṛṣṇa-candra*—Lord Kṛṣṇa.

TRANSLATION

"The word 'aṅghri-padma-sudhā' means 'associating intimately with Kṛṣṇa.' One can attain such perfection only by spontaneous love of God. One cannot obtain Kṛṣṇa in Goloka Vṛndāvana simply by serving the Lord according to regulative principles.

TEXT 227

নায়ং সুখাপো ভগবান্ দেহিনাং গোপিকাসুতঃ।
জ্ঞানিনাঞ্চাত্মভূতানাং যথা ভক্তিমতামিহ ॥ ২২৭ ॥

nāyaṁ sukhāpo bhagavān
dehināṁ gopikā-sutaḥ
jñānināṁ cātma-bhūtānāṁ
yathā bhakti-matām iha

na—not; *ayam*—this Lord Śrī Kṛṣṇa; *sukha-āpaḥ*—easily available; *bhagavān*—the Supreme Personality of Godhead; *dehinām*—for materialistic persons who have accepted the body as the self; *gopikā-sutaḥ*—the son of mother Yaśodā; *jñāninām*—for persons addicted to mental speculation; *ca*—and; *ātma-bhūtānām*—for persons performing severe austerities and penances; *yathā*—as; *bhakti-matām*—for persons engaged in spontaneous devotional service; *iha*—in this world.

TRANSLATION

"'The Supreme Personality of Godhead, Kṛṣṇa, the son of mother Yaśodā, is accessible to those devotees engaged in spontaneous loving service, but He is not as easily accessible to mental speculators, to those striving for self-realization by severe austerities and penances, or to those who consider the body the same as the self.'

PURPORT

This verse from *Śrīmad-Bhāgavatam* (10.9.21) is spoken by Śrīla Śukadeva Gosvāmī. It appears within a passage in which he glorifies mother Yaśodā and other devotees of Kṛṣṇa by describing how they can subjugate Him with their love.

TEXT 228

অতএব গোপীভাব করি অঙ্গীকার।
রাত্রি-দিন চিন্তে রাধাকৃষ্ণের বিহার ॥ ২২৮ ॥

ataeva gopī-bhāva kari aṅgīkāra
rātri-dina cinte rādhā-kṛṣṇera vihāra

ataeva—therefore; *gopī-bhāva*—the loving mood of the *gopīs; kari*—making; *aṅgīkāra*—acceptance; *rātri-dina*—day and night; *cinte*—one thinks; *rādhā-kṛṣṇera*—of Rādhā and Kṛṣṇa; *vihāra*—the pastimes.

TRANSLATION

"Therefore one should accept the mood of the gopīs in their service. In such a transcendental mood, one should always think of the pastimes of Śrī Rādhā and Kṛṣṇa.

TEXT 229

সিদ্ধদেহে চিন্তি' করে তাহাঁঞি সেবন।
সখীভাবে পায় রাধাকৃষ্ণের চরণ ॥ ২২৯ ॥

siddha-dehe cinti' kare tāhāṅñi sevana
sakhī-bhāve pāya rādhā-kṛṣṇera caraṇa

siddha-dehe—in the perfected stage; *cinti'*—by remembering; *kare*—does; *tāhāṅñi*—in the spiritual world; *sevana*—service; *sakhī-bhāve*—in mood of the *gopīs; pāya*—gets; *rādhā-kṛṣṇera*—of Rādhā and Kṛṣṇa; *caraṇa*—the lotus feet.

TRANSLATION

"After thinking of Rādhā and Kṛṣṇa and Their pastimes for a long time and after getting completely free from material contamination, one is transferred to the spiritual world. There the devotee attains an opportunity to serve Rādhā and Kṛṣṇa as one of the gopīs.

PURPORT

Śrīla Bhaktisiddhānta Sarasvatī Ṭhākura comments that the word *siddha-deha,* "perfected spiritual body," refers to a body beyond the material gross body composed of five elements and the subtle astral body composed of mind, intelligence and false ego. In other words, one attains a completely spiritual body fit to render service to the transcendental couple Rādhā and Kṛṣṇa: *sarvopādhi-vinirmuktaṁ tat-paratvena nirmalam.*

When one is situated in his spiritual body, which is beyond this gross and subtle material body, he is fit to serve Rādhā and Kṛṣṇa. That body is called *siddha-deha.* The living entity attains a particular type of gross body in accordance with his past activities and mental condition. In this life the mental condition changes in different ways, and the same living entity gets another body in the next life according to his desires. The mind, intelligence and false ego are always engaged in an attempt to dominate material nature. According to that subtle astral body, one attains a gross body to enjoy the objects of one's desires. According to the activities of the present body, one prepares another subtle body. And according to the subtle body, one attains another gross body. This is the process of material existence. However, when one is spiritually situated and does not desire a gross or subtle body, he attains his original spiritual body. As confirmed by the *Bhagavad-gītā* (4.9): *tyaktvā dehaṁ punar janma naiti mām eti so 'rjuna.*

One is elevated to the spiritual world by the spiritual body and is situated either in Goloka Vṛndāvana or in another Vaikuṇṭha planet. In the spiritual body there are no longer material desires, and one is fully satisfied by rendering service to the Supreme Personality of Godhead, Rādhā and Kṛṣṇa. This is the platform of *bhakti* (*hṛṣīkeṇa hṛṣīkeśa-sevanaṁ bhaktir ucyate*). When the spiritual body, mind and senses are completely purified, one can render service to the Supreme Personality of Godhead and His consort. In Vaikuṇṭha the consort is Lakṣmī, and in Goloka Vṛndāvana the consort is Śrīmatī Rādhārāṇī. In the spiritual body, free from material contamination, one can serve Rādhā-Kṛṣṇa and Lakṣmī-Nārāyaṇa. When one is thus spiritually situated, he no longer thinks of his own personal sense gratification. This spiritual body is called *siddha-deha,* the body by which one can render transcendental service unto Rādhā and Kṛṣṇa. The process is that of engaging the transcendental senses in loving devotional service. This verse specifically mentions, *sakhī-bhāve pāya rādhā-kṛṣṇera caraṇa:* only transcendentally elevated persons in the mood of the *gopīs* can engage in the service of the lotus feet of Rādhā and Kṛṣṇa.

TEXT 230

গোপী-আনুগত্য বিনা ঐশ্বর্যজ্ঞানে ।
ভজিলেহ নাহি পায় ব্রজেন্দ্রনন্দনে ॥ ২৩০ ॥

gopī-ānugatya vinā aiśvarya-jñāne
bhajileha nāhi pāya vrajendra-nandane

gopī-ānugatya—subservience to the *gopīs; vinā*—without; *aiśvarya-jñāne*—in the knowledge of opulence; *bhajileha*—if serving the Supreme Lord; *nāhi*—not; *pāya*—gets; *vrajendra-nandane*—the son of Mahārāja Nanda, Kṛṣṇa.

TRANSLATION

"Unless one follows in the footsteps of the gopīs, he cannot attain the service of the lotus feet of Kṛṣṇa, the son of Nanda Mahārāja. If one is overcome by knowledge of the Lord's opulence, he cannot attain the Lord's lotus feet, even though he is engaged in devotional service.

PURPORT

One can worship Lakṣmī-Nārāyaṇa by the process of *vidhi-mārga,* worshiping the Lord with regulative principles according to the instructions of the *śāstra* and the spiritual master. But the Supreme Personality of Godhead, Rādhā-Kṛṣṇa, cannot be directly worshiped by this process. The dealings between Rādhā and Kṛṣṇa and the *gopīs* are devoid of the opulences of Lakṣmī-Nārāyaṇa. The process of *vidhi-mārga,* following the regulative principles, is utilized in the worship of Lakṣmī-Nārāyaṇa, whereas the process of spontaneous service—following in the footsteps of the *gopīs,* who are the denizens of Vṛndāvana—is transcendentally more advanced and is the process whereby Rādhā and Kṛṣṇa are worshiped. One cannot attain this elevated position while worshiping the Lord in His opulence. Those attracted by the conjugal love between Rādhā and Kṛṣṇa must follow in the footsteps of the *gopīs.* Only then is it possible to enter into the Lord's service in Goloka Vṛndāvana and directly associate with Rādhā and Kṛṣṇa.

TEXT 231

তাহাতে দৃষ্টান্ত — লক্ষ্মী করিল ভজন ।
তথাপি না পাইল ব্রজে ব্রজেন্দ্রনন্দন ॥ ২৩১ ॥

tāhāte dṛṣṭānta — lakṣmī karila bhajana
tathāpi nā pāila vraje vrajendra-nandana

tāhāte — in that; *dṛṣṭānta* — the evidence; *lakṣmī* — the goddess of fortune; *karila* — did; *bhajana* — worship; *tathāpi* — still; *nā* — not; *pāila* — got; *vraje* — in Vṛndāvana; *vrajendra-nandana* — the son of Mahārāja Nanda, Kṛṣṇa.

TRANSLATION

"The unspoken example in this connection is the goddess of fortune, who worshiped Lord Kṛṣṇa in order to attain His pastimes in Vṛndāvana. But due to her opulent life-style, she could not attain the service of Kṛṣṇa in Vṛndāvana.

TEXT 232

নায়ং শ্রিয়োঽঙ্গ উ নিতান্তরতেঃ প্রসাদঃ
স্বর্যোষিতাং নলিনগন্ধরুচাং কুতোঽন্যাঃ ।
রাসোৎসবেঽস্য ভুজদণ্ডগৃহীতকণ্ঠ-
লব্ধাশিষাং য উদগাদ্ব্রজসুন্দরীণাম্ ॥ ২৩২ ॥

nāyaṁ śriyo 'ṅga u nitānta-rateḥ prasādaḥ
svar-yoṣitāṁ nalina-gandha-rucāṁ kuto 'nyāḥ
rāsotsave 'sya bhuja-daṇḍa-gṛhīta-kaṇṭha-
labdhāśiṣāṁ ya udagād vraja-sundarīṇām

na — not; *ayam* — this; *śriyaḥ* — of the goddess of fortune; *aṅge* — on the chest; *u* — alas; *nitānta-rateḥ* — who is very intimately related; *prasādaḥ* — the favor; *svaḥ* — of the heavenly planets; *yoṣitām* — of women; *nalina* — of the lotus flower; *gandha* — having the fragrance; *rucām* — and bodily luster; *kutaḥ* — much less; *anyāḥ* — others; *rāsa-*

utsave—in the festival of the *rāsa* dance; *asya*—of Lord Śrī Kṛṣṇa; *bhuja-daṇḍa*—by the arms; *gṛhīta*—embraced; *kaṇṭha*—their necks; *labdha-āśiṣām*—who achieved such a blessing; *yaḥ*—which; *udagāt*—became manifest; *vraja-sundarīṇām*—of the beautiful *gopīs,* the transcendental girls of Vrajabhūmi.

TRANSLATION

"'When Lord Śrī Kṛṣṇa was dancing with the gopīs in the rāsa-līlā, the gopīs were embraced around the neck by the Lord's arms. This transcendental favor was never bestowed upon the goddess of fortune or the other consorts in the spiritual world. Nor was such a thing ever imagined by the most beautiful girls in the heavenly planets, girls whose bodily luster and aroma resemble the beauty and fragrance of lotus flowers. And what to speak of worldly women, who may be very, very beautiful according to material estimation?'"

PURPORT

This is a quotation from *Śrīmad-Bhāgavatam* (10.47.60).

TEXT 233

এত শুনি' প্রভু তাঁরে কৈল আলিঙ্গন ।
দুই জনে গলাগলি করেন ক্রন্দন ॥ ২৩৩ ॥

eta śuni' prabhu tāṅre kaila āliṅgana
dui jane galāgali karena krandana

eta śuni'—hearing so much; *prabhu*—Lord Śrī Caitanya Mahāprabhu; *tāṅre*—unto Rāmānanda Rāya; *kaila*—did; *āliṅgana*—embracing; *dui jane*—both of them; *galāgali*—embracing shoulder to shoulder; *karena*—did; *krandana*—crying.

TRANSLATION

After hearing this, Lord Śrī Caitanya Mahāprabhu embraced Rāmānanda Rāya, and both of them, embracing shoulder to shoulder, began to cry.

TEXT 234

এইমত প্রেমাবেশে রাত্রি গোঙাইলা ।
প্রাতঃকালে নিজ-নিজ-কার্যে দুঁহে গেলা ॥ ২৩৪ ॥

ei-mata premāveśe rātri goṅāilā
prātaḥ-kāle nija-nija-kārye duṅhe gelā

ei-mata—in this way; *prema-āveśe*—in ecstatic love of Godhead; *rātri*—the night; *goṅāilā*—passed; *prātaḥ-kāle*—in the morning; *nija-nija-kārye*—to their own respective duties; *duṅhe*—both of them; *gelā*—departed.

TRANSLATION

The entire night was passed in this way, in ecstatic love of Godhead. In the morning they both departed to tend to their respective duties.

TEXT 235

বিদায়-সময়ে প্রভুর চরণে ধরিয়া ।
রামানন্দ রায় কহে বিনতি করিয়া ॥ ২৩৫ ॥

vidāya-samaye prabhura caraṇe dhariyā
rāmānanda rāya kahe vinati kariyā

vidāya-samaye—at the point of departure; *prabhura caraṇe*—the lotus feet of Lord Śrī Caitanya Mahāprabhu; *dhariyā*—capturing; *rāmānanda rāya*—Rāmānanda Rāya; *kahe*—says; *vinati kariyā*—with great humility.

TRANSLATION

Before departing from Śrī Caitanya Mahāprabhu, Rāmānanda Rāya fell to the ground and caught hold of the Lord's lotus feet. He then spoke submissively as follows.

TEXT 236

'মোরে কৃপা করিতে তোমার ইহাঁ আগমন ।
দিন দশ রহি' শোধ মোর দুষ্ট মন ॥ ২৩৬ ॥

'more kṛpā karite tomāra ihāṅ āgamana
dina daśa rahi' śodha mora duṣṭa mana

more—unto me; *kṛpā*—mercy; *karite*—to do; *tomāra*—Your; *ihāṅ*—here; *āgamana*—coming; *dina daśa rahi'*—remaining at least ten days; *śodha*—purify; *mora*—my; *duṣṭa mana*—polluted mind.

TRANSLATION

Śrī Rāmānanda Rāya said, "You have come here just to show me Your causeless mercy. Therefore stay here for at least ten days and purify my polluted mind.

TEXT 237

তোমা বিনা অন্য নাহি জীব উদ্ধারিতে।
তোমা বিনা অন্য নাহি কৃষ্ণপ্রেম দিতে ॥' ২৩৭ ॥

tomā vinā anya nāhi jīva uddhārite
tomā vinā anya nāhi kṛṣṇa-prema dite'

tomā vinā—without You; *anya*—anyone else; *nāhi*—there is not; *jīva*—the living entity; *uddhārite*—to liberate; *tomā vinā*—without You; *anya*—anyone else; *nāhi*—there is not; *kṛṣṇa-prema dite*—to bestow love of Kṛṣṇa.

TRANSLATION

"But for You, there is no one who can deliver all the living entities, for You alone can deliver love of Kṛṣṇa."

TEXT 238

প্রভু কহে,—আইলাঙ শুনি' তোমার গুণ।
কৃষ্ণকথা শুনি, শুদ্ধ করাইতে মন ॥ ২৩৮ ॥

prabhu kahe,—āilāṅa śuni' tomāra guṇa
kṛṣṇa-kathā śuni, śuddha karāite mana

prabhu kahe—the Lord said; *āilāṅa*—I have come; *śuni'*—hearing; *tomāra*—your; *guṇa*—qualities; *kṛṣṇa-kathā*—these topics about

Kṛṣṇa; *śuni*—I hear; *śuddha karāite*—just to make pure; *mana*—the mind.

TRANSLATION

The Lord replied, "Having heard about your good qualities, I have come here. I have come to hear about Kṛṣṇa from you and thus purify My mind.

TEXT 239

যৈছে শুনিলুঁ, তৈছে দেখিলুঁ তোমার মহিমা।
রাধাকৃষ্ণ-প্রেমরস-জ্ঞানের তুমি সীমা ॥ ২৩৯ ॥

yaiche śuniluṅ, taiche dekhiluṅ tomāra mahimā
rādhā-kṛṣṇa-premarasa-jñānera tumi sīmā

yaiche—as much; *śuniluṅ*—as I have heard; *taiche*—that much; *dekhiluṅ*—I have seen; *tomāra mahimā*—your glories; *rādhā-kṛṣṇa-prema-rasa-jñānera*—of transcendental knowledge about the loving affairs of Rādhā and Kṛṣṇa; *tumi*—you; *sīmā*—the ultimate goal.

TRANSLATION

"Now that I have actually seen your glories, what I heard about you is confirmed. As far as the pastimes of Rādhā and Kṛṣṇa in a loving mood are concerned, you are the limit of knowledge."

PURPORT

Śrī Caitanya Mahāprabhu found Rāmānanda Rāya to be the best authority in transcendental knowledge of the loving affairs between Rādhā and Kṛṣṇa. In this verse the Lord actually states that Rāmānanda Rāya was the limit of this knowledge.

TEXT 240

দশ দিনের কা-কথা যাবৎ আমি জীব'।
তাবৎ তোমার সঙ্গ ছাড়িতে নারিব ॥ ২৪০ ॥

daśa dinera kā-kathā yāvat āmi jība'
tāvat tomāra saṅga chāḍite nāriba

daśa dinera—of ten days; *kā-kathā*—what to speak; *yāvat*—as long as; *āmi*—I; *jība'*—shall live; *tāvat*—that long; *tomāra*—of you; *saṅga*—the association; *chāḍite*—to give up; *nāriba*—I shall not be able.

TRANSLATION

Śrī Caitanya Mahāprabhu continued, "To say nothing of ten days, as long as I live I shall find it impossible to give up your company.

TEXT 241

নীলাচলে তুমি-আমি থাকিব এক-সঙ্গে।
সুখে গোঙাইব কাল কৃষ্ণকথা-রঙ্গে ॥ ২৪১ ॥

nīlācale tumi-āmi thākiba eka-saṅge
sukhe goṅāiba kāla kṛṣṇa-kathā-raṅge

nīlācale—in Jagannātha Purī; *tumi*—you; *āmi*—I; *thākiba*—shall stay; *eka-saṅge*—together; *sukhe*—in happiness; *goṅāiba*—will pass; *kāla*—time; *kṛṣṇa-kathā-raṅge*—in the joy of talking about Kṛṣṇa.

TRANSLATION

"You and I shall remain together at Jagannātha Purī. We shall pass our time together in joy, talking about Kṛṣṇa and His pastimes."

TEXT 242

এত বলি' দুঁহে নিজ-নিজ কার্যে গেলা।
সন্ধ্যাকালে রায় পুনঃ আসিয়া মিলিলা ॥ ২৪২ ॥

eta bali' duṅhe nija-nija kārye gelā
sandhyā-kāle rāya punaḥ āsiyā mililā

eta bali'—saying this; *duṅhe*—both of them; *nija-nija*—their own respective; *kārye*—in the duties; *gelā*—departed; *sandhyā-kāle*—in the evening; *rāya*—Rāmānanda Rāya; *punaḥ*—again; *āsiyā*—coming there; *mililā*—met.

TRANSLATION

In this way they both departed to perform their respective duties. Then, in the evening, Rāmānanda Rāya returned to see Lord Caitanya Mahāprabhu.

TEXT 243

অন্যোন্যে মিলি' দুঁহে নিভৃতে বসিয়া।
প্রশ্নোত্তর-গোষ্ঠী কহে আনন্দিত হঞা॥ ২৪৩॥

anyonye mili' duṅhe nibhṛte vasiyā
praśnottara-goṣṭhī kahe ānandita hañā

anyonye—each other; *mili'*—meeting; *duṅhe*—both of them; *nibhṛte*—in a secluded place; *vasiyā*—sitting; *praśna-uttara*—of questions and answers; *goṣṭhī*—a discussion; *kahe*—spoke; *ānandita*—jubilant; *hañā*—becoming.

TRANSLATION

Thus they met time and time again, sitting in a secluded place and jubilantly discussing devotional service by the question-and-answer process.

TEXT 244

প্রভু পুছে, রামানন্দ করেন উত্তর।
এই মত সেই রাত্রে কথা পরস্পর॥ ২৪৪॥

prabhu puche, rāmānanda karena uttara
ei mata sei rātre kathā paraspara

prabhu puche—the Lord inquires; *rāmānanda*—Rāya Rāmānanda; *karena*—gives; *uttara*—answers; *ei mata*—in this way; *sei rātre*—on that night; *kathā*—discussion; *paraspara*—mutual.

TRANSLATION

Śrī Caitanya Mahāprabhu asked the questions, and Śrī Rāmānanda Rāya gave the answers. In this way they were engaged in discussion throughout the night.

TEXT 245

প্রভু কহে, — "কোন্ বিদ্যা বিদ্যা-মধ্যে সার ?"
রায় কহে, — "কৃষ্ণভক্তি বিনা বিদ্যা নাহি আর ॥" ২৪৫ ॥

prabhu kahe, — "kon vidyā vidyā-madhye sāra?"
rāya kahe, — "kṛṣṇa-bhakti vinā vidyā nāhi āra"

prabhu kahe — the Lord inquired; *kon* — what; *vidyā* — knowledge; *vidyā-madhye* — in the midst of knowledge; *sāra* — the most important; *rāya kahe* — Rāmānanda Rāya answered; *kṛṣṇa-bhakti* — devotional service to Kṛṣṇa; *vinā* — except; *vidyā* — education; *nāhi* — there is not; *āra* — any other.

TRANSLATION

On one occasion the Lord inquired, "Of all types of education, which is the most important?"

Rāmānanda Rāya replied, "No education is important other than the transcendental devotional service of Kṛṣṇa."

PURPORT

Texts 245 to 257 are all questions and answers between Śrī Caitanya Mahāprabhu and Rāmānanda Rāya. In these exchanges there is an attempt to show the difference between material and spiritual existence. Education in Kṛṣṇa consciousness is always transcendental and is the best of all forms of education. Material education aims at increasing the activities of material sense gratification. Beyond material sense gratification is another negative form of knowledge called *brahma-vidyā,* or impersonal transcendental knowledge. But beyond that *brahma-vidyā,* or knowledge of the impersonal Brahman, is knowledge of devotional service to the Supreme Lord, Viṣṇu. This knowledge is higher. And higher still is devotional service to Lord Kṛṣṇa, which is the topmost form of education. According to *Śrīmad-Bhāgavatam* (4.29.49), *tat karma hari-toṣaṁ yat sā vidyā tan-matir yayā:* "Work meant for pleasing the Supreme Lord is the best, and education that enhances one's Kṛṣṇa consciousness is the best."

Also, according to *Śrīmad-Bhāgavatam* (7.5.23–24):

śravaṇaṁ kīrtanaṁ viṣṇoḥ smaraṇaṁ pāda-sevanam
arcanaṁ vandanaṁ dāsyaṁ sakhyam ātma-nivedanam
iti puṁsārpitā viṣṇau bhaktiś cen nava-lakṣaṇā
kriyeta bhagavaty addhā tan manye 'dhītam uttamam

This is a statement given by Prahlāda Mahārāja in answer to a question raised by his father. Prahlāda Mahārāja said, "To hear or chant about Lord Viṣṇu, to remember Him, to serve His lotus feet, to worship Him, to offer prayers to Him, to become His servant and His friend, to sacrifice everything for His service—all these are varieties of devotional service. One who is engaged in such activities is understood to be educated to the topmost perfection."

TEXT 246

'কীর্তিগণংমধ্যে জীবের কোন্ বড় কীর্তি ?'
'কৃষ্ণভক্ত বলিয়া যাঁহার হয় খ্যাতি ॥' ২৪৬ ॥

'kīrti-gaṇa-madhye jīvera kon baḍa kīrti?'
'kṛṣṇa-bhakta baliyā yāṅhāra haya khyāti'

kīrti-gaṇa-madhye—among glorious activities; *jīvera*—of the living entity; *kon*—which; *baḍa*—greatest; *kīrti*—glory; *kṛṣṇa-bhakta*—a devotee of Lord Kṛṣṇa; *baliyā*—as; *yāṅhāra*—of whom; *haya*—there is; *khyāti*—the reputation.

TRANSLATION

Śrī Caitanya Mahāprabhu then asked Rāmānanda Rāya, "Out of all glorious activities, which is the most glorious?"

Rāmānanda Rāya replied, "That person who is reputed to be a devotee of Lord Kṛṣṇa enjoys the utmost fame and glory."

PURPORT

The greatest reputation a living being can have is to be a devotee of Kṛṣṇa and to act in Kṛṣṇa consciousness. In the material world everyone is trying to be famous by accumulating a large bank balance or material opulence. There is a steady competition among *karmīs* attempting to advance in a wealthy society. The whole world is turning in accordance with that competitive mood. But this kind of name and fame is temporary, for it lasts only as long as the temporary material body exists. One may become famous as a *brahma-jñānī,* an impersonalist scholar, or one may become a materially opulent person. In either case, such reputations are inferior to the reputation of Kṛṣṇa's devotee. In the *Garuḍa Purāṇa* it is said:

kalau bhāgavataṁ nāma durlabhaṁ naiva labhyate
brahma-rudra-padotkṛṣṭaṁ guruṇā kathitaṁ mama

"In this Age of Kali, the fame of one who is known as a great devotee is very rare. However, such a position is superior to that of the great demigods like Brahmā and Mahādeva. This is the opinion of all spiritual masters."

In the *Itihāsa-samuccaya,* Nārada tells Puṇḍarīka:

janmāntara-sahasreṣu yasya syād buddhir īdṛśī
dāso 'haṁ vāsudevasya sarvāl̐ lokān samuddharet

"After many, many births, when a person realizes that he is the eternal servant of Vāsudeva, he can deliver all the worlds."

In the *Ādi Purāṇa,* in a conversation between Kṛṣṇa and Arjuna, it is said, *bhaktānām anugacchanti muktayaḥ śrutibhiḥ saha:* "The most exalted position of liberation is given by Vedic knowledge. Everyone follows in the footsteps of the devotee." Similarly, in the *Bṛhan-nāradīya Purāṇa* it is further stated, *adyāpi ca muni-śreṣṭhā brahmādyā api devatāḥ:* "Until now, even the great demigods like Brahmā and Lord Śiva did not know the influence of a devotee." The *Garuḍa Purāṇa* similarly states:

brāhmaṇānāṁ sahasrebhyaḥ satra-yājī viśiṣyate
satra-yājī-sahasrebhyaḥ sarva-vedānta-pāragaḥ
sarva-vedānta-vit-koṭyā viṣṇu-bhakto viśiṣyate
vaiṣṇavānāṁ sahasrebhya ekānty eko viśiṣyate

"It is said that out of thousands of *brāhmaṇas,* one is qualified to perform sacrifices, and out of many thousands of such qualified *brāhmaṇas* expert in sacrificial offerings, one learned *brāhmaṇa* may have passed beyond all Vedic knowledge. He is considered the best among all these *brāhmaṇas.* And yet, out of thousands of such *brāhmaṇas* who have surpassed Vedic knowledge, one person may be a *viṣṇu-bhakta,* and he is most famous. Out of many thousands of such Vaiṣṇavas, one who is completely fixed in the service of Lord Kṛṣṇa is most famous. Indeed, a person who is completely devoted to the service of the Lord certainly returns home, back to Godhead."

There is also the following statement in *Śrīmad-Bhāgavatam* (3.13.4):

śrutasya puṁsāṁ sucira-śramasya
nanv añjasā sūribhir īḍito 'rthaḥ
tat-tad-guṇānuśravaṇaṁ mukunda-
pādāravindaṁ hṛdayeṣu yeṣām

"After much hard labor, a person highly learned in Vedic literature certainly becomes very famous. However, one who is always hearing and chanting the glories of the lotus feet of Mukunda within his heart is certainly superior."

In the *Nārāyaṇa-vyūha-stava* it is said:

nāhaṁ brahmāpi bhūyāsaṁ tvad-bhakti-rahito hare
tvayi bhaktas tu kīṭo 'pi bhūyāsaṁ janma-janmasu

"I do not aspire to take birth as a Brahmā if that Brahmā is not a devotee of the Lord. I shall be satisfied simply to take birth as an insect if I am given a chance to remain in the house of a devotee."

There are many similar verses in *Śrīmad-Bhāgavatam,* especially 3.25.38, 4.24.29, 4.31.22, 7.9.24 and 10.14.30.

It was Lord Śiva who said, "I do not know the truth about Kṛṣṇa, but a devotee of Lord Kṛṣṇa knows all the truth. Out of all the devotees of Lord Kṛṣṇa, Prahlāda is the greatest."

Above Prahlāda, the Pāṇḍavas are supposedly more advanced. Above the Pāṇḍavas are the members of the Yadu dynasty, who are even more advanced. In the Yadu dynasty, Uddhava is the furthest advanced, and above Uddhava are the damsels of Vraja-dhāma, the *gopīs* themselves.

In the *Bṛhad-vāmana Purāṇa,* Lord Brahmā tells Bhṛgu:

ṣaṣṭi-varṣa-sahasrāṇi mayā taptaṁ tapaḥ purā
nanda-gopa-vraja-strīṇāṁ pāda-reṇūpalabdhaye

"I underwent meditation and austerities for sixty thousand years just to understand the dust of the lotus feet of the *gopīs.* Still, I could not understand it. To say nothing of me, even Lord Śiva, Lord Śeṣa and the goddess of fortune, Lakṣmī, could not understand it."

In the *Ādi Purāṇa* the Supreme Personality of Godhead Himself says:

na tathā me priyatamo brahmā rudraś ca pārthiva
na ca lakṣmīr na cātmā ca yathā gopī-jano mama

"Lord Brahmā, Lord Śiva, the goddess of fortune and even My own self are not as dear to Me as the *gopīs.*" Of all the *gopīs,* Śrīmatī Rādhārāṇī is the topmost. Rūpa Gosvāmī and Sanātana Gosvāmī are the most exalted servitors of Śrīmatī Rādhārāṇī and Lord Śrī Caitanya Mahāprabhu. Those who adhere to their service are known as *rūpānuga* devotees. The *Caitanya-candrāmṛta* (26) gives the following statement about Śrīla Rūpa Gosvāmī:

āstāṁ vairāgya-koṭir bhavatu śama-dama-kṣānti-maitry-ādi-koṭis
tattvānudhyāna-koṭir bhavatu bhavatu vā vaiṣṇavī bhakti-koṭiḥ
koṭy-aṁśo 'py asya na syāt tad api guṇa-gaṇo yaḥ svataḥ-siddha āste
śrīmac-caitanyacandra-priya-caraṇa-nakha-jyotir āmoda-bhājām

The qualities of one engaged in the service of Lord Śrī Caitanya Mahāprabhu—such as reputation, austerities, penances and knowledge—are not to be compared to the good qualities of others. Such is the perfection of a devotee always engaged in the service of Śrī Caitanya Mahāprabhu.

TEXT 247

'সম্পত্তির মধ্যে জীবের কোন্ সম্পত্তি গণি ?'
'রাধাকৃষ্ণে প্রেম যাঁর, সেই বড় ধনী ॥' ২৪৭ ॥

'sampattira madhye jīvera kon sampatti gaṇi?'
'rādhā-kṛṣṇe prema yāṅra, sei baḍa dhanī'

sampattira—riches; *madhye*—among; *jīvera*—of the living entities; *kon*—what; *sampatti*—the wealth; *gaṇi*—we accept; *rādhā-kṛṣṇe*—to Śrīmatī Rādhārāṇī and Kṛṣṇa; *prema*—loving service; *yāṅra*—whose; *sei*—he; *baḍa*—very great; *dhanī*—capitalist.

TRANSLATION

Śrī Caitanya Mahāprabhu asked, "Of the many capitalists who possess great riches, who is the topmost?"

Rāmānanda Rāya replied, "He who is richest in love for Rādhā and Kṛṣṇa is the greatest capitalist."

PURPORT

Everyone in this material world is attempting to acquire riches to satisfy the senses. Actually no one cares for anything other than acquiring material possessions and maintaining them. The wealthy are generally accepted as the most important personalities in this material world, but when we compare a material man of wealth to one wealthy in devotional service to Rādhā and Kṛṣṇa, the latter is found to be the greatest capitalist. According to *Śrīmad-Bhāgavatam* (10.39.2):

kim alabhyaṁ bhagavati prasanne śrī-niketane
tathāpi tat-parā rājan na hi vāñchanti kiñcana

"What is difficult for the devotees of Lord Kṛṣṇa, who is the shelter of the goddess of fortune? Although such devotees can obtain anything, O King, they do not desire anything."

TEXT 248

'দুঃখ-মধ্যে কোন দুঃখ হয় গুরুতর ?'
'কৃষ্ণভক্ত-বিরহ বিনা দুঃখ নাহি দেখি পর ॥' ২৪৮ ॥

'duḥkha-madhye kona duḥkha haya gurutara?'
'kṛṣṇa-bhakta-viraha vinā duḥkha nāhi dekhi para'

duḥkha-madhye—among the miserable conditions of life; *kona*—what; *duḥkha*—misery; *haya*—is; *gurutara*—more painful; *kṛṣṇa-bhakta-viraha*—separation from the devotee of Lord Kṛṣṇa; *vinā*—besides; *duḥkha*—unhappiness; *nāhi*—there is not; *dekhi*—I see; *para*—other.

TRANSLATION

Śrī Caitanya Mahāprabhu asked, "Of all kinds of distress, what is the most painful?"

Śrī Rāmānanda Rāya replied, "Apart from separation from the devotee of Kṛṣṇa, I know of no unbearable unhappiness."

PURPORT

Concerning this, the Lord states in the Vedic literature:

mām anārādhya duḥkhārtaḥ kuṭumbāsakta-mānasaḥ
sat-saṅga-rahito martyo vṛddha-sevā-paricyutaḥ

"A person who does not worship Me, who is unduly attached to family and who does not stick to devotional service must be considered a most unhappy person. Similarly, one who does not associate with Vaiṣṇavas, or who does not render service to his superior, is also a most unhappy person."

There is also the following statement in the *Bṛhad-bhāgavatāmṛta* (1.5.44):

sva-jīvanādhikaṁ prārthyaṁ śrī-viṣṇu-jana-saṅgataḥ
vicchedena kṣaṇaṁ cātra na sukhāṁśaṁ labhāmahe

"Out of all kinds of desirable things experienced in the life of a living entity, association with the devotees of the Lord is the greatest. When we are separated from a devotee even for a moment, we cannot enjoy happiness."

TEXT 249

'মুক্ত-মধ্যে কোন্ জীব মুক্ত করি' মানি ?'
'কৃষ্ণপ্রেম যাঁর, সেই মুক্ত-শিরোমণি ॥' ২৪৯ ॥

'mukta-madhye kon jīva mukta kari' māni?'
'kṛṣṇa-prema yāṅra, sei mukta-śiromaṇi'

mukta-madhye—among the liberated; *kon*—what; *jīva*—living entity; *mukta*—liberated; *kari'*—considering as; *māni*—We accept; *kṛṣṇa-prema*—one who loves Kṛṣṇa; *yāṅra*—of whom; *sei*—such a person; *mukta-śiromaṇi*—the topmost of all liberated souls.

TRANSLATION

Śrī Caitanya Mahāprabhu then inquired, "Out of all liberated persons, who should be accepted as the greatest?"

Rāmānanda Rāya replied, "He who has love for Kṛṣṇa has attained the topmost liberation."

PURPORT

In *Śrīmad-Bhāgavatam* (6.14.5), it is said:

muktānām api siddhānāṁ nārāyaṇa-parāyaṇaḥ
su-durlabhaḥ praśāntātmā kotiṣv api mahā-mune

"O great sage, of the many millions of liberated persons and of the millions who have attained perfection, he who is a devotee of Lord Nārāyaṇa is very, very rare. Indeed, he is the most perfect and peaceful person."

TEXT 250

'গান-মধ্যে কোন্ গান — জীবের নিজ ধর্ম ?'
'রাধাকৃষ্ণের প্রেমকেলি' — যেই গীতের মর্ম' ॥ ২৫০ ॥

'gāna-madhye kona gāna — jīvera nija dharma?'
'rādhā-kṛṣṇera prema-keli — yei gītera marma'

gāna-madhye — among songs; *kona gāna* — which song; *jīvera* — of the living entity; *nija* — his own; *dharma* — religion; *rādhā-kṛṣṇera prema-keli* — the loving affairs of Rādhā and Kṛṣṇa; *yei* — which; *gītera* — of the song; *marma* — purport.

TRANSLATION

Śrī Caitanya Mahāprabhu next asked Rāmānanda Rāya, "Among many songs, which song is to be considered the actual religion of the living entity?"

Rāmānanda Rāya replied, "That song describing the loving affairs of Śrī Rādhā and Kṛṣṇa is superior to all other songs."

PURPORT

As stated in *Śrīmad-Bhāgavatam* (10.33.36):

anugrahāya bhaktānāṁ mānuṣaṁ deham āsthitaḥ
bhajate tādṛśīḥ krīḍā yāḥ śrutvā tat-paro bhavet

"Lord Kṛṣṇa descends apparently as a human being, and He exhibits His transcendental pastimes in Vṛndāvana so that the conditioned soul may be attracted to hearing His transcendental activities." Nondevotees are strictly prohibited from participating in songs celebrating the loving affairs of Rādhā and Kṛṣṇa. Unless one is a devotee, it is very dangerous to hear the songs about the pastimes of Rādhā and Kṛṣṇa that were written by Jayadeva Gosvāmī, Caṇḍīdāsa and other exalted devotees. Lord Śiva drank an ocean of poison, but one should not imitate this. One must first become a pure devotee of Lord Kṛṣṇa. Only then can one enjoy hearing the songs of Jayadeva and relish transcendental bliss. If one simply imitates the activities of Lord Śiva and drinks poison, one will certainly meet with death.

The talks between Lord Śrī Caitanya Mahāprabhu and Rāmānanda Rāya are meant for advanced devotees only. Those who are on the mundane platform and who study these talks in order to put forward some thesis for a Ph.D. will not be able to understand them. Instead, these conversations will have a poisonous effect.

TEXT 251

'শ্রেয়ো-মধ্যে কোন্ শ্রেয়ঃ জীবের হয় সার ?'
'কৃষ্ণভক্ত-সঙ্গ বিনা শ্রেয়ঃ নাহি আর ৷৷' ২৫১ ৷৷

'śreyo-madhye kona śreyaḥ jīvera haya sāra?'
'kṛṣṇa-bhakta-saṅga vinā śreyaḥ nāhi āra'

śreyaḥ-madhye—among beneficial activities; *kona*—which; *śreyaḥ*—beneficial function; *jīvera*—of the living entity; *haya*—is; *sāra*—the essence; *kṛṣṇa-bhakta-saṅga*—for associating with the devotees of Lord Kṛṣṇa; *vinā*—except; *śreyaḥ*—beneficial activity; *nāhi*—there is not; *āra*—another.

TRANSLATION

Then Śrī Caitanya Mahāprabhu asked, "Out of all auspicious and beneficial activities, which is best for the living entity?"

Rāmānanda Rāya replied, "The only auspicious activity is association with the devotees of Kṛṣṇa."

PURPORT

According to *Śrīmad-Bhāgavatam* (11.2.30):

ata ātyantikaṁ kṣemaṁ pṛcchāmo bhavato 'naghāḥ
saṁsāre 'smin kṣaṇārdho 'pi sat-saṅgaḥ śevadhir nṛṇām

"We are asking you to tell us what is the most perfect welfare activity. I think that in this material world, association with devotees—even if it be for a moment—is the greatest treasure house for mankind."

TEXT 252

'কাঁহার স্মরণ জীব করিবে অনুক্ষণ ?'
'কৃষ্ণ'-নাম-গুণ-লীলা — প্রধান স্মরণ ॥' ২৫২ ॥

'kāṅhāra smaraṇa jīva karibe anukṣaṇa?'
'kṛṣṇa'-nāma-guṇa-līlā—pradhāna smaraṇa'

kāṅhāra—of whom; *smaraṇa*—remembering; *jīva*—the living entity; *karibe*—should do; *anukṣaṇa*—constantly; *kṛṣṇa-nāma*—the holy name of Lord Kṛṣṇa; *guṇa-līlā*—His qualities and pastimes; *pradhāna smaraṇa*—most important remembrance.

TRANSLATION

Śrī Caitanya Mahāprabhu asked, "What should all living entities constantly remember?"

Rāmānanda Rāya replied, "The chief objects of remembrance are always the Lord's holy name, qualities and pastimes."

PURPORT

Śrīmad-Bhāgavatam (2.2.36) states:

tasmāt sarvātmanā rājan hariḥ sarvatra sarvadā
śrotavyaḥ kīrtitavyaś ca smartavyo bhagavān nṛṇām

Śukadeva Gosvāmī concludes, "The business of the living entity is to always remember the Supreme Personality of Godhead in every circumstance. The Lord should be heard about, glorified and remembered by all human beings."

TEXT 253

'ধ্যেয়-মধ্যে জীবের কর্তব্য কোন্ ধ্যান ?'
'রাধাকৃষ্ণপদাম্বুজ-ধ্যান — প্রধান ॥' ২৫৩ ॥

'dhyeya-madhye jīvera kartavya kon dhyāna?'
'rādhā-kṛṣṇa-padāmbuja-dhyāna — pradhāna'

dhyeya-madhye — out of all types of meditation; *jīvera* — of the living entity; *kartavya* — the duty; *kon* — what; *dhyāna* — meditation; *rādhā-kṛṣṇa-pada-ambuja* — on the lotus feet of Rādhā and Kṛṣṇa; *dhyāna* — meditation; *pradhāna* — is the chief.

TRANSLATION

Śrī Caitanya Mahāprabhu further inquired, "Out of many types of meditation, which is required for all living entities?"

Śrīla Rāmānanda Rāya replied, "The chief duty of every living entity is to meditate upon the lotus feet of Rādhā and Kṛṣṇa."

PURPORT

Śrīmad-Bhāgavatam (1.2.14) states:

tasmād ekena manasā bhagavān sātvatāṁ patiḥ
śrotavyaḥ kīrtitavyaś ca dhyeyaḥ pūjyaś ca nityadā

Sūta Gosvāmī replied to the sages headed by Śaunaka, "Everyone should very attentively listen to the pastimes of the Supreme Personality of Godhead. One should glorify His activities and meditate upon Him regularly."

TEXT 254

'সর্ব ত্যজি' জীবের কর্তব্য কাহাঁ বাস ?'
'ব্রজভূমি বৃন্দাবন যাহাঁ লীলারাস ॥' ২৫৪ ॥

'sarva tyaji' jīvera kartavya kāhāṅ vāsa?'
'vraja-bhūmi vṛndāvana yāhāṅ līlā-rāsa'

sarva — everything; *tyaji'* — giving up; *jīvera* — of the living entity; *kartavya* — to be done; *kāhāṅ* — where; *vāsa* — residence; *vraja-bhūmi* — the land known as Vrajabhūmi; *vṛndāvana* — the holy place named Vṛndāvana; *yāhāṅ*—where; *līlā-rāsa*—Lord Kṛṣṇa performed His *rāsa* dance.

TRANSLATION

Śrī Caitanya Mahāprabhu asked, "Where should the living entity live, abandoning all other places?"

Rāmānanda Rāya replied, "He should live in the holy place known as Vṛndāvana or Vrajabhūmi, where the Lord performed His rāsa dance."

PURPORT

According to *Śrīmad-Bhāgavatam* (10.47.61):

āsām aho caraṇa-reṇu-juṣām ahaṁ syāṁ
vṛndāvane kim api gulma-latauṣadhīnām
yā dustyajaṁ sva-janam ārya-pathaṁ ca hitvā
bhejur mukunda-padavīṁ śrutibhir vimṛgyām

Uddhava said, "Let me become one of Vṛndāvana's herbs and plants that are trampled by the *gopīs,* who gave up all connections with family and friends and decided to worship the lotus feet of Mukunda. Those lotus feet are sought by all great saintly persons expert in the study of Vedic literature."

TEXT 255

'শ্রবণমধ্যে জীবের কোন্ শ্রেষ্ঠ শ্রবণ ?'
'রাধাকৃষ্ণ-প্রেমকেলি কর্ণ-রসায়ন ॥' ২৫৫ ॥

'śravaṇa-madhye jīvera kon śreṣṭha śravaṇa?'
'rādhā-kṛṣṇa-prema-keli karṇa-rasāyana'

śravaṇa-madhye—out of all topics for hearing; *jīvera*—of the living entity; *kon*—what; *śreṣṭha*—most important; *śravaṇa*—topic of hearing; *rādhā-kṛṣṇa-prema-keli*—the loving affairs between Rādhā and Kṛṣṇa; *karṇa-rasa-ayana*—most pleasing to the ear.

TRANSLATION

Śrī Caitanya Mahāprabhu asked, "Out of all topics people listen to, which is best for all living entities?"

Rāmānanda Rāya replied, "Hearing about the loving affairs between Rādhā and Kṛṣṇa is most pleasing to the ear."

PURPORT

According to *Śrīmad-Bhāgavatam* (10.33.39):

vikrīḍitaṁ vraja-vadhūbhir idaṁ ca viṣṇoḥ
śraddhānvito 'nuśṛṇuyād atha varṇayed yaḥ
bhaktiṁ parāṁ bhagavati pratilabhya kāmaṁ
hṛd-rogam āśv apahinoty acireṇa dhīraḥ

"He who faithfully hears about the dealings between Lord Kṛṣṇa and the *gopīs* in the *rāsa* dance and he who describes these activities attain to the perfectional stage of devotional service and simultaneously lose material, lusty desires."

A liberated person who hears about the loving affairs of Rādhā and Kṛṣṇa is not inclined to have lusty desires. One mundane rogue once said that when the Vaiṣṇavas chant the name "Rādhā, Rādhā," he simply remembers a barber's wife named Rādhā. This is a practical example. Unless one is liberated, he should not try to hear about the loving affairs between Rādhā and Kṛṣṇa. If one is not liberated and listens to a relation of the *rāsa* dance, he may remember his own mundane activities and illicit connections with some woman whose name may also be Rādhā. In the conditioned stage one should not even try to remember such things. By practicing the regulative principles, one should rise to the platform of spontaneous attraction for Kṛṣṇa. Then and only then should one hear about *rādhā-kṛṣṇa-līlā.* Although these affairs may be very pleasing both to conditioned and to liberated souls, the conditioned soul should not try to hear them. The talks between Rāmānanda Rāya and Śrī Caitanya Mahāprabhu are conducted on the platform of liberation.

TEXT 256

'উপাস্যের মধ্যে কোন্ উপাস্য প্রধান ?'
'শ্রেষ্ঠ উপাস্য — যুগল 'রাধাকৃষ্ণ' নাম ॥' ২৫৬ ॥

'upāsyera madhye kon upāsya pradhāna?'
'śreṣṭha upāsya — yugala 'rādhā-kṛṣṇa' nāma'

upāsyera—objects of worship; *madhye*—among; *kon*—which; *upāsya*—worshipable object; *pradhāna*—the chief; *śreṣṭha*—the chief; *upāsya*—worshipable object; *yugala*—the couple; *rādhā-kṛṣṇa nāma*—the holy name of Rādhā-Kṛṣṇa, or Hare Kṛṣṇa.

TRANSLATION

Śrī Caitanya Mahāprabhu asked, "Among all worshipable objects, which is the chief?"

Rāmānanda Rāya replied, "The chief worshipable object is the holy name of Rādhā and Kṛṣṇa, the Hare Kṛṣṇa mantra."

PURPORT

According to *Śrīmad-Bhāgavatam* (6.3.22):

etāvān eva loke 'smin puṁsāṁ dharmaḥ paraḥ smṛtaḥ
bhakti-yogo bhagavati tan-nāma-grahaṇādibhiḥ

"In this material world the living entity's only business is to accept the path of *bhakti-yoga* and chant the holy name of the Lord."

TEXT 257

'মুক্তি, ভুক্তি বাঞ্ছে যেই, কাহাঁ দুঁহার গতি ?'
'স্থাবরদেহ, দেবদেহ যৈছে অবস্থিতি ॥' ২৫৭ ॥

'mukti, bhukti vāñche yei, kāhāṅ duṅhāra gati?'
'sthāvara-deha, deva-deha yaiche avasthiti'

mukti—liberation; *bhukti*—sense enjoyment; *vāñche*—desires; *yei*—one who; *kāhāṅ*—where; *duṅhāra*—of both of them; *gati*—the destination; *sthāvara-deha*—the body of a tree; *deva-deha*—the body of a demigod; *yaiche*—just as; *avasthiti*—situated.

TRANSLATION

"And what is the destination of those who desire liberation and those who desire sense gratification?" Śrī Caitanya Mahāprabhu asked.

Rāmānanda Rāya replied, "Those who attempt to merge into the existence of the Supreme Lord will have to accept bodies like those of

trees. And those who are overly inclined toward sense gratification will attain the bodies of demigods."

PURPORT

Those who desire liberation by merging into the existence of God do not desire sense gratification within the material world. On the other hand, they have no information about serving the lotus feet of the Lord. Consequently, they are doomed to stand like trees for many thousands of years. Although trees are living entities, they are nonmoving. The liberated soul who merges into the existence of the Lord is no better than the trees. Trees also stand in the Lord's existence because material energy and the Lord's energy are the same. Similarly, the Brahman effulgence is also the energy of the Supreme Lord. It is the same whether one remains in the Brahman effulgence or in the material energy because in neither is there spiritual activity. Better situated are those who desire sense gratification and promotion to the heavenly planets. Such people want to enjoy themselves like denizens of heaven in the gardens of paradise. They at least retain their individuality in order to enjoy life. But the impersonalists, who try to lose their individuality, also lose both material and spiritual pleasure. The last destination of the Buddhist philosophers is to become just like a stone, which is immovable and has neither material nor spiritual activity. As far as the hard-working *karmīs* are concerned, *Śrīmad-Bhāgavatam* states (11.10.23):

iṣṭveha devatā yajñaiḥ svar-lokaṁ yāti yājñikaḥ
bhuñjīta deva-vat tatra bhogān divyān nijārjitān

"After performing various sacrificial rituals for elevation to the heavenly planets, the *karmīs* go there and enjoy themselves with the demigods to the extent that they have obtained the results of pious activities."

In the *Bhagavad-gītā* (9.20–21) Lord Kṛṣṇa states:

trai-vidyā māṁ soma-pāḥ pūta-pāpā
yajñair iṣṭvā svar-gatiṁ prārthayante
te puṇyam āsādya surendra-lokam
aśnanti divyān divi deva-bhogān

te taṁ bhuktvā svarga-lokaṁ viśālaṁ
kṣīṇe puṇye martya-lokaṁ viśanti

evaṁ trayī-dharmam anuprapannā
gatāgataṁ kāma-kāmā labhante

"Those who study the *Vedas* and drink *soma* juice, seeking the heavenly planets, worship Me indirectly. Purified of sinful reactions, they take birth on the pious, heavenly planet of Indra, where they enjoy godly delights. When they have thus enjoyed vast heavenly sense pleasure and the results of their pious activities are exhausted, they return to this mortal planet again. Thus those who seek sense enjoyment by adhering to the principles of the three *Vedas* achieve only repeated birth and death."

Therefore after finishing the results of pious activities, the *karmīs* return to this planet in the form of rain, and they begin their life as grass and plants in the evolutionary process.

TEXT 258

অরসজ্ঞ কাক চূষে জ্ঞান-নিম্বফলে।
রসজ্ঞ কোকিল খায় প্রেমাম্র-মুকুলে ॥ ২৫৮ ॥

arasa-jña kāka cūṣe jñāna-nimba-phale
rasa-jña kokila khāya premāmra-mukule

arasa-jña—those who are without mellows; *kāka*—the crows; *cūṣe*—suck; *jñāna*—of knowledge; *nimba-phale*—on the bitter *nimba* fruit; *rasa-jña*—those who enjoy transcendental mellows; *kokila*—the cuckoos; *khāya*—eat; *prema-āmra-mukule*—the buds of the mango of love of Godhead.

TRANSLATION

Rāmānanda Rāya continued, "Those who are devoid of all transcendental mellows are like the crows that suck the juice from the bitter fruits of the nimba tree of knowledge, whereas those who enjoy mellows are like the cuckoos who eat the buds of the mango tree of love of Godhead."

PURPORT

The speculative process of empiric philosophy is as bitter as the fruit of the *nimba* tree. Tasting this fruit is the business of crows. In other words, the philosophical process of realizing the Absolute Truth is a process taken up by crowlike men. But the cuckoolike devotees have very sweet voices with which to chant the holy name of the Lord and taste the sweet fruit of the mango tree of love of Godhead. Such devotees relish sweet mellows with the Lord.

TEXT 259

অভাগিয়া জ্ঞানী আস্বাদয়ে শুষ্ক জ্ঞান ।
কৃষ্ণ-প্রেমামৃত পান করে ভাগ্যবান্ ॥ ২৫৯ ॥

abhāgiyā jñānī āsvādaye śuṣka jñāna
kṛṣṇa-premāmṛta pāna kare bhāgyavān

abhāgiyā—unfortunate; *jñānī*—the philosophical speculators; *āsvādaye*—taste; *śuṣka*—dry; *jñāna*—empiric knowledge; *kṛṣṇa-prema-amṛta*—the nectar of love of Kṛṣṇa; *pāna*—drinking; *kare*—do; *bhāgyavān*—the fortunate.

TRANSLATION

Rāmānanda Rāya concluded, "The unfortunate empiric philosophers taste the dry process of philosophical knowledge, whereas the devotees regularly drink the nectar of love of Kṛṣṇa. Therefore they are the most fortunate of all."

TEXT 260

এইমত দুই জন কৃষ্ণকথা-রসে ।
নৃত্য-গীত-রোদনে হৈল রাত্রি-শেষে ॥ ২৬০ ॥

ei-mata dui jana kṛṣṇa-kathā-rase
nṛtya-gīta-rodane haila rātri-śeṣe

ei-mata—in this way; *dui jana*—both of them (Lord Caitanya and Rāmānanda Rāya); *kṛṣṇa-kathā-rase*—in the mellows of discussing topics about Kṛṣṇa; *nṛtya-gīta*—in dancing and chanting; *rodane*—in crying; *haila*—there was; *rātri-śeṣe*—the end of the night.

TRANSLATION

In this way Caitanya Mahāprabhu and Rāmānanda Rāya passed the whole night relishing the mellows of kṛṣṇa-kathā, topics about Kṛṣṇa. While they were chanting, dancing and crying, the night ended.

TEXT 261

দোঁহে নিজ-নিজ-কার্যে চলিলা বিহানে।
সন্ধ্যাকালে রায় আসি' মিলিলা আর দিনে ॥ ২৬১ ॥

doṅhe nija-nija-kārye calilā vihāne
sandhyā-kāle rāya āsi' mililā āra dine

doṅhe—both of them; *nija-nija-kārye*—in their respective duties; *calilā*—departed; *vihāne*—in the morning; *sandhyā-kāle*—in the evening; *rāya*—Rāmānanda Rāya; *āsi'*—coming again; *mililā*—met; *āra*—next; *dine*—on the day.

TRANSLATION

The next morning they both departed to perform their respective duties, but in the evening Rāmānanda Rāya returned to meet the Lord again.

TEXT 262

ইষ্ট-গোষ্ঠী কৃষ্ণকথা কহি' কতক্ষণ।
প্রভুপদ ধরি' রায় করে নিবেদন ॥ ২৬২ ॥

iṣṭa-goṣṭhī kṛṣṇa-kathā kahi' kata-kṣaṇa
prabhu-pada dhari' rāya kare nivedana

iṣṭa-goṣṭhī—spiritual discussion; *kṛṣṇa-kathā*—topics of Kṛṣṇa; *kahi'*—talking; *kata-kṣaṇa*—for some time; *prabhu-pada*—the lotus feet of the Lord; *dhari'*—catching; *rāya*—Rāmānanda Rāya; *kare*—makes; *nivedana*—submission.

TRANSLATION

That evening, after discussing the topics of Kṛṣṇa for some time, Rāmānanda Rāya caught hold of the lotus feet of the Lord and spoke as follows.

TEXT 263

'কৃষ্ণতত্ত্ব', 'রাধাতত্ত্ব', 'প্রেমতত্ত্বসার'।
'রসতত্ত্ব' 'লীলাতত্ত্ব' বিবিধ প্রকার ॥ ২৬৩ ॥

'kṛṣṇa-tattva', 'rādhā-tattva', 'prema-tattva-sāra'
'rasa-tattva' 'līlā-tattva' vividha prakāra

kṛṣṇa-tattva—the truth about Kṛṣṇa; *rādhā-tattva*—the truth about Rādhā; *prema-tattva-sāra*—the essence of Their loving affairs; *rasa-tattva*—the truth about transcendental mellows; *līlā-tattva*—the truth about the pastimes of the Lord; *vividha prakāra*—of different varieties.

TRANSLATION

"There is a variety of transcendental truths—the truth about Kṛṣṇa, the truth about Rādhārāṇī, the truth about Their loving affairs, the truth about transcendental humors, and the truth about the Lord's pastimes.

TEXT 264

এত তত্ত্ব মোর চিত্তে কৈলে প্রকাশন।
ব্রহ্মাকে বেদ যেন পড়াইল নারায়ণ ॥ ২৬৪ ॥

eta tattva mora citte kaile prakāśana
brahmāke veda yena paḍāila nārāyaṇa

eta tattva—all these varieties of truth; *mora citte*—in my heart; *kaile*—You did; *prakāśana*—manifesting; *brahmāke*—unto Lord Brahmā; *veda*—the Vedic knowledge; *yena*—as; *paḍāila*—taught; *nārāyaṇa*—the Supreme Lord.

TRANSLATION

"You have manifested all these transcendental truths in my heart. This is exactly the way Nārāyaṇa educated Lord Brahmā."

PURPORT

The heart of Brahmā was enlightened by the Supreme Personality of Godhead. This is Vedic information given in the *Śvetāśvatara Upaniṣad* (6.18):

yo brahmāṇaṁ vidadhāti pūrvaṁ
yo vai vedāṁś ca prahiṇoti tasmai
taṁ ha devam ātma-buddhi-prakāśaṁ
mumukṣur vai śaraṇam ahaṁ prapadye

"Because I desire liberation, let me surrender unto the Supreme Personality of Godhead, who first enlightened Lord Brahmā in Vedic knowledge through Lord Brahmā's heart. The Lord is the original source of all enlightenment and spiritual advancement." In this connection one may also refer to *Śrīmad-Bhāgavatam* 2.9.30–35, 11.14.3, 12.4.40 and 12.13.19.

TEXT 265

অন্তর্যামী ঈশ্বরের এই রীতি হয়ে।
বাহিরে না কহে, বস্তু প্রকাশে হৃদয়ে ॥ ২৬৫ ॥

antaryāmī īśvarera ei rīti haye
bāhire nā kahe, vastu prakāśe hṛdaye

antaryāmī—the Supersoul; *īśvarera*—of the Personality of Godhead; *ei*—this; *rīti*—the system; *haye*—is; *bāhire*—externally; *nā kahe*—does not speak; *vastu*—the facts; *prakāśe*—manifests; *hṛdaye*—within the heart.

TRANSLATION

Rāmānanda Rāya continued, "The Supersoul within everyone's heart speaks not externally but from within. He instructs the devotees in all respects, and that is His way of instruction."

PURPORT

Here Śrī Rāmānanda Rāya admits that Śrī Caitanya Mahāprabhu is the Supersoul. It is the Supersoul that inspires the devotee; therefore He is the original source of the Gāyatrī *mantra,* which states, *oṁ bhūr bhuvaḥ svaḥ tat savitur vareṇyaṁ bhargo devasya dhīmahi dhiyo yo naḥ pracodayāt.* Savitā is the original source of all intelligence. That Savitā is Lord Caitanya Mahāprabhu. This is confirmed in *Śrīmad-Bhāgavatam* (2.4.22):

pracoditā yena purā sarasvatī
vitanvatājasya satīṁ smṛtiṁ hṛdi
sva-lakṣaṇā prādurabhūt kilāsyataḥ
sa me ṛṣīṇām ṛṣabhaḥ prasīdatām

"May the Lord, who in the beginning of the creation amplified the potent knowledge of Brahmā from within his heart and inspired him with full knowledge of creation and His own self, and who appeared to be generated from the mouth of Brahmā, be pleased with me." This was spoken by Śukadeva Gosvāmī when he invoked the blessing of the Supreme Personality of Godhead before delivering *Śrīmad-Bhāgavatam* to Mahārāja Parīkṣit.

TEXT 266

জন্মাদ্যস্য যতোঽন্বয়াদিতরতশ্চার্থেষ্বভিজ্ঞঃ স্বরাট্
তেনে ব্রহ্ম হৃদা য আদিকবয়ে মুহ্যন্তি যৎ সূরয়ঃ ।
তেজোবারিমৃদাং যথা বিনিময়ো যত্র ত্রিসর্গোঽমৃষা
ধাম্না স্বেন সদা নিরস্তকুহকং সত্যং পরং ধীমহি ॥ ২৬৬ ॥

janmādy asya yato 'nvayād itarataś cārtheṣv abhijñaḥ sva-rāṭ
tene brahma hṛdā ya ādi-kavaye muhyanti yat sūrayaḥ
tejo-vāri-mṛdāṁ yathā vinimayo yatra tri-sargo 'mṛṣā
dhāmnā svena sadā nirasta-kuhakaṁ satyaṁ paraṁ dhīmahi

janma-ādi—creation, maintenance and dissolution; *asya*—of this (the universe); *yataḥ*—from whom; *anvayāt*—directly from the spiritual connection; *itarataḥ*—indirectly from the lack of material contact; *ca*—also; *artheṣu*—in all affairs; *abhijñaḥ*—perfectly cognizant; *sva-rāṭ*—independent; *tene*—imparted; *brahma*—the Absolute Truth; *hṛdā*—through the heart; *yaḥ*—who; *ādi-kavaye*—unto Lord Brahmā; *muhyanti*—are bewildered; *yat*—in whom; *sūrayaḥ*—great personalities like Lord Brahmā and other demigods or great *brāhmaṇas; tejaḥ-vāri-mṛdām*—of fire, water and earth; *yathā*—as; *vinimayaḥ*—the exchange; *yatra*—in whom; *tri-sargaḥ*—the material creation of three modes; *amṛṣā*—factual; *dhāmnā*—with the abode; *svena*—His own personal; *sadā*—always; *nirasta-kuhakam*—devoid of all illusion; *satyam*—the truth; *param*—absolute; *dhīmahi*—let us meditate upon.

TRANSLATION

"'O my Lord, Śrī Kṛṣṇa, son of Vasudeva, O all-pervading Personality of Godhead, I offer my respectful obeisances unto You. I meditate upon Lord Śrī Kṛṣṇa because He is the Absolute Truth and the primeval cause of all causes of the creation, sustenance and destruction of the manifested universes. He is directly and indirectly conscious of all manifestations, and He is independent because there is no other cause beyond Him. It is He only who first imparted the Vedic knowledge unto the heart of Brahmājī, the original living being. By Him even the great sages and demigods are placed into illusion, as one is bewildered by the illusory representations of water seen in fire, or land seen on water. Only because of Him do the material universes, temporarily manifested by the reactions of the three modes of nature, appear factual, although they are unreal. I therefore meditate upon Him, Lord Śrī Kṛṣṇa, who is eternally existent in the transcendental abode, which is forever free from the illusory representations of the material world. I meditate upon Him, for He is the Absolute Truth.'"

PURPORT

This verse is the opening invocation of *Śrīmad-Bhāgavatam* (1.1.1).

TEXT 267

এক সংশয় মোর আছয়ে হৃদয়ে ।
কৃপা করি' কহ মোরে তাহার নিশ্চয়ে ॥ ২৬৭ ॥

eka saṁśaya mora āchaye hṛdaye
kṛpā kari' kaha more tāhāra niścaye

eka saṁśaya—one doubt; *mora*—my; *āchaye*—there is; *hṛdaye*—in the heart; *kṛpā kari'*—being merciful; *kaha*—please say; *more*—unto me; *tāhāra*—of that; *niścaye*—the ascertainment.

TRANSLATION

Rāmānanda Rāya then said that he had but one doubt within his heart, and he petitioned the Lord, "Please be merciful upon me and just remove my doubt."

TEXT 268

পহিলে দেখিলুঁ তোমার সন্ন্যাসি-স্বরূপ ।
এবে তোমা দেখি মুঞি শ্যাম-গোপরূপ ॥ ২৬৮ ॥

pahile dekhiluṅ tomāra sannyāsi-svarūpa
ebe tomā dekhi muñi śyāma-gopa-rūpa

pahile—in the beginning; *dekhiluṅ*—I saw; *tomāra*—Your; *sannyāsi-svarūpa*—form as a person in the renounced order; *ebe*—now; *tomā*—You; *dekhi*—see; *muñi*—I; *śyāma-gopa-rūpa*—form as Śyāmasundara, the cowherd boy.

TRANSLATION

Rāmānanda Rāya then told Lord Śrī Caitanya Mahāprabhu, "At first I saw You appear like a sannyāsī, but now I am seeing You as Śyāmasundara, the cowherd boy.

TEXT 269

তোমার সম্মুখে দেখি কাঞ্চন-পঞ্চালিকা ।
তাঁর গৌরকান্ত্যে তোমার সর্ব অঙ্গ ঢাকা ॥ ২৬৯ ॥

tomāra sammukhe dekhi kāñcana-pañcālikā
tāṅra gaura-kāntye tomāra sarva aṅga ḍhākā

tomāra—of You; *sammukhe*—in front; *dekhi*—I see; *kāñcana-pañcālikā*—a doll made of gold; *tāṅra*—of it; *gaura-kāntye*—by a golden complexion; *tomāra*—Your; *sarva*—all; *aṅga*—body; *ḍhākā*—covering.

TRANSLATION

"I now see You appearing like a golden doll, and Your entire body appears covered by a golden luster.

PURPORT

Śyāmasundara is blackish, but here Rāmānanda Rāya says that he saw Śrī Caitanya Mahāprabhu appear golden. The lustrous body of

Śrī Caitanya Mahāprabhu was covered by the bodily complexion of Śrīmatī Rādhārāṇī.

TEXT 270

তাহাতে প্রকট দেখোঁ স-বংশী বদন।
নানা ভাবে চঞ্চল তাহে কমল-নয়ন ॥ ২৭০ ॥

tāhāte prakaṭa dekhoṅ sa-vaṁśī vadana
nānā bhāve cañcala tāhe kamala-nayana

tāhāte—in that; *prakaṭa*—manifested; *dekhoṅ*—I see; *sa-vaṁśī*—with the flute; *vadana*—the face; *nānā bhāve*—in various modes; *cañcala*—restless; *tāhe*—in that; *kamala-nayana*—the lotus eyes.

TRANSLATION

"I see that You are holding a flute to Your mouth, and Your lotus eyes are moving very restlessly due to various ecstasies.

TEXT 271

এইমত তোমা দেখি' হয় চমৎকার।
অকপটে কহ, প্রভু, কারণ ইহার ॥ ২৭১ ॥

ei-mata tomā dekhi' haya camatkāra
akapaṭe kaha, prabhu, kāraṇa ihāra

ei-mata—in this way; *tomā*—You; *dekhi'*—seeing; *haya*—there is; *camatkāra*—wonder; *akapaṭe*—without duplicity; *kaha*—please tell; *prabhu*—my Lord; *kāraṇa*—the cause; *ihāra*—of this.

TRANSLATION

"I actually see You in this way, and this is very wonderful. My Lord, please tell me without duplicity what is causing this."

TEXT 272

প্রভু কহে, —কৃষ্ণে তোমার গাঢ়প্রেম হয়।
প্রেমার স্বভাব এই জানিহ নিশ্চয় ॥ ২৭২ ॥

prabhu kahe,—kṛṣṇe tomāra gāḍha-prema haya
premāra svabhāva ei jāniha niścaya

prabhu kahe—the Lord replied; *kṛṣṇe*—unto Kṛṣṇa; *tomāra*—your; *gāḍha-prema*—deep love; *haya*—there is; *premāra*—of such transcendental love; *svabhāva*—the nature; *ei*—this; *jāniha*—please know; *niścaya*—certainly.

TRANSLATION

Lord Śrī Caitanya Mahāprabhu replied, "You have a deep love for Kṛṣṇa, and one who has such deep ecstatic love for the Lord naturally sees things in such a way. Please take this from Me to be certain.

TEXT 273

মহাভাগবত দেখে স্থাবর-জঙ্গম।
তাহাঁ তাহাঁ হয় তাঁর শ্রীকৃষ্ণ-স্ফুরণ ॥ ২৭৩ ॥

mahā-bhāgavata dekhe sthāvara-jaṅgama
tāhāṅ tāhāṅ haya tāṅra śrī-kṛṣṇa-sphuraṇa

mahā-bhāgavata—a first-class advanced devotee; *dekhe*—sees; *sthāvara-jaṅgama*—the movable and inert; *tāhāṅ tāhāṅ*—here and there; *haya*—is; *tāṅra*—his; *śrī-kṛṣṇa-sphuraṇa*—manifestation of Lord Kṛṣṇa.

TRANSLATION

"A devotee advanced on the spiritual platform sees everything movable and inert as the Supreme Lord. For him, everything he sees here and there is but a manifestation of Lord Kṛṣṇa.

TEXT 274

স্থাবর-জঙ্গম দেখে, না দেখে তার মূর্তি।
সর্বত্র হয় নিজ ইষ্টদেব-স্ফুর্তি ॥ ২৭৪ ॥

sthāvara-jaṅgama dekhe, nā dekhe tāra mūrti
sarvatra haya nija iṣṭa-deva-sphūrti

sthāvara-jaṅgama—movable and inert; *dekhe*—he sees; *nā*—not; *dekhe*—sees; *tāra*—its; *mūrti*—form; *sarvatra*—everywhere; *haya*—there is; *nija*—his own; *iṣṭa-deva*—worshipable Lord; *sphūrti*—manifestation.

TRANSLATION

"The mahā-bhāgavata, the advanced devotee, certainly sees everything mobile and immobile, but he does not exactly see their forms. Rather, everywhere he immediately sees manifest the form of the Supreme Lord."

PURPORT

Due to his deep ecstatic love for Kṛṣṇa, the *mahā-bhāgavata* sees Kṛṣṇa everywhere and nothing else. This is confirmed in the *Brahma-saṁhitā* (5.38): *premāñjana-cchurita-bhakti-vilocanena santaḥ sadaiva hṛdayeṣu vilokayanti.*

As soon as a devotee sees something—be it movable or inert—he immediately remembers Kṛṣṇa. An advanced devotee is advanced in knowledge. This knowledge is very natural to a devotee, for he has already read in the *Bhagavad-gītā* how to awaken Kṛṣṇa consciousness. According to Lord Kṛṣṇa in the *Bhagavad-gītā* (7.8):

raso 'ham apsu kaunteya prabhāsmi śaśi-sūryayoḥ
praṇavaḥ sarva-vedeṣu śabdaḥ khe pauruṣaṁ nṛṣu

"O son of Kuntī [Arjuna], I am the taste of water, the light of the sun and the moon, the syllable *oṁ* in the Vedic *mantras;* I am the sound in ether and ability in man."

Thus when a devotee drinks water or any other liquid, he immediately remembers Kṛṣṇa. For a devotee there is no difficulty in awakening Kṛṣṇa consciousness twenty-four hours a day. Caitanya Mahāprabhu therefore says here:

sthāvara jaṅgama dekhe nā dekhe tāra mūrti
sarvatra haya nija iṣṭa-deva-sphūrti

A saintly person, an advanced devotee, sees Kṛṣṇa twenty-four hours a day and nothing else. As far as movable and inert things are concerned, a devotee sees them all as transformations of Kṛṣṇa's energy. As Lord Kṛṣṇa states in the *Bhagavad-gītā* (7.4):

bhūmir āpo 'nalo vāyuḥ khaṁ mano buddhir eva ca
ahaṅkāra itīyaṁ me bhinnā prakṛtir aṣṭadhā

"Earth, water, fire, air, ether, mind, intelligence and false ego—all together these eight constitute My separated material energies."

Actually nothing is separate from Kṛṣṇa. When a devotee sees a tree, he knows that the tree is a combination of two energies—material and spiritual. The inferior energy, which is material, forms the body of the tree; however, within the tree is the living entity, the spiritual spark, which is part and parcel of Kṛṣṇa. This is the superior energy of Kṛṣṇa within this world. Whatever living thing we see is simply a combination of these two energies. When an advanced devotee thinks of these energies, he immediately understands that they are manifestations of the Supreme Lord. As soon as we see the sun rise in the morning, we arise and set about doing our morning duties. Similarly, as soon as a devotee sees the energy of the Lord, he immediately remembers Lord Śrī Kṛṣṇa. This is explained in this verse: *sarvatra haya nija iṣṭa-deva-sphūrti.*

A devotee who has purified his existence through devotional service sees only Kṛṣṇa in every step of life. This is also explained in the next verse, which is a quotation from *Śrīmad-Bhāgavatam* (11.2.45).

TEXT 275

সর্বভূতেষু যঃ পশ্যেদ্ভগবদ্ভাবমাত্মনঃ ।
ভূতানি ভগবত্যাত্মন্যেষ ভাগবতোত্তমঃ ॥ ২৭৫ ॥

sarva-bhūteṣu yaḥ paśyed
bhagavad-bhāvam ātmanaḥ
bhūtāni bhagavaty ātmany
eṣa bhāgavatottamaḥ

sarva-bhūteṣu—in all objects (in matter, spirit and combinations of matter and spirit); *yaḥ*—anyone who; *paśyet*—sees; *bhagavat-bhāvam*—the ability to be engaged in the service of the Lord; *ātmanaḥ*—of the supreme spirit soul or the Transcendence beyond the material conception of life; *bhūtāni*—all beings; *bhagavati*—in the Supreme Personality of Godhead; *ātmani*—the basic principle of all existence; *eṣaḥ*—this; *bhāgavata-uttamaḥ*—a person advanced in devotional service.

TRANSLATION

Śrī Caitanya Mahāprabhu continued, "'A person advanced in devotional service sees within everything the soul of souls, the Supreme Personality of Godhead, Śrī Kṛṣṇa. Consequently he always sees the form of the Supreme Personality of Godhead as the cause of all causes and understands that all things are situated in Him.'

TEXT 276

বনলতাস্তরব আত্মনি বিষ্ণুং ব্যঞ্জয়ন্ত্য ইব পুষ্পফলাঢ্যাঃ ।
প্রণতভারবিটপা মধুধারাঃ প্রেমহৃষ্টতনবো ববৃষুঃ স্ম ॥ ২৭৬ ॥

vana-latās tarava ātmani viṣṇuṁ
vyañjayantya iva puṣpa-phalāḍhyāḥ
praṇata-bhāra-viṭapā madhu-dhārāḥ
prema-hṛṣṭa-tanavo vavṛṣuḥ sma

vana-latāḥ—the herbs and plants; *taravaḥ*—the trees; *ātmani*—in the Supreme Soul; *viṣṇum*—the Supreme Personality of Godhead; *vyañjayantyaḥ*—manifesting; *iva*—like; *puṣpa-phala-āḍhyāḥ*—filled with luxuriant fruits and flowers; *praṇata-bhāra*—bowed down because of loads; *viṭapāḥ*—the trees; *madhu-dhārāḥ*—showers of honey; *prema-hṛṣṭa*—inspired by love of Godhead; *tanavaḥ*—whose bodies; *vavṛṣuḥ*—constantly rained; *sma*—certainly.

TRANSLATION

"'The plants, creepers and trees were full of fruits and flowers due to ecstatic love of Kṛṣṇa. Indeed, being so full, they were bowing down. They were inspired by such deep love for Kṛṣṇa that they were constantly pouring showers of honey. In this way the gopīs saw all the forests of Vṛndāvana.'"

PURPORT

This verse (*Bhāg.* 10.35.9) is one of the songs the *gopīs* sang during Kṛṣṇa's absence. In Kṛṣṇa's absence the *gopīs* were always absorbed in thought of Him. Similarly, the *mahā-bhāgavata,* the advanced devotee, sees everything as potentially serving the Lord. Śrīla Rūpa Gosvāmī states:

prāpañcikatayā buddhyā hari-sambandhi-vastunaḥ
mumukṣubhiḥ parityāgo vairāgyaṁ phalgu kathyate
(*Bhakti-rasāmṛta-sindhu* 1.2.126)

The advanced devotee does not see anything as unconnected with Kṛṣṇa. Unlike the Māyāvādī philosophers, a devotee does not see the material world as false, because he knows that everything in the material world is connected to Kṛṣṇa. A devotee knows how to utilize everything in the service of the Lord, and this is characteristic of the *mahā-bhāgavata.* The *gopīs* saw the plants, creepers and forest trees loaded with fruits and flowers and ready to serve Kṛṣṇa. In this way they immediately remembered their worshipable Lord Śrī Kṛṣṇa. They did not simply see plants, creepers and trees the way a mundaner sees them.

TEXT 277

রাধাকৃষ্ণে তোমার মহাপ্রেম হয়।
যাহাঁ তাহাঁ রাধাকৃষ্ণ তোমারে স্ফুরয় ॥ ২৭৭ ॥

rādhā-kṛṣṇe tomāra mahā-prema haya
yāhāṅ tāhāṅ rādhā-kṛṣṇa tomāre sphuraya

rādhā-kṛṣṇe—unto Rādhā and Kṛṣṇa; *tomāra*—your; *mahā-prema*—great love; *haya*—there is; *yāhāṅ tāhāṅ*—anywhere and everywhere; *rādhā-kṛṣṇa*—Lord Kṛṣṇa and Śrīmatī Rādhārāṇī; *tomāre*—unto you; *sphuraya*—appear.

TRANSLATION

Lord Caitanya Mahāprabhu continued, "My dear Rāya, you are an advanced devotee and are always filled with ecstatic love for

Rādhā and Kṛṣṇa. Therefore whatever you see—anywhere and everywhere—simply awakens your Kṛṣṇa consciousness."

TEXT 278

রায় কহে,—প্রভু তুমি ছাড় ভারিভূরি ।
মোর আগে নিজরূপ না করিহ চুরি ॥ ২৭৮ ॥

rāya kahe,—prabhu tumi chāḍa bhāri-bhūri
mora āge nija-rūpa nā kariha curi

rāya kahe—Rāmānanda Rāya replied; *prabhu*—my Lord; *tumi*—You; *chāḍa*—give up; *bhāri-bhūri*—these grave talks; *mora*—of me; *āge*—in front; *nija-rūpa*—Your real form; *nā*—not; *kariha*—do; *curi*—stealing.

TRANSLATION

Rāmānanda Rāya replied, "My dear Lord, please give up all these serious talks. Please do not conceal Your real form from me."

TEXT 279

রাধিকার ভাবকান্তি করি' অঙ্গীকার ।
নিজরস আস্বাদিতে করিয়াছ অবতার ॥ ২৭৯ ॥

rādhikāra bhāva-kānti kari' aṅgīkāra
nija-rasa āsvādite kariyācha avatāra

rādhikāra—of Śrīmatī Rādhārāṇī; *bhāva-kānti*—ecstatic love and luster; *kari'*—making; *aṅgīkāra*—acceptance; *nija-rasa*—Your own transcendental mellow; *āsvādite*—to taste; *kariyācha*—You have made; *avatāra*—incarnation.

TRANSLATION

Rāmānanda Rāya continued, "My dear Lord, I can understand that You have assumed the ecstasy and bodily complexion of Śrīmatī Rādhārāṇī. By accepting this, You are tasting Your own personal transcendental humor and have therefore appeared as Śrī Caitanya Mahāprabhu.

TEXT 280

নিজগূঢ়কার্য তোমার — প্রেম আস্বাদন।
আনুষঙ্গে প্রেমময় কৈলে ত্রিভুবন ॥ ২৮০ ॥

nija-gūḍha-kārya tomāra — prema āsvādana
ānuṣaṅge prema-maya kaile tribhuvana

nija-gūḍha-kārya — own confidential business; *tomāra* — Your; *prema* — transcendental love; *āsvādana* — tasting; *ānuṣaṅge* — simultaneously; *prema-maya* — transformed into love of God; *kaile* — You have made; *tri-bhuvana* — all the world.

TRANSLATION

"My dear Lord, You have descended in this incarnation of Lord Caitanya for Your own personal reasons. You have come to taste Your own spiritual bliss, and at the same time You are transforming the whole world by spreading the ecstasy of love of Godhead.

TEXT 281

আপনে আইলে মোরে করিতে উদ্ধার।
এবে কপট কর, — তোমার কোন ব্যবহার ॥ ২৮১ ॥

āpane āile more karite uddhāra
ebe kapaṭa kara, — tomāra kona vyavahāra

āpane — personally; *āile* — You have come; *more* — unto me; *karite* — to make; *uddhāra* — deliverance; *ebe* — now; *kapaṭa* — duplicity; *kara* — You do; *tomāra* — Your; *kona* — what; *vyavahāra* — behavior.

TRANSLATION

"My dear Lord, by Your causeless mercy You have appeared before me to grant me liberation. Now You are playing in a duplicitous way. What is the reason for this behavior?"

TEXT 282

তবে হাসি' তাঁরে প্রভু দেখাইল স্বরূপ ।
'রসরাজ', 'মহাভাব' — দুই এক রূপ ॥ ২৮২ ॥

tabe hāsi' tāṅre prabhu dekhāila svarūpa
'rasa-rāja', 'mahābhāva'—dui eka rūpa

tabe—therefore; *hāsi'*—smiling; *tāṅre*—unto him (Rāmānanda Rāya); *prabhu*—the Lord; *dekhāila*—showed; *svarūpa*—His personal form; *rasa-rāja*—the king of all transcendental humors; *mahā-bhāva*—the condition of ecstatic love; *dui*—two; *eka*—one; *rūpa*—form.

TRANSLATION

Lord Śrī Kṛṣṇa is the reservoir of all pleasure, and Śrīmatī Rādhārāṇī is the personification of ecstatic love of Godhead. These two forms had combined as one in Śrī Caitanya Mahāprabhu. This being the case, Lord Śrī Caitanya Mahāprabhu revealed His real form to Rāmānanda Rāya.

PURPORT

This is described as *rādhā-bhāva-dyuti-suvalitaṁ naumi kṛṣṇa-svarūpam.* Lord Śrī Kṛṣṇa was absorbed in the features of Śrīmatī Rādhārāṇī. This was disclosed to Rāmānanda Rāya when he saw Lord Śrī Caitanya Mahāprabhu. An advanced devotee can understand *śrī-kṛṣṇa-caitanya, rādhā-kṛṣṇa nahe anya.* Śrī Caitanya Mahāprabhu, being a combination of Kṛṣṇa and Rādhā, is nondifferent from Rādhā-Kṛṣṇa combined. This is explained by Svarūpa Dāmodara Gosvāmī:

rādhā kṛṣṇa-praṇaya-vikṛtir hlādinī śaktir asmād
ekātmānāv api bhuvi purā deha-bhedaṁ gatau tau
caitanyākhyaṁ prakaṭam adhunā tad-dvayaṁ caikyam āptaṁ
rādhā-bhāva-dyuti-suvalitaṁ naumi kṛṣṇa-svarūpam

(Cc. *Ādi* 1.5)

Rādhā-Kṛṣṇa is one. Rādhā-Kṛṣṇa is Kṛṣṇa and Kṛṣṇa's pleasure potency combined. When Kṛṣṇa exhibits His pleasure potency, He appears to be two—Rādhā and Kṛṣṇa. Otherwise, Rādhā and Kṛṣṇa are one. This oneness may be perceived by advanced devotees through the grace of Śrī Caitanya Mahāprabhu. This was the case with Rāmānanda Rāya. One may aspire to attain such a position, but one should not try to imitate the *mahā-bhāgavata.*

TEXT 283

দেখি' রামানন্দ হৈলা আনন্দে মূর্চ্ছিতে ।
ধরিতে না পারে দেহ, পড়িলা ভূমিতে ॥ ২৮৩ ॥

dekhi' rāmānanda hailā ānande mūrcchite
dharite nā pāre deha, paḍilā bhūmite

dekhi'—seeing this form; *rāmānanda*—Rāmānanda Rāya; *hailā*—there was; *ānande*—in ecstasy; *mūrcchite*—fainting; *dharite*—to hold him; *nā*—not; *pāre*—able; *deha*—the body; *paḍilā*—fell down; *bhūmite*—on the ground.

TRANSLATION

Upon seeing this form, Rāmānanda Rāya lost consciousness in transcendental bliss. Unable to remain standing, he fell to the ground.

TEXT 284

প্রভু তাঁরে হস্ত স্পর্শি' করাইলা চেতন ।
সন্ন্যাসীর বেষ দেখি' বিস্মিত হৈল মন ॥ ২৮৪ ॥

prabhu tāṅre hasta sparśi' karāilā cetana
sannyāsīra veṣa dekhi' vismita haila mana

prabhu—the Lord; *tāṅre*—unto Rāmānanda Rāya; *hasta*—the hand; *sparśi'*—touching; *karāilā*—made; *cetana*—conscious; *sannyāsīra*—of the *sannyāsī; veṣa*—the dress; *dekhi'*—seeing; *vismita*—struck with wonder; *haila*—became; *mana*—the mind.

TRANSLATION

When Rāmānanda Rāya fell to the ground unconscious, Caitanya Mahāprabhu touched his hand, and he immediately regained consciousness. But when he saw Lord Caitanya in the dress of a sannyāsī, he was struck with wonder.

TEXT 285

আলিঙ্গন করি' প্রভু কৈল আশ্বাসন।
তোমা বিনা এইরূপ না দেখে অন্যজন ॥ ২৮৫ ॥

āliṅgana kari' prabhu kaila āśvāsana
tomā vinā ei-rūpa nā dekhe anya-jana

āliṅgana kari'—embracing him; *prabhu*—the Lord; *kaila*—did; *āśvāsana*—pacifying; *tomā vinā*—but for you; *ei-rūpa*—this form; *nā*—not; *dekhe*—sees; *anya-jana*—anyone else.

TRANSLATION

After embracing Rāmānanda Rāya, the Lord pacified him, informing him, "But for you, no one has ever seen this form."

PURPORT

In the *Bhagavad-gītā* (7.25) Lord Kṛṣṇa states:

nāhaṁ prakāśaḥ sarvasya yoga-māyā-samāvṛtaḥ
mūḍho 'yaṁ nābhijānāti loko mām ajam avyayam

"I am never manifest to the foolish and unintelligent. For them I am covered by My internal potency [*yogamāyā*], and so they do not know Me, who am unborn and infallible."

The Lord always reserves the right of not being exposed to everyone. The devotees, however, are always engaged in the service of the Lord, serving with the tongue by chanting the Hare Kṛṣṇa *mantra* and tasting *mahā-prasādam.* Gradually the sincere devotee pleases the Supreme Personality of Godhead, and the Supreme Lord reveals Himself. One cannot see the Supreme Lord by making personal efforts. Rather, when the Lord is pleased by the service of a devotee, He reveals Himself.

TEXT 286

মোর তত্ত্বলীলা-রস তোমার গোচরে।
অতএব এইরূপ দেখাইলুঁ তোমারে ॥ ২৮৬ ॥

mora tattva-līlā-rasa tomāra gocare
ataeva ei-rūpa dekhāiluṅ tomāre

mora—My; *tattva-līlā*—truth and pastimes; *rasa*—and mellows; *tomāra*—of you; *gocare*—within the knowledge; *ataeva*—therefore; *ei-rūpa*—this form; *dekhāiluṅ*—I have shown; *tomāre*—unto you.

TRANSLATION

Śrī Caitanya Mahāprabhu confirmed, "All the truths about My pastimes and mellows are within your knowledge. Therefore I have shown this form to you.

TEXT 287

গৌর অঙ্গ নহে মোর — রাধাঙ্গ-স্পর্শন।
গোপেন্দ্রসুত বিনা তেঁহো না স্পর্শে অন্যজন ॥ ২৮৭ ॥

gaura aṅga nahe mora—rādhāṅga-sparśana
gopendra-suta vinā teṅho nā sparśe anya-jana

gaura—fair; *aṅga*—body; *nahe*—not; *mora*—My; *rādhā-aṅga*—of the body of Śrīmatī Rādhārāṇī; *sparśana*—the touching; *gopendra-suta*—the son of Nanda Mahārāja; *vinā*—except; *teṅho*—Śrīmatī Rādhārāṇī; *nā*—not; *sparśe*—touches; *anya-jana*—anyone else.

TRANSLATION

"Actually My body does not have a fair complexion. It only appears so because it has touched the body of Śrīmatī Rādhārāṇī. However, She does not touch anyone but the son of Nanda Mahārāja.

TEXT 288

তাঁর ভাবে ভাবিত করি' আত্ম-মন।
তবে নিজ-মাধুর্য করি আস্বাদন ॥ ২৮৮ ॥

tāṅra bhāve bhāvita kari' ātma-mana
tabe nija-mādhurya kari āsvādana

tāṅra—of Śrīmatī Rādhārāṇī; *bhāve*—in the ecstasy; *bhāvita*—enlightened; *kari'*—making; *ātma-mana*—body and mind; *tabe*—thereupon; *nija-mādhurya*—My own transcendental humor; *kari*—I do; *āsvādana*—tasting.

TRANSLATION

"I have now converted My body and mind into the ecstasy of Śrīmatī Rādhārāṇī; thus I am tasting My own personal sweetness in that form."

PURPORT

Gaurasundara here informed Śrī Rāmānanda Rāya, "My dear Rāmānanda Rāya, you were actually seeing a separate person with a fair-complexioned body. Actually I am not fair. Being Śrī Kṛṣṇa, the son of Nanda Mahārāja, I am blackish, but when I come in touch with Śrīmatī Rādhārāṇī I become fair-complexioned externally. Śrīmatī Rādhārāṇī does not touch the body of anyone but Kṛṣṇa. I taste My own transcendental features by accepting the complexion of Śrīmatī Rādhārāṇī. Without Rādhārāṇī, one cannot taste the transcendental pleasure of Kṛṣṇa's conjugal love." In this regard, Śrīla Bhaktisiddhānta Sarasvatī Ṭhākura comments on the *prākṛta-sahajiyā-sampradāya,* which considers Kṛṣṇa and Lord Caitanya to possess different bodies. They misinterpret the words *gaura aṅga nahe mora* in text 287. From that verse and the present verse we can understand that Lord Caitanya Mahāprabhu is nondifferent from Kṛṣṇa. Both are the same Supreme Personality of Godhead. In the form of Kṛṣṇa, the Lord enjoys spiritual bliss and remains the shelter of all devotees, *viṣaya-vigraha.* And in His Gaurāṅga feature Kṛṣṇa tastes separation from Kṛṣṇa in the ecstasy of Śrīmatī Rādhārāṇī. This ecstatic form is Śrī Kṛṣṇa Caitanya. Śrī Kṛṣṇa is always the transcendental reservoir of all pleasure, and He is technically called *dhīra-lalita.* Śrīmatī Rādhārāṇī is the embodiment of spiritual energy, personified as ecstatic love for Kṛṣṇa; therefore only Kṛṣṇa can touch Her. The *dhīra-lalita* aspect is not seen in any other form of the Lord, including Viṣṇu and Nārāyaṇa. Śrīmatī Rādhārāṇī is therefore known as Govinda-nandinī and Govinda-mohinī, for She is the only source of transcendental pleasure for Śrī Kṛṣṇa and the only person who can enchant His mind.

TEXT 289

তোমার ঠাঞি আমার কিছু গুপ্ত নাহি কর্ম।
লুকাইলে প্রেম-বলে জান সর্বমর্ম ॥ ২৮৯ ॥

tomāra ṭhāñi āmāra kichu gupta nāhi karma
lukāile prema-bale jāna sarva-marma

tomāra ṭhāñi—before you; *āmāra*—My; *kichu*—anything; *gupta*—hidden; *nāhi*—is not; *karma*—action; *lukāile*—even if I conceal; *prema-bale*—by the force of your love; *jāna*—you know; *sarva-marma*—everything in detail.

TRANSLATION

Lord Caitanya Mahāprabhu then admitted to His pure devotee, Rāmānanda Rāya, "Now there is no confidential activity unknown to you. Even though I try to conceal My activities, you can understand everything in detail by virtue of your advanced love for Me."

TEXT 290

গুপ্তে রাখিহ, কাহাঁ না করিও প্রকাশ।
আমার বাতুল-চেষ্টা লোকে উপহাস ॥ ২৯০ ॥

gupte rākhiha, kāhāṅ nā kario prakāśa
āmāra bātula-ceṣṭā loke upahāsa

gupte—in secret; *rākhiha*—keep; *kāhāṅ*—anywhere; *nā*—not; *kario*—make; *prakāśa*—exposure; *āmāra*—My; *bātula-ceṣṭā*—activities like a madman; *loke*—among the general people; *upahāsa*—laughter.

TRANSLATION

The Lord then requested Rāmānanda Rāya, "Keep all these talks a secret. Please do not expose them anywhere and everywhere. Since My activities appear to be like those of a madman, people may take them lightly and laugh."

TEXT 291

আমি — এক বাতুল, তুমি দ্বিতীয় — বাতুল।
অতএব তোমায় আমায় হই সমতুল ॥ ২৯১ ॥

āmi — eka bātula, tumi — dvitīya bātula
ataeva tomāya āmāya ha-i sama-tula

āmi — I; *eka* — one; *bātula* — madman; *tumi* — you; *dvitīya* — second; *bātula* — madman; *ataeva* — therefore; *tomāya* — you; *āmāya* — Me; *ha-i* — are; *sama-tula* — on an equal level.

TRANSLATION

Caitanya Mahāprabhu then said, "Indeed, I am a madman, and you are also a madman. Therefore we are on the same platform."

PURPORT

All these conversations between Rāmānanda Rāya and Śrī Caitanya Mahāprabhu appear ludicrous to a common man who is not a devotee. The entire world is filled with material conceptions, and people are unable to understand these conversations due to the conditioning of mundane philosophy. Those who are overly attached to mundane activities cannot understand the ecstatic conversations between Rāmānanda Rāya and Caitanya Mahāprabhu. Consequently the Lord requested that Rāmānanda Rāya keep all these conversations secret and not expose them to the general populace. If one is actually advanced in Kṛṣṇa consciousness, he can understand these confidential talks; otherwise they appear crazy. Śrī Caitanya Mahāprabhu therefore informed Rāmānanda Rāya that they both appeared like madmen and were therefore on the same platform. It is confirmed in the *Bhagavad-gītā* (2.69):

yā niśā sarva-bhūtānāṁ tasyāṁ jāgarti saṁyamī
yasyāṁ jāgrati bhūtāni sā niśā paśyato muneḥ

"What is night for all beings is the time of awakening for the self-controlled, and the time of awakening for all beings is night for the introspective sage."

Sometimes Kṛṣṇa consciousness appears like a type of madness to mundane people, just as the activities of mundaners are considered a form of madness by Kṛṣṇa conscious men.

TEXT 292

এইরূপ দশরাত্রি রামানন্দ-সঙ্গে।
সুখে গোঙাইলা প্রভু কৃষ্ণকথা-রঙ্গে ॥ ২৯২ ॥

ei-rūpa daśa-rātri rāmānanda-saṅge
sukhe goṅāilā prabhu kṛṣṇa-kathā-raṅge

ei-rūpa—in this way; *daśa-rātri*—ten nights; *rāmānanda saṅge*—with Śrī Rāmānanda Rāya; *sukhe*—in great happiness; *goṅāilā*—passed; *prabhu*—Lord Śrī Caitanya Mahāprabhu; *kṛṣṇa-kathā-raṅge*—in transcendental pleasure by discussing talks of Kṛṣṇa.

TRANSLATION

For ten nights Lord Caitanya Mahāprabhu and Rāmānanda Rāya spent a happy time discussing the pastimes of Kṛṣṇa.

TEXT 293

নিগূঢ় ব্রজের রস-লীলার বিচার।
অনেক কহিল, তার না পাইল পার ॥ ২৯৩ ॥

nigūḍha vrajera rasa-līlāra vicāra
aneka kahila, tāra nā pāila pāra

nigūḍha—very confidential; *vrajera*—of Vṛndāvana, or Vrajabhūmi; *rasa-līlāra*—of the pastimes of conjugal love between Kṛṣṇa and the *gopīs; vicāra*—consideration; *aneka*—various; *kahila*—spoke; *tāra*—of that; *nā*—not; *pāila*—got; *pāra*—the limit.

TRANSLATION

The conversations between Rāmānanda Rāya and Śrī Caitanya Mahāprabhu contain the most confidential subject matters, touching

on the conjugal love between Rādhā and Kṛṣṇa in Vṛndāvana [Vrajabhūmi]. Although they talked at great length about these pastimes, they could not reach the limit of discussion.

TEXT 294

তামা, কাঁসা, রূপা, সোনা, রত্নচিন্তামণি ।
কেহ যদি কাহাঁ পোতা পায় একখানি ॥ ২৯৪ ॥

tāmā, kāṅsā, rūpā, sonā, ratna-cintāmaṇi
keha yadi kāhāṅ potā pāya eka-khāni

tāmā—copper; *kāṅsā*—bell metal; *rūpā*—silver; *sonā*—gold; *ratna-cintāmaṇi*—touchstone, the basis of all metals; *keha*—somebody; *yadi*—if; *kāhāṅ*—somewhere; *potā*—buried; *pāya*—finds; *eka-khāni*—in one place.

TRANSLATION

Actually, these conversations are like a great mine where, from a single place, one can extract all kinds of metals—copper, bell metal, silver and gold—and also touchstone, the basis of all metals.

PURPORT

Śrīla Bhaktivinoda Ṭhākura gives the following summary of the conversations between Rāmānanda Rāya and Śrī Caitanya Mahāprabhu. Rāmānanda Rāya replied to five questions of Śrī Caitanya Mahāprabhu, and these questions and their replies are recorded in verses 57–67. The first answer is compared to copper, the second to a better metal, bell metal, the third to a still better metal, silver, and the fourth to the best metal of all, gold. But the fifth answer is compared to the most valuable gem, touchstone, because it deals with unalloyed devotion, the ultimate goal of devotional life, and illuminates the preceding four subordinate answers.

Śrīla Bhaktisiddhānta Sarasvatī Ṭhākura points out that in Vrajabhūmi there is the Yamunā River with its sandy banks. There are *kadamba* trees, cows, Kṛṣṇa's sticks with which He herds cows, and Kṛṣṇa's flute. All of these belong to *śānta-rasa*, the mellow of neutrality in devotional service. There are also the direct servants of Kṛṣṇa, such as Citraka, Patraka and Raktaka, and these are the embodiments of service in the mellow of servitude. There are also friends like Śrīdāmā and Sudāmā, who embody service in fraternity. Nanda Mahārāja and mother Yaśodā are the embodiments of parental love. Above all of these are Śrīmatī Rādhārāṇī and Her assistants, the *gopīs* Lalitā, Viśākhā and others, who embody conjugal love. In this way all five mellows—*śānta, dāsya, sakhya, vātsalya* and *mādhurya*—exist eternally in Vrajabhūmi. They are also compared, respectively, to copper, bell metal, silver, gold and touchstone, the basis of all metals. Śrīla Kavirāja Gosvāmī therefore refers to a mine eternally existing in Vṛndāvana, Vrajabhūmi.

TEXT 295

ক্রমে উঠাইতে সেই উত্তম বস্তু পায় ।
ঐছে প্রশ্নোত্তর কৈল প্রভু-রামরায় ॥ ২৯৫ ॥

krame uṭhāite sei uttama vastu pāya
aiche praśnottara kaila prabhu-rāmarāya

krame—gradually; *uṭhāite*—to raise; *sei*—that person; *uttama*—best; *vastu*—metal; *pāya*—gets; *aiche*—so also; *praśna-uttara*—the questions and answers; *kaila*—have done; *prabhu*—Śrī Caitanya Mahāprabhu; *rāma-rāya*—and Rāmānanda Rāya.

TRANSLATION

Śrī Caitanya Mahāprabhu and Rāmānanda Rāya worked like miners, excavating all kinds of valuable metals, each one better than the other. Their questions and answers are exactly like that.

TEXT 296

আর দিন রায়-পাশে বিদায় মাগিলা ।
বিদায়ের কালে তাঁরে এই আজ্ঞা দিলা ॥ ২৯৬ ॥

āra dina rāya-pāśe vidāya māgilā
vidāyera kāle tāṅre ei ājñā dilā

āra dina—the next day; *rāya-pāśe*—before Rāmānanda Rāya; *vidāya māgilā*—begged farewell; *vidāyera kāle*—at the time of departure; *tāṅre*—unto him; *ei*—this; *ājñā*—order; *dilā*—gave.

TRANSLATION

The next day Śrī Caitanya Mahāprabhu begged Rāmānanda Rāya to give Him permission to leave, and at the time of farewell the Lord gave him the following orders.

TEXT 297

বিষয় ছাড়িয়া তুমি যাহ নীলাচলে।
আমি তীর্থ করি' তাঁহা আসিব অল্পকালে ॥ ২৯৭ ॥

viṣaya chāḍiyā tumi yāha nīlācale
āmi tīrtha kari' tāṅhā āsiba alpa-kāle

viṣaya—material engagement; *chāḍiyā*—giving up; *tumi*—you; *yāha*—go; *nīlācale*—to Jagannātha Purī; *āmi*—I; *tīrtha kari'*—finishing My touring and pilgrimage; *tāṅhā*—there; *āsiba*—shall return; *alpa-kāle*—very soon.

TRANSLATION

Śrī Caitanya Mahāprabhu told him, "Give up all material engagements and come to Jagannātha Purī. I will return there very soon after finishing My tour and pilgrimage.

TEXT 298

দুইজনে নীলাচলে রহিব একসঙ্গে।
সুখে গোঙাইব কাল কৃষ্ণকথা-রঙ্গে ॥ ২৯৮ ॥

dui-jane nīlācale rahiba eka-saṅge
sukhe goṅāiba kāla kṛṣṇa-kathā-raṅge

dui-jane—both of us; *nīlācale*—at Jagannātha Purī; *rahiba*—shall stay; *eka-saṅge*—together; *sukhe*—in happiness; *goṅāiba*—shall pass; *kāla*—time; *kṛṣṇa-kathā-raṅge*—in the pleasure of discussing topics about Kṛṣṇa.

TRANSLATION

"The two of us shall remain together at Jagannātha Purī and happily pass our time discussing Kṛṣṇa."

TEXT 299

এত বলি' রামানন্দে করি' আলিঙ্গন ।
তাঁরে ঘরে পাঠাইয়া করিল শয়ন ॥ ২৯৯ ॥

eta bali' rāmānande kari' āliṅgana
tāṅre ghare pāṭhāiyā karila śayana

eta bali'—saying this; *rāmānande*—to Śrī Rāmānanda Rāya; *kari'*—doing; *āliṅgana*—embracing; *tāṅre*—him; *ghare*—to his home; *pāṭhāiyā*—sending; *karila*—did; *śayana*—lying down.

TRANSLATION

Śrī Caitanya Mahāprabhu then embraced Śrī Rāmānanda Rāya, and after sending him back to his home, the Lord took rest.

TEXT 300

প্রাতঃকালে উঠি' প্রভু দেখি' হনুমান্ ।
তাঁরে নমস্করি' প্রভু দক্ষিণে করিলা প্রয়াণ ॥ ৩০০ ॥

prātaḥ-kāle uṭhi' prabhu dekhi' hanumān
tāṅre namaskari' prabhu dakṣiṇe karilā prayāṇa

prātaḥ-kāle—in the morning; *uṭhi'*—rising; *prabhu*—Lord Śrī Caitanya Mahāprabhu; *dekhi'*—visiting; *hanumān*—the village deity Hanumān; *tāṅre*—unto him; *namaskari'*—offering obeisances; *prabhu*—Śrī Caitanya Mahāprabhu; *dakṣiṇe*—to the south; *karilā*—made; *prayāṇa*—departure.

TRANSLATION

After rising from bed the next morning, Śrī Caitanya Mahāprabhu visited the local temple, where there was a deity of Hanumān. After offering him obeisances, the Lord departed for South India.

PURPORT

In almost all the cities and towns of India there are temples of Hanumānjī, the eternal servant of Lord Rāmacandra. There is even a temple of Hanumān near Govindajī temple in Vṛndāvana. Formerly this temple was in front of the Gopālajī temple, but the Gopālajī Deity went to Orissa to remain as Sākṣi-gopāla. Being the eternal servant of Lord Rāmacandra, Hanumānjī has been respectfully worshiped for many hundreds and thousands of years. Here even Lord Śrī Caitanya Mahāprabhu set the example in showing how one should offer respects to Hanumānjī.

TEXT 301

'বিদ্যাপুরে' নানা-মত লোক বৈসে যত।
প্রভু-দর্শনে 'বৈষ্ণব' হৈল ছাড়ি' নিজমত ॥ ৩০১ ॥

'vidyāpūre' nānā-mata loka vaise yata
prabhu-darśane 'vaiṣṇava' haila chāḍi' nija-mata

vidyāpūre—in the town of Vidyānagara; *nānā-mata*—various opinions; *loka*—people; *vaise*—reside; *yata*—all; *prabhu-darśane*—in seeing Śrī Caitanya Mahāprabhu; *vaiṣṇava*—devotees of Lord Viṣṇu; *haila*—became; *chāḍi'*—giving up; *nija-mata*—own opinions.

TRANSLATION

All the residents of Vidyānagara were of different faiths, but after seeing Śrī Caitanya Mahāprabhu, they abandoned their own faiths and became Vaiṣṇavas.

TEXT 302

রামানন্দ হৈলা প্রভুর বিরহে বিহ্বল।
প্রভুর ধ্যানে রহে বিষয় ছাড়িয়া সকল ॥ ৩০২ ॥

rāmānanda hailā prabhura virahe vihvala
prabhura dhyāne rahe viṣaya chāḍiyā sakala

rāmānanda—Śrīla Rāmānanda Rāya; *hailā*—became; *prabhura*—of Lord Śrī Caitanya Mahāprabhu; *virahe*—in separation;

vihvala—overwhelmed; *prabhura dhyāne*—in meditation on Śrī Caitanya Mahāprabhu; *rahe*—remains; *viṣaya*—worldly business; *chāḍiyā*—giving up; *sakala*—all.

TRANSLATION

When Rāmānanda Rāya began to feel separation from Śrī Caitanya Mahāprabhu, he was overwhelmed. Meditating on the Lord, he gave up all his material business.

TEXT 303

সংক্ষেপে কহিলুঁ রামানন্দের মিলন।
বিস্তারি' বর্ণিতে নারে সহস্র-বদন ॥ ৩০৩ ॥

saṅkṣepe kahiluṅ rāmānandera milana
vistāri' varṇite nāre sahasra-vadana

saṅkṣepe—in brief; *kahiluṅ*—I have described; *rāmānandera milana*—meeting with Śrīla Rāmānanda Rāya; *vistāri'*—expanding; *varṇite*—to describe; *nāre*—not able; *sahasra-vadana*—Lord Śeṣa Nāga, who has thousands of hoods.

TRANSLATION

I have briefly described the meeting between Śrī Caitanya Mahāprabhu and Rāmānanda Rāya. No one can actually describe this meeting exhaustively. It is even impossible for Lord Śeṣa Nāga, who has thousands of hoods.

TEXT 304

সহজে চৈতন্যচরিত্র — ঘনদুগ্ধপূর।
রামানন্দ-চরিত্র তাহে খণ্ড প্রচুর ॥ ৩০৪ ॥

sahaje caitanya-caritra—ghana-dugdha-pūra
rāmānanda-caritra tāhe khaṇḍa pracura

sahaje—generally; *caitanya-caritra*—the activities of Śrī Caitanya Mahāprabhu; *ghana-dugdha-pūra*—like condensed milk;

rāmānanda-caritra—the story of Rāmānanda Rāya; *tāhe*—in that; *khaṇḍa*—sugar candy; *pracura*—a large quantity.

TRANSLATION

The activities of Śrī Caitanya Mahāprabhu are like condensed milk, and the activities of Rāmānanda Rāya are like large quantities of sugar candy.

TEXT 305

রাধাকৃষ্ণলীলা — তাতে কর্পূর-মিলন।
ভাগ্যবান্ যেই, সেই করে আস্বাদন ॥ ৩০৫ ॥

rādhā-kṛṣṇa-līlā — tāte karpūra-milana
bhāgyavān yei, sei kare āsvādana

rādhā-kṛṣṇa-līlā—the pastimes of Śrī Rādhā and Kṛṣṇa; *tāte*—in that composition; *karpūra*—the camphor; *milana*—mixture; *bhāgyavān*—fortunate; *yei*—one who; *sei*—that person; *kare*—does; *āsvādana*—tasting.

TRANSLATION

Their meeting is exactly like a mixture of condensed milk and sugar candy. When they talk of the pastimes of Rādhā and Kṛṣṇa, camphor is added. One who tastes this combined preparation is most fortunate.

TEXT 306

যে ইহা একবার পিয়ে কর্ণদ্বারে।
তার কর্ণ লোভে ইহা ছাড়িতে না পারে ॥ ৩০৬ ॥

ye ihā eka-bāra piye karṇa-dvāre
tāra karṇa lobhe ihā chāḍite nā pāre

ye—anyone; *ihā*—this; *eka-bāra*—once; *piye*—drinks; *karṇa-dvāre*—through aural reception; *tāra*—his; *karṇa*—ears; *lobhe*—in greed; *ihā*—this; *chāḍite*—to give up; *nā*—not; *pāre*—are able.

TRANSLATION

This wonderful preparation has to be taken aurally. If one takes it, he becomes greedy to relish it even further.

TEXT 307

'রসতত্ত্ব-জ্ঞান' হয় ইহার শ্রবণে।
'প্রেমভক্তি' হয় রাধাকৃষ্ণের চরণে ॥ ৩০৭ ॥

'rasa-tattva-jñāna' haya ihāra śravaṇe
'prema-bhakti' haya rādhā-kṛṣṇera caraṇe

rasa-tattva-jñāna—transcendental knowledge of the humors of conjugal love between Rādhā and Kṛṣṇa; *haya*—is; *ihāra*—of this; *śravaṇe*—by hearing; *prema-bhakti*—pure love of Godhead; *haya*—becomes possible; *rādhā-kṛṣṇera caraṇe*—at the lotus feet of Rādhā and Kṛṣṇa.

TRANSLATION

By hearing the talks between Rāmānanda Rāya and Śrī Caitanya Mahāprabhu, one becomes enlightened with the transcendental knowledge of the mellows of Rādhā and Kṛṣṇa's pastimes. Thus one can develop unalloyed love for the lotus feet of Rādhā and Kṛṣṇa.

TEXT 308

চৈতন্যের গূঢ়তত্ত্ব জানি ইহা হৈতে।
বিশ্বাস করি' শুন, তর্ক না করিহ চিত্তে ॥ ৩০৮ ॥

caitanyera gūḍha-tattva jāni ihā haite
viśvāsa kari' śuna, tarka nā kariha citte

caitanyera—of Lord Śrī Caitanya Mahāprabhu; *gūḍha-tattva*—the confidential truth; *jāni*—we can learn; *ihā haite*—from these talks; *viśvāsa kari'*—having firm faith; *śuna*—hear; *tarka*—arguments; *nā*—not; *kariha*—do; *citte*—within the heart.

TRANSLATION

The author requests every reader to hear these talks with faith and without argument. By studying them in this way, one will be able to understand the confidential truth of Śrī Caitanya Mahāprabhu.

TEXT 309

অলৌকিক লীলা এই পরম নিগূঢ় ।
বিশ্বাসে পাইয়ে, তর্কে হয় বহুদূর ॥ ৩০৯ ॥

alaukika līlā ei parama nigūḍha
viśvāse pāiye, tarke haya bahu-dūra

alaukika—uncommon; *līlā*—pastimes; *ei*—this; *parama*—most; *nigūḍha*—confidential; *viśvāse*—by faith; *pāiye*—we can get; *tarke*—by argument; *haya*—is; *bahu-dūra*—far away.

TRANSLATION

This part of Śrī Caitanya Mahāprabhu's pastimes is most confidential. One can derive benefit quickly only by faith; otherwise, by arguing one will always remain far away.

TEXT 310

শ্রীচৈতন্য-নিত্যানন্দ-অদ্বৈত-চরণ ।
যাঁহার সর্বস্ব, তাঁরে মিলে এই ধন ॥ ৩১০ ॥

śrī-caitanya-nityānanda-advaita-caraṇa
yāṅhāra sarvasva, tāṅre mile ei dhana

śrī-caitanya—of Lord Śrī Caitanya Mahāprabhu; *nityānanda*—of Lord Nityānanda; *advaita-caraṇa*—and the lotus feet of Śrī Advaita Prabhu; *yāṅhāra sarva-sva*—whose everything; *tāṅre*—him; *mile*—meets; *ei*—this; *dhana*—treasure.

TRANSLATION

He who has accepted as everything the lotus feet of Śrī Caitanya Mahāprabhu, Nityānanda Prabhu and Advaita Prabhu can attain this transcendental treasure.

PURPORT

Śrī Bhaktisiddhānta Sarasvatī Ṭhākura says that Kṛṣṇa is obtainable for the faithful, but for those who are accustomed to argue, Kṛṣṇa is far, far away. Similarly, these talks between Rāmānanda Rāya and Śrī Caitanya Mahāprabhu can be understood by a person who has firm faith. Those who are not in the disciplic succession, the *asauta-panthīs,* cannot have faith in these talks. They are always doubting and engaging in mental concoctions. These talks cannot be understood by such whimsical people. Transcendental topics remain far, far away from those engaged in mundane arguments. In this regard, the Vedic *mantras* in the *Kaṭha Upaniṣad* (1.2.9) state, *naiṣā tarkeṇa matir āpaneyā proktānyenaiva su-jñānāya preṣṭha.* According to the *Muṇḍaka Upaniṣad* (3.2.3):

nāyam ātmā pravacanena labhyo
na medhayā na bahunā śrutena
yam evaiṣa vṛṇute tena labhyas
tasyaiṣa ātmā vivṛṇute tanūṁ svām

And according to the *Brahma-sūtra* (2.1.11), *tarkāpratiṣṭhānāt.*

All Vedic literatures declare that transcendental subjects cannot be understood simply by argument or logic. Spiritual matters are far above experimental knowledge. Only by Kṛṣṇa's mercy can one who is interested in His transcendental loving affairs understand them. If one tries to understand these transcendental topics simply by using one's material brain substance, the attempt will be futile. Whether one is a *prākṛta-sahajiyā* or a mundane opportunist or scholar, one's labor to understand these topics by mundane means will ultimately be frustrated. One therefore has to give up all mundane attempts and try to become a pure devotee of Lord Viṣṇu. When a devotee follows the regulative principles, the truth of these talks will be revealed to him. This is confirmed in the *Bhakti-rasāmṛta-sindhu* (1.2.234):

ataḥ śrī-kṛṣṇa-nāmādi na bhaved grāhyam indriyaiḥ
sevonmukhe hi jihvādau svayam eva sphuraty adaḥ

One cannot understand the Lord's holy name, pastimes, form, qualities or entourage with one's blunt material senses. However, when the senses are purified by the constant rendering of service, the spiritual truth of the pastimes of Rādhā and Kṛṣṇa is revealed. As confirmed in the *Muṇḍaka Upaniṣad, yam evaiṣa vṛṇute tena labhyas.* Only one who is favored by the Supreme Personality of Godhead can understand the transcendental features of Śrī Caitanya Mahāprabhu.

TEXT 311

রামানন্দ রায়ে মোর কোটী নমস্কার ।
যাঁর মুখে কৈল প্রভু রসের বিস্তার ॥ ৩১১ ॥

rāmānanda rāye mora koṭī namaskāra
yāṅra mukhe kaila prabhu rasera vistāra

rāmānanda rāye—unto Śrī Rāmānanda Rāya; *mora*—my; *koṭī*—ten million; *namaskāra*—obeisances; *yāṅra mukhe*—in whose mouth; *kaila*—did; *prabhu*—Śrī Caitanya Mahāprabhu; *rasera vistāra*—the expansion of transcendental mellows.

TRANSLATION

I offer ten million obeisances unto the lotus feet of Śrī Rāmānanda Rāya because from his mouth much spiritual information has been expanded by Śrī Caitanya Mahāprabhu.

TEXT 312

দামোদর-স্বরূপের কড়চা-অনুসারে ।
রামানন্দ-মিলন-লীলা করিল প্রচারে ॥ ৩১২ ॥

dāmodara-svarūpera kaḍacā-anusāre
rāmānanda-milana-līlā karila pracāre

dāmodara-svarūpera—of Svarūpa Dāmodara Gosvāmī; *kaḍacā*—with the notebooks; *anusāre*—in accordance; *rāmānanda-milana-līlā*—the pastimes of the meeting with Rāmānanda; *karila*—have done; *pracāre*—distribution.

TRANSLATION

I have tried to preach the pastimes of Lord Śrī Caitanya Mahāprabhu's meeting with Rāmānanda Rāya in accordance with the notebooks of Śrī Svarūpa Dāmodara.

PURPORT

At the end of every chapter, the author admits the value of the disciplic succession. He never claims to have written this transcendental literature by carrying out research work. He simply admits his indebtedness to the notes taken by Svarūpa Dāmodara, Raghunātha dāsa Gosvāmī and other authoritative persons. This is the way of writing transcendental literatures, which are never meant for so-called scholars and research workers. The process is *mahā-jano yena gataḥ sa panthāḥ:* one has to strictly follow great personalities and *ācāryas. Ācārya-vān puruṣo veda:* one who has the favor of the *ācārya* knows everything. This statement made by Kavirāja Gosvāmī is very valuable for all pure devotees. Sometimes the *prākṛtā sahajiyās* claim that they have heard the truth from their *guru.* But one cannot have transcendental knowledge simply by hearing from a *guru* who is not bona fide. The *guru* must be bona fide, and he must have heard from his own bona fide *guru.* Only then will his message be accepted as bona fide. Lord Kṛṣṇa confirms this in the *Bhagavad-gītā* (4.1):

śrī-bhagavān uvāca
imaṁ vivasvate yogaṁ proktavān aham avyayam
vivasvān manave prāha manur ikṣvākave 'bravīt

"The Supreme Lord said, 'I instructed this imperishable science of *yoga* to the sun-god, Vivasvān, and Vivasvān instructed it to Manu, the father of mankind, and Manu in turn instructed it to Ikṣvāku.'"

In this way the message is transmitted in the bona fide spiritual disciplic succession from bona fide spiritual master to bona fide student. Śrīla Kavirāja Gosvāmī therefore as usual concludes this chapter by reasserting his faith in the lotus feet of the six Gosvāmīs. Thus he is able to set forth this transcendental literature, *Śrī Caitanya-caritāmṛta.*

TEXT 313

শ্রীরূপ-রঘুনাথ-পদে যার আশ।
চৈতন্যচরিতামৃত কহে কৃষ্ণদাস ॥ ৩১৩ ॥

śrī-rūpa-raghunātha-pade yāra āśa
caitanya-caritāmṛta kahe kṛṣṇadāsa

śrī-rūpa—Śrīla Rūpa Gosvāmī; *raghunātha*—Śrīla Raghunātha dāsa Gosvāmī; *pade*—at the lotus feet; *yāra*—whose; *āśa*—expectation; *caitanya-caritāmṛta*—the book named *Caitanya-caritāmṛta; kahe*—describes; *kṛṣṇa-dāsa*—Śrīla Kṛṣṇadāsa Kavirāja Gosvāmī.

TRANSLATION

Praying at the lotus feet of Śrī Rūpa and Śrī Raghunātha, always desiring their mercy, I, Kṛṣṇadāsa, narrate Śrī Caitanya-caritāmṛta, following in their footsteps.

Thus end the Bhaktivedanta purports to Śrī Caitanya-caritāmṛta, Madhya-līlā, *Eighth Chapter, describing the talks between Śrī Caitanya Mahāprabhu and Rāmānanda Rāya.*

CHAPTER NINE

Lord Śrī Caitanya Mahāprabhu's Travels to the Holy Places

A summary of the Ninth Chapter is given by Śrīla Bhaktivinoda Ṭhākura. After leaving Vidyānagara, Śrī Caitanya Mahāprabhu visited such places of pilgrimage as Gautamī-gaṅgā, Mallikārjuna, Ahovala-nṛsiṁha, Siddhavaṭa, Skanda-kṣetra, Trimaṭha, Vṛddhakāśī, Bauddha-sthāna, Tirupati, Tirumala, Pānā-nṛsiṁha, Śiva-kāñcī, Viṣṇu-kāñcī, Trikāla-hasti, Vṛddhakola, Śiyālī-bhairavī, the Kāverī River and Kumbhakarṇa-kapāla.

Finally the Lord went to Śrī Raṅga-kṣetra, where He converted a *brāhmaṇa* named Veṅkaṭa Bhaṭṭa, who, along with his family, took up devotional service to Kṛṣṇa. After leaving Śrī Raṅga, Caitanya Mahāprabhu reached Ṛṣabha-parvata, where He met Paramānanda Purī, who later arrived at Jagannātha Purī. Lord Śrī Caitanya Mahāprabhu then proceeded farther, arriving at Setubandha Rāmeśvara. At Śrī Śaila-parvata, the Lord met Lord Śiva and his wife Durgā in the dress of a *brāhmaṇa* and *brāhmaṇī.* From there He went to Kāmakoṣṭhī-purī and later arrived at southern Mathurā. A *brāhmaṇa* devotee of Lord Rāmacandra talked with Him. Then the Lord took His bath in the river Kṛtamālā. On the hill known as Mahendra-śaila, the Lord saw Paraśurāma. Then the Lord went to Setubandha and took His bath at Dhanus-tīrtha. He also visited Rāmeśvara, where He collected some papers connected with Sītādevī, whose illusory form had been kidnapped by Rāvaṇa. The Lord next visited the places known as Pāṇḍya-deśa, the Tāmraparṇī River, Naya-tripati, Ciyaḍatalā, Tila-kāñcī, Gajendra-mokṣaṇa, Pānāgaḍi, Cāmtāpura, Śrī Vaikuṇṭha, Malaya-parvata and Kanyā-kumārī. The Lord then confronted the Bhaṭṭathāris at Mallāra-deśa and saved Kālā Kṛṣṇadāsa from their clutches. The Lord also collected the *Brahma-saṁhitā,* Fifth Chapter, on the banks of the Payasvinī River. He then visited Payasvinī, Śṛṅgavera-purī-maṭha and Matsya-tīrtha. At the village of Uḍupī He saw the Gopāla Deity installed by Śrī Madhvācārya. He then defeated the Tattvavādīs in śāstric conversation. The Lord next visited Phalgu-tīrtha, Tritakūpa, Pañcāpsarā, Sūrpāraka and Kolāpura. At Pāṇḍarapura the Lord received news from Śrī Raṅga Purī that Śaṅkarāraṇya (Viśvarūpa) had disappeared there. He then went to the banks of the Kṛṣṇa-veṇvā River, where He collected from among the Vaiṣṇava *brāhmaṇas* a book written by Bilvamaṅgala Ṭhākura, *Śrī Kṛṣṇa-karṇāmṛta.* The Lord then visited Tāpī, Māhiṣmatī-pura, the Narmadā River and Ṛṣyamūka-parvata. He entered Daṇḍakāraṇya and liberated seven palm trees. From there He visited a place known as Pampā-sarovara and visited Pañcavaṭī, Nāsika, Brahmagiri and also the source of the Godāvarī River, Kuśāvarta. Thus the Lord visited almost all the holy places in South India. He finally returned to Jagannātha Purī by taking the same route, after visiting Vidyānagara again.

TEXT 1

নানামতগ্রাহগ্রস্তান্ দাক্ষিণাত্যজনদ্বিপান্ ।
কৃপারিণা বিমুচ্যৈতান্ গৌরশ্চক্রে স বৈষ্ণবান্ ॥ ১ ॥

nānā-mata-grāha-grastān
dākṣiṇātya-jana-dvipān
kṛpāriṇā vimucyaitān
gauraś cakre sa vaiṣṇavān

nānā-mata—by various philosophies; *grāha*—like crocodiles; *grastān*—captured; *dākṣiṇātya-jana*—the inhabitants of South India; *dvipān*—like elephants; *kṛpā-ariṇā*—by His disc of mercy; *vimucya*—liberating; *etān*—all these; *gauraḥ*—Śrī Caitanya Mahāprabhu; *cakre*—converted; *saḥ*—He; *vaiṣṇavān*—to the Vaiṣṇava cult.

TRANSLATION

Lord Śrī Caitanya Mahāprabhu converted the inhabitants of South India. These people were as strong as elephants, but they were

in the clutches of the crocodiles of various philosophies, such as the Buddhist, Jain and Māyāvāda philosophies. With His disc of mercy the Lord delivered them all by converting them into Vaiṣṇavas, devotees of the Lord.

PURPORT

Śrī Caitanya Mahāprabhu's converting the people of South India into Vaiṣṇavas is compared herein to Lord Viṣṇu's delivering Gajendra the elephant from the attack of a crocodile. When Śrī Caitanya Mahāprabhu visited southern India, almost all the residents were within the jaws of the crocodiles of Buddhist, Jain and Māyāvāda philosophy. Here Kavirāja Gosvāmī states that although these people were as strong as elephants, they were almost in the clutches of death because they were being attacked by the crocodiles of various philosophies. However, just as Śrī Caitanya Mahāprabhu in the form of Viṣṇu saved the elephant Gajendra from the clutches of a crocodile, so He saved all the people of South India from the clutches of various philosophies by converting them into Vaiṣṇavas.

TEXT 2

জয় জয় শ্রীচৈতন্য জয় নিত্যানন্দ ।
জয়াদ্বৈতচন্দ্র জয় গৌরভক্তবৃন্দ ॥ ২ ॥

jaya jaya śrī-caitanya jaya nityānanda
jayādvaita-candra jaya gaura-bhakta-vṛnda

jaya jaya—all glories; *śrī-caitanya*—to Lord Caitanya Mahāprabhu; *jaya*—all glories; *nityānanda*—unto Nityānanda Prabhu; *jaya advaita-candra*—all glories to Advaita Prabhu; *jaya*—all glories; *gaura-bhakta-vṛnda*—to the devotees of Lord Śrī Caitanya Mahāprabhu.

TRANSLATION

All glories to Lord Śrī Caitanya Mahāprabhu! All glories to Lord Nityānanda Prabhu! All glories to Śrī Advaita Prabhu! And all glories to all the devotees of Śrī Caitanya Mahāprabhu!

TEXT 3

দক্ষিণগমন প্রভুর অতি বিলক্ষণ।
সহস্র সহস্র তীর্থ কৈল দরশন ॥ ৩ ॥

dakṣiṇa-gamana prabhura ati vilakṣaṇa
sahasra sahasra tīrtha kaila daraśana

dakṣiṇa-gamana—touring in South India; *prabhura*—of the Lord; *ati*—very; *vilakṣaṇa*—extraordinary; *sahasra sahasra*—thousands and thousands; *tīrtha*—holy places; *kaila*—did; *daraśana*—visit.

TRANSLATION

Śrī Caitanya Mahāprabhu's tour of South India was certainly very extraordinary because He visited many thousands of places of pilgrimage there.

TEXT 4

সেই সব তীর্থ স্পর্শি' মহাতীর্থ কৈল।
সেই ছলে সেই দেশের লোক নিস্তারিল ॥ ৪ ॥

sei saba tīrtha sparśi' mahā-tīrtha kaila
sei chale sei deśera loka nistārila

sei saba—all those; *tīrtha*—holy places; *sparśi'*—touching; *mahā-tīrtha*—into great places of pilgrimage; *kaila*—made them; *sei chale*—under that plea; *sei deśera*—of those countries; *loka*—the people; *nistārila*—He delivered.

TRANSLATION

On the plea of visiting all those holy places, the Lord converted many thousands of residents and thus delivered them. Simply by touching the holy places, He made them into great places of pilgrimage.

PURPORT

It is said, *tīrthī-kurvanti tīrthāni.* A *tīrtha,* or holy place, is a place where great saintly personalities visit or reside. Although the holy places were already places of pilgrimage, they were all purified by Śrī Caitanya Mahāprabhu's visit. Many people go to these holy places and leave their sinful activities there, thus becoming free from contamination. When these contaminations pile up, they are counteracted by the visit of great personalities like Śrī Caitanya Mahāprabhu and His strict followers. Many kinds of patients come to a hospital, which may be infected by many types of diseases. Actually the hospital is always infected, but the expert physician keeps the hospital sterilized by his expert presence and management. Similarly, places of pilgrimage are always infected by the sins left by the sinners who go there, but when a personality like Śrī Caitanya Mahāprabhu visits such a place, all contaminations vanish.

TEXT 5

সেই সব তীর্থের ক্রম কহিতে না পারি ।
দক্ষিণ-বামে তীর্থ-গমন হয় ফেরাফেরি ॥ ৫ ॥

sei saba tīrthera krama kahite nā pāri
dakṣiṇa-vāme tīrtha-gamana haya pherāpheri

sei saba—all those; *tīrthera*—of holy places; *krama*—the chronological order; *kahite*—to tell of; *nā pāri*—I am unable; *dakṣiṇa-vāme*—left and right; *tīrtha-gamana*—visiting the holy places; *haya*—is; *pherāpheri*—going and coming back.

TRANSLATION

I cannot chronologically record all the places of pilgrimage visited by Lord Śrī Caitanya Mahāprabhu. I can only summarize everything by saying that the Lord visited all holy places right and left, coming and going.

TEXT 6

অতএব নাম-মাত্র করিয়ে গণন ।
কহিতে না পারি তার যথা অনুক্রম ॥ ৬ ॥

ataeva nāma-mātra kariye gaṇana
kahite nā pāri tāra yathā anukrama

ataeva—therefore; *nāma-mātra*—only as a token record; *kariye gaṇana*—I count; *kahite*—to tell; *nā pāri*—I am unable; *tāra*—of that; *yathā*—as; *anukrama*—chronological order.

TRANSLATION

Because it is impossible for me to record all these places in chronological order, I will simply make a token gesture of recording them.

TEXTS 7–8

পূর্ব্ববৎ পথে যাইতে যে পায় দরশন।
যেই গ্রামে যায়, সে গ্রামের যত জন ॥ ৭ ॥
সবেই বৈষ্ণব হয়, কহে 'কৃষ্ণ' 'হরি'।
অন্য গ্রাম নিস্তারয়ে সেই 'বৈষ্ণব' করি' ॥ ৮ ॥

pūrvavat pathe yāite ye pāya daraśana
yei grāme yāya, se grāmera yata jana

sabei vaiṣṇava haya, kahe 'kṛṣṇa' 'hari'
anya grāma nistāraye sei 'vaiṣṇava' kari'

pūrva-vat—as done previously; *pathe*—on the way; *yāite*—while going; *ye*—anyone who; *pāya*—gets; *daraśana*—audience; *yei*—which; *grāme*—in the village; *yāya*—Lord Śrī Caitanya Mahāprabhu goes; *se*—that; *grāmera*—of the village; *yata*—all; *jana*—people; *sabei*—all of them; *vaiṣṇava haya*—become devotees; *kahe*—say; *kṛṣṇa hari*—the holy names of Lord Kṛṣṇa and Hari; *anya grāma*—other villages; *nistāraye*—delivers; *sei*—He; *vaiṣṇava*—devotees; *kari'*—making.

TRANSLATION

As previously stated, all the residents of the villages visited by Lord Caitanya became Vaiṣṇavas and began to chant Hari and Kṛṣṇa. In this way, in all the villages visited by the Lord, everyone became a Vaiṣṇava, a devotee.

PURPORT

The holy names of Kṛṣṇa and Hari, or the chanting of the Hare Kṛṣṇa *mahā-mantra,* are so spiritually powerful that even today, as our preachers go to remote parts of the world, people immediately begin chanting Hare Kṛṣṇa. Śrī Caitanya Mahāprabhu was the Supreme Personality of Godhead Himself. There cannot be anyone who can compare to Him or His potencies. However, because we are following in His footsteps and are also chanting the Hare Kṛṣṇa *mahā-mantra,* the effect is almost as potent as during the time of Lord Caitanya Mahāprabhu. Our preachers mainly belong to European and American countries, yet by the grace of Lord Caitanya they have tremendous success wherever they go to open branches. Indeed, everywhere people are very seriously chanting Hare Kṛṣṇa, Hare Kṛṣṇa, Kṛṣṇa Kṛṣṇa, Hare Hare/ Hare Rāma, Hare Rāma, Rāma Rāma, Hare Hare.

TEXT 9

দক্ষিণ দেশের লোক অনেক প্রকার।
কেহ জ্ঞানী, কেহ কর্মী, পাষণ্ডী অপার ॥ ৯ ॥

dakṣiṇa deśera loka aneka prakāra
keha jñānī, keha karmī, pāṣaṇḍī apāra

dakṣiṇa deśera—of South India; *loka*—people; *aneka*—many; *prakāra*—varieties; *keha*—someone; *jñānī*—philosophical speculator; *keha*—someone; *karmī*—fruitive worker; *pāṣaṇḍī*—nondevotees; *apāra*—innumerable.

TRANSLATION

In South India there were many types of people. Some were philosophical speculators, and some were fruitive workers, but in any case there were innumerable nondevotees.

TEXT 10

সেই সব লোক প্রভুর দর্শনপ্রভাবে।
নিজ-নিজ-মত ছাড়ি' হইল বৈষ্ণবে ॥ ১০ ॥

sei saba loka prabhura darśana-prabhāve
nija-nija-mata chāḍi' ha-ila vaiṣṇave

sei saba loka—all those people; *prabhura*—of Lord Śrī Caitanya Mahāprabhu; *darśana-prabhāve*—by the influence of His visit; *nija-nija*—their own; *mata*—opinion; *chāḍi'*—giving up; *ha-ila*—became; *vaiṣṇave*—devotees.

TRANSLATION

By the influence of Śrī Caitanya Mahāprabhu, all these people abandoned their own opinions and became Vaiṣṇavas, devotees of Kṛṣṇa.

TEXT 11

বৈষ্ণবের মধ্যে রাম-উপাসক সব।
কেহ 'তত্ত্ববাদী', কেহ হয় 'শ্রীবৈষ্ণব' ॥ ১১ ॥

vaiṣṇavera madhye rāma-upāsaka saba
keha 'tattvavādī', keha haya 'śrī-vaiṣṇava'

vaiṣṇavera madhye—amongst Vaiṣṇavas; *rāma-upāsaka saba*—all worshipers of Lord Śrī Rāmacandra; *keha*—someone; *tattva-vādī*—followers of Madhvācārya; *keha*—someone; *haya*—is; *śrī-vaiṣṇava*—devotees following the disciplic succession of Śrī Rāmānujācārya.

TRANSLATION

At the time, all the South Indian Vaiṣṇavas were worshipers of Lord Rāmacandra. Some were Tattvavādīs, and some were followers of Rāmānujācārya.

PURPORT

Śrīla Bhaktisiddhānta Sarasvatī Ṭhākura points out that the word "Tattvavādī" refers to the followers of Śrīla Madhvācārya. To distinguish his disciplic succession from the Māyāvādī followers of Śaṅkarācārya, Śrīla Madhvācārya named his party the Tattvavādīs. Impersonal monists are always attacked by these Tattvavādīs, who attempt to defeat their philosophy of impersonalism. Generally, they establish the supremacy of the Supreme Personality of Godhead. Actually the disciplic succession of Madhvācārya is known as the Brahmā Vaiṣṇava sect; that is the sect coming down from Lord Brahmā. Consequently the Tattvavādīs, or followers of Madhvācārya, do not accept the incident of Lord Brahmā's illusion, which is recorded in the Tenth Canto of *Śrīmad-Bhāgavatam.* Śrīla Madhvācārya has purposefully avoided commenting on that portion of *Śrīmad-Bhāgavatam* in which *brahma-mohana,* the illusion of Lord Brahmā, is mentioned. Śrīla Mādhavendra Purī was one of the *ācāryas* in the Tattvavāda disciplic succession, and he established the ultimate goal of transcendentalism to be attainment of pure devotional service, love of Godhead. Those Vaiṣṇavas belonging to the Gauḍīya-sampradāya, the disciplic succession following Śrī Caitanya Mahāprabhu, are distinct from the Tattvavādīs, although they belong to the same Tattvavāda-sampradāya. The followers of Śrī Caitanya Mahāprabhu are therefore known as the Madhva-Gauḍīya-sampradāya.

The word *pāṣaṇḍī* refers to those who are opposed to pure devotional service. In particular, these are the Māyāvādīs, the impersonalists. A definition of *pāṣaṇḍī* is given in the *Hari-bhakti-vilāsa* (1.73), wherein it is stated:

> *yas tu nārāyaṇaṁ devaṁ brahma-rudrādi-daivataiḥ*
> *samatvenaiva vīkṣeta sa pāṣaṇḍī bhaved dhruvam*

A *pāṣaṇḍī* is one who thinks that the Supreme Lord Nārāyaṇa, the Personality of Godhead, is on the same level with the demigods, headed by Lord Brahmā and Lord Śiva. A devotee never considers Lord Nārāyaṇa to be on the same platform with Lord Brahmā and Lord Śiva. The Madhvācārya-sampradāya and Rāmānuja-sampradāya are mainly worshipers of Lord Rāmacandra, although the Śrī Vaiṣṇavas are supposed to be worshipers of Lord Nārāyaṇa and Lakṣmī and the Tattvavādīs are supposed to be worshipers of Lord Kṛṣṇa. At present, in most of the monasteries belonging to the Madhva-sampradāya, Lord Rāmacandra is worshiped.

In the book known as *Adhyātma-rāmāyaṇa,* there are statements in Chapters Twelve to Fifteen about worshiping the Deities of Śrī

Rāmacandra and Sītā. There it is stated that during Lord Rāmacandra's time there was a *brāhmaṇa* who took a vow to fast until he saw Lord Rāmacandra. Sometimes, due to business, Lord Rāmacandra was absent from His capital for a full week and could not be seen by the citizens during that time. Because of his vow, the *brāhmaṇa* could not take even a drop of water during that week. Later, after eight or nine days, when the *brāhmaṇa* could see Lord Rāmacandra personally, he would break his fast. Upon observing the *brāhmaṇa's* rigid vow, Lord Śrī Rāmacandra ordered His younger brother Lakṣmaṇa to deliver a pair of Sītā-Rāma Deities to the *brāhmaṇa.* The *brāhmaṇa* received the Deities from Śrī Lakṣmaṇajī and worshiped Them faithfully as long as he lived. At the time of his death, he delivered the Deities to Śrī Hanumānjī, who, for many years, hung Them around his neck and served Them with all devotion. After many years, when Hanumānjī departed on the hill known as Gandha-mādana, he delivered the Deities to Bhīmasena, one of the Pāṇḍavas, and Bhīmasena brought Them to his palace, where he kept Them very carefully. The last king of the Pāṇḍavas, Kṣemakānta, worshiped the Deities in that palace. Later, the same Deities were kept in the custody of the kings of Orissa known as Gajapatis. One of the *ācāryas,* known as Narahari Tīrtha, who was in the disciplic succession of Madhvācārya, received these Deities from the King of Orissa.

It may be noted that these particular Deities of Rāma and Sītā have been worshiped from the time of King Ikṣvāku. Indeed, they were worshiped by the royal princes even before the appearance of Lord Rāmacandra. Later, during Lord Rāmacandra's presence, the Deities were worshiped by Lakṣmaṇa. It is said that just three months before his disappearance, Śrī Madhvācārya received these Deities and installed them in the Uḍupī temple. Since then the Deities have been worshiped by the Madhvācārya-sampradāya at that monastery. As far as the Śrī Vaiṣṇavas are concerned, beginning with Rāmānujācārya, they also worshiped Deities of Sītā-Rāma. Sītā-Rāma Deities are also being worshiped in Tirupati and other places. From the Śrī Rāmānuja-sampradāya there is another branch known as Rāmānandī or Rāmāt, and the followers of that branch also worship Deities of Sītā-Rāma very rigidly. The Rāmānuja-sampradāya Vaiṣṇavas prefer the worship of Lord Rāmacandra to that of Rādhā-Kṛṣṇa.

TEXT 12

সেই সব বৈষ্ণব মহাপ্রভুর দর্শনে।
কৃষ্ণ-উপাসক হৈল, লয় কৃষ্ণনামে ॥ ১২॥

sei saba vaiṣṇava mahāprabhura darśane
kṛṣṇa-upāsaka haila, laya kṛṣṇa-nāme

sei saba—all those; *vaiṣṇava*—devotees; *mahāprabhura*—of Śrī Caitanya Mahāprabhu; *darśane*—by seeing; *kṛṣṇa-upāsaka*—devotees of Lord Kṛṣṇa; *haila*—became; *laya*—took; *kṛṣṇa-nāme*—the holy name of Lord Kṛṣṇa.

TRANSLATION

After meeting Śrī Caitanya Mahāprabhu, all those different Vaiṣṇavas became devotees of Kṛṣṇa and began chanting the Hare Kṛṣṇa mahā-mantra.

TEXT 13

রাম! রাঘব! রাম! রাঘব! রাম! রাঘব! পাহি মাম্।
কৃষ্ণ! কেশব! কৃষ্ণ! কেশব! কৃষ্ণ! কেশব! রক্ষ মাম্॥ ১৩ ॥

rāma! rāghava! rāma! rāghava! rāma! rāghava! pāhi mām
kṛṣṇa! keśava! kṛṣṇa! keśava! kṛṣṇa! keśava! rakṣa mām

rāma—O Rāma; *rāghava*—O descendant of Raghu; *pāhi*—please protect; *mām*—me; *kṛṣṇa*—O Kṛṣṇa; *keśava*—O killer of Keśī; *rakṣa*—protect; *mām*—me.

TRANSLATION

"'O Lord Rāmacandra, descendant of Mahārāja Raghu, kindly protect me! O Lord Kṛṣṇa, killer of the Keśī demon, kindly protect me!'"

TEXT 14

এই শ্লোক পথে পড়ি' করিলা প্রয়াণ।
গৌতমী-গঙ্গায় যাই' কৈল গঙ্গাস্নান ॥ ১৪ ॥

ei śloka pathe paḍi' karilā prayāṇa
gautamī-gaṅgāya yāi' kaila gaṅgā-snāna

ei śloka—this Sanskrit verse; *pathe*—on the way; *paḍi'*—reciting; *karilā*—did; *prayāṇa*—going; *gautamī-gaṅgāya*—to the bank of the Gautamī-gaṅgā; *yāi'*—going; *kaila*—did; *gaṅgā-snāna*—bathing in the Ganges.

TRANSLATION

While walking on the road, Śrī Caitanya Mahāprabhu used to chant this Rāma Rāghava mantra. Chanting in this way, He arrived at the banks of the Gautamī-gaṅgā and took His bath there.

PURPORT

The Gautamī-gaṅgā is a branch of the river Godāvarī. Formerly a great sage named Gautama Ṛṣi used to live on the bank of this river opposite the city of Rājamahendrī, and consequently this branch was called the Gautamī-gaṅgā.

Śrīla Bhaktivinoda Ṭhākura says that Śrīla Kavirāja Gosvāmī has recorded the names of the holy places visited by Śrī Caitanya Mahāprabhu but that there is no chronological order of the places visited. However, there is a notebook of Govinda dāsa's containing a chronological order and references to geographical positions. Śrīla Bhaktivinoda Ṭhākura requests the readers to refer to that book. According to Govinda dāsa, Śrī Caitanya Mahāprabhu went to Trimanda from the Gautamī-gaṅgā. From there He went to Ḍhuṇḍirāma-tīrtha, another place of pilgrimage. According to *Śrī Caitanya-caritāmṛta,* after visiting the Gautamī-gaṅgā, Śrī Caitanya Mahāprabhu went to Mallikārjuna-tīrtha.

TEXT 15

মল্লিকার্জুন-তীর্থে যাই' মহেশ দেখিল ।
তাহাঁ সব লোকে কৃষ্ণনাম লওয়াইল ॥ ১৫ ॥

mallikārjuna-tīrthe yāi' maheśa dekhila
tāhāṅ saba loke kṛṣṇa-nāma laoyāila

mallikārjuna-tīrthe—to the holy place known as Mallikārjuna; *yāi'*—going; *maheśa*—the deity of Lord Śiva; *dekhila*—He saw; *tāhāṅ*—there; *saba loke*—all the people; *kṛṣṇa-nāma*—Lord Kṛṣṇa's holy name; *laoyāila*—He induced to chant.

TRANSLATION

Śrī Caitanya Mahāprabhu then went to Mallikārjuna-tīrtha and saw the deity of Lord Śiva there. He also induced all the people to chant the Hare Kṛṣṇa mahā-mantra.

PURPORT

Mallikārjuna is also known as Śrī Saila. It is situated about one hundred miles northeast of Karṇula on the southern bank of the Kṛṣṇā River. There are great walls all around the village, and within the walls resides the deity known as Mallikārjuna. It is a deity of Lord Śiva and is one of the Jyotir-liṅgas.

TEXT 16

রামদাস মহাদেবে করিল দরশন ।
অহোবল-নৃসিংহেরে করিলা গমন ॥ ১৬ ॥

rāmadāsa mahādeve karila daraśana
ahovala-nṛsiṁhere karilā gamana

rāma-dāsa—Rāmadāsa; *mahā-deve*—of Mahādeva; *karila*—did; *daraśana*—seeing; *ahovala-nṛsiṁhere*—to Ahovala-nṛsiṁha; *karilā*—did; *gamana*—going.

TRANSLATION

There He saw Lord Mahādeva [Śiva], the servant of Lord Rāma. He then went to Ahovala-nṛsiṁha.

TEXT 17

নৃসিংহ দেখিয়া তাঁরে কৈল নতি-স্তুতি ।
সিদ্ধবট গেলা যাহাঁ মূর্তি সীতাপতি ॥ ১৭ ॥

nṛsiṁha dekhiyā tāṅre kaila nati-stuti
siddhavaṭa gelā yāhāṅ mūrti sītāpati

nṛsiṁha dekhiyā—after seeing the Lord Nṛsiṁha Deity; *tāṅre*—unto Him; *kaila*—did; *nati-stuti*—offering of various prayers; *siddhavaṭa*—to Siddhavaṭa; *gelā*—He went; *yāhāṅ*—where; *mūrti*—the Deity; *sītā-pati*—Lord Rāmacandra.

TRANSLATION

Upon seeing the Ahovala-nṛsiṁha Deity, Caitanya Mahāprabhu offered many prayers unto the Lord. He then went to Siddhavaṭa, where He saw the Deity of Rāmacandra, the Lord of Sītādevī.

PURPORT

Siddhavaṭa, also known as Sidhauṭa, is ten miles east of the village of Kuḍāpā. Previously this place was also known as the southern Benares. There is a great banyan tree there, and it is therefore known as Siddhavaṭa. *Vaṭa* means banyan tree.

TEXT 18

রঘুনাথ দেখি' কৈল প্রণতি স্তবন ।
তাহাঁ এক বিপ্র প্রভুর কৈল নিমন্ত্রণ ॥ ১৮ ॥

raghunātha dekhi' kaila praṇati stavana
tāhāṅ eka vipra prabhura kaila nimantraṇa

raghu-nātha dekhi'—after seeing Lord Rāmacandra, the descendant of Mahārāja Raghu; *kaila*—offered; *praṇati*—obeisances; *stavana*—prayers; *tāhāṅ*—there; *eka*—one; *vipra*—*brāhmaṇa; prabhura*—to Lord Śrī Caitanya Mahāprabhu; *kaila*—did; *nimantraṇa*—invitation.

TRANSLATION

Upon seeing the Deity of Lord Rāmacandra, the descendant of King Raghu, the Lord offered His prayers and obeisances. Then a brāhmaṇa invited the Lord to take lunch.

TEXT 19

সেই বিপ্র রামনাম নিরন্তর লয় ।
'রাম' 'রাম' বিনা অন্য বাণী না কহয় ॥ ১৯ ॥

sei vipra rāma-nāma nirantara laya
'rāma' 'rāma' vinā anya vāṇī nā kahaya

sei vipra—that *brāhmaṇa; rāma-nāma*—the holy name of Lord Rāmacandra; *nirantara*—constantly; *laya*—chants; *rāma rāma*—the holy names Rāma Rāma; *vinā*—without; *anya*—other; *vāṇī*—vibration; *nā*—does not; *kahaya*—speak.

TRANSLATION

That brāhmaṇa constantly chanted the holy name of Rāmacandra. Indeed, but for chanting Lord Rāmacandra's holy name, that brāhmaṇa did not speak a word.

TEXT 20

সেই দিন তাঁর ঘরে রহি' ভিক্ষা করি' ।
তাঁরে কৃপা করি' আগে চলিলা গৌরহরি ॥ ২০ ॥

sei dina tāṅra ghare rahi' bhikṣā kari'
tāṅre kṛpā kari' āge calilā gaurahari

sei dina—on that day; *tāṅra ghare*—the house of that *brāhmaṇa; rahi'*—staying; *bhikṣā kari'*—accepting *prasādam; tāṅre*—unto him; *kṛpā kari'*—showing mercy; *āge*—ahead; *calilā*—departed; *gaura-hari*—Lord Śrī Caitanya Mahāprabhu.

TRANSLATION

That day, Lord Caitanya remained there and accepted prasādam at his house. After bestowing mercy upon him in this way, the Lord proceeded ahead.

TEXT 21

স্কন্দক্ষেত্র-তীর্থে কৈল স্কন্দ দরশন ।
ত্রিমঠ আইলা, তাঁহা দেখি' ত্রিবিক্রম ॥ ২১ ॥

skanda-kṣetra-tīrthe kaila skanda daraśana
trimaṭha āilā, tāhāṅ dekhi' trivikrama

skanda-kṣetra-tīrthe—in the holy place known as Skanda-kṣetra; *kaila*—did; *skanda daraśana*—visiting Lord Skanda (Kārttikeya, son of Lord Śiva); *trimaṭha*—at Trimaṭha; *āilā*—arrived; *tāhāṅ*—there; *dekhi'*—seeing; *trivikrama*—a form of Lord Viṣṇu, Trivikrama.

TRANSLATION

At the holy place known as Skanda-kṣetra, Lord Śrī Caitanya Mahāprabhu visited the temple of Skanda. From there He went to Trimaṭha, where He saw the Viṣṇu Deity Trivikrama.

TEXT 22

পুনঃ সিদ্ধবট আইলা সেই বিপ্র-ঘরে ।
সেই বিপ্র কৃষ্ণনাম লয় নিরন্তরে ॥ ২২ ॥

punaḥ siddhavaṭa āilā sei vipra-ghare
sei vipra kṛṣṇa-nāma laya nirantare

punaḥ—again; *siddha-vaṭa*—to the place known as Siddhavaṭa; *āilā*—returned; *sei*—that; *vipra-ghare*—in the house of the *brāhmaṇa; sei vipra*—that *brāhmaṇa; kṛṣṇa-nāma*—the holy name of Lord Kṛṣṇa; *laya*—chants; *nirantare*—constantly.

TRANSLATION

After visiting the temple of Trivikrama, the Lord returned to Siddhavaṭa, where He again visited the house of the brāhmaṇa, who was now constantly chanting the Hare Kṛṣṇa mahā-mantra.

TEXT 23

ভিক্ষা করি' মহাপ্রভু তাঁরে প্রশ্ন কৈল ।
"কহ বিপ্র, এই তোমার কোন্ দশা হৈল ॥ ২৩ ॥

bhikṣā kari' mahāprabhu tāṅre praśna kaila
"kaha vipra, ei tomāra kon daśā haila

bhikṣā kari'—after accepting lunch; *mahāprabhu*—Śrī Caitanya Mahāprabhu; *tāṅre*—unto him; *praśna kaila*—asked a question; *kaha vipra*—My dear *brāhmaṇa* friend, please say; *ei*—this; *tomāra*—your; *kon*—what; *daśā*—situation; *haila*—became.

TRANSLATION

After finishing His lunch there, Śrī Caitanya Mahāprabhu asked the brāhmaṇa, "My dear friend, kindly tell Me what your position is now.

TEXT 24

পূর্বে তুমি নিরন্তর লৈতে রামনাম।
এবে কেনে নিরন্তর লও কৃষ্ণনাম ॥" ২৪ ॥

pūrve tumi nirantara laite rāma-nāma
ebe kene nirantara lao kṛṣṇa-nāma"

pūrve—formerly; *tumi*—you; *nirantara*—constantly; *laite*—used to chant; *rāma-nāma*—the holy name of Lord Rāmacandra; *ebe*—now; *kene*—why; *nirantara*—constantly; *lao*—you chant; *kṛṣṇa-nāma*—the holy name of Kṛṣṇa.

TRANSLATION

"Formerly you were constantly chanting the holy name of Lord Rāma. Why are you now constantly chanting the holy name of Kṛṣṇa?"

TEXT 25

বিপ্র বলে, —এই তোমার দর্শন-প্রভাবে।
তোমা দেখি' গেল মোর আজন্ম স্বভাবে ॥ ২৫ ॥

vipra bale,—ei tomāra darśana-prabhāve
tomā dekhi' gela mora ājanma svabhāve

vipra bale—the *brāhmaṇa* replied; *ei*—this; *tomāra darśana-prabhāve*—by the influence of Your visit; *tomā dekhi'*—after seeing You; *gela*—went; *mora*—my; *ā-janma*—from childhood; *svabhāve*—nature.

TRANSLATION

The brāhmaṇa replied, "This is all due to Your influence, Sir. After seeing You, I have lost my lifelong practice.

TEXT 26

বাল্যাবধি রামনাম-গ্রহণ আমার ।
তোমা দেখি' কৃষ্ণনাম আইল একবার ॥ ২৬ ॥

bālyāvadhi rāma-nāma-grahaṇa āmāra
tomā dekhi' kṛṣṇa-nāma āila eka-bāra

bālya-avadhi—since the days of my childhood; *rāma-nāma-grahaṇa*—chanting the holy name of Lord Rāmacandra; *āmāra*—my; *tomā dekhi'*—upon seeing You; *kṛṣṇa-nāma*—the holy name of Lord Kṛṣṇa; *āila*—came; *eka-bāra*—once only.

TRANSLATION

"From my childhood I have been chanting the holy name of Lord Rāmacandra, but upon seeing You I chanted the holy name of Lord Kṛṣṇa just once.

TEXT 27

সেই হৈতে কৃষ্ণনাম জিহ্বাতে বসিলা ।
কৃষ্ণনাম স্ফুরে, রামনাম দূরে গেলা ॥ ২৭ ॥

sei haite kṛṣṇa-nāma jihvāte vasilā
kṛṣṇa-nāma sphure, rāma-nāma dūre gelā

sei haite—since that time; *kṛṣṇa-nāma*—the holy name of Lord Kṛṣṇa; *jihvāte*—on the tongue; *vasilā*—was seated tightly; *kṛṣṇa-nāma*—the holy name of Lord Kṛṣṇa; *sphure*—automatically comes; *rāma-nāma*—the holy name of Lord Rāmacandra; *dūre*—far away; *gelā*—went.

TRANSLATION

"Since then, the holy name of Kṛṣṇa has been tightly fixed upon my tongue. Indeed, since I have been chanting the holy name of Kṛṣṇa, the holy name of Lord Rāmacandra has gone far away.

TEXT 28

বাল্যকাল হৈতে মোর স্বভাব এক হয়।
নামের মহিমা-শাস্ত্র করিয়ে সঞ্চয় ॥ ২৮ ॥

bālya-kāla haite mora svabhāva eka haya
nāmera mahimā-śāstra kariye sañcaya

bālya-kāla haite—from my childhood; *mora*—my; *svabhāva*—practice; *eka*—one; *haya*—there is; *nāmera*—of the holy name; *mahimā*—concerning the glories; *śāstra*—the revealed scriptures; *kariye sañcaya*—I collect.

TRANSLATION

"From my childhood I have been collecting the glories of the holy name from revealed scriptures.

TEXT 29

রমন্তে যোগিনোঽনন্তে সত্যানন্দে চিদাত্মনি।
ইতি রামপদেনাসৌ পরং ব্রহ্মাভিধীয়তে ॥ ২৯ ॥

ramante yogino 'nante
satyānande cid-ātmani
iti rāma-padenāsau
paraṁ brahmābhidhīyate

ramante—take pleasure; *yoginaḥ*—transcendentalists; *anante*—in the unlimited; *satya-ānande*—real pleasure; *cit-ātmani*—in spiritual existence; *iti*—thus; *rāma*—Rāma; *padena*—by the word; *asau*—He; *param*—supreme; *brahma*—truth; *abhidhīyate*—is called.

TRANSLATION

"'The Supreme Absolute Truth is called Rāma because the transcendentalists take pleasure in the unlimited true pleasure of spiritual existence.'

PURPORT

This is the eighth verse of the *Śata-nāma-stotra* of Lord Rāmacandra, which is found in the *Padma Purāṇa.*

TEXT 30

কৃষির্ভূবাচকঃ শব্দো ণশ্চ নির্বৃতিবাচকঃ ।
তয়োরৈক্যং পরং ব্রহ্ম কৃষ্ণ ইত্যভিধীয়তে ॥ ৩০ ॥

kṛṣir bhū-vācakaḥ śabdo
ṇaś ca nirvṛti-vācakaḥ
tayor aikyaṁ paraṁ brahma
kṛṣṇa ity abhidhīyate

kṛṣiḥ—the verbal root *kṛṣ; bhū*—attractive existence; *vācakaḥ*—signifying; *śabdaḥ*—word; *ṇaḥ*—the syllable *ṇa; ca*—and; *nirvṛti*—spiritual pleasure; *vācakaḥ*—indicating; *tayoḥ*—of both; *aikyam*—amalgamation; *param*—supreme; *brahma*—Absolute Truth; *kṛṣṇaḥ*—Lord Kṛṣṇa; *iti*—thus; *abhidhīyate*—is called.

TRANSLATION

"'The word "kṛṣ" is the attractive feature of the Lord's existence, and "ṇa" means spiritual pleasure. When the verb "kṛṣ" is added to the affix "ṇa," it becomes "Kṛṣṇa," which indicates the Absolute Truth.'

PURPORT

This is a verse from the *Mahābhārata* (*Udyoga-parva* 71.4).

TEXT 31

পরংব্রহ্ম দুই নাম সমান হইল ।
পুনঃ আর শাস্ত্রে কিছু বিশেষ পাইল ॥ ৩১ ॥

paraṁ brahma dui-nāma samāna ha-ila
punaḥ āra śāstre kichu viśeṣa pāila

param brahma—the Absolute Truth; *dui-nāma*—two names (Rāma and Kṛṣṇa); *samāna*—on an equal level; *ha-ila*—were; *punaḥ*—again; *āra*—further; *śāstre*—in revealed scriptures; *kichu*—some; *viśeṣa*—specification; *pāila*—is found.

TRANSLATION

"As far as the holy names of Rāma and Kṛṣṇa are concerned, they are on an equal level, but for further advancement we receive some specific information from the revealed scriptures.

TEXT 32

রাম রামেতি রামেতি রমে রামে মনোরমে ।
সহস্রনামভিস্তুল্যং রামনাম বরাননে ॥ ৩২ ॥

rāma rāmeti rāmeti
rame rāme manorame
sahasra-nāmabhis tulyaṁ
rāma-nāma varānane

rāma—Rāma; *rāma*—Rāma; *iti*—thus; *rāma*—Rāma; *iti*—thus; *rame*—I enjoy; *rāme*—in the holy name of Rāma; *manaḥ-rame*—most beautiful; *sahasra-nāmabhiḥ*—with the one thousand names; *tulyam*—equal; *rāma-nāma*—the holy name of Rāma; *vara-ānane*—O lovely-faced woman.

TRANSLATION

"[Lord Śiva addressed his wife, Durgā:] 'O Varānanā, I chant the holy name of Rāma, Rāma, Rāma and thus enjoy this beautiful sound. This holy name of Rāmacandra is equal to one thousand holy names of Lord Viṣṇu.'

PURPORT

This is a verse from the *Bṛhad-viṣṇu-sahasranāma-stotra* in the *Uttara-khaṇḍa* of the *Padma Purāṇa* (72.335).

TEXT 33

সহস্রনাম্নাং পুণ্যানাং ত্রিরাবৃত্ত্যা তু যৎ ফলম্ ।
একাবৃত্ত্যা তু কৃষ্ণস্য নামৈকং তৎ প্রযচ্ছতি ॥ ৩৩ ॥

sahasra-nāmnāṁ puṇyānāṁ
trir-āvṛttyā tu yat phalam

ekāvṛttyā tu kṛṣṇasya
nāmaikaṁ tat prayacchati

sahasra-nāmnām—of one thousand names; *puṇyānām*—holy; *triḥ-āvṛttyā*—by thrice chanting; *tu*—but; *yat*—which; *phalam*—result; *eka-āvṛttyā*—by one repetition; *tu*—but; *kṛṣṇasya*—of Lord Kṛṣṇa; *nāma*—holy name; *ekam*—only one; *tat*—that result; *prayacchati*—gives.

TRANSLATION

"'The pious results derived from chanting the thousand holy names of Viṣṇu three times can be attained by only one utterance of the holy name of Kṛṣṇa.'

PURPORT

This verse from the *Brahmāṇḍa Purāṇa* is found in the *Laghu-bhāgavatāmṛta* (1.5.354), by Rūpa Gosvāmī. Simply by chanting the name of Kṛṣṇa once, one can attain the same results achieved by chanting the holy name of Rāma three times.

TEXT 34

এই বাক্যে কৃষ্ণ নামের মহিমা অপার ।
তথাপি লইতে নারি, শুন হেতু তার ॥ ৩৪ ॥

ei vākye kṛṣṇa-nāmera mahimā apāra
tathāpi la-ite nāri, śuna hetu tāra

ei vākye—in this statement; *kṛṣṇa-nāmera*—of the holy name of Kṛṣṇa; *mahimā*—glories; *apāra*—unlimited; *tathāpi*—still; *la-ite*—to chant; *nāri*—I am unable; *śuna*—just hear; *hetu*—the reason; *tāra*—of that.

TRANSLATION

"According to this statement of the śāstras, the glories of the holy name of Kṛṣṇa are unlimited. Still I could not chant His holy name. Please hear the reason for this.

TEXT 35

ইষ্টদেব রাম, তাঁর নামে সুখ পাই।
সুখ পাঞা রামনাম রাত্রিদিন গাই ॥ ৩৫ ॥

iṣṭa-deva rāma, tāṅra nāme sukha pāi
sukha pāñā rāma-nāma rātri-dina gāi

iṣṭa-deva—my worshipable Lord; *rāma*—Lord Śrī Rāmacandra; *tāṅra nāme*—in His holy name; *sukha pāi*—I get happiness; *sukha pāñā*—getting such transcendental happiness; *rāma-nāma*—the holy name of Lord Rāma; *rātri-dina*—day and night; *gāi*—I chant.

TRANSLATION

"My worshipable Lord has been Lord Rāmacandra, and by chanting His holy name I received happiness. Because I received such happiness, I chanted the holy name of Lord Rāma day and night.

TEXT 36

তোমার দর্শনে যবে কৃষ্ণনাম আইল।
তাহার মহিমা তবে হৃদয়ে লাগিল ॥ ৩৬ ॥

tomāra darśane yabe kṛṣṇa-nāma āila
tāhāra mahimā tabe hṛdaye lāgila

tomāra darśane—by meeting You; *yabe*—when; *kṛṣṇa-nāma*—the holy name of Kṛṣṇa; *āila*—appeared; *tāhāra*—His; *mahimā*—glories; *tabe*—at that time; *hṛdaye*—in the heart; *lāgila*—became fixed.

TRANSLATION

"By Your appearance, Lord Kṛṣṇa's holy name also appeared, and at that time the glories of Kṛṣṇa's name awoke in my heart.

TEXT 37

সেই কৃষ্ণ তুমি সাক্ষাৎ—ইহা নির্ধারিল।
এত কহি' বিপ্র প্রভুর চরণে পড়িল ॥ ৩৭ ॥

sei kṛṣṇa tumi sākṣāt—ihā nirdhārila
eta kahi' vipra prabhura caraṇe paḍila

sei—that; *kṛṣṇa*—the Personality of Godhead, Kṛṣṇa; *tumi*—You; *sākṣāt*—directly; *ihā*—this; *nirdhārila*—concluded; *eta kahi'*—saying this; *vipra*—the *brāhmaṇa; prabhura*—of Lord Caitanya Mahāprabhu; *caraṇe*—at the lotus feet; *paḍila*—fell down.

TRANSLATION

"Sir, You are that Lord Kṛṣṇa Himself. This is my conclusion." Saying this, the brāhmaṇa fell down at the lotus feet of Śrī Caitanya Mahāprabhu.

TEXT 38

তাঁরে কৃপা করি' প্রভু চলিলা আর দিনে ।
বৃদ্ধকাশী আসি' কৈল শিব-দরশনে ॥ ৩৮ ॥

tāṅre kṛpā kari' prabhu calilā āra dine
vṛddhakāśī āsi' kaila śiva-daraśane

tāṅre—unto him; *kṛpā kari'*—showing mercy; *prabhu*—Lord Śrī Caitanya Mahāprabhu; *calilā*—traveled; *āra dine*—the next day; *vṛddhakāśī*—to Vṛddhakāśī; *āsi'*—coming; *kaila*—did; *śiva-daraśane*—visiting Lord Śiva's temple.

TRANSLATION

After showing mercy to the brāhmaṇa, Lord Śrī Caitanya Mahāprabhu left the next day and arrived at Vṛddhakāśī, where He visited the temple of Lord Śiva.

PURPORT

Vṛddhakāśī's present name is Vṛddhācalam. It is situated in the southern Arcot district on the bank of the river Maṇimukha. This place is also known as Kālahastipura. Lord Śiva's temple there was worshiped for many years by Govinda, the cousin of Rāmānujācārya.

TEXT 39

তাহাঁ হৈতে চলি' আগে গেলা এক গ্রামে ।
ব্রাহ্মণ-সমাজ তাহাঁ, করিল বিশ্রামে ॥ ৩৯ ॥

tāhāṅ haite cali' āge gelā eka grāme
brāhmaṇa-samāja tāhāṅ, karila viśrāme

tāhāṅ haite—from there; *cali'*—going; *āge*—forward; *gelā*—went; *eka*—one; *grāme*—to a village; *brāhmaṇa-samāja*—assembly of *brāhmaṇas; tāhāṅ*—there; *karila viśrāme*—He rested.

TRANSLATION

Śrī Caitanya Mahāprabhu then left Vṛddhakāśī and proceeded further. In one village He saw that most of the residents were brāhmaṇas, and He took His rest there.

TEXT 40

প্রভুর প্রভাবে লোক আইল দরশনে ।
লক্ষার্বুদ লোক আইসে না যায় গণনে ॥ ৪০ ॥

prabhura prabhāve loka āila daraśane
lakṣārbuda loka āise nā yāya gaṇane

prabhura—of Lord Śrī Caitanya Mahāprabhu; *prabhāve*—by the influence; *loka*—people; *āila*—came; *daraśane*—to see Him; *lakṣa-arbuda*—many millions; *loka*—persons; *āise*—came; *nā*—not; *yāya gaṇane*—can be counted.

TRANSLATION

Due to the influence of Lord Caitanya Mahāprabhu, many millions of men came just to see Him. Indeed, the assembly being unlimited, its members could not be counted.

TEXT 41

গোসাঞির সৌন্দর্য দেখি' তাতে প্রেমাবেশ ।
সবে 'কৃষ্ণ' কহে, 'বৈষ্ণব' হৈল সর্বদেশ ॥ ৪১ ॥

gosāñira saundarya dekhi' tāte premāveśa
sabe 'kṛṣṇa' kahe, 'vaiṣṇava' haila sarva-deśa

gosāñira—of the Lord; *saundarya*—the beauty; *dekhi'*—seeing; *tāte*—in that; *prema-āveśa*—ecstatic love; *sabe*—everyone; *kṛṣṇa kahe*—uttered the holy name of Kṛṣṇa; *vaiṣṇava*—Vaiṣṇava devotees; *haila*—became; *sarva-deśa*—everyone.

TRANSLATION

The Lord's bodily features were very beautiful, and in addition He was always in the ecstasy of love of Godhead. Simply by seeing Him, everyone began chanting the holy name of Kṛṣṇa, and thus everyone became a Vaiṣṇava devotee.

TEXT 42

তার্কিক-মীমাংসক, যত মায়াবাদিগণ।
সাংখ্য, পাতঞ্জল, স্মৃতি, পুরাণ, আগম॥ ৪২॥

tārkika-mīmāṁsaka, yata māyāvādi-gaṇa
sāṅkhya, pātañjala, smṛti, purāṇa, āgama

tārkika—logicians; *mīmāṁsaka*—followers of Mīmāṁsā philosophy; *yata*—all; *māyāvādi-gaṇa*—followers of Śaṅkarācārya; *sāṅkhya*—followers of Kapila; *pātañjala*—followers of mystic *yoga; smṛti*—supplementary Vedic literatures; *purāṇa—Purāṇas; āgama*—the *tantra-śāstras.*

TRANSLATION

There are many kinds of philosophers. Some are logicians who follow Gautama or Kaṇāda. Some follow the Mīmāṁsā philosophy of Jaimini. Some follow the Māyāvāda philosophy of Śaṅkarācārya, and others follow Kapila's Sāṅkhya philosophy or the mystic yoga system of Patañjali. Some follow the smṛti-śāstra composed of twenty religious scriptures, and others follow the Purāṇas and the tantra-śāstra. In this way there are many different types of philosophers.

TEXT 43

নিজ-নিজ-শাস্ত্রোদ্গ্রাহে সবাই প্রচণ্ড ।
সর্ব মত দুষি' প্রভু করে খণ্ড খণ্ড ॥ ৪৩ ॥

nija-nija-śāstrodgrāhe sabāi pracaṇḍa
sarva mata duṣi' prabhu kare khaṇḍa khaṇḍa

nija-nija—their own; *śāstra*—of the scripture; *udgrāhe*—to establish the conclusion; *sabāi*—all of them; *pracaṇḍa*—very powerful; *sarva*—all; *mata*—opinions; *duṣi'*—condemning; *prabhu*—Śrī Caitanya Mahāprabhu; *kare*—does; *khaṇḍa khaṇḍa*—breaking to pieces.

TRANSLATION

All of these adherents of various scriptures were ready to present the conclusions of their respective scriptures, but Śrī Caitanya Mahāprabhu broke all their opinions to pieces and established His own cult of bhakti based on the Vedas, Vedānta, the Brahma-sūtra and the philosophy of acintya-bhedābheda-tattva.

TEXT 44

সর্বত্র স্থাপয় প্রভু বৈষ্ণবসিদ্ধান্তে ।
প্রভুর সিদ্ধান্ত কেহ না পারে খণ্ডিতে ॥ ৪৪ ॥

sarvatra sthāpaya prabhu vaiṣṇava-siddhānte
prabhura siddhānta keha nā pāre khaṇḍite

sarvatra—everywhere; *sthāpaya*—establishes; *prabhu*—Śrī Caitanya Mahāprabhu; *vaiṣṇava-siddhānte*—the conclusion of the Vaiṣṇavas; *prabhura*—of Lord Śrī Caitanya Mahāprabhu; *siddhānta*—conclusion; *keha*—anyone; *nā pāre*—is not able; *khaṇḍite*—to defy.

TRANSLATION

Śrī Caitanya Mahāprabhu established the devotional cult everywhere. No one could defeat Him.

TEXT 45

হারি' হারি' প্রভুমতে করেন প্রবেশ।
এইমতে 'বৈষ্ণব' প্রভু কৈল দক্ষিণ দেশ ॥ ৪৫ ॥

hāri' hāri' prabhu-mate karena praveśa
ei-mate 'vaiṣṇava' prabhu kaila dakṣiṇa deśa

hāri' hāri'—being defeated; *prabhu-mate*—into the cult of Śrī Caitanya Mahāprabhu; *karena praveśa*—enter; *ei-mate*—in this way; *vaiṣṇava*—Vaiṣṇava devotees; *prabhu*—Lord Śrī Caitanya Mahāprabhu; *kaila*—made; *dakṣiṇa*—South India; *deśa*—country.

TRANSLATION

Being thus defeated by Lord Śrī Caitanya Mahāprabhu, all these philosophers and their followers entered into His cult. In this way Lord Caitanya made South India into a country of Vaiṣṇavas.

TEXT 46

পাষণ্ডী আইল যত পাণ্ডিত্য শুনিয়া।
গর্ব করি' আইল সঙ্গে শিষ্যগণ লঞা ॥ ৪৬ ॥

pāṣaṇḍī āila yata pāṇḍitya śuniyā
garva kari' āila saṅge śiṣya-gaṇa lañā

pāṣaṇḍī—nonbelievers; *āila*—came there; *yata*—all; *pāṇḍitya*—erudition; *śuniyā*—hearing; *garva kari'*—with great pride; *āila*—came there; *saṅge*—with; *śiṣya-gaṇa*—disciples; *lañā*—taking.

TRANSLATION

When the nonbelievers heard of the erudition of Śrī Caitanya Mahāprabhu, they came to Him with great pride, bringing their disciples with them.

TEXT 47

বৌদ্ধাচার্য মহাপণ্ডিত নিজ নবমতে।
প্রভুর আগে উদ্গ্রাহ করি' লাগিলা বলিতে ॥ ৪৭ ॥

bauddhācārya mahā-paṇḍita nija nava-mate
prabhura āge udgrāha kari' lāgilā balite

bauddha-ācārya—the leader in Buddhist philosophy; *mahā-paṇḍita*—greatly learned scholar; *nija*—own; *nava*—nine; *mate*—philosophical conclusions; *prabhura āge*—before Lord Śrī Caitanya Mahāprabhu; *udgrāha*—argument; *kari'*—making; *lāgilā*—began; *balite*—to speak.

TRANSLATION

One of them was a leader of the Buddhist cult and was a very learned scholar. To establish the nine philosophical conclusions of Buddhism, he came before the Lord and began to speak.

TEXT 48

যদ্যপি অসম্ভাষ্য বৌদ্ধ অযুক্ত দেখিতে।
তথাপি বলিলা প্রভু গর্ব খণ্ডাইতে ॥ ৪৮ ॥

yadyapi asambhāṣya bauddha ayukta dekhite
tathāpi balilā prabhu garva khaṇḍāite

yadyapi—although; *asambhāṣya*—not fit for discussion; *bauddha*—followers of Buddha's philosophy; *ayukta*—not fit; *dekhite*—to see; *tathāpi*—still; *balilā*—spoke; *prabhu*—Lord Śrī Caitanya Mahāprabhu; *garva*—pride; *khaṇḍāite*—to diminish.

TRANSLATION

Although the Buddhists are unfit for discussion and should not be seen by Vaiṣṇavas, Caitanya Mahāprabhu spoke to them just to decrease their false pride.

TEXT 49

তর্ক-প্রধান বৌদ্ধশাস্ত্র 'নব মতে'।
তর্কেই খণ্ডিল প্রভু, না পারে স্থাপিতে ॥ ৪৯ ॥

tarka-pradhāna bauddha-śāstra 'nava mate'
tarkei khaṇḍila prabhu, nā pāre sthāpite

tarka-pradhāna—argumentative; *bauddha-śāstra*—scriptures of the Buddhist cult; *nava mate*—in nine basic principles; *tarkei*—by argument; *khaṇḍila*—refuted; *prabhu*—Śrī Caitanya Mahāprabhu; *nā*—not; *pāre*—can; *sthāpite*—establish.

TRANSLATION

The scriptures of the Buddhist cult are chiefly based on argument and logic, and they contain nine chief principles. Because Śrī Caitanya Mahāprabhu defeated the Buddhists in their argument, they could not establish their cult.

PURPORT

Śrīla Bhaktivinoda Ṭhākura states that according to the Buddhist cult there are two ways of understanding philosophy. One is called Hīnāyāna, and the other is called Mahāyāna. Along the Buddhist path there are nine principles: (1) The creation is eternal; therefore there is no need to accept a creator. (2) This cosmic manifestation is false. (3) "I am" is the truth. (4) There is repetition of birth and death. (5) Lord Buddha is the only source of understanding the truth. (6) The principle of *nirvāṇa,* or annihilation, is the ultimate goal. (7) The philosophy of Buddha is the only philosophical path. (8) The *Vedas* are compiled by human beings. (9) Pious activities, showing mercy to others and so on are advised.

No one can attain the Absolute Truth by argument. One may be very expert in logic, and another person may be even more expert in the art of argument. Because there is so much word jugglery in logic, one can never come to the real conclusion about the Absolute Truth by argument. The followers of the Vedic principles understand this. However, it is seen here that Śrī Caitanya Mahāprabhu defeated the Buddhist philosophy by argument. Those who are preachers in ISKCON will certainly meet many people who believe in intellectual arguments. Most of these people do not believe in the authority of the *Vedas.* Nevertheless, they accept intellectual speculation and argument. Therefore the preachers of Kṛṣṇa consciousness should be prepared to defeat others by argument, just as Śrī Caitanya Mahāprabhu did. In this verse it is clearly said, *tarkei khaṇḍila prabhu.* Lord Śrī Caitanya Mahāprabhu put forward such a strong argument that the Buddhists could not counter Him to establish their cult.

Their first principle is that the creation has always existed. But if this were the case, there could be no theory of annihilation. The Buddhists maintain that annihilation, or dissolution, is the highest truth. If the creation eternally exists, there is no question of dissolution or annihilation. This argument is not very strong because by practical experience we see that material things have a beginning, a middle and an end. The ultimate aim of the Buddhist philosophy is to dissolve the body. This is proposed because the body has a beginning. Similarly, the entire cosmic manifestation is also a gigantic body, but if we accept the fact that it will always exist, there can be no question of annihilation. Therefore the attempt to annihilate everything in order to attain zero is an absurdity. By our own practical experience we have to accept the beginning of creation, and when we accept the beginning, we must accept a creator. Such a creator must possess an all-pervasive body, as pointed out in the *Bhagavad-gītā* (13.14):

sarvataḥ pāṇi-pādaṁ tat sarvato-'kṣi-śiro-mukham
sarvataḥ śruti-mal loke sarvam āvṛtya tiṣṭhati

"Everywhere are His hands and legs, His eyes, heads and faces, and He has ears everywhere. In this way the Supersoul exists, pervading everything."

The Supreme Person must be present everywhere. His bodyexisted before the creation; otherwise He could not be the creator. If the Supreme Person is a created being, there can be no question of a creator. The conclusion is that the cosmic manifestation is certainly created at a certain time, and the creator existed before the creation; therefore the creator is not a created being. The creator is Parabrahman, or the Supreme Spirit. Matter is not only subordinate to spirit but is actually created on the basis of spirit. When the spirit soul enters the womb of a mother, the body is created by material ingredients supplied by the mother. Everything is created in the material world, and consequently there must be a creator who is the Supreme Spirit and who is distinct from matter. It is confirmed in the *Bhagavad-gītā* that the material energy is inferior and that the spiritual energy is the living entity. Both inferior and superior energies belong to a supreme person.

The Buddhists argue that the world is false, but this is not valid. The world is temporary, but it is not false. As long as we have the body, we must suffer the pleasures and pains of the body, even though we are not the body. We may not take these pleasures and pains very seriously, but they are factual nonetheless. We cannot actually say that they are false. If the bodily pains and pleasures were false, the creation would be false also, and consequently no one would take very much interest in it. The conclusion is that the material creation is not false or imaginary, but it is temporary.

The Buddhists maintain that the principle "I am" is the ultimate truth, but this excludes the individuality of "I" and "you." If there is no "I" and "you," or individuality, there is no possibility of argument. The Buddhist philosophy depends on argument, but there can be no argument if one simply depends on "I am." There must be a "you," or another person also. The philosophy of duality—the existence of the individual soul and the Supersoul—must be there. This is confirmed in the Second Chapter of the *Bhagavad-gītā* (2.12), wherein the Lord says:

na tv evāhaṁ jātu nāsaṁ na tvaṁ neme janādhipāḥ
na caiva na bhaviṣyāmaḥ sarve vayam ataḥ param

"Never was there a time when I did not exist, nor you, nor all these kings; nor in the future shall any of us cease to be."

We existed in the past in different bodies, and after the annihilation of this body we shall exist in another body. The principle of the soul is eternal, and it exists in this body or in another body. Even in this lifetime we experience existence in a child's body, a youth's body, a man's body and an old body. After the annihilation of the body, we acquire another body. The Buddhist cult also accepts the philosophy of transmigration, but the Buddhists do not properly explain the next birth. There are 8,400,000 species of life, and our next birth may be in any one of them; therefore this human body is not guaranteed.

According to the Buddhists' fifth principle, Lord Buddha is the only source for the attainment of knowledge. We cannot accept this, for Lord Buddha rejected the principles of Vedic knowledge. One must accept a principle of standard knowledge because one cannot attain the Absolute Truth simply by intellectual speculation. If everyone is an authority, or if everyone accepts his own intelligence as the ultimate criterion—as is presently fashionable—the scriptures will be interpreted in many different ways, and everyone will claim that his own philosophy is supreme. This has become a very great problem, and everyone is interpreting scripture in his own way and setting up his own basis of authority. *Yata mata tata patha.* Now everybody and anybody is trying to establish his own theory as the ultimate truth. The Buddhists theorize that annihilation, or *nirvāṇa,* is the ultimate goal. Annihilation applies to the body, but the spirit soul transmigrates from one body to another. If this were not the case, how can so many multifarious bodies come into existence? If the next birth is a fact, the next bodily form is also a fact. As soon as we accept a material body, we must accept the fact that body will be annihilated and that we will have to accept another body. If all material bodies are doomed to annihilation, we must obtain a nonmaterial body, or a spiritual body, if we wish the next birth to be anything but false. How the spiritual body is attained is explained by Lord Kṛṣṇa in the *Bhagavad-gītā* (4.9):

janma karma ca me divyam evaṁ yo vetti tattvataḥ
tyaktvā dehaṁ punar janma naiti mām eti so 'rjuna

"One who knows the transcendental nature of My appearance and activities does not, upon leaving the body, take his birth again in this material world, but attains My eternal abode, O Arjuna."

This is the highest perfection—to give up one's material body and not accept another but to return home, back to Godhead. It is not that perfection means one's existence becomes void or zero. Existence continues, but if we positively want to annihilate the material body, we have to accept a spiritual body; otherwise there can be no eternality for the soul.

We cannot accept the theory that the Buddhist philosophy is the only way, for there are so many defects in that philosophy. A perfect philosophy is one that has no defects, and that is Vedānta philosophy. No one can point out any defects in Vedānta philosophy, and therefore we can conclude that Vedānta is the supreme philosophical way of understanding the truth. According to the Buddhist cult, the *Vedas* are compiled by ordinary human beings. If this were the case, they would not be authoritative. From the Vedic literatures we understand that shortly after the creation Lord Brahmā was instructed in the *Vedas.*

It is not that the *Vedas* were created by Brahmā, although Brahmā is the original person in the universe. If Brahmā did not create the *Vedas* but he is acknowledged as the first created being, wherefrom did Vedic knowledge come to Brahmā? Obviously the *Vedas* did not come from an ordinary person born in this material world. According to *Śrīmad-Bhāgavatam, tene brahma hṛdā ya ādi-kavaye:* after the creation, the Supreme Person imparted Vedic knowledge within the heart of Brahmā. There was no person in the beginning of the creation other than Brahmā, yet he did not compile the *Vedas;* therefore the conclusion is that the *Vedas* were not compiled by any created being. Vedic knowledge was given by the Supreme Personality of Godhead, who created this material world. This is also accepted by Śaṅkarācārya, although he is not a Vaiṣṇava.

It is stated that mercy is one of the qualities of a Buddhist, but mercy is a relative thing. We show our mercy to a subordinate or to one who is suffering more than ourselves. However, if there is a superior person present, the superior person cannot be the object of our mercy. Rather, we are objects for the mercy of the superior person. Therefore showing compassion and mercy is a relative activity. It is not the Absolute Truth. Apart from this, we also must know what actual mercy is. To give a sick man something forbidden for him to eat is not mercy. Rather, it is cruelty. Unless we know what mercy really is, we may create an undesirable situation. If we wish to show real mercy, we will preach Kṛṣṇa consciousness in order to revive the lost consciousness of human beings, the living entity's original consciousness. Since the Buddhist philosophy does not admit the existence of the spirit soul, the so-called mercy of the Buddhists is defective.

TEXT 50

বৌদ্ধাচার্য 'নব প্রশ্ন' সব উঠাইল ।
দৃঢ় যুক্তি-তর্কে প্রভু খণ্ড খণ্ড কৈল ॥ ৫০ ॥

bauddhācārya 'nava praśna' saba uṭhāila
dṛḍha yukti-tarke prabhu khaṇḍa khaṇḍa kaila

bauddha-ācārya—the teacher of the Buddhist cult; *nava praśna*—nine different types of questions; *saba*—all; *uṭhāila*—raised;

dṛḍha—strong; *yukti*—argument; *tarke*—with logic; *prabhu*—Lord Śrī Caitanya Mahāprabhu; *khaṇḍa khaṇḍa kaila*—broke into pieces.

TRANSLATION

The teacher of the Buddhist cult set forth the nine principles, but Śrī Caitanya Mahāprabhu broke them to pieces with His strong logic.

TEXT 51

দার্শনিক পণ্ডিত সবাই পাইল পরাজয় ।
লোকে হাস্য করে, বৌদ্ধ পাইল লজ্জা-ভয় ॥ ৫১ ॥

dārśanika paṇḍita sabāi pāila parājaya
loke hāsya kare, bauddha pāila lajjā-bhaya

dārśanika—philosophical speculators; *paṇḍita*—scholars; *sabāi*—all of them; *pāila parājaya*—were defeated; *loke*—people in general; *hāsya kare*—laugh; *bauddha*—the Buddhists; *pāila*—got; *lajjā*—shame; *bhaya*—fear.

TRANSLATION

All mental speculators and learned scholars were defeated by Śrī Caitanya Mahāprabhu, and when the people began to laugh, the Buddhist philosophers felt both shame and fear.

PURPORT

These philosophers were all atheists, for they did not believe in the existence of God. Atheists may be very expert in mental speculation and may be so-called great philosophers, but they can be defeated by a Vaiṣṇava firmly situated in his conviction and God consciousness. Following in the footsteps of Śrī Caitanya Mahāprabhu, all the preachers engaged in the service of ISKCON should be very expert in putting forward strong arguments and defeating all types of atheists.

TEXT 52

প্রভুকে বৈষ্ণব জানি' বৌদ্ধ ঘরে গেল ।
সকল বৌদ্ধ মিলি' তবে কুমন্ত্রণা কৈল ॥ ৫২ ॥

prabhuke vaiṣṇava jāni' bauddha ghare gela
sakala bauddha mili' tabe kumantraṇā kaila

prabhuke—Lord Śrī Caitanya Mahāprabhu; *vaiṣṇava jāni'*—knowing to be a Vaiṣṇava; *bauddha*—the Buddhists; *ghare gela*—returned home; *sakala bauddha*—all the Buddhists; *mili'*—coming together; *tabe*—thereafter; *ku-mantraṇā*—plot; *kaila*—made.

TRANSLATION

The Buddhists could understand that Lord Śrī Caitanya Mahāprabhu was a Vaiṣṇava, and they returned home very unhappy. Later, however, they began to plot against the Lord.

TEXT 53

অপবিত্র অন্ন এক থালিতে ভরিয়া ।
প্রভু-আগে নিল 'মহাপ্রসাদ' বলিয়া ॥ ৫৩ ॥

apavitra anna eka thālite bhariyā
prabhu-āge nila 'mahā-prasāda' baliyā

apavitra—polluted; *anna*—food; *eka*—one; *thālite*—plate; *bhariyā*—filling; *prabhu-āge*—in front of Lord Śrī Caitanya Mahāprabhu; *nila*—brought; *mahā-prasāda baliyā*—calling it *mahā-prasādam.*

TRANSLATION

Having made their plot, the Buddhists brought a plate of untouchable food before Lord Śrī Caitanya Mahāprabhu and called it mahā-prasādam.

PURPORT

The word *apavitra anna* refers to food that is unacceptable for a Vaiṣṇava. In other words, a Vaiṣṇava cannot accept any food offered by an *avaiṣṇava* in the name of *mahā-prasādam.* This should be a principle for all Vaiṣṇavas. When asked, "What is the behavior of a Vaiṣṇava?" Śrī Caitanya Mahāprabhu replied, "A Vaiṣṇava must avoid the company of an *avaiṣṇava* [*asat*]." The word *asat* refers to an *avaiṣṇava,* that is, one who is not a Vaiṣṇava. *Asat-saṅga-tyāga,—ei vaiṣṇava-ācāra* (Cc.

Madhya 22.87). A Vaiṣṇava must be very strict in this respect and should not at all cooperate with an *avaiṣṇava.* If an *avaiṣṇava* offers food in the name of *mahā-prasādam,* it should not be accepted. Such food cannot be *prasādam* because an *avaiṣṇava* cannot offer anything to the Lord. Sometimes preachers in the Kṛṣṇa consciousness movement have to accept food in a home where the householder is an *avaiṣṇava;* however, if this food is offered to the Deity, it can be taken. Ordinary food cooked by an *avaiṣṇava* should not be accepted by a Vaiṣṇava. Even if an *avaiṣṇava* cooks food without fault, he cannot offer it to Lord Viṣṇu, and it cannot be accepted as *mahā-prasādam.* According to Lord Kṛṣṇa in the *Bhagavad-gītā* (9.26):

patraṁ puṣpaṁ phalaṁ toyaṁ yo me bhaktyā prayacchati
tad ahaṁ bhakty-upahṛtam aśnāmi prayatātmanaḥ

"If one offers Me with love and devotion a leaf, a flower, a fruit or water, I will accept it."

Kṛṣṇa can accept anything offered by His devotee with devotion. An *avaiṣṇava* may be a vegetarian and a very clean cook, but because he cannot offer Viṣṇu the food he cooks, it cannot be accepted as *mahā-prasādam.* It is better that a Vaiṣṇava abandon such food as untouchable.

TEXT 54

হেন কালে মহাকায় এক পক্ষী আইল ।
ঠোঁটে করি' অন্নসহ থালি লঞা গেল ॥ ৫৪ ॥

hena-kāle mahā-kāya eka pakṣī āila
ṭhoṅṭe kari' anna-saha thāli lañā gela

hena-kāle—at this time; *mahā-kāya*—having a large body; *eka*—one; *pakṣī*—bird; *āila*—appeared there; *ṭhoṅṭe kari'*—by the beak; *anna-saha*—with food; *thāli*—the plate; *lañā*—taking; *gela*—went away.

TRANSLATION

When the contaminated food was offered to Śrī Caitanya Mahāprabhu, a very large bird appeared on the spot, picked up the plate in its beak and flew away.

TEXT 55

বৌদ্ধগণের উপরে অন্ন পড়ে অমেধ্য হৈয়া ।
বৌদ্ধাচার্যের মাথায় থালি পড়িল বাজিয়া ॥ ৫৫ ॥

bauddha-gaṇera upare anna paḍe amedhya haiyā
bauddhācāryera māthāya thāli paḍila bājiyā

bauddha-gaṇera—all the Buddhists; *upare*—upon; *anna*—the food; *paḍe*—began to fall down; *amedhya*—untouchable; *haiyā*—being; *bauddha-ācāryera*—of the teacher of the Buddhists; *māthāya*—on the head; *thāli*—the plate; *paḍila*—fell down; *bājiyā*—making a loud sound.

TRANSLATION

Indeed, the untouchable food fell upon the Buddhists, and the large bird dropped the plate on the head of the chief Buddhist teacher. When it fell on his head, it made a loud sound.

TEXT 56

তেরছে পড়িল থালি, —মাথা কাটি' গেল ।
মূর্চ্ছিত হঞা আচার্য ভূমিতে পড়িল ॥ ৫৬ ॥

terache paḍila thāli,—māthā kāṭi' gela
mūrcchita hañā ācārya bhūmite paḍila

terache—at an angle; *paḍila*—fell down; *thāli*—the plate; *māthā*—the head; *kāṭi'*—cutting; *gela*—went; *mūrcchita*—unconscious; *hañā*—becoming; *ācārya*—the teacher; *bhūmite*—on the ground; *paḍila*—fell down.

TRANSLATION

The plate was made of metal, and when its edge hit the head of the teacher, it cut him, and the teacher immediately fell to the ground unconscious.

TEXT 57

হাহাকার করি' কান্দে সব শিষ্যগণ ।
সবে আসি' প্রভু-পদে লইল শরণ ॥ ৫৭ ॥

hāhākāra kari' kānde saba śiṣya-gaṇa
sabe āsi' prabhu-pade la-ila śaraṇa

hāhā-kāra—a roaring sound; *kari'*—making; *kānde*—cry; *saba*—all; *śiṣya-gaṇa*—disciples; *sabe*—all of them; *āsi'*—coming; *prabhu-pade*—to the lotus feet of Lord Caitanya Mahāprabhu; *la-ila*—took; *śaraṇa*—shelter.

TRANSLATION

When the teacher fell unconscious, his Buddhist disciples cried aloud and ran to the lotus feet of Śrī Caitanya Mahāprabhu for shelter.

TEXT 58

তুমি ত' ঈশ্বর সাক্ষাৎ, ক্ষম অপরাধ।
জীয়াও আমার গুরু, করহ প্রসাদ ॥ ৫৮ ॥

tumi ta' īśvara sākṣāt, kṣama aparādha
jīyāo āmāra guru, karaha prasāda

tumi—You; *ta'*—indeed; *īśvara*—the Supreme Personality of Godhead; *sākṣāt*—directly; *kṣama*—please excuse; *aparādha*—offense; *jīyāo*—bring back to consciousness; *āmāra*—our; *guru*—spiritual master; *karaha*—do; *prasāda*—this mercy.

TRANSLATION

They all prayed to Lord Śrī Caitanya Mahāprabhu, addressing Him as the Supreme Personality of Godhead Himself and saying, "Sir, please excuse our offense. Please have mercy upon us and bring our spiritual master back to life."

TEXT 59

প্রভু কহে,—সবে কহ 'কৃষ্ণ' 'কৃষ্ণ' 'হরি'।
গুরুকর্ণে কহ কৃষ্ণনাম উচ্চ করি' ॥ ৫৯ ॥

prabhu kahe,—sabe kaha 'kṛṣṇa' 'kṛṣṇa' 'hari'
guru-karṇe kaha kṛṣṇa-nāma ucca kari'

prabhu kahe—Lord Śrī Caitanya Mahāprabhu said; *sabe*—all of you; *kaha*—chant; *kṛṣṇa kṛṣṇa hari*—the holy names of Lord Kṛṣṇa and Hari; *guru-karṇe*—near the ear of your spiritual master; *kaha*—chant; *kṛṣṇa-nāma*—the holy name of Lord Kṛṣṇa; *ucca kari'*—very loudly.

TRANSLATION

The Lord then replied to the Buddhist disciples, "You should all chant the names of Kṛṣṇa and Hari very loudly near the ear of your spiritual master.

TEXT 60

তোমা-সবার 'গুরু' তবে পাইবে চেতন।
সব বৌদ্ধ মিলি' করে কৃষ্ণসঙ্কীর্তন ॥ ৬০ ॥

tomā-sabāra 'guru' tabe pāibe cetana
saba bauddha mili' kare kṛṣṇa-saṅkīrtana

tomā-sabāra—all of you; *guru*—the spiritual master; *tabe*—then; *pāibe*—will get; *cetana*—consciousness; *saba bauddha*—all the Buddhist disciples; *mili'*—coming together; *kare*—do; *kṛṣṇa-saṅkīrtana*—chanting of the Hare Kṛṣṇa *mantra.*

TRANSLATION

"By this method your spiritual master will regain his consciousness." Following Śrī Caitanya Mahāprabhu's advice, all the Buddhist disciples began to chant the holy name of Kṛṣṇa congregationally.

TEXT 61

গুরু-কর্ণে কহে সবে 'কৃষ্ণ' 'রাম' 'হরি'।
চেতন পাঞা আচার্য বলে 'হরি' 'হরি' ॥ ৬১ ॥

guru-karṇe kahe sabe 'kṛṣṇa' 'rāma' 'hari'
cetana pāñā ācārya bale 'hari' 'hari'

guru-karṇe—into the ear of the spiritual master; *kahe*—they said; *sabe*—all together; *kṛṣṇa rāma hari*—the holy names of the Lord, namely "Kṛṣṇa," "Rāma" and "Hari"; *cetana*—consciousness; *pāñā*—getting; *ācārya*—the teacher; *bale*—chanted; *hari hari*—the name of Lord Hari.

TRANSLATION

When all the disciples chanted the holy names Kṛṣṇa, Rāma and Hari, the Buddhist teacher regained consciousness and immediately began to chant the holy name of Lord Hari.

PURPORT

Śrī Bhaktisiddhānta Sarasvatī Ṭhākura comments that all the Buddhist disciples were actually initiated by Śrī Caitanya Mahāprabhu into the chanting of the holy name of Kṛṣṇa, and when they chanted, they actually became different persons. At that time they were not Buddhists or atheists but Vaiṣṇavas. Consequently they immediately accepted Śrī Caitanya Mahāprabhu's order. Their original Kṛṣṇa consciousness was revived, and they were immediately able to chant Hare Kṛṣṇa and begin worshiping the Supreme Lord Viṣṇu.

It is the spiritual master who delivers the disciple from the clutches of *māyā* by initiating him into the chanting of the Hare Kṛṣṇa *mahā-mantra.* In this way a sleeping human being can revive his consciousness by chanting Hare Kṛṣṇa, Hare Kṛṣṇa, Kṛṣṇa Kṛṣṇa, Hare Hare/ Hare Rāma, Hare Rāma, Rāma Rāma, Hare Hare. In other words, the spiritual master awakens the sleeping living entity to his original consciousness so that he can worship Lord Viṣṇu. This is the purpose of *dīkṣā,* or initiation. Initiation means receiving the pure knowledge of spiritual consciousness.

One point to note in this regard is that the spiritual master of the Buddhists did not initiate his disciples. Rather, his disciples were initiated by Śrī Kṛṣṇa Caitanya Mahāprabhu, and they in turn were able to initiate their so-called spiritual master. This is the *paramparā* system. The so-called spiritual master of the Buddhists was actually in the position of a disciple, and after his disciples were initiated by Śrī Caitanya Mahāprabhu, they acted as his spiritual masters. This was possible only because the disciples of the Buddhist *ācārya* received the mercy of Lord Śrī Caitanya Mahāprabhu. Unless one is favored by

Śrī Caitanya Mahāprabhu in the disciplic succession, one cannot act as a spiritual master. We should take the instructions of Śrī Caitanya Mahāprabhu, the spiritual master of the whole universe, to understand how one becomes a spiritual master and a disciple.

TEXT 62

কৃষ্ণ বলি' আচার্য প্রভুরে করেন বিনয়।
দেখিয়া সকল লোক হইল বিস্ময় ॥ ৬২ ॥

kṛṣṇa bali' ācārya prabhure karena vinaya
dekhiyā sakala loka ha-ila vismaya

kṛṣṇa bali'—chanting the holy name of Kṛṣṇa; *ācārya*—the so-called spiritual master of the Buddhists; *prabhure*—unto Lord Śrī Caitanya Mahāprabhu; *karena*—does; *vinaya*—submission; *dekhiyā*—seeing this; *sakala loka*—all the people; *ha-ila*—became; *vismaya*—astonished.

TRANSLATION

When the spiritual master of the Buddhists began to chant the holy name of Kṛṣṇa and submitted to Lord Śrī Caitanya Mahāprabhu, all the people who were gathered there were astonished.

TEXT 63

এইরূপে কৌতুক করি' শচীর নন্দন।
অন্তর্ধান কৈল, কেহ না পায় দর্শন ॥ ৬৩ ॥

ei-rūpe kautuka kari' śacīra nandana
antardhāna kaila, keha nā pāya darśana

ei-rūpe—in this way; *kautuka kari'*—making fun; *śacīra nandana*—the son of mother Śacī; *antardhāna kaila*—disappeared; *keha*—anyone; *nā*—does not; *pāya*—get; *darśana*—audience.

TRANSLATION

Śrī Caitanya Mahāprabhu, the son of Śacīdevī, then suddenly and playfully disappeared from everyone's sight, and it was impossible for anyone to find Him.

TEXT 64

মহাপ্রভু চলি' আইলা ত্রিপতি-ত্রিমল্লে।
চতুর্ভুজ মূর্তি দেখি' ব্যেঙ্কটাদ্রে চলে ॥ ৬৪ ॥

mahāprabhu cali' āilā tripati-trimalle
catur-bhuja mūrti dekhi' vyeṅkaṭādrye cale

mahāprabhu—Lord Śrī Caitanya Mahāprabhu; *cali' āilā*—arrived by walking; *tripati-trimalle*—at the holy places named Tirupati and Tirumala; *catur-bhuja*—four-handed; *mūrti*—Deity; *dekhi'*—seeing; *vyeṅkaṭa-adrye*—to the holy place Veṅkaṭa Hill; *cale*—began to proceed.

TRANSLATION

Śrī Caitanya Mahāprabhu next arrived at Tirupati and Tirumala, where He saw a four-handed Deity. Then He proceeded toward Veṅkaṭa Hill.

PURPORT

Śrīla Bhaktisiddhānta Sarasvatī Ṭhākura has actually described the chronological order of Lord Caitanya Mahāprabhu's visit. The Tirupati temple is sometimes called Tirupaṭura. It is situated on the northern side of Arcot in the district of Candragiri. It is a famous holy place of pilgrimage. In pursuance of His name, Veṅkaṭeśvara, the four-handed Lord Viṣṇu, the Deity of Bālājī, with His potencies named Śrī and Bhū, is located on Veṅkaṭa Hill, about eight miles from Tirupati. This Veṅkaṭeśvara Deity is in the form of Lord Viṣṇu, and the place where He is situated is known as Veṅkaṭa-kṣetra. There are many temples in southern India, but this Bālājī temple is especially opulent. A great fair is held there in the month of Āśvina (September–October). There is a railway station called Tirupati on the Southern railway. Nimna-tirupati is located in the valley of Veṅkaṭa Hill. There are several temples there also, among which are those of Govindarāja and Lord Rāmacandra.

TEXT 65

ত্রিপতি আসিয়া কৈল শ্রীরাম দরশন।
রঘুনাথ-আগে কৈল প্রণাম স্তবন ॥ ৬৫ ॥

tripati āsiyā kaila śrī-rāma daraśana
raghunātha-āge kaila praṇāma stavana

tripati āsiyā—coming to Tirupati; *kaila śrī-rāma daraśana*—visited the temple of Rāmacandra; *raghunātha-āge*—before Lord Rāmacandra; *kaila*—did; *praṇāma*—obeisances; *stavana*—offering prayers.

TRANSLATION

After arriving at Tirupati, Lord Śrī Caitanya Mahāprabhu visited the temple of Lord Rāmacandra. He offered His prayers and obeisances before Rāmacandra, the descendant of King Raghu.

TEXT 66

স্বপ্রভাবে লোক-সবার করাঞা বিস্ময় ।
পানা-নৃসিংহে আইলা প্রভু দয়াময় ॥ ৬৬ ॥

sva-prabhāve loka-sabāra karāñā vismaya
pānā-nṛsiṁhe āilā prabhu dayā-maya

sva-prabhāve—by His own influence; *loka-sabāra*—of all the people; *karāñā*—inducing; *vismaya*—astonishment; *pānā-nṛsiṁhe*—to the Lord named Pānā-nṛsiṁha; *āilā*—came; *prabhu*—Lord Śrī Caitanya Mahāprabhu; *dayā-maya*—the most merciful.

TRANSLATION

Everywhere Śrī Caitanya Mahāprabhu went, His influence astonished everyone. He next arrived at the temple of Pānā-nṛsiṁha. The Lord is so merciful.

PURPORT

Pānā-nṛsiṁha, or Pānākal-narasiṁha, is located in the district of Krishna, in the hills known as Maṅgalagiri, about seven miles from a city known as Vijayawada. One must climb six hundred steps to reach the temple. It is said that when the Lord is offered food with syrup here, He does not take more than half. Within this temple is a conchshell presented by the late king of Tanjore, and it is said that this shell was used by Lord Kṛṣṇa Himself. During the month of March, a great fair takes place in this temple.

TEXT 67

নৃসিংহে প্রণতি-স্তুতি প্রেমাবেশে কৈল ।
প্রভুর প্রভাবে লোক চমৎকার হৈল ॥ ৬৭ ॥

nṛsiṁhe praṇati-stuti premāveśe kaila
prabhura prabhāve loka camatkāra haila

nṛsiṁhe—unto Lord Nṛsiṁha; *praṇati-stuti*—obeisances and prayers; *prema-āveśe*—in ecstatic love; *kaila*—offered; *prabhura*—of the Lord; *prabhāve*—by the influence; *loka*—the people; *camatkāra haila*—were astonished.

TRANSLATION

In great ecstatic love, Śrī Caitanya Mahāprabhu offered obeisances and prayers unto Lord Nṛsiṁha. The people were astonished to see Lord Caitanya's influence.

TEXT 68

শিবকাঞ্চী আসিয়া কৈল শিব দরশন ।
প্রভাবে 'বৈষ্ণব' কৈল সব শৈবগণ ॥ ৬৮ ॥

śiva-kāñcī āsiyā kaila śiva daraśana
prabhāve 'vaiṣṇava' kaila saba śaiva-gaṇa

śiva-kāñcī—to the holy place named Śiva-kāñcī; *āsiyā*—coming; *kaila*—did; *śiva daraśana*—visiting the temple of Lord Śiva; *prabhāve*—by His influence; *vaiṣṇava kaila*—turned into Vaiṣṇavas; *saba*—all; *śaiva-gaṇa*—the devotees of Lord Śiva.

TRANSLATION

Arriving at Śiva-kāñcī, Caitanya Mahāprabhu visited the deity of Lord Śiva. By His influence, He converted all the devotees of Lord Śiva into Vaiṣṇavas.

PURPORT

Śiva-kāñcī is also known as Kāñcīpuram, or the Benares of southern India. In Śiva-kāñcī there are hundreds of temples containing symbolic representations of Lord Śiva, and one of these temples is said to be very, very old.

TEXT 69

বিষ্ণুকাঞ্চী আসি' দেখিল লক্ষ্মী-নারায়ণ ।
প্রণাম করিয়া কৈল বহুত স্তবন ॥ ৬৯ ॥

viṣṇu-kāñcī āsi' dekhila lakṣmī-nārāyaṇa
praṇāma kariyā kaila bahuta stavana

viṣṇu-kāñcī—to the holy place named Viṣṇu-kāñcī; *āsi'*—coming; *dekhila*—the Lord saw; *lakṣmī-nārāyaṇa*—the Deity of Lord Nārāyaṇa with mother Lakṣmī, the goddess of fortune; *praṇāma kariyā*—after offering obeisances; *kaila*—made; *bahuta stavana*—many prayers.

TRANSLATION

The Lord then visited a holy place known as Viṣṇu-kāñcī. There He saw Lakṣmī-Nārāyaṇa Deities, and He offered His respects and many prayers to please Them.

PURPORT

Viṣṇu-kāñcī is situated about five miles away from Kāñcīpuram. It is here that Lord Varadarāja, another form of Lord Viṣṇu, resides. There is also a big lake known as Ananta-sarovara.

TEXT 70

প্রেমাবেশে নৃত্য-গীত বহুত করিল ।
দিন-দুই রহি' লোকে 'কৃষ্ণভক্ত' কৈল ॥ ৭০ ॥

premāveśe nṛtya-gīta bahuta karila
dina-dui rahi' loke 'kṛṣṇa-bhakta' kaila

prema-āveśe—in ecstatic love; *nṛtya-gīta*—dancing and chanting; *bahuta*—much; *karila*—performed; *dina-dui*—for two days; *rahi'*—staying; *loke*—the people in general; *kṛṣṇa-bhakta*—devotees of Lord Kṛṣṇa; *kaila*—made.

TRANSLATION

When Śrī Caitanya Mahāprabhu stayed at Viṣṇu-kāñcī for two days, He danced and performed kīrtana in ecstasy. When all the people saw Him, they were converted into devotees of Lord Kṛṣṇa.

TEXT 71

ত্রিমলয় দেখি' গেলা ত্রিকালহস্তি-স্থানে।
মহাদেব দেখি' তাঁরে করিল প্রণামে ॥ ৭১ ॥

trimalaya dekhi' gelā trikāla-hasti-sthāne
mahādeva dekhi' tāṅre karila praṇāme

trimalaya dekhi'—after seeing Trimalaya; *gelā*—went; *trikāla-hasti-sthāne*—to the place named Trikāla-hasti; *mahādeva*—Lord Śiva; *dekhi'*—seeing; *tāṅre*—unto him; *karila praṇāme*—offered obeisances.

TRANSLATION

After visiting Trimalaya, Śrī Caitanya Mahāprabhu went to see Trikāla-hasti. There He saw Lord Śiva and offered him all respects and obeisances.

PURPORT

Trikāla-hasti, or Śrī Kāla-hasti, is situated about twenty-two miles east of Tirupati. On its western side is a river known as Suvarṇa-mukhī. The temple of Trikāla-hasti is located on the southern side of the river. The place is generally known as Śrī Kālahasti or Kālahasti and is famous for its temple of Lord Śiva. There he is called Vāyu-liṅga Śiva.

TEXT 72

পক্ষিতীর্থ দেখি' কৈল শিব দরশন।
বৃদ্ধকোল-তীর্থে তবে করিলা গমন ॥ ৭২ ॥

pakṣi-tīrtha dekhi' kaila śiva daraśana
vṛddhakola-tīrthe tabe karilā gamana

pakṣi-tīrtha dekhi'—after visiting the place known as Pakṣi-tīrtha; *kaila*—did; *śiva daraśana*—visiting the temple of Lord Śiva; *vṛddhakola-tīrthe*—to the holy place known as Vṛddhakola; *tabe*—then; *karilā gamana*—went.

TRANSLATION

At Pakṣi-tīrtha, Lord Śrī Caitanya Mahāprabhu visited the temple of Lord Śiva. Then He went to the Vṛddhakola place of pilgrimage.

PURPORT

Pakṣi-tīrtha, also called Tirukāḍi-kuṇḍam, is located nine miles southeast of Ciṁlipaṭ. It has a five-hundred-foot elevation and is situated in a chain of hills known as Vedagiri or Vedācalam. There is a temple of Lord Śiva there, and the deity is known as Vedagirīśvara. Two birds come there daily to receive food from the temple priest, and it is claimed that they have been coming since time immemorial.

TEXT 73

শ্বেতবরাহ দেখি, তাঁরে নমস্করি' ।
পীতাম্বর-শিব-স্থানে গেলা গৌরহরি ॥ ৭৩ ॥

śveta-varāha dekhi, tāṅre namaskari'
pītāmbara-śiva-sthāne gelā gaurahari

śveta-varāha—the white boar incarnation; *dekhi*—seeing; *tāṅre*—unto Him; *namaskari'*—offering respect; *pīta-ambara*—dressed with yellow garments; *śiva-sthāne*—to the temple of Lord Śiva; *gelā*—went; *gaurahari*—Lord Śrī Caitanya Mahāprabhu.

TRANSLATION

At Vṛddhakola, Lord Śrī Caitanya Mahāprabhu visited the temple of Śveta-varāha, the white boar incarnation. After offering Him respects,

the Lord visited the temple of Lord Śiva, wherein the deity is dressed with yellow garments.

PURPORT

The temple of the white boar incarnation is situated at Vṛddhakola, or Śrī Muṣṇam. The temple is made of stone and is located about one mile south of an oasis known as Balipīṭham. There is a Deity of the white boar incarnation, above whose head Śeṣa Nāga serves as an umbrella.

The temple of Lord Śiva mentioned here is situated in Pītāmbara, or Cidāmbaram, which lies twenty-six miles south of Cuddalore. The deity of Lord Śiva there is known as Ākāśaliṅga. The temple is situated on about thirty-nine acres of land, and all this land is surrounded by a wall and by a road that is about sixty feet wide.

TEXT 74

শিয়ালী ভৈরবী দেবী করি' দরশন।
কাবেরীর তীরে আইলা শচীর নন্দন ॥ ৭৪ ॥

śiyālī bhairavī devī kari' daraśana
kāverīra tīre āilā śacīra nandana

śiyālī bhairavī—Śiyālī-bhairavī; *devī*—goddess; *kari' daraśana*—visiting; *kāverīra tīre*—on the bank of the river Kāverī; *āilā*—came; *śacīra nandana*—the son of mother Śacī.

TRANSLATION

After visiting the temple of Śiyālī-bhairavī [a form of the goddess Durgā], Śrī Caitanya Mahāprabhu, the son of mother Śacī, went to the bank of the river Kāverī.

PURPORT

The temple of Śiyālī-bhairavī is located in the Tanjore district, about forty-eight miles northeast of Tanjore City. There is a very much celebrated temple of Lord Śiva there and also a very large lake. It is said that once a small boy who was a devotee of Lord Śiva came to that temple, and goddess Durgā, known as Bhairavī, gave him her breast to suck. After visiting this temple, Śrī Caitanya Mahāprabhu went to the bank of the river Kāverī (Kolirana) via the district of Tiruchchirāpalli. The Kāverī is mentioned in *Śrīmad-Bhāgavatam* (11.5.40) as a very pious river.

TEXT 75

গো-সমাজে শিব দেখি' আইলা বেদাবন।
মহাদেব দেখি' তাঁরে করিলা বন্দন ॥ ৭৫ ॥

go-samāje śiva dekhi' āilā vedāvana
mahādeva dekhi' tāṅre karilā vandana

go-samāje—at the place named Go-samāja; *śiva dekhi'*—seeing the deity of Lord Śiva; *āilā vedāvana*—He arrived at Vedāvana; *mahādeva dekhi'*—seeing Lord Śiva; *tāṅre*—unto him; *karilā vandana*—offered prayers.

TRANSLATION

The Lord then visited a place known as Go-samāja, where He saw Lord Śiva's temple. He then arrived at Vedāvana, where He saw another deity of Lord Śiva and offered him prayers.

PURPORT

Go-samāja is a place of pilgrimage for the devotees of Lord Śiva. It is very important and is located near Vedāvana.

TEXT 76

অমৃতলিঙ্গ-শিব দেখি' বন্দন করিল।
সব শিবালয়ে শৈব 'বৈষ্ণব' হইল ॥ ৭৬ ॥

amṛtaliṅga-śiva dekhi' vandana karila
saba śivālaye śaiva 'vaiṣṇava' ha-ila

amṛta-liṅga-śiva—the Lord Śiva deity named Amṛta-liṅga; *dekhi'*—seeing; *vandana karila*—offered obeisances; *saba śiva-ālaye*—in all the temples of Lord Śiva; *śaiva*—devotees of Lord Śiva; *vaiṣṇava ha-ila*—became devotees of Lord Kṛṣṇa.

TRANSLATION

Seeing the Śiva deity named Amṛta-liṅga, Lord Caitanya Mahāprabhu offered His obeisances. Thus He visited all the temples of Lord Śiva and converted the devotees of Lord Śiva into Vaiṣṇavas.

TEXT 77

দেবস্থানে আসি' কৈল বিষ্ণু দরশন ।
শ্রী-বৈষ্ণবের সঙ্গে তাহাঁ গোষ্ঠী অনুক্ষণ ॥ ৭৭ ॥

deva-sthāne āsi' kaila viṣṇu daraśana
śrī-vaiṣṇavera saṅge tāhāṅ goṣṭhī anukṣaṇa

deva-sthāne—to the place known as Devasthāna; *āsi'*—coming; *kaila*—did; *viṣṇu daraśana*—visiting the temple of Lord Viṣṇu; *śrī-vaiṣṇavera saṅge*—with the Vaiṣṇavas in the disciplic succession of Rāmānuja; *tāhāṅ*—there; *goṣṭhī*—discussion; *anukṣaṇa*—always.

TRANSLATION

At Devasthāna, Caitanya Mahāprabhu visited the temple of Lord Viṣṇu, and there He talked with the Vaiṣṇavas in the disciplic succession of Rāmānujācārya. These Vaiṣṇavas are known as Śrī Vaiṣṇavas.

TEXT 78

কুম্ভকর্ণ-কপালে দেখি' সরোবর ।
শিব-ক্ষেত্রে শিব দেখে গৌরাঙ্গসুন্দর ॥ ৭৮ ॥

kumbhakarṇa-kapāle dekhi' sarovara
śiva-kṣetre śiva dekhe gaurāṅga-sundara

kumbhakarṇa-kapāle—at Kumbhakarṇa-kapāla; *dekhi'*—after seeing; *sarovara*—the lake; *śiva-kṣetre*—at Śiva-kṣetra; *śiva*—Lord Śiva; *dekhe*—sees; *gaurāṅga-sundara*—Lord Śrī Caitanya Mahāprabhu.

TRANSLATION

At Kumbhakarṇa-kapāla, Śrī Caitanya Mahāprabhu saw a great lake and then the holy place named Śiva-kṣetra, where a temple of Lord Śiva is located.

PURPORT

Kumbhakarṇa is the name of the brother of Rāvaṇa. At the present moment the city of Kumbhakarṇa-kapāla is known as Kumbhakonam; it is situated twenty-four miles northeast of the city of Tanjore. There are twelve temples of Lord Śiva located at Kumbhakonam, as well as four Viṣṇu temples and one temple of Lord Brahmā. Śiva-kṣetra, within the city of Tanjore, is situated near a big lake known as Śiva-gaṅgā. At this place is a large temple of Lord Śiva known as Bṛhatīśvara-śiva-mandira.

TEXT 79

পাপনাশনে বিষ্ণু কৈল দরশন ।
শ্রীরঙ্গক্ষেত্রে তবে করিলা গমন ॥ ৭৯ ॥

pāpa-nāśane viṣṇu kaila daraśana
śrī-raṅga-kṣetre tabe karilā gamana

pāpa-nāśane—at the place named Pāpanāśana; *viṣṇu*—Lord Viṣṇu; *kaila*—did; *daraśana*—visiting; *śrī-raṅga-kṣetre*—to the holy place named Śrī Raṅga-kṣetra; *tabe*—then; *karilā*—did; *gamana*—departure.

TRANSLATION

After visiting the holy place named Śiva-kṣetra, Caitanya Mahāprabhu arrived at Pāpanāśana and there saw the temple of Lord Viṣṇu. Then He finally reached Śrī Raṅga-kṣetra.

PURPORT

There are two holy places known as Pāpanāśana: one is located eight miles southwest of Kumbhakonam, and the other lies near the river Tāmraparṇī, in the district of Tirunelveli, twenty miles west of the city of Tirunelveli (Pālamakoṭā).

Śrī Raṅga-kṣetra (Śrī Raṅgam) is a very famous place. It lies in the district of Tiruchchirāpalli, about ten miles west of Kumbhakonam and near the city of Tiruchchirāpalli, on an island in the Kāverī River. The Śrī Raṅgam temple is the largest in India, and there are seven walls surrounding it. There are also seven roads leading to Śrī Raṅgam.

The ancient names of these roads are the road of Dharma, the road of Rājamahendra, the road of Kulaśekhara, the road of Ālināḍana, the road of Tiruvikrama, the Tirubiḍi road of Māḍamāḍi-gāisa, and the road of Aḍa-iyāvala-indāna. The temple was founded before the reign of Dharmavarma, who reigned before Rājamahendra. Many celebrated kings like Kulaśekhara and Yāmunācārya (Ālabandāru) resided in the temple of Śrī Raṅgam. Yāmunācārya, Śrī Rāmānuja, Sudarśanācārya and others also supervised this temple.

The incarnation of the goddess of fortune known as Godādevī or Śrī Āṇḍāl was one of the twelve Ālvārs, liberated persons known as *divya-sūris.* She was married to the Deity of Lord Śrī Raṅganātha, and later she entered into the body of the Lord. An incarnation of Kārmuka named Tirumaṅga (also one of the Ālvārs) acquired some money by stealing and built the fourth boundary wall of Śrī Raṅgam. It is said that in the year 289 of the Age of Kali, the Ālvār of the name Toṇḍaraḍippaḍi was born. While engaged in devotional service he fell victim to a prostitute, and Śrī Raṅganātha, seeing His devotee so degraded, sent one of His servants with a golden plate to that prostitute. When the golden plate was discovered missing from the temple, there was a search, and it was found in the prostitute's house. When the devotee saw Raṅganātha's mercy upon this prostitute, his mistake was rectified. He then prepared the third boundary wall of the Raṅganātha temple and cultivated a *tulasī* garden there.

There was also a celebrated disciple of Rāmānujācārya's known as Kūreśa. Śrī Rāmapillāi was the son of Kūreśa, and his son was Vāgvijaya Bhaṭṭa, whose son was Vedavyāsa Bhaṭṭa, or Śrī Sudarśanācārya. When Sudarśanācārya was an old man, the Muslims attacked the temple of Raṅganātha and killed about twelve hundred Śrī Vaiṣṇavas. At that time the Deity of Raṅganātha was transferred to the temple of Tirupati, in the kingdom of Vijaya-nagara. The governor of Gingee, Goppaṇārya, brought Śrī Raṅganātha from the temple of Tirupati to a place known as Siṁha-brahma, where the Lord was situated for three years. In the year 1293 Śaka (A.D. 1371) the Deity was reinstalled in the Raṅganātha temple. On the eastern wall of the Raṅganātha temple is an inscription written by Vedānta-deśika relating how Raṅganātha was returned to the temple.

TEXT 80

কাবেরীতে স্নান করি' দেখি' রঙ্গনাথ।
স্তুতি-প্রণতি করি' মানিলা কৃতার্থ॥ ৮০॥

kāverīte snāna kari' dekhi' raṅganātha
stuti-praṇati kari' mānilā kṛtārtha

kāverīte—in the river known as Kāverī; *snāna kari'*—after bathing; *dekhi'*—visiting; *raṅga-nātha*—the temple of Raṅganātha; *stuti*—prayers; *praṇati*—obeisances; *kari'*—offering; *mānilā*—thought Himself; *kṛta-artha*—very successful.

TRANSLATION

After bathing in the river Kāverī, Śrī Caitanya Mahāprabhu saw the temple of Raṅganātha and offered His ardent prayers and obeisances. Thus He felt Himself successful.

TEXT 81

প্রেমাবেশে কৈল বহুত গান নর্তন।
দেখি' চমৎকার হৈল সব লোকের মন॥ ৮১॥

premāveśe kaila bahuta gāna nartana
dekhi' camatkāra haila saba lokera mana

prema-āveśe—in the ecstasy of love; *kaila*—did; *bahuta*—various; *gāna*—songs; *nartana*—dancing; *dekhi'*—seeing which; *camatkāra*—astonished; *haila*—were; *saba*—all; *lokera*—of persons; *mana*—minds.

TRANSLATION

In the temple of Raṅganātha, Śrī Caitanya Mahāprabhu chanted and danced in ecstatic love of Godhead. Seeing His performance, everyone was struck with wonder.

TEXT 82

শ্রী-বৈষ্ণব এক, — 'ব্যেঙ্কট ভট্ট' নাম।
প্রভুরে নিমন্ত্রণ কৈল করিয়া সম্মান॥ ৮২॥

śrī-vaiṣṇava eka,—'vyeṅkaṭa bhaṭṭa' nāma
prabhure nimantraṇa kaila kariyā sammāna

śrī-vaiṣṇava eka—a devotee belonging to the Rāmānuja-sampradāya; *vyeṅkaṭa bhaṭṭa*—Veṅkaṭa Bhaṭṭa; *nāma*—named; *prabhure*—unto Lord Caitanya Mahāprabhu; *nimantraṇa*—invitation; *kaila*—did; *kariyā*—offering; *sammāna*—great respect.

TRANSLATION

A Vaiṣṇava known as Veṅkaṭa Bhaṭṭa then invited Śrī Caitanya Mahāprabhu to his home with great respect.

PURPORT

Śrī Veṅkaṭa Bhaṭṭa was a Vaiṣṇava *brāhmaṇa* and an inhabitant of Śrī Raṅga-kṣetra. He belonged to the disciplic succession of Śrī Rāmānujācārya. Śrī Raṅga is one of the places of pilgrimage in the province of Tamil Nadu. The inhabitants of that province do not retain the name "Veṅkaṭa." It is therefore supposed that Veṅkaṭa Bhaṭṭa did not belong to that province, although he may have been residing there for a very long time. Veṅkaṭa Bhaṭṭa was in a branch of the Rāmānuja-sampradāya known as Baḍagala-i. He had a brother in the Rāmānuja-sampradāya known as Śrīpāda Prabodhānanda Sarasvatī. The son of Veṅkaṭa Bhaṭṭa was later known in the Gauḍīya-sampradāya as Gopāla Bhaṭṭa Gosvāmī, and he established the Rādhāramaṇa temple in Vṛndāvana. More information about him may be found in a book known as the *Bhakti-ratnākara,* by Narahari Cakravartī.

TEXT 83

নিজ-ঘরে লঞা কৈল পাদপ্রক্ষালন।
সেই জল লঞা কৈল সবংশে ভক্ষণ ॥ ৮৩ ॥

nija-ghare lañā kaila pāda-prakṣālana
sei jala lañā kaila sa-vaṁśe bhakṣaṇa

nija-ghare—to his own home; *lañā*—bringing; *kaila*—did; *pāda-prakṣālana*—washing of the feet; *sei jala*—that water;

lañā—taking; *kaila*—did; *sa-vaṁśe*—with all the family members; *bhakṣaṇa*—drinking.

TRANSLATION

Śrī Veṅkaṭa Bhaṭṭa took Śrī Caitanya Mahāprabhu to his home. After he washed the Lord's feet, all the members of his family drank the water.

TEXT 84

ভিক্ষা করাঞা কিছু কৈল নিবেদন ।
চাতুর্মাস্য আসি' প্রভু, হৈল উপসন্ন ॥ ৮৪ ॥

bhikṣā karāñā kichu kaila nivedana
cāturmāsya āsi' prabhu, haila upasanna

bhikṣā karāñā—after offering lunch; *kichu*—some; *kaila*—did; *nivedana*—submission; *cāturmāsya*—the period of Cāturmāsya; *āsi'*—coming; *prabhu*—my Lord; *haila upasanna*—has already arrived.

TRANSLATION

After offering lunch to the Lord, Veṅkaṭa Bhaṭṭa submitted that the period of Cāturmāsya had already arrived.

TEXT 85

চাতুর্মাস্যে কৃপা করি' রহ মোর ঘরে ।
কৃষ্ণকথা কহি' কৃপায় উদ্ধার' আমারে ॥ ৮৫ ॥

cāturmāsye kṛpā kari' raha mora ghare
kṛṣṇa-kathā kahi' kṛpāya uddhāra' āmāre

cāturmāsye—during this period of Cāturmāsya; *kṛpā kari'*—being merciful; *raha*—please stay; *mora ghare*—at my place; *kṛṣṇa-kathā*—topics of Lord Kṛṣṇa; *kahi'*—speaking; *kṛpāya*—by Your mercy; *uddhāra' āmāre*—kindly deliver me.

TRANSLATION

Veṅkaṭa Bhaṭṭa said, "Please be merciful to me and stay at my house during Cāturmāsya. Speak about Lord Kṛṣṇa's pastimes and kindly deliver me by Your mercy."

TEXT 86

তাঁর ঘরে রহিলা প্রভু কৃষ্ণকথা-রসে ।
ভট্টসঙ্গে গোঙাইল সুখে চারি মাসে ॥ ৮৬ ॥

tāṅra ghare rahilā prabhu kṛṣṇa-kathā-rase
bhaṭṭa-saṅge goṅāila sukhe cāri māse

tāṅra ghare—in his home; *rahilā*—stayed; *prabhu*—Lord Śrī Caitanya Mahāprabhu; *kṛṣṇa-kathā-rase*—enjoying the transcendental mellow of discussing Lord Kṛṣṇa's pastimes; *bhaṭṭa-saṅge*—with Veṅkaṭa Bhaṭṭa; *goṅāila*—passed; *sukhe*—in happiness; *cāri māse*—four months.

TRANSLATION

Śrī Caitanya Mahāprabhu remained at the house of Veṅkaṭa Bhaṭṭa for four continuous months. The Lord passed His days in great happiness, enjoying the transcendental mellow of discussing Lord Kṛṣṇa's pastimes.

TEXT 87

কাবেরীতে স্নান করি' শ্রীরঙ্গ দর্শন ।
প্রতিদিন প্রেমাবেশে করেন নর্তন ॥ ৮৭ ॥

kāverīte snāna kari' śrī-raṅga darśana
pratidina premāveśe karena nartana

kāverīte—in the river known as Kāverī; *snāna kari'*—taking a bath; *śrī-raṅga darśana*—visiting the temple of Śrī Raṅga; *prati-dina*—every day; *prema-āveśe*—in great happiness; *karena*—does perform; *nartana*—dancing.

TRANSLATION

While there, Śrī Caitanya Mahāprabhu took His bath in the river Kāverī and visited the temple of Śrī Raṅga. Every day the Lord also danced in ecstasy.

TEXT 88

সৌন্দর্যাদি প্রেমাবেশ দেখি, সর্বলোক।
দেখিবারে আইসে, দেখে, খণ্ডে দুঃখ-শোক ॥ ৮৮ ॥

saundaryādi premāveśa dekhi, sarva-loka
dekhibāre āise, dekhe, khaṇḍe duḥkha-śoka

saundarya-ādi—the beauty of the body, etc.; *prema-āveśa*—His ecstatic love; *dekhi*—seeing; *sarva-loka*—all men; *dekhibāre*—to see; *āise*—come there; *dekhe*—and see; *khaṇḍe duḥkha-śoka*—are relieved from all unhappiness and distress.

TRANSLATION

The beauty of Lord Caitanya's body and His ecstatic love of God were witnessed by everyone. Many people used to come see Him, and as soon as they saw Him, all their unhappiness and distress vanished.

TEXT 89

লক্ষ লক্ষ লোক আইল নানা-দেশ হৈতে।
সবে কৃষ্ণনাম কহে প্রভুকে দেখিতে ॥ ৮৯ ॥

lakṣa lakṣa loka āila nānā-deśa haite
sabe kṛṣṇa-nāma kahe prabhuke dekhite

lakṣa lakṣa—many hundreds of thousands; *loka*—of people; *āila*—came there; *nānā-deśa*—different countries; *haite*—from; *sabe*—all of them; *kṛṣṇa-nāma kahe*—chant the Hare Kṛṣṇa *mahā-mantra; prabhuke*—the Lord; *dekhite*—seeing.

TRANSLATION

Many hundreds of thousands of people from various countries came to see the Lord, and after seeing Him they all chanted the Hare Kṛṣṇa mahā-mantra.

TEXT 90

কৃষ্ণনাম বিনা কেহ নাহি কহে আর ।
সবে কৃষ্ণভক্ত হৈল, — লোকে চমৎকার ॥ ৯০ ॥

kṛṣṇa-nāma vinā keha nāhi kahe āra
sabe kṛṣṇa-bhakta haila, — loke camatkāra

kṛṣṇa-nāma vinā — without chanting the Hare Kṛṣṇa *mahā-mantra; keha* — anyone; *nāhi* — does not; *kahe* — speak; *āra* — anything else; *sabe* — all of them; *kṛṣṇa-bhakta* — Lord Kṛṣṇa's devotees; *haila* — became; *loke* — the people; *camatkāra* — astonished.

TRANSLATION

Indeed, they did not chant anything but the Hare Kṛṣṇa mahā-mantra, and all of them became Lord Kṛṣṇa's devotees. Thus the general populace was astonished.

TEXT 91

শ্রীরঙ্গক্ষেত্রে বৈসে যত বৈষ্ণব-ব্রাহ্মণ ।
এক এক দিন সবে কৈল নিমন্ত্রণ ॥ ৯১ ॥

śrī-raṅga-kṣetre vaise yata vaiṣṇava-brāhmaṇa
eka eka dina sabe kaila nimantraṇa

śrī-raṅga-kṣetre — in Śrī Raṅga-kṣetra; *vaise* — residing; *yata* — all; *vaiṣṇava-brāhmaṇa* — Vaiṣṇava *brāhmaṇas; eka eka dina* — every day; *sabe* — all of them; *kaila nimantraṇa* — invited the Lord.

TRANSLATION

All the Vaiṣṇava brāhmaṇas residing in Śrī Raṅga-kṣetra invited the Lord to their homes. Indeed, He had an invitation every day.

TEXT 92

এক এক দিনে চাতুর্মাস্য পূর্ণ হৈল ।
কতক ব্রাহ্মণ ভিক্ষা দিতে না পাইল ॥ ৯২ ॥

eka eka dine cāturmāsya pūrṇa haila
kataka brāhmaṇa bhikṣā dite nā pāila

eka eka dine—day by day; *cāturmāsya*—the period of Cāturmāsya; *pūrṇa haila*—became filled; *kataka brāhmaṇa*—some of the *brāhmaṇas; bhikṣā dite*—to offer Him lunch; *nā*—did not; *pāila*—get the opportunity.

TRANSLATION

Each day the Lord was invited by a different brāhmaṇa, but some of the brāhmaṇas did not get the opportunity to offer Him lunch because the period of Cāturmāsya came to an end.

TEXT 93

সেই ক্ষেত্রে রহে এক বৈষ্ণব-ব্রাহ্মণ ।
দেবালয়ে আসি' করে গীতা আবর্তন ॥ ৯৩ ॥

sei kṣetre rahe eka vaiṣṇava-brāhmaṇa
devālaye āsi' kare gītā āvartana

sei kṣetre—in that holy place; *rahe*—there was; *eka*—one; *vaiṣṇava-brāhmaṇa*—a *brāhmaṇa* following the Vaiṣṇava cult; *deva-ālaye*—in the temple; *āsi'*—coming; *kare*—does; *gītā*—of the *Bhagavad-gītā; āvartana*—recitation.

TRANSLATION

In the holy place of Śrī Raṅga-kṣetra, a brāhmaṇa Vaiṣṇava used to visit the temple daily and recite the entire text of the Bhagavad-gītā.

TEXT 94

অষ্টাদশাধ্যায় পড়ে আনন্দ-আবেশে ।
অশুদ্ধ পড়েন, লোক করে উপহাসে ॥ ৯৪ ॥

aṣṭādaśādhyāya paḍe ānanda-āveśe
aśuddha paḍena, loka kare upahāse

aṣṭādaśa-adhyāya—eighteen chapters; *paḍe*—reads; *ānanda-āveśe*—in great ecstasy; *aśuddha paḍena*—could not pronounce the text correctly; *loka*—people in general; *kare*—do; *upahāse*—joking.

TRANSLATION

The brāhmaṇa regularly read the eighteen chapters of the Bhagavad-gītā in great transcendental ecstasy, but because he could not pronounce the words correctly, people used to joke about him.

TEXT 95

কেহ হাসে, কেহ নিন্দে, তাহা নাহি মানে।
আবিষ্ট হঞা গীতা পড়ে আনন্দিত-মনে ॥ ৯৫ ॥

keha hāse, keha ninde, tāhā nāhi māne
āviṣṭa hañā gītā paḍe ānandita-mane

keha hāse—someone laughs; *keha ninde*—someone criticizes; *tāhā*—that; *nāhi māne*—he does not care for; *āviṣṭa hañā*—being in great ecstasy; *gītā paḍe*—reads the *Bhagavad-gītā; ānandita*—in great happiness; *mane*—his mind.

TRANSLATION

Due to his incorrect pronunciation, people sometimes criticized him and laughed at him, but he did not care. He was full of ecstasy due to reading the Bhagavad-gītā and was personally very happy.

TEXT 96

পুলকাশ্রু, কম্প, স্বেদ, —যাবৎ পঠন।
দেখি' আনন্দিত হৈল মহাপ্রভুর মন ॥ ৯৬ ॥

pulakāśru, kampa, sveda,—yāvat paṭhana
dekhi' ānandita haila mahāprabhura mana

pulaka—standing of the hairs of the body; *aśru*—tears; *kampa*—trembling; *sveda*—perspiration; *yāvat*—during; *paṭhana*—the reading of the book; *dekhi'*—seeing this; *ānandita*—very happy;

haila—became; *mahāprabhura*—of Śrī Caitanya Mahāprabhu; *mana*—the mind.

TRANSLATION

While reading the book, the brāhmaṇa experienced transcendental bodily transformations. The hairs on his body stood on end, tears welled up in his eyes, and his body trembled and perspired as he read. Seeing this, Śrī Caitanya Mahāprabhu became very happy.

PURPORT

Although the *brāhmaṇa* could not pronounce the words very well due to illiteracy, he still experienced ecstatic symptoms while reading the *Bhagavad-gītā.* Śrī Caitanya Mahāprabhu was very pleased to observe these symptoms, and this indicates that the Supreme Personality of Godhead is pleased by devotion, not by erudite scholarship. Even though the words were imperfectly pronounced, Śrī Caitanya Mahāprabhu, Lord Kṛṣṇa Himself, did not think this very serious. Rather, the Lord was pleased by the *bhāva* (devotion). In *Śrīmad-Bhāgavatam* (1.5.11) this is confirmed:

tad-vāg-visargo janatāgha-viplavo
yasmin prati-ślokam abaddhavaty api
nāmāny anantasya yaśo-'ṅkitāni yat
śṛṇvanti gāyanti gṛṇanti sādhavaḥ

"On the other hand, that literature which is full of descriptions of the transcendental glories of the name, fame, forms and pastimes of the unlimited Supreme Lord is a different creation, full of transcendental words directed toward bringing about a revolution in the impious lives of this world's misdirected civilization. Such transcendental literatures, even though imperfectly composed, are heard, sung and accepted by purified men who are thoroughly honest."

The purport to this verse may be considered for further information on this subject.

TEXT 97

মহাপ্রভু পুছিল তাঁরে, শুন, মহাশয়।
কোন্ অর্থ জানি' তোমার এত সুখ হয়॥ ৯৭॥

mahāprabhu puchila tāṅre, śuna, mahāśaya
kon artha jāni' tomāra eta sukha haya

mahāprabhu—Śrī Caitanya Mahāprabhu; *puchila*—inquired; *tāṅre*—from him; *śuna*—please hear; *mahā-āśaya*—My dear sir; *kon*—what; *artha*—meaning; *jāni'*—knowing; *tomāra*—your; *eta*—so great; *sukha*—happiness; *haya*—is.

TRANSLATION

Śrī Caitanya Mahāprabhu asked the brāhmaṇa, "My dear sir, why are you in such ecstatic love? Which portion of the Bhagavad-gītā gives you such transcendental pleasure?"

TEXT 98

বিপ্র কহে, —মূর্খ আমি, শব্দার্থ না জানি ।
শুদ্ধাশুদ্ধ গীতা পড়ি, গুরু-আজ্ঞা মানি' ॥ ৯৮ ॥

vipra kahe,—mūrkha āmi, śabdārtha nā jāni
śuddhāśuddha gītā paḍi, guru-ājñā māni'

vipra kahe—the *brāhmaṇa* replied; *mūrkha āmi*—I am illiterate; *śabda-artha*—the meaning of the words; *nā jāni*—I do not know; *śuddha-aśuddha*—sometimes correct and sometimes not correct; *gītā*—the *Bhagavad-gītā; paḍi*—I read; *guru-ājñā*—the order of my spiritual master; *māni'*—accepting.

TRANSLATION

The brāhmaṇa replied, "I am illiterate and therefore do not know the meaning of the words. Sometimes I read the Bhagavad-gītā correctly and sometimes incorrectly, but in any case I am doing this in compliance with the orders of my spiritual master."

PURPORT

This is a good example of a person who had become so successful that he was able to capture the attention of Śrī Caitanya Mahāprabhu even while reading the *Bhagavad-gītā* incorrectly. His spiritual activities did not depend on material things such as correct pronunciation. Rather, his success depended on strictly following the instructions of his spiritual master.

yasya deve parā bhaktir yathā deve tathā gurau
tasyaite kathitā hy arthāḥ prakāśante mahātmanaḥ

"Only unto those great souls who have implicit faith in both the Lord and the spiritual master are all the imports of Vedic knowledge automatically revealed."(*Śvetāśvatara Up.* 6.23)

Actually the meaning of the words of the *Bhagavad-gītā* or *Śrīmad-Bhāgavatam* are revealed to one strictly following the orders of the spiritual master. They are also revealed to one who has equal faith in the Supreme Personality of Godhead. In other words, being faithful to both Kṛṣṇa and the spiritual master is the secret of success in spiritual life.

TEXT 99

অর্জুনের রথে কৃষ্ণ হয় রজ্জুধর ।
বসিয়াছে হাতে তোত্র শ্যামল সুন্দর ॥ ৯৯ ॥

arjunera rathe kṛṣṇa haya rajju-dhara
vasiyāche hāte totra śyāmala sundara

arjunera—of Arjuna; *rathe*—in the chariot; *kṛṣṇa*—Lord Kṛṣṇa; *haya*—is; *rajju-dhara*—holding the reins; *vasiyāche*—He was sitting there; *hāte*—in the hand; *totra*—a bridle; *śyāmala*—blackish; *sundara*—very beautiful.

TRANSLATION

The brāhmaṇa continued, "Actually I see only Lord Kṛṣṇa sitting on a chariot as Arjuna's charioteer. Taking the reins in His hands, He appears very beautiful and blackish.

TEXT 100

অর্জুনেরে কহিতেছেন হিত-উপদেশ ।
তাঁরে দেখি' হয় মোর আনন্দ-আবেশ ॥ ১০০ ॥

arjunere kahitechena hita-upadeśa
tāṅre dekhi' haya mora ānanda-āveśa

arjunere—unto Arjuna; *kahitechena*—He is speaking; *hita-upadeśa*—good instruction; *tāṅre*—Him; *dekhi'*—seeing; *haya*—there is; *mora*—my; *ānanda*—transcendental happiness; *āveśa*—ecstasy.

TRANSLATION

"While seeing Lord Kṛṣṇa sitting in a chariot and instructing Arjuna, I am filled with ecstatic happiness.

TEXT 101

যাবৎ পড়োঁ, তাবৎ পাঙ তাঁর দরশন।
এই লাগি' গীতা-পাঠ না ছাড়ে মোর মন ॥ ১০১ ॥

yāvat paḍoṅ, tāvat pāṅa tāṅra daraśana
ei lāgi' gītā-pāṭha nā chāḍe mora mana

yāvat—as long as; *paḍoṅ*—I read; *tāvat*—so long; *pāṅa*—I get; *tāṅra*—His; *daraśana*—audience; *ei lāgi'*—for this reason; *gītā-pāṭha*—reading the *Bhagavad-gītā; nā chāḍe*—does not quit; *mora mana*—my mind.

TRANSLATION

"As long as I read the Bhagavad-gītā, I simply see the Lord's beautiful features. It is for this reason that I am reading the Bhagavad-gītā, and my mind cannot be distracted from this."

TEXT 102

প্রভু কহে,—গীতা-পাঠে তোমারই অধিকার।
তুমি সে জানহ এই গীতার অর্থ-সার ॥ ১০২ ॥

prabhu kahe,—gītā-pāṭhe tomārā-i adhikāra
tumi se jānaha ei gītāra artha-sāra

prabhu kahe—the Lord replied; *gītā-pāṭhe*—in reading the *Bhagavad-gītā; tomārāi adhikāra*—you have the proper authority;

tumi—you; *se*—that; *jānaha*—know; *ei*—this; *gītāra*—of the *Bhagavad-gītā; artha-sāra*—the real purport.

TRANSLATION

Śrī Caitanya Mahāprabhu told the brāhmaṇa, "Indeed, you are an authority in the reading of the Bhagavad-gītā. Whatever you know constitutes the real purport of the Bhagavad-gītā."

PURPORT

According to the *śāstras: bhaktyā bhāgavataṁ grāhyaṁ na buddhyā na ca ṭīkayā.* One should understand the *Bhagavad-gītā* and *Śrīmad-Bhāgavatam* by hearing them from a real devotee. One cannot understand them simply by erudite scholarship or sharp intelligence. It is also said:

gītādhītā ca yenāpi bhakti-bhāvena cetasā
veda-śāstra-purāṇāni tenādhītāni sarvaśaḥ

To one who reads the *Bhagavad-gītā* with faith and devotion, the essence of Vedic knowledge is revealed. And according to the *Śvetāśvatara Upaniṣad* (6.23):

yasya deve parā bhaktir yathā deve tathā gurau
tasyaite kathitā hy arthāḥ prakāśante mahātmanaḥ

"Only unto those great souls who have implicit faith in both the Lord and the spiritual master are all the imports of Vedic knowledge automatically revealed."

All Vedic literatures are to be understood with faith and devotion, not by mundane scholarship. We have therefore presented *Bhagavad-gītā As It Is.* There are many so-called scholars and philosophers who read the *Bhagavad-gītā* in a scholarly way. They simply waste their time and mislead those who read their commentaries.

TEXT 103

এত বলি' সেই বিপ্রে কৈল আলিঙ্গন।
প্রভু-পদ ধরি' বিপ্র করেন রোদন॥ ১০৩॥

eta bali' sei vipre kaila āliṅgana
prabhu-pada dhari' vipra karena rodana

eta bali'—saying this; *sei vipre*—that *brāhmaṇa; kaila āliṅgana*—He embraced; *prabhu-pada*—the lotus feet of Lord Śrī Caitanya Mahāprabhu; *dhari'*—catching; *vipra*—the *brāhmaṇa; karena*—does; *rodana*—crying.

TRANSLATION

After saying this, Lord Caitanya Mahāprabhu embraced the brāhmaṇa, and the brāhmaṇa, catching the lotus feet of the Lord, began to cry.

TEXT 104

তোমা দেখি' তাহা হৈতে দ্বিগুণ সুখ হয়।
সেই কৃষ্ণ তুমি, — হেন মোর মনে লয় ॥ ১০৪ ॥

tomā dekhi' tāhā haite dvi-guṇa sukha haya
sei kṛṣṇa tumi,—hena mora mane laya

tomā dekhi'—by seeing You; *tāhā haite*—than the vision of Lord Kṛṣṇa; *dvi-guṇa*—twice as much; *sukha*—happiness; *haya*—there is; *sei kṛṣṇa*—that Lord Kṛṣṇa; *tumi*—You are; *hena*—such; *mora*—my; *mane*—in the mind; *laya*—takes.

TRANSLATION

The brāhmaṇa said, "Upon seeing You, my happiness is doubled. I take it that You are the same Lord Kṛṣṇa."

TEXT 105

কৃষ্ণস্ফূর্ত্যে তাঁর মন হঞাছে নির্মল।
অতএব প্রভুর তত্ত্ব জানিল সকল ॥ ১০৫ ॥

kṛṣṇa-sphūrtye tāṅra mana hañāche nirmala
ataeva prabhura tattva jānila sakala

kṛṣṇa-sphūrtye—by revelation of Lord Kṛṣṇa; *tāṅra*—his; *mana*—mind; *hañāche*—did become; *nirmala*—purified; *ataeva*—therefore;

prabhura—of Lord Śrī Caitanya Mahāprabhu; *tattva*—truth; *jānila*—could understand; *sakala*—all.

TRANSLATION

The mind of the brāhmaṇa was purified by the revelation of Lord Kṛṣṇa, and therefore he could understand the truth of Śrī Caitanya Mahāprabhu in all details.

TEXT 106

তবে মহাপ্রভু তাঁরে করাইল শিক্ষণ।
এই বাৎ কাহাঁ না করিহ প্রকাশন ॥ ১০৬ ॥

tabe mahāprabhu tāṅre karāila śikṣaṇa
ei bāt kāhāṅ nā kariha prakāśana

tabe—then; *mahāprabhu*—Śrī Caitanya Mahāprabhu; *tāṅre*—unto the *brāhmaṇa; karāila*—made; *śikṣaṇa*—instruction; *ei bāt*—this version; *kāhāṅ*—anywhere; *nā*—do not; *kariha*—do; *prakāśana*—revelation.

TRANSLATION

Śrī Caitanya Mahāprabhu then taught the brāhmaṇa very thoroughly and requested him not to disclose the fact that He was Lord Kṛṣṇa Himself.

TEXT 107

সেই বিপ্র মহাপ্রভুর বড় ভক্ত হৈল।
চারি মাস প্রভু-সঙ্গ কভু না ছাড়িল ॥ ১০৭ ॥

sei vipra mahāprabhura baḍa bhakta haila
cāri māsa prabhu-saṅga kabhu nā chāḍila

sei vipra—that *brāhmaṇa; mahāprabhura*—of Śrī Caitanya Mahāprabhu; *baḍa*—big; *bhakta*—devotee; *haila*—became; *cāri māsa*—for four months; *prabhu-saṅga*—association of the Lord; *kabhu*—at any time; *nā*—did not; *chāḍila*—give up.

TRANSLATION

That brāhmaṇa became a great devotee of Śrī Caitanya Mahāprabhu, and for four continuous months he did not give up the Lord's company.

TEXT 108

এইমত ভট্টগৃহে রহে গৌরচন্দ্র ।
নিরন্তর ভট্ট-সঙ্গে কৃষ্ণকথানন্দ ॥ ১০৮ ॥

ei-mata bhaṭṭa-gṛhe rahe gauracandra
nirantara bhaṭṭa-saṅge kṛṣṇa-kathānanda

ei-mata—in this way; *bhaṭṭa-gṛhe*—in the house of Veṅkaṭa Bhaṭṭa; *rahe*—remained; *gauracandra*—Śrī Caitanya Mahāprabhu; *nirantara*—constantly; *bhaṭṭa-saṅge*—with Veṅkaṭa Bhaṭṭa; *kṛṣṇa-kathā-ānanda*—the transcendental bliss of talking about Kṛṣṇa.

TRANSLATION

Śrī Caitanya Mahāprabhu remained at the house of Veṅkaṭa Bhaṭṭa and constantly talked with him about Lord Kṛṣṇa. In this way He was very happy.

TEXT 109

'শ্রী-বৈষ্ণব' ভট্ট সেবে লক্ষ্মী-নারায়ণ ।
তাঁর ভক্তি দেখি' প্রভুর তুষ্ট হৈল মন ॥ ১০৯ ॥

śrī-vaiṣṇava' bhaṭṭa seve lakṣmī-nārāyaṇa
tāṅra bhakti dekhi' prabhura tuṣṭa haila mana

śrī-vaiṣṇava—a devotee of the Rāmānuja-sampradāya; *bhaṭṭa*—Veṅkaṭa Bhaṭṭa; *seve*—used to worship; *lakṣmī-nārāyaṇa*—the Deities of Lord Nārāyaṇa and the goddess of fortune, Lakṣmī; *tāṅra*—his; *bhakti*—devotion; *dekhi'*—seeing; *prabhura*—of Lord Śrī Caitanya Mahāprabhu; *tuṣṭa*—happy; *haila*—became; *mana*—the mind.

TRANSLATION

Being a Vaiṣṇava in the Rāmānuja-sampradāya, Veṅkaṭa Bhaṭṭa worshiped the Deities of Lakṣmī and Nārāyaṇa. Seeing his pure devotion, Śrī Caitanya Mahāprabhu was very satisfied.

TEXT 110

নিরন্তর তাঁর সঙ্গে হৈল সখ্যভাব।
হাস্য-পরিহাসে দুঁহে সখ্যের স্বভাব ॥ ১১০ ॥

nirantara tāṅra saṅge haila sakhya-bhāva
hāsya-parihāse duṅhe sakhyera svabhāva

nirantara—constantly; *tāṅra saṅge*—being associated with him; *haila*—there was; *sakhya-bhāva*—a friendly relationship; *hāsya*—laughing; *parihāse*—joking; *duṅhe*—both of them; *sakhyera*—of fraternity; *svabhāva*—nature.

TRANSLATION

Constantly associating with each other, Śrī Caitanya Mahāprabhu and Veṅkaṭa Bhaṭṭa gradually developed a friendly relationship. Indeed, sometimes they laughed and joked together.

TEXT 111

প্রভু কহে,—ভট্ট, তোমার লক্ষ্মী-ঠাকুরাণী।
কান্ত-বক্ষঃস্থিতা, পতিব্রতা-শিরোমণি ॥ ১১১ ॥

prabhu kahe,—bhaṭṭa, tomāra lakṣmī-ṭhākurāṇī
kānta-vakṣaḥ-sthitā, pativratā-śiromaṇi

prabhu kahe—Lord Śrī Caitanya Mahāprabhu said; *bhaṭṭa*—My dear Bhaṭṭācārya; *tomāra*—your; *lakṣmī-ṭhākurāṇī*—goddess of fortune; *kānta*—of her husband, Nārāyaṇa; *vakṣaḥ-sthitā*—situated on the chest; *pati-vratā*—chaste woman; *śiromaṇi*—the topmost.

TRANSLATION

Śrī Caitanya Mahāprabhu told the Bhaṭṭācārya, "Your worshipable goddess of fortune, Lakṣmī, always remains on the chest of Nārāyaṇa, and she is certainly the most chaste woman in the creation.

TEXT 112

আমার ঠাকুর কৃষ্ণ — গোপ, গো-চারক।
সাধ্বী হঞা কেনে চাহে তাঁহার সঙ্গম ॥ ১১২ ॥

āmāra ṭhākura kṛṣṇa — gopa, go-cāraka
sādhvī hañā kene cāhe tāṅhāra saṅgama

āmāra ṭhākura — My worshipable Deity; *kṛṣṇa* — Lord Kṛṣṇa; *gopa* — cowherd; *go-cāraka* — a tender of cows; *sādhvī hañā* — being so chaste; *kene* — why; *cāhe* — wants; *tāṅhāra* — His; *saṅgama* — association.

TRANSLATION

"However, My Lord is Lord Śrī Kṛṣṇa, a cowherd boy who is engaged in tending cows. Why is it that Lakṣmī, being such a chaste wife, wants to associate with My Lord?

TEXT 113

এই লাগি' সুখভোগ ছাড়ি' চিরকাল।
ব্রত-নিয়ম করি' তপ করিল অপার ॥ ১১৩ ॥

ei lāgi' sukha-bhoga chāḍi' cira-kāla
vrata-niyama kari' tapa karila apāra

ei lāgi' — for this reason; *sukha-bhoga* — the enjoyment of Vaikuṇṭha; *chāḍi'* — giving up; *cira-kāla* — for a long time; *vrata-niyama* — vows and regulative principles; *kari'* — accepting; *tapa* — austerity; *karila apāra* — performed unlimitedly.

TRANSLATION

"Just to associate with Kṛṣṇa, Lakṣmī abandoned all transcendental happiness in Vaikuṇṭha and for a long time accepted vows and regulative principles and performed unlimited austerities."

TEXT 114

কস্যানুভাবোঽস্য ন দেব বিদ্মহে, তবাঙ্ঘ্রি রেণুস্পরশাধিকারঃ।
যদ্বাঞ্ছয়া শ্রীর্ললনাচরত্তপো, বিহায় কামান্ সুচিরং ধৃতব্রতা ॥ ১১৪ ॥

kasyānubhāvo 'sya na deva vidmahe
tavāṅghri-reṇu-sparaśādhikāraḥ
yad-vāñchayā śrīr lalanācarat tapo
vihāya kāmān su-ciraṁ dhṛta-vratā

kasya—of what; *anubhāvaḥ*—a result; *asya*—of the serpent (Kāliya); *na*—not; *deva*—O Lord; *vidmahe*—we know; *tava aṅghri*—of Your lotus feet; *reṇu*—of the dust; *sparaśa*—for touching; *adhikāraḥ*—qualification; *yat*—which; *vāñchayā*—by desiring; *śrīḥ*—the goddess of fortune; *lalanā*—the topmost woman; *acarat*—performed; *tapaḥ*—austerity; *vihāya*—giving up; *kāmān*—all desires; *su-ciram*—for a long time; *dhṛta*—a law upheld; *vratā*—as a vow.

TRANSLATION

Caitanya Mahāprabhu then said, "'O Lord, we do not know how the serpent Kāliya attained such an opportunity to be touched by the dust of Your lotus feet. Even the goddess of fortune, for this end, performed austerities for centuries, giving up all other desires and observing austere vows. Indeed, we do not know how the serpent Kāliya got such an opportunity.'"

PURPORT

This verse from *Śrīmad-Bhāgavatam* (10.16.36) was spoken by the wives of the Kāliya serpent.

TEXT 115

ভট্ট কহে, কৃষ্ণ-নারায়ণ — একই স্বরূপ।
কৃষ্ণেতে অধিক লীলা-বৈদগ্ধ্যাদিরূপ ॥ ১১৫ ॥

bhaṭṭa kahe, kṛṣṇa-nārāyaṇa—eka-i svarūpa
kṛṣṇete adhika līlā-vaidagdhyādi-rūpa

bhaṭṭa kahe—Veṅkaṭa Bhaṭṭa said; *kṛṣṇa-nārāyaṇa*—Kṛṣṇa and Nārāyaṇa; *eka-i svarūpa*—one and the same; *kṛṣṇete*—in Lord Kṛṣṇa; *adhika*—more; *līlā*—pastimes; *vaidagdhya-ādi-rūpa*—sportive nature.

TRANSLATION

Veṅkaṭa Bhaṭṭa then said, "Lord Kṛṣṇa and Lord Nārāyaṇa are one and the same, but the pastimes of Kṛṣṇa are more relishable due to their sportive nature.

TEXT 116

তার স্পর্শে নাহি যায় পতিব্রতা-ধর্ম।
কৌতুকে লক্ষ্মী চাহেন কৃষ্ণের সঙ্গম ॥ ১১৬ ॥

tāra sparśe nāhi yāya pativratā-dharma
kautuke lakṣmī cāhena kṛṣṇera saṅgama

tāra sparśe—by the touching of Kṛṣṇa by Lakṣmī; *nāhi*—does not; *yāya*—disappear; *pati-vratā-dharma*—the vow of chastity; *kautuke*—in great fun; *lakṣmī*—the goddess of fortune; *cāhena*—wants; *kṛṣṇera*—of Lord Kṛṣṇa; *saṅgama*—association.

TRANSLATION

"Since Kṛṣṇa and Nārāyaṇa are the same personality, Lakṣmī's association with Kṛṣṇa does not break her vow of chastity. Rather, it was in great fun that the goddess of fortune wanted to associate with Lord Kṛṣṇa."

PURPORT

This is the answer to Lord Śrī Caitanya Mahāprabhu's question, and from this we can understand that Veṅkaṭa Bhaṭṭa knew the truth. He told Śrī Caitanya Mahāprabhu that Nārāyaṇa is a form of Kṛṣṇa associated with transcendental opulence. Although Kṛṣṇa is two-armed and Nārāyaṇa four-armed, there is no difference in the person. They are one and the same. Nārāyaṇa is as beautiful as Kṛṣṇa, but Kṛṣṇa's pastimes are more sportive. It is not that the sportive pastimes of Kṛṣṇa make Him different from Nārāyaṇa. Lakṣmī's desiring to associate with

Kṛṣṇa was perfectly natural. In other words, it is understandable that a chaste woman wants to associate with her husband in all his different dresses. Therefore one should not criticize Lakṣmī for wanting to associate with Kṛṣṇa.

TEXT 117

সিদ্ধান্ততস্ত্বভেদেঽপি শ্রীশ-কৃষ্ণস্বরূপয়োঃ ।
রসেনোৎকৃষ্যতে কৃষ্ণরূপমেষা রসস্থিতিঃ ॥ ১১৭ ॥

siddhāntatas tv abhede 'pi
śrīśa-kṛṣṇa-svarūpayoḥ
rasenotkṛṣyate kṛṣṇa-
rūpam eṣā rasa-sthitiḥ

siddhāntataḥ—in reality; *tu*—but; *abhede*—no difference; *api*—although; *śrī-īśa*—of the husband of Lakṣmī, Nārāyaṇa; *kṛṣṇa*—of Lord Kṛṣṇa; *svarūpayoḥ*—between the forms; *rasena*—by transcendental mellows; *utkṛṣyate*—is superior; *kṛṣṇa-rūpam*—the form of Lord Kṛṣṇa; *eṣā*—this; *rasa-sthitiḥ*—reservoir of pleasure.

TRANSLATION

Veṅkaṭa Bhaṭṭa continued, "'According to transcendental realization, there is no difference between the forms of Nārāyaṇa and Kṛṣṇa. Yet in Kṛṣṇa there is a special transcendental attraction due to the conjugal mellow, and consequently He surpasses Nārāyaṇa. This is the conclusion of transcendental mellows.'

PURPORT

This verse quoted by Veṅkaṭa Bhaṭṭa is also found in the *Bhakti-rasāmṛta-sindhu* (1.2.59).

TEXT 118

কৃষ্ণসঙ্গে পতিব্রতা-ধর্ম নহে নাশ ।
অধিক লাভ পাইয়ে, আর রাসবিলাস ॥ ১১৮ ॥

kṛṣṇa-saṅge pativratā-dharma nahe nāśa
adhika lābha pāiye, āra rāsa-vilāsa

kṛṣṇa-saṅge—in the association of Lord Kṛṣṇa; *pati-vratā*—of chastity; *dharma*—vow; *nahe*—is not; *nāśa*—lost; *adhika*—more; *lābha*—profit; *pāiye*—I get; *āra*—also; *rāsa-vilāsa*—the enjoyment in the *rāsa* dance.

TRANSLATION

"The goddess of fortune considered that her vow of chastity would not be damaged by her relationship with Kṛṣṇa. Rather, by associating with Kṛṣṇa she could enjoy the benefit of the rāsa dance."

TEXT 119

বিনোদিনী লক্ষ্মীর হয় কৃষ্ণে অভিলাষ।
ইহাতে কি দোষ, কেনে কর পরিহাস॥ ১১৯॥

vinodinī lakṣmīra haya kṛṣṇe abhilāṣa
ihāte ki doṣa, kene kara parihāsa

vinodinī—the enjoyer; *lakṣmīra*—of the goddess of fortune; *haya*—there is; *kṛṣṇe*—for Lord Kṛṣṇa; *abhilāṣa*—desire; *ihāte*—in this; *ki*—what; *doṣa*—fault; *kene*—why; *kara*—You do; *parihāsa*—joking.

TRANSLATION

Veṅkaṭa Bhaṭṭa further explained, "Mother Lakṣmī, the goddess of fortune, is also an enjoyer of transcendental bliss; therefore if she wanted to enjoy herself with Kṛṣṇa, what fault is there? Why are You joking so about this?"

TEXT 120

প্রভু কহে,—দোষ নাহি, ইহা আমি জানি।
রাস না পাইল লক্ষ্মী, শাস্ত্রে ইহা শুনি॥ ১২০॥

prabhu kahe,—doṣa nāhi, ihā āmi jāni
rāsa nā pāila lakṣmī, śāstre ihā śuni

prabhu kahe—the Lord replied; *doṣa nāhi*—there is no fault; *ihā āmi jāni*—this I know; *rāsa nā pāila lakṣmī*—Lakṣmī, the goddess of fortune, could not join the *rāsa* dance; *śāstre ihā śuni*—we get this information from revealed scriptures.

TRANSLATION

Lord Caitanya Mahāprabhu replied, "I know that there is no fault on the part of the goddess of fortune, but still she could not enter into the rāsa dance. We hear this from the revealed scriptures.

TEXT 121

নায়ং শ্রিয়োঽঙ্গ উ নিতান্তরতেঃ প্রসাদঃ ।
স্বর্যোষিতাং নলিনগন্ধরুচাং কুতোঽন্যাঃ ।
রাসোৎসবেঽস্য ভুজদণ্ডগৃহীতকণ্ঠ-
লব্ধাশিষাং য উদগাদ্‌ব্রজসুন্দরীণাম্‌ ॥ ১২১ ॥

nāyaṁ śriyo 'ṅga u nitānta-rateḥ prasādaḥ
svar-yoṣitāṁ nalina-gandha-rucāṁ kuto 'nyāḥ
rāsotsave 'sya bhuja-daṇḍa-gṛhīta-kaṇṭha-
labdhāśiṣāṁ ya udagād vraja-sundarīṇām

na—not; *ayam*—this; *śriyaḥ*—of the goddess of fortune; *aṅge*—on the chest; *u*—alas; *nitānta-rateḥ*—one who is very intimately related; *prasādaḥ*—the favor; *svaḥ*—of the heavenly planets; *yoṣitām*—of women; *nalina*—of the lotus flower; *gandha*—having the aroma; *rucām*—and bodily luster; *kutaḥ*—much less; *anyāḥ*—others; *rāsa-utsave*—in the festival of the *rāsa* dance; *asya*—of Lord Śrī Kṛṣṇa; *bhuja-daṇḍa*—by the arms; *gṛhīta*—embraced; *kaṇṭha*—their necks; *labdha-āśiṣām*—who achieved such a blessing; *yaḥ*—which; *udagāt*—became manifest; *vraja-sundarīṇām*—of the beautiful *gopīs,* the transcendental girls of Vrajabhūmi.

TRANSLATION

"'When Lord Śrī Kṛṣṇa was dancing with the gopīs in the rāsa-līlā, the gopīs were embraced around the neck by the Lord's arms. This transcendental favor was never bestowed upon the goddess of fortune

or the other consorts in the spiritual world. Nor was such a thing ever imagined by the most beautiful girls in the heavenly planets, girls whose bodily luster and aroma exactly resemble the beauty and fragrance of lotus flowers. And what to speak of worldly women, who may be very, very beautiful according to material estimation?'

PURPORT

This is a verse from *Śrīmad-Bhāgavatam* (10.47.60).

TEXT 122

লক্ষ্মী কেনে না পাইল, ইহার কি কারণ।
তপ করি' কৈছে কৃষ্ণ পাইল শ্রুতিগণ ॥ ১২২ ॥

lakṣmī kene nā pāila, ihāra ki kāraṇa
tapa kari' kaiche kṛṣṇa pāila śruti-gaṇa

lakṣmī—the goddess of fortune; *kene*—why; *nā*—did not; *pāila*—get; *ihāra*—of this; *ki*—what; *kāraṇa*—cause; *tapa kari'*—undergoing severe austerities; *aiche*—how; *kṛṣṇa*—Lord Kṛṣṇa; *pāila*—attained; *śruti-gaṇa*—Vedic authorities.

TRANSLATION

"But can you tell Me why the goddess of fortune, Lakṣmī, could not enter the rāsa dance? The authorities of Vedic knowledge could enter the dance and associate with Kṛṣṇa.

TEXT 123

নিভৃতমরুন্মনোঽক্ষদৃঢ়যোগযুজো হৃদি য-
ন্মুনয় উপাসতে তদরয়োঽপি যযুঃ স্মরণাৎ।
স্ত্রিয় উরগেন্দ্র-ভোগভুজদণ্ডবিষক্ত-ধিয়ো
বয়মপি তে সমাঃ সমদৃশোঽঙ্ঘ্রিসরোজসুধাঃ ॥ ১২৩ ॥

nibhṛta-marun-mano-'kṣa-dṛḍha-yoga-yujo hṛdi yan-
munaya upāsate tad arayo 'pi yayuḥ smaraṇāt
striya uragendra-bhoga-bhuja-daṇḍa-viṣakta-dhiyo
vayam api te samāḥ samadṛśo 'ṅghri-saroja-sudhāḥ

nibhṛta—controlled; *marut*—the life air; *manaḥ*—the mind; *akṣa*—the senses; *dṛḍha*—strong; *yoga*—in the mystic *yoga* process; *yujaḥ*—who are engaged; *hṛdi*—within the heart; *yat*—who; *munayaḥ*—the great sages; *upāsate*—worship; *tat*—that; *arayaḥ*—the enemies; *api*—also; *yayuḥ*—obtain; *smaraṇāt*—from remembering; *striyaḥ*—the *gopīs; uraga-indra*—of serpents; *bhoga*—like the bodies; *bhuja*—the arms; *daṇḍa*—like rods; *viṣakta*—fastened to; *dhiyaḥ*—whose minds; *vayam api*—we also; *te*—Your; *samāḥ*—equal to them; *sama-dṛśaḥ*—having the same ecstatic emotions; *aṅghri-saroja*—of the lotus feet; *sudhāḥ*—the nectar.

TRANSLATION

"'Great sages conquer the mind and senses by practicing the mystic yoga system and controlling the breath. Thus engaging in mystic yoga, they see the Supersoul within their hearts and ultimately enter into impersonal Brahman. But even the enemies of the Supreme Personality of Godhead attain that position simply by thinking of the Supreme Lord. However, the damsels of Vraja, the gopīs, being attracted by the beauty of Kṛṣṇa, simply wanted to embrace Him and His arms, which are like serpents. Thus the gopīs ultimately tasted the nectar of the lotus feet of the Lord. Similarly, we Upaniṣads can also taste the nectar of His lotus feet by following in the footsteps of the gopīs.'"

PURPORT

This verse is from *Śrīmad-Bhāgavatam* (10.87.23).

TEXT 124

শ্রুতি পায়, লক্ষ্মী না পায়, ইথে কি কারণ।
ভট্ট কহে,—ইহা প্রবেশিতে নারে মোর মন ॥ ১২৪ ॥

śruti pāya, lakṣmī nā pāya, ithe ki kāraṇa
bhaṭṭa kahe,—ihā praveśite nāre mora mana

śruti pāya—the Vedic authorities got admission; *lakṣmī nā pāya*—and the goddess of fortune could not get admission; *ithe ki kāraṇa*—what must be the reason for this; *bhaṭṭa kahe*—Veṅkaṭa Bhaṭṭa replied; *ihā*—this; *praveśite*—to enter; *nāre*—is not able; *mora*—my; *mana*—mind.

TRANSLATION

Having been asked by Caitanya Mahāprabhu why the goddess of fortune could not enter into the rāsa dance whereas the authorities on Vedic knowledge could, Veṅkaṭa Bhaṭṭa replied, "I cannot enter into the mysteries of this behavior."

TEXT 125

আমি জীব, —ক্ষুদ্রবুদ্ধি, সহজে অস্থির।
ঈশ্বরের লীলা —কোটিসমুদ্র-গম্ভীর ॥ ১২৫ ॥

āmi jīva,—kṣudra-buddhi, sahaje asthira
īśvarera līlā—koṭi-samudra-gambhīra

āmi jīva—I am an ordinary living being; *kṣudra-buddhi*—possessing limited intelligence; *sahaje asthira*—very easily agitated; *īśvarera līlā*—the pastimes of the Lord; *koṭi-samudra*—as millions of oceans; *gambhīra*—as deep.

TRANSLATION

Veṅkaṭa Bhaṭṭa then said, "I am an ordinary human being. Since my intelligence is very limited and I am easily agitated, my mind cannot enter within the deep ocean of the pastimes of the Lord.

TEXT 126

তুমি সাক্ষাৎ সেই কৃষ্ণ, জান নিজকর্ম।
যারে জানাহ, সেই জানে তোমার লীলামর্ম ॥ ১২৬ ॥

tumi sākṣāt sei kṛṣṇa, jāna nija-karma
yāre jānāha, sei jāne tomāra līlā-marma

tumi—You; *sākṣāt*—directly; *sei*—that; *kṛṣṇa*—the Supreme Personality of Godhead; *jāna*—You know; *nija-karma*—Your activities; *yāre jānāha*—and unto whom You make it known; *sei*—that person; *jāne*—knows; *tomāra*—Your; *līlā-marma*—the purport of the pastimes.

TRANSLATION

"You are the Supreme Personality of Godhead, Kṛṣṇa Himself. You know the purpose of Your activities, and the person whom You enlighten can also understand Your pastimes."

PURPORT

The Supreme Personality of Godhead Kṛṣṇa and His pastimes cannot be understood by blunt material senses. One has to purify the senses by rendering transcendental loving service unto the Lord. When the Lord is pleased and reveals Himself, one can understand the transcendental form, name, qualities and pastimes of the Lord. This is confirmed in the *Kaṭha Upaniṣad* (2.23) and *Muṇḍaka Upaniṣad* (3.2.3): *yam evaiṣa vṛṇute tena labhyas tasyaiṣa ātmā vivṛṇute tanūṁ svām.* "Anyone who is favored by the Supreme Personality of Godhead can understand His transcendental name, qualities, form and pastimes."

TEXT 127

প্রভু কহে, —কৃষ্ণের এক স্বভাব বিলক্ষণ।
স্বমাধুর্যে সর্ব চিত্ত করে আকর্ষণ ॥ ১২৭ ॥

prabhu kahe,—kṛṣṇera eka svabhāva vilakṣaṇa
sva-mādhurye sarva citta kare ākarṣaṇa

prabhu kahe—the Lord replied; *kṛṣṇera*—of Lord Kṛṣṇa; *eka*—one; *svabhāva*—characteristic; *vilakṣaṇa*—special; *sva-mādhurye*—His conjugal love; *sarva*—all; *citta*—hearts; *kare*—does; *ākarṣaṇa*—attraction.

TRANSLATION

The Lord replied, "Lord Kṛṣṇa has a special characteristic: He attracts everyone's heart by the mellow of His personal conjugal love.

TEXT 128

ব্রজলোকের ভাবে পাইয়ে তাঁহার চরণ।
তাঁরে ঈশ্বর করি' নাহি জানে ব্রজজন ॥ ১২৮ ॥

vraja-lokera bhāve pāiye tāṅhāra caraṇa
tāṅre īśvara kari' nāhi jāne vraja-jana

vraja-lokera—of the inhabitants of Goloka Vṛndāvana; *bhāve*—in the ecstasy; *pāiye*—one gets; *tāṅhāra*—Lord Kṛṣṇa's; *caraṇa*—lotus feet; *tāṅre*—unto Him; *īśvara*—the Supreme Person; *kari'*—accepting; *nāhi*—do not; *jāne*—know; *vraja-jana*—the inhabitants of Vrajabhūmi.

TRANSLATION

"By following in the footsteps of the inhabitants of the planet known as Vrajaloka or Goloka Vṛndāvana, one can attain the shelter of the lotus feet of Śrī Kṛṣṇa. However, in that planet the inhabitants do not know that Lord Kṛṣṇa is the Supreme Personality of Godhead.

TEXT 129

কেহ তাঁরে পুত্র-জ্ঞানে উদুখলে বান্ধে।
কেহ সখা-জ্ঞানে জিনি' চড়ে তাঁর কান্ধে ॥ ১২৯ ॥

keha tāṅre putra-jñāne udukhale bāndhe
keha sakhā-jñāne jini' caḍe tāṅra kāndhe

keha—someone; *tāṅre*—Him; *putra-jñāne*—by accepting as a son; *udukhale*—to a big mortar; *bāndhe*—ties; *keha*—someone; *sakhā-jñāne*—by accepting as a friend; *jini'*—conquering; *caḍe*—gets up; *tāṅra*—His; *kāndhe*—on the shoulder.

TRANSLATION

"There someone may accept Him as a son and sometimes bind Him to a grinding mortar. Someone else may accept Him as an intimate friend and, attaining victory over Him, playfully mount His shoulders.

TEXT 130

'ব্রজেন্দ্রনন্দন' বলি' তাঁরে জানে ব্রজজন ।
ঐশ্বর্যজ্ঞানে নাহি কোন সম্বন্ধ-মানন ॥ ১৩০ ॥

'vrajendra-nandana' bali' tāṅre jāne vraja-jana
aiśvarya-jñāne nāhi kona sambandha-mānana

vrajendra-nandana—the son of Nanda Mahārāja, the King of Vrajabhūmi; *bali'*—as; *tāṅre*—Him; *jāne*—know; *vraja-jana*—the inhabitants of Vrajabhūmi; *aiśvarya-jñāne*—in opulence; *nāhi*—there is not; *kona*—any; *sambandha*—relationship; *mānana*—regarding.

TRANSLATION

"The inhabitants of Vrajabhūmi know Kṛṣṇa as the son of Mahārāja Nanda, the King of Vrajabhūmi, and they consider that they can have no relationship with the Lord in the rasa of opulence.

TEXT 131

ব্রজলোকের ভাবে যেই করয়ে ভজন ।
সেই জন পায় ব্রজে ব্রজেন্দ্রনন্দন ॥ ১৩১ ॥

vraja-lokera bhāve yei karaye bhajana
sei jana pāya vraje vrajendra-nandana

vraja-lokera—of the inhabitants of Vrajabhūmi; *bhāve*—in the ecstasy; *yei*—anyone who; *karaye*—does; *bhajana*—worship; *sei jana*—that person; *pāya*—attains; *vraje*—in Vraja; *vrajendra-nandana*—Lord Kṛṣṇa, the son of Mahārāja Nanda.

TRANSLATION

"One who worships the Lord by following in the footsteps of the inhabitants of Vrajabhūmi attains Him in the transcendental planet of Vraja, where He is known as the son of Mahārāja Nanda."

PURPORT

The inhabitants of Vrajabhūmi, or Goloka Vṛndāvana, know Kṛṣṇa as the son of Mahārāja Nanda. They do not accept Him as the Supreme

Personality of Godhead, as people in general do. The Lord is the supreme maintainer of everyone and the chief personality among all personalities. In Vrajabhūmi Kṛṣṇa is certainly the central point of love, but no one knows Him there as the Supreme Personality of Godhead. Rather, a person may know Him as a friend, son, lover or master. In any case, the center is Kṛṣṇa. The inhabitants of Vrajabhūmi are related to the Lord in servitude, friendship, parental love and conjugal love. A person engaged in devotional service may accept any one of these transcendental relationships, which are known as mellows. When such a person reaches the perfectional stage, he returns home, back to Kṛṣṇa, in his pure spiritual identity.

TEXT 132

নায়ং সুখাপো ভগবান্ দেহিনাং গোপিকাসুতঃ ।
জ্ঞানিনাং চাত্মভূতানাং যথা ভক্তিমতামিহ ॥ ১৩২ ॥

nāyaṁ sukhāpo bhagavān
dehināṁ gopikā-sutaḥ
jñānināṁ cātma-bhūtānāṁ
yathā bhakti-matām iha

na—not; *ayam*—this Lord Śrī Kṛṣṇa; *sukha-āpaḥ*—easily available; *bhagavān*—the Supreme Personality of Godhead; *dehinām*—for materialistic persons who have accepted the body as the self; *gopikā-sutaḥ*—the son of mother Yaśodā; *jñāninām*—for persons addicted to mental speculation; *ca*—and; *ātma-bhūtānām*—for persons performing severe austerities and penances; *yathā*—as; *bhakti-matām*—for persons engaged in spontaneous devotional service; *iha*—in this world.

TRANSLATION

Caitanya Mahāprabhu then quoted, "'The Supreme Personality of Godhead, Kṛṣṇa, the son of mother Yaśodā, is accessible to those devotees engaged in spontaneous loving service, but He is not as easily accessible to mental speculators, to those striving for self-realization by severe austerities and penances, or to those who consider the body the same as the self.'

PURPORT

This verse, also given in *Madhya-līlā* 8.227, is quoted from *Śrīmad-Bhāgavatam* (10.9.21).

TEXT 133

শ্রুতিগণ গোপীগণের অনুগত হঞা ।
ব্রজেশ্বরীসুত ভজে গোপীভাব লঞা ॥ ১৩৩ ॥

śruti-gaṇa gopī-gaṇera anugata hañā
vrajeśvarī-suta bhaje gopī-bhāva lañā

śruti-gaṇa—the authorities of Vedic hymns; *gopī-gaṇera*—of the *gopīs; anugata hañā*—following in the footsteps; *vrajeśvarī-suta*—the son of mother Yaśodā; *bhaje*—worship; *gopī-bhāva*—the ecstasy of the *gopīs; lañā*—accepting.

TRANSLATION

"The authorities in the Vedic literature who are known as the śruti-gaṇas worshiped Lord Kṛṣṇa in the ecstasy of the gopīs and followed in their footsteps.

PURPORT

The authorities in the Vedic literature who are known as the *śruti-gaṇas* desired to enter into Lord Śrī Kṛṣṇa's *rāsa* dance; therefore they began to worship the Lord in the ecstasy of the *gopīs.* In the beginning, however, they were unsuccessful. When they could not enter the dance simply by thinking of Kṛṣṇa in the ecstasy of the *gopīs,* they actually accepted bodies like those of the *gopīs.* They even took birth in Vrajabhūmi just like the *gopīs* and consequently became engrossed in the ecstasy of the *gopīs'* love. In this way they were allowed to enter into the *rāsa-līlā* dance of the Lord.

TEXT 134

বাহ্যান্তরে গোপীদেহ ব্রজে যবে পাইল ।
সেই দেহে কৃষ্ণসঙ্গে রাসক্রীড়া কৈল ॥ ১৩৪ ॥

bāhyāntare gopī-deha vraje yabe pāila
sei dehe kṛṣṇa-saṅge rāsa-krīḍā kaila

bāhya-antare—externally and internally; *gopī-deha*—the body of a *gopī; vraje*—in Vrajabhūmi; *yabe*—when; *pāila*—they got; *sei dehe*—in that body; *kṛṣṇa-saṅge*—with Kṛṣṇa; *rāsa-krīḍā*—pastimes of the *rāsa* dance; *kaila*—performed.

TRANSLATION

"The personified authorities on the Vedic hymns acquired bodies like those of the gopīs and took birth in Vrajabhūmi. In those bodies they were allowed to enter into the Lord's rāsa-līlā dance.

TEXT 135

গোপজাতি কৃষ্ণ, গোপী — প্রেয়সী তাঁহার ।
দেবী বা অন্য স্ত্রী কৃষ্ণ না করে অঙ্গীকার ॥ ১৩৫ ॥

gopa-jāti kṛṣṇa, gopī—preyasī tāṅhāra
devī vā anya strī kṛṣṇa nā kare aṅgīkāra

gopa-jāti—belonging to the cowherd community; *kṛṣṇa*—Lord Kṛṣṇa; *gopī*—the damsels of Vrajabhūmi, the *gopīs; preyasī*—dearmost; *tāṅhāra*—His; *devī*—the wives of the demigods; *vā*—or; *anya*—other; *strī*—women; *kṛṣṇa*—Lord Kṛṣṇa; *nā*—does not; *kare*—do; *aṅgīkāra*—acceptance.

TRANSLATION

"Lord Kṛṣṇa belongs to the cowherd community, and the gopīs are the dearmost lovers of Kṛṣṇa. Although the wives of the denizens of the heavenly planets are most opulent within the material world, neither they nor any other women in the material universe can acquire Kṛṣṇa's association.

TEXT 136

লক্ষ্মী চাহে সেই দেহে কৃষ্ণের সঙ্গম ।
গোপিকা-অনুগা হঞা না কৈল ভজন ॥ ১৩৬ ॥

lakṣmī cāhe sei dehe kṛṣṇera saṅgama
gopikā-anugā hañā nā kaila bhajana

lakṣmī—the goddess of fortune; *cāhe*—wants; *sei*—that; *dehe*—in the body; *kṛṣṇera saṅgama*—the association of Kṛṣṇa; *gopikā*—of the *gopīs;* *anugā*—follower; *hañā*—becoming; *nā*—did not; *kaila*—perform; *bhajana*—worship.

TRANSLATION

"The goddess of fortune, Lakṣmī, wanted to enjoy Kṛṣṇa and at the same time retain her spiritual body in the form of Lakṣmī. However, she did not follow in the footsteps of the gopīs in her worship of Kṛṣṇa.

TEXT 137

অন্য দেহে না পাইয়ে রাসবিলাস।
অতএব 'নায়ং' শ্লোক কহে বেদব্যাস ॥ ১৩৭ ॥

anya dehe nā pāiye rāsa-vilāsa
ataeva 'nāyaṁ' śloka kahe veda-vyāsa

anya dehe—in a body other than those of the *gopīs;* *nā*—not; *pāiye*—one gets; *rāsa-vilāsa*—the pastimes of the *rāsa* dance; *ataeva*—therefore; *nāyam*—beginning with the word *nāyam;* *śloka*—the Sanskrit verse; *kahe*—says; *veda-vyāsa*—Dvaipāyana Vedavyāsa.

TRANSLATION

"Vyāsadeva, the supreme authority on Vedic literature, composed the verse beginning 'nāyaṁ sukhāpo bhagavān' because no one can enter into the rāsa-līlā dance in any body other than that of a gopī."

PURPORT

This verse confirms a verse of the *Bhagavad-gītā* (9.25):

yānti deva-vratā devān pitṝn yānti pitṛ-vratāḥ
bhūtāni yānti bhūtejyā yānti mad-yājino 'pi mām

Lord Kṛṣṇa said, "Those who worship the demigods will take birth among the demigods, those who worship the ancestors go to the ancestors, those who worship ghosts and spirits will take birth among such beings, and those who worship Me will live with Me."

In the material world, every conditioned soul changes his material body again and again, but when the spirit soul is purified of all material coverings, there is no longer a chance of his accepting a material body. Such a soul then remains in his original, spiritual identity, a state that is possible to achieve only by understanding Kṛṣṇa in truth through the practice of Kṛṣṇa consciousness. As Kṛṣṇa says in the *Bhagavad-gītā* (4.9),

janma karma ca me divyam evaṁ yo vetti tattvataḥ
tyaktvā dehaṁ punar janma naiti mām eti so 'rjuna

"One who knows the transcendental nature of My appearance and activities does not, upon leaving the body, take his birth again in this material world, but attains My eternal abode, O Arjuna."

Only when one regains his original spiritual body can he enter into the spiritual kingdom. As far as the *rāsa-līlā* pastimes of the Lord are concerned, it is futile for one who is within the material world to attempt to imitate the Lord's dances. One has to attain a spiritual body like that of a *gopī* to enter into the pastimes of the *rāsa-līlā*. In the *nāyaṁ sukhāpo* verse, the devotees are referred to as *bhaktimat,* that is, fully engaged in devotional service and devoid of material contamination. One cannot enter into Kṛṣṇa's *rāsa-līlā* dance simply by artificially imitating it or artificially thinking oneself a *sakhī* and dressing up like one. Kṛṣṇa's *rāsa-līlā* dance is completely spiritual; it has nothing to do with material contamination. Therefore no one can enter into this pastime by artificial, material means. That is the instruction of the *nāyaṁ sukhāpo* verse, and it must be strictly understood.

TEXT 138

পূর্বে ভট্টের মনে এক ছিল অভিমান ।
'শ্রীনারায়ণ' হয়েন স্বয়ং-ভগবান্ ॥ ১৩৮ ॥

pūrve bhaṭṭera mane eka chila abhimāna
'śrī-nārāyaṇa' hayena svayaṁ-bhagavān

pūrve—before this; *bhaṭṭera*—of Veṅkaṭa Bhaṭṭa; *mane*—in the mind; *eka*—one; *chila*—there was; *abhimāna*—an impression; *śrī-nārāyaṇa*—the form of the Lord as Nārāyaṇa; *hayena*—is; *svayam*—personally; *bhagavān*—the Supreme Personality of Godhead.

TRANSLATION

Before this explanation was given by Śrī Caitanya Mahāprabhu, Veṅkaṭa Bhaṭṭa thought that Śrī Nārāyaṇa was the Supreme Personality of Godhead.

TEXT 139

তাঁহার ভজন সর্বোপরি-কক্ষা হয়।
'শ্রী-বৈষ্ণবে'র ভজন এই সর্বোপরি হয় ॥ ১৩৯ ॥

tāṅhāra bhajana sarvopari-kakṣā haya
śrī-vaiṣṇave'ra bhajana ei sarvopari haya

tāṅhāra bhajana—worship of Nārāyaṇa; *sarva-upari*—topmost; *kakṣā*—department; *haya*—is; *śrī-vaiṣṇavera*—of the followers of Rāmānujācārya; *bhajana*—worship; *ei*—this; *sarva-upari haya*—is the topmost.

TRANSLATION

Thinking in this way, Veṅkaṭa Bhaṭṭa believed that worship of Nārāyaṇa was the supreme form of worship, superior to all other processes of devotional service, for it was followed by the Śrī Vaiṣṇava disciples of Rāmānujācārya.

TEXT 140

এই তাঁর গর্ব প্রভু করিতে খণ্ডন।
পরিহাসদ্বারে উঠায় এতেক বচন ॥ ১৪০ ॥

ei tāṅra garva prabhu karite khaṇḍana
parihāsa-dvāre uṭhāya eteka vacana

ei—this; *tāṅra*—his (Veṅkaṭa Bhaṭṭa's); *garva*—pride; *prabhu*—Lord Caitanya Mahāprabhu; *karite khaṇḍana*—to curb; *parihāsa-dvāre*—by joking; *uṭhāya*—raises; *eteka*—so many; *vacana*—words.

TRANSLATION

Śrī Caitanya Mahāprabhu had understood this misconception of Veṅkaṭa Bhaṭṭa's, and to correct it the Lord talked so much in a joking way.

TEXT 141

প্রভু কহে,—ভট্ট, তুমি না করিহ সংশয় ।
'স্বয়ং-ভগবান্' কৃষ্ণ এই ত' নিশ্চয় ॥ ১৪১ ॥

prabhu kahe,—bhaṭṭa, tumi nā kariha saṁśaya
'svayaṁ-bhagavān' kṛṣṇa ei ta' niścaya

prabhu kahe—the Lord said; *bhaṭṭa*—My dear Veṅkaṭa Bhaṭṭa; *tumi*—you; *nā kariha*—do not do; *saṁśaya*—doubt; *svayam-bhagavān*—the Supreme Personality of Godhead; *kṛṣṇa*—is Lord Kṛṣṇa; *ei ta' niścaya*—this is the conclusion.

TRANSLATION

The Lord then continued, "My dear Veṅkaṭa Bhaṭṭa, please do not continue doubting. Lord Kṛṣṇa is the Supreme Personality of Godhead, and this is the conclusion of the Vedic literatures

TEXT 142

কৃষ্ণের বিলাস-মূর্তি—শ্রীনারায়ণ ।
অতএব লক্ষ্মী-আদ্যের হরে তেঁহ মন ॥ ১৪২ ॥

kṛṣṇera vilāsa-mūrti—śrī-nārāyaṇa
ataeva lakṣmī-ādyera hare teṅha mana

kṛṣṇera—of Lord Kṛṣṇa; *vilāsa-mūrti*—form for enjoyment; *śrī-nārāyaṇa*—Lord Nārāyaṇa; *ataeva*—therefore; *lakṣmī-ādyera*—of the goddess of fortune and her followers; *hare*—attracts; *teṅha*—He (Lord Nārāyaṇa); *mana*—the mind.

TRANSLATION

"Lord Nārāyaṇa, the opulent form of Kṛṣṇa, attracts the minds of the goddess of fortune and her followers.

TEXT 143

এতে চাংশকলাঃ পুংসঃ কৃষ্ণস্তু ভগবান্ স্বয়ম্ ।
ইন্দ্রারিব্যাকুলং লোকং মৃড়য়ন্তি যুগে যুগে ॥ ১৪৩ ॥

ete cāṁśa-kalāḥ puṁsaḥ
kṛṣṇas tu bhagavān svayam
indrāri-vyākulaṁ lokaṁ
mṛḍayanti yuge yuge

ete—these; *ca*—and; *aṁśa*—plenary portions; *kalāḥ*—parts of plenary portions; *puṁsaḥ*—of the *puruṣa-avatāras; kṛṣṇaḥ*—Lord Kṛṣṇa; *tu*—but; *bhagavān*—the Supreme Personality of Godhead; *svayam*—Himself; *indra-ari*—the enemies of Lord Indra; *vyākulam*—full of; *lokam*—the world; *mṛḍayanti*—make happy; *yuge yuge*—at the right time in each age.

TRANSLATION

"'All these incarnations of Godhead are either plenary portions or parts of the plenary portions of the puruṣa-avatāras. But Kṛṣṇa is the Supreme Personality of Godhead Himself. In every age He protects the world through His different features when the world is disturbed by the enemies of Indra.'

PURPORT

This is a verse from *Śrīmad-Bhāgavatam* (1.3.28).

TEXT 144

নারায়ণ হৈতে কৃষ্ণের অসাধারণ গুণ ।
অতএব লক্ষ্মীর কৃষ্ণে তৃষ্ণা অনুক্ষণ ॥ ১৪৪ ॥

nārāyaṇa haite kṛṣṇera asādhāraṇa guṇa
ataeva lakṣmīra kṛṣṇe tṛṣṇā anukṣaṇa

nārāyaṇa haite—over and above Nārāyaṇa; *kṛṣṇera*—of Lord Kṛṣṇa; *asādhāraṇa guṇa*—uncommon qualities; *ataeva*—therefore; *lakṣmīra*—of the goddess of fortune; *kṛṣṇe*—unto Kṛṣṇa; *tṛṣṇā*—desire; *anukṣaṇa*—always.

TRANSLATION

"Because Kṛṣṇa has four extraordinary qualities not possessed by Lord Nārāyaṇa, the goddess of fortune, Lakṣmī, always desires His company.

PURPORT

Lord Nārāyaṇa has sixty transcendental qualities. Over and above these, Kṛṣṇa has four extraordinary transcendental qualities absent in Lord Nārāyaṇa. These four qualities are (1) His wonderful pastimes, which are compared to an ocean, (2) His association in the circle of the supreme devotees in conjugal love (the *gopīs*), (3) His playing on the flute, whose vibration attracts the three worlds, and (4) His extraordinary beauty, which surpasses the beauty of the three worlds. Lord Kṛṣṇa's beauty is unequaled and unsurpassed.

TEXT 145

তুমি যে পড়িলা শ্লোক, সে হয় প্রমাণ ।
সেই শ্লোকে আইসে 'কৃষ্ণ — স্বয়ং ভগবান্' ॥ ১৪৫ ॥

tumi ye paḍilā śloka, se haya pramāṇa
sei śloke āise 'kṛṣṇa — svayaṁ bhagavān'

tumi—you; *ye*—which; *paḍilā*—have recited; *śloka*—verse; *se*—that; *haya*—is; *pramāṇa*—evidence; *sei śloke*—in that verse; *āise kṛṣṇa*—Kṛṣṇa is; *svayam bhagavān*—the Supreme Personality of Godhead.

TRANSLATION

"You have recited the śloka beginning with 'siddhāntatas tv abhede 'pi.' That very verse is evidence that Kṛṣṇa is the Supreme Personality of Godhead.

TEXT 146

সিদ্ধান্ততস্ত্বভেদেঽপি শ্রীশ-কৃষ্ণস্বরূপয়োঃ।
রসেনোৎকৃষ্যতে কৃষ্ণরূপমেষা রসস্থিতিঃ॥ ১৪৬॥

siddhāntatas tv abhede 'pi
śrīśa-kṛṣṇa-svarūpayoḥ
rasenotkṛṣyate kṛṣṇa-
rūpam eṣā rasa-sthitiḥ

siddhāntataḥ—in reality; *tu*—but; *abhede*—no difference; *api*—although; *śrī-īśa*—of the husband of Lakṣmī, Nārāyaṇa; *kṛṣṇa*—of Lord Kṛṣṇa; *svarūpayoḥ*—between the forms; *rasena*—by transcendental mellows; *utkṛṣyate*—is superior; *kṛṣṇa-rūpam*—the form of Lord Kṛṣṇa; *eṣā*—this; *rasa-sthitiḥ*—the reservoir of pleasure.

TRANSLATION

"'According to transcendental realization, there is no difference between the forms of Kṛṣṇa and Nārāyaṇa. Yet in Kṛṣṇa there is a special transcendental attraction due to the conjugal mellow, and consequently He surpasses Nārāyaṇa. This is the conclusion of transcendental mellows.'

PURPORT

This is a verse from the *Bhakti-rasāmṛta-sindhu* (1.2.59). Here Śrīla Kṛṣṇadāsa Kavirāja says that Lord Caitanya spoke the verse to Veṅkaṭa Bhaṭṭa, and earlier he said that Veṅkaṭa Bhaṭṭa spoke it to the Lord. But since their conversation took place long, long before the *Bhakti-rasāmṛta-sindhu* was composed, the question my be raised as to how either of them quoted the verse. Śrīla Bhaktivinoda Ṭhākura explains that this verse and many others like it were current among devotees long before the *Bhakti-rasāmṛta-sindhu* was composed. Thus devotees would always quote them and explain their purport in ecstasy.

TEXT 147

'স্বয়ং ভগবান্ 'কৃষ্ণ' হরে লক্ষ্মীর মন।
গোপিকার মন হরিতে নারে 'নারায়ণ'॥ ১৪৭॥

svayaṁ bhagavān 'kṛṣṇa' hare lakṣmīra mana
gopikāra mana harite nāre 'nārāyaṇa'

svayam bhagavān—the Supreme Personality of Godhead; *kṛṣṇa*—is Lord Kṛṣṇa; *hare*—attracts; *lakṣmīra*—of the goddess of fortune; *mana*—the mind; *gopikāra*—of the *gopīs; mana*—the minds; *harite*—to attract; *nāre*—is not able; *nārāyaṇa*—Lord Nārāyaṇa.

TRANSLATION

"The Supreme Personality of Godhead, Kṛṣṇa, attracts the mind of the goddess of fortune, but Lord Nārāyaṇa cannot attract the minds of the gopīs. This proves the superexcellence of Kṛṣṇa.

TEXT 148

নারায়নের কা কথা, শ্রীকৃষ্ণ আপনে।
গোপিকারে হাস্য করাইতে হয় 'নারায়ণে' ॥ ১৪৮ ॥

nārāyaṇera kā kathā, śrī-kṛṣṇa āpane
gopikāre hāsya karāite haya 'nārāyaṇe'

nārāyaṇera—of Lord Nārāyaṇa; *kā kathā*—what to speak; *śrī-kṛṣṇa*—Lord Śrī Kṛṣṇa; *āpane*—Himself; *gopikāre*—the *gopīs; hāsya karāite*—to make them jubilant; *haya*—becomes; *nārāyaṇe*—in the form of Nārāyaṇa.

TRANSLATION

"To say nothing of Lord Nārāyaṇa personally, Lord Kṛṣṇa Himself appeared as Nārāyaṇa just to play a joke on the gopīs.

TEXT 149

'চতুর্ভুজ-মূর্তি' দেখায় গোপীগণের আগে।
সেই 'কৃষ্ণে' গোপিকার নহে অনুরাগে ॥ ১৪৯ ॥

'catur-bhuja-mūrti' dekhāya gopī-gaṇera āge
sei 'kṛṣṇe' gopikāra nahe anurāge

catur-bhuja-mūrti—a four-handed form; *dekhāya*—exhibits; *gopī-gaṇera*—of the *gopīs; āge*—in front; *sei kṛṣṇe*—unto that Kṛṣṇa; *gopikāra*—of the *gopīs; nahe*—not; *anurāge*—attraction.

TRANSLATION

"Although Kṛṣṇa assumed the four-armed form of Nārāyaṇa, He could not attract the serious attention of the gopīs in ecstatic love.

TEXT 150

গোপীনাং পশুপেন্দ্রনন্দনজুষো ভাবস্য কস্তাং কৃতী
বিজ্ঞাতুং ক্ষমতে দুরূহপদবীসঞ্চারিণঃ প্রক্রিয়াম্ ।
আবিষ্কুর্বতি বৈষ্ণবীমপি তনুং তস্মিন্ ভুজৈর্জিষ্ণুভি-
র্যাসাং হন্ত চতুর্ভিরদ্ভুতরুচিং রাগোদয়ঃ কুঞ্চতি ॥ ১৫০ ॥

gopīnāṁ paśupendra-nandana-juṣo bhāvasya kas tāṁ kṛtī
vijñātuṁ kṣamate durūha-padavī-sañcāriṇaḥ prakriyām
āviṣkurvati vaiṣṇavīm api tanuṁ tasmin bhujair jiṣṇubhir
yāsāṁ hanta caturbhir adbhuta-ruciṁ rāgodayaḥ kuñcati

gopīnām—of the *gopīs; paśupa-indra-nandana-juṣaḥ*—of the service of the son of Vraja's King, Mahārāja Nanda; *bhāvasya*—ecstatic; *kaḥ*—what; *tām*—that; *kṛtī*—learned man; *vijñātum*—to understand; *kṣamate*—is able; *durūha*—very difficult to understand; *padavī*—the position; *sañcāriṇaḥ*—which provokes; *prakriyām*—activity; *āviṣkurvati*—He manifests; *vaiṣṇavīm*—of Viṣṇu; *api*—certainly; *tanum*—the body; *tasmin*—in that; *bhujaiḥ*—with arms; *jiṣṇubhiḥ*—very beautiful; *yāsām*—of whom (the *gopīs*); *hanta*—alas; *caturbhiḥ*—four; *adbhuta*—wonderfully; *rucim*—beautiful; *rāga-udayaḥ*—the evoking of ecstatic feelings; *kuñcati*—cripples.

TRANSLATION

"'Once Lord Śrī Kṛṣṇa playfully manifested Himself as Nārāyaṇa, with four victorious hands and a very beautiful form. When the gopīs saw this exalted form, however, their ecstatic feelings were crippled. A learned scholar, therefore, cannot understand the gopīs' ecstatic

feelings, which are firmly fixed upon the original form of Lord Kṛṣṇa as the son of Nanda Mahārāja. The wonderful feelings of the gopīs in ecstatic parama-rasa with Kṛṣṇa constitute the greatest mystery in spiritual life.'"

PURPORT

This is a verse spoken by Nārada Muni in the *Lalita-mādhava-nāṭaka* (6.14), a drama written by Śrīla Rūpa Gosvāmī.

TEXT 151

এত কহি' প্রভু তাঁর গর্ব চূর্ণ করিয়া ।
তাঁরে সুখ দিতে কহে সিদ্ধান্ত ফিরাইয়া ॥ ১৫১ ॥

eta kahi' prabhu tāṅra garva cūrṇa kariyā
tāṅre sukha dite kahe siddhānta phirāiyā

eta kahi'—saying this; *prabhu*—Lord Śrī Caitanya Mahāprabhu; *tāṅra*—his (of Veṅkaṭa Bhaṭṭa); *garva*—pride; *cūrṇa kariyā*—smashing into pieces; *tāṅre*—unto him; *sukha dite*—to give happiness; *kahe*—says; *siddhānta phirāiyā*—turning the whole conversation.

TRANSLATION

In this way Lord Śrī Caitanya Mahāprabhu deflated the pride of Veṅkaṭa Bhaṭṭa, but just to make him happy again, He spoke as follows.

TEXT 152

দুঃখ না ভাবিহ, ভট্ট, কৈলুঁ পরিহাস ।
শাস্ত্রসিদ্ধান্ত শুন, যাতে বৈষ্ণব-বিশ্বাস ॥ ১৫২ ॥

duḥkha nā bhāviha, bhaṭṭa, kailuṅ parihāsa
śāstra-siddhānta śuna, yāte vaiṣṇava-viśvāsa

duḥkha—unhappiness; *nā*—do not; *bhāviha*—bear; *bhaṭṭa*—My dear Veṅkaṭa Bhaṭṭa; *kailuṅ parihāsa*—I was simply making a joke; *śāstra-siddhānta*—the conclusion of the revealed scriptures;

śuna—hear; *yāte*—in which; *vaiṣṇava-viśvāsa*—the faith of the Vaiṣṇavas.

TRANSLATION

The Lord pacified Veṅkaṭa Bhaṭṭa by saying, "Actually whatever I have said is by way of jest. Now you can hear from Me the conclusion of the śāstras, in which every Vaiṣṇava devotee has firm faith.

TEXT 153

কৃষ্ণ-নারায়ণ, যৈছে একই স্বরূপ।
গোপী-লক্ষ্মী-ভেদ নাহি হয় একরূপ ॥ ১৫৩ ॥

kṛṣṇa-nārāyaṇa, yaiche eka-i svarūpa
gopī-lakṣmī-bheda nāhi haya eka-rūpa

kṛṣṇa-nārāyaṇa—Lord Kṛṣṇa and Lord Nārāyaṇa; *yaiche*—as; *eka-i*—one; *svarūpa*—form; *gopī*—the *gopīs; lakṣmī*—the goddess of fortune; *bheda*—difference; *nāhi*—there is not; *haya*—there is; *eka-rūpa*—one form.

TRANSLATION

"There is no difference between Lord Kṛṣṇa and Lord Nārāyaṇa, for They are of the same form. Similarly, there is no difference between the gopīs and the goddess of fortune, for they also are of the same form.

TEXT 154

গোপীদ্বারে লক্ষ্মী করে কৃষ্ণসঙ্গাস্বাদ।
ঈশ্বরত্বে ভেদ মানিলে হয় অপরাধ ॥ ১৫৪ ॥

gopī-dvāre lakṣmī kare kṛṣṇa-saṅgāsvāda
īśvaratve bheda mānile haya aparādha

gopī-dvāre—through the *gopīs; lakṣmī*—the goddess of fortune; *kare*—does; *kṛṣṇa-saṅga-āsvāda*—tasting the sweetness of the association of Lord Kṛṣṇa; *īśvaratve*—in the Supreme Personality of

Godhead; *bheda*—difference; *mānile*—if one considers; *haya*—there is; *aparādha*—offense.

TRANSLATION

"The goddess of fortune enjoys the association of Kṛṣṇa through the gopīs. One should not differentiate between the forms of the Lord, for such a conception is offensive.

TEXT 155

এক ঈশ্বর — ভক্তের ধ্যান-অনুরূপ ।
একই বিগ্রহে করে নানাকার রূপ ॥ ১৫৫ ॥

eka īśvara—bhaktera dhyāna-anurūpa
eka-i vigrahe kare nānākāra rūpa

eka īśvara—the Lord is one; *bhaktera*—of the devotees; *dhyāna*—meditation; *anurūpa*—according to; *eka-i*—one; *vigrahe*—in form; *kare*—exhibits; *nānā-ākāra*—different; *rūpa*—forms.

TRANSLATION

"There is no difference between the transcendental forms of the Lord. Different forms are manifested due to different attachments of different devotees. Actually the Lord is one, but He appears in different forms just to satisfy His devotees.

PURPORT

In the *Brahma-saṁhitā* (5.33) it is stated:

advaitam acyutam anādim ananta-rūpam
ādyaṁ purāṇa-puruṣaṁ nava-yauvanaṁ ca

The Lord is *advaita,* without differentiation. There is no difference between the forms of Kṛṣṇa, Rāma, Nārāyaṇa and Viṣṇu. All of Them are one. Sometimes foolish people ask whether when we chant "Rāma" in the Hare Kṛṣṇa *mantra* we refer to Lord Rāmacandra or Lord Balarāma. If a devotee says that the name Rāma in the Hare Kṛṣṇa *mahā-mantra* refers to Balarāma, a foolish person may become angry because to him the name Rāma refers to Lord Rāmacandra. Actually there is no difference between Balarāma and Lord Rāma. It does not matter whether one refers to Balarāma or to Lord Rāmacandra when chanting Hare Rāma, for there is no difference between Them. However, it is offensive to think that Balarāma is superior to Lord Rāmacandra or vice versa. Neophyte devotees do not understand this śāstric conclusion, and consequently they unnecessarily create an offensive situation. In text 154 Śrī Caitanya Mahāprabhu clarified this in a very lucid way: *īśvaratve bheda mānile haya aparādha.* "It is offensive for one to differentiate between the forms of the Lord." On the other hand, one should not think that the forms of the Lord are the same as the forms of the demigods. This is certainly offensive, as confirmed by the *Vaiṣṇava-tantra:*

yas tu nārāyaṇaṁ devaṁ brahma-rudrādi-daivataiḥ
samatvenaiva vīkṣeta sa pāṣaṇḍī bhaved dhruvam

"A *pāṣaṇḍī* is one who considers the great demigods such as Lord Brahmā and Lord Śiva equal to the Supreme Personality of Godhead, Nārāyaṇa." (*Hari-bhakti-vilāsa* 7.117)

The conclusion is that we should neither differentiate between the forms of the Lord nor equate the forms of the Lord with the forms of demigods or human beings. For instance, sometimes foolish *sannyāsīs,* thinking the body of the Lord to be material, equate *daridra-nārāyaṇa* with Nārāyaṇa, and this is certainly offensive. Unless one is instructed by a bona fide spiritual master, he cannot perfectly understand these different forms. The *Brahma-saṁhitā* confirms, *vedeṣu durlabham adurlabham ātma-bhaktau.* One cannot understand the differences between the forms of the Lord simply by academic study or by reading Vedic literature. One must learn from a realized devotee. Only then can one learn how to distinguish between one form of the Lord and another. The conclusion is that there is no difference between the forms of the Lord, but there is a difference between His forms and those of the demigods.

TEXT 156

মণির্যথা বিভাগেন নীলপীতাদিভির্যুতঃ ।
রূপভেদমবাপ্নোতি ধ্যানভেদাত্তথাচ্যুতঃ ॥ ১৫৬ ॥

maṇir yathā vibhāgena
nīla-pītādibhir yutaḥ
rūpa-bhedam avāpnoti
dhyāna-bhedāt tathācyutaḥ

maṇiḥ—jewel, specifically the jewel known as *vaidūrya; yathā*—as; *vibhāgena*—separately; *nīla*—blue; *pīta*—yellow; *ādibhiḥ*—and with other colors; *yutaḥ*—joined; *rūpa-bhedam*—difference of form; *avāpnoti*—gets; *dhyāna-bhedāt*—by different types of meditation; *tathā*—similarly; *acyutaḥ*—the infallible Supreme Personality of Godhead.

TRANSLATION

"'When the jewel known as vaidūrya touches various other materials, it appears to be separated into different colors, and consequently its forms also appear different. Similarly, according to the meditational ecstasy of the devotee, the Lord, who is known as Acyuta ["the infallible one"], appears in different forms, although He is essentially one.'"

PURPORT

This verse is quoted from *Śrī Nārada-pañcarātra.*

TEXT 157

ভট্ট কহে, —কাহাঁ আমি জীব পামর ।
কাহাঁ তুমি সেই কৃষ্ণ, —সাক্ষাৎ ঈশ্বর ॥ ১৫৭ ॥

bhaṭṭa kahe,—kāhāṅ āmi jīva pāmara
kāhāṅ tumi sei kṛṣṇa,—sākṣāt īśvara

bhaṭṭa kahe—Veṅkaṭa Bhaṭṭa said; *kāhāṅ*—whereas; *āmi*—I; *jīva*—an ordinary living being; *pāmara*—fallen; *kāhāṅ*—whereas; *tumi*—You; *sei kṛṣṇa*—the same Supreme Personality of Godhead, Kṛṣṇa; *sākṣāt īśvara*—directly the Lord.

TRANSLATION

Veṅkaṭa Bhaṭṭa then said, "I am an ordinary fallen living entity, but You are Kṛṣṇa, the Supreme Personality of Godhead Himself.

TEXT 158

অগাধ ঈশ্বর-লীলা কিছুই না জানি।
তুমি যেই কহ, সেই সত্য করি' মানি ॥ ১৫৮ ॥

agādha īśvara-līlā kichui nā jāni
tumi yei kaha, sei satya kari' māni

agādha—unfathomable; *īśvara-līlā*—pastimes of the Lord; *kichui*—anything; *nā jāni*—I do not know; *tumi*—You; *yei*—whatever; *kaha*—say; *sei satya*—that is right; *kari' māni*—I accept.

TRANSLATION

"The transcendental pastimes of the Lord are unfathomable, and I do not know anything about them. Whatever You say I accept as the truth.

PURPORT

This is the way to understand the truth about the Supreme Personality of Godhead. After hearing the *Bhagavad-gītā,* Arjuna said very much the same thing:

sarvam etad ṛtaṁ manye yan māṁ vadasi keśava
na hi te bhagavan vyaktiṁ vidur devā na dānavāḥ

"O Kṛṣṇa, I totally accept as truth all that You have told me. Neither the demigods nor the demons, O Lord, can understand Your personality." (Bg. 10.14)

It is not possible to understand the truth about the pastimes of the Lord simply by using our own logic, argument and academic education. We must receive bona fide information from the Supreme Personality of Godhead, just as Arjuna received information when Kṛṣṇa spoke the *Bhagavad-gītā.* We have to accept the *Bhagavad-gītā* or any other Vedic literature in good faith. These Vedic literatures are the only source of knowledge about the Lord. We must understand that we cannot comprehend the Absolute Truth by the speculative process.

TEXT 159

মোরে পূর্ণ কৃপা কৈল লক্ষ্মী-নারায়ণ ।
তাঁর কৃপায় পাইনু তোমার চরণ-দরশন ॥ ১৫৯ ॥

more pūrṇa kṛpā kaila lakṣmī-nārāyaṇa
tāṅra kṛpāya pāinu tomāra caraṇa-daraśana

more—unto me; *pūrṇa*—complete; *kṛpā*—mercy; *kaila*—did; *lakṣmī-nārāyaṇa*—the Deity of mother goddess of fortune and Nārāyaṇa; *tāṅra kṛpāya*—by Their mercy; *pāinu*—I have gotten; *tomāra*—Your; *caraṇa-daraśana*—vision of the lotus feet.

TRANSLATION

"I have been engaged in the service of Lakṣmī-Nārāyaṇa, and it is due to Their mercy that I have been able to see Your lotus feet.

TEXT 160

কৃপা করি' কহিলে মোরে কৃষ্ণের মহিমা ।
যাঁর রূপ-গুণৈশ্বর্যের কেহ না পায় সীমা ॥ ১৬০ ॥

kṛpā kari' kahile more kṛṣṇera mahimā
yāṅra rūpa-guṇaiśvaryera keha nā pāya sīmā

kṛpā kari'—showing causeless mercy; *kahile*—You have spoken; *more*—unto me; *kṛṣṇera*—of Lord Kṛṣṇa; *mahimā*—the glories; *yāṅra*—whose; *rūpa-guṇa-aiśvaryera*—of forms, qualities and opulence; *keha*—anyone; *nā*—not; *pāya*—gets; *sīmā*—the limit.

TRANSLATION

"Out of Your causeless mercy You have told me of the glories of Lord Kṛṣṇa. No one can reach the end of the opulence, qualities and forms of the Lord.

TEXT 161

এবে সে জানিনু কৃষ্ণভক্তি সর্বোপরি ।
কৃতার্থ করিলে, মোরে কহিলে কৃপা করি' ॥ ১৬১ ॥

ebe se jāninu kṛṣṇa-bhakti sarvopari
kṛtārtha karile, more kahile kṛpā kari'

ebe—now; *se*—that; *jāninu*—I understand; *kṛṣṇa-bhakti*—devotional service to Lord Kṛṣṇa; *sarva-upari*—above all; *kṛta-artha*—successful; *karile*—You have made; *more*—unto me; *kahile*—You have spoken; *kṛpā kari'*—by Your causeless mercy.

TRANSLATION

"I can now understand that devotional service unto Lord Kṛṣṇa is the supreme form of worship. Out of Your causeless mercy You have made my life successful simply by explaining the facts."

TEXT 162

এত বলি' ভট্ট পড়িলা প্রভুর চরণে।
কৃপা করি' প্রভু তাঁরে কৈলা আলিঙ্গনে ॥ ১৬২ ॥

eta bali' bhaṭṭa paḍilā prabhura caraṇe
kṛpā kari' prabhu tāṅre kailā āliṅgane

eta bali'—saying this; *bhaṭṭa*—Veṅkaṭa Bhaṭṭa; *paḍilā*—fell down; *prabhura caraṇe*—at the lotus feet of the Lord; *kṛpā kari'*—showing him mercy; *prabhu*—Lord Śrī Caitanya Mahāprabhu; *tāṅre*—unto him; *kailā*—did; *āliṅgane*—embracing.

TRANSLATION

After saying this, Veṅkaṭa Bhaṭṭa fell down before the lotus feet of the Lord, and the Lord, out of His causeless mercy, embraced him.

TEXT 163

চাতুর্মাস্য পূর্ণ হৈল, ভট্ট-আজ্ঞা লঞা।
দক্ষিণ চলিলা প্রভু শ্রীরঙ্গ দেখিয়া ॥ ১৬৩ ॥

cāturmāsya pūrṇa haila, bhaṭṭa-ājñā lañā
dakṣiṇa calilā prabhu śrī-raṅga dekhiyā

cāturmāsya—the period of Cāturmāsya; *pūrṇa haila*—became completed; *bhaṭṭa-ājñā lañā*—taking permission from Veṅkaṭa Bhaṭṭa; *dakṣiṇa*—south; *calilā*—proceeded; *prabhu*—Śrī Caitanya Mahāprabhu; *śrī-raṅga dekhiyā*—visiting Śrī Raṅga.

TRANSLATION

When the period of Cāturmāsya was completed, Śrī Caitanya Mahāprabhu took permission to leave from Veṅkaṭa Bhaṭṭa, and after visiting Śrī Raṅga, He proceeded further toward southern India.

TEXT 164

সঙ্গেতে চলিলা ভট্ট, না যায় ভবনে।
তাঁরে বিদায় দিলা প্রভু অনেক যতনে ॥ ১৬৪ ॥

saṅgete calilā bhaṭṭa, nā yāya bhavane
tāṅre vidāya dilā prabhu aneka yatane

saṅgete—along with Him; *calilā*—began to go; *bhaṭṭa*—Veṅkaṭa Bhaṭṭa; *nā yāya bhavane*—does not return to his home; *tāṅre*—unto him; *vidāya dilā*—gave farewell; *prabhu*—Śrī Caitanya Mahāprabhu; *aneka yatane*—with great endeavor.

TRANSLATION

Veṅkaṭa Bhaṭṭa did not want to return home but also wanted to go with the Lord. It was with great endeavor that Śrī Caitanya Mahāprabhu bade him farewell.

TEXT 165

প্রভুর বিয়োগে ভট্ট হৈল অচেতন।
এই রঙ্গলীলা করে শচীর নন্দন ॥ ১৬৫ ॥

prabhura viyoge bhaṭṭa haila acetana
ei raṅga-līlā kare śacīra nandana

prabhura viyoge—on account of separation from Śrī Caitanya Mahāprabhu; *bhaṭṭa*—Veṅkaṭa Bhaṭṭa; *haila*—became; *acetana*—

unconscious; *ei*—this; *raṅga-līlā*—pastime at Śrī Raṅga-kṣetra; *kare*—does; *śacīra nandana*—the son of mother Śacī.

TRANSLATION

When He did so, Veṅkaṭa Bhaṭṭa fell down unconscious. Such are the pastimes of Lord Śrī Caitanya Mahāprabhu, the son of mother Śacī, at Śrī Raṅga-kṣetra.

TEXT 166

ঋষভ-পর্বতে চলি' আইলা গৌরহরি।
নারায়ণ দেখিলা তাঁহা নতি-স্তুতি করি' ॥ ১৬৬ ॥

ṛṣabha-parvate cali' āilā gaurahari
nārāyaṇa dekhilā tāṅhā nati-stuti kari'

ṛṣabha-parvate—to the Ṛṣabha Hill; *cali'*—walking; *āilā*—arrived; *gaurahari*—Lord Śrī Caitanya Mahāprabhu; *nārāyaṇa*—the Deity of Lord Nārāyaṇa; *dekhilā*—saw; *tāṅhā*—there; *nati-stuti kari'*—offering obeisances and prayers.

TRANSLATION

When the Lord arrived at Ṛṣabha Hill, He saw the temple of Lord Nārāyaṇa and offered obeisances and various prayers.

PURPORT

Ṛṣabha Hill (Ānāgaḍa-malaya-parvata) is situated twelve miles north of Madurai City, in the district of Madurai, in southern Tamil Nadu. It is one of the mountains known as the Kuṭakācalas. Nearby Ṛṣabha Hill is the forest where Lord Ṛṣabhadeva burned Himself to ashes.

TEXT 167

পরমানন্দপুরী তাহাঁ রহে চতুর্মাস।
শুনি' মহাপ্রভু গেলা পুরী-গোসাঞির পাশ ॥ ১৬৭ ॥

paramānanda-purī tāhāṅ rahe catur-māsa
śuni' mahāprabhu gelā purī-gosāñira pāśa

paramānanda-purī—Paramānanda Purī; *tāhāṅ*—there; *rahe*—remained; *catur-māsa*—four months; *śuni'*—hearing; *mahāprabhu*—Śrī Caitanya Mahāprabhu; *gelā*—went; *purī*—Paramānanda Purī; *gosāñira*—the spiritual master; *pāśa*—near.

TRANSLATION

Paramānanda Purī had stayed at Ṛṣabha Hill during the four months of the rainy season, and when Śrī Caitanya Mahāprabhu heard this, He immediately went to see him.

TEXT 168

পুরী-গোসাঞির প্রভু কৈল চরণ-বন্দন।
প্রেমে পুরী গোসাঞি তাঁরে কৈল আলিঙ্গন ॥ ১৬৮ ॥

purī-gosāñira prabhu kaila caraṇa vandana
preme purī gosāñi tāṅre kaila āliṅgana

purī-gosāñira—of Paramānanda Purī; *prabhu*—Śrī Caitanya Mahāprabhu; *kaila*—did; *caraṇa vandana*—worship of the lotus feet; *preme*—in ecstasy; *purī gosāñi*—Paramānanda Purī; *tāṅre*—unto Him; *kaila*—did; *āliṅgana*—embracing.

TRANSLATION

Upon meeting Paramānanda Purī, Śrī Caitanya Mahāprabhu offered him all respects, touching his lotus feet, and Paramānanda Purī embraced the Lord in ecstasy.

TEXT 169

তিনদিন প্রেমে দোঁহে কৃষ্ণকথা-রঙ্গে।
সেই বিপ্র-ঘরে দোঁহে রহে-একসঙ্গে ॥ ১৬৯ ॥

tina-dina preme doṅhe kṛṣṇa-kathā-raṅge
sei vipra-ghare doṅhe rahe eka-saṅge

tina-dina—three days; *preme*—in ecstasy; *doṅhe*—both; *kṛṣṇa-kathā*—discussing topics of Kṛṣṇa; *raṅge*—in jubilation; *sei vipra-*

ghare—in the home of a *brāhmaṇa; doṅhe*—both of them; *rahe*—stayed; *eka-saṅge*—together.

TRANSLATION

Śrī Caitanya Mahāprabhu stayed with Paramānanda Purī in the brāhmaṇa's house where he was residing. The two of them passed three days there discussing topics of Kṛṣṇa.

TEXT 170

পুরী-গোসাঞি বলে,—আমি যাব পুরুষোত্তমে ।
পুরুষোত্তম দেখি' গৌড়ে যাব গঙ্গাস্নানে ॥ ১৭০ ॥

purī-gosāñi bale,—āmi yāba puruṣottame
puruṣottama dekhi' gauḍe yāba gaṅgā-snāne

purī-gosāñi—Paramānanda Purī; *bale*—said; *āmi*—I; *yāba*—shall go; *puruṣottame*—to Jagannātha Purī; *puruṣottama dekhi'*—after visiting Jagannātha Purī; *gauḍe yāba*—I shall go to Bengal; *gaṅgā-snāne*—for bathing in the Ganges.

TRANSLATION

Paramānanda Purī informed Śrī Caitanya Mahāprabhu that he was going to see Puruṣottama at Jagannātha Purī. After seeing Lord Jagannātha there, he would go to Bengal to bathe in the Ganges.

TEXT 171

প্রভু কহে,—তুমি পুনঃ আইস নীলাচলে ।
আমি সেতুবন্ধ হৈতে আসিব অল্পকালে ॥ ১৭১ ॥

prabhu kahe,—tumi punaḥ āisa nīlācale
āmi setubandha haite āsiba alpa-kāle

prabhu kahe—the Lord said; *tumi*—you; *punaḥ*—again; *āisa*—come; *nīlācale*—to Jagannātha Purī; *āmi*—I; *setubandha haite*—from Rāmeśvara; *āsiba*—shall return; *alpa-kāle*—very soon.

TRANSLATION

Śrī Caitanya Mahāprabhu then told him, "Please return to Jagannātha Purī, for I will return there very soon from Rāmeśvara [Setubandha].

TEXT 172

তোমার নিকটে রহি, — হেন বাঞ্ছা হয়।
নীলাচলে আসিবে মোরে হঞা সদয় ॥ ১৭২ ॥

tomāra nikaṭe rahi, — hena vāñchā haya
nīlācale āsibe more hañā sadaya

tomāra nikaṭe — with you; *rahi* — I may stay; *hena* — such; *vāñchā haya* — is My desire; *nīlācale* — to Jagannātha Purī; *āsibe* — please come; *more* — unto Me; *hañā* — being; *sa-daya* — merciful.

TRANSLATION

"It is My desire to stay with you, and therefore if you would return to Jagannātha Purī, you would show great mercy to Me."

TEXT 173

এত বলি' তাঁর ঠাঞি এই আজ্ঞা লঞা।
দক্ষিণে চলিলা প্রভু হরষিত হঞা ॥ ১৭৩ ॥

eta bali' tāṅra ṭhāñi ei ājñā lañā
dakṣiṇe calilā prabhu haraṣita hañā

eta bali' — saying this; *tāṅra ṭhāñi* — from him; *ei ājñā lañā* — taking permission; *dakṣiṇe calilā* — departed for southern India; *prabhu* — Lord Śrī Caitanya Mahāprabhu; *haraṣita hañā* — being very pleased.

TRANSLATION

After talking in this way with Paramānanda Purī, the Lord took his permission to leave and, very pleased, departed for southern India.

TEXT 174

পরমানন্দ পুরী তবে চলিলা নীলাচলে ।
মহাপ্রভু চলি চলি আইলা শ্রীশৈলে ॥ ১৭৪ ॥

paramānanda purī tabe calilā nīlācale
mahāprabhu cali cali āilā śrī-śaile

paramānanda purī—Paramānanda Purī; *tabe*—then; *calilā nīlācale*—departed for Jagannātha Purī; *mahāprabhu*—Śrī Caitanya Mahāprabhu; *cali cali*—walking; *āilā*—came; *śrī-śaile*—to Śrī Śaila.

TRANSLATION

Thus Paramānanda Purī started for Jagannātha Purī, and Śrī Caitanya Mahāprabhu began walking toward Śrī Śaila.

PURPORT

Śrīla Bhaktisiddhānta Sarasvatī Ṭhākura remarks, "Which Śrī Śaila is being indicated by Kṛṣṇadāsa Kavirāja Gosvāmī is not clearly understood. There is no temple of Mallikārjuna in this area because the Śrī Śaila located in the district of Dhārwād cannot possibly be there. That Śrī Śaila is on the southern side of Belgaum, and the Śiva temple of Mallikārjuna is located there. (Refer to text 15 of this chapter.) It is said that on that hill Lord Śiva lived with Devī. Also, Lord Brahmā lived there with all the demigods."

TEXT 175

শিব-দুর্গা রহে তাহাঁ ব্রাহ্মণের বেশে ।
মহাপ্রভু দেখি' দোঁহার হইল উল্লাসে ॥ ১৭৫ ॥

śiva-durgā rahe tāhāṅ brāhmaṇera veśe
mahāprabhu dekhi' doṅhāra ha-ila ullāse

śiva-durgā—Lord Śiva and his wife, Durgā; *rahe tāhāṅ*—stayed there; *brāhmaṇera veśe*—in the dress of *brāhmaṇas; mahāprabhu dekhi'*—seeing Śrī Caitanya Mahāprabhu; *doṅhāra*—of both of them; *ha-ila*—there was; *ullāse*—great pleasure.

TRANSLATION

In Śrī Śaila Lord Śiva and his wife Durgā lived in the dress of brāhmaṇas, and when they saw Śrī Caitanya Mahāprabhu, they became very pleased.

TEXT 176

তিন দিন ভিক্ষা দিল করি' নিমন্ত্রণ ।
নিভৃতে বসি' গুপ্তবার্তা কহে দুই জন ॥ ১৭৬ ॥

tina dina bhikṣā dila kari' nimantraṇa
nibhṛte vasi' gupta-vārtā kahe dui jana

tina dina—for three days; *bhikṣā dila*—offered alms; *kari' nimantraṇa*—inviting Him; *nibhṛte*—in a solitary place; *vasi'*—sitting together; *gupta-vārtā*—confidential talks; *kahe*—speak; *dui jana*—both of them.

TRANSLATION

Lord Śiva, dressed like a brāhmaṇa, gave alms to Śrī Caitanya Mahāprabhu and invited Him to spend three days in a solitary place. Sitting there together, they talked very confidentially.

TEXT 177

তাঁর সঙ্গে মহাপ্রভু করি ইষ্টগোষ্ঠী ।
তাঁর আজ্ঞা লঞা আইলা পুরী কামকোষ্ঠী ॥ ১৭৭ ॥

tāṅra saṅge mahāprabhu kari iṣṭagoṣṭhī
tāṅra ājñā lañā āilā purī kāmakoṣṭhī

tāṅra saṅge—with him; *mahāprabhu*—Śrī Caitanya Mahāprabhu; *kari iṣṭa-goṣṭhī*—discussing spiritual subject matter; *tāṅra*—his; *ājñā*—order; *lañā*—taking; *āilā*—came; *purī kāmakoṣṭhī*—to Kāmakoṣṭhī-purī.

TRANSLATION

After talking with Lord Śiva, Śrī Caitanya Mahāprabhu took his permission to leave and went to Kāmakoṣṭhī-purī.

TEXT 178

দক্ষিণ-মথুরা আইলা কামকোষ্ঠী হৈতে।
তাহাঁ দেখা হৈল এক ব্রাহ্মণ-সহিতে ॥ ১৭৮ ॥

dakṣiṇa-mathurā āilā kāmakoṣṭhī haite
tāhāṅ dekhā haila eka brāhmaṇa-sahite

dakṣiṇa-mathurā—at southern Mathurā; *āilā*—arrived; *kāmakoṣṭhī haite*—from Kāmakoṣṭhī; *tāhāṅ*—there; *dekhā haila*—He met; *eka*—one; *brāhmaṇa-sahite*—with a *brāhmaṇa.*

TRANSLATION

When Śrī Caitanya Mahāprabhu arrived at southern Mathurā from Kāmakoṣṭhī, He met a brāhmaṇa.

PURPORT

Southern Mathurā, presently known as Madurai, is situated on the banks of the Bhāgāi River. This place of pilgrimage is specifically meant for the devotees of Lord Śiva; therefore it is called Śaiva-kṣetra, that is, the place where Lord Śiva is worshiped. In this area there are mountains and forests. There are also two Śiva temples, one known as Rāmeśvara and the other known as Sundareśvara. There is also a temple to Devī called the Mīnākṣī-devī temple, which displays very great architectural craftsmanship. It was built under the supervision of the kings of the Pāṇḍya Dynasty, and when the Muslims attacked this temple, as well as the temple of Sundareśvara, great damage was done. In the Christian year 1372, a king named Kampanna Udaiyara reigned on the throne of Madurai. Long ago, Emperor Kulaśekhara ruled this area, and during his reign he established a colony of *brāhmaṇas.* A well-known king named Anantaguṇa Pāṇḍya is an eleventh-generation descendant of Emperor Kulaśekhara.

TEXT 179

সেই বিপ্র মহাপ্রভুকে কৈল নিমন্ত্রণ।
রামভক্ত সেই বিপ্র — বিরক্ত মহাজন ॥ ১৭৯ ॥

sei vipra mahāprabhuke kaila nimantraṇa
rāma-bhakta sei vipra—virakta mahājana

sei vipra—that *brāhmaṇa; mahāprabhuke*—unto Lord Śrī Caitanya Mahāprabhu; *kaila*—did; *nimantraṇa*—invitation; *rāma-bhakta*—devotee of Lord Rāmacandra; *sei*—that; *vipra*—*brāhmaṇa; virakta*—very much detached; *mahājana*—a great devotee and authority.

TRANSLATION

The brāhmaṇa who met Śrī Caitanya Mahāprabhu invited the Lord to his home. This brāhmaṇa was a great devotee and an authority on Lord Śrī Rāmacandra. He was always detached from material activities.

TEXT 180

কৃতমালায় স্নান করি' আইলা তাঁর ঘরে।
ভিক্ষা কি দিবেন বিপ্র,—পাক নাহি করে॥ ১৮০॥

kṛtamālāya snāna kari' āilā tāṅra ghare
bhikṣā ki dibena vipra,—pāka nāhi kare

kṛtamālāya—in the Kṛtamālā River; *snāna kari'*—bathing; *āilā*—came; *tāṅra*—of the *brāhmaṇa; ghare*—to the home; *bhikṣā*—offering of alms; *ki dibena*—what shall give; *vipra*—the *brāhmaṇa; pāka*—cooking; *nāhi kare*—did not do.

TRANSLATION

After bathing in the river Kṛtamālā, Śrī Caitanya Mahāprabhu went to the brāhmaṇa's house to take lunch, but He saw that the food was unprepared because the brāhmaṇa had not cooked it.

TEXT 181

মহাপ্রভু কহে তাঁরে,—শুন মহাশয়।
মধ্যাহ্ন হৈল, কেনে পাক নাহি হয়॥ ১৮১॥

mahāprabhu kahe tāṅre,—śuna mahāśaya
madhyāhna haila, kene pāka nāhi haya

mahāprabhu kahe—Śrī Caitanya Mahāprabhu said; *tāṅre*—unto him; *śuna mahāśaya*—please hear, My dear sir; *madhya-ahna haila*—it is already noon; *kene*—why; *pāka nāhi haya*—you did not cook.

TRANSLATION

Seeing this, Śrī Caitanya Mahāprabhu said, "My dear sir, please tell Me why you have not cooked. It is already noon."

TEXT 182

বিপ্র কহে, —প্রভু, মোর অরণ্যে বসতি।
পাকের সামগ্রী বনে না মিলে সম্প্রতি ॥ ১৮২ ॥

vipra kahe,—prabhu, mora araṇye vasati
pākera sāmagrī vane nā mile samprati

vipra kahe—the *brāhmaṇa* replied; *prabhu*—O Lord; *mora*—my; *araṇye*—in the forest; *vasati*—residence; *pākera sāmagrī*—the ingredients for cooking; *vane*—in the forest; *nā mile*—are not available; *samprati*—at this time.

TRANSLATION

The brāhmaṇa replied, "My dear Lord, we are living in the forest. For the time being we cannot get all the ingredients for cooking.

TEXT 183

বন্য শাক-ফল-মূল আনিবে লক্ষ্মণ।
তবে সীতা করিবেন পাক-প্রয়োজন ॥ ১৮৩ ॥

vanya śāka-phala-mūla ānibe lakṣmaṇa
tabe sītā karibena pāka-prayojana

vanya—of the forest; *śāka*—vegetables; *phala-mūla*—fruits and roots; *ānibe*—will bring; *lakṣmaṇa*—Lakṣmaṇa; *tabe*—that time; *sītā*—mother Sītā; *karibena*—will do; *pāka-prayojana*—the necessary cooking.

TRANSLATION

"When Lakṣmaṇa brings all the vegetables, fruits and roots from the forest, Sītā will do the necessary cooking."

TEXT 184

তাঁর উপাসনা শুনি' প্রভু তুষ্ট হৈলা ।
আস্তে-ব্যস্তে সেই বিপ্র রন্ধন করিলা ॥ ১৮৪ ॥

tāṅra upāsanā śuni' prabhu tuṣṭa hailā
āste-vyaste sei vipra randhana karilā

tāṅra—his; *upāsanā*—method of worship; *śuni'*—hearing; *prabhu*—Lord Śrī Caitanya Mahāprabhu; *tuṣṭa hailā*—was very pleased; *āste-vyaste*—with great haste; *sei*—that; *vipra*—*brāhmaṇa; randhana karilā*—began to cook.

TRANSLATION

Śrī Caitanya Mahāprabhu was very satisfied to hear about the brāhmaṇa's method of worship. Finally the brāhmaṇa hastily made arrangements for cooking.

TEXT 185

প্রভু ভিক্ষা কৈল দিনের তৃতীয়প্রহরে ।
নির্বিণ্ণ সেই বিপ্র উপবাস করে ॥ ১৮৫ ॥

prabhu bhikṣā kaila dinera tṛtīya-prahare
nirviṇṇa sei vipra upavāsa kare

prabhu—Lord Caitanya Mahāprabhu; *bhikṣā kaila*—took His luncheon; *dinera*—of the day; *tṛtīya-prahare*—at about three o'clock; *nirviṇṇa*—sorrowful; *sei*—that; *vipra*—*brāhmaṇa; upavāsa kare*—fasted.

TRANSLATION

Śrī Caitanya Mahāprabhu took His lunch at about three o'clock, but the brāhmaṇa, being very sorrowful, fasted.

TEXT 186

প্রভু কহে, —বিপ্র কাঁহে কর উপবাস।
কেনে এত দুঃখ, কেনে করহ হুতাশ ॥ ১৮৬ ॥

prabhu kahe,—vipra kāṅhe kara upavāsa
kene eta duḥkha, kene karaha hutāśa

prabhu kahe—Lord Śrī Caitanya Mahāprabhu said; *vipra*—My dear *brāhmaṇa; kāṅhe*—why; *kara upavāsa*—you are fasting; *kene*—why; *eta*—so much; *duḥkha*—unhappiness; *kene*—why; *karaha hutāśa*—you express so much worry.

TRANSLATION

While the brāhmaṇa was fasting, Śrī Caitanya Mahāprabhu asked him, "Why are you fasting? Why are you so unhappy? Why are you so worried?"

TEXT 187

বিপ্র কহে, —জীবনে মোর নাহি প্রয়োজন।
অগ্নি-জলে প্রবেশিয়া ছাড়িব জীবন ॥ ১৮৭ ॥

vipra kahe,—jīvane mora nāhi prayojana
agni-jale praveśiyā chāḍiba jīvana

vipra kahe—the *brāhmaṇa* said; *jīvane mora*—for my life; *nāhi*—there is not; *prayojana*—necessity; *agni*—in fire; *jale*—in water; *praveśiyā*—entering; *chāḍiba*—I shall give up; *jīvana*—life.

TRANSLATION

The brāhmaṇa replied, "I have no reason to live. I shall give up my life by entering either fire or water.

TEXT 188

জগন্মাতা মহালক্ষ্মী সীতা-ঠাকুরাণী।
রাক্ষসে স্পর্শিল তাঁরে, —ইহা কানে শুনি ॥ ১৮৮ ॥

jagan-mātā mahā-lakṣmī sītā-ṭhākurāṇī
rākṣase sparśila tāṅre, — ihā kāne śuni

jagat-mātā — the mother of the universe; *mahā-lakṣmī* — the supreme goddess of fortune; *sītā-ṭhākurāṇī* — mother Sītā; *rākṣase* — the demon Rāvaṇa; *sparśila* — touched; *tāṅre* — her; *ihā* — this; *kāne śuni* — I have heard.

TRANSLATION

"My dear Sir, mother Sītā is the mother of the universe and the supreme goddess of fortune. She has been touched by the demon Rāvaṇa, and I am troubled upon hearing this news.

TEXT 189

এ শরীর ধরিবারে কভু না যুয়ায় ।
এই দুঃখে জ্বলে দেহ, প্রাণ নাহি যায় ॥ ১৮৯ ॥

e śarīra dharibāre kabhu nā yuyāya
ei duḥkhe jvale deha, prāṇa nāhi yāya

e śarīra — this body; *dharibāre* — to keep; *kabhu* — ever; *nā* — not; *yuyāya* — deserve; *ei duḥkhe* — in this unhappiness; *jvale deha* — my body is burning; *prāṇa* — my life; *nāhi yāya* — does not go away.

TRANSLATION

"Sir, due to my unhappiness I cannot continue living. Although my body is burning, my life is not leaving."

TEXT 190

প্রভু কহে, — এ ভাবনা না করিহ আর ।
পণ্ডিত হঞা কেনে না করহ বিচার ॥ ১৯০ ॥

prabhu kahe, — e bhāvanā nā kariha āra
paṇḍita hañā kene nā karaha vicāra

prabhu kahe — the Lord said; *e bhāvanā* — this kind of thinking; *nā* — do not; *kariha* — do; *āra* — anymore; *paṇḍita hañā* — being a learned *paṇḍita; kena*—why; *nā karaha*—you do not make; *vicāra*—consideration.

TRANSLATION

Śrī Caitanya Mahāprabhu replied, "Please do not think this way any longer. You are a learned paṇḍita. Why don't you consider the case?"

TEXT 191

ঈশ্বর-প্রেয়সী সীতা — চিদানন্দমূর্তি ।
প্রাকৃত-ইন্দ্রিয়ের তাঁরে দেখিতে নাহি শক্তি ॥ ১৯১ ॥

īśvara-preyasī sītā—cid-ānanda-mūrti
prākṛta-indriyera tāṅre dekhite nāhi śakti

īśvara-preyasī—the dearmost wife of the Lord; *sītā*—mother Sītā; *cit-ānanda-mūrti*—spiritual blissful form; *prākṛta*—material; *indriyera*—of the senses; *tāṅre*—her; *dekhite*—to see; *nāhi*—there is not; *śakti*—power.

TRANSLATION

Śrī Caitanya Mahāprabhu continued, "Sītādevī, the dearmost wife of the Supreme Lord Rāmacandra, certainly has a spiritual form full of bliss. No one can see her with material eyes, for no materialist has such power.

TEXT 192

স্পর্শিবার কার্য আছুক, না পায় দর্শন ।
সীতার আকৃতি-মায়া হরিল রাবণ ॥ ১৯২ ॥

sparśibāra kārya āchuka, nā pāya darśana
sītāra ākṛti-māyā harila rāvaṇa

sparśibāra—to touch; *kārya*—business; *āchuka*—let it be; *nā*—does not; *pāya*—get; *darśana*—sight; *sītāra*—of mother Sītā; *ākṛti-māyā*—the form made of *māyā; harila*—took away; *rāvaṇa*—the demon Rāvaṇa.

TRANSLATION

"To say nothing of touching mother Sītā, a person with material senses cannot even see her. When Rāvaṇa kidnapped her, he kidnapped only her material, illusory form.

TEXT 193

রাবণ আসিতেই সীতা অন্তর্ধান কৈল ।
রাবণের আগে মায়া-সীতা পাঠাইল ॥ ১৯৩ ॥

rāvaṇa āsitei sītā antardhāna kaila
rāvaṇera āge māyā-sītā pāṭhāila

rāvaṇa—the demon Rāvaṇa; *āsitei*—as soon as he arrived; *sītā*—mother Sītā; *antardhāna kaila*—disappeared; *rāvaṇera āge*—before the demon Rāvaṇa; *māyā-sītā*—illusory, material form of Sītā; *pāṭhāila*—sent.

TRANSLATION

"As soon as Rāvaṇa arrived before Sītā, she disappeared. Then just to cheat Rāvaṇa she sent an illusory, material form.

TEXT 194

অপ্রাকৃত বস্তু নহে প্রাকৃত-গোচর ।
বেদ-পুরাণেতে এই কহে নিরন্তর ॥ ১৯৪ ॥

aprākṛta vastu nahe prākṛta-gocara
veda-purāṇete ei kahe nirantara

aprākṛta—spiritual; *vastu*—substance; *nahe*—not; *prākṛta*—of matter; *gocara*—within the jurisdiction; *veda-purāṇete*—the *Vedas* and the *Purāṇas; ei*—this; *kahe*—say; *nirantara*—always.

TRANSLATION

"Spiritual substance is never within the jurisdiction of the material conception. This is always the verdict of the Vedas and Purāṇas."

PURPORT

As stated in the *Kaṭha Upaniṣad* (2.3.9, 12):

na sandṛśe tiṣṭhati rūpam asya
na cakṣuṣā paśyati kaścanainam
hṛdā manīṣā manasābhikḷpto
ya etad vidur amṛtās te bhavanti
naiva vācā na manasā
prāptuṁ śakyo na cakṣuṣā

"Spirit is not within the jurisdiction of material eyes, words or mind."

Similarly, *Śrīmad-Bhāgavatam* (10.84.13) states:

yasyātma-buddhiḥ kuṇape tri-dhātuke
sva-dhīḥ kalatrādiṣu bhauma ijya-dhīḥ
yat-tīrtha-buddhiḥ salile na karhicij
janeṣv abhijñeṣu sa eva go-kharaḥ

"A human being who identifies his body made of three elements with his self, who considers the by-products of his body to be his kinsmen, who considers the land of his birth worshipable, and who goes to a place of pilgrimage simply to take a bath rather than to meet men of transcendental knowledge there is to be considered like an ass or a cow."

These are some Vedic statements about spiritual substance. Spiritual substance cannot be seen by the unintelligent, because they do not have the eyes or the mentality to see the spirit soul. Consequently they think that there is no such thing as spirit. But the followers of the Vedic injunctions take their information from Vedic statements, such as the verses from the *Kaṭha Upaniṣad* and *Śrīmad-Bhāgavatam* quoted above.

TEXT 195

বিশ্বাস করহ তুমি আমার বচনে ।
পুনরপি কু-ভাবনা না করিহ মনে ॥ ১৯৫ ॥

viśvāsa karaha tumi āmāra vacane
punarapi ku-bhāvanā nā kariha mane

viśvāsa karaha—believe; *tumi*—you; *āmāra*—My; *vacane*—in the words; *punarapi*—again; *ku-bhāvanā*—misconception; *nā kariha*—do not do; *mane*—in the mind.

TRANSLATION

Śrī Caitanya Mahāprabhu then assured the brāhmaṇa, "Have faith in My words and do not burden your mind any longer with this misconception."

PURPORT

This is the process of spiritual understanding. *Acintyā khalu ye bhāvā na tāṁs tarkeṇa yojayet:* "We should not try to understand things beyond our material conception by argument and counterargument." *Mahā-jano yena gataḥ sa panthāḥ:* "We have to follow in the footsteps of great authorities coming down in the *paramparā* system." If we approach a bona fide *ācārya* and keep faith in his words, spiritual realization will be easy.

TEXT 196

প্রভুর বচনে বিপ্রের হইল বিশ্বাস।
ভোজন করিল, হৈল জীবনের আশ ॥ ১৯৬ ॥

prabhura vacane viprera ha-ila viśvāsa
bhojana karila, haila jīvanera āśa

prabhura vacane—in the words of Lord Śrī Caitanya Mahāprabhu; *viprera*—of the *brāhmaṇa; ha-ila*—was; *viśvāsa*—faith; *bhojana karila*—he took his lunch; *haila*—there was; *jīvanera*—for living; *āśa*—hope.

TRANSLATION

Although the brāhmaṇa was fasting, he had faith in the words of Śrī Caitanya Mahāprabhu and accepted food. In this way his life was saved.

TEXT 197

তাঁরে আশ্বাসিয়া প্রভু করিলা গমন।
কৃতমালায় স্নান করি আইলা দুর্বশন ॥ ১৯৭ ॥

tāṅre āśvāsiyā prabhu karilā gamana
kṛtamālāya snāna kari āilā durvaśana

tāṅre āśvāsiyā—assuring him; *prabhu*—Śrī Caitanya Mahāprabhu; *karilā gamana*—departed; *kṛtamālāya*—in the river known as Kṛtamālā; *snāna kari*—bathing; *āilā*—came; *durvaśana*—to Durvaśana.

TRANSLATION

After thus assuring the brāhmaṇa, Śrī Caitanya Mahāprabhu proceeded further into southern India and finally arrived at Durvaśana, where He bathed in the river Kṛtamālā.

PURPORT

Presently the Kṛtamālā River is known as the river Bhāgāi or Vaigai. This river has three tributaries, named Surulī, Varāha-nadī and Baṭṭilla-guṇḍu. The river Kṛtamālā is also mentioned in *Śrīmad-Bhāgavatam* (11.5.39) by the sage Karabhājana.

TEXT 198

দুর্বশনে রঘুনাথে কৈল দরশন।
মহেন্দ্র-শৈলে পরশুরামের কৈল বন্দন ॥ ১৯৮ ॥

durvaśane raghunāthe kaila daraśana
mahendra-śaile paraśurāmera kaila vandana

durvaśane—at Durvaśana; *raghunāthe*—Lord Rāmacandra; *kaila daraśana*—Śrī Caitanya Mahāprabhu visited; *mahendra-śaile*—on Mahendra-śaila; *paraśu-rāmera*—to Lord Paraśurāma; *kaila vandana*—offered prayers.

TRANSLATION

At Durvaśana Śrī Caitanya Mahāprabhu visited the temple of Lord Rāmacandra, and on the hill known as Mahendra-śaila He saw Lord Paraśurāma.

PURPORT

In Durvaśana, or Darbhaśayana (now known as Tiruppullani), which is seven miles east of Ramnad, there is a temple of Lord Rāmacandra. The hill known as Mahendra-śaila is near Tirunelveli, and at the end of this hill is a city known as Tiruchendur. West of Mahendra-śaila is the territory of Tribāṅkura. There is mention of Mahendra-śaila in the *Rāmāyaṇa.*

TEXT 199

সেতুবন্ধে আসি' কৈল ধনুস্তীর্থে স্নান ।
রামেশ্বর দেখি' তাহাঁ করিল বিশ্রাম ॥ ১৯৯ ॥

setubandhe āsi' kaila dhanus-tīrthe snāna
rāmeśvara dekhi' tāhāṅ karila viśrāma

setubandhe āsi'—coming to Setubandha; *kaila*—did; *dhanuḥ-tīrthe snāna*—bathing at the holy place known as Dhanus-tīrtha; *rāmeśvara dekhi'*—visiting the holy place Rāmeśvara; *tāhāṅ*—there; *karila viśrāma*—took rest.

TRANSLATION

Śrī Caitanya Mahāprabhu then went to Setubandha [Rāmeśvara], where He took His bath at the place called Dhanus-tīrtha. From there He visited the Rāmeśvara temple and then took rest.

PURPORT

The path from Mandapam through the ocean to the island known as Pambam consists partly of sand and partly of water. The island of Pambam is about seventeen miles long and six miles wide. On this island, four miles north of Pambam Harbor, is Setubandha, where the temple of Rāmeśvara is located. This is a temple of Lord Śiva, and the name Rāmeśvara indicates that he is a great personality whose worshipable Deity is Lord Rāma. Thus the Lord Śiva found in the temple of Rāmeśvara is a great devotee of Lord Rāmacandra. It is said, *devī-pattanam ārabhya gaccheyuḥ setu-bandhanam:* "After visiting the temple of the goddess Durgā, one should go to the temple of Rāmeśvara."

In this area there are twenty-four different holy places, one of which is Dhanus-tīrtha, located about twelve miles southeast of Rāmeśvara. It is near the last station of the South Indian Railway, a station called Ramnad. It is said that here, on the request of Rāvaṇa's younger brother Vibhīṣaṇa, Lord Rāmacandra destroyed the bridge to Laṅkā with His bow while returning to His capital. It is also said that one who visits Dhanus-tīrtha is liberated from the cycle of birth and death, and that one who bathes there gets all the fruitive results of performing the *yajña* known as Agniṣṭoma.

TEXT 200

বিপ্র-সভায় শুনে তাঁহা কূর্ম-পুরাণ।
তার মধ্যে আইলা পতিব্রতা-উপাখ্যান ॥ ২০০ ॥

vipra-sabhāya śune tāṅhā kūrma-purāṇa
tāra madhye āilā pativratā-upākhyāna

vipra-sabhāya—among the assembly of *brāhmaṇas; śune*—hears; *tāṅhā*—there; *kūrma-purāṇa*—the *Kūrma Purāṇa; tāra madhye*—within that book; *āilā*—there was; *pati-vratā*—of the chaste woman; *upākhyāna*—narration.

TRANSLATION

There, among the brāhmaṇas, Śrī Caitanya Mahāprabhu listened to the Kūrma Purāṇa, wherein is mentioned the chaste woman's narration.

PURPORT

Śrīla Bhaktisiddhānta Sarasvatī Ṭhākura remarks that only two *khaṇḍas* of the *Kūrma Purāṇa* are now available, namely the *Pūrva-khaṇḍa* and *Uttara-khaṇḍa.* Sometimes it is said that the *Kūrma Purāṇa* contains six thousand verses, but according to *Śrīmad-Bhāgavatam* the original *Kūrma Purāṇa* contains seventeen thousand verses. It is considered the fifteenth of the eighteen *Mahā-purāṇas.*

TEXT 201

পতিব্রতা-শিরোমণি জনক-নন্দিনী ।
জগতের মাতা সীতা — রামের গৃহিণী ॥ ২০১ ॥

pativratā-śiromaṇi janaka-nandinī
jagatera mātā sītā — rāmera gṛhiṇī

pati-vratā — chaste woman; *śiromaṇi* — the topmost; *janaka-nandinī* — is the daughter of King Janaka; *jagatera* — of all the three worlds; *mātā* — the mother; *sītā* — Sītā; *rāmera* — of Lord Rāmacandra; *gṛhiṇī* — wife.

TRANSLATION

Śrīmatī Sītādevī is the mother of the three worlds and the wife of Lord Rāmacandra. Among chaste women she is supreme, and she is the daughter of King Janaka.

TEXT 202

রাবণ দেখিয়া সীতা লৈল অগ্নির শরণ ।
রাবণ হৈতে অগ্নি কৈল সীতাকে আবরণ ॥ ২০২ ॥

rāvaṇa dekhiyā sītā laila agnira śaraṇa
rāvaṇa haite agni kaila sītāke āvaraṇa

rāvaṇa dekhiyā — after seeing Rāvaṇa; *sītā* — mother Sītā; *laila* — took; *agnira* — of fire; *śaraṇa* — shelter; *rāvaṇa* — Rāvaṇa; *haite* — from; *agni* — fire; *kaila* — did; *sītāke* — unto mother Sītā; *āvaraṇa* — covering.

TRANSLATION

When Rāvaṇa came to kidnap mother Sītā and she saw him, she took shelter of the fire-god, Agni. The fire-god covered the body of mother Sītā, and in this way she was protected from the hands of Rāvaṇa.

TEXT 203

'মায়াসীতা'রাবণ নিল, শুনিলা আখ্যানে।
শুনি' মহাপ্রভু হইল আনন্দিত মনে ॥ ২০৩ ॥

'māyā-sītā' rāvaṇa nila, śunilā ākhyāne
śuni' mahāprabhu haila ānandita mane

māyā-sītā—false, illusory Sītā; *rāvaṇa*—the demon Rāvaṇa; *nila*—took; *śunilā*—heard; *ākhyāne*—in the narration of the *Kūrma Purāṇa; śuni'*—hearing this; *mahāprabhu*—Lord Śrī Caitanya Mahāprabhu; *haila*—became; *ānandita*—very happy; *mane*—within the mind.

TRANSLATION

Upon hearing from the Kūrma Purāṇa how Rāvaṇa had kidnapped a false form of mother Sītā, Śrī Caitanya Mahāprabhu became very satisfied.

TEXT 204

সীতা লঞা রাখিলেন পার্বতীর স্থানে।
'মায়াসীতা' দিয়া অগ্নি বঞ্চিলা রাবণে ॥ ২০৪ ॥

sītā lañā rākhilena pārvatīra sthāne
'māyā-sītā' diyā agni vañcilā rāvaṇe

sītā lañā—taking away mother Sītā; *rākhilena*—kept; *pārvatīra sthāne*—with mother Pārvatī, or goddess Durgā; *māyā-sītā*—the false, illusory form of Sītā; *diyā*—delivering; *agni*—fire-god; *vañcilā*—cheated; *rāvaṇe*—the demon Rāvaṇa.

TRANSLATION

The fire-god, Agni, took away the real Sītā and brought her to the place of Pārvatī, goddess Durgā. An illusory form of mother Sītā was then delivered to Rāvaṇa, and in this way Rāvaṇa was cheated.

TEXT 205

রঘুনাথ আসি' যবে রাবণে মারিল।
অগ্নি-পরীক্ষা দিতে যবে সীতারে আনিল ॥ ২০৫ ॥

raghunātha āsi' yabe rāvaṇe mārila
agni-parīkṣā dite yabe sītāre ānila

raghunātha—Lord Rāmacandra; *āsi'*—coming; *yabe*—when; *rāvaṇe*—Rāvaṇa; *mārila*—killed; *agni-parīkṣā*—test by fire; *dite*—to give; *yabe*—when; *sītāre*—Sītā; *ānila*—brought.

TRANSLATION

After Rāvaṇa was killed by Lord Rāmacandra, Sītādevī was brought before the fire and tested.

TEXT 206

তবে মায়াসীতা অগ্নি করি অন্তর্ধান।
সত্য-সীতা আনি' দিল রাম-বিদ্যমান॥ ২০৬॥

tabe māyā-sītā agni kari antardhāna
satya-sītā āni' dila rāma-vidyamāna

tabe—at that time; *māyā-sītā*—the illusory form of Sītā; *agni*—the fire-god; *kari*—doing; *antardhāna*—disappearing; *satya-sītā*—real Sītā; *āni'*—bringing; *dila*—delivered; *rāma*—of Rāmacandra; *vidyamāna*—in the presence.

TRANSLATION

When the illusory Sītā was brought before the fire by Lord Rāmacandra, the fire-god made the illusory form disappear and delivered the real Sītā to Lord Rāmacandra.

TEXT 207

শুনিঞা প্রভুর আনন্দিত হৈল মন।
রামদাস-বিপ্রের কথা হইল স্মরণ॥ ২০৭॥

śuniñā prabhura ānandita haila mana
rāmadāsa-viprera kathā ha-ila smaraṇa

śuniñā—hearing; *prabhura*—of Śrī Caitanya Mahāprabhu; *ānandita*—very pleased; *haila*—became; *mana*—the mind;

rāmadāsa-viprera—of the *brāhmaṇa* known as Rāmadāsa; *kathā*—words; *ha-ila smaraṇa*—He remembered.

TRANSLATION

When Śrī Caitanya Mahāprabhu heard this story, He was very pleased, and He remembered the words of Rāmadāsa Vipra.

TEXT 208

এ-সব সিদ্ধান্ত শুনি' প্রভুর আনন্দ হৈল ।
ব্রাহ্মণের স্থানে মাগি' সেই পত্র নিল ॥ ২০৮ ॥

e-saba siddhānta śuni' prabhura ānanda haila
brāhmaṇera sthāne māgi' sei patra nila

e-saba siddhānta—all these conclusive statements; *śuni'*—hearing; *prabhura*—of Lord Śrī Caitanya Mahāprabhu; *ānanda*—happiness; *haila*—there was; *brāhmaṇera sthāne*—from the *brāhmaṇas; māgi'*—asking; *sei*—those; *patra*—leaves; *nila*—took.

TRANSLATION

Indeed, when Śrī Caitanya Mahāprabhu heard these conclusive statements from the Kūrma Purāṇa, He felt great happiness. After asking the brāhmaṇas' permission, He took possession of the manuscript leaves of the Kūrma Purāṇa.

TEXT 209

নূতন পত্র লেখাঞা পুস্তকে দেওয়াইল ।
প্রতীতি লাগি' পুরাতন পত্র মাগি' নিল ॥ ২০৯ ॥

nūtana patra lekhāñā pustake deoyāila
pratīti lāgi' purātana patra māgi' nila

nūtana—new; *patra*—leaves; *lekhāñā*—getting written; *pustake*—the book; *deoyāila*—He gave; *pratīti lāgi'*—for direct evidence; *purātana*—the old; *patra*—leaves; *māgi'*—requesting; *nila*—He took.

TRANSLATION

Since the Kūrma Purāṇa was very old, the manuscript was also very old. Śrī Caitanya Mahāprabhu took possession of the original leaves in order to have direct evidence. The text was copied onto new leaves in order that the Purāṇa be replaced.

TEXT 210

পত্র লঞা পুনঃ দক্ষিণ-মথুরা আইলা ।
রামদাস বিপ্রে সেই পত্র আনি দিলা ॥ ২১০ ॥

patra lañā punaḥ dakṣiṇa-mathurā āilā
rāmadāsa vipre sei patra āni dilā

patra lañā—taking those leaves; *punaḥ*—again; *dakṣiṇa-mathurā*—to southern Mathurā; *āilā*—came; *rāmadāsa vipre*—unto the *brāhmaṇa* known as Rāmadāsa; *sei patra*—those leaves; *āni*—bringing back; *dilā*—delivered.

TRANSLATION

Śrī Caitanya Mahāprabhu then returned to southern Mathurā [Madurai] and delivered the original manuscript of the Kūrma Purāṇa to Rāmadāsa Vipra.

TEXTS 211–212

সীতয়ারাধিতো বহ্নিশ্ছায়া-সীতামজীজনৎ ।
তাং জহার দশগ্রীবঃ সীতা বহ্নিপুরং গতা ॥ ২১১ ॥
পরীক্ষাংসময়ে বহ্নিং ছায়া-সীতা বিবেশ সা ।
বহ্নিঃ সীতাং সমানীয় তৎপুরস্তাদনীনয়ৎ ॥ ২১২ ॥

sītayārādhito vahniś
chāyā-sītām ajījanat
tāṁ jahāra daśa-grīvaḥ
sītā vahni-puraṁ gatā

parīkṣā-samaye vahniṁ
chāyā-sītā viveśa sā
vahniḥ sītāṁ samānīya
tat-purastād anīnayat

sītayā—by mother Sītā; *ārādhitaḥ*—being called for; *vahniḥ*—the fire-god; *chāyā-sītām*—the illusory form of mother Sītā; *ajījanat*—created; *tām*—her; *jahāra*—kidnapped; *daśa-grīvaḥ*—the ten-faced Rāvaṇa; *sītā*—mother Sītā; *vahni-puram*—to the abode of the fire-god; *gatā*—departed; *parīkṣā-samaye*—at the time of testing; *vahnim*—the fire; *chāyā-sītā*—the illusory form of Sītā; *viveśa*—entered; *sā*—she; *vahniḥ*—the fire-god; *sītām*—the original mother Sītā; *samānīya*—bringing back; *tat-purastāt*—in His presence; *anīnayat*—brought back.

TRANSLATION

"When he was petitioned by mother Sītā, the fire-god, Agni, brought forth an illusory form of Sītā, and Rāvaṇa, who had ten heads, kidnapped the false Sītā. The original Sītā then went to the abode of the fire-god. When Lord Rāmacandra tested the body of Sītā, it was the false, illusory Sītā that entered the fire. At that time the fire-god brought the original Sītā from his abode and delivered her to Lord Rāmacandra."

PURPORT

These two verses are taken from the *Kūrma Purāṇa.*

TEXT 213

পত্র পাঞা বিপ্রের হৈল আনন্দিত মন ।
প্রভুর চরণে ধরি' করয়ে ক্রন্দন ॥ ২১৩ ॥

patra pāñā viprera haila ānandita mana
prabhura caraṇe dhari' karaye krandana

patra pāñā—getting the leaves; *viprera*—of the *brāhmaṇa; haila*—there was; *ānandita*—pleased; *mana*—mind; *prabhura caraṇe*—the lotus feet of Lord Śrī Caitanya Mahāprabhu; *dhari'*—taking; *karaye*—does; *krandana*—crying.

TRANSLATION

Rāmadāsa Vipra was very pleased to receive the original leaf manuscript of the Kūrma Purāṇa, and he immediately fell down before the lotus feet of Śrī Caitanya Mahāprabhu and began to cry.

TEXT 214

বিপ্র কহে, — তুমি সাক্ষাৎ শ্রীরঘুনন্দন ।
সন্ন্যাসীর বেষে মোরে দিলা দরশন ॥ ২১৪ ॥

vipra kahe, — tumi sākṣāt śrī-raghunandana
sannyāsīra veṣe more dilā daraśana

vipra kahe — the *brāhmaṇa* said; *tumi* — You; *sākṣāt* — directly; *śrī-raghunandana* — Lord Śrī Rāmacandra; *sannyāsīra veṣe* — in the dress of a mendicant; *more* — unto me; *dilā* — You gave; *daraśana* — audience.

TRANSLATION

After receiving the manuscript, the brāhmaṇa, being very pleased, said, "Sir, You are Lord Rāmacandra Himself and have come in the dress of a sannyāsī to give me audience.

TEXT 215

মহা-দুঃখ হইতে মোরে করিলা নিস্তার ।
আজি মোর ঘরে ভিক্ষা কর অঙ্গীকার ॥ ২১৫ ॥

mahā-duḥkha ha-ite more karilā nistāra
āji mora ghare bhikṣā kara aṅgīkāra

mahā-duḥkha — great unhappiness; *ha-ite* — from; *more* — me; *karilā nistāra* — You delivered; *āji* — today; *mora* — my; *ghare* — at home; *bhikṣā* — lunch; *kara* — do; *aṅgīkāra* — accept.

TRANSLATION

"My dear Sir, You have delivered me from a very unhappy condition. I request that You take Your lunch at my place. Please accept this invitation.

TEXT 216

মনোদুঃখে ভাল ভিক্ষা না দিল সেই দিনে ।
মোর ভাগ্যে পুনরপি পাইলুঁ দরশনে ॥ ২১৬ ॥

mano-duḥkhe bhāla bhikṣā nā dila sei dine
mora bhāgye punarapi pāiluṅ daraśane

mano-duḥkhe—out of great mental distress; *bhāla bhikṣā*—good lunch; *nā dila*—could not give You; *sei dine*—that day; *mora bhāgye*—because of my good fortune; *punarapi*—again; *pāiluṅ*—I have gotten; *daraśane*—visit.

TRANSLATION

"Due to my mental distress I could not give You a very nice lunch the other day. Now, by good fortune, You have come again to my home."

TEXT 217

এত বলি' সেই বিপ্র সুখে পাক কৈল।
উত্তম প্রকারে প্রভুকে ভিক্ষা করাইল ॥ ২১৭ ॥

eta bali' sei vipra sukhe pāka kaila
uttama prakāre prabhuke bhikṣā karāila

eta bali'—saying this; *sei vipra*—that *brāhmaṇa; sukhe*—in great happiness; *pāka kaila*—cooked; *uttama prakāre*—very nicely; *prabhuke*—unto Lord Śrī Caitanya Mahāprabhu; *bhikṣā*—lunch; *karāila*—gave.

TRANSLATION

Saying this, the brāhmaṇa very happily cooked food, and a first-class dinner was offered to Śrī Caitanya Mahāprabhu.

TEXT 218

সেই রাত্রি তাহাঁ রহি' তাঁরে কৃপা করি'।
পাণ্ড্যদেশে তাম্রপর্ণী গেলা গৌরহরি ॥ ২১৮ ॥

sei rātri tāhāṅ rahi' tāṅre kṛpā kari'
pāṇḍya-deśe tāmraparṇī gelā gaurahari

sei rātri—that night; *tāhāṅ*—there; *rahi'*—staying; *tāṅre*—unto the *brāhmaṇa; kṛpā kari'*—showing mercy; *pāṇḍya-deśe*—in the country known as Pāṇḍya-deśa; *tāmraparṇī*—to the river named Tāmraparṇī; *gelā*—went; *gaurahari*—Lord Śrī Caitanya Mahāprabhu.

TRANSLATION

Śrī Caitanya Mahāprabhu passed that night in the house of the brāhmaṇa. Then, after showing him mercy, the Lord started toward the Tāmraparṇī River in Pāṇḍya-deśa.

PURPORT

Pāṇḍya-deśa is situated in the southern part of India known as Kerala and Cola. In all these areas there were many kings with the title Pāṇḍya who ruled over Madurai and Rāmeśvara. In the *Rāmāyaṇa* the Tāmraparṇī River is mentioned. The Tāmraparṇī, also known as the Puruṇai, flows through Tirunelveli before entering the Bay of Bengal. The Tāmraparṇī River is also mentioned in *Śrīmad-Bhāgavatam* (11.5.39).

TEXT 219

তাম্রপর্ণী স্নান করি' তাম্রপর্ণী-তীরে।
নয় ত্রিপতি দেখি' বুলে কুতূহলে ॥ ২১৯ ॥

tāmraparṇī snāna kari' tāmraparṇī-tīre
naya tripati dekhi' bule kutūhale

tāmraparṇī—in the Tāmraparṇī River; *snāna kari'*—taking a bath; *tāmraparṇī-tīre*—on the bank of the Tāmraparṇī River; *naya tripati*—the place named Naya-tripati; *dekhi'*—after seeing; *bule*—wandered on; *kutūhale*—in great curiosity.

TRANSLATION

There were nine temples of Lord Viṣṇu at Naya-tripati, on the bank of the river Tāmraparṇī, and after bathing in the river, Lord Caitanya Mahāprabhu saw the Deities with great curiosity and wandered on.

PURPORT

The nine Viṣṇu temples known as Naya-tripati (Nava-tirupati) are situated in and around Ālvār Tirunagarai. This is a town about seventeen miles southeast of Tirunelveli. All the Deities of the temples assemble together during a yearly festival in the town.

TEXT 220

চিয়ড়তলা তীর্থে দেখি' শ্রীরাম-লক্ষ্মণ।
তিলকাঞ্চী আসি' কৈল শিব দরশন ॥ ২২০ ॥

ciyaḍatalā tīrthe dekhi' śrī-rāma-lakṣmaṇa
tila-kāñcī āsi' kaila śiva daraśana

ciyaḍatalā—named Ciyaḍatalā; *tīrthe*—at the holy place; *dekhi'*—seeing; *śrī-rāma-lakṣmaṇa*—the Deity of Lord Rāma and Lakṣmaṇa; *tila-kāñcī*—to Tila-kāñcī; *āsi'*—coming; *kaila*—did; *śiva daraśana*—visiting the temple of Lord Śiva.

TRANSLATION

After this, Śrī Caitanya Mahāprabhu went to a holy place known as Ciyaḍatalā, where He saw the Deities of the two brothers Lord Rāmacandra and Lakṣmaṇa. He then proceeded to Tila-kāñcī, where He saw the temple of Lord Śiva.

PURPORT

Ciyaḍatalā is sometimes known as Cheratalā. It is near the city of Kaila, and there is a temple there dedicated to Lord Śrī Rāmacandra and His brother Lakṣmaṇa. Tila-kāñcī (Tenkasi) is about thirty miles northeast of the city of Tirunelveli.

TEXT 221

গজেন্দ্রমোক্ষণ-তীর্থে দেখি বিষ্ণুমূর্তি।
পানাগড়ি-তীর্থে আসি' দেখিল সীতাপতি ॥ ২২১ ॥

gajendra-mokṣaṇa-tīrthe dekhi viṣṇu-mūrti
pānāgaḍi-tīrthe āsi' dekhila sītāpati

gajendra-mokṣaṇa-tīrthe—at the holy place named Gajendra-mokṣaṇa; *dekhi*—seeing; *viṣṇu-mūrti*—the Deity of Lord Viṣṇu;

pānāgaḍi-tīrthe—to the holy place Pānāgaḍi; *āsi'*—coming; *dekhila*—saw; *sītā-pati*—Lord Śrī Rāmacandra and Sītādevī.

TRANSLATION

Lord Śrī Caitanya Mahāprabhu then visited the holy place named Gajendra-mokṣaṇa, where He went to a temple of Lord Viṣṇu. He then came to Pānāgaḍi, a holy place where He saw the Deities of Lord Rāmacandra and Sītā.

PURPORT

The Gajendra-mokṣaṇa temple is sometimes mistaken for a temple of Lord Śiva. It is about two miles south of the city of Kaivera (Nagercoil). Actually the Deity is not of Lord Śiva but of Viṣṇu.

Pānāgaḍi (Pannakudi) is about thirty miles south of Tirunelveli. Formerly the temple there contained the Deity of Śrī Rāmacandra, but later the devotees of Lord Śiva replaced Lord Rāmacandra with a deity of Lord Śiva named Rāmeśvara or Rāma-liṅga Śiva.

TEXT 222

চাম্‌তাপুরে আসি' দেখি' শ্রীরাম-লক্ষ্মণ ।
শ্রীবৈকুণ্ঠে আসি' কৈল বিষ্ণু দরশন ॥ ২২২ ॥

cāmtāpure āsi' dekhi' śrī-rāma-lakṣmaṇa
śrī-vaikuṇṭhe āsi' kaila viṣṇu daraśana

cāmtāpure—to Cāmtāpura; *āsi'*—coming; *dekhi'*—seeing; *śrī-rāma-lakṣmaṇa*—Lord Rāmacandra and Lakṣmaṇa; *śrī-vaikuṇṭhe āsi'*—coming to Śrī Vaikuṇṭha; *kaila*—did; *viṣṇu daraśana*—seeing the temple of Lord Viṣṇu.

TRANSLATION

Later the Lord went to Cāmtāpura, where He saw the Deities of Lord Rāmacandra and Lakṣmaṇa. He then went to Śrī Vaikuṇṭha and saw the temple of Lord Viṣṇu there.

PURPORT

Cāmtāpura (sometimes called Chengannur) is located in the state of Kerala. A temple of Lord Rāmacandra and Lakṣmaṇa is located there. Śrī Vaikuṇṭha—about four miles north of Ālvār Tirunagarai and sixteen miles southeast of Tirunelveli—is situated on the bank of the Tāmraparṇī River.

TEXT 223

মলয়-পর্বতে কৈল অগস্ত্য-বন্দন ।
কন্যাকুমারী তাহাঁ কৈল দরশন ॥ ২২৩ ॥

malaya-parvate kaila agastya-vandana
kanyā-kumārī tāhāṅ kaila daraśana

malaya-parvate—in the Malaya Hills; *kaila*—did; *agastya-vandana*—obeisances to Agastya Muni; *kanyā-kumārī*—Kanyā-kumārī; *tāhāṅ*—there; *kaila daraśana*—visited.

TRANSLATION

Śrī Caitanya Mahāprabhu then went to Malaya-parvata and offered prayers to Agastya Muni. He then visited Kanyā-kumārī [Cape Comorin].

PURPORT

The range of mountains in South India beginning at Kerala and extending to Cape Comorin is called Malaya-parvata. Concerning Agastya, there are four opinions: (1) There is a temple of Agastya Muni in the village of Agastyampallī, in the district of Tanjore. (2) There is a temple of Lord Skanda on a hill known as Śiva-giri, and this temple is said to have been established by Agastya Muni. (3) Some say that the hill near Cape Comorin known as Paṭhiyā served as Agastya Muni's residence. (4) There is a place known as Agastya-malaya, which is a range of hills on both sides of the Tāmraparṇī River. Cape Comorin itself is also known as Kanyā-kumārī.

TEXT 224

আম্‌লিতলায় দেখি' শ্রীরাম গৌরহরি ।
মল্লার-দেশেতে আইলা যথা ভট্টথারি ॥ ২২৪ ॥

āmlitalāya dekhi' śrī-rāma gaurahari
mallāra-deśete āilā yathā bhaṭṭathāri

āmlitalāya—at Āmlitalā; *dekhi'*—seeing; *śrī-rāma*—the Deity of Rāmacandra; *gaurahari*—Śrī Caitanya Mahāprabhu; *mallāra-deśete*—to Mallāra-deśa; *āilā*—came; *yathā*—where; *bhaṭṭathāri*—the Bhaṭṭathāri community.

TRANSLATION

After visiting Kanyā-kumārī, Śrī Caitanya Mahāprabhu came to Āmlitalā, where He saw the Deity of Śrī Rāmacandra. Thereafter He went to a place known as Mallāra-deśa, where a community of Bhaṭṭathāris lived.

PURPORT

North of Mallāra-deśa is South Kanara. To the east are Coorg and Mysore, to the south is Cochin, and to the west is the Arabian Sea. As far as the Bhaṭṭathāris are concerned, they are a nomadic community. They camp wherever they like and have no fixed place of residence. Outwardly they take up the dress of *sannyāsīs,* but their real business is stealing and cheating. They allure others to supply women for their camp, and they cheat many women and keep them within their community. In this way they increase their population. In Bengal also there is a similar community. Actually, all over the world there are nomadic communities whose business is simply to allure, cheat and steal innocent women.

TEXT 225

তমাল-কার্তিক দেখি' আইল বেতাপনি ।
রঘুনাথ দেখি' তাহাঁ বঞ্চিলা রজনী ॥ ২২৫ ॥

tamāla-kārtika dekhi' āila vetāpani
raghunātha dekhi' tāhāṅ vañcilā rajanī

tamāla-kārtika—the place named Tamāla-kārtika; *dekhi'*—seeing; *āila*—came; *vetāpani*—to Vetāpani; *raghunātha dekhi'*—seeing the temple of Lord Rāmacandra; *tāhāṅ*—there; *vañcilā rajanī*—passed the night.

TRANSLATION

After visiting Mallāra-deśa, Śrī Caitanya Mahāprabhu went to Tamāla-kārtika and then to Vetāpani. There He saw the temple of Raghunātha, Lord Rāmacandra, and passed the night.

PURPORT

Tamāla-kārtika is forty-four miles south of Tirunelveli and two miles south of Aramavallī Mountain. It is located within the jurisdiction of Tovalai. At Tamāla-kārtika is a temple of Subrahmaṇya, or Lord Kārtika, the son of Lord Śiva.

Vetāpani, or Vātāpāṇī, is north of Kaila in the Tamil Nadu state. It is also known as Bhūtapaṇḍi and is within the jurisdiction of the Tobala district. It is understood that formerly there was a Deity of Lord Rāmacandra there. Later the Deity was replaced with a deity of Lord Śiva known as Rāmeśvara or Bhūtanātha.

TEXT 226

গোসাঞিঞর সঙ্গে রহে কৃষ্ণদাস ব্রাহ্মণ ।
ভট্টথারি-সহ তাহাঁ হৈল দরশন ॥ ২২৬ ॥

gosāñira saṅge rahe kṛṣṇadāsa brāhmaṇa
bhaṭṭathāri-saha tāhāṅ haila daraśana

gosāñira—the Lord; *saṅge*—with; *rahe*—there was; *kṛṣṇadāsa brāhmaṇa*—a *brāhmaṇa* servant named Kṛṣṇadāsa; *bhaṭṭathāri-saha*—with the Bhaṭṭathāris; *tāhāṅ*—there; *haila*—there was; *daraśana*—a meeting.

TRANSLATION

Śrī Caitanya Mahāprabhu was accompanied by His servant, Kṛṣṇadāsa. He was a brāhmaṇa, but he met with the Bhaṭṭathāris there.

TEXT 227

স্ত্রীধন দেখাঞা তাঁর লোভ জন্মাইল ।
আর্য সরল বিপ্রের বুদ্ধিনাশ কৈল ॥ ২২৭ ॥

strī-dhana dekhāñā tāṅra lobha janmāila
ārya sarala viprera buddhi-nāśa kaila

strī-dhana—women; *dekhāñā*—showing; *tāṅra*—his; *lobha*—attraction; *janmāila*—they created; *ārya*—gentleman; *sarala*—simple; *viprera*—of the *brāhmaṇa; buddhi-nāśa*—loss of intelligence; *kaila*—they made.

TRANSLATION

With women the Bhaṭṭathāris allured the brāhmaṇa Kṛṣṇadāsa, who was simple and gentle. By virtue of their bad association, they polluted his intelligence.

TEXT 228

প্রাতে উঠি' আইলা বিপ্র ভট্টথারি-ঘরে ।
তাহার উদ্দেশে প্রভু আইলা সত্বরে ॥ ২২৮ ॥

prāte uṭhi' āilā vipra bhaṭṭathāri-ghare
tāhāra uddeśe prabhu āilā satvare

prāte—in the morning; *uṭhi'*—rising from bed; *āilā*—came; *vipra*—the *brāhmaṇa* Kṛṣṇadāsa; *bhaṭṭathāri-ghare*—to the place of the Bhaṭṭathāris; *tāhāra uddeśe*—for him; *prabhu*—Lord Caitanya Mahāprabhu; *āilā*—came; *satvare*—very soon.

TRANSLATION

Allured by the Bhaṭṭathāris, Kṛṣṇadāsa went to their place early in the morning. The Lord also went there very quickly just to find him.

TEXT 229

আসিয়া কহেন সব ভট্টথারিগণে ।
আমার ব্রাহ্মণ তুমি রাখ কি কারণে ॥ ২২৯ ॥

āsiyā kahena saba bhaṭṭathāri-gaṇe
āmāra brāhmaṇa tumi rākha ki kāraṇe

āsiyā—coming; *kahena*—He said; *saba*—all; *bhaṭṭathāri-gaṇe*—to the Bhaṭṭathāris; *āmāra*—My; *brāhmaṇa*—*brāhmaṇa* assistant; *tumi*—you; *rākha*—are keeping; *ki*—for what; *kāraṇe*—reason.

TRANSLATION

Upon reaching their community, Śrī Caitanya Mahāprabhu asked the Bhaṭṭathāris, "Why are you keeping My brāhmaṇa assistant?

TEXT 230

আমিহ সন্ন্যাসী দেখ, তুমিহ সন্ন্যাসী।
মোরে দুঃখ দেহ, — তোমার 'ন্যায়' নাহি বাসি' ॥ ২৩০ ॥

āmiha sannyāsī dekha, tumiha sannyāsī
more duḥkha deha, — tomāra 'nyāya' nāhi vāsi

āmiha—I; *sannyāsī*—in the renounced order of life; *dekha*—you see; *tumiha*—you; *sannyāsī*—in the renounced order of life; *more*—unto Me; *duḥkha*—pains; *deha*—you give; *tomāra*—your; *nyāya*—logic; *nāhi vāsi*—I do not find.

TRANSLATION

"I am in the renounced order of life, and so are you. Yet you are purposefully giving Me pain, and I do not see any good logic in this."

TEXT 231

শুনি' সব ভট্টথারি উঠে অস্ত্র লঞা।
মারিবারে আইল সবে চারিদিকে ধাঞা ॥ ২৩১ ॥

śuni' saba bhaṭṭathāri uṭhe astra lañā
māribāre āila sabe cāri-dike dhāñā

śuni'—hearing; *saba*—all; *bhaṭṭathāri*—nomads; *uṭhe*—rise up; *astra*—weapons; *lañā*—taking; *māribāre*—to kill; *āila*—came; *sabe*—all; *cāri-dike*—all around; *dhāñā*—running.

TRANSLATION

Upon hearing Śrī Caitanya Mahāprabhu, all the Bhaṭṭathāris came running from all sides with weapons in their hands, desiring to hurt the Lord.

TEXT 232

তার অস্ত্র তার অঙ্গে পড়ে হাত হৈতে ।
খণ্ড খণ্ড হৈল ভট্টথারি পলায় চারি ভিতে ॥ ২৩২ ॥

tāra astra tāra aṅge paḍe hāta haite
khaṇḍa khaṇḍa haila bhaṭṭathāri palāya cāri bhite

tāra astra—their weapons; *tāra aṅge*—on their bodies; *paḍe*—fall; *hāta haite*—from their hands; *khaṇḍa khaṇḍa*—cut into pieces; *haila*—became; *bhaṭṭathāri*—the nomads; *palāya*—run away; *cāri bhite*—in the four directions.

TRANSLATION

However, their weapons fell from their hands and struck their own bodies. When some of the Bhaṭṭathāris were thus cut to pieces, the others ran away in the four directions.

TEXT 233

ভট্টথারি-ঘরে মহা উঠিল ক্রন্দন ।
কেশে ধরি' বিপ্রে লঞা করিল গমন ॥ ২৩৩ ॥

bhaṭṭathāri-ghare mahā uṭhila krandana
keśe dhari' vipre lañā karila gamana

bhaṭṭathāri-ghare—at the home of the Bhaṭṭathāris; *mahā*—great; *uṭhila*—there arose; *krandana*—crying; *keśe dhari'*—catching by the hair; *vipre*—the *brāhmaṇa* Kṛṣṇadāsa; *lañā*—taking; *karila*—did; *gamana*—departure.

TRANSLATION

While there was much roaring and crying at the Bhaṭṭathāri community, Śrī Caitanya Mahāprabhu grabbed Kṛṣṇadāsa by the hair and took him away.

TEXT 234

সেই দিন চলি' আইলা পয়স্বিনী-তীরে ।
স্নান করি' গেলা আদিকেশব-মন্দিরে ॥ ২৩৪ ॥

sei dina cali' āilā payasvinī-tīre
snāna kari' gelā ādi-keśava-mandire

sei dina—on that very day; *cali'*—walking; *āilā*—came; *payasvinī-tīre*—to the bank of the Payasvinī River; *snāna kari'*—bathing; *gelā*—went; *ādi-keśava-mandire*—to the temple of Ādi-keśava.

TRANSLATION

That very night, Śrī Caitanya Mahāprabhu and His assistant Kṛṣṇadāsa arrived at the bank of the Payasvinī River. They took their bath and then went to see the temple of Ādi-keśava.

TEXT 235

কেশব দেখিয়া প্রেমে আবিষ্ট হৈলা ।
নতি, স্তুতি, নৃত্য, গীত, বহুত করিলা ॥ ২৩৫ ॥

keśava dekhiyā preme āviṣṭa hailā
nati, stuti, nṛtya, gīta, bahuta karilā

keśava dekhiyā—after seeing the Deity of Lord Keśava; *preme*—in ecstasy; *āviṣṭa hailā*—became overwhelmed; *nati*—obeisances; *stuti*—prayer; *nṛtya*—dancing; *gīta*—chanting; *bahuta karilā*—performed in various ways.

TRANSLATION

When the Lord saw the Ādi-keśava temple, He was immediately overwhelmed with ecstasy. Offering various obeisances and prayers, He chanted and danced.

TEXT 236

প্রেম দেখি' লোকে হৈল মহা-চমৎকার ।
সর্বলোক কৈল প্রভুর পরম সৎকার ॥ ২৩৬ ॥

prema dekhi' loke haila mahā-camatkāra
sarva-loka kaila prabhura parama satkāra

prema dekhi'—seeing His ecstatic features; *loke*—people; *haila*—became; *mahā-camatkāra*—greatly astonished; *sarva-loka*—all people; *kaila*—did; *prabhura*—of Lord Śrī Caitanya Mahāprabhu; *parama satkāra*—great reception.

TRANSLATION

All the people there were greatly astonished to see the ecstatic pastimes of Śrī Caitanya Mahāprabhu. They all received the Lord very well.

TEXT 237

মহাভক্তগণসহ তাহাঁ গোষ্ঠী কৈল ।
'ব্রহ্মসংহিতাধ্যায়'-পুঁথি তাহাঁ পাইল ॥ ২৩৭ ॥

mahā-bhakta-gaṇa-saha tāhāṅ goṣṭhī kaila
'brahma-saṁhitādhyāya'-puṅthi tāhāṅ pāila

mahā-bhakta-gaṇa-saha—among highly advanced devotees; *tāhāṅ*—there; *goṣṭhī kaila*—discussed; *brahma-saṁhitā-adhyāya*—one chapter of the *Brahma-saṁhitā* ; *puṅthi*—scripture; *tāhāṅ*—there; *pāila*—found.

TRANSLATION

In the temple of Ādi-keśava, Śrī Caitanya Mahāprabhu discussed spiritual matters among highly advanced devotees. While there, He found a chapter of the Brahma-saṁhitā.

TEXT 238

পুঁথি পাঞা প্রভুর হৈল আনন্দ অপার ।
কম্পাশ্রু-স্বেদ-স্তম্ভ-পুলক বিকার ॥ ২৩৮ ॥

puṅthi pāñā prabhura haila ānanda apāra
kampāśru-sveda-stambha-pulaka vikāra

puṅthi pāñā—getting that scripture; *prabhura*—of Lord Śrī Caitanya Mahāprabhu; *haila*—there was; *ānanda*—happiness; *apāra*—unlimited; *kampa*—trembling; *aśru*—tears; *sveda*—perspiration; *stambha*—being stunned; *pulaka*—jubilation; *vikāra*—transformations.

TRANSLATION

Śrī Caitanya Mahāprabhu was greatly happy to find a chapter of that scripture, and symptoms of ecstatic transformation — trembling, tears, perspiration, trance and jubilation — were manifest in His body.

TEXTS 239–240

সিদ্ধান্ত-শাস্ত্র নাহি 'ব্রহ্মসংহিতা'র সম।
গোবিন্দমহিমা জ্ঞানের পরম কারণ ॥ ২৩৯ ॥
অল্পাক্ষরে কহে সিদ্ধান্ত অপার।
সকল-বৈষ্ণবশাস্ত্র-মধ্যে অতি সার ॥ ২৪০ ॥

siddhānta-śāstra nāhi 'brahma-saṁhitā'ra sama
govinda-mahimā jñānera parama kāraṇa

alpākṣare kahe siddhānta apāra
sakala-vaiṣṇava-śāstra-madhye ati sāra

siddhānta-śāstra—conclusive scripture; *nāhi*—there is not; *brahma-saṁhitāra sama*—like the scripture *Brahma-saṁhitā; govinda-mahimā*—of the glories of Lord Govinda; *jñānera*—of knowledge; *parama*—final; *kāraṇa*—cause; *alpa-akṣare*—briefly; *kahe*—expresses; *siddhānta*—conclusion; *apāra*—unlimited; *sakala*—all; *vaiṣṇava-śāstra*—devotional scriptures; *madhye*—among; *ati sāra*—very essential.

TRANSLATION

There is no scripture equal to the Brahma-saṁhitā as far as the final spiritual conclusion is concerned. Indeed, that scripture is the supreme revelation of the glories of Lord Govinda, for it reveals the topmost knowledge about Him. Since all conclusions are briefly presented in the Brahma-saṁhitā, it is essential among all the Vaiṣṇava literatures.

PURPORT

The *Brahma-saṁhitā* is a very important scripture. Śrī Caitanya Mahāprabhu acquired the Fifth Chapter from the Ādi-keśava temple. In that Fifth Chapter, the philosophical conclusion of *acintya-bhedābheda-tattva* (simultaneous oneness and difference) is presented. The chapter also presents methods of devotional service, the eighteen-syllable Vedic hymn, discourses on the soul, the Supersoul and fruitive activity, an explanation of Kāma-gāyatrī, *kāma-bīja* and the original Mahā-Viṣṇu, and a detailed description of the spiritual world, specifically Goloka Vṛndāvana. The *Brahma-saṁhitā* also explains the demigod Gaṇeśa, Garbhodakaśāyī Viṣṇu, the origin of the Gāyatrī *mantra,* the form of Govinda and His transcendental position and abode, the living entities, the highest goal, the goddess Durgā, the meaning of austerity, the five gross elements, love of Godhead, impersonal Brahman, the initiation of Lord Brahmā, and the vision of transcendental love enabling one to see the Lord. The steps of devotional service are also explained. The mind, *yoga-nidrā,* the goddess of fortune, devotional service in spontaneous ecstasy, incarnations beginning with Lord Rāmacandra, Deities, the conditioned soul and its duties, the truth about Lord Viṣṇu, prayers, Vedic hymns, Lord Śiva, the Vedic literature, personalism and impersonalism, good behavior, and many other subjects are also discussed. There is also a description of the sun and the universal form of the Lord. All these subjects are conclusively explained in a nutshell in the *Brahma-saṁhitā.*

TEXT 241

বহু যত্নে সেই পুঁথি নিল লেখাইয়া ।
'অনন্ত-পদ্মনাভ' আইলা হরষিত হঞা ॥ ২৪১ ॥

bahu yatne sei puṅthi nila lekhāiyā
'ananta padmanābha' āilā haraṣita hañā

bahu yatne—with great attention; *sei puṅthi*—that scripture; *nila*—took; *lekhāiyā*—having it copied; *ananta-padmanābha*—to Ananta Padmanābha; *āilā*—came; *haraṣita*—in great happiness; *hañā*—being.

TRANSLATION

Śrī Caitanya Mahāprabhu had the Brahma-saṁhitā copied, and then with great pleasure He went to a place known as Ananta Padmanābha.

PURPORT

Concerning Ananta Padmanābha, one should refer to *Madhya-līlā,* Chapter One, text 115.

TEXT 242

দিন-দুই পদ্মনাভের কৈল দরশন ।
আনন্দে দেখিতে আইলা শ্রীজনার্দন ॥ ২৪২ ॥

dina-dui padmanābhera kaila daraśana
ānande dekhite āilā śrī-janārdana

dina-dui—two days; *padmanābhera*—of the Deity known as Padmanābha; *kaila daraśana*—visited the temple; *ānande*—in great ecstasy; *dekhite*—to see; *āilā*—came; *śrī-janārdana*—to the temple of Śrī Janārdana.

TRANSLATION

Śrī Caitanya Mahāprabhu remained for two or three days at Ananta Padmanābha and visited the temple there. Then, in great ecstasy He went to see the temple of Śrī Janārdana.

PURPORT

The temple of Śrī Janārdana is situated twenty-six miles north of Trivandrum, near the Varkala railway station.

TEXT 243

দিন-দুই তাহাঁ করি' কীর্তন-নর্তন ।
পয়স্বিনী আসিয়া দেখে শঙ্কর নারায়ণ ॥ ২৪৩ ॥

dina-dui tāhāṅ kari' kīrtana-nartana
payasvinī āsiyā dekhe śaṅkara nārāyaṇa

dina-dui—two days; *tāhāṅ*—there; *kari'*—performing; *kīrtana-nartana*—chanting and dancing; *payasvinī āsiyā*—coming to the bank of the Payasvinī River; *dekhe*—sees; *śaṅkara nārāyaṇa*—the temple of Śaṅkara-nārāyaṇa.

TRANSLATION

Śrī Caitanya Mahāprabhu chanted and danced at Śrī Janārdana for two days. He then went to the bank of the Payasvinī River and visited the temple of Śaṅkara-nārāyaṇa.

TEXT 244

শৃঙ্গেরি-মঠে আইলা শঙ্করাচার্য-স্থানে ।
মৎস্য-তীর্থ দেখি' কৈল তুঙ্গভদ্রায় স্নানে ॥ ২৪৪ ॥

śṛṅgeri-maṭhe āilā śaṅkarācārya-sthāne
matsya-tīrtha dekhi' kaila tuṅgabhadrāya snāne

śṛṅgeri-maṭhe—to the Śṛṅgeri monastery; *āilā*—came; *śaṅkarācārya-sthāne*—at the place of Śaṅkarācārya; *matsya-tīrtha*—the holy place named Matsya-tīrtha; *dekhi'*—seeing; *kaila*—did; *tuṅgabhadrāya snāne*—bathing in the river Tuṅgabhadrā.

TRANSLATION

Then He saw the monastery known as Śṛṅgeri-maṭha, the abode of Ācārya Śaṅkara. He then visited Matsya-tīrtha, a place of pilgrimage, and took a bath in the river Tuṅgabhadrā.

PURPORT

The monastery known as Śṛṅgeri-maṭha is situated in the state of Karnataka, in the district of Chikmagalur. This monastery is located at the confluence of the rivers Tuṅga and Bhadrā, seven miles south of Harihara-pura. The real name of this place is Śṛṅga-giri or Śṛṅgavera-purī, and it is the headquarters of Śaṅkarācārya.

Śaṅkarācārya had four principal disciples, and he established four centers under their management. In North India at Badarikāśrama, the monastery named Jyotir-maṭha was established. At Puruṣottama, the

Bhogavardhana or Govardhana monastery was established. In Dvārakā, the Sāradā monastery was established. And the fourth monastery, established in South India, is known as Śṛṅgeri-maṭha. In the Śṛṅgeri-maṭha, the *sannyāsīs* assume the designations Sarasvatī, Bhāratī and Purī. They are all *ekadaṇḍi-sannyāsīs,* distinguished from the Vaiṣṇava *sannyāsīs,* who are known as *tridaṇḍi-sannyāsīs.* The Śṛṅgeri-maṭha is situated in South India in a portion of the country known as Āndhra, Draviḍa, Karṇāṭa and Kerala. The community is called Bhūrivāra, and the dynasty is called Bhūr-bhuvaḥ. The place is called Rāmeśvara, and the slogan is *ahaṁ brahmāsmi.* The Deity is Lord Varāha, and the energetic power is Kāmākṣī. The *ācārya* is Hastāmalaka, and the *brahmacārī* assistants of the *sannyāsīs* are known as Caitanya. The place of pilgrimage is called Tuṅgabhadrā, and the subject for Vedic study is the *Yajur Veda.*

The list of the disciplic succession from Śaṅkarācārya is available, and the names of the *ācāryas* and the dates of their accepting *sannyāsa,* according to the Śaka Era (or Śakābda), are as follows (for approximate Christian-era dates, add 78 years): Śaṅkarācārya, 622 Śaka; Sureśvarācārya, 630; Bodhanācārya, 680; Jñānadhanācārya, 768; Jñānottama-śivācārya, 827; Jñānagiri Ācārya, 871; Siṁhagiri Ācārya, 958; Īśvara Tīrtha, 1019; Narasiṁha Tīrtha, 1067; Vidyātīrtha Vidyā-śaṅkara, 1150; Bhāratī-kṛṣṇa Tīrtha, 1250; Vidyāraṇya Bhāratī, 1253; Candraśekhara Bhāratī, 1290; Narasiṁha Bhāratī, 1309; Puruṣottama Bhāratī, 1328; Śaṅkarānanda, 1350; Candraśekhara Bhāratī, 1371; Narasiṁha Bhāratī, 1386; Puruṣottama Bhāratī, 1398; Rāmacandra Bhāratī, 1430; Narasiṁha Bhāratī, 1479; Narasiṁha Bhāratī, 1485; Dhanamaḍi-narasiṁha Bhāratī, 1498; Abhinava-narasiṁha Bhāratī, 1521; Saccidānanda Bhāratī, 1544; Narasiṁha Bhāratī, 1585; Saccidānanda Bhāratī, 1627; Abhinava-saccidānanda Bhāratī, 1663; Nṛsiṁha Bhāratī, 1689; Saccidānanda Bhāratī, 1692; Abhinava-saccidānanda Bhāratī, 1730; Narasiṁha Bhāratī, 1739; Saccidānanda Śivābhinava Vidyā-narasiṁha Bhāratī, 1788.

Regarding Śaṅkarācārya, it is understood that he was born in the year 608 of the Śakābda Era, in the month of Vaiśākha, on the third day of the waxing moon, in a place in South India known as Kālāḍi. His father's name was Śivaguru, and he lost his father at an early age. When Śaṅkarācārya was only eight years old, he completed his study of all scriptures and took *sannyāsa* from Govinda, who was residing on the banks of the Narmadā. After accepting *sannyāsa,* Śaṅkarācārya stayed with his spiritual master for some days. He then took his permission to go to Vārāṇasī, and from there he went to Badarikāśrama, where he stayed until his twelfth year. While there, he wrote a commentary on the *Brahma-sūtra,* as well as on ten *Upaniṣads* and the *Bhagavad-gītā.* He also wrote *Sanat-sujātīya* and a commentary on the *Nṛsiṁha-tāpanī.* Among his many disciples, his four chief disciples are Padmapāda, Sureśvara, Hastāmalaka and Troṭaka. After departing from Vārāṇasī, Śaṅkarācārya went to Prayāga, where he met a great learned scholar called Kumārila Bhaṭṭa. Śaṅkarācārya wanted to discuss the authority of the scriptures, but Kumārila Bhaṭṭa, being on his deathbed, sent him to his disciple Maṇḍana, in the city of Māhiṣmatī. It was there that Śaṅkarācārya defeated Maṇḍana Miśra in a discussion of the *śāstras.* Maṇḍana had a wife named Sarasvatī, or Ubhaya-bhāratī, who served as mediator between Śaṅkarācārya and her husband. It is said that she wanted to discuss erotic principles and amorous love with Śaṅkarācārya, but Śaṅkarācārya had been a *brahmacārī* since birth and therefore had no experience in amorous love. He took a month's leave from Ubhaya-bhāratī and, by his mystic power, entered the body of a king who had just died. In this way Śaṅkarācārya experienced the erotic principles. After attaining this experience, he wanted to discuss erotic principles with Ubhaya-bhāratī, but without hearing his discussion she blessed him and assured the continuous existence of the Śṛṅgeri-maṭha. She then took leave of material life. Afterwards, Maṇḍana Miśra took the order of *sannyāsa* from Śaṅkarācārya and became known as Sureśvara. Śaṅkarācārya defeated many scholars throughout India and converted them to his Māyāvāda philosophy. He left his material body at the age of thirty-three.

As far as Matsya-tīrtha is concerned, it was supposedly situated beside the ocean in the district of Malabar.

TEXT 245

মধ্বাচার্য-স্থানে আইলা যাঁহা 'তত্ত্ববাদী'।
উড়ুপীতে 'কৃষ্ণ' দেখি, তাহাঁ হৈল প্রেমোন্মাদী ॥ ২৪৫ ॥

madhvācārya-sthāne āilā yāṅhā 'tattvavādī'
uḍupīte 'kṛṣṇa' dekhi, tāhāṅ haila premonmādī

madhva-ācārya-sthāne—at the place of Madhvācārya; *āilā*—arrived; *yāṅhā*—where; *tattva-vādī*—philosophers known as Tattvavādīs; *uḍupīte*—at the place known as Uḍupī; *kṛṣṇa*—the Deity of Lord Kṛṣṇa; *dekhi*—seeing; *tāhāṅ*—there; *haila*—became; *prema-unmādī*—mad in ecstasy.

TRANSLATION

Caitanya Mahāprabhu next arrived at Uḍupī, the place of Madhvācārya, where the philosophers known as Tattvavādīs resided. There He saw the Deity of Lord Kṛṣṇa and became mad with ecstasy.

PURPORT

Śrīpāda Madhvācārya took his birth near Uḍupī, which is situated in the South Kanara district of South India, just west of Sahyādri. This is the chief city of the South Kanara province and is near the city of Mangalore, which is situated to the south of Uḍupī. Near the city of Uḍupī is a place called Pājakā-kṣetra, where Madhvācārya took his birth in a Śivāllī-brāhmaṇa dynasty as the son of Madhyageha Bhaṭṭa, in the year 1040 Śakābda (A.D. 1118). According to some, he was born in the year 1160 Śakābda (A.D. 1238).

In his childhood Madhvācārya was known as Vāsudeva, and there are some wonderful stories surrounding him. It is said that once when his father had piled up many debts, Madhvācārya converted tamarind seeds into actual coins to pay them off. When he was five years old, he was offered the sacred thread. A demon named Maṇimān lived near his abode in the form of a snake, and at the age of five Madhvācārya killed that snake with the toe of his left foot. When his mother was very much disturbed, he would appear before her in one jump. He was a great scholar even in childhood, and although his father did not agree, he accepted *sannyāsa* at the age of twelve. Upon receiving *sannyāsa* from Acyuta Prekṣa, he received the name Pūrṇaprajña Tīrtha. After traveling all over India, he finally discussed scriptures with Vidyāśaṅkara, the exalted leader of Śṛṅgeri-maṭha. Vidyāśaṅkara was actually diminished in the presence of Madhvācārya. Accompanied by

Satya Tīrtha, Madhvācārya went to Badarikāśrama. It was there that he met Vyāsadeva and explained his commentary on the *Bhagavad-gītā* before him. Thus he became a great scholar by studying before Vyāsadeva.

By the time he came to the Ānanda-maṭha from Badarikāśrama, Madhvācārya had finished his commentary on the *Bhagavad-gītā.* His companion Satya Tīrtha wrote down the entire commentary. When Madhvācārya returned from Badarikāśrama, he went to Gañjāma, which is on the bank of the river Godāvarī. There he met with two learned scholars named Śobhana Bhaṭṭa and Svāmī Śāstrī. Later these scholars became known in the disciplic succession of Madhvācārya as Padmanābha Tīrtha and Narahari Tīrtha. When he returned to Uḍupī, he would sometimes bathe in the ocean. On such an occasion he composed a prayer in five chapters. Once, while sitting beside the sea engrossed in meditation upon Lord Śrī Kṛṣṇa, he saw that a large boat containing goods for Dvārakā was in danger. He gave some signs by which the boat could approach the shore, and it was saved. The owners of the boat wanted to give him a present, and at the time Madhvācārya agreed to take some *gopī-candana.* He received a big lump of *gopī-candana,* and as it was being brought to him, it broke apart and revealed a large Deity of Lord Kṛṣṇa. The Deity had a stick in one hand and a lump of food in the other. As soon as Madhvācārya received the Deity of Kṛṣṇa in this way, he composed a prayer. The Deity was so heavy that not even thirty people could lift it. Yet Madhvācārya personally brought this Deity to Uḍupī. Eight of Madhvācārya's *sannyāsa* disciples became directors of his eight monasteries. Worship of the Lord Kṛṣṇa Deity is still going on at Uḍupī according to the plans Madhvācārya established.

Madhvācārya then for the second time visited Badarikāśrama. While he was passing through Maharashtra, the local king was digging a big lake for the public benefit. As Madhvācārya passed through that area with his disciples, he was also obliged to help in the excavation. After some time, when Madhvācārya visited the king, he engaged the king in that work and departed with his disciples.

Often in the province of Gāṅga-pradeśa there were fights between Hindus and Muslims. The Hindus were on one bank of the river, and the Muslims on the other. Due to the community tension, no boat was available for crossing the river. The Muslim soldiers were always stopping passengers on the other side, but Madhvācārya did not care for these soldiers. He crossed the river anyway, and when he met the soldiers on the other side, he was brought before the king. The Muslim king was so pleased with him that he wanted to give him a kingdom and some money, but Madhvācārya refused. While walking on the road, he was attacked by some dacoits, but by his bodily strength he killed them all. When his companion Satya Tīrtha was attacked by a tiger, Madhvācārya separated them by virtue of his great strength. When he met Vyāsadeva, he received from him the *śālagrāma-śilā* known as Aṣṭamūrti. After this, he summarized the *Mahābhārata.*

Madhvācārya's devotion to the Lord and his erudite scholarship became known throughout India. Consequently the owners of the Śṛṅgeri-maṭha, established by Śaṅkarācārya, became a little perturbed. At that time the followers of Śaṅkarācārya were afraid of Madhvācārya's rising power, and they began to tease Madhvācārya's disciples in many ways. There was even an attempt to prove that the disciplic succession of Madhvācārya was not in line with Vedic principles. A person named Puṇḍarīka Purī, a follower of the Māyāvāda philosophy of Śaṅkarācārya, came before Madhvācārya to discuss the *śāstras.* It is said that all of Madhvācārya's books were taken away, but later they were found with the help of King Jayasiṁha, ruler of Kumla. In discussion, Puṇḍarīka Purī was defeated by Madhvācārya. A great personality named Trivikramācārya, who was a resident of Viṣṇumaṅgala, became Madhvācārya's disciple, and his son later became Nārāyaṇācārya, the composer of *Śrī Madhva-vijaya.* After the death of Trivikramācārya, the younger brother of Nārāyaṇācārya took *sannyāsa* and later became known as Viṣṇu Tīrtha.

It was reputed that there was no limit to the bodily strength of Pūrṇaprajña, Madhvācārya. There was a person named Kaḍañjari who was famed for possessing the strength of thirty men. Madhvācārya placed the big toe of his foot upon the ground and asked the man to separate it from the ground, but the great strong man could not do so even after great effort. Śrīla Madhvācārya passed from this material world at the age of eighty while writing a commentary on the *Aitareya Upaniṣad.* For further information about Madhvācārya, one should read *Madhva-vijaya,* by Nārāyaṇācārya.

The *ācāryas* of the Madhva-sampradāya established Uḍupī as the chief center, and the monastery there was known as Uttararāḍhī-maṭha. A list of the different centers of the Madhvācārya-sampradāya can be found at Uḍupī, and their *maṭha* commanders are (1) Viṣṇu Tīrtha (Śoda-maṭha), (2) Janārdana Tīrtha (Kṛṣṇapura-maṭha), (3) Vāmana Tīrtha (Kanura-maṭha), (4) Narasiṁha Tīrtha (Adamara-maṭha), (5) Upendra Tīrtha (Puttugī-maṭha), (6) Rāma Tīrtha (Śirura-maṭha), (7) Hṛṣīkeśa Tīrtha (Palimara-maṭha), and (8) Akṣobhya Tīrtha (Pejāvara-maṭha). The disciplic succession of the Madhvācārya-sampradāya is as follows (the dates are those of birth in the Śakābda Era; for Christian era dates, add seventy-eight years.): (1) Haṁsa Paramātmā; (2) Caturmukha Brahmā; (3) Sanakādi; (4) Durvāsā; (5) Jñānanidhi; (6) Garuḍa-vāhana; (7) Kaivalya Tīrtha; (8) Jñāneśa Tīrtha; (9) Para Tīrtha; (10) Satyaprajña Tīrtha; (11) Prājña Tīrtha; (12) Acyuta Prekṣācārya Tīrtha; (13) Śrī Madhvācārya, 1040 Śaka; (14) Padmanābha, 1120; Narahari, 1127; Mādhava, 1136; and Akṣobhya, 1159; (15) Jaya Tīrtha, 1167; (16) Vidyādhirāja, 1190; (17) Kavīndra, 1255; (18) Vāgīśa, 1261; (19) Rāmacandra, 1269; (20) Vidyānidhi, 1298; (21) Śrī Raghunātha, 1366; (22) Rayuvarya (who spoke with Śrī Caitanya Mahāprabhu), 1424; (23) Raghūttama, 1471; (24) Vedavyāsa, 1517; (25) Vidyādhīśa, 1541; (26) Vedanidhi, 1553; (27) Satyavrata, 1557; (28) Satyanidhi, 1560; (29) Satyanātha, 1582; (30) Satyābhinava, 1595; (31) Satyapūrṇa, 1628; (32) Satyavijaya, 1648; (33) Satyapriya, 1659; (34) Satyabodha, 1666; (35) Satyasandha, 1705; (36) Satyavara, 1716; (37) Satyadharma, 1719; (38) Satyasaṅkalpa, 1752; (39) Satyasantuṣṭa, 1763; (40) Satyaparāyaṇa, 1763; (41) Satyakāma, 1785; (42) Satyeṣṭa, 1793; (43) Satyaparākrama, 1794; (44) Satyadhīra, 1801; (45) Satyadhīra Tīrtha, 1808.

After the sixteenth *ācārya* (Vidyādhirāja Tīrtha), there was another disciplic succession, including Rājendra Tīrtha, 1254; Vijayadhvaja; Puruṣottama; Subrahmaṇya; and Vyāsa Rāya, 1470–1520. The nineteenth *ācārya,* Rāmacandra Tīrtha, had another disciplic succession, including Vibudhendra, 1218; Jitāmitra, 1348; Raghunandana; Surendra; Vijendra; Sudhīndra; and Rāghavendra Tīrtha, 1545.

To date, in the Uḍupī monastery there are another fourteen Madhva-tīrtha *sannyāsīs.* As stated, Uḍupī is situated beside the sea in South Kanara, about thirty-six miles north of Mangalore.

Most of the information in this purport is available from the *South Kānāḍā Manual* and the *Bombay Gazette.*

TEXT 246

নর্তক গোপাল দেখে পরম-মোহনে ।
মধ্বাচার্যে স্বপ্ন দিয়া আইলা তাঁর স্থানে ॥ ২৪৬ ॥

nartaka gopāla dekhe parama-mohane
madhvācārye svapna diyā āilā tāṅra sthāne

nartaka gopāla—dancing Gopāla; *dekhe*—saw; *parama-mohane*—most beautiful; *madhva-ācārye*—unto Madhvācārya; *svapna diyā*—appearing in a dream; *āilā*—came; *tāṅra*—his; *sthāne*—to the place.

TRANSLATION

While at the Uḍupī monastery, Śrī Caitanya Mahāprabhu saw Nartaka Gopāla ["dancing Gopāla"], a most beautiful Deity. This Deity appeared to Madhvācārya in a dream.

TEXT 247

গোপীচন্দন-তলে আছিল ডিঙ্গাতে ।
মধ্বাচার্য সেই কৃষ্ণ পাইলা কোনমতে ॥ ২৪৭ ॥

gopī-candana-tale āchila ḍiṅgāte
madhvācārya sei kṛṣṇa pāilā kona-mate

gopī-candana-tale—under heaps of *gopī-candana* (yellowish clay used for *tilaka*); *āchila*—came; *ḍiṅgāte*—in a boat; *madhva-ācārya*—Madhvācārya; *sei kṛṣṇa*—that Kṛṣṇa Deity; *pāilā*—got; *kona-mate*—somehow or other.

TRANSLATION

Madhvācārya had somehow or other acquired the Deity of Kṛṣṇa from a heap of gopī-candana that had been transported in a boat.

TEXT 248

মধ্বাচার্য আনি' তাঁরে করিলা স্থাপন।
অদ্যাবধি সেবা করে তত্ত্ববাদিগণ ॥ ২৪৮ ॥

madhvācārya āni' tāṅre karilā sthāpana
adyāvadhi sevā kare tattvavādi-gaṇa

madhva-ācārya—Madhvācārya; *āni'*—bringing; *tāṅre*—Him; *karilā sthāpana*—installed; *adya-avadhi*—to date; *sevā kare*—worship; *tattvavādi-gaṇa*—the Tattvavādīs.

TRANSLATION

Madhvācārya brought this dancing Gopāla Deity to Uḍupī and installed Him in the temple. To date, the followers of Madhvācārya, known as Tattvavādīs, worship this Deity.

TEXT 249

কৃষ্ণমূর্তি দেখি' প্রভু মহাসুখ পাইল।
প্রেমাবেশে বহুক্ষণ নৃত্য-গীত কৈল ॥ ২৪৯ ॥

kṛṣṇa-mūrti dekhi' prabhu mahā-sukha pāila
premāveśe bahu-kṣaṇa nṛtya-gīta kaila

kṛṣṇa-mūrti dekhi'—seeing the Deity of Lord Kṛṣṇa; *prabhu*—Lord Śrī Caitanya Mahāprabhu; *mahā-sukha*—great happiness; *pāila*—got; *prema-āveśe*—in ecstatic love; *bahu-kṣaṇa*—for a long time; *nṛtya-gīta*—dancing and singing; *kaila*—performed.

TRANSLATION

Śrī Caitanya Mahāprabhu received great pleasure in seeing this beautiful form of Gopāla. For a long time He danced and chanted in ecstatic love.

TEXT 250

তত্ত্ববাদিগণ প্রভুকে 'মায়াবাদী' জ্ঞানে।
প্রথম দর্শনে প্রভুকে না কৈল সম্ভাষণে ॥ ২৫০ ॥

tattvavādi-gaṇa prabhuke 'māyāvādī' jñāne
prathama darśane prabhuke nā kaila sambhāṣaṇe

tattvavādi-gaṇa—the Tattvavādīs; *prabhuke*—Śrī Caitanya Mahāprabhu; *māyāvādī jñāne*—considering as a Māyāvādī *sannyāsī; prathama darśane*—in the first meeting; *prabhuke*—Śrī Caitanya Mahāprabhu; *nā*—did not; *kaila*—do; *sambhāṣaṇe*—addressing.

TRANSLATION

When the Tattvavādī Vaiṣṇavas first saw Śrī Caitanya Mahāprabhu, they considered Him a Māyāvādī sannyāsī. Therefore they did not talk to Him.

TEXT 251

পাছে প্রেমাবেশ দেখি' হৈল চমৎকার।
বৈষ্ণব-জ্ঞানে বহুত করিল সৎকার ॥ ২৫১ ॥

pāche premāveśa dekhi' haila camatkāra
vaiṣṇava-jñāne bahuta karila satkāra

pāche—later; *prema-āveśa*—ecstatic love; *dekhi'*—seeing; *haila camatkāra*—became struck with wonder; *vaiṣṇava-jñāne*—understanding as a Vaiṣṇava; *bahuta*—much; *karila*—did; *satkāra*—reception.

TRANSLATION

Later, after seeing Śrī Caitanya Mahāprabhu in ecstatic love, they were struck with wonder. Then, considering Him a Vaiṣṇava, they gave Him a nice reception.

TEXT 252

'বৈষ্ণবতা' সবার অন্তরে গর্ব জানি'।
ঈষৎ হাসিয়া কিছু কহে গৌরমণি ॥ ২৫২ ॥

'vaiṣṇavatā' sabāra antare garva jāni'
īṣat hāsiyā kichu kahe gauramaṇi

vaiṣṇavatā—Vaiṣṇavism; *sabāra*—of all of them; *antare*—within the mind; *garva*—pride; *jāni'*—knowing; *īṣat*—mildly; *hāsiyā*—smiling; *kichu*—something; *kahe*—says; *gaura-maṇi*—Lord Śrī Caitanya Mahāprabhu.

TRANSLATION

Śrī Caitanya Mahāprabhu could understand that the Tattvavādīs were very proud of their Vaiṣṇavism. He therefore smiled and began to speak to them.

TEXT 253

তাঁ-সবার অন্তরে গর্ব জানি গৌরচন্দ্র।
তাঁ-সবা-সঙ্গে গোষ্ঠী করিলা আরম্ভ ॥ ২৫৩ ॥

tāṅ-sabāra antare garva jāni gauracandra
tāṅ-sabā-saṅge goṣṭhī karilā ārambha

tāṅ-sabāra—of all of them; *antare*—within the mind; *garva*—pride; *jāni*—knowing; *gaura-candra*—Śrī Caitanya Mahāprabhu; *tāṅ-sabā-saṅge*—with them; *goṣṭhī*—discussion; *karilā*—made; *ārambha*—beginning.

TRANSLATION

Considering them very proud, Caitanya Mahāprabhu began His discussion.

TEXT 254

তত্ত্ববাদী আচার্য—সব শাস্ত্রেতে প্রবীণ।
তাঁরে প্রশ্ন কৈল প্রভু হঞা যেন দীন ॥ ২৫৪ ॥

tattvavādī ācārya—saba śāstrete pravīṇa
tāṅre praśna kaila prabhu hañā yena dīna

tattvavādī ācārya—the chief preacher of the Tattvavāda community; *saba*—all; *śāstrete*—in revealed scriptures; *pravīṇa*—experienced; *tāṅre*—unto him; *praśna*—question; *kaila*—did; *prabhu*—Śrī

Caitanya Mahāprabhu; *hañā*—becoming; *yena*—as if; *dīna*—very humble.

TRANSLATION

The chief ācārya of the Tattvavāda community was very learned in the revealed scriptures. Śrī Caitanya Mahāprabhu humbly questioned him.

TEXT 255

সাধ্য-সাধন আমি না জানি ভালমতে।
সাধ্য-সাধন-শ্রেষ্ঠ জানাহ আমাতে॥ ২৫৫॥

sādhya-sādhana āmi nā jāni bhāla-mate
sādhya-sādhana-śreṣṭha jānāha āmāte

sādhya-sādhana—the aim of life and how to achieve it; *āmi*—I; *nā*—not; *jāni*—know; *bhāla-mate*—very well; *sādhya-sādhana*—the aim of life and how to achieve it; *śreṣṭha*—the best; *jānāha*—kindly explain; *āmāte*—unto Me.

TRANSLATION

Caitanya Mahāprabhu said, "I do not know very well the aim of life and how to achieve it. Please tell Me of the best ideal for humanity and how to attain it."

TEXT 256

আচার্য কহে, — 'বর্ণাশ্রম-ধর্ম, কৃষ্ণে সমর্পণ'।
এই হয় কৃষ্ণভক্তের শ্রেষ্ঠ 'সাধন'॥ ২৫৬॥

ācārya kahe,—'varṇāśrama-dharma, kṛṣṇe samarpaṇa'
ei haya kṛṣṇa-bhaktera śreṣṭha 'sādhana'

ācārya kahe—the *ācārya* said; *varṇa-āśrama-dharma*—the institution of four castes and four *āśramas; kṛṣṇe*—unto Kṛṣṇa; *samarpaṇa*—to dedicate; *ei haya*—this is; *kṛṣṇa-bhaktera*—of the devotee of Kṛṣṇa; *śreṣṭha sādhana*—the best means of achievement.

TRANSLATION

The ācārya replied, "When the activities of the four castes and the four āśramas are dedicated to Kṛṣṇa, they constitute the best means whereby one can attain the highest goal of life.

TEXT 257

'পঞ্চবিধ মুক্তি' পাঞা বৈকুণ্ঠে গমন।
'সাধ্য-শ্রেষ্ঠ' হয়, — এই শাস্ত্র-নিরূপণ ॥ ২৫৭ ॥

'pañca-vidha mukti' pāñā vaikuṇṭhe gamana
'sādhya-śreṣṭha' haya, — ei śāstra-nirūpaṇa

pañca-vidha mukti — five kinds of liberation; *pāñā* — getting; *vaikuṇṭhe* — to the spiritual world; *gamana* — transference; *sādhya-śreṣṭha haya* — is the highest achievement of the goal of life; *ei* — this; *śāstra-nirūpaṇa* — the verdict of all revealed scriptures.

TRANSLATION

"When one dedicates the duties of varṇāśrama-dharma to Kṛṣṇa, he is eligible for five kinds of liberation. Thus he is transferred to the spiritual world in Vaikuṇṭha. This is the highest goal of life and the verdict of all revealed scriptures."

TEXT 258

প্রভু কহে, — শাস্ত্রে কহে শ্রবণ-কীর্তন।
কৃষ্ণপ্রেমসেবা-ফলের 'পরম সাধন' ॥ ২৫৮ ॥

prabhu kahe, — śāstre kahe śravaṇa-kīrtana
kṛṣṇa-prema-sevā-phalera 'parama-sādhana'

prabhu kahe — Lord Śrī Caitanya Mahāprabhu said; *śāstre kahe* — in the *śāstra* it is said; *śravaṇa-kīrtana* — the process of chanting and hearing; *kṛṣṇa-prema-sevā* — of loving service to Lord Kṛṣṇa; *phalera* — of the result; *parama-sādhana* — best process of achievement.

TRANSLATION

Śrī Caitanya Mahāprabhu said, "According to the verdict of the śāstras, the process of hearing and chanting is the best means to attain loving service to Kṛṣṇa.

PURPORT

According to the Tattvavādīs, the best process for achieving the highest goal of life is to execute the duties of the four *varṇas* and *āśramas.* In the material world, unless one is situated in one of the *varṇas* (*brāhmaṇa, kṣatriya, vaiśya* or *śūdra*) one cannot manage social affairs properly to attain the ultimate goal. One also has to follow the principles of the *āśramas* (*brahmacarya, gṛhastha, vānaprastha* and *sannyāsa*), since these principles are considered essential for the attainment of the highest goal. In this way the Tattvavādīs establish that the execution of the principles of *varṇa* and *āśrama* for the sake of Kṛṣṇa is the best way to attain the topmost goal. The Tattvavādīs thus established their principles in terms of human society. Śrī Caitanya Mahāprabhu, however, differed when He said that the best process is hearing and chanting about Lord Viṣṇu. According to the Tattvavādīs, the highest goal is returning home, back to Godhead, but in Śrī Caitanya Mahāprabhu's opinion the highest goal is attaining love of Godhead, in either the material world or the spiritual world. In the material world this is practiced according to śāstric injunction, and in the spiritual world the real achievement is already there.

TEXTS 259–260

শ্রবণং কীর্তনং বিষ্ণোঃ স্মরণং পাদসেবনম্ ।
অর্চনং বন্দনং দাস্যং সখ্যমাত্মনিবেদনম্ ॥ ২৫৯ ॥
ইতি পুংসার্পিতা বিষ্ণৌ ভক্তিশ্চেন্নবলক্ষণা ।
ক্রিয়েত ভগবত্যদ্ধা তন্মন্যেঽধীতমুত্তমম্ ॥ ২৬০ ॥

śravaṇaṁ kīrtanaṁ viṣṇoḥ
smaraṇaṁ pāda-sevanam
arcanaṁ vandanaṁ dāsyaṁ
sakhyam ātma-nivedanam

iti puṁsārpitā viṣṇau
bhaktiś cen nava-lakṣaṇā
kriyeta bhagavaty addhā
tan manye 'dhītam uttamam

śravaṇam—hearing of the holy name, form, qualities, entourage and pastimes, all of which must pertain to Lord Viṣṇu; *kīrtanam*—vibrating transcendental sounds pertaining to the holy name, form, qualities and entourage, and inquiring about them (these also should be only in relationship to Viṣṇu); *viṣṇoḥ*—of Lord Viṣṇu; *smaraṇam*—remembering the holy name, form and entourage, and inquiring about them, also only for Viṣṇu; *pāda-sevanam*—executing devotional service according to time, circumstances and situation, only in relationship with Viṣṇu; *arcanam*—worshiping the Deity of Lord Kṛṣṇa, Lord Rāmacandra, Lakṣmī-Nārāyaṇa or the other forms of Viṣṇu; *vandanam*—offering prayers to the Supreme Personality of Godhead; *dāsyam*—always thinking oneself an eternal servant of the Supreme Personality of Godhead; *sakhyam*—making friends with the Supreme Personality of Godhead; *ātma-nivedanam*—dedicating everything (body, mind and soul) for the service of the Lord; *iti*—thus; *puṁsā*—by the human being; *arpitā*—dedicated; *viṣṇau*—unto the Supreme Personality of Godhead, Viṣṇu; *bhaktiḥ*—devotional service; *cet*—if; *nava-lakṣaṇā*—possessing nine different systems, as above mentioned; *kriyeta*—one should execute; *bhagavati*—unto the Supreme Personality of Godhead; *addhā*—directly (not indirectly through *karma, jñāna* or *yoga*); *tat*—that; *manye*—I understand; *adhītam*—studied; *uttamam*—first class.

TRANSLATION

"'This process entails hearing, chanting and remembering the holy name, form, pastimes, qualities and entourage of the Lord, offering service according to the time, place and performer, worshiping the Deity, offering prayers, always considering oneself the eternal servant of Kṛṣṇa, making friends with Him and dedicating everything unto Him. These nine items of devotional service, when directly offered to Kṛṣṇa, constitute the highest attainment of life. This is the verdict of the revealed scriptures.'

PURPORT

Śrī Caitanya Mahāprabhu quoted these verses from *Śrīmad-Bhāgavatam* (7.5.23–24).

TEXT 261

শ্রবণ-কীর্তন হইতে কৃষ্ণে হয় 'প্রেমা'।
সেই পঞ্চম পুরুষার্থ — পুরুষার্থের সীমা ॥ ২৬১ ॥

śravaṇa-kīrtana ha-ite kṛṣṇe haya 'premā'
sei pañcama puruṣārtha — puruṣārthera sīmā

śravaṇa-kīrtana — hearing and chanting; *ha-ite* — from; *kṛṣṇe* — unto Lord Kṛṣṇa; *haya* — there is; *premā* — transcendental love; *sei* — that; *pañcama puruṣa-artha* — the fifth platform of perfection of life; *puruṣa-arthera sīmā* — the limit of goals of life.

TRANSLATION

"When one comes to the platform of loving service to Lord Kṛṣṇa by executing these nine processes, beginning with hearing and chanting, he has attained the fifth platform of success and the limit of life's goals.

PURPORT

Everyone is after success in religion, economic development, sense gratification and ultimately merging into the existence of Brahman. These are the general practices of the common man, but according to the strict principles of the *Vedas,* the highest attainment is to rise to the platform of *śravaṇaṁ kīrtanam,* hearing and chanting about the Supreme Personality of Godhead. This is confirmed in *Śrīmad-Bhāgavatam* (1.1.2):

dharmaḥ projjhita-kaitavo 'tra paramo nirmatsarāṇāṁ satāṁ
vedyaṁ vāstavam atra vastu śiva-daṁ tāpa-trayonmūlanam
śrīmad-bhāgavate mahā-muni-kṛte kiṁ vā parair īśvaraḥ
sadyo hṛdy avarudhyate 'tra kṛtibhiḥ śuśrūṣubhis tat-kṣaṇāt

"Completely rejecting all religious activities which are materially motivated, this *Bhāgavata Purāṇa* propounds the highest truth, which is understandable by those devotees who are fully pure in heart. The highest truth is reality distinguished from illusion for the welfare of all. Such truth uproots the threefold miseries. This beautiful *Bhāgavatam,* compiled by the great sage Śrī Vyāsadeva, is sufficient in itself for God realization. What is the need of any other scripture? As soon as one attentively and submissively hears the message of *Bhāgavatam,* by this culture of knowledge the Supreme Lord is established within his heart." This verse of *Śrīmad-Bhāgavatam* rejects as cheating processes all religious activities that aim at achieving materialistic goals, including *dharma, artha, kāma* and even *mokṣa,* or liberation.

According to Śrīdhara Svāmī, the material conception of success (*mokṣa,* or liberation) is desired by those in material existence. Devotees, however, not being situated in material existence, have no desire for liberation.

A devotee is always liberated in all stages of life because he is always engaged in the nine items of devotional service (*śravaṇam, kīrtanam,* etc.). Śrī Caitanya Mahāprabhu's philosophy holds that devotional service to Kṛṣṇa always exists in everyone's heart. It simply has to be awakened by the process of *śravaṇaṁ kīrtanaṁ viṣṇoḥ. Śravaṇādi śuddhacitte karaye udaya* (Cc. *Madhya* 22.107). When a person is actually engaged in devotional service, his eternal relationship with the Lord, the servant-master relationship, is awakened.

TEXT 262

এবংব্রতঃ স্বপ্রিয়নাম-কীর্ত্যা
জাতানুরাগো দ্রুতচিত্ত উচ্চৈঃ ।
হসত্যথো রোদিতি রৌতি গায়-
ত্যুন্মাদবন্নৃত্যতি লোকবাহ্যঃ ॥ ২৬২ ॥

evaṁ-vrataḥ sva-priya-nāma-kīrtyā
jātānurāgo druta-citta uccaiḥ
hasaty atho roditi rauti gāyaty
unmāda-van nṛtyati loka-bāhyaḥ

evam-vrataḥ—when one thus engages in a vow to chant and dance; *sva*—own; *priya*—very dear; *nāma*—holy name; *kīrtyā*—by chanting; *jāta*—in this way develops; *anurāgaḥ*—attachment; *druta-*

cittaḥ—very eagerly; *uccaiḥ*—loudly; *hasati*—laughs; *atho*—also; *roditi*—cries; *rauti*—becomes agitated; *gāyati*—chants; *unmāda-vat*—like a madman; *nṛtyati*—dances; *loka-bāhyaḥ*—without caring for outsiders.

TRANSLATION

"'When one is actually advanced and takes pleasure in chanting the holy name of the Lord, who is very dear to him, he is agitated and loudly chants the holy name. He also laughs, cries, becomes agitated and chants just like a madman, not caring for outsiders.'

PURPORT

This verse is a quotation from *Śrīmad-Bhāgavatam* (11.2.40).

TEXT 263

কর্মনিন্দা, কর্মত্যাগ, সর্বশাস্ত্রে কহে।
কর্ম হৈতে প্রেমভক্তি কৃষ্ণে কভু নহে ॥ ২৬৩ ॥

karma-nindā, karma-tyāga, sarva-śāstre kahe
karma haite prema-bhakti kṛṣṇe kabhu nahe

karma-nindā—condemnation of fruitive activities; *karma-tyāga*—renunciation of fruitive activities; *sarva-śāstre kahe*—is announced in every revealed scripture; *karma haite*—from fruitive activities; *prema-bhakti*—devotional service in ecstatic love; *kṛṣṇe*—for Kṛṣṇa; *kabhu nahe*—can never be achieved.

TRANSLATION

"In every revealed scripture there is condemnation of fruitive activities. It is advised everywhere to give up engagement in fruitive activities, for no one can attain the highest goal of life, love of Godhead, by executing them.

PURPORT

In the *Vedas* there are three *kāṇḍas,* or divisions: *karma-kāṇḍa, jñāna-kāṇḍa* and *upāsanā-kāṇḍa.* The *karma-kāṇḍa* portion stresses the execution of fruitive activities. But ultimately it is advised that one abandon both *karma-kāṇḍa* and *jñāna-kāṇḍa* (speculative knowledge) and accept only *upāsanā-kāṇḍa,* or *bhakti-kāṇḍa.* One cannot attain love of Godhead by executing *karma-kāṇḍa* or *jñāna-kāṇḍa.* But by dedicating one's *karma,* or fruitive activities, to the Supreme Lord, one may be relieved from the polluted mind, and becoming free from mental pollution helps elevate one to the spiritual platform. Then, however, one needs the association of a pure devotee, for only by a pure devotee's association can one become a pure devotee of the Supreme Personality of Godhead, Kṛṣṇa. When one comes to the stage of pure devotional service, the process of *śravaṇaṁ kīrtanam* is very essential. By executing the nine items of devotional service, beginning with *śravaṇaṁ kīrtanam,* one is completely purified. *Anyābhilāṣitā-śūnyaṁ jñāna-karmādy-anāvṛtam* (*Bhakti-rasāmṛta-sindhu* 1.1.11). Only then is one able to execute Kṛṣṇa's orders in the *Bhagavad-gītā* (18.65, 66):

man-manā bhava mad-bhakto mad-yājī māṁ namaskuru
mām evaiṣyasi satyam te pratijāne priyo 'si me

sarva-dharmān parityajya mām ekaṁ śaranaṁ vraja
ahaṁ tvāṁ sarva-pāpebhyo mokṣayiṣyāmi mā śucaḥ

"Always think of Me, become My devotee, worship Me and offer your homage unto Me. Thus you will come to Me without fail. I promise you this because you are My very dear friend. Abandon all varieties of religion and just surrender unto Me. I shall deliver you from all sinful reactions. Do not fear." In this way one develops his original constitutional position of rendering loving service to the Lord.

One cannot be elevated to the highest platform of devotional service by *karma-kāṇḍa* or *jñāna-kāṇḍa.* Pure devotional service can be understood and attained only through the association of pure devotees. In this regard, Śrīla Bhaktisiddhānta Sarasvatī Ṭhākura states that there are two types of *karma-kāṇḍa* activities—pious and impious. Pious activities are certainly better than impious activities, but even pious activities cannot bring about ecstatic love of God, Kṛṣṇa. Pious and impious activities can bring about material happiness and distress, but there is no possibility of one's becoming a pure devotee simply by acting piously or impiously. *Bhakti,* devotional service, means satisfying Kṛṣṇa. In every revealed scripture, whether stressing *jñāna-kāṇḍa* or *karma-kāṇḍa,* the principle of renunciation is always praised. The ripened fruit of Vedic knowledge, *Śrīmad-Bhāgavatam,* is the supreme Vedic evidence. In *Śrīmad-Bhāgavatam* (1.5.12) it is said:

naiṣkarmyam apy acyuta-bhāva-varjitaṁ
na śobhate jñānam alaṁ nirañjanam
kutaḥ punaḥ śaśvad abhadram īśvare
na cārpitaṁ karma yad apy akāraṇam

"Knowledge of self-realization, even though freed from all material affinity, does not look well if devoid of a conception of the Infallible [God]. What, then, is the use of fruitive activities, which are naturally painful from the very beginning and transient by nature, if they are not utilized for the devotional service of the Lord?" This means that even knowledge, which is superior to fruitive activity, is not successful if it is devoid of devotional service. Therefore in *Śrīmad-Bhāgavatam*—in the beginning, middle and end—*karma-kāṇḍa* and *jñāna-kāṇḍa* are condemned. For example, in *Śrīmad-Bhāgavatam* 1.1.2 it is said, *dharmaḥ projjhita-kaitavo 'tra.*

This is explained in the following verses taken from *Śrīmad-Bhāgavatam* (11.11.32) and the *Bhagavad-gītā* (18.66).

TEXT 264

আজ্ঞায়ৈবং গুণান্ দোষান্ময়াদিষ্টানপি স্বকান্ ।
ধর্মান্ সন্ত্যজ্য যঃ সর্বান্মাং ভজেৎ স চ সত্তমঃ ॥ ২৬৪ ॥

ājñāyaivaṁ guṇān doṣān
mayādiṣṭān api svakān
dharmān santyajya yaḥ sarvān
māṁ bhajet sa ca sattamaḥ

ājñāya—knowing perfectly; *evam*—thus; *guṇān*—qualities; *doṣān*—faults; *mayā*—by Me; *ādiṣṭān*—instructed; *api*—although; *svakān*—own; *dharmān*—occupational duties; *santyajya*—giving up; *yaḥ*—anyone who; *sarvān*—all; *mām*—unto Me; *bhajet*—may render service; *saḥ*—he; *ca*—and; *sat-tamaḥ*—first-class person.

TRANSLATION

"'Occupational duties are described in the religious scriptures. If one analyzes them, he can fully understand their qualities and faults and

then give them up completely to render service unto the Supreme Personality of Godhead. A person who does so is considered a first-class man.'

TEXT 265

সর্বধর্মান্ পরিত্যজ্য মামেকং শরণং ব্রজ।
অহং ত্বাং সর্বপাপেভ্যো মোক্ষয়িষ্যামি মা শুচঃ ॥ ২৬৫ ॥

sarva-dharmān parityajya
mām ekaṁ śaranaṁ vraja
ahaṁ tvāṁ sarva-pāpebhyo
mokṣayiṣyāmi mā śucaḥ

sarva-dharmān—all kinds of occupational duties; *parityajya*—giving up; *mām ekam*—unto Me only; *śaraṇam*—as shelter; *vraja*—go; *aham*—I; *tvām*—unto you; *sarva-pāpebhyaḥ*—from all the reactions of sinful life; *mokṣayiṣyāmi*—will give liberation; *mā*—do not; *śucaḥ*—worry.

TRANSLATION

"'Abandon all varieties of religion and just surrender unto Me. I shall deliver you from all sinful reactions. Do not fear.'

TEXT 266

তাবৎ কর্মাণি কুর্বীত ন নির্বিদ্যেত যাবতা।
মৎকথা-শ্রবণাদৌ বা শ্রদ্ধা যাবন্ন জায়তে ॥ ২৬৬ ॥

tāvat karmāṇi kurvīta
na nirvidyeta yāvatā
mat-kathā-śravaṇādau vā
śraddhā yāvan na jāyate

tāvat—up to that time; *karmāṇi*—fruitive activities; *kurvīta*—one should execute; *na nirvidyeta*—is not satiated; *yāvatā*—as long as; *mat-kathā*—of discourses about Me; *śravaṇa-ādau*—in the matter of *śravaṇam, kīrtanam,* and so on; *vā*—or; *śraddhā*—faith; *yāvat*—as long as; *na*—not; *jāyate*—is awakened.

TRANSLATION

"'As long as one is not satiated by fruitive activity and has not awakened his taste for devotional service by śravaṇaṁ kīrtanaṁ viṣṇoḥ, one has to act according to the regulative principles of the Vedic injunctions.'

PURPORT

This is a quotation from *Śrīmad-Bhāgavatam* (11.20.9).

TEXT 267

পঞ্চবিধ মুক্তি ত্যাগ করে ভক্তগণ ।
ফল্গু করি' 'মুক্তি' দেখে নরকের সম ॥ ২৬৭ ॥

pañca-vidha mukti tyāga kare bhakta-gaṇa
phalgu kari' 'mukti' dekhe narakera sama

pañca-vidha—five kinds of; *mukti*—liberation; *tyāga kare*—give up; *bhakta-gaṇa*—devotees; *phalgu*—insignificant; *kari'*—considering; *mukti*—liberation; *dekhe*—see; *narakera*—to hell; *sama*—equal.

TRANSLATION

"Pure devotees reject the five kinds of liberation; indeed, for them liberation is very insignificant because they see it as hellish.

TEXT 268

সালোক্য-সার্ষ্টি-সামীপ্য-সারূপ্যৈকত্বমপ্যুত ।
দীয়মানং ন গৃহ্ণন্তি বিনা মৎসেবনং জনাঃ ॥ ২৬৮ ॥

sālokya-sārṣṭi-sāmīpya-
sārūpyaikatvam apy uta
dīyamānaṁ na gṛhṇanti
vinā mat-sevanaṁ janāḥ

sālokya—to live on the same planet as the Supreme Personality of Godhead; *sārṣṭi*—to possess opulence equal to the Lord's; *sāmīpya*—to always associate with the Supreme Personality of Godhead; *sārūpya*—to possess bodily features like the Lord's;

ekatvam—to merge into the body of the Supreme Personality of Godhead; *api*—even; *uta*—certainly; *dīyamānam*—being offered; *na*—never; *gṛhṇanti*—accept; *vinā*—without; *mat*—My; *sevanam*—devotional service; *janāḥ*—devotees.

TRANSLATION

"'Pure devotees always reject the five kinds of liberation, which include living in the spiritual Vaikuṇṭha planets, possessing the same opulences as those possessed by the Supreme Lord, having the same bodily features as the Lord's, associating with the Lord and merging into the body of the Lord. The pure devotees do not accept these benedictions without the service of the Lord.'

PURPORT

This is a verse from *Śrīmad-Bhāgavatam* (3.29.13).

TEXT 269

যো দুস্ত্যজান্ ক্ষিতিসুতস্বজনার্থদারান্
প্রার্থ্যাং শ্রিয়ং সুরবরৈঃ সদয়াবলোকাম্ ।
নৈচ্ছন্নৃপস্তদুচিতং মহতাং মধুদ্বিট্-
সেবানুরক্তমনসামভবোঽপি ফল্গুঃ ॥ ২৬৯ ॥

yo dustyajān kṣiti-suta-svajanārtha-dārān
prārthyāṁ śriyaṁ sura-varaiḥ sadayāvalokām
naicchan nṛpas tad ucitaṁ mahatāṁ madhu-dviṭ-
sevānurakta-manasām abhavo 'pi phalguḥ

yaḥ—one who; *dustyajān*—very difficult to give up; *kṣiti*—land; *suta*—children; *svajana*—relatives; *artha*—riches; *dārān*—and wife; *prārthyām*—desirable; *śriyam*—fortune; *sura-varaiḥ*—by the best of the demigods; *sa-dayā*—merciful; *avalokām*—whose glance; *na aicchat*—did not desire; *nṛpaḥ*—the King (Mahārāja Bharata); *tat*—that; *ucitam*—is befitting; *mahatām*—of great personalities; *madhu-dviṭ*—of the killer of the demon Madhu; *sevā-anurakta*—engaged in the service; *manasām*—the minds of whom; *abhavaḥ*—cessation of the repetition of birth and death; *api*—even; *phalguḥ*—insignificant.

TRANSLATION

"'It is very difficult to give up material opulence, land, children, society, friends, riches, wife or the blessings of the goddess of fortune, which are desired even by great demigods. But King Bharata did not desire such things, and this was quite befitting his position, because for a pure devotee whose mind is always engaged in the service of the Lord, even liberation, or merging into the existence of the Lord, is insignificant. And what to speak of material opportunities?'

PURPORT

This is a verse from *Śrīmad-Bhāgavatam* (5.14.44) concerning the glorification of King Bharata, whom Śukadeva Gosvāmī was describing to King Parīkṣit.

TEXT 270

নারায়ণপরাঃ সর্বে ন কুতশ্চন বিভ্যতি ।
স্বর্গাপবর্গনরকেষ্বপি তুল্যার্থদর্শিনঃ ॥ ২৭০ ॥

nārāyaṇa-parāḥ sarve
na kutaścana bibhyati
svargāpavarga-narakeṣv
api tulyārtha-darśinaḥ

nārāyaṇa-parāḥ—persons who are devotees of the Supreme Personality of Godhead Nārāyaṇa; *sarve*—all; *na*—never; *kutaścana*—anywhere; *bibhyati*—are afraid; *svarga*—in the heavenly planetary system; *apavarga*—on the path of liberation; *narakeṣu*—or in a hellish condition of life; *api*—even; *tulya*—equal; *artha*—value; *darśinaḥ*—seers of.

TRANSLATION

"'A person who is a devotee of Lord Nārāyaṇa is not afraid of a hellish condition, because he considers it the same as elevation to the heavenly planets or liberation. The devotees of Lord Nārāyaṇa are accustomed to seeing all these things on the same level.'

PURPORT

This is a verse from *Śrīmad-Bhāgavatam* (6.17.28) regarding the personality Citraketu. Once when Citraketu saw the goddess Pārvatī sitting on the lap of Lord Śambhu (Śiva), he criticized Lord Śiva for being shameless and sitting just like an ordinary man with his wife on his lap. For this reason Citraketu was cursed by Pārvatī. Later he became a demon named Vṛtrāsura. Citraketu was a very powerful king and a devotee, and he could certainly retaliate even against Lord Śiva, but when Pārvatī cursed him, he immediately accepted the curse with a bowed head. When he agreed to accept this curse, Lord Śiva praised him and told Pārvatī that a devotee of Lord Nārāyaṇa is never afraid of accepting any position provided there is a chance to serve the Supreme Personality of Godhead. This is the purport of *nārāyaṇa-parāḥ sarve na kutaścana bibhyati.*

TEXT 271

মুক্তি, কর্ম — দুই বস্তু ত্যজে ভক্তগণ।
সেই দুই স্থাপ' তুমি 'সাধ্য', 'সাধন' ॥ ২৭১ ॥

mukti, karma — dui vastu tyaje bhakta-gaṇa
sei dui sthāpa' tumi 'sādhya', 'sādhana'

mukti — liberation; *karma* — fruitive activities; *dui* — two; *vastu* — things; *tyaje* — give up; *bhakta-gaṇa* — the devotees; *sei* — those; *dui* — two; *sthāpa'* — establish; *tumi* — you; *sādhya* — the goal of life; *sādhana* — the process of achievement.

TRANSLATION

"Both liberation and fruitive activity are rejected by devotees. You are trying to establish these things as life's goal and the process for attaining it."

TEXT 272

সন্ন্যাসী দেখিয়া মোরে করহ বঞ্চন।
না কহিলা তেঞি সাধ্য-সাধন-লক্ষণ ॥ ২৭২ ॥

sannyāsī dekhiyā more karaha vañcana
nā kahilā teñi sādhya-sādhana-lakṣaṇa

sannyāsī—a person in the renounced order of life; *dekhiyā*—seeing; *more*—unto Me; *karaha*—you do; *vañcana*—duplicity; *nā kahilā*—did not describe; *teñi*—therefore; *sādhya*—objective; *sādhana*—process of achievement; *lakṣaṇa*—symptoms.

TRANSLATION

Śrī Caitanya Mahāprabhu continued speaking to the Tattvavādī ācārya: "Seeing that I am a mendicant in the renounced order of life, you have been playing with Me in a duplicitous way. You have not actually described the process and ultimate objective."

TEXT 273

শুনি' তত্ত্বাচার্য হৈলা অন্তরে লজ্জিত।
প্রভুর বৈষ্ণবতা দেখি, হইলা বিস্মিত ॥ ২৭৩ ॥

śuni' tattvācārya hailā antare lajjita
prabhura vaiṣṇavatā dekhi, ha-ilā vismita

śuni'—hearing; *tattva-ācārya*—the *ācārya* of the Tattvavāda *sampradāya; hailā*—became; *antare*—within the mind; *lajjita*—ashamed; *prabhura*—of Lord Śrī Caitanya Mahāprabhu; *vaiṣṇavatā*—devotion in Vaiṣṇavism; *dekhi*—seeing; *ha-ilā*—became; *vismita*—struck with wonder.

TRANSLATION

After hearing Śrī Caitanya Mahāprabhu, the ācārya of the Tattvavāda sampradāya became very much ashamed. Upon observing Śrī Caitanya Mahāprabhu's rigid faith in Vaiṣṇavism, he was struck with wonder.

TEXT 274

আচার্য কহে,—তুমি যেই কহ, সেই সত্য হয়।
সর্বশাস্ত্রে বৈষ্ণবের এই সুনিশ্চয় ॥ ২৭৪ ॥

ācārya kahe,—tumi yei kaha, sei satya haya
sarva-śāstre vaiṣṇavera ei suniścaya

ācārya kahe—the Tattvavādī *ācārya* said; *tumi*—You; *yei*—whatever; *kaha*—say; *sei*—that; *satya*—truth; *haya*—is; *sarva-śāstre*—in all revealed scriptures; *vaiṣṇavera*—of the devotees of Lord Viṣṇu; *ei*—this; *su-niścaya*—conclusion.

TRANSLATION

The Tattvavādī ācārya replied, "What You have said is certainly factual. It is the conclusion of all the revealed scriptures of the Vaiṣṇavas.

TEXT 275

তথাপি মধ্বাচার্য যে করিয়াছে নির্বন্ধ।
সেই আচরিয়ে সবে সম্প্রদায়-সম্বন্ধ ॥ ২৭৫ ॥

tathāpi madhvācārya ye kariyāche nirbandha
sei ācariye sabe sampradāya-sambandha

tathāpi—still; *madhva-ācārya*—Madhvācārya; *ye*—whatever; *kariyāche*—formulated; *nirbandha*—rules and regulations; *sei*—that; *ācariye*—we practice; *sabe*—all; *sampradāya*—party; *sambandha*—relationship.

TRANSLATION

"Still, whatever Madhvācārya has established as the formula for our party we practice as a party policy."

TEXT 276

প্রভু কহে,—কর্মী, জ্ঞানী,—দুই ভক্তিহীন।
তোমার সম্প্রদায়ে দেখি সেই দুই চিহ্ন ॥ ২৭৬ ॥

prabhu kahe,—karmī, jñānī,—dui bhakti-hīna
tomāra sampradāye dekhi sei dui cihna

prabhu kahe—Lord Śrī Caitanya Mahāprabhu said; *karmī*—fruitive worker; *jñānī*—mental speculator; *dui*—both of them; *bhakti-*

hīna—nondevotees; *tomāra*—your; *sampradāye*—in the community; *dekhi*—I see; *sei*—those; *dui*—both; *cihna*—symptoms.

TRANSLATION

Śrī Caitanya Mahāprabhu said, "Both the fruitive worker and the speculative philosopher are considered nondevotees. We see both elements present in your sampradāya.

TEXT 277

সবে, এক গুণ দেখি তোমার সম্প্রদায়ে।
সত্যবিগ্রহ করি' ঈশ্বরে করহ নিশ্চয়ে ॥ ২৭৭ ॥

sabe, eka guṇa dekhi tomāra sampradāye
satya-vigraha kari' īśvare karaha niścaye

sabe—in all; *eka*—one; *guṇa*—quality; *dekhi*—I see; *tomāra*—your; *sampradāye*—in the party; *satya-vigraha*—the form of the Lord as truth; *kari'*—accepting; *īśvare*—the Supreme Personality of Godhead; *karaha*—you do; *niścaye*—conviction.

TRANSLATION

"The only qualification that I see in your sampradāya is that you accept the form of the Lord as truth."

PURPORT

Śrī Caitanya Mahāprabhu wanted to point out to the Tattvavādī *ācārya,* who belonged to the Madhvācārya-sampradāya, that the general behavior of the Tattvavādīs did not favor pure devotional service, which must be devoid of the taints of fruitive activity and speculative knowledge. As far as fruitive activity is concerned, the contamination is the desire for elevation to a higher standard of life, and for speculative knowledge the contamination is the desire to merge into the existence of the Absolute Truth. The Tattvavāda *sampradāya* of the Madhvācārya school sticks to the principle of *varṇāśrama-dharma,* which involves fruitive activity. Their ultimate goal (*mukti*) is simply a form of material desire. A pure devotee should be free from all kinds of material desire.

He simply engages in the service of the Lord. Nonetheless, Caitanya Mahāprabhu was pleased that the Madhvācārya-sampradāya, or the Tattvavāda *sampradāya,* accepted the transcendental form of the Lord. This is the great qualification of the Vaiṣṇava *sampradāyas.*

It is the Māyāvāda *sampradāya* that does not accept the transcendental form of the Lord. If a Vaiṣṇava *sampradāya* is also carried away by that impersonal attitude, that *sampradāya* has no position at all. It is a fact that there are many so-called Vaiṣṇavas whose ultimate aim is to merge into the existence of the Lord. For example, the *sahajiyās'* Vaiṣṇava philosophy is to become one with the Supreme. Śrī Caitanya Mahāprabhu points out that Śrī Mādhavendra Purī accepted Madhvācārya only because his *sampradāya* accepted the transcendental form of the Lord.

TEXT 278

এইমত তাঁর ঘরে গর্ব চূর্ণ করি' ।
ফল্গুতীর্থে তবে চলি আইলা গৌরহরি ॥ ২৭৮ ॥

ei-mata tāṅra ghare garva cūrṇa kari'
phalgu-tīrthe tabe cali āilā gaurahari

ei-mata—in this way; *tāṅra ghare*—at his place; *garva*—pride; *cūrṇa*—broken; *kari'*—making; *phalgu-tīrthe*—to the holy place named Phalgu-tīrtha; *tabe*—then; *cali*—walking; *āilā*—came; *gaurahari*—Lord Śrī Caitanya Mahāprabhu.

TRANSLATION

Thus Śrī Caitanya Mahāprabhu broke the pride of the Tattvavādīs to pieces. He then went to the holy place known as Phalgu-tīrtha.

TEXT 279

ত্রিতকূপে বিশালার করি' দরশন ।
পঞ্চাপ্সরা-তীর্থে আইলা শচীর নন্দন ॥ ২৭৯ ॥

tritakūpe viśālāra kari' daraśana
pañcāpsarā-tīrthe āilā śacīra nandana

tritakūpe—to Tritakūpa; *viśālāra*—of the Deity named Viśālā; *kari'*—doing; *daraśana*—visiting; *pañca-apsarā-tīrthe*—to Pañcāpsarā-tīrtha; *āilā*—came; *śacīra nandana*—the son of mother Śacī.

TRANSLATION

Śrī Caitanya Mahāprabhu, the son of mother Śacī, next went to Tritakūpa, and after seeing the Viśālā Deity there, He went to the holy place known as Pañcāpsarā-tīrtha.

PURPORT

The Apsarās, denizens of the heavenly planets, are generally known as dancing girls. The girls in the heavenly planets are exquisitely beautiful, and if a woman on earth is found to be very beautiful, she is compared to the Apsarās. There were five Apsarās named Latā, Budbudā, Samīcī, Saurabheyī and Varṇā. It is said that these five beautiful dancing girls were sent by Indra to break the severe austerity of a saintly person called Acyuta Ṛṣi. This action was typical of Indra, the King of heaven. Whenever Indra discovered someone undergoing severe austerities, he would begin to fear for his post. Indra was always anxious about his position, fearing that if someone became more powerful than he was, he would lose his elevated position. Thus as soon as he would see a saint undergoing severe austerities, he would send dancing girls to distract him. Even the great saint Viśvāmitra Muni fell victim to his plan.

When the five Apsarās went to break Acyuta Ṛṣi's meditation, they were all chastised and cursed by the saint. As a result, the girls turned into crocodiles in a lake that came to be known as Pañcāpsarā. Lord Rāmacandra also visited this place. From Śrī Nārada Muni's narration, it is understood that when Arjuna went to visit the holy places, he learned about the condemnation of the five Apsarās. He delivered them from their abominable condition, and from that day the lake known as Pañcāpsarā became a place of pilgrimage.

TEXT 280

গোকর্ণে শিব দেখি' আইলা দ্বৈপায়নি ।
সূর্পারক-তীর্থে আইলা ন্যাসিশিরোমণি ॥ ২৮০ ॥

gokarṇe śiva dekhi' āilā dvaipāyani
sūrpāraka-tīrthe āilā nyāsi-śiromaṇi

gokarṇe—in the place named Gokarṇa; *śiva*—the temple of Lord Śiva; *dekhi'*—seeing; *āilā*—came; *dvaipāyani*—to Dvaipāyani; *sūrpāraka-tīrthe*—to the holy place named Sūrpāraka; *āilā*—came; *nyāsi-śiromaṇi*—the best of the *sannyāsīs*, Śrī Caitanya Mahāprabhu.

TRANSLATION

After seeing Pañcāpsarā, Śrī Caitanya Mahāprabhu went to Gokarṇa. While there, He visited the temple of Lord Śiva, and then He went to Dvaipāyani. Śrī Caitanya Mahāprabhu, the crown jewel of all sannyāsīs, then went to Sūrpāraka-tīrtha.

PURPORT

Gokarṇa is situated in North Kanara, in the Karnataka state. It is about thirty-three miles southeast of Karwar. This place is very famous for the temple of Lord Śiva known as Mahā-baleśvara. Hundreds and thousands of pilgrims come to see this temple.

Sūrpāraka is about twenty-six miles north of Bombay. In the Maharashtra province, near Bombay, is a district known as Thānā and a place known as Sopārā. Sūrpāraka is mentioned in the *Mahābhārata* (*Śānti-parva,* Chapter 41, verses 66–67).

TEXT 281

কোলাপুরে লক্ষ্মী দেখি' দেখেন ক্ষীর-ভগবতী ।
লাঙ্গ-গণেশ দেখি' দেখেন চোর-পার্বতী ॥ ২৮১ ॥

kolāpure lakṣmī dekhi' dekhena kṣīra-bhagavatī
lāṅga-gaṇeśa dekhi' dekhena cora-pārvatī

kolāpure—at Kolāpura; *lakṣmī*—the goddess of fortune; *dekhi'*—seeing; *dekhena*—He visited; *kṣīra-bhagavatī*—the temple of Kṣīra-bhagavatī; *lāṅga-gaṇeśa*—the deity Lāṅga-gaṇeśa; *dekhi'*—seeing; *dekhena*—He sees; *cora-pārvatī*—the goddess Pārvatī, who is known as a thief.

TRANSLATION

Śrī Caitanya Mahāprabhu then visited the town of Kolāpura, where He saw the goddess of fortune in the temple of Kṣīra-bhagavatī and saw Lāṅga-gaṇeśa in another temple, known as Cora-pārvatī.

PURPORT

Kolāpura is a town in the Maharashtra province, formerly known as Bombay Pradesh. Formerly Kolāpura was a native state, and it is bordered on the north by the district of Sāṅtārā, on the east and south by the district of Belagāma, and on the west by the district of Ratnagiri. In Kolāpura there is a river named Urṇā. From the *Bombay Gazette* it is understood that there were about 250 temples there, out of which six are very famous. These are (1) Ambābāi, or Mahālakṣmī Mandira, (2) Viṭhobā Mandira, (3) Ṭemblāi Mandira, (4) Mahākālī Mandira, (5) Phirāṅga-i, or Pratyaṅgirā Mandira, and (6) Yāllāmmā Mandira.

TEXT 282

তথা হৈতে পাণ্ডরপুরে আইলা গৌরচন্দ্র ।
বিঠ্ঠল-ঠাকুর দেখি' পাইলা আনন্দ ॥ ২৮২ ॥

tathā haite pāṇḍarapure āilā gauracandra
viṭhṭhala-ṭhākura dekhi' pāilā ānanda

tathā haite—from there; *pāṇḍara-pure*—to Pāṇḍarapura; *āilā*—came; *gauracandra*—Lord Śrī Caitanya Mahāprabhu; *viṭhṭhala-ṭhākura*—the Deity known as Viṭhṭhala; *dekhi'*—seeing; *pāilā*—got; *ānanda*—great happiness.

TRANSLATION

From there Śrī Caitanya Mahāprabhu went to Pāṇḍarapura, where He happily saw the temple of Viṭhṭhala Ṭhākura.

PURPORT

The city of Pāṇḍarapura is situated on the river Bhīmā. It is said that Śrī Caitanya Mahāprabhu initiated Tukārāma when He visited Pāṇḍarapura, and thus Tukārāma became His disciple. Tukārāma

Ācārya became very famous in the Maharashtra province, and he spread the *saṅkīrtana* movement all over the province. The *saṅkīrtana* party belonging to Tukārāma is still very popular in Bombay and throughout the province of Maharashtra. Tukārāma's book is known as *Abhaṅga.* His *saṅkīrtana* party exactly resembles the Gauḍīya-Vaiṣṇava *saṅkīrtana* parties, for they chant the holy name of the Lord with *mṛdaṅga* and *karatālas.*

The Lord Viṭhṭhaladeva mentioned in this verse is a form of Lord Viṣṇu with two hands. He is Nārāyaṇa.

TEXT 283

প্রেমাবেশে কৈল বহুত কীর্তন-নর্তন ।
তাহাঁ এক বিপ্র তাঁরে কৈল নিমন্ত্রণ ॥ ২৮৩ ॥

premāveśe kaila bahuta kīrtana-nartana
tāhāṅ eka vipra tāṅre kaila nimantraṇa

prema-āveśe—in the great ecstasy of love; *kaila*—performed; *bahuta*—much; *kīrtana-nartana*—chanting and dancing; *tāhāṅ*—there; *eka*—one; *vipra*—*brāhmaṇa; tāṅre*—unto Him; *kaila*—did; *nimantraṇa*—invitation.

TRANSLATION

Śrī Caitanya Mahāprabhu chanted and danced in various ways as usual. A brāhmaṇa, seeing Him in ecstatic love, was very pleased and invited the Lord to his home for lunch.

TEXT 284

বহুত আদরে প্রভুকে ভিক্ষা করাইল ।
ভিক্ষা করি' তথা এক শুভবার্তা পাইল ॥ ২৮৪ ॥

bahuta ādare prabhuke bhikṣā karāila
bhikṣā kari' tathā eka śubha-vārtā pāila

bahuta ādare—with great love; *prabhuke*—unto Lord Śrī Caitanya Mahāprabhu; *bhikṣā karāila*—offered lunch; *bhikṣā kari'*—after finishing His lunch; *tathā*—there; *eka*—one; *śubha-vārtā*—auspicious news; *pāila*—got.

TRANSLATION

The brāhmaṇa offered Śrī Caitanya Mahāprabhu food with great respect and love. After finishing His lunch, the Lord received auspicious news.

TEXT 285

মাধব-পুরীর শিষ্য 'শ্রীরঙ্গ-পুরী' নাম।
সেই গ্রামে বিপ্রগৃহে করেন বিশ্রাম ॥ ২৮৫ ॥

mādhava-purīra śiṣya 'śrī-raṅga-purī' nāma
sei grāme vipra-gṛhe karena viśrāma

mādhava-purīra śiṣya—a disciple of Mādhavendra Purī; *śrī-raṅga-purī*—Śrī Raṅga Purī; *nāma*—named; *sei grāme*—in that village; *vipra-gṛhe*—in the house of a *brāhmaṇa; karena viśrāma*—rests.

TRANSLATION

Śrī Caitanya Mahāprabhu received word that Śrī Raṅga Purī, one of the disciples of Śrī Mādhavendra Purī, was present in that village at the home of a brāhmaṇa.

TEXT 286

শুনিয়া চলিলা প্রভু তাঁরে দেখিবারে।
বিপ্রগৃহে বসি' আছেন, দেখিলা তাঁহারে ॥ ২৮৬ ॥

śuniyā calilā prabhu tāṅre dekhibāre
vipra-gṛhe vasi' āchena, dekhilā tāṅhāre

śuniyā—hearing; *calilā*—went; *prabhu*—Śrī Caitanya Mahāprabhu; *tāṅre*—him; *dekhibāre*—to see; *vipra-gṛhe*—at the house of the *brāhmaṇa; vasi'*—sitting; *āchena*—was; *dekhilā*—saw; *tāṅhāre*—him.

TRANSLATION

Hearing this news, Śrī Caitanya Mahāprabhu immediately went to see Śrī Raṅga Purī at the brāhmaṇa's home. Upon entering, the Lord saw him sitting there.

TEXT 287

প্রেমাবেশে করে তাঁরে দণ্ড-পরণাম।
অশ্রু, পুলক, কম্প, সর্বাঙ্গে পড়ে ঘাম ॥ ২৮৭ ॥

premāveśe kare tāṅre daṇḍa-paraṇāma
aśru, pulaka, kampa, sarvāṅge paḍe ghāma

prema-āveśe—in ecstatic love; *kare*—does; *tāṅre*—unto him; *daṇḍa-paraṇāma*—obeisances, falling flat; *aśru*—tears; *pulaka*—jubilation; *kampa*—trembling; *sarva-aṅge*—all over the body; *paḍe*—there was; *ghāma*—perspiration.

TRANSLATION

As soon as Śrī Caitanya Mahāprabhu saw Śrī Raṅga Purī, He immediately offered him obeisances in ecstatic love, falling flat on the ground. The symptoms of transcendental transformation were visible — namely, tears, jubilation, trembling and perspiration.

TEXT 288

দেখিয়া বিস্মিত হৈল শ্রীরঙ্গ-পুরীর মন।
'উঠহ শ্রীপাদ' বলি' বলিলা বচন ॥ ২৮৮ ॥

dekhiyā vismita haila śrī-raṅga-purīra mana
'uṭhaha śrīpāda' bali' balilā vacana

dekhiyā—seeing; *vismita*—astonished; *haila*—became; *śrī-raṅga-purīra*—of Śrī Raṅga Purī; *mana*—the mind; *uṭhaha*—get up; *śrī-pāda*—Your Holiness; *bali'*—saying; *balilā vacana*—began to speak.

TRANSLATION

Upon seeing Śrī Caitanya Mahāprabhu in such an ecstatic mood, Śrī Raṅga Purī said, "Your Holiness, please get up.

TEXT 289

শ্রীপাদ, ধর মোর গোসাঞির সম্বন্ধ।
তাহা বিনা অন্যত্র নাহি এই প্রেমার গন্ধ ॥ ২৮৯ ॥

śrīpāda, dhara mora gosāñira sambandha
tāhā vinā anyatra nāhi ei premāra gandha

śrī-pāda—O Your Holiness; *dhara*—You hold; *mora*—my; *gosāñira*—with Śrī Mādhavendra Purī; *sambandha*—relationship; *tāhā vinā*—without him; *anyatra*—elsewhere; *nāhi*—there is not; *ei*—this; *premāra*—of ecstasy; *gandha*—fragrance.

TRANSLATION

"Your Holiness is certainly related to Śrī Mādhavendra Purī, without whom there is no fragrance of ecstatic love."

PURPORT

Śrīla Bhaktisiddhānta Sarasvatī Ṭhākura remarks that up to the advent of His Holiness Śrīpāda Lakṣmīpati Tīrtha, it was the system in the disciplic succession of Madhvācārya to worship Lord Kṛṣṇa alone. After Śrīla Mādhavendra Purī, worship of both Rādhā and Kṛṣṇa was established. For this reason Śrī Mādhavendra Purī is accepted as the root of worship in ecstatic love. Unless one is connected to the disciplic succession of Mādhavendra Purī, there is no possibility of awakening the symptoms of ecstatic love. The word *gosāñi* is significant in this connection. The spiritual master who is fully surrendered unto the Supreme Personality of Godhead and has no business other than the Lord's service is called the best of the *paramahaṁsas.* A *paramahaṁsa* has no program for sense gratification; he is interested only in satisfying the senses of the Lord. One who has control of the senses in this way is called a *gosāñi* or a *gosvāmī,* master of the senses. The senses cannot be controlled unless one is engaged in the service of the Lord; therefore the bona fide spiritual master, who has full control over his senses, engages twenty-four hours a day in the Lord's service. He can therefore be addressed as *gosāñi* or *gosvāmī.* The title *gosvāmī* cannot be inherited but can be given only to a bona fide spiritual master.

There were six great Gosvāmīs of Vṛndāvana—Śrīla Rūpa, Sanātana, Bhaṭṭa Raghunātha, Śrī Jīva, Gopāla Bhaṭṭa and Dāsa Raghunātha—and none of them inherited the title of *gosvāmī.* All the Gosvāmīs of Vṛndāvana were bona fide spiritual masters situated on the highest platform of devotional service, and for that reason they were called *gosvāmīs.* All the temples of Vṛndāvana were certainly started by the six Gosvāmīs. Later the worship in the temples was entrusted to some householder disciples of the Gosvāmīs, and since then the hereditary title of *gosvāmī* has been used. However, only one who is a bona fide spiritual master expanding the cult of Śrī Caitanya Mahāprabhu, the Kṛṣṇa consciousness movement, and who is in full control of his senses can be addressed as a *gosvāmī.* Unfortunately, the hereditary process is going on; therefore at the present moment, in most cases the title is being misused due to ignorance of the word's etymology.

TEXT 290

এত বলি' প্রভুকে উঠাঞা কৈল আলিঙ্গন।
গলাগলি করি' দুঁহে করেন ক্রন্দন ॥ ২৯০ ॥

eta bali' prabhuke uṭhāñā kaila āliṅgana
galāgali kari' duṅhe karena krandana

eta bali'—saying this; *prabhuke*—Lord Śrī Caitanya Mahāprabhu; *uṭhāñā*—lifting up; *kaila*—did; *āliṅgana*—embracing; *galāgali*—shoulder to shoulder; *kari'*—doing; *duṅhe*—both of them; *karena*—do; *krandana*—crying.

TRANSLATION

After saying this, Śrī Raṅga Purī lifted Śrī Caitanya Mahāprabhu up and embraced Him. As they embraced shoulder to shoulder, they both began to cry in ecstasy.

TEXT 291

ক্ষণেকে আবেশ ছাড়ি' দুঁহার ধৈর্য হৈল।
ঈশ্বর-পুরীর সম্বন্ধ গোসাঞি জানাইল ॥ ২৯১ ॥

kṣaṇeke āveśa chāḍi' duṅhāra dhairya haila
īśvara-purīra sambandha gosāñi jānāila

kṣaṇeke—after just a few moments; *āveśa*—ecstasy; *chāḍi'*—giving up; *duṅhāra*—of both of them; *dhairya*—patience; *haila*—there was; *īśvara-purīra*—of Īśvara Purī; *sambandha*—relationship; *gosāñi*—Śrī Caitanya Mahāprabhu; *jānāila*—disclosed.

TRANSLATION

After some moments, they came to their senses and became patient. Śrī Caitanya Mahāprabhu then informed Śrī Raṅga Purī about His relationship with Īśvara Purī.

TEXT 292

অদ্ভুত প্রেমের বন্যা দুঁহার উথলিল।
দুঁহে মান্য করি' দুঁহে আনন্দে বসিল ॥ ২৯২ ॥

adbhuta premera vanyā duṅhāra uthalila
duṅhe mānya kari' duṅhe ānande vasila

adbhuta—wonderful; *premera*—of love of Godhead; *vanyā*—inundation; *duṅhāra*—of both of them; *uthalila*—arose; *duṅhe*—both of them; *mānya kari'*—offering respect; *duṅhe*—both of them; *ānande*—with great happiness; *vasila*—sat down.

TRANSLATION

They were both inundated by the wonderful ecstasy of love that was aroused in them. Finally they sat down and respectfully began to converse.

TEXT 293

দুই জনে কৃষ্ণকথা কহে রাত্রি-দিনে।
এইমতে গোঙাইল পাঁচ-সাত দিনে ॥ ২৯৩ ॥

dui jane kṛṣṇa-kathā kahe rātri-dine
ei-mate goṅāila pāṅca-sāta dine

dui jane—both the persons; *kṛṣṇa-kathā*—topics of Kṛṣṇa; *kahe*—speak; *rātri-dine*—day and night; *ei-mate*—in this way; *goṅāila*—passed; *pāṅca-sāta*—five to seven; *dine*—days.

TRANSLATION

In this way they discussed topics about Lord Kṛṣṇa continually for five to seven days.

TEXT 294

কৌতুকে পুরী তাঁরে পুছিল জন্মস্থান
গোসাঞি কৌতুকে কহেন 'নবদ্বীপ' নাম ॥ ২৯৪ ॥

kautuke purī tāṅre puchila janma-sthāna
gosāñi kautuke kahena 'navadvīpa' nāma

kautuke—out of curiosity; *purī*—Śrī Raṅga Purī; *tāṅre*—Him; *puchila*—asked; *janma-sthāna*—the place of birth; *gosāñi*—Śrī Caitanya Mahāprabhu; *kautuke*—as a matter of course; *kahena*—said; *nava-dvīpa*—Navadvīpa; *nāma*—name.

TRANSLATION

Out of curiosity, Śrī Raṅga Purī asked Śrī Caitanya Mahāprabhu about His birthplace, and the Lord informed him that it was Navadvīpa-dhāma.

TEXT 295

শ্রীমাধব-পুরীর সঙ্গে শ্রীরঙ্গ-পুরী।
পূর্বে আসিয়াছিলা তেঁহো নদীয়া-নগরী ॥ ২৯৫ ॥

śrī-mādhava-purīra saṅge śrī-raṅga-purī
pūrve āsiyāchilā teṅho nadīyā-nagarī

śrī-mādhava-purīra saṅge—with Śrī Mādhavendra Purī; *śrī-raṅga-purī*—Śrī Raṅga Purī; *pūrve*—formerly; *āsiyāchilā*—came; *teṅho*—he; *nadīyā-nagarī*—to the city of Nadia.

TRANSLATION

Śrī Raṅga Purī had formerly gone to Navadvīpa with Śrī Mādhavendra Purī, and he therefore remembered the incidents that had taken place there.

TEXT 296

জগন্নাথমিশ্র-ঘরে ভিক্ষা যে করিল।
অপূর্ব মোচার ঘণ্ট তাহাঁ যে খাইল ॥ ২৯৬ ॥

jagannātha-miśra-ghare bhikṣā ye karila
apūrva mocāra ghaṇṭa tāhāṅ ye khāila

jagannātha-miśra-ghare—in the house of Śrī Jagannātha Miśra; *bhikṣā*—lunch; *ye*—that; *karila*—took; *apūrva*—unprecedented; *mocāra ghaṇṭa*—curry made of plantain flowers; *tāhāṅ*—there; *ye*—that; *khāila*—ate.

TRANSLATION

As soon as Śrī Raṅga Purī recalled Navadvīpa, he also recalled accompanying Śrī Mādhavendra Purī to the house of Jagannātha Miśra, where Śrī Raṅga Purī had taken lunch. He even remembered the taste of an unprecedented curry made of banana flowers.

TEXT 297

জগন্নাথের ব্রাহ্মণী, তেঁহ — মহা-পতিব্রতা ।
বাৎসল্যে হয়েন তেঁহ যেন জগন্মাতা ॥ ২৯৭ ॥

jagannāthera brāhmaṇī, teṅha — mahā-pativratā
vātsalye hayena teṅha yena jagan-mātā

jagannāthera—of Jagannātha Miśra; *brāhmaṇī*—wife; *teṅha*—she; *mahā*—great; *pati-vratā*—devoted to her husband; *vātsalye*—in affection; *hayena*—was; *teṅha*—she; *yena*—as if; *jagat-mātā*—the mother of the whole universe.

TRANSLATION

Śrī Raṅga Purī also remembered the wife of Jagannātha Miśra. She was very devoted and chaste. As for her affection, she was exactly like the mother of the universe.

TEXT 298

রন্ধনে নিপুণা তাঁ-সম নাহি ত্রিভুবনে ।
পুত্রসম স্নেহ করেন সন্ন্যাসি-ভোজনে ॥ ২৯৮ ॥

randhane nipuṇā tāṅ-sama nāhi tribhuvane
putra-sama sneha karena sannyāsi-bhojane

randhane—in cooking; *nipuṇā*—very expert; *tāṅ-sama*—like her; *nāhi*—there is none; *tri-bhuvane*—in the three worlds; *putra-sama*—like to her own sons; *sneha karena*—she was affectionate; *sannyāsi-bhojane*—in feeding the *sannyāsīs.*

TRANSLATION

He also remembered how Śrī Jagannātha Miśra's wife, Śacīmātā, was expert in cooking. He recalled that she was very affectionate toward the sannyāsīs and fed them exactly like her own sons.

TEXT 299

তাঁর এক যোগ্য পুত্র করিয়াছে সন্ন্যাস।
'শঙ্করারণ্য' নাম তাঁর অল্প বয়স ॥ ২৯৯ ॥

tāṅra eka yogya putra kariyāche sannyāsa
'śaṅkarāraṇya' nāma tāṅra alpa vayasa

tāṅra—her; *eka*—one; *yogya*—deserving; *putra*—son; *kariyāche*—has accepted; *sannyāsa*—the renounced order of life; *śaṅkarāraṇya*—Śaṅkarāraṇya; *nāma*—named; *tāṅra*—his; *alpa*—little; *vayasa*—age.

TRANSLATION

Śrī Raṅga Purī also remembered that one of her deserving sons had accepted the renounced order at a very young age. His name was Śaṅkarāraṇya.

TEXT 300

এই তীর্থে শঙ্করারণ্যের সিদ্ধিপ্রাপ্তি হৈল।
প্রস্তাবে শ্রীরঙ্গ-পুরী এতেক কহিল ॥ ৩০০ ॥

ei tīrthe śaṅkarāraṇyera siddhi-prāpti haila
prastāve śrī-raṅga-purī eteka kahila

ei tīrthe—in this holy place; *śaṅkarāraṇyera*—of Śaṅkarāraṇya; *siddhi-prāpti*—attainment of perfection; *haila*—became fulfilled;

prastāve—in the course of conversation; *śrī-raṅga-purī*—Śrī Raṅga Purī; *eteka*—thus; *kahila*—spoke.

TRANSLATION

Śrī Raṅga Purī informed Śrī Caitanya Mahāprabhu that the sannyāsī named Śaṅkarāraṇya had attained perfection in that holy place, Pāṇḍarapura.

PURPORT

Śrī Caitanya Mahāprabhu's elder brother was named Viśvarūpa. He left home before Śrī Caitanya Mahāprabhu and accepted the *sannyāsa* order under the name of Śaṅkarāraṇya Svāmī. He traveled all over the country and finally went to Pāṇḍarapura, where he passed away after attaining perfection. In other words, he entered the spiritual world after giving up his mortal body at Pāṇḍarapura. Śrī Raṅga Purī, a disciple of Śrī Mādhavendra Purī and Godbrother of Īśvara Purī, disclosed this important news to Śrī Caitanya Mahāprabhu.

TEXT 301

প্রভু কহে, — পূর্বাশ্রমে তেঁহ মোর ভ্রাতা ।
জগন্নাথ মিশ্র — পূর্বাশ্রমে মোর পিতা ॥ ৩০১ ॥

prabhu kahe,—pūrvāśrame teṅha mora bhrātā
jagannātha miśra—pūrvāśrame mora pitā

prabhu kahe—the Lord replied; *pūrva-āśrame*—in My previous *āśrama; teṅha*—he; *mora bhrātā*—My brother; *jagannātha miśra*—Jagannātha Miśra; *pūrva-āśrame*—in My previous *āśrama; mora pitā*—My father.

TRANSLATION

Śrī Caitanya Mahāprabhu said, "In My previous āśrama, Śaṅkarāraṇya was My brother and Jagannātha Miśra was My father."

TEXT 302

এইমত দুইজনে ইষ্টগোষ্ঠী করি' ।
দ্বারকা দেখিতে চলিলা শ্রীরঙ্গপুরী ॥ ৩০২ ॥

ei-mata dui-jane iṣṭa-goṣṭhī kari'
dvārakā dekhite calilā śrī-raṅga-purī

ei-mata—in this way; *dui-jane*—both of them; *iṣṭa-goṣṭhī kari'*—discussing many topics; *dvārakā dekhite*—to see Dvārakā; *calilā*—started; *śrī-raṅga-purī*—Śrī Raṅga Purī.

TRANSLATION

After finishing his talks with Śrī Caitanya Mahāprabhu, Śrī Raṅga Purī started for Dvārakā-dhāma.

TEXT 303

দিন চারি তথা প্রভুকে রাখিল ব্রাহ্মণ।
ভীমানদী স্নান করি' করেন বিঠ্ঠল দর্শন ॥ ৩০৩ ॥

dina cāri tathā prabhuke rākhila brāhmaṇa
bhīmā-nadī snāna kari' karena viṭhṭhala darśana

dina—days; *cāri*—four; *tathā*—there; *prabhuke*—Lord Caitanya Mahāprabhu; *rākhila*—kept; *brāhmaṇa*—the *brāhmaṇa; bhīmā-nadī*—in the river Bhīmā; *snāna kari'*—bathing; *karena*—does; *viṭhṭhala darśana*—visit the temple of Viṭhṭhala.

TRANSLATION

After Śrī Raṅga Purī departed for Dvārakā, Śrī Caitanya Mahāprabhu remained with the brāhmaṇa at Pāṇḍarapura for four more days. He took His bath in the Bhīmā River and visited the temple of Viṭhṭhala.

TEXT 304

তবে মহাপ্রভু আইলা কৃষ্ণবেণ্বা-তীরে।
নানা তীর্থ দেখি' তাহাঁ দেবতা-মন্দিরে ॥ ৩০৪ ॥

tabe mahāprabhu āilā kṛṣṇa-veṇvā-tīre
nānā tīrtha dekhi' tāhāṅ devatā-mandire

tabe—thereafter; *mahāprabhu*—Śrī Caitanya Mahāprabhu; *āilā*—came; *kṛṣṇa-veṇvā-tīre*—to the bank of the river Kṛṣṇa-veṇvā;

nānā—various; *tīrtha*—holy places; *dekhi'*—seeing; *tāhāṅ*—there; *devatā-mandire*—in the temples of some gods.

TRANSLATION

Śrī Caitanya Mahāprabhu next went to the bank of the Kṛṣṇa-veṇvā River, where He visited many holy places and the temples of various gods.

PURPORT

This river is a branch of the river Kṛṣṇā. It is said that Ṭhākura Bilvamaṅgala resided on the banks of this river, which is also called the Vīnā, the Veṇī, the Sinā and the Bhīmā.

TEXT 305

ব্রাহ্মণ-সমাজ সব —বৈষ্ণব-চরিত।
বৈষ্ণব সকল পড়ে 'কৃষ্ণকর্ণামৃত' ॥ ৩০৫ ॥

brāhmaṇa-samāja saba—vaiṣṇava-carita
vaiṣṇava sakala paḍe 'kṛṣṇa-karṇāmṛta'

brāhmaṇa-samāja—the community of *brāhmaṇas; saba*—all; *vaiṣṇava-carita*—pure devotees; *vaiṣṇava sakala*—all the Vaiṣṇavas; *paḍe*—study; *kṛṣṇa-karṇāmṛta*—the *Kṛṣṇa-karṇāmṛta* of Bilvamaṅgala Ṭhākura.

TRANSLATION

The brāhmaṇa community there was composed of pure devotees. They regularly studied a book entitled Kṛṣṇa-karṇāmṛta, which was composed by Bilvamaṅgala Ṭhākura.

PURPORT

This book was composed by Bilvamaṅgala Ṭhākura in 112 verses. There are two or three other books bearing the same name, and there are also two commentaries on Bilvamaṅgala's book. One commentary was written by Kṛṣṇadāsa Kavirāja Gosvāmī and the other by Caitanya dāsa Gosvāmī.

TEXT 306

কৃষ্ণকর্ণামৃত শুনি' প্রভুর আনন্দ হৈল।
আগ্রহ করিয়া পুঁথি লেখাঞা লৈল ॥ ৩০৬ ॥

kṛṣṇa-karṇāmṛta śuni' prabhura ānanda haila
āgraha kariyā puṅthi lekhāñā laila

kṛṣṇa-karṇāmṛta śuni'—after hearing the *Kṛṣṇa-karnāmṛta; prabhura*—of Lord Śrī Caitanya Mahāprabhu; *ānanda haila*—there was great happiness; *āgraha kariya*—with great eagerness; *puṅthi*—the book; *lekhāñā*—getting copied; *laila*—took.

TRANSLATION

Śrī Caitanya Mahāprabhu was very pleased to hear the book Kṛṣṇa-karṇāmṛta, and with great eagerness He had it copied and took it with Him.

TEXT 307

'কর্ণামৃত'-সম বস্তু নাহি ত্রিভুবনে।
যাহা হৈতে হয় কৃষ্ণে শুদ্ধপ্রেমজ্ঞানে ॥ ৩০৭ ॥

'karṇāmṛta'-sama vastu nāhi tribhuvane
yāhā haite haya kṛṣṇe śuddha-prema-jñāne

karṇāmṛta—the *Kṛṣṇa-karṇāmṛta; sama*—like; *vastu nāhi*—there is nothing; *tri-bhuvane*—in the three worlds; *yāhā haite*—from which; *haya*—there is; *kṛṣṇe*—unto Lord Kṛṣṇa; *śuddha-prema-jñāne*—knowledge of pure devotional service.

TRANSLATION

There is no comparison to the Kṛṣṇa-karṇāmṛta within the three worlds. By studying this book, one is elevated to the knowledge of pure devotional service to Kṛṣṇa.

TEXT 308

সৌন্দর্য-মাধুর্য-কৃষ্ণলীলার অবধি।
সেই জানে, যে 'কর্ণামৃত' পড়ে নিরবধি ॥ ৩০৮ ॥

saundarya-mādhurya-kṛṣṇa-līlāra avadhi
sei jāne, ye 'karṇāmṛta' paḍe niravadhi

saundarya—beauty; *mādhurya*—sweetness; *kṛṣṇa-līlāra*—of the pastimes of Lord Kṛṣṇa; *avadhi*—limit; *sei jāne*—he knows; *ye*—one who; *karṇāmṛta*—the book *Kṛṣṇa-karṇāmṛta; paḍe*—studies; *niravadhi*—constantly.

TRANSLATION

One who constantly reads the Kṛṣṇa-karṇāmṛta can fully understand the beauty and melodious taste of the pastimes of Lord Kṛṣṇa.

TEXT 309

'ব্রহ্মসংহিতা', 'কর্ণামৃত' দুই পুঁথি পাঞা।
মহারত্নপ্রায় পাই আইলা সঙ্গে লঞা ॥ ৩০৯ ॥

'brahma-saṁhitā', 'karṇāmṛta' dui puṅthi pāñā
mahā-ratna-prāya pāi āilā saṅge lañā

brahma-saṁhitā—the book *Brahma-saṁhitā; karṇāmṛta*—the book *Kṛṣṇa-karṇāmṛta; dui*—two; *puṅthi*—books; *pāñā*—getting; *mahā-ratna-prāya*—like the most valuable jewels; *pāi*—getting; *āilā*—came back; *saṅge*—with Him; *lañā*—taking.

TRANSLATION

The Brahma-saṁhitā and Kṛṣṇa-karṇāmṛta were two books that Śrī Caitanya Mahāprabhu considered to be most valuable jewels. Therefore He took them with Him on His return trip.

TEXT 310

তাপী স্নান করি' আইলা মাহিষ্মতীপুরে।
নানা তীর্থ দেখি তাহাঁ নর্মদার তীরে ॥ ৩১০ ॥

tāpī snāna kari' āilā māhiṣmatī-pure
nānā tīrtha dekhi tāhāṅ narmadāra tīre

tāpī—in the Tāpī River; *snāna kari'*—taking a bath; *āilā*—arrived; *māhiṣmatī-pure*—at Māhiṣmatī-pura; *nānā tīrtha*—many holy places; *dekhi*—seeing; *tāhāṅ*—there; *narmadāra tīre*—on the bank of the river Narmadā.

TRANSLATION

Śrī Caitanya Mahāprabhu next arrived at the banks of the river Tāpī. After bathing there, He went to Māhiṣmatī-pura. While there, He saw many holy places on the banks of the river Narmadā.

PURPORT

The river Tāpī is also known as Tāpti. The river's source is a mountain called Multāi, and the river flows westward through the state of Saurāṣṭra and into the Arabian Sea.

Māhiṣmatī-pura (Maheshwar) is mentioned in *Mahābhārata* in connection with Sahadeva's victory. Sahadeva, the youngest brother of the Pāṇḍavas, conquered that part of the country. As stated in the *Mahābhārata:*

tato ratnāny upādāya purīṁ māhiṣmatīṁ yayau
tatra nīlena rājñā sa cakre yuddhaṁ nararṣabhaḥ

"After acquiring jewels, Sahadeva went to the city of Māhiṣmatī, where he fought with a king called Nīla."

TEXT 311

ধনুস্তীর্থ দেখি' করিলা নির্বিন্ধ্যাতে স্নানে ।
ঋষ্যমূক-গিরি আইলা দণ্ডকারণ্যে ॥ ৩১১ ॥

dhanus-tīrtha dekhi' karilā nirvindhyāte snāne
ṛṣyamūka-giri āilā daṇḍakāraṇye

dhanuḥ-tīrtha—Dhanus-tīrtha; *dekhi'*—seeing; *karilā*—did; *nirvindhyāte*—in the river Nirvindhyā; *snāne*—bathing; *ṛṣyamūka-giri*—at the Ṛṣyamūka Mountain; *āilā*—arrived; *daṇḍaka-araṇye*—in the forest known as Daṇḍakāraṇya.

TRANSLATION

The Lord next arrived at Dhanus-tīrtha, where He took His bath in the river Nirvindhyā. He then arrived at Ṛṣyamūka Mountain and then went to Daṇḍakāraṇya.

PURPORT

According to some opinions, Ṛṣyamūka is a chain of mountains beginning at the village of Hāmpi-grāma in the district of Belāri. The mountain chain begins along the bank of the river Tuṅgabhadrā, which gradually reaches the state of Hyderabad. According to other opinions, this hill is situated in Madhya Pradesh and bears the present name of Rāmpa. Daṇḍakāraṇya is a spacious tract of land which begins north of Khāndeśa and extends up to the southern Āhammada-nagara through Nāsika and Āuraṅgābāda. The Godāvarī River flows through this tract of land, and there is a great forest there where Lord Rāmacandra lived.

TEXT 312

'সপ্ততাল-বৃক্ষ' দেখে কানন-ভিতর ।
অতি বৃদ্ধ, অতি স্থূল, অতি উচ্চতর ॥ ৩১২ ॥

'saptatāla-vṛkṣa' dekhe kānana-bhitara
ati vṛddha, ati sthūla, ati uccatara

sapta-tāla-vṛkṣa—seven palm trees; *dekhe*—sees; *kānana bhitara*—within the forest; *ati vṛddha*—very old; *ati sthūla*—very bulky; *ati uccatara*—very high.

TRANSLATION

Within the Daṇḍakāraṇya forest Śrī Caitanya Mahāprabhu then visited a place called Saptatāla. The seven palm trees there were very old, very bulky and very high.

PURPORT

The name Saptatāla is mentioned in the *Kiṣkindhyā* section of the *Rāmāyaṇa* and is described in the eleventh and twelfth chapters of that section.

TEXT 313

সপ্ততাল দেখি' প্রভু আলিঙ্গন কৈল ।
সশরীরে সপ্ততাল বৈকুণ্ঠে চলিল ॥ ৩১৩ ॥

saptatāla dekhi' prabhu āliṅgana kaila
saśarīre saptatāla vaikuṇṭhe calila

sapta-tāla dekhi'—upon seeing the seven palm trees; *prabhu*—Lord Caitanya Mahāprabhu; *āliṅgana kaila*—embraced; *sa-śarīre*—with their bodies; *sapta-tāla*—the seven palm trees; *vaikuṇṭhe calila*—returned to Vaikuṇṭhaloka.

TRANSLATION

Upon seeing the seven palm trees, Śrī Caitanya Mahāprabhu embraced them. As a result, they all returned to Vaikuṇṭhaloka, the spiritual world.

TEXT 314

শূন্যস্থল দেখি' লোকের হৈল চমৎকার ।
লোকে কহে, এ সন্ন্যাসী — রাম-অবতার ॥ ৩১৪ ॥

śūnya-sthala dekhi' lokera haila camatkāra
loke kahe, e sannyāsī — rāma-avatāra

śūnya-sthala—the vacant place; *dekhi'*—seeing; *lokera*—of the people in general; *haila*—there was; *camatkāra*—astonishment; *loke kahe*—all people began to say; *e sannyāsī*—this *sannyāsī; rāma-avatāra*—incarnation of Lord Rāmacandra.

TRANSLATION

After the seven palm trees had departed for Vaikuṇṭha, everyone was astonished to see that they were gone. The people then began to say, "This sannyāsī called Śrī Caitanya Mahāprabhu must be an incarnation of Lord Rāmacandra.

TEXT 315

সশরীরে তাল গেল শ্রীবৈকুণ্ঠ-ধাম ।
ঐছে শক্তি কার হয়, বিনা এক রাম ॥ ৩১৫ ॥

saśarīre tāla gela śrī-vaikuṇṭha-dhāma
aiche śakti kāra haya, vinā eka rāma

sa-śarīre—with the material body; *tāla*—the palm trees; *gela*—went; *śrī-vaikuṇṭha-dhāma*—to the spiritual kingdom, known as Vaikuṇṭha; *aiche*—such; *śakti*—power; *kāra*—whose; *haya*—is; *vinā*—without; *eka*—one; *rāma*—Lord Rāmacandra.

TRANSLATION

"Only Lord Rāmacandra has the power to send seven palm trees to the spiritual Vaikuṇṭha planets."

TEXT 316

প্রভু আসি' কৈল পম্পা-সরোবরে স্নান ।
পঞ্চবটী আসি, তাহাঁ করিল বিশ্রাম ॥ ৩১৬ ॥

prabhu āsi' kaila pampā-sarovare snāna
pañcavaṭī āsi, tāhāṅ karila viśrāma

prabhu—Śrī Caitanya Mahāprabhu; *āsi'*—coming; *kaila*—did; *pampā-sarovare*—in the lake known as Pampā; *snāna*—bathing; *pañcavaṭī āsi*—then coming to Pañcavaṭī; *tāhāṅ*—there; *karila*—took; *viśrāma*—rest.

TRANSLATION

Eventually Śrī Caitanya Mahāprabhu arrived at a lake known as Pampā, where He took His bath. He then went to a place called Pañcavaṭī, where He rested.

PURPORT

According to some, the old name of the Tuṅgabhadrā River was Pambā. According to others, Vijaya-nagara, the capital of the state, was known as Pampātīrtha. According to still others, the lake near Anāguṇḍi, in the direction of Hyderabad, is Pampā-sarovara. The river Tuṅgabhadrā also flows through there. There are many different opinions about the lake called Pampā-sarovara.

TEXT 317

নাসিকে ত্র্যম্বক দেখি' গেলা ব্রহ্মগিরি ।
কুশাবর্তে আইলা যাহাঁ জন্মিলা গোদাবরী ॥ ৩১৭ ॥

nāsike tryambaka dekhi' gelā brahmagiri
kuśāvarte āilā yāhāṅ janmilā godāvarī

nāsike—at the holy place Nāsika; *tryambaka*—a deity of Lord Śiva; *dekhi'*—after seeing; *gelā*—went; *brahmagiri*—to the place known as Brahmagiri; *kuśāvarte āilā*—then He came to the holy place known as Kuśāvarta; *yāhāṅ*—where; *janmilā*—took birth; *godāvarī*—the river Godāvarī.

TRANSLATION

Śrī Caitanya Mahāprabhu then visited Nāsika, where He saw the deity of Tryambaka [Lord Śiva]. He then went to Brahma-giri and then to Kuśāvarta, the source of the river Godāvarī.

PURPORT

Kuśāvarta is located in the western *ghāṭa,* at Sahyādri. It is near Nāsika, a holy place, but according to some it was situated in the valley of Vindhya.

TEXT 318

সপ্ত গোদাবরী আইলা করি' তীর্থ বহুতর ।
পুনরপি আইলা প্রভু বিদ্যানগর ॥ ৩১৮ ॥

sapta godāvarī āilā kari' tīrtha bahutara
punarapi āilā prabhu vidyānagara

sapta godāvarī—to the place known as Sapta-godāvarī; *āilā*—came; *kari' tīrtha bahutara*—visiting various holy places; *punarapi*—again; *āilā*—came back; *prabhu*—Śrī Caitanya Mahāprabhu; *vidyānagara*—to the place where He met Rāmānanda Rāya.

TRANSLATION

After visiting many other holy places, the Lord went to Sapta-godāvarī. At last He returned to Vidyānagara.

PURPORT

In this way Śrī Caitanya Mahāprabhu traveled from the source of the Godāvarī River and eventually visited the northern side of Hyderabad state. He finally arrived at the state of Kaliṅga.

TEXT 319

রামানন্দ রায় শুনি প্রভুর আগমন ।
আনন্দে আসিয়া কৈল প্রভুসহ মিলন ॥ ৩১৯ ॥

rāmānanda rāya śuni' prabhura āgamana
ānande āsiyā kaila prabhu-saha milana

rāmānanda rāya—Rāmānanda Rāya; *śuni'*—hearing; *prabhura*—of Lord Caitanya Mahāprabhu; *āgamana*—return; *ānande*—in great happiness; *āsiyā*—coming; *kaila*—did; *prabhu-saha*—with Lord Caitanya Mahāprabhu; *milana*—meeting.

TRANSLATION

When Rāmānanda Rāya heard that Śrī Caitanya Mahāprabhu had arrived, he was very pleased, and he immediately went to see Him.

TEXT 320

দণ্ডবৎ হঞা পড়ে চরণে ধরিয়া ।
আলিঙ্গন কৈল প্রভু তাঁরে উঠাঞা ॥ ৩২০ ॥

daṇḍavat hañā paḍe caraṇe dhariyā
āliṅgana kaila prabhu tāṅre uṭhāñā

daṇḍavat hañā—like a stick; *paḍe*—fell; *caraṇe*—the lotus feet; *dhariyā*—catching; *āliṅgana*—embracing; *kaila*—did; *prabhu*—Śrī Caitanya Mahāprabhu; *tāṅre*—him; *uṭhāñā*—getting up.

TRANSLATION

When Rāmānanda Rāya fell flat, touching the lotus feet of Śrī Caitanya Mahāprabhu, the Lord immediately raised him to his feet and embraced him.

TEXT 321

দুই জনে প্রেমাবেশে করেন ক্রন্দন ।
প্রেমানন্দে শিথিল হৈল দুঁহাকার মন ॥ ৩২১ ॥

dui jane premāveśe karena krandana
premānande śithila haila duṅhākāra mana

dui jane—both of them; *prema-āveśe*—in ecstatic love; *karena*—do; *krandana*—crying; *prema-ānande*—in ecstatic love; *śithila haila*—became slackened; *duṅhākāra*—of both of them; *mana*—minds.

TRANSLATION

In great ecstatic love they both began to cry, and thus their minds were slackened.

TEXT 322

কতক্ষণে দুই জনা সুস্থির হঞা।
নানা ইষ্টগোষ্ঠী করে একত্র বসিয়া ॥ ৩২২ ॥

kata-kṣaṇe dui janā susthira hañā
nānā iṣṭa-goṣṭhī kare ekatra vasiyā

kata-kṣaṇe—after some time; *dui*—two; *janā*—people; *susthira hañā*—coming to their senses; *nānā*—various; *iṣṭa-goṣṭhī*—discussions; *kare*—do; *ekatra*—together; *vasiyā*—sitting.

TRANSLATION

After some time they regained their senses and sat together to discuss various subjects.

TEXT 323

তীর্থ-যাত্রা-কথা প্রভু সকল কহিলা।
কর্ণামৃত, ব্রহ্মসংহিতা, —দুই পুঁথি দিলা ॥ ৩২৩ ॥

tīrtha-yātrā-kathā prabhu sakala kahilā
karnāmṛta, brahma-saṁhitā,—dui puṅthi dilā

tīrtha-yātrā-kathā—topics of His pilgrimage; *prabhu*—Lord Śrī Caitanya Mahāprabhu; *sakala kahilā*—described everything; *karṇāmṛta*—the book named *Kṛṣṇa-karṇāmṛta; brahma-saṁhitā*—the book named *Brahma-saṁhitā; dui*—two; *puṅthi*—scriptures; *dilā*—delivered.

TRANSLATION

Śrī Caitanya Mahāprabhu gave Rāmānanda Rāya a vivid description of His travels to the holy places and told him how He had acquired the two books named Kṛṣṇa-karṇāmṛta and Brahma-saṁhitā. The Lord delivered the books to Rāmānanda Rāya.

TEXT 324

প্রভু কহে, — তুমি যেই সিদ্ধান্ত কহিলে ।
এই দুই পুঁথি সেই সব সাক্ষী দিলে ॥ ৩২৪ ॥

prabhu kahe, — tumi yei siddhānta kahile
ei dui puṅthi sei saba sākṣī dile

prabhu kahe — the Lord said; *tumi* — you; *yei* — whatever; *siddhānta* — conclusion; *kahile* — informed; *ei dui* — these two; *puṅthi* — books; *sei* — that; *saba* — everything; *sākṣī* — evidence; *dile* — gave.

TRANSLATION

The Lord said, "Whatever you have told Me about devotional service is all supported by these two books."

TEXT 325

রায়ের আনন্দ হৈল পুস্তক পাইয়া ।
প্রভু-সহ আস্বাদিল, রাখিল লিখিয়া ॥ ৩২৫ ॥

rāyera ānanda haila pustaka pāiyā
prabhu-saha āsvādila, rākhila likhiyā

rāyera — of Rāya Rāmānanda; *ānanda* — happiness; *haila* — there was; *pustaka pāiyā* — getting those two books; *prabhu-saha* — with the Lord; *āsvādila* — tasted; *rākhila* — kept; *likhiyā* — writing.

TRANSLATION

Rāmānanda Rāya was very happy to receive these books. He tasted their contents along with the Lord and made a copy of each.

TEXT 326

'গোসাঞি আইলা' গ্রামে হইল কোলাহল।
প্রভুকে দেখিতে লোক আইল সকল ॥ ৩২৬ ॥

'gosāñi āilā' grāme haila kolāhala
prabhuke dekhite loka āila sakala

gosāñi—Śrī Caitanya Mahāprabhu; *āilā'*—has returned; *grāme*—in the village; *haila*—there was; *kolāhala*—commotion; *prabhuke*—Lord Śrī Caitanya Mahāprabhu; *dekhite*—to see; *loka*—people; *āila*—came there; *sakala*—all.

TRANSLATION

News spread in the village of Vidyānagara about the arrival of Śrī Caitanya Mahāprabhu, and everyone came to see Him once again.

TEXT 327

লোক দেখি' রামানন্দ গেলা নিজ-ঘরে।
মধ্যাহ্নে উঠিলা প্রভু ভিক্ষা করিবারে ॥ ৩২৭ ॥

loka dehki' rāmānanda gelā nija-ghare
madhyāhne uṭhilā prabhu bhikṣā karibāre

loka dekhi'—seeing the people; *rāmānanda*—Rāya Rāmānanda; *gelā*—departed; *nija-ghare*—to his own home; *madhyāhne*—at noon; *uṭhilā prabhu*—Śrī Caitanya Mahāprabhu got up; *bhikṣā karibāre*—to take His lunch.

TRANSLATION

After seeing the people who gathered there, Śrī Rāmānanda Rāya returned to his own home. At noon, Śrī Caitanya Mahāprabhu got up to take His lunch.

TEXT 328

রাত্রিকালে রায় পুনঃ কৈল আগমন।
দুই জনে কৃষ্ণকথায় কৈল জাগরণ ॥ ৩২৮ ॥

rātri-kāle rāya punaḥ kaila āgamana
dui jane kṛṣṇa-kathāya kaila jāgaraṇa

rātri-kāle—at night; *rāya*—Rāmānanda Rāya; *punaḥ*—again; *kaila*—did; *āgamana*—coming; *dui jane*—the two of them; *kṛṣṇa-kathāya*—in discourses on topics of Kṛṣṇa; *kaila*—did; *jāgaraṇa*—keeping awake through the night.

TRANSLATION

Śrī Rāmānanda Rāya returned at night, and he and the Lord discussed topics concerning Kṛṣṇa. Thus they passed the night.

TEXT 329

দুই জনে কৃষ্ণকথা কহে রাত্রি-দিনে।
পরম-আনন্দে গেল পাঁচ-সাত দিনে ॥ ৩২৯ ॥

dui jane kṛṣṇa-kathā kahe rātri-dine
parama-ānande gela pāṅca-sāta dine

dui jane—both of them; *kṛṣṇa-kathā*—topics of Kṛṣṇa; *kahe*—speak; *rātri-dine*—day and night; *parama-ānande*—in great happiness; *gela*—passed; *pāṅca-sāta dine*—five to seven days.

TRANSLATION

Rāmānanda Rāya and Śrī Caitanya Mahāprabhu discussed Kṛṣṇa day and night, and thus they passed from five to seven days in great happiness.

TEXT 330

রামানন্দ কহে,—প্রভু, তোমার আজ্ঞা পাঞা।
রাজাকে লিখিলুঁ আমি বিনয় করিয়া ॥ ৩৩০ ॥

rāmānanda kahe,—prabhu, tomāra ājñā pāñā
rājāke likhiluṅ āmi vinaya kariyā

rāmānanda kahe—Rāmānanda Rāya said; *prabhu*—my dear Lord; *tomāra ājñā*—Your permission; *pāñā*—getting; *rājāke likhiluṅ*—have written a letter to the King; *āmi*—I; *vinaya kariyā*—with great humility.

TRANSLATION

Rāmānanda Rāya said, "My dear Lord, with Your permission I have already written a letter to the King with great humility.

TEXT 331

রাজা মোরে আজ্ঞা দিল নীলাচলে যাইতে।
চলিবার উদ্‌যোগ আমি লাগিয়াছি করিতে ॥ ৩৩১ ॥

rājā more ājñā dila nīlācale yāite
calibāra udyoga āmi lāgiyāchi karite

rājā—the King; *more*—unto me; *ājñā dila*—has given an order; *nīlācale yāite*—to go to Jagannātha Purī; *calibāra*—to go; *udyoga*—arrangement; *āmi*—I; *lāgiyāchi*—began; *karite*—to do.

TRANSLATION

"The King has already given me an order to return to Jagannātha Purī, and I am making arrangements to do this."

TEXT 332

প্রভু কহে,—এথা মোর এ-নিমিত্তে আগমন।
তোমা লঞা নীলাচলে করিব গমন ॥ ৩৩২ ॥

prabhu kahe,—ethā mora e-nimitte āgamana
tomā lañā nīlācale kariba gamana

prabhu kahe—Lord Śrī Caitanya Mahāprabhu said; *ethā*—here; *mora*—My; *e-nimitte*—for this reason; *āgamana*—coming back; *tomā lañā*—taking you; *nīlācale*—to Jagannātha Purī; *kariba*—I shall do; *gamana*—going.

TRANSLATION

Śrī Caitanya Mahāprabhu then said, "It is for this purpose alone that I have returned. I want to take you with Me to Jagannātha Purī."

TEXT 333

রায় কহে,—প্রভু, আগে চল নীলাচলে।
মোর সঙ্গে হাতী-ঘোড়া, সৈন্য-কোলাহলে ॥ ৩৩৩ ॥

rāya kahe,—prabhu, āge cala nīlācale
mora saṅge hātī-ghoḍā, sainya-kolāhale

rāya kahe—Rāmānanda Rāya replied; *prabhu*—Lord; *āge cala*—You go ahead; *nīlācale*—to Jagannātha Purī; *mora saṅge*—with me; *hātī-ghoḍā*—elephants and horses; *sainya*—soldiers; *kolāhale*—tumultuous roaring.

TRANSLATION

Rāmānanda Rāya said, "My dear Lord, it is better that You proceed to Jagannātha Purī alone because with me there will be many horses, elephants and soldiers, all roaring tumultuously.

TEXT 334

দিন-দশে ইহা-সবার করি' সমাধান।
তোমার পাছে পাছে আমি করিব প্রয়াণ ॥ ৩৩৪ ॥

dina-daśe ihā-sabāra kari' samādhāna
tomāra pāche pāche āmi kariba prayāṇa

dina-daśe—within ten days; *ihā-sabāra*—of all of this; *kari' samādhāna*—making adjustment; *tomāra*—You; *pāche pāche*—following; *āmi*—I; *kariba*—shall do; *prayāṇa*—going.

TRANSLATION

"I shall make arrangements within ten days. Following You, I shall go to Nīlācala without delay."

TEXT 335

তবে মহাপ্রভু তাঁরে আসিতে আজ্ঞা দিয়া।
নীলাচলে চলিলা প্রভু আনন্দিত হঞা ॥ ৩৩৫ ॥

tabe mahāprabhu tāṅre āsite ājñā diyā
nīlācale calilā prabhu ānandita hañā

tabe—then; *mahāprabhu*—Śrī Caitanya Mahāprabhu; *tāṅre*—unto him; *āsite*—to come; *ājñā diyā*—giving an order; *nīlācale*—to Jagannātha Purī; *calilā*—departed; *prabhu*—Lord Śrī Caitanya Mahāprabhu; *ānandita hañā*—with great pleasure.

TRANSLATION

Giving orders to Rāmānanda Rāya to come to Nīlācala, Śrī Caitanya Mahāprabhu departed for Jagannātha Purī with great pleasure.

TEXT 336

যেই পথে পূর্বে প্রভু কৈলা আগমন।
সেই পথে চলিলা দেখি, সর্ব বৈষ্ণবগণ ॥ ৩৩৬ ॥

yei pathe pūrve prabhu kailā āgamana
sei pathe calilā dekhi, sarva vaiṣṇava-gaṇa

yei pathe—the path by which; *pūrve*—formerly; *prabhu*—Lord Śrī Caitanya Mahāprabhu; *kailā āgamana*—came; *sei pathe*—by that way; *calilā*—departed; *dekhi*—seeing; *sarva*—all; *vaiṣṇava-gaṇa*—Vaiṣṇavas.

TRANSLATION

Śrī Caitanya Mahāprabhu returned by the same road He had formerly taken to Vidyānagara, and all the Vaiṣṇavas along the way saw Him again.

TEXT 337

যাহাঁ যায়, লোক উঠে হরিধ্বনি করি'।
দেখি' আনন্দিত-মন হৈলা গৌরহরি ॥ ৩৩৭ ॥

yāhāṅ yāya, loka uṭhe hari-dhvani kari'
dekhi' ānandita-mana hailā gaurahari

yāhāṅ yāya—wherever He goes; *loka uṭhe*—people stand up; *hari-dhvani kari'*—vibrating the holy name of the Hare Kṛṣṇa *mantra; dekhi'*—by seeing; *ānandita*—happy; *mana*—in mind; *hailā*—became; *gaurahari*—Lord Śrī Caitanya Mahāprabhu.

TRANSLATION

Wherever Śrī Caitanya Mahāprabhu went, the holy name of Śrī Hari was vibrated. Seeing this, the Lord became very happy.

TEXT 338

আলালনাথে আসি' কৃষ্ণদাসে পাঠাইল।
নিত্যানন্দ-আদি নিজগণে বোলাইল ॥ ৩৩৮ ॥

ālālanāthe āsi' kṛṣṇadāse pāṭhāila
nityānanda-ādi nija-gaṇe bolāila

ālālanāthe—to the place known as Ālālanātha; *āsi'*—coming; *kṛṣṇadāse*—Kṛṣṇadāsa, His assistant; *pāṭhāila*—sent ahead; *nityānanda*—Lord Nityānanda; *ādi*—and others; *nija-gaṇe*—personal associates; *bolāila*—called for.

TRANSLATION

When the Lord reached Ālālanātha, He sent His assistant Kṛṣṇadāsa ahead to call for Nityānanda Prabhu and other personal associates.

TEXT 339

প্রভুর আগমন শুনি' নিত্যানন্দ রায়।
উঠিয়া চলিলা, প্রেমে থেহ নাহি পায় ॥ ৩৩৯ ॥

prabhura āgamana śuni' nityānanda rāya
uṭhiyā calilā, preme theha nāhi pāya

prabhura—of Lord Śrī Caitanya Mahāprabhu; *āgamana*—arrival; *śuni'*—hearing; *nityānanda rāya*—Lord Nityānanda; *uṭhiyā calilā*—got up and started; *preme*—in great ecstasy; *theha*—patience; *nāhi pāya*—does not get.

TRANSLATION

As soon as Nityānanda Prabhu received news of the arrival of Śrī Caitanya Mahāprabhu, He immediately got up and started out to see Him. Indeed, He was very impatient in His great ecstasy.

TEXT 340

জগদানন্দ, দামোদর-পণ্ডিত, মুকুন্দ ।
নাচিয়া চলিলা, দেহে না ধরে আনন্দ ॥ ৩৪০ ॥

jagadānanda, dāmodara-paṇḍita, mukunda
nāciyā calilā, dehe nā dhare ānanda

jagadānanda—Jagadānanda; *dāmodara-paṇḍita*—Dāmodara Paṇḍita; *mukunda*—Mukunda; *nāciyā*—dancing; *calilā*—departed; *dehe*—the body; *nā dhare*—does not hold; *ānanda*—happiness.

TRANSLATION

Śrī Nityānanda Rāya, Jagadānanda, Dāmodara Paṇḍita and Mukunda all became ecstatic in their happiness, and dancing along the way, they went to meet the Lord.

TEXT 341

গোপীনাথাচার্য চলিলা আনন্দিত হঞা ।
প্রভুরে মিলিলা সবে পথে লাগ্ পাঞা ॥ ৩৪১ ॥

gopīnāthācārya calilā ānandita hañā
prabhure mililā sabe pathe lāg pāñā

gopīnātha-ācārya—Gopīnātha Ācārya; *calilā*—departed; *ānandita*—in happiness; *hañā*—being; *prabhure*—Lord Śrī Caitanya Mahāprabhu; *mililā*—met; *sabe*—all; *pathe*—along the way; *lāg*—contact; *pāñā*—getting.

TRANSLATION

Gopīnātha Ācārya also went in a very happy mood. They all went to meet the Lord, and they finally contacted Him on the way.

TEXT 342

প্রভু প্রেমাবেশে সবায় কৈল আলিঙ্গন।
প্রেমাবেশে সবে করে আনন্দ-ক্রন্দন ॥ ৩৪২ ॥

prabhu premāveśe sabāya kaila āliṅgana
premāveśe sabe kare ānanda-krandana

prabhu—Lord Śrī Caitanya Mahāprabhu; *prema-āveśe*—in ecstatic love; *sabāya*—all of them; *kaila āliṅgana*—embraced; *prema-āveśe*—in ecstatic love; *sabe kare*—all of them did; *ānanda-krandana*—crying in pleasure.

TRANSLATION

The Lord was also filled with ecstatic love, and He embraced them all. Out of their love, they began to cry with pleasure.

TEXT 343

সার্বভৌম ভট্টাচার্য আনন্দে চলিলা।
সমুদ্রের তীরে আসি' প্রভুরে মিলিলা ॥ ৩৪৩ ॥

sārvabhauma bhaṭṭācārya ānande calilā
samudrera tīre āsi' prabhure mililā

sārvabhauma bhaṭṭācārya—Sārvabhauma Bhaṭṭācārya; *ānande*—in pleasure; *calilā*—went; *samudrera tīre*—on the beach by the ocean; *āsi'*—coming; *prabhure mililā*—met the Lord.

TRANSLATION

Sārvabhauma Bhaṭṭācārya also went to see the Lord with great pleasure, and he met Him on the beach by the sea.

TEXT 344

সার্বভৌম মহাপ্রভুর পড়িলা চরণে।
প্রভু তাঁরে উঠাঞা কৈল আলিঙ্গনে ॥ ৩৪৪ ॥

sārvabhauma mahāprabhura paḍilā caraṇe
prabhu tāṅre uṭhāñā kaila āliṅgane

sārvabhauma—Sārvabhauma Bhaṭṭācārya; *mahāprabhura*—of Lord Śrī Caitanya Mahāprabhu; *paḍilā*—fell down; *caraṇe*—at the feet; *prabhu*—Śrī Caitanya Mahāprabhu; *tāṅre*—him; *uṭhāñā*—getting up; *kaila āliṅgane*—embraced.

TRANSLATION

Sārvabhauma Bhaṭṭācārya fell down at the lotus feet of the Lord, and the Lord pulled him up and embraced him.

TEXT 345

প্রেমাবেশে সার্বভৌম করিলা রোদনে ।
সবা-সঙ্গে আইলা প্রভু ঈশ্বর-দরশনে ॥ ৩৪৫ ॥

premāveśe sārvabhauma karilā rodane
sabā-saṅge āilā prabhu īśvara-daraśane

prema-āveśe—in ecstatic love; *sārvabhauma*—Sārvabhauma; *karilā rodane*—cried; *sabā-saṅge*—with all of them; *āilā*—came; *prabhu*—Śrī Caitanya Mahāprabhu; *īśvara-daraśane*—to see the Jagannātha temple.

TRANSLATION

Sārvabhauma Bhaṭṭācārya cried in great ecstatic love. Then the Lord, accompanied by them all, went to the temple of Jagannātha.

TEXT 346

জগন্নাথ-দরশন প্রেমাবেশে কৈল ।
কম্প-স্বেদ-পুলকাশ্রুতে শরীর ভাসিল ॥ ৩৪৬ ॥

jagannātha-daraśana premāveśe kaila
kampa-sveda-pulakāśrute śarīra bhāsila

jagannātha-daraśana—visiting Lord Jagannātha; *prema-āveśe*—in ecstatic love; *kaila*—made; *kampa*—trembling; *sveda*—perspiration; *pulaka*—jubilation; *aśrute*—with tears; *śarīra*—the whole body; *bhāsila*—was inundated.

TRANSLATION

Due to ecstatic love experienced upon visiting Lord Jagannātha, inundations of trembling, perspiration, tears and jubilation swept the body of Śrī Caitanya Mahāprabhu.

TEXT 347

বহু নৃত্যগীত কৈল প্রেমাবিষ্ট হঞা ।
পাণ্ডাপাল আইল সবে মালা-প্রসাদ লঞা ॥ ৩৪৭ ॥

bahu nṛtya-gīta kaila premāviṣṭa hañā
pāṇḍā-pāla āila sabe mālā-prasāda lañā

bahu—much; *nṛtya-gīta*—dancing and chanting; *kaila*—performed; *prema-āviṣṭa*—in ecstatic love; *hañā*—being; *pāṇḍā-pāla*—the priests and attendants; *āila*—came; *sabe*—all; *mālā-prasāda*—a garland and remnants of the food of Jagannātha; *lañā*—offering.

TRANSLATION

In ecstatic love Śrī Caitanya Mahāprabhu danced and chanted. At that time all the attendants and priests came to offer Him a garland and the remnants of Lord Jagannātha's food.

PURPORT

Those who are priests engaged in Lord Jagannātha's service are called *pāṇḍās* or *paṇḍitas,* and they are *brāhmaṇas.* The attendants who look after the temple's external affairs are called *pālas.* The priests and attendants went together to see Śrī Caitanya Mahāprabhu.

TEXT 348

মালা-প্রসাদ পাঞা প্রভু সুস্থির হইলা ।
জগন্নাথের সেবক সব আনন্দে মিলিলা ॥ ৩৪৮ ॥

mālā-prasāda pāñā prabhu susthira ha-ilā
jagannāthera sevaka saba ānande mililā

mālā-prasāda—the garland and *prasādam; pāñā*—getting; *prabhu*—Śrī Caitanya Mahāprabhu; *su-sthira ha-ilā*—became patient; *jagannāthera*—of Lord Jagannātha; *sevaka*—servants; *saba*—all; *ānande mililā*—met Him in great pleasure.

TRANSLATION

Śrī Caitanya Mahāprabhu became patient after receiving the garland and prasādam of Lord Jagannātha. All the servants of Lord Jagannātha met Śrī Caitanya Mahāprabhu with great pleasure.

TEXT 349

কাশীমিশ্র আসি' প্রভুর পড়িলা চরণে ।
মান্য করি' প্রভু তাঁরে কৈল আলিঙ্গনে ॥ ৩৪৯ ॥

kāśī-miśra āsi' prabhura paḍilā caraṇe
mānya kari' prabhu tāṅre kaila āliṅgane

kāśī-miśra—Kāśī Miśra; *āsi'*—coming; *prabhura*—of the Lord; *paḍilā*—fell down; *caraṇe*—at the feet; *mānya kari'*—with great respect; *prabhu*—Lord Śrī Caitanya Mahāprabhu; *tāṅre*—unto him; *kaila*—did; *āliṅgane*—embracing.

TRANSLATION

Afterward, Kāśī Miśra came and fell down at the lotus feet of the Lord, and the Lord respectfully embraced him.

TEXT 350

প্রভু লঞা সার্বভৌম নিজ-ঘরে গেলা ।
মোর ঘরে ভিক্ষা বলি' নিমন্ত্রণ কৈলা ॥ ৩৫০ ॥

prabhu lañā sārvabhauma nija-ghare gelā
mora ghare bhikṣā bali' nimantraṇa kailā

prabhu lañā—taking Lord Śrī Caitanya Mahāprabhu; *sārvabhauma*—Sārvabhauma Bhaṭṭācārya; *nija-ghare*—to his own home; *gelā*—went; *mora*—my; *ghare*—at home; *bhikṣā*—luncheon; *bali'*—saying; *nimantraṇa kailā*—invited.

TRANSLATION

Sārvabhauma Bhaṭṭācārya then took the Lord with him to his home, saying, "Today's luncheon will be at my home." In this way he invited the Lord.

TEXT 351

দিব্য মহাপ্রসাদ অনেক আনাইল।
পীঠা-পানা আদি জগন্নাথ যে খাইল ॥ ৩৫১ ॥

divya mahā-prasāda aneka ānāila
pīṭhā-pānā ādi jagannātha ye khāila

divya—very nice; *mahā-prasāda*—remnants of food from Jagannātha; *aneka*—various; *ānāila*—brought; *pīṭhā-pānā ādi*—such as cakes and condensed milk; *jagannātha*—Lord Jagannātha; *ye*—which; *khāila*—ate.

TRANSLATION

Sārvabhauma Bhaṭṭācārya brought various types of food remnants that had been left by Lord Jagannātha. He brought all kinds of cakes and condensed-milk preparations.

TEXT 352

মধ্যাহ্ন করিলা প্রভু নিজগণ লঞা।
সার্বভৌম-ঘরে ভিক্ষা করিলা আসিয়া ॥ ৩৫২ ॥

madhyāhna karilā prabhu nija-gaṇa lañā
sārvabhauma-ghare bhikṣā karilā āsiyā

madhyāhna—noon lunch; *karilā*—performed; *prabhu*—Śrī Caitanya Mahāprabhu; *nija-gaṇa lañā*—accompanied by associates; *sārvabhauma-ghare*—at the home of Sārvabhauma Bhaṭṭācārya; *bhikṣā*—lunch; *karilā*—performed; *āsiyā*—coming.

TRANSLATION

Accompanied by all His associates, Śrī Caitanya Mahāprabhu went to Sārvabhauma Bhaṭṭācārya's house and took His noon lunch there.

TEXT 353

ভিক্ষা করাঞা তাঁরে করাইল শয়ন।
আপনে সার্বভৌম করে পাদসম্বাহন ॥ ৩৫৩ ॥

bhikṣā karāñā tāṅre karāila śayana
āpane sārvabhauma kare pāda-saṁvāhana

bhikṣā karāñā—after giving lunch; *tāṅre*—Him; *karāila*—made; *śayana*—lie down to rest; *āpane*—personally; *sārvabhauma*—Sārvabhauma Bhaṭṭācārya; *kare*—does; *pāda-saṁvāhana*—massaging the legs.

TRANSLATION

After offering food to Śrī Caitanya Mahāprabhu, Sārvabhauma Bhaṭṭācārya made Him lie down to rest, and he personally began to massage the legs of the Lord.

TEXT 354

প্রভু তাঁরে পাঠাইল ভোজন করিতে।
সেই রাত্রি তাঁর ঘরে রহিলা তাঁর প্রীতে ॥ ৩৫৪ ॥

prabhu tāṅre pāṭhāila bhojana karite
sei rātri tāṅra ghare rahilā tāṅra prīte

prabhu—Śrī Caitanya Mahāprabhu; *tāṅre*—him; *pāṭhāila*—sent; *bhojana karite*—to take lunch; *sei rātri*—that night; *tāṅra ghare*—at his home; *rahilā*—remained; *tāṅra prīte*—just to satisfy him.

TRANSLATION

Śrī Caitanya Mahāprabhu then sent Sārvabhauma Bhaṭṭācārya to take his lunch, and the Lord remained that night in his home just to please him.

TEXT 355

সার্বভৌম-সঙ্গে আর লঞা নিজগণ।
তীর্থযাত্রা-কথা কহি' কৈল জাগরণ ॥ ৩৫৫ ॥

sārvabhauma-saṅge āra lañā nija-gaṇa
tīrtha-yātrā-kathā kahi' kaila jāgaraṇa

sārvabhauma-saṅge—with Sārvabhauma Bhaṭṭācārya; *āra*—and; *lañā nija-gaṇa*—taking His own associates; *tīrtha-yātrā-kathā*—topics of the pilgrimage; *kahi'*—telling; *kaila*—did; *jāgaraṇa*—keeping awake through the night.

TRANSLATION

Śrī Caitanya Mahāprabhu and His personal associates remained with Sārvabhauma Bhaṭṭācārya. They all stayed awake the entire night as the Lord spoke of His pilgrimage.

TEXT 356

প্রভু কহে, — এত তীর্থ কৈলুঁ পর্যটন ।
তোমা-সম বৈষ্ণব না দেখিলুঁ একজন ॥ ৩৫৬ ॥

prabhu kahe,—eta tīrtha kailuṅ paryaṭana
tomā-sama vaiṣṇava nā dekhiluṅ eka-jana

prabhu kahe—the Lord said; *eta tīrtha*—to so many holy places; *kailuṅ paryaṭana*—I have traveled; *tomā-sama*—like you; *vaiṣṇava*—devotee; *nā*—not; *dekhiluṅ*—I could see; *eka-jana*—one man.

TRANSLATION

The Lord told Sārvabhauma Bhaṭṭācārya, "I have traveled to many holy places, but I could not find a Vaiṣṇava as good as you anywhere."

TEXT 357

এক রামানন্দ রায় বহু সুখ দিল ।
ভট্ট কহে, — এই লাগি' মিলিতে কহিল ॥ ৩৫৭ ॥

eka rāmānanda rāya bahu sukha dila
bhaṭṭa kahe,—ei lāgi' milite kahila

eka—one; *rāmānanda rāya*—Rāmānanda Rāya; *bahu sukha*—much pleasure; *dila*—gave; *bhaṭṭa kahe*—Sārvabhauma

Bhaṭṭācārya replied; *ei lāgi'*—for this reason; *milite*—to meet; *kahila*—I requested.

TRANSLATION

Śrī Caitanya Mahāprabhu continued, "I received much pleasure from the talks of Rāmānanda Rāya."

The Bhaṭṭācārya replied, "For this reason I requested that You meet him."

PURPORT

In the *Śrī Caitanya-candrodaya* (beginning of the eighth act) Śrī Caitanya Mahāprabhu says, "Sārvabhauma, I have traveled to many holy places, but I cannot find a Vaiṣṇava as good as you anywhere. However, I must admit that Rāmānanda Rāya is wonderful."

Sārvabhauma Bhaṭṭācārya replies, "Therefore, my Lord, I requested that You see him."

Śrī Caitanya Mahāprabhu then says, "There are, of course, many Vaiṣṇavas in these holy places, and most of them worship Lord Nārāyaṇa. Others, who are called Tattvavādīs, are also Lakṣmī-Nārāyaṇa worshipers, but they do not belong to the pure Vaiṣṇava cult. There are many worshipers of Lord Śiva, and there are also many atheists. Regardless, My dear Bhaṭṭācārya, I very much like Rāmānanda Rāya and his opinions."

TEXT 358

তীর্থযাত্রা-কথা এই কৈলুঁ সমাপন ।
সংক্ষেপে কহিলুঁ, বিস্তার না যায় বর্ণন ॥ ৩৫৮ ॥

tīrtha-yātrā-kathā ei kailuṅ samāpana
saṅkṣepe kahiluṅ, vistāra nā yāya varṇana

tīrtha-yātrā-kathā—topics of the pilgrimage; *ei*—these; *kailuṅ samāpana*—I have finished; *saṅkṣepe kahiluṅ*—I have described in brief; *vistāra*—expansively; *nā yāya varṇana*—it is not possible to describe.

TRANSLATION

Thus I have ended my narration about Śrī Caitanya Mahāprabhu's pilgrimage, describing it in brief. It cannot be described very broadly.

PURPORT

Śrīla Bhaktisiddhānta Sarasvatī Ṭhākura points out that in the seventy-fourth verse of this chapter it is stated that Śrī Caitanya Mahāprabhu visited the temple of Śiyālī-bhairavī, but actually at Śiyālī Śrī Caitanya Mahāprabhu visited the temple of Śrī Bhū-varāha. Near Śiyālī and Cidambaram there is a temple known as Śrī Muṣṇam. In this temple there is a Deity of Śrī Bhū-varāha. In the jurisdiction of Cidambaram there is a district known as southern Ārkaṭa. The town of Śiyālī is in that district. There is a temple of Śrī Bhū-varāhadeva nearby, not Bhairavī-devī. This is Śrīla Bhaktisiddhānta Sarasvatī Ṭhākura's conclusion.

TEXT 359

অনন্ত চৈতন্যলীলা কহিতে না জানি ।
লোভে লজ্জা খাঞা তার করি টানাটানি ॥ ৩৫৯ ॥

ananta caitanya-līlā kahite nā jāni
lobhe lajjā khāñā tāra kari ṭānāṭāni

ananta—unlimited; *caitanya-līlā*—pastimes of Lord Caitanya; *kahite*—to speak; *nā jāni*—I do not know; *lobhe*—out of greed; *lajjā khāñā*—becoming shameless; *tāra*—of them; *kari*—I do; *ṭānāṭāni*—some attempt only.

TRANSLATION

The pastimes of Lord Caitanya are unlimited. No one can properly describe His activities, yet I make the attempt out of greed. This but reveals my shamelessness.

TEXT 360

প্রভুর তীর্থযাত্রা-কথা শুনে যেই জন ।
চৈতন্যচরণে পায় গাঢ় প্রেমধন ॥ ৩৬০ ॥

prabhura tīrtha-yātrā-kathā śune yei jana
caitanya-caraṇe pāya gāḍha prema-dhana

prabhura—of Lord Śrī Caitanya Mahāprabhu; *tīrtha-yātrā*—touring of sacred places of pilgrimage; *kathā*—topics about; *śune*—hears; *yei*—who; *jana*—person; *caitanya-caraṇe*—at the lotus feet of Śrī Caitanya Mahāprabhu; *pāya*—gets; *gāḍha*—deep; *prema-dhana*—riches of ecstatic love.

TRANSLATION

Whoever hears of Śrī Caitanya Mahāprabhu's pilgrimage to various holy places attains the riches of very deep ecstatic love.

PURPORT

Śrīla Bhaktisiddhānta Sarasvatī Ṭhākura remarks, "The impersonalists imagine some forms of the Absolute Truth through the direct perception of their senses. The impersonalists worship such imaginary forms, but neither *Śrīmad-Bhāgavatam* nor Śrī Caitanya Mahāprabhu accepts this sense gratificatory worship to be of any spiritual significance." The Māyāvādīs imagine themselves to be the Supreme. They imagine that the Supreme has no personal form and that all His forms are imaginary like the will-o'-the-wisp or a flower in the sky. Both Māyāvādīs and those who imagine forms of God are misguided. According to them, worship of the Deity or any other form of the Lord is a result of the conditioned soul's illusion. However, Śrī Caitanya Mahāprabhu confirms the conclusion of *Śrīmad-Bhāgavatam* on the strength of His philosophy of *acintya-bhedābheda-tattva.* That philosophy holds that the Supreme Lord is simultaneously one with and different from His creation. That is to say, there is unity in diversity. In this way Śrī Caitanya Mahāprabhu proved the impotence of fruitive workers, speculative empiric philosophers and mystic *yogīs.* The realization of such men is simply a waste of time and energy.

To set the example, Śrī Caitanya Mahāprabhu personally visited temples in various holy places. Wherever He visited, He immediately exhibited His ecstatic love for the Supreme Personality of Godhead. When a Vaiṣṇava visits the temple of a demigod, his vision of that demigod is different from the vision of the impersonalists and

Māyāvādīs. The *Brahma-saṁhitā* supports this. A Vaiṣṇava's visit to the temple of Lord Śiva, for example, is different from a nondevotee's visit. The nondevotee considers the deity of Lord Śiva an imaginary form because he ultimately thinks that the Supreme Absolute Truth is void. However, a Vaiṣṇava sees Lord Śiva as being simultaneously one with and different from the Supreme Lord. In this regard, the example of milk and yogurt is given. Yogurt is actually nothing but milk, but at the same time it is not milk. It is simultaneously one with milk yet different from it. This is the philosophy of Śrī Caitanya Mahāprabhu, and it is confirmed by Lord Kṛṣṇa in the *Bhagavad-gītā* (9.4):

mayā tatam idaṁ sarvaṁ jagad avyakta-mūrtinā
mat-sthāni sarva-bhūtāni na cāhaṁ teṣv avasthitaḥ

"By Me, in My unmanifested form, this entire universe is pervaded. All beings are in Me, but I am not in them."

The Absolute Truth, God, is everything, but this does not mean that everything is God. For this reason Śrī Caitanya Mahāprabhu and His followers visited the temples of all the demigods, but they did not see them in the same way an impersonalist sees them. Everyone should follow in the footsteps of Śrī Caitanya Mahāprabhu and visit all temples. Sometimes mundane *sahajiyās* suppose that the *gopīs* visited the temple of Kātyāyanī in the same way mundane people visit the temple of Devī. However, the *gopīs* prayed to Kātyāyanī to grant them Kṛṣṇa as their husband, whereas mundaners visit the temple of Kātyāyanī to receive some material profit. That is the difference between a Vaiṣṇava's visit and a nondevotee's visit.

Not understanding the process of disciplic succession, so-called logicians put forward the theory of *pañcopāsanā,* in which a person worships one of five deities—namely Viṣṇu, Śiva, Durgā, the sun-god or Ganeśa. In this conception the impersonalists imagine one of these five deities as supreme and reject the others. Such philosophical speculation, which is certainly idol worship, is not accepted by Śrī Caitanya Mahāprabhu or by Vaiṣṇavas. This imaginary deity worship has recently been transformed into Māyāvāda impersonalism. For want of Kṛṣṇa consciousness, people are victimized by the Māyāvāda philosophy, and consequently they sometimes become staunch atheists. However, Śrī Caitanya Mahāprabhu established the process of self-realization by His own personal behavior. As stated in the *Caitanya-caritāmṛta* (*Madhya* 8.274):

sthāvara-jaṅgama dekhe, nā dekhe tāra mūrti
sarvatra haya nija iṣṭa-deva-sphūrti

"A Vaiṣṇava never sees the material form of anything, moving or nonmoving. Rather, everywhere he looks he sees the energy of the Supreme Personality of Godhead, and immediately he remembers the transcendental form of the Lord."

TEXT 361

চৈতন্যচরিত শুন শ্রদ্ধা-ভক্তি করি' ।
মাৎসর্য ছাড়িয়া মুখে বল 'হরি' 'হরি' ॥ ৩৬১ ॥

caitanya-carita śuna śraddhā-bhakti kari'
mātsarya chāḍiyā mukhe bala 'hari' 'hari'

caitanya-carita—the activities of Lord Śrī Caitanya Mahāprabhu; *śuna*—hear; *śraddhā*—faith; *bhakti*—devotion; *kari'*—accepting; *mātsarya*—envy; *chāḍiyā*—giving up; *mukhe*—by the mouth; *bala*—say; *hari hari*—the holy name of the Lord (Hari, Hari).

TRANSLATION

Please hear the transcendental pastimes of Lord Śrī Caitanya Mahāprabhu with faith and devotion. Giving up envy of the Lord, everyone chant the Lord's holy name, Hari.

TEXT 362

এই কলিকালে আর নাহি কোন ধর্ম ।
বৈষ্ণব, বৈষ্ণবশাস্ত্র, এই কহে মর্ম ॥ ৩৬২ ॥

ei kali-kāle āra nāhi kona dharma
vaiṣṇava, vaiṣṇava-śāstra, ei kahe marma

ei kali-kāle—in this Age of Kali; *āra*—other; *nāhi kona*—there is not any; *dharma*—religious principle; *vaiṣṇava*—devotee; *vaiṣṇava-śāstra*—devotional literature; *ei kahe marma*—this is the purport.

TRANSLATION

In this Age of Kali there are no genuine religious principles other than those established by Vaiṣṇava devotees and the Vaiṣṇava scriptures. This is the sum and substance of everything.

PURPORT

One must have firm faith in the process of devotional service and the scriptures that support it. If one hears the activities of Śrī Caitanya Mahāprabhu with this faith, he can be freed from his envious position. *Śrīmad-Bhāgavatam* is meant for such nonenvious persons (*nirmatsarāṇāṁ satām*). In this age a person should not envy Śrī Caitanya Mahāprabhu's movement but should chant the holy names of Hari and Kṛṣṇa, the *mahā-mantra.* That is the sum and substance of the eternal religion, known as *sanātana-dharma.* In this verse the word *vaiṣṇava* refers to a pure devotee and fully realized soul, and the word *vaiṣṇava-śāstra* refers to *śruti,* or the *Vedas,* which are called *śabda-pramāṇa,* the evidence of transcendental sound. One who strictly follows the Vedic literature and chants the holy name of the Supreme Personality of Godhead will actually be situated in the transcendental disciplic succession. Those who want to attain life's ultimate goal must follow this principle. In *Śrīmad-Bhāgavatam* (11.19.17), it is said:

śrutiḥ pratyakṣam aitihyam anumānaṁ catuṣṭayam
pramāṇeṣv anavasthānād vikalpāt sa virajyate

"Vedic literature, direct perception, history and hypothesis are the four kinds of evidential proofs. Everyone should stick to these principles for the realization of the Absolute Truth."

TEXT 363

চৈতন্যচন্দ্রের লীলা — অগাধ, গম্ভীর ।
প্রবেশ করিতে নারি, — স্পর্শি রহি' তীর ॥ ৩৬৩ ॥

caitanya-candrera līlā — agādha, gambhīra
praveśa karite nāri, — sparśi rahi' tīra

caitanya-candrera līlā — the pastimes of Lord Śrī Caitanya Mahāprabhu; *agādha* — unfathomable; *gambhīra* — deep; *praveśa karite*—to enter into; *nāri*—I am unable; *sparśi*—I touch; *rahi' tīra*—standing on the bank.

TRANSLATION

The pastimes of Śrī Caitanya Mahāprabhu are just like an unfathomable ocean. It is not possible for me to enter into it. Simply standing on the shore, I am but touching the water.

TEXT 364

চৈতন্যচরিত শ্রদ্ধায় শুনে যেই জন ।
যতেক বিচারে, তত পায় প্রেমধন ॥ ৩৬৪ ॥

caitanya-carita śraddhāya śune yei jana
yateka vicāre, tata pāya prema-dhana

caitanya-carita—the pastimes of Śrī Caitanya Mahāprabhu; *śraddhāya*—with faith; *śune*—hears; *yei jana*—which person; *yateka vicāre*—as far as he analytically studies; *tata*—so far; *pāya*—he gets; *prema-dhana*—the riches of ecstatic love.

TRANSLATION

The more one hears the pastimes of Śrī Caitanya Mahāprabhu with faith, analytically studying them, the more one attains the ecstatic riches of love of Godhead.

TEXT 365

শ্রীরূপ-রঘুনাথ-পদে যার আশ ।
চৈতন্যচরিতামৃত কহে কৃষ্ণদাস ॥ ৩৬৫ ॥

śrī-rūpa-raghunātha-pade yāra āśa
caitanya-caritāmṛta kahe kṛṣṇadāsa

śrī-rūpa—Śrīla Rūpa Gosvāmī; *raghunātha*—Śrīla Raghunātha dāsa Gosvāmī; *pade*—at the lotus feet; *yāra*—whose; *āśa*—expectation; *caitanya-caritāmṛta*—the book named *Caitanya-caritāmṛta;* *kahe*—describes; *kṛṣṇadāsa*—Śrīla Kṛṣṇadāsa Kavirāja Gosvāmī.

TRANSLATION

Praying at the lotus feet of Śrī Rūpa and Śrī Raghunātha, always desiring their mercy, I, Kṛṣṇadāsa, narrate Śrī Caitanya-caritāmṛta, following in their footsteps.

PURPORT

As usual the author concludes the chapter by reciting the names of Śrī Rūpa and Raghunātha and reinstating himself at their lotus feet.

Thus end the Bhaktivedanta purports to Śrī Caitanya-caritāmṛta, Madhya-līlā, *Ninth Chapter, describing Śrī Caitanya Mahāprabhu's travels to many holy places in South India.*

CHAPTER TEN

The Lord's Return to Jagannātha Purī

While Śrī Caitanya Mahāprabhu was traveling in South India, Sārvabhauma Bhaṭṭācārya had many talks with King Pratāparudra. When Mahārāja Pratāparudra requested the Bhaṭṭācārya to arrange an interview with the Lord, the Bhaṭṭācārya assured him that he would try to do so as soon as Caitanya Mahāprabhu returned from South India. When the Lord returned to Jagannātha Purī from His South Indian tour, He lived at the home of Kāśī Miśra. Sārvabhauma Bhaṭṭācārya introduced many Vaiṣṇavas to Śrī Caitanya Mahāprabhu after His return. The father of Rāmānanda Rāya, Bhavānanda Rāya, offered another son named Vāṇīnātha Paṭṭanāyaka for the Lord's service. Śrī Caitanya Mahāprabhu informed His associates about the pollution of Kṛṣṇadāsa brought about by his association with the Bhaṭṭathāris, and thus the Lord proposed to give him leave. Nityānanda Prabhu sent Kṛṣṇadāsa to Bengal to inform the Navadvīpa devotees about the Lord's return to Jagannātha Purī. All the devotees of Navadvīpa thus began arranging to come to Jagannātha Purī. At this time Paramānanda Purī was at Navadvīpa, and immediately upon hearing news of the Lord's return, he started for Jagannātha Purī accompanied by a *brāhmaṇa* named Kamalākānta. Puruṣottama Bhaṭṭācārya, a resident of Navadvīpa, was educated at Vārāṇasī. He accepted the renounced order from Caitanyānanda, but he took the name of Svarūpa. Thus he arrived at the lotus feet of Śrī Caitanya Mahāprabhu. After the demise of Śrī Īśvara Purī, his disciple Govinda, following his instructions, went to serve Caitanya Mahāprabhu. Due to his relationship with Keśava

Bhāratī, Brahmānanda Bhāratī was also respectfully received by Śrī Caitanya Mahāprabhu. When he arrived at Jagannātha Purī, he was advised to give up the deerskin clothing he wore. When Brahmānanda understood Śrī Caitanya Mahāprabhu correctly, he accepted Him as Kṛṣṇa himself. However, when Sārvabhauma Bhaṭṭācārya addressed Śrī Caitanya Mahāprabhu as Kṛṣṇa, the Lord immediately protested. In the meantime, Kāśīśvara Gosvāmī also came to see Caitanya Mahāprabhu. In this chapter, devotees from many different areas come to see Caitanya Mahāprabhu, and they are exactly like many rivers that come from many places to finally flow into the sea.

TEXT 1

তং বন্দে গৌরজলদং স্বস্য যো দর্শনামৃতৈঃ।
বিচ্ছেদাবগ্রহম্লান-ভক্তশস্যান্যজীবয়ৎ ॥ ১ ॥

taṁ vande gaura-jaladaṁ
svasya yo darśanāmṛtaiḥ
vicchedāvagraha-mlāna-
bhakta-śasyāny ajīvayat

tam—unto Him; *vande*—I offer my respectful obeisances; *gaura*—Śrī Caitanya Mahāprabhu; *jala-dam*—rain cloud; *svasya*—of Himself; *yaḥ*—He who; *darśana-amṛtaiḥ*—by the nectar of the audience; *viccheda*—because of separation; *avagraha*—scarcity of rain; *mlāna*—morose, dried up; *bhakta*—devotees; *śasyāni*—food grains; *ajīvayat*—saved.

TRANSLATION

I offer my respectful obeisances unto Lord Śrī Caitanya Mahāprabhu, who is compared to a cloud that pours water on fields of grain, which are like devotees suffering due to a shortage of rain. Separation from Śrī Caitanya Mahāprabhu is like a drought, but when the Lord returns, His presence is like a nectarean rain that falls on all the grains and saves them from perishing.

TEXT 2

জয় জয় শ্রীচৈতন্য জয় নিত্যানন্দ।
জয়াদ্বৈতচন্দ্র জয় গৌরভক্তবৃন্দ ॥ ২ ॥

jaya jaya śrī-caitanya jaya nityānanda
jayādvaita-candra jaya gaura-bhakta-vṛnda

jaya jaya—all glories; *śrī-caitanya*—to Lord Śrī Caitanya Mahāprabhu; *jaya*—all glories; *nityānanda*—to Nityānanda Prabhu; *jaya*—all glories; *advaita-candra*—to Advaita Ācārya; *jaya*—all glories; *gaura-bhakta-vṛnda*—to all the devotees of Śrī Caitanya Mahāprabhu.

TRANSLATION

All glories to Lord Caitanya! All glories to Nityānanda Prabhu! All glories to Advaitacandra! And all glories to all the devotees of Lord Caitanya!

TEXT 3

পূর্বে যবে মহাপ্রভু চলিলা দক্ষিণে।
প্রতাপরুদ্র রাজা তবে বোলাইল সার্বভৌমে ॥ ৩ ॥

pūrve yabe mahāprabhu calilā dakṣiṇe
pratāparudra rājā tabe bolāila sārvabhaume

pūrve—formerly; *yabe*—when; *mahāprabhu*—Śrī Caitanya Mahāprabhu; *calilā*—departed; *dakṣiṇe*—for His South Indian tour; *pratāparudra*—Pratāparudra; *rājā*—the King; *tabe*—at that time; *bolāila*—called for; *sārvabhaume*—Sārvabhauma Bhaṭṭācārya.

TRANSLATION

When Śrī Caitanya Mahāprabhu departed for South India, King Pratāparudra called Sārvabhauma Bhaṭṭācārya to his palace.

TEXT 4

বসিতে আসন দিল করি' নমস্কারে।
মহাপ্রভুর বার্তা তবে পুছিল তাঁহারে ॥ ৪ ॥

vasite āsana dila kari' namaskāre
mahāprabhura vārtā tabe puchila tāṅhāre

vasite—to sit; *āsana*—sitting place; *dila*—offered; *kari'*—doing; *namaskāre*—obeisances; *mahāprabhura*—of Śrī Caitanya

Mahāprabhu; *vārtā*—news; *tabe*—at that time; *puchila*—inquired; *tāṅhāre*—from him.

TRANSLATION

When Sārvabhauma Bhaṭṭācārya met with the King, the King offered him a seat with all respects and inquired about news of Śrī Caitanya Mahāprabhu.

TEXT 5

শুনিলাঙ তোমার ঘরে এক মহাশয় ।
গৌড় হইতে আইলা, তেঁহো মহা-কৃপাময় ॥ ৫ ॥

śunilāṅa tomāra ghare eka mahāśaya
gauḍa ha-ite āilā, teṅho mahā-kṛpāmaya

śunilāṅa—I have heard; *tomāra*—your; *ghare*—at home; *eka*—one; *mahāśaya*—great personality; *gauḍa ha-ite*—from Bengal; *āilā*—has come; *teṅho*—He; *mahā-kṛpā-maya*—very merciful.

TRANSLATION

The King said to the Bhaṭṭācārya, "I have heard that a great personality has come from Bengal and is staying at your home. I have also heard that He is very, very merciful.

TEXT 6

তোমারে বহু কৃপা কৈলা, কহে সর্বজন ।
কৃপা করি' করাহ মোরে তাঁহার দর্শন ॥ ৬ ॥

tomāre bahu kṛpā kailā, kahe sarva-jana
kṛpā kari' karāha more tāṅhāra darśana

tomāre—unto you; *bahu kṛpā*—great mercy; *kailā*—showed; *kahe*—says; *sarva-jana*—everyone; *kṛpā kari'*—being merciful; *karāha*—arrange; *more*—for me; *tāṅhāra*—His; *darśana*—interview.

TRANSLATION

"I have also heard that this great personality has shown you great favor. At any rate, this is what I hear from many different people. Now,

being merciful upon me, you should do me the favor of arranging an interview."

TEXT 7

ভট্ট কহে, — যে শুনিলা সব সত্য হয়।
তাঁর দর্শন তোমার ঘটন না হয় ॥ ৭ ॥

bhaṭṭa kahe,—ye śunilā saba satya haya
tāṅra darśana tomāra ghaṭana nā haya

bhaṭṭa kahe—the Bhaṭṭācārya replied; *ye*—what; *śunilā*—you have heard; *saba*—all; *satya*—true; *haya*—is; *tāṅra darśana*—His interview; *tomāra*—of you; *ghaṭana*—happening; *nā haya*—is not.

TRANSLATION

The Bhaṭṭācārya replied, "All that you have heard is true, but as far as an interview is concerned, it is very difficult to arrange.

TEXT 8

বিরক্ত সন্ন্যাসী তেঁহো রহেন নির্জনে।
স্বপ্নেহ না করেন তেঁহো রাজদরশনে ॥ ৮ ॥

virakta sannyāsī teṅho rahena nirjane
svapneha nā karena teṅho rāja-daraśane

virakta—detached; *sannyāsī*—in the renounced order; *teṅho*—He; *rahena*—keeps Himself; *nirjane*—in a solitary place; *svapneha*—even in dreams; *nā*—does not; *karena*—do; *teṅho*—He; *rāja-daraśane*—interview with a king.

TRANSLATION

"Śrī Caitanya Mahāprabhu is in the renounced order and is very much detached from worldly affairs. He stays in solitary places, and even in dreams He does not grant interviews to a king.

TEXT 9

তথাপি প্রকারে তোমা করাইতাম দরশন।
সম্প্রতি করিলা তেঁহো দক্ষিণ গমন ॥ ৯ ॥

tathāpi prakāre tomā karāitāma daraśana
samprati karilā teṅho dakṣiṇa gamana

tathāpi—yet; *prakāre*—somehow or other; *tomā*—you; *karāitāma*—I would have arranged; *daraśana*—interview; *samprati*—recently; *karilā*—has done; *teṅho*—He; *dakṣiṇa*—to the southern part of India; *gamana*—departure.

TRANSLATION

"Still, I would have tried to arrange your interview, but He has recently left to tour South India."

TEXT 10

রাজা কহে, — জগন্নাথ ছাড়ি' কেনে গেলা।
ভট্ট কহে, — মহান্তের এই এক লীলা ॥ ১০ ॥

rājā kahe,—jagannātha chāḍi' kene gelā
bhaṭṭa kahe,—mahāntera ei eka līlā

rājā kahe—the King said; *jagannātha chāḍi'*—leaving the place of Lord Jagannātha; *kene gelā*—why did He leave; *bhaṭṭa kahe*—Sārvabhauma Bhaṭṭācārya replied; *mahāntera*—of a great person; *ei*—this; *eka*—one; *līlā*—pastime.

TRANSLATION

The King asked, "Why has He left Jagannātha Purī?"

The Bhaṭṭācārya replied, "Such are the pastimes of a great personality.

TEXT 11

তীর্থ পবিত্র করিতে করে তীর্থ ভ্রমণ।
সেই ছলে নিস্তারয়ে সাংসারিক জন ॥ ১১ ॥

tīrtha pavitra karite kare tīrtha-bhramaṇa
sei chale nistāraye sāṁsārika jana

tīrtha—holy places; *pavitra karite*—to purify; *kare*—does; *tīrtha-bhramaṇa*—touring in places of pilgrimage; *sei chale*—on that plea; *nistāraye*—delivers; *sāṁsārika*—conditioned; *jana*—souls.

TRANSLATION

"Great saints go to holy places of pilgrimage in order to purify them. For that reason Caitanya Mahāprabhu is visiting many tīrthas and delivering many, many conditioned souls.

TEXT 12

ভবদ্বিধা ভাগবতাস্তীর্থীভূতাঃ স্বয়ং বিভো ।
তীর্থীকুর্বন্তি তীর্থানি স্বান্তঃস্থেন গদাভৃতা ॥ ১২ ॥

bhavad-vidhā bhāgavatās
tīrthī-bhūtāḥ svayaṁ vibho
tīrthī-kurvanti tīrthāni
svāntaḥ-sthena gadā-bhṛtā

bhavat—your good self; *vidhāḥ*—like; *bhāgavatāḥ*—devotees; *tīrthī*—as holy places of pilgrimage; *bhūtāḥ*—existing; *svayam*—themselves; *vibho*—O almighty one; *tīrthī-kurvanti*—make into holy places of pilgrimage; *tīrthāni*—the holy places; *sva-antaḥ-sthena*—being situated in their hearts; *gadā-bhṛtā*—by the Personality of Godhead.

TRANSLATION

"'Saints of your caliber are themselves places of pilgrimage. Because of their purity, they are constant companions of the Lord, and therefore they can purify even the places of pilgrimage.'

PURPORT

This verse, spoken by Mahārāja Yudhiṣṭhira to Vidura in *Śrīmad-Bhāgavatam* (1.13.10), is also quoted in the *Ādi-līlā* (1.63).

TEXT 13

বৈষ্ণবের এই হয় এক স্বভাব নিশ্চল ।
তেঁহো জীব নহেন, হন স্বতন্ত্র ঈশ্বর ॥ ১৩ ॥

vaiṣṇavera ei haya eka svabhāva niścala
teṅho jīva nahena, hana svatantra īśvara

vaiṣṇavera—of great devotees; *ei*—this; *haya*—is; *eka*—one; *svabhāva*—nature; *niścala*—unflinching; *teṅho*—He; *jīva*— conditioned soul; *nahena*—is not; *hana*—is; *svatantra*—independent; *īśvara*—controller.

TRANSLATION

"A Vaiṣṇava travels to places of pilgrimage to purify them and reclaim fallen conditioned souls. This is one of the duties of a Vaiṣṇava. Actually, Śrī Caitanya Mahāprabhu is not a living entity but the Supreme Personality of Godhead Himself. Consequently, He is a fully independent controller, yet in His position as a devotee, He carries out the activities of a devotee."

PURPORT

Śrīla Bhaktisiddhānta Sarasvatī Ṭhākura points out that because there are many permanent residents in holy places who do not precisely follow the rules and regulations governing living in a sacred place, exalted devotees have to go to these places to reclaim such persons. This is the business of a Vaiṣṇava. A Vaiṣṇava is unhappy to see others materially enmeshed. Śrī Caitanya Mahāprabhu taught these activities of a Vaiṣṇava although He is the worshipable Deity of all Vaiṣṇavas, the complete and independent Supreme Personality of Godhead. He is *pūrṇaḥ śuddho nitya-muktaḥ*—complete, completely uncontaminated and eternally liberated. He is *sanātana,* for He has no beginning or end.

TEXT 14

রাজা কহে, —তাঁরে তুমি যাইতে কেনে দিলে।
পায় পড়ি' যত্ন করি' কেনে না রাখিলে ॥ ১৪ ॥

rājā kahe,—tāṅre tumi yāite kene dile
pāya paḍi' yatna kari' kene nā rākhile

rājā kahe—the King said; *tāṅre*—Him; *tumi*—you; *yāite*—to go; *kene*—why; *dile*—allowed; *pāya*—at His lotus feet; *paḍi'*—falling; *yatna kari'*—endeavoring very much; *kene*—why; *nā*—not; *rākhile*—kept.

TRANSLATION

Upon hearing this, the King replied, "Why did you allow Him to leave? Why didn't you fall at His lotus feet and keep Him here?"

TEXT 15

ভট্টাচার্য কহে, — তেঁহো স্বয়ং ঈশ্বর স্বতন্ত্র ।
সাক্ষাৎ শ্রীকৃষ্ণ, তেঁহো নহে পরতন্ত্র ॥ ১৫ ॥

bhaṭṭācārya kahe, — teṅho svayaṁ īśvara svatantra
sākṣāt śrī-kṛṣṇa, teṅho nahe para-tantra

bhaṭṭācārya kahe — Sārvabhauma replied; *teṅho* — He; *svayam* — personally; *īśvara* — the Supreme Personality of Godhead; *svatantra* — independent; *sākṣāt* — directly; *śrī-kṛṣṇa* — Lord Kṛṣṇa; *teṅho* — He; *nahe* — is not; *para-tantra* — dependent on anyone.

TRANSLATION

Sārvabhauma Bhaṭṭācārya replied, "Śrī Caitanya Mahāprabhu is the Supreme Personality of Godhead Himself and is completely independent. Being Lord Kṛṣṇa Himself, He is not dependent on anyone.

TEXT 16

তথাপি রাখিতে তাঁরে বহু যত্ন কৈলুঁ ।
ঈশ্বরের স্বতন্ত্র ইচ্ছা, রাখিতে নারিলুঁ ॥ ১৬ ॥

tathāpi rākhite tāṅre bahu yatna kailuṅ
īśvarera svatantra icchā, rākhite nāriluṅ

tathāpi — still; *rākhite* — to keep; *tāṅre* — Him; *bahu* — various; *yatna* — endeavors; *kailuṅ* — I made; *īśvarera* — of the Supreme Personality of Godhead; *svatantra* — independent; *icchā* — desire; *rākhite* — to keep; *nāriluṅ* — I was unable.

TRANSLATION

"Still, I endeavored very hard to keep Him here, but because He is the Supreme Personality of Godhead and completely independent, I was not successful."

TEXT 17

রাজা কহে, —ভট্ট তুমি বিজ্ঞশিরোমণি।
তুমি তাঁরে 'কৃষ্ণ' কহ, তাতে সত্য মানি ॥ ১৭ ॥

rājā kahe, — bhaṭṭa tumi vijña-śiromaṇi
tumi tāṅre 'kṛṣṇa' kaha, tāte satya māni

rājā kahe — the King said; *bhaṭṭa* — Sārvabhauma Bhaṭṭācārya; *tumi* — you; *vijña-śiromaṇi* — the most experienced learned scholar; *tumi* — you; *tāṅre* — Him; *kṛṣṇa kaha* — address as Lord Kṛṣṇa; *tāte* — your statement; *satya māni* — I accept as true.

TRANSLATION

The King said, "Bhaṭṭācārya, you are the most learned and experienced person I know. Therefore when you address Śrī Caitanya Mahāprabhu as Lord Kṛṣṇa, I accept this as the truth.

PURPORT

This is the way to advance in spiritual science. One must accept the words of an *ācārya,* a bona fide spiritual master, to clear the path for spiritual advancement. This is the secret of success. However, one's guide must be a spiritual master who is actually an unalloyed devotee strictly following the instructions of the previous *ācārya* without deviation. Whatever the spiritual master says must be accepted by the disciple. Only then is success certain. This is the Vedic system.

Sārvabhauma Bhaṭṭācārya was a *brāhmaṇa* and a realized soul, whereas Pratāparudra was a *kṣatriya. Kṣatriya* kings used to obey very faithfully the orders of learned *brāhmaṇas* and saintly persons, and in this way they would rule their country. Similarly, *vaiśyas* used to follow the king's orders, and *śūdras* used to serve the three higher castes. In this way the *brāhmaṇas, kṣatriyas, vaiśyas* and *śūdras* used to live cooperatively, performing their respective duties. Consequently society was peaceful, and people were able to discharge the duties of Kṛṣṇa consciousness. Thus they were happy in this life and able to return home, back to Godhead.

TEXT 18

পুনরপি ইহাঁ তাঁর হৈলে আগমন ।
একবার দেখি' করি সফল নয়ন ॥ ১৮ ॥

punarapi ihāṅ tāṅra haile āgamana
eka-bāra dekhi' kari saphala nayana

punarapi—again; *ihāṅ*—here; *tāṅra*—His; *haile*—when there is; *āgamana*—arrival; *eka-bāra*—once; *dekhi'*—seeing; *kari*—I make; *sa-phala*—fruitful; *nayana*—my eyes.

TRANSLATION

"When Śrī Caitanya Mahāprabhu returns, I wish to see Him just once in order to make my eyes perfect."

TEXT 19

ভট্টাচার্য কহে, — তেঁহো আসিবে অল্পকালে ।
রহিতে তাঁরে এক স্থান চাহিয়ে বিরলে ॥ ১৯ ॥

bhaṭṭācārya kahe,—teṅho āsibe alpa-kāle
rahite tāṅre eka sthāna cāhiye virale

bhaṭṭācārya kahe—Sārvabhauma Bhaṭṭācārya replied; *teṅho*—He; *āsibe*—will come; *alpa-kāle*—very soon; *rahite*—to keep; *tāṅre*—Him; *eka*—one; *sthāna*—place; *cāhiye*—I want; *virale*—secluded.

TRANSLATION

Sārvabhauma Bhaṭṭācārya replied, "His Holiness Lord Śrī Caitanya Mahāprabhu will return very soon. I wish to have a nice place ready for Him, a place solitary and peaceful.

TEXT 20

ঠাকুরের নিকট, আর হইবে নির্জনে ।
এমত নির্ণয় করি' দেহ এক স্থানে ॥ ২০ ॥

ṭhākurera nikaṭa, āra ha-ibe nirjane
e-mata nirṇaya kari' deha' eka sthāne

ṭhākurera nikaṭa—near the place of Lord Jagannātha; *āra*—also; *haibe*—must be; *nirjane*—secluded; *e-mata*—in this way; *nirṇaya kari'*—considering carefully; *deha'*—please give; *eka sthāne*—one place.

TRANSLATION

"Lord Caitanya's residence should be very secluded and also near the temple of Jagannātha. Please consider this proposal and give me a nice place for Him."

TEXT 21

রাজা কহে, — ঐছে কাশীমিশ্রের ভবন।
ঠাকুরের নিকট, হয় পরম নির্জন ॥ ২১ ॥

rājā kahe,—aiche kāśī-miśrera bhavana
ṭhākurera nikaṭa, haya parama nirjana

rājā kahe—the King replied; *aiche*—exactly like that; *kāśī-miśrera bhavana*—the house of Kāśī Miśra; *ṭhākurera nikaṭa*—near Lord Jagannātha; *haya*—is; *parama*—very; *nirjana*—secluded.

TRANSLATION

The King replied, "Kāśī Miśra's house is exactly what you require. It is near the temple and is very secluded, calm and quiet."

TEXT 22

এত কহি' রাজা রহে উৎকণ্ঠিত হঞা।
ভট্টাচার্য কাশীমিশ্রে কহিল আসিয়া ॥ ২২ ॥

eta kahi' rājā rahe utkaṇṭhita hañā
bhaṭṭācārya kāśī-miśre kahila āsiyā

eta kahi'—saying this; *rājā*—the King; *rahe*—remained; *utkaṇṭhita*—very anxious; *hañā*—being; *bhaṭṭācārya*—Sārvabhauma Bhaṭṭācārya; *kāśī-miśre*—unto Kāśī Miśra; *kahila*—said; *āsiyā*—coming.

TRANSLATION

After saying this, the King became very anxious for the Lord to return. Sārvabhauma Bhaṭṭācārya then went to Kāśī Miśra to convey the King's desire.

TEXT 23

কাশীমিশ্র কহে, — আমি বড় ভাগ্যবান্ ।
মোর গৃহে 'প্রভুপাদের' হবে অবস্থান ॥ ২৩ ॥

kāśī-miśra kahe, — āmi baḍa bhāgyavān
mora gṛhe 'prabhu-pādera' habe avasthāna

kāśī-miśra kahe — Kāśī Miśra said; *āmi* — I; *baḍa* — very; *bhāgyavān* — fortunate; *mora gṛhe* — in my home; *prabhu-pādera* — of the Lord of the *prabhus*; *habe* — there will be; *avasthāna* — staying.

TRANSLATION

When Kāśī Miśra heard the proposal, he said, "I am very fortunate that Śrī Caitanya Mahāprabhu, the Lord of all prabhus, will stay at my home."

PURPORT

In this verse the word *prabhupāda,* referring to Śrī Caitanya Mahāprabhu, is significant. Regarding this, Śrīla Bhaktisiddhānta Sarasvatī Gosvāmī Prabhupāda comments, "Śrī Caitanya Mahāprabhu is the Supreme Personality of Godhead Himself, Śrī Kṛṣṇa, and all His servants address Him as Prabhupāda. This means that there are many *prabhus* taking shelter under His lotus feet." The pure Vaiṣṇava is addressed as *prabhu,* and this address is an etiquette observed between Vaiṣṇavas. When many *prabhus* remain under the shelter of the lotus feet of another *prabhu,* the address Prabhupāda is given. Śrī Nityānanda Prabhu and Śrī Advaita Prabhu are also addressed as Prabhupāda. Śrī Caitanya Mahāprabhu, Śrī Advaita Prabhu and Śrī Nityānanda Prabhu are all *viṣṇu-tattva,* the Supreme Personality of Godhead, Lord Viṣṇu. Therefore all living entities are under Their lotus feet. Lord Viṣṇu is the eternal Lord of everyone, and the representative of Lord Viṣṇu is the Lord's confidential servant. Such a person acts as the spiritual master for neophyte Vaiṣṇavas; therefore the spiritual master is as respectable as Śrī Kṛṣṇa Caitanya or Lord Viṣṇu Himself. For this reason the spiritual master is addressed as Oṁ Viṣṇupāda or Prabhupāda. The *ācārya,* the spiritual master, is generally respected by others as Śrīpāda, and the initiated Vaiṣṇavas are addressed as Prabhu. Prabhu, Prabhupāda and Viṣṇupāda are described in revealed scriptures like *Śrīmad-Bhāgavatam, Śrī Caitanya-caritāmṛta* and *Śrī Caitanya-bhāgavata.* In this regard, these scriptures present evidence accepted by unalloyed devotees.

The *prākṛta-sahajiyās* are not even worthy of being called Vaiṣṇavas. They think that only caste *gosvāmīs* should be called Prabhupāda. Such ignorant *sahajiyās* call themselves *vaiṣṇava-dāsa-anudāsa,* which means the servant of the Vaiṣṇavas. However, they are opposed to addressing a pure Vaiṣṇava as Prabhupāda. In other words, they are envious of a bona fide spiritual master who is addressed as Prabhupāda, and they commit offenses by considering a bona fide spiritual master an ordinary human being or a member of a certain caste. Śrīla Bhaktisiddhānta Sarasvatī Ṭhākura describes such *sahajiyās* as most unfortunate. Because of their misconceptions, they fall into a hellish condition.

TEXT 24

এইমত পুরুষোত্তমবাসী যত জন ।
প্রভুকে মিলিতে সবার উৎকণ্ঠিত মন ॥ ২৪ ॥

ei-mata puruṣottama-vāsī yata jana
prabhuke milite sabāra utkaṇṭhita mana

ei-mata—in this way; *puruṣottama-vāsī*—the residents of Jagannātha Purī; *yata*—all; *jana*—persons; *prabhuke*—Lord Śrī Caitanya Mahāprabhu; *milite*—to meet; *sabāra*—of everyone; *utkaṇṭhita*—anxious; *mana*—mind.

TRANSLATION

Thus all the residents of Jagannātha Purī, which is also known as Puruṣottama, became anxious to meet Śrī Caitanya Mahāprabhu again.

TEXT 25

সর্বলোকের উৎকণ্ঠা যবে অত্যন্ত বাড়িল ।
মহাপ্রভু দক্ষিণ হৈতে তবহি আইল ॥ ২৫ ॥

sarva-lokera utkaṇṭhā yabe atyanta bāḍila
mahāprabhu dakṣiṇa haite tabahi āila

sarva-lokera—of all people; *utkaṇṭhā*—anxieties; *yabe*—when; *atyanta*—very much; *bāḍila*—increased; *mahāprabhu*—Śrī Caitanya Mahāprabhu; *dakṣiṇa haite*—from South India; *tabahi*—at that very time; *āila*—returned.

TRANSLATION

When all the residents of Jagannātha Purī became extremely anxious to meet the Lord again, He returned from South India.

TEXT 26

শুনি' আনন্দিত হৈল সবাকার মন ।
সবে আসি' সার্বভৌমে কৈল নিবেদন ॥ ২৬ ॥

śuni' ānandita haila sabākāra mana
sabe āsi' sārvabhaume kaila nivedana

śuni'—hearing; *ānandita*—happy; *haila*—were; *sabākāra*—of everyone; *mana*—the minds; *sabe āsi'*—everyone coming; *sārvabhaume*—unto Sārvabhauma Bhaṭṭācārya; *kaila*—did; *nivedana*—submission.

TRANSLATION

Hearing of the Lord's return, everyone became very happy, and they all went to Sārvabhauma Bhaṭṭācārya and spoke to him as follows.

TEXT 27

প্রভুর সহিত আমা-সবার করাহ মিলন ।
তোমার প্রসাদে পাই প্রভুর চরণ ॥ ২৭ ॥

prabhura sahita āmā-sabāra karāha milana
tomāra prasāde pāi prabhura caraṇa

prabhura sahita—with Śrī Caitanya Mahāprabhu; *āmā-sabāra*—of all of us; *karāha*—arrange; *milana*—meeting; *tomāra*—your; *prasāde*—by mercy; *pāi*—we get; *prabhura caraṇa*—the lotus feet of the Lord.

TRANSLATION

"Please arrange our meeting with Śrī Caitanya Mahāprabhu. It is only by your mercy that we can attain the shelter of the lotus feet of the Lord."

TEXT 28

ভট্টাচার্য কহে, — কালি কাশীমিশ্রের ঘরে।
প্রভু যাইবেন, তাহাঁ মিলাব সবারে ॥ ২৮ ॥

bhaṭṭācārya kahe, — kāli kāśī-miśrera ghare
prabhu yāibena, tāhāṅ milāba sabāre

bhaṭṭācārya kahe — the Bhaṭṭācārya replied; *kāli* — tomorrow; *kāśī-miśrera ghare* — in the house of Kāśī Miśra; *prabhu* — the Lord; *yāibena* — will go; *tāhāṅ* — there; *milāba sabāre* — I shall arrange for a meeting with all of you.

TRANSLATION

The Bhaṭṭācārya replied to the people, "Tomorrow the Lord will be at the house of Kāśī Miśra. I shall arrange for you all to meet Him."

TEXT 29

আর দিন মহাপ্রভু ভট্টাচার্যের সঙ্গে।
জগন্নাথ দরশন কৈল মহারঙ্গে ॥ ২৯ ॥

āra dina mahāprabhu bhaṭṭācāryera saṅge
jagannātha daraśana kaila mahā-raṅge

āra dina — the next day; *mahāprabhu* — Śrī Caitanya Mahāprabhu; *bhaṭṭācāryera saṅge* — with Sārvabhauma Bhaṭṭācārya; *jagannātha* — of Lord Jagannātha; *daraśana* — visiting the temple; *kaila* — did; *mahā-raṅge* — with great enthusiasm.

TRANSLATION

The next day Śrī Caitanya Mahāprabhu arrived and went with Sārvabhauma Bhaṭṭācārya, with great enthusiasm, to see the temple of Lord Jagannātha.

TEXT 30

মহাপ্রসাদ দিয়া তাহাঁ মিলিলা সেবকগণ ।
মহাপ্রভু সবাকারে কৈল আলিঙ্গন ॥ ৩০ ॥

mahā-prasāda diyā tāhān̐ mililā sevaka-gaṇa
mahāprabhu sabākāre kaila āliṅgana

mahā-prasāda — remnants of the food of Lord Jagannātha; *diyā* — delivering; *tāhān̐* — there; *mililā* — met; *sevaka-gaṇa* — the servants of Lord Jagannātha; *mahāprabhu* — Śrī Caitanya Mahāprabhu; *sabākāre* — unto all of them; *kaila* — did; *āliṅgana* — embracing.

TRANSLATION

All the servants of Lord Jagannātha delivered remnants of the Lord's food to Śrī Caitanya Mahāprabhu. In return, Caitanya Mahāprabhu embraced them all.

TEXT 31

দর্শন করি' মহাপ্রভু চলিলা বাহিরে ।
ভট্টাচার্য আনিল তাঁরে কাশীমিশ্র-ঘরে ॥ ৩১ ॥

darśana kari' mahāprabhu calilā bāhire
bhaṭṭācārya ānila tān̐re kāśī-miśra-ghare

darśana kari' — seeing Lord Jagannātha; *mahāprabhu* — Śrī Caitanya Mahāprabhu; *calilā* — departed; *bāhire* — outside; *bhaṭṭācārya* — Sārvabhauma Bhaṭṭācārya; *ānila* — brought; *tān̐re* — Him; *kāśī-miśra-ghare* — to the house of Kāśī Miśra.

TRANSLATION

After seeing Lord Jagannātha, Śrī Caitanya Mahāprabhu left the temple. The Bhaṭṭācārya then took Him to the house of Kāśī Miśra.

TEXT 32

কাশীমিশ্র আসি' পড়িল প্রভুর চরণে ।
গৃহ-সহিত আত্মা তাঁরে কৈল নিবেদনে ॥ ৩২ ॥

kāśī-miśra āsi' paḍila prabhura caraṇe
gṛha-sahita ātmā tāṅre kaila nivedane

kāśī-miśra—Kāśī Miśra; *āsi'*—coming; *paḍila*—fell down; *prabhura*—of Lord Śrī Caitanya Mahāprabhu; *caraṇe*—at the lotus feet; *gṛha-sahita*—with his house; *ātmā*—his personal self; *tāṅre*—unto Him; *kaila*—did; *nivedane*—submission.

TRANSLATION

When Śrī Caitanya Mahāprabhu arrived at his house, Kāśī Miśra immediately fell down at His lotus feet and surrendered himself and all his possessions.

TEXT 33

প্রভু চতুর্ভুজ-মূর্তি তাঁরে দেখাইল।
আত্মসাৎ করি' তারে আলিঙ্গন কৈল ॥ ৩৩ ॥

prabhu catur-bhuja-mūrti tāṅre dekhāila
ātmasāt kari' tāre āliṅgana kaila

prabhu—Śrī Caitanya Mahāprabhu; *catur-bhuja-mūrti*—four-armed form; *tāṅre*—unto him; *dekhāila*—showed; *ātmasāt kari'*—accepting; *tāre*—him; *āliṅgana kaila*—embraced.

TRANSLATION

Śrī Caitanya Mahāprabhu then showed Kāśī Miśra His four-armed form. Then, accepting him for His service, the Lord embraced him.

TEXT 34

তবে মহাপ্রভু তাহাঁ বসিলা আসনে।
চৌদিকে বসিলা নিত্যানন্দাদি ভক্তগণে ॥ ৩৪ ॥

tabe mahāprabhu tāhāṅ vasilā āsane
caudike vasilā nityānandādi bhakta-gaṇe

tabe—at that time; *mahāprabhu*—Śrī Caitanya Mahāprabhu; *tāhāṅ*—there; *vasilā*—sat down; *āsane*—on His seat; *cau-dike*—on four sides; *vasilā*—sat down; *nityānanda-ādi*—headed by Lord Nityānanda; *bhakta-gaṇe*—all the devotees.

TRANSLATION

Śrī Caitanya Mahāprabhu next sat down at the place prepared for Him, and all the devotees, headed by Lord Nityānanda Prabhu, surrounded Him.

TEXT 35

সুখী হৈলা দেখি' প্রভু বাসার সংস্থান ।
যেই বাসায় হয় প্রভুর সর্ব-সমাধান ॥ ৩৫ ॥

sukhī hailā dekhi' prabhu vāsāra saṁsthāna
yei vāsāya haya prabhura sarva-samādhāna

sukhī hailā—became very happy; *dekhi'*—by seeing; *prabhu*—Śrī Caitanya Mahāprabhu; *vāsāra*—of the residential quarters; *saṁsthāna*—situation; *yei vāsāya*—at which place; *haya*—there is; *prabhura*—of Śrī Caitanya Mahāprabhu; *sarva-samādhāna*—fulfillment of all necessities.

TRANSLATION

Śrī Caitanya Mahāprabhu was very happy to see His residential quarters, in which all His necessities were taken care of.

TEXT 36

সার্বভৌম কহে,—প্রভু, যোগ্য তোমার বাসা ।
তুমি অঙ্গীকার কর,—কাশীমিশ্রের আশা ॥ ৩৬ ॥

sārvabhauma kahe,—prabhu, yogya tomāra vāsā
tumi aṅgīkāra kara,—kāśī-miśrera āśā

sārvabhauma—Sārvabhauma Bhaṭṭācārya; *kahe*—said; *prabhu*—my dear Lord; *yogya*—just befitting; *tomāra*—Your; *vāsā*—residential quarters; *tumi*—You; *aṅgīkāra kara*—accept; *kāśī-miśrera āśā*—the hope of Kāśī Miśra.

TRANSLATION

Sārvabhauma Bhaṭṭācārya said, "This place is just befitting You. Please accept it. It is the hope of Kāśī Miśra that You do."

TEXT 37

প্রভু কহে, — এই দেহ তোমা-সবাকার ।
যেই তুমি কহ, সেই সম্মত আমার ॥ ৩৭ ॥

prabhu kahe,—ei deha tomā-sabākāra
yei tumi kaha, sei sammata āmāra

prabhu kahe—Śrī Caitanya Mahāprabhu said; *ei deha*—this body; *tomā-sabākāra*—belongs to all of you; *yei*—whatever; *tumi*—you; *kaha*—say; *sei*—that; *sammata āmāra*—accepted by Me.

TRANSLATION

Śrī Caitanya Mahāprabhu said, "My body belongs to all of you. Therefore I agree to whatever you say."

TEXT 38

তবে সার্বভৌম প্রভুর দক্ষিণ-পার্শ্বে বসি' ।
মিলাইতে লাগিলা সব পুরুষোত্তমবাসী ॥ ৩৮ ॥

tabe sārvabhauma prabhura dakṣiṇa-pārśve vasi'
milāite lāgilā saba puruṣottama-vāsī

tabe—thereafter; *sārvabhauma*—Sārvabhauma; *prabhura*—of Śrī Caitanya Mahāprabhu; *dakṣiṇa-pārśve*—by the right side; *vasi'*—sitting; *milāite*—to introduce; *lāgilā*—began; *saba*—all; *puruṣottama-vāsī*—residents of Puruṣottama (Jagannātha Purī).

TRANSLATION

After this, Sārvabhauma Bhaṭṭācārya, sitting at the right hand of the Lord, began to introduce all the inhabitants of Puruṣottama, Jagannātha Purī.

TEXT 39

এই সব লোক, প্রভু, বৈসে নীলাচলে ।
উৎকণ্ঠিত হঞাছে সবে তোমা মিলিবারে ॥ ৩৯ ॥

ei saba loka, prabhu, vaise nīlācale
utkaṇṭhita hañāche sabe tomā milibāre

ei saba loka—all these people; *prabhu*—my Lord; *vaise*—reside; *nīlācale*—at Jagannātha Purī; *utkaṇṭhita hañāche*—they have become very anxious; *sabe*—all; *tomā*—You; *milibāre*—to meet.

TRANSLATION

The Bhaṭṭācārya said, "My dear Lord, all these people who are residents of Nīlācala, Jagannātha Purī, have been very anxious to meet You.

TEXT 40

তৃষিত চাতক যৈছে করে হাহাকার ।
তৈছে এই সব, —সবে কর অঙ্গীকার ॥ ৪০ ॥

tṛṣita cātaka yaiche kare hāhākāra
taiche ei saba,—sabe kara aṅgīkāra

tṛṣita—thirsty; *cātaka*—the cātaka bird; *yaiche*—just as; *kare*—does; *hāhā-kāra*—vibration of disappointment; *taiche*—similarly; *ei saba*—all of these; *sabe*—all of them; *kara aṅgīkāra*—kindly accept.

TRANSLATION

"In Your absence all these people have been exactly like thirsty cātaka birds crying in disappointment. Kindly accept them."

TEXT 41

জগন্নাথ-সেবক এই, নাম—জনার্দন ।
অনবসরে করে প্রভুর শ্রীঅঙ্গ-সেবন ॥ ৪১ ॥

jagannātha-sevaka ei, nāma—janārdana
anavasare kare prabhura śrī-aṅga-sevana

jagannātha-sevaka—servitor of Lord Jagannātha; *ei*—this; *nāma*—named; *janārdana*—Janārdana; *anavasare*—during the time of renovation; *kare*—does; *prabhura*—of the Lord; *śrī-aṅga*—of the transcendental body; *sevana*—service.

TRANSLATION

Sārvabhauma Bhaṭṭācārya first introduced Janārdana, saying, "Here is Janārdana, servant of Lord Jagannātha. He renders service to the Lord when it is time to renovate His transcendental body."

PURPORT

During Anavasara, after the Snāna-yātrā ceremony, Lord Jagannātha is absent from the temple for fifteen days so He can be renovated. This occurs annually. Janārdana, who is here being introduced to Śrī Caitanya Mahāprabhu, was rendering this service at the time. The renovation of Lord Jagannātha is also known as Nava-yauvana, which indicates that the Jagannātha Deity is being fully restored to youth.

TEXT 42

কৃষ্ণদাস-নাম এই সুবর্ণ-বেত্রধারী।
শিখি মাহাতি-নাম এই লিখনাধিকারী ॥ ৪২ ॥

kṛṣṇadāsa-nāma ei suvarṇa-vetra-dhārī
śikhi māhāti-nāma ei likhanādhikārī

kṛṣṇadāsa—Kṛṣṇadāsa; *nāma*—named; *ei*—this; *suvarṇa*—golden; *vetra-dhārī*—carrier of the cane; *śikhi māhāti*—Śikhi Māhiti; *nāma*—named; *ei*—this; *likhana-adhikārī*—entrusted with writing.

TRANSLATION

Sārvabhauma Bhaṭṭācārya continued, "This is Kṛṣṇadāsa, who carries a golden cane, and here is Śikhi Māhiti, who is in charge of writing.

PURPORT

The person in charge of writing is also called *deula-karaṇa-pada-prāpta karmacārī.* He is employed especially to write a calendar called *Mātalā-pāñji.*

TEXT 43

প্রদ্যুম্নমিশ্র ইঁহ বৈষ্ণব প্রধান।
জগন্নাথের মহা-সোয়ার ইঁহ 'দাস' নাম ॥ ৪৩ ॥

pradyumna-miśra iṅha vaiṣṇava pradhāna
jagannāthera mahā-soyāra iṅha 'dāsa' nāma

pradyumna-miśra—Pradyumna Miśra; *iṅha*—this person; *vaiṣṇava pradhāna*—chief of all the Vaiṣṇavas; *jagannāthera*—of Lord Jagannātha; *mahā-soyāra*—great servitor; *iṅha*—this; *dāsa nāma*—designated as Dāsa.

TRANSLATION

"This is Pradyumna Miśra, who is chief of all Vaiṣṇavas. He is a great servitor of Jagannātha, and his name is Dāsa.

PURPORT

In Orissa most of the *brāhmaṇas* have the title Dāsa. Generally it is understood that the word *dāsa* refers to those other than the *brāhmaṇas,* but in Orissa the *brāhmaṇas* use the Dāsa title. This is confirmed by Culli Bhaṭṭa. Actually, everyone is *dāsa* because everyone is a servant of the Supreme Personality of Godhead. In that sense, the bona fide *brāhmaṇa* has first claim to the appellation *dāsa.* Therefore in this case the designation *dāsa* is not incompatible.

TEXT 44

মুরারি মাহাতি ইঁহ — শিখিমাহাতির ভাই।
তোমার চরণ বিনু আর গতি নাই ॥ ৪৪ ॥

murāri māhāti iṅha—śikhi-māhātira bhāi
tomāra caraṇa vinu āra gati nāi

murāri māhāti—Murāri Māhiti; *iṅha*—this; *śikhi-māhātira*—of Śikhi Māhiti; *bhāi*—younger brother; *tomāra*—Your; *caraṇa*—lotus feet; *vinu*—without; *āra*—any other; *gati*—destination; *nāi*—he does not have.

TRANSLATION

"This is Murāri Māhiti, the brother of Śikhi Māhiti. He has nothing other than Your lotus feet.

TEXT 45

চন্দনেশ্বর, সিংহেশ্বর, মুরারি ব্রাহ্মণ।
বিষ্ণুদাস, —ইঁহ ধ্যায়ে তোমার চরণ ॥ ৪৫ ॥

candaneśvara, siṁheśvara, murāri brāhmaṇa
viṣṇudāsa, —iṅha dhyāye tomāra caraṇa

candaneśvara—Candaneśvara; *siṁheśvara*—Siṁheśvara; *murāri brāhmaṇa*—the *brāhmaṇa* named Murāri; *viṣṇudāsa*—Viṣṇudāsa; *iṅha*—all of them; *dhyāye*—meditate; *tomāra*—Your; *caraṇa*—on the lotus feet.

TRANSLATION

"Here are Candaneśvara, Siṁheśvara, Murāri Brāhmaṇa and Viṣṇudāsa. They are all constantly engaged in meditating on Your lotus feet.

TEXT 46

প্রহররাজ মহাপাত্র ইঁহ মহামতি।
পরমানন্দ মহাপাত্র ইঁহার সংহতি ॥ ৪৬ ॥

prahararāja mahāpātra iṅha mahā-mati
paramānanda mahāpātra iṅhāra saṁhati

prahararāja—Prahararāja; *mahāpātra*—Mahāpātra; *iṅha*—this; *mahā-mati*—very intelligent; *paramānanda mahāpātra*—Paramānanda Mahāpātra; *iṅhāra*—of him; *saṁhati*—combination.

TRANSLATION

"This is Paramānanda Prahararāja, who is also known as Mahāpātra. He is very, very intelligent.

PURPORT

Prahararāja is a designation given to *brāhmaṇas* who represent the king when the throne is vacant. In Orissa, between the time of a king's death and the enthronement of another king, a representative must sit on the throne. This representative is called Praharарāja. The Praharарāja is generally selected from a family of priests close to the king. During the time of Śrī Caitanya Mahāprabhu, the Praharарāja was Paramānanda Praharарāja.

TEXT 47

এ-সব বৈষ্ণব — এই ক্ষেত্রের ভূষণ ।
একান্তভাবে চিন্তে সবে তোমার চরণ ॥ ৪৭ ॥

e-saba vaiṣṇava — ei kṣetrera bhūṣaṇa
ekānta-bhāve cinte sabe tomāra caraṇa

e-saba vaiṣṇava — all these pure devotees; *ei kṣetrera* — of this holy place; *bhūṣaṇa* — ornaments; *ekānta-bhāve* — without deviation; *cinte* — meditate; *sabe* — all; *tomāra caraṇa* — on Your lotus feet.

TRANSLATION

"All these pure devotees serve as ornaments to Jagannātha Purī. They are always undeviatingly meditating upon Your lotus feet."

TEXT 48

তবে সবে ভূমে পড়ে দণ্ডবৎ হঞা ।
সবা আলিঙ্গিলা প্রভু প্রসাদ করিয়া ॥ ৪৮ ॥

tabe sabe bhūme paḍe daṇḍavat hañā
sabā āliṅgilā prabhu prasāda kariyā

tabe — thereafter; *sabe* — all of them; *bhūme* — on the ground; *paḍe* — fell down; *daṇḍa-vat* — flat like rods; *hañā* — becoming; *sabā* — all of them; *āliṅgilā* — embraced; *prabhu* — Śrī Caitanya Mahāprabhu; *prasāda kariyā* — being very merciful.

TRANSLATION

After this introduction, everyone fell to the ground like rods. Being very merciful upon them all, Śrī Caitanya Mahāprabhu embraced each one of them.

TEXT 49

হেনকালে আইলা তথা ভবানন্দ রায় ।
চারিপুত্র-সঙ্গে পড়ে মহাপ্রভুর পায় ॥ ৪৯ ॥

hena-kāle āilā tathā bhavānanda rāya
cāri-putra-saṅge paḍe mahāprabhura pāya

hena-kāle—at this time; *āilā*—came; *tathā*—there; *bhavānanda rāya*—Bhavānanda Rāya; *cāri-putra-saṅge*—with four of his sons; *paḍe*—fell down; *mahāprabhura pāya*—at the lotus feet of Śrī Caitanya Mahāprabhu.

TRANSLATION

At this time Bhavānanda Rāya appeared with four of his sons, and all of them fell down at the lotus feet of Śrī Caitanya Mahāprabhu.

PURPORT

Bhavānanda Rāya had five sons, one of whom was the exalted personality known as Rāmānanda Rāya. Bhavānanda Rāya first met Śrī Caitanya Mahāprabhu after His return from South India. At that time Rāmānanda Rāya was still serving at his government post; therefore when Bhavānanda Rāya went to see Śrī Caitanya Mahāprabhu, he went with his other four sons. They were named Vāṇīnātha, Gopīnātha, Kalānidhi and Sudhānidhi. A description of Bhavānanda Rāya and his five sons is given in the *Ādi-līlā* (10.133–34).

TEXT 50

সার্বভৌম কহে, — এই রায় ভবানন্দ ।
ইঁহার প্রথম পুত্র — রায় রামানন্দ ॥ ৫০ ॥

sārvabhauma kahe,—ei rāya bhavānanda
iṅhāra prathama putra—rāya rāmānanda

sārvabhauma kahe—Sārvabhauma Bhaṭṭācārya continued to speak; *ei*—this person; *rāya bhavānanda*—Bhavānanda Rāya; *iṅhāra*—his; *prathama putra*—first son; *rāya rāmānanda*—Rāmānanda Rāya.

TRANSLATION

Sārvabhauma Bhaṭṭācārya continued, "This is Bhavānanda Rāya, the father of Śrī Rāmānanda Rāya, who is his first son."

TEXT 51

তবে মহাপ্রভু তাঁরে কৈল আলিঙ্গন।
স্তুতি করি' কহে রামানন্দ-বিবরণ ॥ ৫১ ॥

tabe mahāprabhu tāṅre kaila āliṅgana
stuti kari' kahe rāmānanda-vivaraṇa

tabe—thereupon; *mahāprabhu*—Śrī Caitanya Mahāprabhu; *tāṅre*—unto him; *kaila*—did; *āliṅgana*—embracing; *stuti kari'*—praising very highly; *kahe*—said; *rāmānanda*—of Rāmānanda Rāya; *vivaraṇa*—description.

TRANSLATION

Śrī Caitanya Mahāprabhu embraced Bhavānanda Rāya and with great respect spoke of his son Rāmānanda Rāya.

TEXT 52

রামানন্দ-হেন রত্ন যাঁহার তনয়।
তাঁহার মহিমা লোকে কহন না যায় ॥ ৫২ ॥

rāmānanda-hena ratna yāṅhāra tanaya
tāṅhāra mahimā loke kahana nā yāya

rāmānanda-hena—like Rāmānanda Rāya; *ratna*—jewel; *yāṅhāra*—whose; *tanaya*—son; *tāṅhāra*—his; *mahimā*—glorification; *loke*—within this world; *kahana*—to describe; *nā*—not; *yāya*—is possible.

TRANSLATION

Śrī Caitanya Mahāprabhu honored Bhavānanda Rāya by saying, "The glories of a person who has a jewel of a son like Rāmānanda Rāya cannot be described within this mortal world.

TEXT 53

সাক্ষাৎ পাণ্ডু তুমি, তোমার পত্নী কুন্তী ।
পঞ্চপাণ্ডব তোমার পঞ্চপুত্র মহামতি ॥ ৫৩ ॥

sākṣāt pāṇḍu tumi, tomāra patnī kuntī
pañca-pāṇḍava tomāra pañca-putra mahā-mati

sākṣāt pāṇḍu—directly Mahārāja Pāṇḍu; *tumi*—you; *tomāra*—your; *patnī*—wife; *kuntī*—like Kuntīdevī; *pañca-pāṇḍava*—five Pāṇḍavas; *tomāra*—your; *pañca-putra*—five sons; *mahā-mati*—all highly intellectual.

TRANSLATION

"You are Mahārāja Pāṇḍu himself, and your wife is Kuntīdevī herself. All your highly intellectual sons are representatives of the five Pāṇḍavas."

TEXT 54

রায় কহে,—আমি শূদ্র, বিষয়ী, অধম ।
তবু তুমি স্পর্শ,—এই ঈশ্বর-লক্ষণ ॥ ৫৪ ॥

rāya kahe,—āmi śūdra, viṣayī, adhama
tabu tumi sparśa,—ei īśvara-lakṣaṇa

rāya kahe—Bhavānanda Rāya replied; *āmi śūdra*—I belong to the fourth class of the social divisions; *viṣayī*—engaged in mundane affairs; *adhama*—very fallen; *tabu*—still; *tumi*—You; *sparśa*—touch; *ei*—this; *īśvara-lakṣaṇa*—sign of the Supreme Personality of Godhead.

TRANSLATION

After hearing Śrī Caitanya Mahāprabhu's praise, Bhavānanda Rāya submitted, "I am in the fourth class of the social order, and I engage in mundane affairs. Although I am very fallen, You have still touched me. This is proof that You are the Supreme Personality of Godhead."

PURPORT

As stated in the *Bhagavad-gītā* (5.18):

vidyā-vinaya-sampanne brāhmaṇe gavi hastini
śuni caiva śva-pāke ca paṇḍitāḥ sama-darśinaḥ

"The humble sages, by virtue of true knowledge, see with equal vision a learned and gentle *brāhmaṇa,* a cow, an elephant, a dog and a dog-eater [outcaste]."

Those who are highly advanced in spiritual understanding do not care about a person's material condition. A spiritually advanced person sees the spiritual identity of every living being, and consequently he makes no distinction between a learned *brāhmaṇa,* a dog, a *caṇḍāla* or anyone else. He is not influenced by the material body but sees a person's spiritual identity. Consequently Bhavānanda Rāya appreciated Śrī Caitanya Mahāprabhu's statement, which showed that the Lord did not consider the social position of Bhavānanda Rāya, who belonged to the *śūdra* caste engaged in mundane activities. Rather, the Lord considered the spiritual position of Bhavānanda Rāya, along with that of Rāmānanda Rāya and his brothers. The servant of the Lord is also similarly inclined. He gives shelter to any person—any living entity—regardless of whether he belongs to a *brāhmaṇa* family or a *caṇḍāla* family. The spiritual master reclaims all people and encourages everyone in spiritual life. By taking shelter of such a devotee, one can make his life successful. As confirmed in *Śrīmad-Bhāgavatam* (2.4.18):

kirāta-hūṇāndhra-pulinda-pulkaśā
ābhīra-śumbhā yavanāḥ khasādayaḥ
ye 'nye ca pāpā yad-apāśrayāśrayāḥ
śudhyanti tasmai prabhaviṣṇave namaḥ

"Kirātas, Hūṇas, Āndhras, Pulindas, Pulkaśas, Ābhīras, Śumbhas, Yavanas and members of the Khaśa races, and even others who are addicted to sinful acts, can be purified by taking shelter of the devotees of the Lord, due to His being the supreme power. I beg to offer my respectful obeisances unto Him."

Whoever takes shelter of the Supreme Personality of Godhead or His pure devotee is elevated to the spiritual order and purified from material contamination. This is also confirmed by Kṛṣṇa in the *Bhagavad-gītā* (9.32):

māṁ hi pārtha vyapāśritya ye 'pi syuḥ pāpa-yonayaḥ
striyo vaiśyās tathā śūdrās te 'pi yānti parāṁ gatim

"O son of Pṛthā, those who take shelter in Me, though they be of lower birth—women, *vaiśyas* [merchants] and *śūdras* [workers]—can attain the supreme destination."

TEXT 55

নিজ-গৃহ-বিত্ত-ভৃত্য-পঞ্চপুত্র-সনে।
আত্মা সমর্পিলুঁ আমি তোমার চরণে ॥ ৫৫ ॥

nija-gṛha-vitta-bhṛtya-pañca-putra-sane
ātmā samarpiluṅ āmi tomāra caraṇe

nija—own; *gṛha*—house; *vitta*—wealth; *bhṛtya*—servants; *pañca-putra*—five sons; *sane*—with; *ātmā*—self; *samarpiluṅ*—surrender; *āmi*—I; *tomāra*—Your; *caraṇe*—at the lotus feet.

TRANSLATION

Appreciating Śrī Caitanya Mahāprabhu's favor, Bhavānanda Rāya also said, "Along with my home, riches, servants and five sons, I surrender myself at Your lotus feet.

PURPORT

This is the process of surrender. As Śrīla Bhaktivinoda Ṭhākura sings:

mānasa, deha, geha, yo kichu mora
arpiluṅ tuyā pade nanda-kiśora!

(*Śaraṇāgati*)

When one surrenders unto the lotus feet of the Lord, he does so with everything in his possession—his house, his body, his mind and whatever else he possesses. If there is any obstruction to this surrendering process, one should immediately give it up without attachment. If one can surrender with all his family members, there is no need to take *sannyāsa*. However, if the surrendering process is hampered by so-called family members, one should immediately give them up to complete the surrendering process.

TEXT 56

এই বাণীনাথ রহিবে তোমার চরণে।
যবে যেই আজ্ঞা, তাহা করিবে সেবনে ॥ ৫৬ ॥

ei vāṇīnātha rahibe tomara caraṇe
yabe yei ājñā, tāhā karibe sevane

ei vāṇīnātha—this Vāṇīnātha; *rahibe*—will remain; *tomāra caraṇe*—at Your lotus feet; *yabe*—when; *yei*—whatever; *ājñā*—order; *tāhā*—that; *karibe*—will execute; *sevane*—service.

TRANSLATION

"This son Vāṇīnātha will remain at Your lotus feet to always immediately attend to Your orders and serve You.

TEXT 57

আত্মীয়-জ্ঞানে মোরে সঙ্কোচ না করিবে।
যেই যবে ইচ্ছা, তবে সেই আজ্ঞা দিবে ॥ ৫৭ ॥

ātmīya-jñāne more saṅkoca nā karibe
yei yabe icchā, tabe sei ājñā dibe

ātmīya-jñāne—by considering as a relative; *more*—me; *saṅkoca*—hesitation; *nā*—do not; *karibe*—do; *yei*—whatever; *yabe*—whenever; *icchā*—Your desire; *tabe*—then; *sei*—that; *ājñā*—order; *dibe*—kindly give.

TRANSLATION

"My dear Lord, please consider me Your relative. Do not hesitate to order whatever You desire at any time You desire it."

TEXT 58

প্রভু কহে,—কি সঙ্কোচ, তুমি নহ পর।
জন্মে জন্মে তুমি আমার সবংশে কিঙ্কর ॥ ৫৮ ॥

prabhu kahe,—ki saṅkoca, tumi naha para
janme janme tumi āmāra savaṁśe kiṅkara

prabhu kahe—the Lord replied; *ki saṅkoca*—what hesitation; *tumi*—you; *naha*—are not; *para*—outsider; *janme janme*—birth after birth; *tumi*—you; *āmāra*—My; *sa-vaṁśe*—with family members; *kiṅkara*—servant.

TRANSLATION

Śrī Caitanya Mahāprabhu accepted Bhavānanda Rāya's offer, saying, "I accept without hesitation because you are not an outsider. Birth after birth you have been My servant, along with your family members.

TEXT 59

দিন-পাঁচ-সাত ভিতরে আসিবে রামানন্দ ।
তাঁর সঙ্গে পূর্ণ হবে আমার আনন্দ ॥ ৫৯ ॥

dina-pāṅca-sāta bhitare āsibe rāmānanda
tāṅra saṅge pūrṇa habe āmāra ānanda

dina-pāṅca-sāta—five or seven days; *bhitare*—within; *āsibe*—will come; *rāmānanda*—Rāmānanda; *tāṅra saṅge*—with him; *pūrṇa habe*—will be full; *āmāra*—My; *ānanda*—pleasure.

TRANSLATION

"Śrī Rāmānanda Rāya is coming within five to seven days. As soon as he arrives, My desires will be fulfilled. I take great pleasure in his company."

TEXT 60

এত বলি' প্রভু তাঁরে কৈল আলিঙ্গন ।
তাঁর পুত্র সব শিরে ধরিল চরণ ॥ ৬০ ॥

eta bali' prabhu tāṅre kaila āliṅgana
tāṅra putra saba śire dharila caraṇa

eta bali'—saying this; *prabhu*—Śrī Caitanya Mahāprabhu; *tāṅre*—unto him; *kaila*—did; *āliṅgana*—embracing; *tāṅra putra*—his sons; *saba*—all; *śire*—on the head; *dharila*—kept; *caraṇa*—His feet.

TRANSLATION

Saying this, Śrī Caitanya Mahāprabhu embraced Bhavānanda Rāya. The Lord then touched the heads of his sons with His lotus feet.

TEXT 61

তবে মহাপ্রভু তাঁরে ঘরে পাঠাইল।
বাণীনাথ-পট্টনায়কে নিকটে রাখিল ॥ ৬১ ॥

tabe mahāprabhu tāṅre ghare pāṭhāila
vāṇīnātha-paṭṭanāyake nikaṭe rākhila

tabe—thereafter; *mahāprabhu*—Śrī Caitanya Mahāprabhu; *tāṅre*—him (Bhavānanda Rāya); *ghare*—to his home; *pāṭhāila*—sent back; *vāṇīnātha-paṭṭanāyake*—Vāṇīnātha Paṭṭanāyaka; *nikaṭe*—near; *rākhila*—kept.

TRANSLATION

Śrī Caitanya Mahāprabhu then sent Bhavānanda Rāya back to his home, and He kept only Vāṇīnātha Paṭṭanāyaka in His personal service.

TEXT 62

ভট্টাচার্য সব লোকে বিদায় করাইল।
তবে প্রভু কালা-কৃষ্ণদাসে বোলাইল ॥ ৬২ ॥

bhaṭṭācārya saba loke vidāya karāila
tabe prabhu kālā-kṛṣṇadāse bolāila

bhaṭṭācārya—Sārvabhauma Bhaṭṭācārya; *saba loke*—all persons; *vidāya karāila*—asked to leave; *tabe*—at that time; *prabhu*—Śrī Caitanya Mahāprabhu; *kālā-kṛṣṇadāse*—Kālā Kṛṣṇadāsa; *bolāila*—called for.

TRANSLATION

Sārvabhauma Bhaṭṭācārya then asked all the people to leave. Afterward, Śrī Caitanya Mahāprabhu called for Kālā Kṛṣṇadāsa, who had accompanied the Lord during His South Indian tour.

TEXT 63

প্রভু কহে,—ভট্টাচার্য, শুনহ ইঁহার চরিত।
দক্ষিণ গিয়াছিল ইঁহ আমার সহিত ॥ ৬৩ ॥

prabhu kahe,—bhaṭṭācārya, śunaha iṅhāra carita
dakṣiṇa giyāchila iṅha āmāra sahita

prabhu kahe—Śrī Caitanya Mahāprabhu said; *bhaṭṭācārya*—My dear Bhaṭṭācārya; *śunaha*—just hear; *iṅhāra carita*—his character; *dakṣiṇa giyāchila*—went to South India; *iṅha*—this man; *āmāra sahita*—with Me.

TRANSLATION

Śrī Caitanya Mahāprabhu said, "My dear Bhaṭṭācārya, just consider the character of this man who went with Me to South India.

TEXT 64

ভট্টথারি-কাছে গেলা আমারে ছাড়িয়া।
ভট্টথারি হৈতে ইঁহারে আনিলুঁ উদ্ধারিয়া ॥ ৬৪ ॥

bhaṭṭathāri-kāche gelā āmāre chāḍiyā
bhaṭṭathāri haite iṅhāre āniluṅ uddhāriyā

bhaṭṭathāri-kāche—in the association of the Bhaṭṭathāris; *gelā*—he went; *āmāre chāḍiyā*—giving up My company; *bhaṭṭathāri haite*—from the Bhaṭṭathāris; *iṅhāre*—him; *āniluṅ*—I brought; *uddhāriyā*—after rescuing.

TRANSLATION

"He left My company to associate with the Bhaṭṭathāris, but I rescued him from their company and brought him here.

TEXT 65

এবে আমি ইহাঁ আনি' করিলাঙ বিদায়।
যাহাঁ ইচ্ছা, যাহ, আমা-সনে নাহি আর দায় ॥ ৬৫ ॥

ebe āmi ihāṅ āni' karilāṅa vidāya
yāhāṅ icchā, yāha, āmā-sane nāhi āra dāya

ebe—now; *āmi*—I; *ihāṅ*—here; *āni'*—bringing; *karilāṅa vidāya*—have asked to go away; *yāhāṅ icchā*—wherever he likes; *yāha*—go; *āmā-sane*—with Me; *nāhi āra*—there is no more; *dāya*—responsibility.

TRANSLATION

"Now that I have brought him here, I am asking him to leave. Now he can go wherever he likes, for I am no longer responsible for him."

PURPORT

Kālā Kṛṣṇadāsa was influenced and allured by nomads or gypsies, who enticed him with women. *Māyā* is so strong that Kālā Kṛṣṇadāsa left Śrī Caitanya Mahāprabhu's company to join gypsy women. Even though a person may associate with Śrī Caitanya Mahāprabhu, he can be allured by *māyā* and leave the Lord's company due to his slight independence. Only one who is overwhelmed by *māyā* can be so unfortunate as to leave Śrī Caitanya Mahāprabhu's company, yet unless one is very conscientious, the influence of *māyā* can drag one away, even though he be the personal assistant of Śrī Caitanya Mahāprabhu. And what to speak of others? The Bhaṭṭathāris used to increase their numbers by using women to allure outsiders. This is factual evidence showing that it is possible at any time to fall down from the Lord's association. One need only misuse his little independence. Once fallen and separated from the Supreme Personality of Godhead's association, one becomes a candidate for suffering in the material world. Although rejected by Śrī Caitanya Mahāprabhu, Kālā Kṛṣṇadāsa was given another chance, as the following verses relate.

TEXT 66

এত শুনি' কৃষ্ণদাস কান্দিতে লাগিল ।
মধ্যাহ্ন করিতে মহাপ্রভু চলি' গেল ॥ ৬৬ ॥

eta śuni' kṛṣṇadāsa kāndite lāgila
madhyāhna karite mahāprabhu cali' gela

eta śuni'—hearing this; *kṛṣṇadāsa*—Kālā Kṛṣṇadāsa; *kāndite lāgila*—began to cry; *madhyāhna*—noon lunch; *karite*—to execute; *mahāprabhu*—Śrī Caitanya Mahāprabhu; *cali' gela*—left.

TRANSLATION

Hearing the Lord reject him, Kālā Kṛṣṇadāsa began to cry. However, Śrī Caitanya Mahāprabhu, not caring for him, immediately left to take His noon lunch.

TEXT 67

নিত্যানন্দ, জগদানন্দ, মুকুন্দ, দামোদর।
চারিজনে যুক্তি তবে করিলা অন্তর ॥ ৬৭ ॥

nityānanda, jagadānanda, mukunda, dāmodara
cāri-jane yukti tabe karilā antara

nityānanda — Lord Nityānanda Prabhu; *jagadānanda* — Jagadānanda; *mukunda* — Mukunda; *dāmodara* — Dāmodara; *cāri-jane* — four persons; *yukti* — plan; *tabe* — thereupon; *karilā* — did; *antara* — within the mind.

TRANSLATION

After this, the other devotees — headed by Nityānanda Prabhu, Jagadānanda, Mukunda and Dāmodara — began to consider a certain plan.

PURPORT

Even though a person is rejected by the Supreme Personality of Godhead, the devotees of the Lord do not reject him; therefore the Lord's devotees are more merciful than the Lord Himself. Śrīla Narottama dāsa Ṭhākura thus sings, *chāḍiyā vaiṣṇava-sevā nistāra peyeche kebā:* one cannot be relieved from the material clutches without engaging in the service of pure devotees. The Lord Himself may sometimes be very hard, but the devotees are always kind. Thus Kālā Kṛṣṇadāsa received the mercy of the four devotees mentioned above.

TEXT 68

গৌড়দেশে পাঠাইতে চাহি একজন।
'আই'কে কহিবে যাই, প্রভুর আগমন ॥ ৬৮ ॥

gauḍa-deśe pāṭhāite cāhi eka-jana
'āi'ke kahibe yāi, prabhura āgamana

gauḍa-deśe — to Bengal; *pāṭhāite* — to send; *cāhi* — we want; *eka-jana* — one person; *āike* — mother Śacīdevī; *kahibe* — will inform; *yāi* — going; *prabhura* — of Śrī Caitanya Mahāprabhu; *āgamana* — arrival.

TRANSLATION

The Lord's four devotees considered, "We want a person to go to Bengal just to inform Śacīmātā about Śrī Caitanya Mahāprabhu's arrival at Jagannātha Purī.

TEXT 69

অদ্বৈত-শ্রীবাসাদি যত ভক্তগণ ।
সবেই আসিবে শুনি' প্রভুর আগমন ॥ ৬৯ ॥

advaita-śrīvāsādi yata bhakta-gaṇa
sabei āsibe śuni' prabhura āgamana

advaita—Advaita Prabhu; *śrīvāsa-ādi*—and all the devotees like Śrīvāsa; *yata*—all; *bhakta-gaṇa*—devotees; *sabei*—all; *āsibe*—will come; *śuni'*—hearing; *prabhura*—of Śrī Caitanya Mahāprabhu; *āgamana*—arrival.

TRANSLATION

"After hearing news of Śrī Caitanya Mahāprabhu's arrival, devotees like Advaita and Śrīvāsa will certainly come to see Him.

TEXT 70

এই কৃষ্ণদাসে দিব গৌড়ে পাঠাঞা ।
এত কহি' তারে রাখিলেন আশ্বাসিয়া ॥ ৭০॥

ei kṛṣṇadāse diba gauḍe pāṭhāñā
eta kahi' tāre rākhilena āśvāsiyā

ei—this; *kṛṣṇadāse*—Kālā Kṛṣṇadāsa; *diba*—away; *gauḍe*—to Bengal; *pāṭhāñā*—let us send; *eta kahi'*—saying this; *tāre*—him; *rākhilena*—they kept; *āśvāsiyā*—giving assurance.

TRANSLATION

"Let us therefore send Kṛṣṇadāsa to Bengal." Saying this, they kept Kṛṣṇadāsa engaged in the service of the Lord and gave him assurance.

PURPORT

Because Śrī Caitanya Mahāprabhu rejected him, Kālā Kṛṣṇadāsa became very, very sorry and began to cry. Therefore the Lord's devotees took compassion upon him, gave him assurance and encouraged him to continue to engage in the Lord's service.

TEXT 71

আর দিনে প্রভুস্থানে কৈল নিবেদন।
আজ্ঞা দেহ' গৌড়-দেশে পাঠাই একজন ॥ ৭১ ॥

āra dine prabhu-sthāne kaila nivedana
ājñā deha' gauḍa-deśe pāṭhāi eka-jana

āra dine—next day; *prabhu-sthāne*—before Lord Śrī Caitanya Mahāprabhu; *kaila*—did; *nivedana*—submission; *ājñā deha'*—please give permission; *gauḍa-deśe*—to Bengal; *pāṭhāi*—we may send; *eka-jana*—one person.

TRANSLATION

The next day, all the devotees asked Śrī Caitanya Mahāprabhu, "Please give permission for a person to go to Bengal.

TEXT 72

তোমার দক্ষিণ-গমন শুনি' শচী 'আই'।
অদ্বৈতাদি ভক্ত সব আছে দুঃখ পাই' ॥ ৭২ ॥

tomāra dakṣiṇa-gamana śuni' śacī 'āi'
advaitādi bhakta saba āche duḥkha pāi'

tomāra—Your; *dakṣiṇa-gamana*—South Indian tour; *śuni'*—hearing; *śacī āi*—mother Śacī; *advaita-ādi*—Śrī Advaita Prabhu and others; *bhakta*—devotees; *saba*—all; *āche*—remain; *duḥkha pāi'*—in great unhappiness.

TRANSLATION

"Mother Śacī and all the devotees headed by Advaita Prabhu are all very unhappy due to not receiving news about Your return from Your South Indian tour.

TEXT 73

একজন যাই' কহুক্ শুভ সমাচার ।
প্রভু কহে, — সেই কর, যে ইচ্ছা তোমার ॥ ৭৩ ॥

eka-jana yāi' kahuk śubha samācāra
prabhu kahe, — sei kara, ye icchā tomāra

eka-jana — one person; *yāi'* — going; *kahuk* — may inform; *śubha samācāra* — this auspicious news; *prabhu kahe* — the Lord replied; *sei kara* — do that; *ye* — whatever; *icchā* — desire; *tomāra* — your.

TRANSLATION

"One person should go to Bengal and inform them about the auspicious news of Your return to Jagannātha Purī."

Upon hearing this, Śrī Caitanya Mahāprabhu replied, "Do whatever you decide."

TEXT 74

তবে সেই কৃষ্ণদাসে গৌড়ে পাঠাইল ।
বৈষ্ণব-সবাকে দিতে মহাপ্রসাদ দিল ॥ ৭৪ ॥

tabe sei kṛṣṇadāse gauḍe pāṭhāila
vaiṣṇava-sabāke dite mahā-prasāda dila

tabe — thereafter; *sei* — that; *kṛṣṇadāse* — Kṛṣṇadāsa; *gauḍe* — to Bengal; *pāṭhāila* — sent; *vaiṣṇava-sabāke* — to all the Vaiṣṇavas; *dite* — to deliver; *mahā-prasāda* — the remnants of Jagannātha's food; *dila* — they gave.

TRANSLATION

In this way Kālā Kṛṣṇadāsa was sent to Bengal, and he was given sufficient quantities of Lord Jagannātha's food remnants to distribute there.

TEXT 75

তবে গৌড়দেশে আইলা কালা-কৃষ্ণদাস ।
নবদ্বীপে গেল তেঁহ শচী-আই-পাশ ॥ ৭৫ ॥

tabe gauḍa-deśe āilā kālā-kṛṣṇadāsa
navadvīpe gela teṅha śacī-āi-pāśa

tabe—then; *gauḍa-deśe*—to Bengal; *āilā*—came; *kālā-kṛṣṇadāsa*—Kālā Kṛṣṇadāsa; *navadvīpe*—to Navadvīpa; *gela*—went; *teṅha*—he; *śacī-āi-pāśa*—before mother Śacī.

TRANSLATION

Thus Kālā Kṛṣṇadāsa went to Bengal, and he first went to Navadvīpa to see mother Śacī.

TEXT 76

মহাপ্রসাদ দিয়া তাঁরে কৈল নমস্কার ।
দক্ষিণ হৈতে আইলা প্রভু, —কহে সমাচার ॥ ৭৬ ॥

mahā-prasāda diyā tāṅre kaila namaskāra
dakṣiṇa haite āilā prabhu,—kahe samācāra

mahā-prasāda diyā—delivering the *mahā-prasādam; tāṅre*—unto Śacīmātā; *kaila namaskāra*—he offered respects by bowing down; *dakṣiṇa haite*—from the South India tour; *āilā*—came back; *prabhu*—Lord Śrī Caitanya Mahāprabhu; *kahe samācāra*—he delivered this news.

TRANSLATION

Upon reaching mother Śacī, Kālā Kṛṣṇadāsa first offered his obeisances and delivered the food remnants [mahā-prasādam]. He then informed her of the good news that Śrī Caitanya Mahāprabhu had returned from His South Indian tour.

TEXT 77

শুনিয়া আনন্দিত হৈল শচীমাতার মন ।
শ্রীবাসাদি আর যত যত ভক্তগণ ॥ ৭৭ ॥

śuniyā ānandita haila śacīmātāra mana
śrīvāsādi āra yata yata bhakta-gaṇa

śuniyā—hearing; *ānandita*—very happy; *haila*—became; *śacī-mātāra*—of mother Śacī; *mana*—mind; *śrīvāsa-ādi*—headed by Śrīvāsa; *āra*—and others; *yata yata*—all; *bhakta-gaṇa*—devotees.

TRANSLATION

This good news gave much pleasure to mother Śacī, as well as to all the devotees of Navadvīpa, headed by Śrīvāsa Ṭhākura.

TEXT 78

শুনিয়া সবার হৈল পরম উল্লাস।
অদ্বৈত-আচার্য-গৃহে গেলা কৃষ্ণদাস ॥ ৭৮ ॥

śuniyā sabāra haila parama ullāsa
advaita-ācārya-gṛhe gelā kṛṣṇadāsa

śuniyā—hearing; *sabāra*—of all; *haila*—there was; *parama*—supreme; *ullāsa*—happiness; *advaita-ācārya*—of Advaita Ācārya Prabhu; *gṛhe*—to the home; *gelā*—went; *kṛṣṇadāsa*—Kṛṣṇadāsa.

TRANSLATION

Hearing of Lord Caitanya's return to Purī, everyone became very glad. Kṛṣṇadāsa next went to the house of Advaita Ācārya.

TEXT 79

আচার্যেরে প্রসাদ দিয়া করি' নমস্কার।
সম্যক্ কহিল মহাপ্রভুর সমাচার ॥ ৭৯ ॥

ācāryere prasāda diyā kari' namaskāra
samyak kahila mahāprabhura samācāra

ācāryere—unto Śrī Advaita Ācārya; *prasāda*—the remnants of Jagannātha's food; *diyā*—delivering; *kari'*—making; *namaskāra*—obeisances; *samyak*—completely; *kahila*—informed; *mahāprabhura*—of Śrī Caitanya Mahāprabhu; *samācāra*—news.

TRANSLATION

After paying Him respectful obeisances, Kṛṣṇadāsa offered mahāprasādam to Advaita Ācārya. He then informed Him of the news of Lord Caitanya in complete detail.

TEXT 80

শুনি' আচার্য-গোসাঞির আনন্দ হইল।
প্রেমাবেশে হুঙ্কার বহু নৃত্য-গীত কৈল ॥ ৮০ ॥

śuni' ācārya-gosāñira ānanda ha-ila
premāveśe huṅkāra bahu nṛtya-gīta kaila

śuni'—hearing; *ācārya*—Advaita Ācārya; *gosāñira*—of the spiritual master; *ānanda ha-ila*—there was much jubilation; *prema-āveśe*—in great ecstasy; *huṅkāra*—rumbling sound; *bahu*—various; *nṛtya-gīta*—chanting and dancing; *kaila*—performed.

TRANSLATION

When Advaita Ācārya Gosvāmī heard of Śrī Caitanya Mahāprabhu's return, He became very pleased. In His great ecstasy of love, He made a rumbling sound and danced and chanted for a long time.

TEXT 81

হরিদাস ঠাকুরের হৈল পরম আনন্দ।
বাসুদেব দত্ত, গুপ্ত মুরারি, সেন শিবানন্দ ॥ ৮১ ॥

haridāsa ṭhākurera haila parama ānanda
vāsudeva datta, gupta murāri, sena śivānanda

haridāsa ṭhākurera—of Haridāsa Ṭhākura; *haila*—was; *parama*—topmost; *ānanda*—ecstasy; *vāsudeva datta*—Vāsudeva Datta; *gupta murāri*—Murāri Gupta; *sena śivānanda*—Śivānanda Sena.

TRANSLATION

Also hearing this auspicious news, Haridāsa Ṭhākura became very pleased. So also did Vāsudeva Datta, Murāri Gupta and Śivānanda Sena.

TEXT 82

আচার্যরত্ন, আর পণ্ডিত বক্রেশ্বর।
আচার্যনিধি, আর পণ্ডিত গদাধর ॥ ৮২ ॥

ācāryaratna, āra paṇḍita vakreśvara
ācāryanidhi, āra paṇḍita gadādhara

ācāryaratna—Ācāryaratna; *āra*—and; *paṇḍita vakreśvara*—Vakreśvara Paṇḍita; *ācāryanidhi*—Ācāryanidhi; *āra*—also; *paṇḍita gadādhara*—Gadādhara Paṇḍita.

TRANSLATION

Ācāryaratna, Vakreśvara Paṇḍita, Ācāryanidhi and Gadādhara Paṇḍita were all very pleased to hear this news.

TEXT 83

শ্রীরাম পণ্ডিত আর পণ্ডিত দামোদর ।
শ্রীমান্ পণ্ডিত, আর বিজয়, শ্রীধর ॥ ৮৩ ॥

śrīrāma paṇḍita āra paṇḍita dāmodara
śrīmān paṇḍita, āra vijaya, śrīdhara

śrī-rāma paṇḍita—Śrīrāma Paṇḍita; *āra*—and; *paṇḍita dāmodara*—Dāmodara Paṇḍita; *śrīmān paṇḍita*—Śrīmān Paṇḍita; *āra*—and; *vijaya*—Vijaya; *śrīdhara*—Śrīdhara.

TRANSLATION

Śrīrāma Paṇḍita, Dāmodara Paṇḍita, Śrīmān Paṇḍita, Vijaya and Śrīdhara were also very pleased to hear it.

TEXT 84

রাঘবপণ্ডিত, আর আচার্য নন্দন ।
কতেক কহিব আর যত প্রভুর গণ ॥ ৮৪ ॥

rāghava-paṇḍita, āra ācārya nandana
kateka kahiba āra yata prabhura gaṇa

rāghava-paṇḍita—Rāghava Paṇḍita; *āra*—and; *ācārya nandana*—the son of Advaita Ācārya; *kateka*—how many; *kahiba*—shall I describe; *āra*—other; *yata*—all; *prabhura gaṇa*—associates of Śrī Caitanya Mahāprabhu.

TRANSLATION

Rāghava Paṇḍita, the son of Advaita Ācārya and all the devotees became very satisfied. How many can I describe?

TEXT 85

শুনিয়া সবার হৈল পরম উল্লাস।
সবে মেলি' গেলা শ্রীঅদ্বৈতের পাশ ॥ ৮৫ ॥

śuniyā sabāra haila parama ullāsa
sabe meli' gelā śrī-advaitera pāśa

śuniyā—hearing; *sabāra*—of everyone; *haila*—there was; *parama ullāsa*—great ecstasy; *sabe meli'*—all together; *gelā*—went; *śrī-advaitera pāśa*—to the house of Śrī Advaita Ācārya.

TRANSLATION

Everyone was very pleased, and they all gathered together at the house of Advaita Ācārya.

TEXT 86

আচার্যের সবে কৈল চরণ বন্দন।
আচার্য-গোসাঁই সবারে কৈল আলিঙ্গন ॥ ৮৬ ॥

ācāryera sabe kaila caraṇa vandana
ācārya-gosāṅi sabāre kaila āliṅgana

ācāryera—of Advaita Ācārya; *sabe*—all; *kaila*—did; *caraṇa vandana*—offering obeisances at the lotus feet; *ācārya-gosāṅi*—Advaita Ācārya; *sabāre*—to all; *kaila*—did; *āliṅgana*—embracing.

TRANSLATION

All the devotees offered respectful obeisances at the lotus feet of Advaita Ācārya, and in return Advaita Ācārya embraced them all.

TEXT 87

দিন দুই-তিন আচার্য মহোৎসব কৈল।
নীলাচল যাইতে আচার্য যুক্তি দৃঢ় কৈল ॥ ৮৭ ॥

dina dui-tina ācārya mahotsava kaila
nīlācala yāite ācārya yukti dṛḍha kaila

dina dui-tina—for two or three days; *ācārya*—Advaita Ācārya; *mahotsava*—festival; *kaila*—performed; *nīlācala*—to Jagannātha Purī; *yāite*—to go; *ācārya*—Advaita Ācārya; *yukti*—consideration; *dṛḍha*—firm; *kaila*—made.

TRANSLATION

Advaita Ācārya then held a festival that lasted two or three days. Thereafter, they all made a firm decision to go to Jagannātha Purī.

TEXT 88

সবে মেলি' নবদ্বীপে একত্র হঞা।
নীলাদ্রি চলিল শচীমাতার আজ্ঞা লঞা ॥ ৮৮ ॥

sabe meli' navadvīpe ekatra hañā
nīlādri calila śacīmātāra ājñā lañā

sabe—all; *meli'*—meeting; *navadvīpe*—at Navadvīpa; *ekatra hañā*—being together; *nīlādri*—to Jagannātha Purī; *calila*—departed; *śacīmātāra*—of mother Śacī; *ājñā*—permission; *lañā*—taking.

TRANSLATION

All the devotees met together at Navadvīpa and, with mother Śacī's permission, departed for Nīlādri, Jagannātha Purī.

TEXT 89

প্রভুর সমাচার শুনি' কুলীনগ্রামবাসী।
সত্যরাজ-রামানন্দ মিলিলা সবে আসি' ॥ ৮৯ ॥

prabhura samācāra śuni' kulīna-grāma-vāsī
satyarāja-rāmānanda mililā sabe āsi'

prabhura—of Śrī Caitanya Mahāprabhu; *samācāra*—news; *śuni'*—hearing; *kulīna-grāma-vāsī*—the inhabitants of Kulīna-grāma; *satyarāja*—Satyarāja; *rāmānanda*—Rāmānanda; *mililā*—met; *sabe*—all; *āsi'*—coming.

TRANSLATION

The inhabitants of Kulīna-grāma — Satyarāja, Rāmānanda and all the other devotees there — came and joined Advaita Ācārya.

TEXT 90

মুকুন্দ, নরহরি, রঘুনন্দন খণ্ড হৈতে।
আচার্যের ঠাঞি আইলা নীলাচল যাইতে ॥ ৯০ ॥

mukunda, narahari, raghunandana khaṇḍa haite
ācāryera ṭhāñi āilā nīlācala yāite

mukunda — Mukunda; *narahari* — Narahari; *raghunandana* — Raghunandana; *khaṇḍa haite* — from the place known as Khaṇḍa; *ācāryera ṭhāñi* — to Advaita Ācārya; *āilā* — came; *nīlācala yāite* — to go to Nīlācala (Jagannātha Purī).

TRANSLATION

Mukunda, Narahari, Raghunandana and all the others came from Khaṇḍa to Advaita Ācārya's home to accompany Him to Jagannātha Purī.

TEXT 91

সেকালে দক্ষিণ হৈতে পরমানন্দপুরী।
গঙ্গাতীরে-তীরে আইলা নদীয়া নগরী ॥ ৯১ ॥

se-kāle dakṣiṇa haite paramānanda-purī
gaṅgā-tīre-tīre āilā nadīyā nagarī

se-kāle — at that time; *dakṣiṇa haite* — from the South; *paramānanda-purī* — Paramānanda Purī; *gaṅgā-tīre-tīre* — along the bank of the Ganges; *āilā* — came; *nadīyā nagarī* — to the town of Nadia.

TRANSLATION

At that time Paramānanda Purī came from South India. Traveling along the banks of the Ganges, he ultimately reached the town of Nadia.

TEXT 92

আইর মন্দিরে সুখে করিলা বিশ্রাম ।
আই তাঁরে ভিক্ষা দিলা করিয়া সম্মান ॥ ৯২ ॥

āira mandire sukhe karilā viśrāma
āi tāṅre bhikṣā dilā kariyā sammāna

āira mandire—at the house of Śacīmātā; *sukhe*—in happiness; *karilā*—took; *viśrāma*—lodging; *āi*—mother Śacī; *tāṅre*—unto him; *bhikṣā dilā*—gave boarding; *kariyā sammāna*—with great respect.

TRANSLATION

At Navadvīpa, Paramānanda Purī took his board and lodging at the house of Śacīmātā. She provided him with everything very respectfully.

TEXT 93

প্রভুর আগমন তেঁহ তাহাঁঞি শুনিল ।
শীঘ্র নীলাচল যাইতে তাঁর ইচ্ছা হৈল ॥ ৯৩ ॥

prabhura āgamana teṅha tāhāññi śunila
śīghra nīlācala yāite tāṅra icchā haila

prabhura āgamana—Śrī Caitanya Mahāprabhu's return; *teṅha*—he; *tāhāññi*—there; *śunila*—heard; *śīghra*—very soon; *nīlācala*—to Jagannātha Purī; *yāite*—to go; *tāṅra*—his; *icchā*—desire; *haila*—became.

TRANSLATION

While residing at the house of Śacīmātā, Paramānanda Purī heard the news of Śrī Caitanya Mahāprabhu's return to Jagannātha Purī. He therefore decided to go there as soon as possible.

TEXT 94

প্রভুর এক ভক্ত — 'দ্বিজ কমলাকান্ত' নাম ।
তাঁরে লঞা নীলাচলে করিলা প্রয়াণ ॥ ৯৪ ॥

prabhura eka bhakta—'dvija kamalākānta' nāma
tāṅre lañā nīlācale karilā prayāṇa

prabhura—of Śrī Caitanya Mahāprabhu; *eka bhakta*—one devotee; *dvija kamalākānta*—Dvija Kamalākānta; *nāma*—named; *tāṅre*—him; *lañā*—accepting as his companion; *nīlācale*—to Jagannātha Purī; *karilā*—did; *prayāṇa*—departure.

TRANSLATION

There was a devotee of Śrī Caitanya Mahāprabhu's named Dvija Kamalākānta, whom Paramānanda Purī took with him to Jagannātha Purī.

TEXT 95

সত্বরে আসিয়া তেঁহ মিলিলা প্রভুরে।
প্রভুর আনন্দ হৈল পাঞা তাঁহারে ॥ ৯৫ ॥

satvare āsiyā teṅha mililā prabhure
prabhura ānanda haila pāñā tāṅhāre

satvare—very soon; *āsiyā*—coming; *teṅha*—he; *mililā*—met; *prabhure*—Śrī Caitanya Mahāprabhu; *prabhura*—of Śrī Caitanya Mahāprabhu; *ānanda*—happiness; *haila*—was; *pāñā*—getting; *tāṅhāre*—him.

TRANSLATION

Paramānanda Purī very soon arrived at Śrī Caitanya Mahāprabhu's place. The Lord was very happy to see him.

TEXT 96

প্রেমাবেশে কৈল তাঁর চরণ বন্দন।
তেঁহ প্রেমাবেশে কৈল প্রভুরে আলিঙ্গন ॥ ৯৬ ॥

premāveśe kaila tāṅra caraṇa vandana
teṅha premāveśe kaila prabhure āliṅgana

prema-āveśe—in great ecstasy; *kaila*—did; *tāṅra*—his; *caraṇa vandana*—worshiping the feet; *teṅha*—Paramānanda Purī; *prema-āveśe*—in great ecstasy; *kaila*—did; *prabhure*—unto Śrī Caitanya Mahāprabhu; *āliṅgana*—embracing.

TRANSLATION

In the great ecstasy of love, the Lord worshiped the lotus feet of Paramānanda Purī, and in turn Paramānanda Purī embraced the Lord in great ecstasy.

TEXT 97

প্রভু কহে, — তোমা-সঙ্গে রহিতে বাঞ্ছা হয়।
মোরে কৃপা করি' কর নীলাদ্রি আশ্রয় ॥ ৯৭ ॥

prabhu kahe, — tomā-saṅge rahite vāñchā haya
more kṛpā kari' kara nīlādri āśraya

prabhu kahe — Śrī Caitanya Mahāprabhu said; *tomā-saṅge* — with you; *rahite* — to stay; *vāñchā haya* — I desire; *more* — unto Me; *kṛpā kari'* — doing a favor; *kara* — accept; *nīlādri* — at Jagannātha Purī; *āśraya* — shelter.

TRANSLATION

Śrī Caitanya Mahāprabhu said, "Please stay with Me and thus show Me favor, accepting the shelter of Jagannātha Purī."

TEXT 98

পুরী কহে, — তোমা-সঙ্গে রহিতে বাঞ্ছা করি'।
গৌড় হৈতে চলি' আইলাঙ নীলাচল-পুরী ॥ ৯৮ ॥

purī kahe, — tomā-saṅge rahite vāñchā kari'
gauḍa haite cali' āilāṅa nīlācala-purī

purī kahe — Paramānanda Purī replied; *tomā-saṅge* — with You; *rahite* — to stay; *vāñchā kari'* — desiring; *gauḍa haite* — from Bengal; *cali'* — traveling; *āilāṅa* — I have come; *nīlācala-purī* — to Jagannātha Purī.

TRANSLATION

Paramānanda Purī replied, "I also wish to stay with You. Therefore I have come from Bengal, Gauḍa, to Jagannātha Purī.

TEXT 99

দক্ষিণ হৈতে শুনি' তোমার আগমন।
শচী আনন্দিত, আর যত ভক্তগণ॥ ৯৯॥

dakṣiṇa haite śuni' tomāra āgamana
śacī ānandita, āra yata bhakta-gaṇa

dakṣiṇa haite—from South India; *śuni'*—hearing; *tomāra āgamana*—Your return; *śacī*—mother Śacī; *ānandita*—very happy; *āra*—and; *yata*—all; *bhakta-gaṇa*—devotees.

TRANSLATION

"At Navadvīpa, mother Śacī and all the other devotees were very glad to hear about Your return from South India.

TEXT 100

সবে আসিতেছেন তোমারে দেখিতে।
তাঁ-সবার বিলম্ব দেখি' আইলাঙ ত্বরিতে॥ ১০০॥

sabe āsitechena tomāre dekhite
tāṅ-sabāra vilamba dekhi' āilāṅa tvarite

sabe—all; *āsitechena*—are coming; *tomāre*—You; *dekhite*—to see; *tāṅ-sabāra*—of all of them; *vilamba*—delay; *dekhi'*—seeing; *āilāṅa*—I have come; *tvarite*—very quickly.

TRANSLATION

"They are all coming here to see You, but seeing that they were delayed, I came alone very quickly."

TEXT 101

কাশীমিশ্রের আবাসে নিভৃতে এক ঘর।
প্রভু তাঁরে দিল, আর সেবার কিঙ্কর॥ ১০১॥

kāśī-miśrera āvāse nibhṛte eka ghara
prabhu tāṅre dila, āra sevāra kiṅkara

kāśī-miśrera—of Kāśī Miśra; *āvāse*—at the house; *nibhṛte*—solitary; *eka*—one; *ghara*—room; *prabhu*—Śrī Caitanya Mahāprabhu; *tāṅre*—unto Paramānanda Purī; *dila*—gave; *āra*—and; *sevāra*—to serve him; *kiṅkara*—one servant.

TRANSLATION

There was a solitary room at Kāśī Miśra's house, and Śrī Caitanya Mahāprabhu gave it to Paramānanda Purī. He also gave him a servant.

TEXT 102

আর দিনে আইলা স্বরূপ দামোদর ।
প্রভুর অত্যন্ত মর্মী, রসের সাগর ॥ ১০২ ॥

āra dine āilā svarūpa dāmodara
prabhura atyanta marmī, rasera sāgara

āra dine—next day; *āilā*—came; *svarūpa dāmodara*—Svarūpa Dāmodara; *prabhura*—of Śrī Caitanya Mahāprabhu; *atyanta*—very; *marmī*—intimate friend; *rasera*—of transcendental mellows; *sāgara*—ocean.

TRANSLATION

Svarūpa Dāmodara also arrived the next day. He was a very intimate friend of Śrī Caitanya Mahāprabhu's, and he was an ocean of transcendental mellows.

PURPORT

"Svarūpa" is one of the names of a *brahmacārī* in Śaṅkarācārya's disciplic succession. In the Vedic discipline there are ten names for *sannyāsīs,* and it is customary for a *brahmacārī* assisting a *sannyāsī* of the designation Tīrtha or Āśrama to receive the title Svarūpa. Dāmodara Svarūpa was formerly a resident of Navadvīpa, and his name was Puruṣottama Ācārya. When he went to Vārāṇasī, he took *sannyāsa* from a *sannyāsī* designated Tīrtha. Although he received the title Svarūpa in his *brahmacārī* stage, he did not change his name when he took *sannyāsa.* Actually as a *sannyāsī* he should have been called Tīrtha, but he chose to retain his original *brahmacārī* title of Svarūpa.

TEXT 103

'পুরুষোত্তম আচার্য' তাঁর নাম পূর্বাশ্রমে ।
নবদ্বীপে ছিলা তেঁহ প্রভুর চরণে ॥ ১০৩ ॥

'puruṣottama ācārya' tāṅra nāma pūrvāśrame
navadvīpe chilā teṅha prabhura caraṇe

puruṣottama ācārya—Puruṣottama Ācārya; *tāṅra*—his; *nāma*—name; *pūrva-āśrame*—in the previous āśrama; *navadvīpe*—at Navadvīpa; *chilā*—was; *teṅha*—he; *prabhura*—of Śrī Caitanya Mahāprabhu; *caraṇe*—at the feet.

TRANSLATION

When Svarūpa Dāmodara was residing at Navadvīpa under the shelter of Śrī Caitanya Mahāprabhu, his name was Puruṣottama Ācārya.

TEXT 104

প্রভুর সন্ন্যাস দেখি' উন্মত্ত হঞা ।
সন্ন্যাস গ্রহণ কৈল বারাণসী গিয়া ॥ ১০৪ ॥

prabhura sannyāsa dekhi' unmatta hañā
sannyasa grahaṇa kaila vārāṇasī giyā

prabhura—of Lord Śrī Caitanya Mahāprabhu; *sannyāsa dekhi'*—when he saw the *sannyāsa* order; *unmatta hañā*—he became just like a madman; *sannyāsa grahaṇa kaila*—he also accepted the renounced order of life; *vārāṇasī*—to Vārāṇasī; *giyā*—going.

TRANSLATION

After seeing that Śrī Caitanya Mahāprabhu accepted the renounced order, Puruṣottama Ācārya became like a madman and immediately went to Vārāṇasī to take sannyāsa.

TEXT 105

'চৈতন্যানন্দ' গুরু তাঁর আজ্ঞা দিলেন তাঁরে ।
বেদান্ত পড়িয়া পড়াও সমস্ত লোকেরে ॥ ১০৫ ॥

'caitanyānanda' guru tāṅra ājñā dilena tāṅre
vedānta paḍiyā paḍāo samasta lokere

caitanya-ānanda—of the name Caitanyānanda Bhāratī; *guru*—spiritual master; *tāṅra*—his; *ājñā*—order; *dilena*—gave; *tāṅre*—to him; *vedānta paḍiyā*—reading the *Vedānta-sūtra; paḍāo*—teach; *samasta*—all; *lokere*—people.

TRANSLATION

At the conclusion of his sannyāsa, his spiritual master, Caitanyānanda Bhāratī, ordered him, "Read the Vedānta-sūtra and teach it to all others."

TEXT 106

পরম বিরক্ত তেঁহ পরম পণ্ডিত।
কায়মনে আশ্রিয়াছে শ্রীকৃষ্ণ চরিত॥ ১০৬॥

parama virakta teṅha parama paṇḍita
kāya-mane āśriyāche śrī-kṛṣṇa-carita

parama—very; *virakta*—renounced; *teṅha*—he; *parama*—great; *paṇḍita*—learned scholar; *kāya-mane*—with body and mind; *āśriyāche*—took shelter of; *śrī-kṛṣṇa-carita*—the Personality of Godhead Śrī Kṛṣṇa.

TRANSLATION

Svarūpa Dāmodara was a great renunciant as well as a great learned scholar. With heart and soul he took shelter of the Supreme Personality of Godhead, Śrī Kṛṣṇa.

TEXT 107

'নিশ্চিন্তে কৃষ্ণ ভজিব' এই ত' কারণে।
উন্মাদে করিল তেঁহ সন্ন্যাস গ্রহণে॥ ১০৭॥

'niścinte kṛṣṇa bhajiba' ei ta' kāraṇe
unmāde karila teṅha sannyāsa grahaṇe

niścinte—without disturbance; *kṛṣṇa*—Lord Kṛṣṇa; *bhajiba*—I shall worship; *ei*—for this; *ta'*—certainly; *kāraṇe*—reason;

unmāde—ecstatic; *karila*—did; *teṅha*—he; *sannyāsa*—the renounced order of life; *grahaṇe*—taking.

TRANSLATION

He was very enthusiastic to worship Śrī Kṛṣṇa without disturbance, and therefore, almost in madness, he accepted the sannyāsa order.

TEXT 108

সন্ন্যাস করিলা শিখা-সূত্রত্যাগ-রূপ।
যোগপট্ট না নিল, নাম হৈল 'স্বরূপ' ॥ ১০৮ ॥

sannyāsa karilā śikhā-sūtra-tyāga-rūpa
yoga-paṭṭa nā nila, nāma haila 'svarūpa'

sannyāsa karilā—accepted the *sannyāsa* order; *śikhā*—tuft of hair; *sūtra*—sacred thread; *tyāga*—giving up; *rūpa*—in the form of; *yoga-paṭṭa*—saffron-colored dress; *nā nila*—did not accept; *nāma*—name; *haila*—was; *svarūpa*—Svarūpa.

TRANSLATION

Upon accepting sannyāsa, Puruṣottama Ācārya followed the regulative principles by giving up his tuft of hair and sacred thread, but he did not accept the saffron-colored dress. Also, he did not accept a sannyāsī title but remained as a naiṣṭhika-brahmacārī.

PURPORT

There are regulative principles governing the renounced order. One has to perform eight kinds of *śrāddha.* One must offer oblations to one's forefathers and perform the sacrifice of *virajā-homa.* Then one must cut off the tuft of hair called a *śikhā* and also give up the sacred thread. These are preliminary processes in the acceptance of *sannyāsa,* and Svarūpa Dāmodara accepted all these. However, Puruṣottama Ācārya did not accept the saffron color, a *sannyāsī* name or a *daṇḍa,* and for this reason he retained his *brahmacārī* name. Actually Puruṣottama Ācārya did not accept the *sannyāsa* order formally, but he renounced worldly life. He did not want to be disturbed by the formality of the *sannyāsa* order. He simply wanted to worship Lord Śrī Kṛṣṇa without disturbance; therefore with heart and soul he took up the renounced order but not the formalities accompanying it. Renunciation means not doing anything but serving the Supreme Personality of Godhead, Śrī Kṛṣṇa. When one acts on this platform, trying to please the Supreme Personality of Godhead, one is both a *sannyāsī* and a *yogī.* This is confirmed in the *Bhagavad-gītā* (6.1):

śrī-bhagavān uvāca
anāśritaḥ karma-phalaṁ kāryaṁ karma karoti yaḥ
sa sannyāsī ca yogī ca na niragnir na cākriyaḥ

"The Supreme Personality of Godhead said, 'One who is unattached to the fruits of his work and who works as he is obligated is in the renounced order of life, and he is the true mystic, not he who lights no fire and performs no work.'"

TEXT 109

গুরু-ঠাঞি আজ্ঞা মাগি' আইলা নীলাচলে ।
রাত্রিদিনে কৃষ্ণপ্রেম-আনন্দ-বিহ্বলে ॥ ১০৯ ॥

guru-ṭhāñi ājñā māgi' āilā nīlācale
rātri-dine kṛṣṇa-prema-ānanda-vihvale

guru-ṭhāñi—from his spiritual master; *ājñā māgi'*—asking permission; *āilā*—came; *nīlācale*—to Jagannātha Purī; *rātri-dine*—day and night; *kṛṣṇa-prema-ānanda*—by ecstatic love of Kṛṣṇa; *vihvale*—overwhelmed.

TRANSLATION

After taking permission from his sannyāsa-guru, Svarūpa Dāmodara went to Nīlācala and accepted the shelter of Śrī Caitanya Mahāprabhu. Then all day and night, in ecstatic love of Kṛṣṇa, he enjoyed transcendental mellows in the loving service of the Lord.

TEXT 110

পাণ্ডিত্যের অবধি, বাক্য নাহি কারো সনে ।
নির্জনে রহয়ে, লোক সব নাহি জানে ॥ ১১০ ॥

pāṇḍityera avadhi, vākya nāhi kāro sane
nirjane rahaye, loka saba nāhi jāne

pāṇḍityera avadhi—the limit of learned scholarship; *vākya nāhi*—no word; *kāro sane*—with anyone; *nirjane*—in a solitary place; *rahaye*—stays; *loka*—people in general; *saba*—all; *nāhi jāne*—do not know.

TRANSLATION

Svarūpa Dāmodara was the limit of all learned scholarship, but he did not exchange words with anyone. He simply remained in a solitary place, and no one could understand where he was.

TEXT 111

কৃষ্ণরস-তত্ত্ব-বেত্তা, দেহ — প্রেমরূপ।
সাক্ষাৎ মহাপ্রভুর দ্বিতীয় স্বরূপ ॥ ১১১ ॥

kṛṣṇa-rasa-tattva-vettā, deha—prema-rūpa
sākṣāt mahāprabhura dvitīya svarūpa

kṛṣṇa-rasa—of transcendental mellows in relationship with Kṛṣṇa; *tattva*—of the truth; *vettā*—cognizant; *deha*—body; *prema-rūpa*—personified *prema; sākṣāt*—directly; *mahāprabhura*—of Śrī Caitanya Mahāprabhu; *dvitīya*—second; *svarūpa*—representation.

TRANSLATION

Śrī Svarūpa Dāmodara was the personification of ecstatic love, fully cognizant of the transcendental mellows in relationship with Kṛṣṇa. He directly represented Śrī Caitanya Mahāprabhu as His second expansion.

TEXT 112

গ্রন্থ, শ্লোক, গীত কেহ প্রভু-পাশে আনে।
স্বরূপ পরীক্ষা কৈলে, পাছে প্রভু শুনে ॥ ১১২ ॥

grantha, śloka, gīta keha prabhu-pāśe āne
svarūpa parīkṣā kaile, pāche prabhu śune

grantha—scriptures; *śloka*—verses; *gīta*—songs; *keha*—anyone; *prabhu-pāśe*—to Śrī Caitanya Mahāprabhu; *āne*—brings; *svarūpa*—Svarūpa Dāmodara; *parīkṣā kaile*—after he examined; *pāche*—later; *prabhu*—Śrī Caitanya Mahāprabhu; *śune*—hears.

TRANSLATION

If someone wrote a book or composed verses and songs and wanted to recite them before Śrī Caitanya Mahāprabhu, Svarūpa Dāmodara would first examine them and then correctly present them. Only then would Śrī Caitanya Mahāprabhu agree to listen.

TEXT 113

ভক্তিসিদ্ধান্ত-বিরুদ্ধ, আর রসাভাস।
শুনিতে না হয় প্রভুর চিত্তের উল্লাস ॥ ১১৩ ॥

bhakti-siddhānta-viruddha, āra rasābhāsa
śunite nā haya prabhura cittera ullāsa

bhakti-siddhānta — conclusive statements about the science of devotional service; *viruddha* — opposing; *āra* — and; *rasa-ābhāsa* — overlapping of transcendental mellows; *śunite* — to hear; *nā* — not; *haya* — becomes; *prabhura* — of Śrī Caitanya Mahāprabhu; *cittera* — of the heart; *ullāsa* — jubilation.

TRANSLATION

Śrī Caitanya Mahāprabhu was never pleased to hear books or verses opposed to the conclusive statements of devotional service. The Lord did not like hearing rasābhāsa, the overlapping of transcendental mellows.

PURPORT

Bhakti-siddhānta-viruddha refers to that which is against the principle of unity in diversity, philosophically known as *acintya-bhedābheda* — simultaneous oneness and difference — whereas *rasābhāsa* is something that may appear to be a transcendental mellow but actually is not. Those who are pure Vaiṣṇavas should avoid both these things opposed to devotional service. These misconceptions practically parallel the Māyāvāda philosophy. If one indulges in Māyāvāda philosophy, he gradually falls down from the platform of devotional service. By overlapping mellows (*rasābhāsa*) one eventually becomes a *prākṛta-sahajiyā* and takes everything to be very easy. One may also become a member of the *bāula* community and gradually become attracted to material activities. Śrī Caitanya Mahāprabhu has therefore advised us to avoid *bhakti-siddhānta-viruddha* and *rasābhāsa.* In this way the devotee can remain pure and free from falldowns. Everyone should try to remain aloof from *bhakti-siddhānta-viruddha* and *rasābhāsa.*

TEXT 114

অতএব স্বরূপ আগে করে পরীক্ষণ।
শুদ্ধ হয় যদি, প্রভুরে করা'ন শ্রবণ ॥ ১১৪ ॥

ataeva svarūpa āge kare parīkṣaṇa
śuddha haya yadi, prabhure karā'na śravaṇa

ataeva—therefore; *svarūpa*—Svarūpa Dāmodara; *āge*—at first; *kare*—does; *parīkṣaṇa*—examination; *śuddha*—pure; *haya*—is; *yadi*—if; *prabhure*—unto Lord Śrī Caitanya Mahāprabhu; *karā'na*—causes; *śravaṇa*—hearing.

TRANSLATION

It was the practice of Svarūpa Dāmodara Gosvāmī to examine all literatures to find out whether their conclusions were correct. Only then would he allow them to be heard by Śrī Caitanya Mahāprabhu.

PURPORT

Śrīla Bhaktisiddhānta Sarasvatī Ṭhākura says that if something impedes the execution of devotional service, it should be understood to be impure. Pure devotees of the Lord do not accept impure principles. Impure devotees accept *rasābhāsa,* or overlapping, contradictory mellows, and other principles opposed to the *bhakti* path. The followers of such impure principles are never accepted as pure devotees. There are many parties following the path of *rasābhāsa,* and the followers are sometimes adored by ordinary men. Those who adopt the conclusions of *rasābhāsa* and *bhakti-siddhānta-viruddha* are never accepted as devotees of Śrī Caitanya Mahāprabhu. Svarūpa Dāmodara Gosvāmī never approved such followers as Gauḍīya Vaiṣṇavas, nor did he allow them even to meet the Supreme Lord, Śrī Caitanya Mahāprabhu.

TEXT 115

বিদ্যাপতি, চণ্ডীদাস, শ্রীগীতগোবিন্দ।
এই তিন গীতে করা'ন প্রভুর আনন্দ ॥ ১১৫ ॥

vidyāpati, caṇḍīdāsa, śrī-gīta-govinda
ei tina gīte karā'na prabhura ānanda

vidyāpati—an old Vaiṣṇava poet from the province of Mithilā; *caṇḍīdāsa*—a Bengali Vaiṣṇava poet born in the village of Nānnura, in the Birbhum district; *śrī-gīta-govinda*—a celebrated poem by Jayadeva Gosvāmī; *ei*—these; *tina*—three; *gīte*—songs; *karā'na*—cause; *prabhura*—of Śrī Caitanya Mahāprabhu; *ānanda*—happiness.

TRANSLATION

Śrī Svarūpa Dāmodara used to read the poems of Vidyāpati and Caṇḍīdāsa and Jayadeva Gosvāmī's Śrī Gīta-govinda. He used to make Śrī Caitanya Mahāprabhu very happy by singing these songs.

TEXT 116

সঙ্গীতে — গন্ধর্ব-সম, শাস্ত্রে বৃহস্পতি।
দামোদর-সম আর নাহি মহামতি ॥ ১১৬ ॥

saṅgīte—gandharva-sama, śāstre bṛhaspati
dāmodara-sama āra nāhi mahā-mati

saṅgīte—in music; *gandharva-sama*—just like the Gandharvas; *śāstre*—in discussions of the revealed scriptures; *bṛhaspati*—like Bṛhaspati, the priest of the heavenly demigods; *dāmodara-sama*—equal to Svarūpa Dāmodara; *āra*—anyone else; *nāhi*—there is not; *mahā-mati*—great personality.

TRANSLATION

Svarūpa Dāmodara was as expert a musician as the Gandharvas, and in scriptural discussion he was just like Bṛhaspati, the priest of the heavenly gods. Therefore it is to be concluded that there was no great personality quite like Svarūpa Dāmodara.

PURPORT

Svarūpa Dāmodara Gosvāmī was very expert in music as well as the Vedic scriptures. Śrī Caitanya Mahāprabhu used to call him Dāmodara because of his expert singing and musical skills. The name Dāmodara was given by Śrī Caitanya Mahāprabhu and added to the name given by his *sannyāsa-guru.* He was therefore known as Svarūpa Dāmodara, or Dāmodara Svarūpa. He compiled a book of music named *Saṅgīta-dāmodara.*

TEXT 117

অদ্বৈত-নিত্যানন্দের পরম প্রিয়তম।
শ্রীবাসাদি ভক্তগণের হয় প্রাণ-সম ॥ ১১৭ ॥

advaita-nityānandera parama priyatama
śrīvāsādi bhakta-gaṇera haya prāṇa-sama

advaita—of Advaita Ācārya; *nityānandera*—of Lord Nityānanda Prabhu; *parama*—very; *priya-tama*—dear; *śrīvāsa-ādi*—beginning with Śrīvāsa; *bhakta-gaṇera*—of the devotees; *haya*—is; *prāṇa-sama*—exactly like the life and soul.

TRANSLATION

Śrī Svarūpa Dāmodara was very dear to Advaita Ācārya and Nityānanda Prabhu, and he was the life and soul of all the devotees, headed by Śrīvāsa Ṭhākura.

TEXT 118

সেই দামোদর আসি' দণ্ডবৎ হৈলা।
চরণে পড়িয়া শ্লোক পড়িতে লাগিলা ॥ ১১৮ ॥

sei dāmodara āsi' daṇḍavat hailā
caraṇe paḍiyā śloka paḍite lāgilā

sei dāmodara—that Svarūpa Dāmodara; *āsi'*—coming; *daṇḍa-vat hailā*—fell flat to offer obeisances; *caraṇe paḍiyā*—falling down at the lotus feet; *śloka*—a verse; *paḍite lāgilā*—began to recite.

TRANSLATION

When Svarūpa Dāmodara came to Jagannātha Purī, he fell flat before the lotus feet of Śrī Caitanya Mahāprabhu, offering Him obeisances and reciting a verse.

TEXT 119

হেলোদ্ধূনিত-খেদয়া বিশদয়া প্রোন্মীলদামোদয়া
শাম্যচ্ছাস্ত্রবিবাদয়া রসদয়া চিত্তার্পিতোন্মাদয়া ।
শশ্বদ্ভক্তিবিনোদয়া স-মদয়া মাধুর্যমর্যাদয়া
শ্রীচৈতন্য দয়ানিধে তব দয়া ভূয়াদমন্দোদয়া ॥ ১১৯ ॥

heloddhūnita-khedayā viśadayā pronmīlad-āmodayā
śāmyac-chāstra-vivādayā rasa-dayā cittārpitonmādayā
śaśvad-bhakti-vinodayā sa-madayā mādhurya-maryādayā
śrī-caitanya dayā-nidhe tava dayā bhūyād amandodayā

helā—very easily; *uddhūnita*—driven away; *khedayā*—lamentation; *viśadayā*—which purifies everything; *pronmīlat*—awakening; *āmodayā*—transcendental bliss; *śāmyat*—mitigating; *śāstra*—of revealed scriptures; *vivādayā*—disagreements; *rasa-dayā*—distributing all transcendental mellows; *citta*—in the heart; *arpita*—fixed; *unmādayā*—jubilation; *śaśvat*—always; *bhakti*—devotional service; *vinodayā*—stimulating; *sa-madayā*—full of ecstasy; *mādhurya*—of conjugal love; *maryādayā*—the limit; *śrī-caitanya*—O Lord Śrī Caitanya Mahāprabhu; *dayā-nidhe*—ocean of mercy; *tava*—Your; *dayā*—mercy; *bhūyāt*—let it be; *amanda*—of good fortune; *udayā*—in which there is awakening.

TRANSLATION

"O ocean of mercy, Śrī Caitanya Mahāprabhu! Let there be an awakening of Your auspicious mercy, which easily drives away all kinds of material lamentation by making everything pure and blissful. Indeed, Your mercy awakens transcendental bliss and covers all material pleasures. By Your auspicious mercy, quarrels and disagreements arising among different scriptures are vanquished. Your auspicious mercy pours forth transcendental mellows and thus causes the heart to jubilate. Your mercy, which is full of joy, always stimulates devotional service and

glorifies conjugal love of God. May transcendental bliss be awakened within my heart by Your causeless mercy."

PURPORT

This important verse (*Śrī Caitanya-candrodaya-nāṭaka* 8.10) specifically describes the Lord's causeless mercy. Śrīla Bhaktisiddhānta Sarasvatī Ṭhākura explains that Śrī Caitanya Mahāprabhu, who is the most magnanimous Personality of Godhead, distributes His causeless mercy in three ways to the conditioned soul. Every living entity is morose in the material world because he is always in want. He undergoes a great struggle for existence and tries to minimize his miserable condition by squeezing the utmost pleasure out of this world. But the living entity is never successful in this endeavor. While in a miserable condition, a person sometimes seeks the favor of the Supreme Personality of Godhead, but this is very difficult for materialistic people to obtain. However, when one becomes Kṛṣṇa conscious by the grace of the Lord,the fragrance of the lotus feet of the Lord expands, and in this way a materialist may gain freedom from his miseries. Actually his mind is cleansed by his transcendental connection with the lotus feet of the Lord. At such a time one is enlightened by the loving service of the Lord.

There are many different kinds of scriptures, and by reading them one often becomes puzzled. But when one receives the mercy of the Lord, his confusion is mitigated. Not only are scriptural disparities resolved, but a kind of transcendental bliss is awakened, and in this way one is fully satisfied. The transcendental loving service of the Lord constantly engages the conditioned soul in serving the Lord's lotus feet. Through such fortunate engagement, one's transcendental love for Kṛṣṇa is increased. One's position is thus completely purified, and one is filled with transcendental bliss accompanied by the spirit soul's jubilation.

Thus the transcendental causeless mercy of Lord Kṛṣṇa is manifested in the heart of the devotee. At such a time, material needs no longer exist. The lamentation that invariably accompanies material desires also vanishes. By the grace of the Lord one is elevated to the transcendental position, and then the transcendental mellows of the spiritual world are manifested in him. One's devotional service then becomes firm, and one engages in the Lord's transcendental loving service with great determination. All these combine to fully awaken the devotee's heart with love of Kṛṣṇa.

In the beginning, a conditioned soul is bereft of Kṛṣṇa consciousness and is always morose in his material activities. Later, by associating with a pure devotee, one becomes inquisitive to know the Absolute Truth. In this way one begins to engage in the transcendental service of the Lord. Next, by the Lord's grace all misconceptions are vanquished and the heart is cleansed of all material dirt. It is only then that the pleasure of transcendental bliss is awakened. By the Lord's mercy one is completely convinced of the value of devotional service. When one can see the pastimes of the Lord everywhere, he is firmly situated in transcendental bliss. Such a devotee is relieved of all kinds of material desires, and he preaches the glories of the Lord all over the world. These Kṛṣṇa conscious activities separate him from material activities and the desire for liberation, because at every step the devotee feels himself connected with the Supreme Personality of Godhead. Although such a devotee may sometimes be involved in household life, he is untouched by material existence due to his constant engagement in devotional service. Thus everyone is advised to take shelter of devotional service to become happy and liberated.

TEXT 120

উঠাঞা মহাপ্রভু কৈল আলিঙ্গন ।
দুইজনে প্রেমাবেশে হৈল অচেতন ॥ ১২০ ॥

uṭhāñā mahāprabhu kaila āliṅgana
dui-jane premāveśe haila acetana

uṭhāñā—after raising him; *mahāprabhu*—Lord Śrī Caitanya Mahāprabhu; *kaila*—made; *āliṅgana*—embracing; *dui-jane*—two persons; *prema-āveśe*—in the ecstasy of love; *haila*—became; *acetana*—unconscious.

TRANSLATION

Śrī Caitanya Mahāprabhu raised Svarūpa Dāmodara to his feet and embraced him. They both became ecstatic in love and fell unconscious.

TEXT 121

কতক্ষণে দুই জনে স্থির যবে হৈলা ।
তবে মহাপ্রভু তাঁরে কহিতে লাগিলা ॥ ১২১ ॥

kata-kṣaṇe dui jane sthira yabe hailā
tabe mahāprabhu tāṅre kahite lāgilā

kata-kṣaṇe—after some time; *dui jane*—both persons; *sthira*—patient; *yabe*—when; *hailā*—became; *tabe*—at that time; *mahāprabhu*—Śrī Caitanya Mahāprabhu; *tāṅre*—unto him; *kahite*—to speak; *lāgilā*—began.

TRANSLATION

After they had regained their patience, Śrī Caitanya Mahāprabhu began to speak.

TEXT 122

তুমি যে আসিবে, আজি স্বপ্নেতে দেখিল ।
ভাল হৈল, অন্ধ যেন দুই নেত্র পাইল ॥ ১২২ ॥

tumi ye āsibe, āji svapnete dekhila
bhāla haila, andha yena dui netra pāila

tumi—you; *ye*—that; *āsibe*—will come; *āji*—today; *svapnete*—in dream; *dekhila*—I saw; *bhāla haila*—it is very good; *andha*—a blind man; *yena*—as if; *dui*—two; *netra*—eyes; *pāila*—got back.

TRANSLATION

Śrī Caitanya Mahāprabhu said, "I saw in a dream that you were coming, and so this is very auspicious. I have been like a blind man, but your coming here restores My vision."

TEXT 123

স্বরূপ কহে, —প্রভু, মোর ক্ষম' অপরাধ ।
তোমা ছাড়ি' অন্যত্র গেনু, করিনু প্রমাদ ॥ ১২৩ ॥

svarūpa kahe,—prabhu, mora kṣama' aparādha
tomā chāḍi' anyatra genu, karinu pramāda

svarūpa kahe—Svarūpa Dāmodara said; *prabhu*—my Lord; *mora*—my; *kṣama'*—please excuse; *aparādha*—offense; *tomā*—You; *chāḍi'*—giving up; *anyatra*—elsewhere; *genu*—I went; *karinu*—I have done; *pramāda*—great mistake.

TRANSLATION

Svarūpa said, "My dear Lord, please excuse my offense. I gave up Your company to go elsewhere, and that was my great mistake.

TEXT 124

তোমার চরণে মোর নাহি প্রেম-লেশ ।
তোমা ছাড়ি' পাপী মুঞি গেনু অন্য দেশ ॥ ১২৪ ॥

tomāra caraṇe mora nāhi prema-leśa
tomā chāḍi' pāpī muñi genu anya deśa

tomāra caraṇe—for Your lotus feet; *mora*—my; *nāhi*—there is not; *prema-leśa*—a trace of love; *tomā*—You; *chāḍi'*—giving up; *pāpī*—sinful; *muñi*—I; *genu*—went; *anya deśa*—to another country.

TRANSLATION

"My dear Lord, I do not possess even a trace of love for Your lotus feet. If I did, how could I have gone to another country? I am therefore a most sinful man.

TEXT 125

মুঞি তোমা ছাড়িল, তুমি মোরে না ছাড়িলা ।
কৃপা-পাশ গলে বান্ধি' চরণে আনিলা ॥ ১২৫ ॥

muñi tomā chāḍila, tumi more nā chāḍilā
kṛpā-pāśa gale bāndhi' caraṇe ānilā

muñi—I; *tomā*—You; *chādila*—gave up; *tumi*—You; *more*—me; *nā*—did not; *chāḍilā*—give up; *kṛpā*—of mercy; *pāśa*—by the rope; *gale*—by the neck; *bāndhi'*—binding; *caraṇe*—at Your lotus feet; *ānilā*—You brought back.

TRANSLATION

"I gave up Your company, but You did not give me up. By Your rope of mercy You have bound me by the neck and brought me back again to Your lotus feet."

TEXT 126

তবে স্বরূপ কৈল নিতাইর চরণ বন্দন ।
নিত্যানন্দপ্রভু কৈল প্রেম-আলিঙ্গন ॥ ১২৬ ॥

tabe svarūpa kaila nitāira caraṇa vandana
nityānanda-prabhu kaila prema-āliṅgana

tabe—thereafter; *svarūpa*—Svarūpa Dāmodara; *kaila*—did; *nitāira*—of Nityānanda Prabhu; *caraṇa*—of the lotus feet; *vandana*—worship; *nityānanda-prabhu*—Lord Nityānanda; *kaila*—did; *prema-āliṅgana*—embracing in love.

TRANSLATION

Svarūpa Dāmodara then worshiped the lotus feet of Nityānanda Prabhu, and Nityānanda Prabhu in turn embraced him in the ecstasy of love.

TEXT 127

জগদানন্দ, মুকুন্দ, শঙ্কর, সার্বভৌম ।
সবা-সঙ্গে যথাযোগ্য করিল মিলন ॥ ১২৭ ॥

jagadānanda, mukunda, śaṅkara, sārvabhauma
sabā-saṅge yathā-yogya karila milana

jagadānanda—Jagadānanda; *mukunda*—Mukunda; *śaṅkara*—Śaṅkara; *sārvabhauma*—Sārvabhauma; *sabā-saṅge*—with all; *yathā-yogya*—as is befitting; *karila*—did; *milana*—meeting.

TRANSLATION

After worshiping Nityānanda Prabhu, Svarūpa Dāmodara met Jagadānanda, Mukunda, Śaṅkara and Sārvabhauma, as was befitting.

TEXT 128

পরমানন্দ পুরীর কৈল চরণ বন্দন ।
পুরী-গোসাঞি তাঁরে কৈল প্রেম-আলিঙ্গন ॥ ১২৮ ॥

paramānanda purīra kaila caraṇa vandana
purī-gosāñi tāṅre kaila prema-āliṅgana

paramānanda purīra—of Paramānanda Purī; *kaila*—he did; *caraṇa vandana*—worshiping the lotus feet; *purī-gosāñi*—Paramānanda Purī; *tāṅre*—unto him; *kaila*—did; *prema-āliṅgana*—embracing in love.

TRANSLATION

Svarūpa Dāmodara also offered his worshipful prayers at the lotus feet of Paramānanda Purī, who, in return, embraced him in ecstatic love.

TEXT 129

মহাপ্রভু দিল তাঁরে নিভৃতে বাসাঘর ।
জলাদি-পরিচর্যা লাগি' দিল এক কিঙ্কর ॥ ১২৯ ॥

mahāprabhu dila tāṅre nibhṛte vāsā-ghara
jalādi-paricaryā lāgi' dila eka kiṅkara

mahāprabhu—Śrī Caitanya Mahāprabhu; *dila*—gave; *tāṅre*—unto him; *nibhṛte*—in a solitary place; *vāsā-ghara*—residential quarters; *jala-ādi*—supplying water, etc.; *paricaryā*—service; *lāgi'*—for the purpose of; *dila*—gave; *eka*—one; *kiṅkara*—servant.

TRANSLATION

Śrī Caitanya Mahāprabhu then gave Svarūpa Dāmodara residence in a solitary place and ordered a servant to serve him with a supply of water and other necessities.

TEXT 130

আর দিন সার্বভৌম-আদি ভক্ত-সঙ্গে ।
বসিয়া আছেন মহাপ্রভু কৃষ্ণকথা-রঙ্গে ॥ ১৩০ ॥

āra dina sārvabhauma-ādi bhakta-saṅge
vasiyā āchena mahāprabhu kṛṣṇa-kathā-raṅge

āra dina—the next day; *sārvabhauma-ādi*—headed by Sārvabhauma Bhaṭṭācārya; *bhakta-saṅge*—with the devotees; *vasiyā āchena*—was sitting; *mahāprabhu*—Śrī Caitanya Mahāprabhu; *kṛṣṇa-kathā-raṅge*—engaged in discussions of topics concerning Kṛṣṇa.

TRANSLATION

The next day Śrī Caitanya Mahāprabhu sat with all the devotees, headed by Sārvabhauma Bhaṭṭācārya, and they discussed the pastimes of Kṛṣṇa.

TEXT 131

হেনকালে গোবিন্দের হৈল আগমন।
দণ্ডবৎ করি' কহে বিনয়-বচন ॥ ১৩১ ॥

hena-kāle govindera haila āgamana
daṇḍavat kari' kahe vinaya-vacana

hena-kāle—at that time; *govindera*—of Govinda; *haila*—there was; *āgamana*—arrival; *daṇḍavat kari'*—offering obeisances; *kahe*—says; *vinaya-vacana*—submissive words.

TRANSLATION

At that time Govinda appeared on the scene, offered his respectful obeisances and spoke submissively.

TEXT 132

ঈশ্বর-পুরীর ভৃত্য, — 'গোবিন্দ' মোর নাম।
পুরী-গোসাঞির আজ্ঞায় আইনু তোমার স্থান ॥ ১৩২ ॥

īśvara-purīra bhṛtya,—'govinda' mora nāma
purī-gosāñira ājñāya āinu tomāra sthāna

īśvara-purīra bhṛtya—servant of Īśvara Purī; *govinda mora nāma*—my name is Govinda; *purī-gosāñira*—of Īśvara Purī; *ājñāya*—on the order; *āinu*—I have come; *tomāra*—to Your; *sthāna*—place.

TRANSLATION

"I am the servant of Īśvara Purī. My name is Govinda, and following the orders of my spiritual master, I have come here.

TEXT 133

সিদ্ধিপ্রাপ্তিকালে গোসাঞি আজ্ঞা কৈল মোরে।
কৃষ্ণচৈতন্য-নিকটে রহি সেবিহ তাঁহারে ॥ ১৩৩ ॥

siddha-prāpti-kāle gosāñi ājñā kaila more
kṛṣṇa-caitanya-nikaṭe rahi seviha tāṅhāre

siddhi-prāpti-kāle—at the time of his departure from this mortal world to achieve the highest perfection of life; *gosāñi*—my spiritual master; *ājñā*—order; *kaila*—made; *more*—unto me; *kṛṣṇa-caitanya-nikaṭe*—at the place of Śrī Kṛṣṇa Caitanya; *rahi*—remaining; *seviha*—render service; *tāṅhāre*—unto Him.

TRANSLATION

"Just before his departure from this mortal world to attain the highest perfection, Īśvara Purī told me that I should go to Śrī Caitanya Mahāprabhu and render service unto Him.

TEXT 134

কাশীশ্বর আসিবেন সব তীর্থ দেখিয়া।
প্রভু-আজ্ঞায় মুঞি আইনু তোমা-পদে ধাঞা ॥ ১৩৪ ॥

kāśīśvara āsibena saba tīrtha dekhiyā
prabhu-ājñāya muñi āinu tomā-pade dhāñā

kāśīśvara—Kāśīśvara; *āsibena*—will come; *saba*—all; *tīrtha*—holy places; *dekhiyā*—visiting; *prabhu-ājñāya*—under the order of my spiritual master; *muñi*—I; *āinu*—have come; *tomā*—to Your; *pade*—lotus feet; *dhāñā*—running.

TRANSLATION

"Kāśīśvara will also come here after visiting all the holy places. However, following the orders of my spiritual master, I have hastily come to be present at Your lotus feet."

TEXT 135

গোসাঞি কহিল, 'পুরীশ্বর' বাৎসল্য করে মোরে।
কৃপা করি' মোর ঠাঞি পাঠাইলা তোমারে ॥ ১৩৫ ॥

gosāñi kahila, 'purīśvara' vātsalya kare more
kṛpā kari' mora ṭhāñi pāṭhāilā tomāre

gosāñi kahila—Śrī Caitanya Mahāprabhu replied; *purīśvara*—Īśvara Purī; *vātsalya*—paternal affection; *kare*—does; *more*—unto Me; *kṛpā kari'*—being merciful; *mora ṭhāñi*—to My place; *pāṭhāilā*—sent; *tomāre*—you.

TRANSLATION

Śrī Caitanya Mahāprabhu replied, "My spiritual master, Īśvara Purī, always favors Me with paternal affection. Therefore, out of his causeless mercy, he has sent you here."

TEXT 136

এত শুনি' সার্বভৌম প্রভুরে পুছিল।
পুরী-গোসাঞি শূদ্র-সেবক কাঁহে ত' রাখিল ॥ ১৩৬ ॥

eta śuni' sārvabhauma prabhure puchila
purī-gosāñi śūdra-sevaka kāṅhe ta' rākhila

eta śuni'—hearing this; *sārvabhauma*—Sārvabhauma Bhaṭṭācārya; *prabhure*—unto the Lord; *puchila*—inquired; *purī-gosāñi*—Īśvara Purī; *śūdra-sevaka*—a servant who is a *śūdra; kāṅhe ta'*—why; *rākhila*—kept.

TRANSLATION

After hearing this, Sārvabhauma Bhaṭṭācārya asked Śrī Caitanya Mahāprabhu, "Why did Īśvara Purī keep a servant who comes from a śūdra family?"

PURPORT

Both Kāśīśvara and Govinda were personal servants of Īśvara Purī. After Īśvara Purī's demise, Kāśīśvara went to visit all the holy places of India. Following the orders of his spiritual master, Govinda immediately went to Śrī Caitanya Mahāprabhu for shelter. Govinda came from a *śūdra* family, but because he was initiated by Īśvara Purī, he was certainly a *brāhmaṇa.* Sārvabhauma Bhaṭṭācārya here asked Śrī Caitanya Mahāprabhu why Īśvara Purī accepted a disciple from a *śūdra* family. According to the *smṛti-śāstra,* which gives directions for the management of the *varṇāśrama* institution, a *brāhmaṇa* cannot accept a disciple from the lower castes. In other words, a *kṣatriya, vaiśya* or *śūdra* cannot be accepted as a servant. If a spiritual master accepts such a person, he is contaminated. Sārvabhauma Bhaṭṭācārya therefore asked why Īśvara Purī accepted a servant or disciple born of a *śūdra* family.

In answer to this question, Śrī Caitanya Mahāprabhu replied that His spiritual master, Īśvara Purī, was so empowered that he was as good as the Supreme Personality of Godhead. As such, Īśvara Purī was the spiritual master of the whole world. He was not a servant of any mundane rule or regulation. An empowered spiritual master like Īśvara Purī can bestow his mercy upon anyone, irrespective of caste or creed. The conclusion is that an empowered spiritual master is authorized by Kṛṣṇa and his own *guru* and should therefore be considered as good as the Supreme Personality of Godhead Himself. That is the verdict of Viśvanātha Cakravartī: *sākṣād-dharitvena.* An authorized spiritual master is as good as Hari, the Supreme Personality of Godhead. As Hari is free to act as He likes, the empowered spiritual master is also free. As Hari is not subject to mundane rules and regulations, the spiritual master empowered by Him is also not subject. According to the *Caitanya-caritāmṛta* (*Antya-līlā* 7.11), *kṛṣṇa-śakti vinā nahe tāra pravartana.* An authorized spiritual master empowered by Kṛṣṇa can spread the glories of the holy name of the Lord, for he has power of attorney from the Supreme Personality of Godhead. In the mundane world, anyone possessing his master's power of attorney can act on behalf of his master. Similarly, a spiritual master empowered by Kṛṣṇa through his own bona fide spiritual master should be considered as good as the Supreme Personality of Godhead Himself. That is the meaning of *sākṣād-dharitvena.* Śrī Caitanya Mahāprabhu therefore describes the activities of the Supreme Personality of Godhead and the bona fide spiritual master as follows.

TEXT 137

প্রভু কহে, —ঈশ্বর হয় পরম স্বতন্ত্র।
ঈশ্বরের কৃপা নহে বেদ-পরতন্ত্র ॥ ১৩৭ ॥

prabhu kahe,—īśvara haya parama svatantra
īśvarera kṛpā nahe veda-paratantra

prabhu kahe—Śrī Caitanya Mahāprabhu said; *īśvara*—the Supreme Personality of Godhead or Īśvara Purī; *haya*—is; *parama*—supremely; *svatantra*—independent; *īśvarera*—of the Supreme Personality of Godhead or of Īśvara Purī; *kṛpā*—the mercy; *nahe*—is not; *veda-paratantra*—subject to the Vedic rules.

TRANSLATION

Śrī Caitanya Mahāprabhu said, "Both the Supreme Personality of Godhead and My spiritual master, Īśvara Purī, are completely independent. Therefore neither the mercy of the Supreme Personality of Godhead nor that of Īśvara Purī is subject to any Vedic rules and regulations.

TEXT 138

ঈশ্বরের কৃপা জাতি-কুলাদি না মানে।
বিদুরের ঘরে কৃষ্ণ করিলা ভোজনে ॥ ১৩৮ ॥

īśvarera kṛpā jāti-kulādi nā māne
vidurera ghare kṛṣṇa karilā bhojane

īśvarera kṛpā—the mercy of the Lord; *jāti*—caste; *kula-ādi*—family, etc.; *nā māne*—does not obey; *vidurera*—of Vidura; *ghare*—at the home; *kṛṣṇa*—Lord Kṛṣṇa; *karilā*—did; *bhojane*—eating.

TRANSLATION

"The mercy of the Supreme Personality of Godhead is not restricted to the jurisdiction of caste and creed. Vidura was a śūdra, yet Kṛṣṇa accepted lunch at his home.

TEXT 139

স্নেহ-লেশাপেক্ষা মাত্র শ্রীকৃষ্ণ-কৃপার।
স্নেহবশ হঞা করে স্বতন্ত্র আচার ॥ ১৩৯ ॥

sneha-leśāpekṣā mātra śrī-kṛṣṇa-kṛpāra
sneha-vaśa hañā kare svatantra ācāra

sneha—of affection; *leśa*—on a trace; *apekṣā*—reliance; *mātra*—only; *śrī-kṛṣṇa*—of Lord Śrī Kṛṣṇa; *kṛpāra*—of the mercy; *sneha-vaśa*—obliged by affection; *hañā*—being; *kare*—does; *svatantra*—independent; *ācāra*—behavior.

TRANSLATION

"Lord Kṛṣṇa's mercy is dependent only on affection. Being obliged only by affection, Lord Kṛṣṇa acts very independently.

PURPORT

Lord Śrī Kṛṣṇa, the Supreme Personality of Godhead, is merciful, but His mercy does not depend on mundane rules and regulations. He is dependent only on affection and nothing else. Service to Lord Kṛṣṇa can be rendered in two ways. One can serve the Lord in affection or in veneration. When service is rendered in affection, it is the Lord's special mercy. When service is rendered in veneration, it is doubtful whether Kṛṣṇa's mercy is actually involved. If Kṛṣṇa's mercy is there, it is not dependent on any prescribed caste or creed. Śrī Caitanya Mahāprabhu wanted to inform Sārvabhauma Bhaṭṭācārya that Lord Kṛṣṇa is the spiritual master of everyone, and He does not care for mundane caste or creed. Therefore Śrī Caitanya Mahāprabhu cited the example of Lord Kṛṣṇa's accepting food at the house of Vidura, who was a *śūdra* by birth. By the same token, Īśvara Purī, an empowered spiritual master, could show mercy to anyone. As such, he accepted Govinda, although the boy was born in a *śūdra* family. When Govinda was initiated, he became a *brāhmaṇa* and was accepted as Īśvara Purī's personal servant. In the *Hari-bhakti-vilāsa,* Śrī Sanātana Gosvāmī states that one who is initiated by a bona fide spiritual master immediately becomes a *brāhmaṇa.* A pseudo spiritual master cannot transform a person into a *brāhmaṇa,* but an authorized spiritual master can do so. This is the verdict of *śāstra,* Śrī Caitanya Mahāprabhu and all the Gosvāmīs.

TEXT 140

মর্যাদা হৈতে কোটি সুখ স্নেহ-আচরণে।
পরমানন্দ হয় যার নাম-শ্রবণে ॥ ১৪০ ॥

maryādā haite koṭi sukha sneha-ācaraṇe
paramānanda haya yāra nāma-śravaṇe

maryādā haite—greater than veneration and awe; *koṭi*—millions of times; *sukha*—happiness; *sneha*—with affection; *ācaraṇe*—in dealings; *parama-ānanda*—transcendental bliss; *haya*—there is; *yāra*—whose; *nāma*—holy name; *śravaṇe*—by hearing.

TRANSLATION

"In conclusion, dealings in affection with the Supreme Personality of Godhead bring happiness many millions of times greater than dealings with Him in awe and veneration. Simply by hearing the holy name of the Lord, the devotee is merged in transcendental bliss."

TEXT 141

এত বলি' গোবিন্দেরে কৈল আলিঙ্গন।
গোবিন্দ করিল প্রভুর চরণ বন্দন ॥ ১৪১ ॥

eta bali' govindere kaila āliṅgana
govinda karila prabhura caraṇa vandana

eta bali'—saying this; *govindere*—unto Govinda; *kaila*—did; *āliṅgana*—embracing; *govinda*—Govinda; *karila*—did; *prabhura*—of Lord Śrī Caitanya Mahāprabhu; *caraṇa vandana*—worshiping the lotus feet.

TRANSLATION

After saying this, Śrī Caitanya Mahāprabhu embraced Govinda, and Govinda in turn offered his respectful obeisances unto Śrī Caitanya Mahāprabhu's lotus feet.

TEXT 142

প্রভু কহে, — ভট্টাচার্য, করহ বিচার।
গুরুর কিঙ্কর হয় মান্য সে আমার ॥ ১৪২ ॥

prabhu kahe, — bhaṭṭācārya, karaha vicāra
gurura kiṅkara haya mānya se āmāra

prabhu kahe—Śrī Caitanya Mahāprabhu said; *bhaṭṭācārya*—My dear Bhaṭṭācārya; *karaha vicāra*—just consider; *gurura kiṅkara*—the servant of the spiritual master; *haya*—is; *mānya*—respectable; *se*—he; *āmāra*—to Me.

TRANSLATION

Śrī Caitanya Mahāprabhu then continued speaking to Sārvabhauma Bhaṭṭācārya: "Consider this point. The servant of the spiritual master is always respectable for Me.

TEXT 143

তাঁহারে আপন-সেবা করাইতে না যুয়ায়।
গুরু আজ্ঞা দিয়াছেন, কি করি উপায় ॥ ১৪৩ ॥

tāṅhāre āpana-sevā karāite nā yuyāya
guru ājñā diyāchena, ki kari upāya

tāṅhāre—him; *āpana-sevā*—personal service; *karāite*—to engage to do; *nā yuyāya*—is not befitting; *guru*—the spiritual master; *ājñā*—order; *diyāchena*—has given; *ki*—what; *kari*—can I do; *upāya*—remedy.

TRANSLATION

"As such, it is not befitting that the guru's servant should engage in My personal service. Yet My spiritual master has given this order. What shall I do?"

PURPORT

A *guru's* servants or disciples are all Godbrothers to one another, and as such they should all respect one another as *prabhu,* or master. No one should disrespect his Godbrother. For this reason Śrī Caitanya

Mahāprabhu asked Sārvabhauma Bhaṭṭācārya what to do about Govinda. Govinda was the personal servant of Īśvara Purī, Śrī Caitanya Mahāprabhu's spiritual master, and now Īśvara Purī had ordered Govinda to become Śrī Caitanya Mahāprabhu's personal servant. So what was to be done? This was the inquiry Śrī Caitanya Mahāprabhu placed before Sārvabhauma Bhaṭṭācārya, an experienced friend.

TEXT 144

ভট্ট কহে, — গুরুর আজ্ঞা হয় বলবান্।
গুরু-আজ্ঞা না লঙ্ঘিয়ে, শাস্ত্র — প্রমাণ ॥ ১৪৪ ॥

bhaṭṭa kahe, — gurura ājñā haya balavān
guru-ājñā nā laṅghiye, śāstra — pramāṇa

bhaṭṭa kahe — Sārvabhauma Bhaṭṭācārya said; *gurura ājñā* — the order of the spiritual master; *haya* — is; *balavān* — strong; *guru-ājñā* — the order of the spiritual master; *nā* — not; *laṅghiye* — we can disobey; *śāstra* — scriptural; *pramāṇa* — injunction.

TRANSLATION

Sārvabhauma Bhaṭṭācārya said, "The order of the spiritual master is very strong and cannot be disobeyed. That is the injunction of the śāstras, the revealed scriptures.

TEXT 145

স শুশ্রুবান্মাতরি ভার্গবেণ পিতুর্নিয়োগাৎ প্রহৃতং দ্বিষদ্বৎ।
প্রত্যগৃহীদগ্রজশাসনং তদাজ্ঞা গুরূণাং হ্যবিচারণীয়া ॥ ১৪৫ ॥

sa śuśruvān mātari bhārgaveṇa
pitur niyogāt prahṛtaṁ dviṣad-vat
pratyagṛhīd agraja-śāsanaṁ tad
ājñā gurūṇāṁ hy avicāraṇīyā

saḥ — He (Lakṣmaṇa, the brother of Lord Rāmacandra); *śuśruvān* — hearing; *mātari* — unto the mother; *bhārgaveṇa* — by Paraśurāma; *pituḥ* — of the father; *niyogāt* — by the order; *prahṛtam* — killing; *dviṣat-vat* — like an enemy; *pratyagṛhīt* — accepted; *agraja-*

śāsanam—the order of the elder brother; *tat*—that; *ājñā*—order; *gurūṇām*—of superior persons, such as the spiritual master or father; *hi*—because; *avicāraṇīyā*—to be obeyed without consideration.

TRANSLATION

"'Being ordered by his father, Paraśurāma killed his mother, Reṇukā, just as if she were an enemy. When Lakṣmaṇa, the younger brother of Lord Rāmacandra, heard of this, He immediately engaged Himself in the service of His elder brother and accepted His orders. The order of the spiritual master must be obeyed without consideration.'

PURPORT

This is a quotation from the *Raghu-vaṁśa* (14.46). Lord Rāmacandra's statement to Sītā given below is from the *Rāmāyaṇa* (*Ayodhyā-kāṇḍa* 22.9).

TEXT 146

নির্বিচারং গুরোরাজ্ঞা ময়া কার্যা মহাত্মনঃ ।
শ্রেয়ো হ্যেবং ভবত্যাশ্চ মম চৈব বিশেষতঃ ॥ ১৪৬ ॥

nirvicāraṁ guror ājñā
mayā kāryā mahātmanaḥ
śreyo hy evaṁ bhavatyāś ca
mama caiva viśeṣataḥ

nirvicāram—to be obeyed without consideration; *guroḥ*—of the spiritual master; *ājñā*—the order; *mayā*—by Me; *kāryā*—must be done; *mahā-ātmanaḥ*—of the great soul; *śreyaḥ*—good fortune; *hi*—indeed; *evam*—thus; *bhavatyāḥ*—for you; *ca*—and; *mama*—for Me; *ca*—also; *eva*—certainly; *viśeṣataḥ*—specifically.

TRANSLATION

"'The order of a great personality like a father must be executed without consideration because there is good fortune in such an order for both of us. In particular, there is good fortune for Me.'"

TEXT 147

তবে মহাপ্রভু তাঁরে কৈল অঙ্গীকার।
আপন-শ্রীঅঙ্গ-সেবায় দিল অধিকার ॥ ১৪৭ ॥

tabe mahāprabhu tāṅre kaila aṅgīkāra
āpana-śrī-aṅga-sevāya dila adhikāra

tabe—after that; *mahāprabhu*—Śrī Caitanya Mahāprabhu; *tāṅre*—unto Govinda; *kaila*—did; *aṅgīkāra*—acceptance; *āpana*—personal; *śrī-aṅga*—of the transcendental body; *sevāya*—in the service; *dila*—gave; *adhikāra*—responsibility.

TRANSLATION

After Sārvabhauma Bhaṭṭācārya said this, Śrī Caitanya Mahāprabhu embraced Govinda and engaged him in the service of His personal body.

TEXT 148

প্রভুর প্রিয় ভৃত্য করি' সবে করে মান।
সকল বৈষ্ণবের গোবিন্দ করে সমাধান ॥ ১৪৮ ॥

prabhura priya bhṛtya kari' sabe kare māna
sakala vaiṣṇavera govinda kare samādhāna

prabhura—of Lord Śrī Caitanya Mahāprabhu; *priya*—dear; *bhṛtya*—servant; *kari'*—understanding; *sabe*—all; *kare*—do; *māna*—respect; *sakala*—all; *vaiṣṇavera*—of devotees; *govinda*—Govinda; *kare*—does; *samādhāna*—service.

TRANSLATION

Everyone respected Govinda as the dearest servant of Śrī Caitanya Mahāprabhu, and Govinda served all the Vaiṣṇavas and saw to their needs.

TEXT 149

ছোট-বড়-কীর্তনীয়া — দুই হরিদাস।
রামাই, নন্দাই রহে গোবিন্দের পাশ ॥ ১৪৯ ॥

choṭa-baḍa-kīrtanīyā — dui haridāsa
rāmāi, nandāi rahe govindera pāśa

choṭa-baḍa — junior and senior; *kīrtanīyā* — musicians; *dui* — two; *haridāsa* — Haridāsas; *rāmāi* — Rāmāi; *nandāi* — Nandāi; *rahe* — stay; *govindera pāśa* — with Govinda.

TRANSLATION

Both Haridāsa senior and Haridāsa junior, who were musicians, as well as Rāmāi and Nandāi, used to stay with Govinda.

TEXT 150

গোবিন্দের সঙ্গে করে প্রভুর সেবন।
গোবিন্দের ভাগ্যসীমা না যায় বর্ণন ॥ ১৫০ ॥

govindera saṅge kare prabhura sevana
govindera bhāgya-sīmā nā yāya varṇana

govindera saṅge — with Govinda; *kare* — do; *prabhura* — of Śrī Caitanya Mahāprabhu; *sevana* — service; *govindera* — of Govinda; *bhāgya-sīmā* — the limit of good fortune; *nā* — not; *yāya varṇana* — can be described.

TRANSLATION

They all remained with Govinda to serve Śrī Caitanya Mahāprabhu; therefore no one could estimate the good fortune of Govinda.

TEXT 151

আর দিনে মুকুন্দদত্ত কহে প্রভুর স্থানে।
ব্রহ্মানন্দ-ভারতী আইলা তোমার দরশনে ॥ ১৫১ ॥

āra dine mukunda-datta kahe prabhura sthāne
brahmānanda-bhāratī āilā tomāra daraśane

āra dine — the next day; *mukunda-datta* — Mukunda Datta; *kahe* — said; *prabhura* — of Śrī Caitanya Mahāprabhu; *sthāne* — at the place; *brahmānanda-bhāratī* — Brahmānanda Bhāratī; *āilā* — has come; *tomāra daraśane* — to see You.

TRANSLATION

The next day Mukunda Datta informed Śrī Caitanya Mahāprabhu, "Brahmānanda Bhāratī has come to see You."

TEXT 152

আজ্ঞা দেহ' যদি তাঁরে আনিয়ে এথাই।
প্রভু কহে,—গুরু তেঁহ, যাব তাঁর ঠাঞি ॥ ১৫২ ॥

ājñā deha' yadi tāṅre āniye ethāi
prabhu kahe,—guru teṅha, yāba tāṅra ṭhāñi

ājñā deha'—order; *yadi*—if; *tāṅre*—him; *āniye*—I can bring; *ethāi*—here; *prabhu kahe*—Śrī Caitanya Mahāprabhu said; *guru teṅha*—he is My spiritual master; *yāba*—I shall go; *tāṅra ṭhāñi*—to his place.

TRANSLATION

Mukunda Datta then asked the Lord, "Shall I bring him here?"

Śrī Caitanya Mahāprabhu said, "Brahmānanda Bhāratī is like My spiritual master. It is better that I go to him."

TEXT 153

এত বলি' মহাপ্রভু ভক্তগণ-সঙ্গে।
চলি' আইলা ব্রহ্মানন্দ-ভারতীর আগে ॥ ১৫৩ ॥

eta bali' mahāprabhu bhakta-gaṇa-saṅge
cali' āilā brahmānanda-bhāratīra āge

eta bali'—saying this; *mahāprabhu*—Śrī Caitanya Mahāprabhu; *bhakta-gaṇa-saṅge*—with the devotees; *cali'*—walking; *āilā*—came; *brahmānanda-bhāratīra*—of Brahmānanda Bhāratī; *āge*—in the presence.

TRANSLATION

After saying this, Śrī Caitanya Mahāprabhu and His devotees came into the presence of Brahmānanda Bhāratī.

TEXT 154

ব্রহ্মানন্দ পরিয়াছে মৃগচর্মাম্বর ।
তাহা দেখি' প্রভু দুঃখ পাইলা অন্তর ॥ ১৫৪ ॥

brahmānanda pariyāche mṛga-carmāmbara
tāhā dekhi' prabhu duḥkha pāilā antara

brahmānanda—Brahmānanda; *pariyāche*—did wear; *mṛga-carma-ambara*—a garment made of deerskin; *tāhā dekhi'*—seeing that; *prabhu*—Śrī Caitanya Mahāprabhu; *duḥkha*—unhappiness; *pāilā*—got; *antara*—within Himself.

TRANSLATION

When Śrī Caitanya Mahāprabhu and His devotees approached him, they saw that he was covered with a deerskin. Seeing this, Śrī Caitanya Mahāprabhu became very unhappy.

PURPORT

Brahmānanda Bhāratī belonged to the Śaṅkara-sampradāya. (The title Bhāratī indicates a member of one of that *sampradāya's* ten classes of *sannyāsīs.*) It is customary for a person who has renounced the world to cover his body with a deerskin or the bark of a tree. This is enjoined by the *Manu-saṁhitā.* But if a *sannyāsī* who has renounced the world simply wears a deerskin and does not spiritually advance, he is bewildered by false prestige. Śrī Caitanya Mahāprabhu did not like to see Brahmānanda Bhāratī wearing a deerskin.

TEXT 155

দেখিয়া ত' ছদ্ম কৈল যেন দেখে নাঞি ।
মুকুন্দেরে পুছে,—কাহাঁ ভারতী-গোসাঞি ॥ ১৫৫ ॥

dekhiyā ta' chadma kaila yena dekhe nāñi
mukundere puche,—kāhāṅ bhāratī-gosāñi

dekhiyā—seeing; *ta'*—certainly; *chadma kaila*—pretended; *yena*—as if; *dekhe*—sees; *nāñi*—not; *mukundere puche*—inquired from Mukunda; *kāhāṅ*—where; *bhāratī-gosāñi*—Brahmānanda Bhāratī, My spiritual master.

TRANSLATION

Seeing Brahmānanda Bhāratī wearing the deerskin, Caitanya Mahāprabhu pretended not to see him. Instead, He asked Mukunda Datta, "Where is Brahmānanda Bhāratī, My spiritual master?"

TEXT 156

মুকুন্দ কহে, — এই আগে দেখ বিদ্যমান ।
প্রভু কহে, — তেঁহ নহেন, তুমি অগেয়ান ॥ ১৫৬ ॥

mukunda kahe, — ei āge dekha vidyamāna
prabhu kahe, — teṅha nahena, tumi ageyāna

mukunda kahe — Mukunda said; *ei āge* — here in front; *dekha* — see; *vidyamāna* — present; *prabhu kahe* — Śrī Caitanya Mahāprabhu replied; *teṅha nahena* — he is not; *tumi ageyāna* — you are incorrect.

TRANSLATION

Mukunda Datta replied, "Here is Brahmānanda Bhāratī, in Your presence."

The Lord replied, "You are incorrect. This is not Brahmānanda Bhāratī.

TEXT 157

অন্যেরে অন্য কহ, নাহি তোমার জ্ঞান ।
ভারতী-গোসাঞি কেনে পরিবেন চাম ॥ ১৫৭ ॥

anyere anya kaha, nāhi tomāra jñāna
bhāratī-gosāñi kene paribena cāma

anyere — another; *anya kaha* — you talk of someone else; *nāhi* — there is not; *tomāra* — your; *jñāna* — knowledge; *bhāratī* — Brahmānanda Bhāratī; *gosāñi* — My spiritual master; *kene* — why; *paribena* — should wear; *cāma* — skin.

TRANSLATION

"You must be talking of someone else, for this is surely not Brahmānanda Bhāratī. You simply have no knowledge. Why should Brahmānanda Bhāratī wear a deerskin?"

TEXT 158

শুনি' ব্রহ্মানন্দ করে হৃদয়ে বিচারে।
মোর চর্মাম্বর এই না ভায় ইঁহারে ॥ ১৫৮ ॥

śuni' brahmānanda kare hṛdaye vicāre
mora carmāmbara ei nā bhāya iṅhāre

śuni'—hearing; *brahmānanda*—Brahmānanda; *kare*—does; *hṛdaye*—within himself; *vicāre*—consideration; *mora*—my; *carma-ambara*—deerskin garment; *ei*—this; *nā*—not; *bhāya*—is approved; *iṅhāre*—by Śrī Caitanya Mahāprabhu.

TRANSLATION

When Brahmānanda Bhāratī heard this, he thought, "My deerskin is not approved by Śrī Caitanya Mahāprabhu."

TEXT 159

ভাল কহেন, — চর্মাম্বর দম্ভ লাগি' পরি।
চর্মাম্বর-পরিধানে সংসার না তরি ॥ ১৫৯ ॥

bhāla kahena,—carmāmbara dambha lāgi' pari
carmāmbara-paridhāne saṁsāra nā tari

bhāla—well; *kahena*—He said; *carma-ambara*—the garment of deerskin; *dambha*—prestige; *lāgi'*—for the matter of; *pari*—I put on; *carma-ambara-paridhāne*—by putting on a garment of skin; *saṁsāra*—the material world; *nā tari*—I cannot cross.

TRANSLATION

Thus admitting his mistake, Brahmānanda Bhāratī thought, "He spoke well. I put on this deerskin only for prestige. I cannot cross over the ocean of nescience simply by wearing a deerskin.

TEXT 160

আজি হৈতে না পরিব এই চর্মাম্বর।
প্রভু বহির্বাস আনাইলা জানিয়া অন্তর ॥ ১৬০ ॥

āji haite nā pariba ei carmāmbara
prabhu bahirvāsa ānāilā jāniyā antara

āji haite—from today; *nā pariba*—I shall not put on; *ei*—this; *carma-ambara*—deerskin garment; *prabhu*—Śrī Caitanya Mahāprabhu; *bahir-vāsa*—the cloth of a *sannyāsī; ānāilā*—had someone bring; *jāniyā*—knowing; *antara*—his contemplation.

TRANSLATION

"From today on I shall not wear this deerskin." As soon as Brahmānanda Bhāratī decided this, Śrī Caitanya Mahāprabhu, understanding his mind, immediately sent for the robes of a sannyāsī.

TEXT 161

চর্মাম্বর ছাড়ি' ব্রহ্মানন্দ পরিল বসন ।
প্রভু আসি' কৈল তাঁর চরণ বন্দন ॥ ১৬১ ॥

carmāmbara chāḍi' brahmānanda parila vasana
prabhu āsi' kaila tāṅra caraṇa vandana

carma-ambara chāḍi'—giving up the deerskin garment; *brahmānanda*—Brahmānanda Bhāratī; *parila*—put on; *vasana*—cloth garment; *prabhu*—Śrī Caitanya Mahāprabhu; *āsi'*—coming; *kaila*—did; *tāṅra*—his; *caraṇa vandana*—worshiping the feet.

TRANSLATION

As soon as Brahmānanda Bhāratī gave up his deerskin and covered himself with sannyāsī robes, Śrī Caitanya Mahāprabhu came and offered His respects at his lotus feet.

TEXT 162

ভারতী কহে,—তোমার আচার লোক শিখাইতে ।
পুনঃ না করিবে নতি, ভয় পাঙ চিত্তে ॥ ১৬২ ॥

bhāratī kahe,—tomāra ācāra loka śikhāite
punaḥ nā karibe nati, bhaya pāṅa citte

bhāratī kahe—Brahmānanda Bhāratī said; *tomāra*—Your; *ācāra*— behavior; *loka*—people in general; *śikhāite*—to teach; *punaḥ*—again; *nā*—not; *karibe*—will do; *nati*—obeisances; *bhaya*—fear; *pāṅa*—I get; *citte*—within the mind.

TRANSLATION

Brahmānanda Bhāratī said, "You instruct the general populace by Your behavior. I will not do anything against Your wishes; otherwise You will not offer me respects but will neglect me. I am afraid of this.

TEXT 163

সাম্প্রতিক 'দুই ব্রহ্ম' ইহাঁ 'চলাচল'।
জগন্নাথ — অচল ব্রহ্ম, তুমি ত' সচল ॥ ১৬৩ ॥

sāmpratika 'dui brahma' ihāṅ 'calācala'
jagannātha—acala brahma, tumi ta' sacala

sāmpratika—at the present moment; *dui brahma*—two Brahmans, or spiritual identities; *ihāṅ*—here; *cala-acala*—moving and not moving; *jagannātha*—Lord Jagannātha; *acala brahma*—not moving Brahman; *tumi*—You; *ta'*—but; *sa-cala*—moving Brahman

TRANSLATION

"At the present moment I see two Brahmans. One Brahman is Lord Jagannātha, who does not move, and the other Brahman, who is moving, is You. Lord Jagannātha is the arcā-vigraha, the worshipable Deity, and it is He who is the nonmoving Brahman. But You are Lord Śrī Caitanya Mahāprabhu, and You are moving here and there. The two of You are the same Brahman, master of the material nature, but You are playing two parts—one moving and one not moving. In this way two Brahmans are now residing at Jagannātha Purī, Puruṣottama.

TEXT 164

তুমি — গৌরবর্ণ, তেঁহ — শ্যামলবরণ।
দুই ব্রহ্মে কৈল সব জগৎ-তারণ ॥ ১৬৪ ॥

tumi — gaura-varṇa, teṅha — śyāmala-varṇa
dui brahme kaila saba jagat-tāraṇa

tumi — You; *gaura-varṇa* — having a golden or fair complexion; *teṅha* — He; *śyāmala-varṇa* — having a blackish complexion; *dui brahme* — both Brahmans; *kaila* — performed; *saba jagat* — of the whole world; *tāraṇa* — deliverance.

TRANSLATION

"Of the two Brahmans, You are fair-complexioned, and the other, Lord Jagannātha, is blackish. Both of You are delivering the whole world."

TEXT 165

প্রভু কহে, — সত্য কহি, তোমার আগমনে।
দুই ব্রহ্ম প্রকটিল শ্রীপুরুষোত্তমে ॥ ১৬৫ ॥

prabhu kahe, — satya kahi, tomara āgamane
dui brahma prakaṭila śrī-puruṣottame

prabhu kahe — Lord Śrī Caitanya Mahāprabhu said; *satya kahi* — I speak the truth; *tomāra āgamane* — by your presence; *dui brahma* — two Brahmans; *prakaṭila* — appeared; *śrī-puruṣottame* — at Jagannātha Purī.

TRANSLATION

Lord Śrī Caitanya Mahāprabhu replied, "Actually, to tell you the truth, due to your presence there are now two Brahmans at Jagannātha Purī.

TEXT 166

'ব্রহ্মানন্দ' নাম তুমি — গৌর-ব্রহ্ম 'চল'।
শ্যামবর্ণ জগন্নাথ বসিয়াছেন 'অচল' ॥ ১৬৬ ॥

'brahmānanda' nāma tumi — gaura-brahma 'cala'
śyāma-varṇa jagannātha vasiyāchena 'acala'

brahmānanda — Brahmānanda; *nāma tumi* — your name; *gaura-brahma* — the Brahman of the name Gaura; *cala* — both of them are moving; *śyāma-varṇa*—of blackish hue; *jagannātha*—Lord Jagannātha; *vasiyāchena*—is sitting; *acala*—without movement.

TRANSLATION

"Both Brahmānanda and Gaurahari are moving, whereas the blackish Lord Jagannātha is sitting tight and immobile."

PURPORT

Brahmānanda Bhāratī wanted to prove that there is no difference between the Supreme Lord and the *jīva,* whereas Caitanya Mahāprabhu wanted to prove that He and Brahmānanda Bhāratī were *jīvas* and that although the *jīvas* are Brahman, they are many but the Supreme Lord, the Supreme Brahman, is one. On the other hand, Brahmānanda Bhāratī also wanted to prove that Jagannātha and Śrī Caitanya Mahāprabhu are one, the Supreme Personality of Godhead, but that to fulfill His mission Śrī Caitanya Mahāprabhu appeared to be moving whereas Lord Jagannātha appeared to be inert. Thus this jolly argument was going on. Finally, Brahmānanda Bhāratī referred the whole matter to Sārvabhauma Bhaṭṭācārya for a final decision.

TEXT 167

ভারতী কহে,—সার্বভৌম, মধ্যস্থ হঞা।
ইঁহার সনে আমার 'ন্যায়' বুঝ' মন দিয়া॥ ১৬৭॥

bhāratī kahe,—sārvabhauma, madhyastha hañā
iṅhāra sane āmāra 'nyāya' bujha' mana diyā

bhāratī kahe—Brahmānanda Bhāratī said; *sārvabhauma*—O Sārvabhauma Bhaṭṭācārya; *madhya-stha hañā*—becoming a mediator; *iṅhāra sane*—with Lord Śrī Caitanya Mahāprabhu; *āmāra*—my; *nyāya*—logic; *bujha'*—try to understand; *mana diyā*—with attention.

TRANSLATION

Brahmānanda Bhāratī said, "My dear Sārvabhauma Bhaṭṭācārya, please become the mediator in this logical argument between Śrī Caitanya Mahāprabhu and me."

TEXT 168

‘ব্যাপ্য’ ‘ব্যাপক’-ভাবে ‘জীব’-‘ব্রহ্মে’ জানি।
জীব — ব্যাপ্য, ব্রহ্ম — ব্যাপক, শাস্ত্রেতে বাখানি ॥ ১৬৮ ॥

‘vyāpya’ ‘vyāpaka’-bhāve ‘jīva’-‘brahme’ jāni
jīva — vyāpya, brahma — vyāpaka, śāstrete vākhāni

vyāpya—localized; *vyāpaka*—all-pervading; *bhāve*—in this way; *jīva*—living entity; *brahme*—the Supreme Lord; *jāni*—I know; *jīva*—the living entity; *vyāpya*—localized; *brahma*—the Supreme Lord; *vyāpaka*—all-pervading; *śāstrete*—in the revealed scripture; *vākhāni*—description.

TRANSLATION

Brahmānanda Bhāratī continued, “The living entity is localized, whereas the Supreme Brahman is all-pervading. That is the verdict of the revealed scriptures.

PURPORT

Brahmānanda Bhāratī drew Sārvabhauma Bhaṭṭācārya’s attention because he wanted him to judge the argument. He then stated that Brahman, the Supreme Lord, is all-pervading. This is confirmed by Lord Kṛṣṇa in the *Bhagavad-gītā* (13.3):

kṣetra-jñaṁ cāpi māṁ viddhi sarva-kṣetreṣu bhārata
kṣetra-kṣetrajñayor jñānaṁ yat taj jñānaṁ mataṁ mama

“O scion of Bharata, you should understand that I am also the knower in all bodies, and to understand this body and its knower is called knowledge. That is My opinion.”

The Supreme Personality of Godhead in His Paramātmā feature is expanded everywhere. The *Brahma-saṁhitā* says, *aṇḍāntara-stha-paramāṇu-cayāntara-stham:* by virtue of His all-pervasive nature, the Supreme Lord is within the universe as well as within all elements of the universe. He is even within the atom. In this way the Supreme Lord Govinda is all-pervasive. On the other hand, the living entities are very, very small. It is said that the living entity is one ten-thousandth of the tip of a hair. Therefore the living entity is localized.

Living entities rest on the Brahman effulgence, the bodily rays of the Supreme Personality of Godhead.

TEXT 169

চর্ম ঘুচাঞা কৈল আমারে শোধন ।
দোঁহার ব্যাপ্য-ব্যাপকত্বে এই ত' কারণ ॥ ১৬৯ ॥

carma ghucāñā kaila āmāre śodhana
doṅhāra vyāpya-vyāpakatve ei ta' kāraṇa

carma—deerskin; *ghucāñā*—taking away; *kaila*—did; *āmāre*—unto me; *śodhana*—purification; *doṅhāra*—of both of us; *vyāpya*—being localized; *vyāpakatve*—being all-pervasive; *ei*—this; *ta'*—indeed; *kāraṇa*—the cause.

TRANSLATION

"Śrī Caitanya Mahāprabhu purified me by taking away my deerskin. This is proof that He is all-pervasive and all-powerful and that I am subordinate to Him.

PURPORT

Brahmānanda Bhāratī herein asserts that Śrī Caitanya Mahāprabhu is the Supreme Brahman and that he is the subordinate Brahman. This is confirmed in the *Vedas: nityo nityānāṁ cetanaś cetanānām.* The Supreme Personality of Godhead is Brahman or Parambrahman, the chief of all living entities. Both the Supreme Brahman, or the Personality of Godhead, and the living entities are persons, but the Supreme Brahman is the predominator, whereas the living entities are predominated.

TEXT 170

সুবর্ণবর্ণো হেমাঙ্গো বরাঙ্গশ্চন্দনাঙ্গদী ।
সন্ন্যাসকৃচ্ছমঃ শান্তো নিষ্ঠা-শান্তি-পরায়ণঃ ॥ ১৭০ ॥

suvarṇa-varṇo hemāṅgo
varāṅgaś candanāṅgadī
sannyāsa-kṛc chamaḥ śānto
niṣṭhā-śānti-parāyaṇaḥ

suvarṇa—of gold; *varṇaḥ*—having the color; *hema-aṅgaḥ*—whose body was like molten gold; *vara-aṅgaḥ*—having a most beautiful body; *candana-aṅgadī*—whose body was smeared with sandalwood; *sannyāsa-kṛt*—practicing the renounced order of life; *śamaḥ*—equipoised; *śāntaḥ*—peaceful; *niṣṭhā*—of devotion; *śānti*—and of peace; *parāyaṇaḥ*—the highest resort.

TRANSLATION

"'His bodily hue is golden, and His whole body is like molten gold. Every part of His body is very beautifully constructed and smeared with sandalwood pulp. Accepting the renounced order, the Lord is always equipoised. He is firmly fixed in His mission of chanting the Hare Kṛṣṇa mantra, and He is firmly situated in His dualistic conclusion and in His peace.'

PURPORT

This is a quote from the *Mahābhārata's Viṣṇu-sahasra-nāma-stotra.*

TEXT 171

এই সব নামের ইঁহ হয় নিজাস্পদ।
চন্দনাক্ত প্রসাদ-ডোর — শ্রীভুজে অঙ্গদ ॥ ১৭১ ॥

ei saba nāmera iṅha haya nijāspada
candanākta prasāda-ḍora — śrī-bhuje aṅgada

ei saba—all these; *nāmera*—of names; *iṅha*—Śrī Caitanya Mahāprabhu; *haya*—is; *nija-āspada*—the reservoir; *candana-akta*—smeared with the pulp of sandalwood; *prasāda-ḍora*—the thread received from the Jagannātha temple; *śrī-bhuje*—on His arms; *aṅgada*—ornaments.

TRANSLATION

"All the symptoms mentioned in the verse from the Viṣṇu-sahasra-nāma-stotra are visible in the body of Śrī Caitanya Mahāprabhu. His arms are decorated with sandalwood pulp and the thread received from the Śrī Jagannātha Deity, and these are His ornamental bangles."

TEXT 172

ভট্টাচার্য কহে,—ভারতী, দেখি তোমার জয়।
প্রভু কহে,—যেই কহ, সেই সত্য হয়॥ ১৭২॥

bhaṭṭācārya kahe,—bhāratī, dekhi tomāra jaya
prabhu kahe,—yei kaha, sei satya haya

bhaṭṭācārya kahe—the Bhaṭṭācārya said; *bhāratī*—O Brahmānanda Bhāratī; *dekhi*—I see; *tomāra jaya*—your victory; *prabhu kahe*—Lord Caitanya Mahāprabhu said; *yei kaha*—whatever you say; *sei*—that; *satya*—true; *haya*—is.

TRANSLATION

After hearing this, Sārvabhauma Bhaṭṭācārya rendered his judgment, saying, "Brahmānanda Bhāratī, I see that you are victorious."

Śrī Caitanya Mahāprabhu immediately said, "I accept whatever Brahmānanda Bhāratī has said. It is quite all right with Me."

TEXT 173

গুরু-শিষ্য-ন্যায়ে সত্য শিষ্যের পরাজয়।
ভারতী কহে,—এহো নহে, অন্য হেতু হয়॥ ১৭৩॥

guru-śiṣya-nyāye satya śiṣyera parājaya
bhāratī kahe,—eho nahe, anya hetu haya

guru-śiṣya-nyāye—when there is a logical argument between the spiritual master and the disciple; *satya*—certainly; *śiṣyera*—of the disciple; *parājaya*—defeat; *bhāratī kahe*—Brahmānanda Bhāratī said; *eho nahe*—in this case it is not the fact; *anya hetu*—another cause; *haya*—there is.

TRANSLATION

Śrī Caitanya Mahāprabhu thus posed Himself as a disciple and accepted Brahmānanda Bhāratī as His spiritual master. He then said, "The disciple is certainly defeated in an argument with the spiritual master."

Brahmānanda Bhāratī immediately countered these words, saying, "This is not the cause of Your defeat. There is another cause.

TEXT 174

ভক্ত ঠাঞি হার' তুমি, — এ তোমার স্বভাব ।
আর এক শুন তুমি আপন প্রভাব ॥ ১৭৪ ॥

bhakta ṭhāñi hāra' tumi, — e tomāra svabhāva
āra eka śuna tumi āpana prabhāva

bhakta ṭhāñi — in the presence of a devotee; *hāra'* — become defeated; *tumi* — You; *e* — this; *tomāra* — Your; *svabhāva* — nature; *āra* — another; *eka* — one; *śuna* — hear; *tumi* — You; *āpana prabhāva* — Your own influence.

TRANSLATION

"It is Your natural characteristic to accept defeat at the hands of Your devotee. There is also another glory of Yours, which I ask You to hear attentively.

TEXT 175

আজন্ম করিনু মুঞি 'নিরাকার'-ধ্যান ।
তোমা দেখি' 'কৃষ্ণ' হৈল মোর বিদ্যমান ॥ ১৭৫ ॥

ājanma karinu muñi 'nirākāra'-dhyāna
tomā dekhi' 'kṛṣṇa' haila mora vidyamāna

ā-janma — since my birth; *karinu* — have done; *muñi* — I; *nirākāra-dhyāna* — meditation on impersonal Brahman; *tomā dekhi'* — by seeing You; *kṛṣṇa* — Lord Kṛṣṇa; *haila* — became; *mora* — my; *vidyamāna* — experience.

TRANSLATION

"I have been meditating on the impersonal Brahman since my birth, but since I have seen You, I have fully experienced Kṛṣṇa."

PURPORT

Brahmānanda Bhāratī admitted that when there is an argument between the spiritual master and the disciple, the spiritual master is naturally victorious, although the disciple may put forward a strong argument. In other words, it is customary that the words of the spiritual master are more worshipable than the words of a disciple. Under the circumstances, since Brahmānanda Bhāratī was in the position of a spiritual master, he emerged victorious over Śrī Caitanya Mahāprabhu, who considered Himself Brahmānanda Bhāratī's disciple. However, Brahmānanda Bhāratī reversed the argument and took the position of a devotee, stating that Śrī Caitanya Mahāprabhu was the Supreme Personality of Godhead, Kṛṣṇa. This means that the Lord was voluntarily defeated out of affection for His devotee. He was defeated voluntarily, because no one can defeat the Supreme Lord. Concerning this, the words of Bhīṣma in *Śrīmad-Bhāgavatam* (1.9.37) are important:

sva-nigamam apahāya mat-pratijñām
ṛtam adhikartum avapluto ratha-sthaḥ
dhṛta-ratha-caraṇo 'bhyayāc calad-gur
harir iva hantum ibhaṁ gatottarīyaḥ

"Fulfilling my desire and sacrificing His own promise, He got down from the chariot, took up its wheel and ran toward me hurriedly, just as a lion goes to kill an elephant. He even dropped His outer garment on the way."

Kṛṣṇa promised not to fight in the Battle of Kurukṣetra, but Bhīṣma, in order to break Kṛṣṇa's promise, attacked Arjuna in such a vigorous way that Kṛṣṇa was obliged to take up a chariot wheel and attack Bhīṣma. The Lord did this to show that His devotee was being maintained at the sacrifice of His own promise. Brahmānanda Bhāratī said, "Since the beginning of my life I was attached to impersonal Brahman realization, but as soon as I saw You, I became very much attached to the Personality of Godhead, Kṛṣṇa." Therefore Śrī Caitanya Mahāprabhu is Lord Kṛṣṇa Himself, and thus Brahmānanda Bhāratī became His devotee.

TEXT 176

কৃষ্ণনাম স্ফুরে মুখে, মনে নেত্রে কৃষ্ণ ।
তোমাকে তদ্রূপ দেখি' হৃদয় — সতৃষ্ণ ॥ ১৭৬ ॥

kṛṣṇa-nāma sphure mukhe, mane netre kṛṣṇa
tomāke tad-rūpa dekhi' hṛdaya—satṛṣṇa

kṛṣṇa-nāma—the holy name of Lord Kṛṣṇa; *sphure*—is manifest; *mukhe*—in the mouth; *mane*—in the mind; *netre*—before the eyes; *kṛṣṇa*—the presence of Lord Kṛṣṇa; *tomāke*—You; *tat-rūpa*—His form; *dekhi'*—I see; *hṛdaya*—my heart; *sa-tṛṣṇa*—very eager.

TRANSLATION

Brahmānanda Bhāratī continued, "Since I have seen You, I have been feeling Lord Kṛṣṇa's presence in my mind and have been seeing Him before my eyes. I now want to chant the holy name of Lord Kṛṣṇa. Over and above this, within my heart I consider You to be Kṛṣṇa, and I am therefore very eager to serve You.

TEXT 177

বিল্বমঙ্গল কৈল যৈছে দশা আপনার ।
ইহাঁ দেখি' সেই দশা হইল আমার ॥ ১৭৭ ॥

bilvamaṅgala kaila yaiche daśā āpanāra
ihāṅ dekhi' sei daśā ha-ila āmāra

bilvamaṅgala—Bilvamaṅgala; *kaila*—did; *yaiche*—as; *daśā*—condition; *āpanāra*—his own; *ihāṅ*—here; *dekhi'*—I see; *sei daśā*—that condition; *ha-ila*—became; *āmāra*—mine.

TRANSLATION

"Bilvamaṅgala Ṭhākura abandoned his impersonal realization for the realization of the Personality of Godhead. I now see that my condition is similar to his, for it has already changed."

PURPORT

In his early life, Bilvamaṅgala Ṭhākura was an impersonalistic monist, and he used to meditate upon the impersonal Brahman effulgence. Later he became a devotee of Lord Kṛṣṇa, and his explanation for this change is given in a verse (text 178) that is quoted in the *Bhakti-rasāmṛta-sindhu.* Sometimes a devotee gradually comes to the stage of Bhagavān realization, realization of the Supreme Person, after having attained the lower stages of realization—impersonal Brahman realization and localized Paramātmā realization. The condition of such a devotee is described in the *Caitanya-candrāmṛta* (5), by Prabodhānanda Sarasvatī:

kaivalyaṁ narakāyate tridaśa-pūr ākāśa-puṣpāyate
durdāntendriya-kāla-sarpa-paṭalī protkhāta-daṁṣṭrāyate
viśvaṁ pūrṇa-sukhāyate vidhi-mahendrādiś ca kīṭāyate
yat-kāruṇya-kaṭākṣa-vaibhava-vatāṁ taṁ gauram eva stumaḥ

Kaivalya, oneness in the effulgence of Brahman, appears hellish to the devotee. The heavenly planets, the abodes of the demigods, appear to a devotee like phantasmagoria. The *yogīs* meditate for sense control, but for the devotee the senses appear like serpents with broken teeth. The devotee doesn't have to control his senses, for his senses are already engaged in the Lord's service. Consequently there is no possibility that the senses will act like serpents. In the material condition, the senses are as strong as poisonous snakes. But when the senses are engaged in the Lord's service, they are like poisonous snakes with their fangs removed, and so they are no longer dangerous. The entire world is a replica of Vaikuṇṭha for the devotee because he has no anxiety. He sees that everything belongs to Kṛṣṇa, and he does not want to enjoy anything for himself. He does not even aspire for the position of Lord Brahmā or Indra. He simply wants to engage everything in the service of the Lord; therefore he has no problem. He stands in his original constitutional position. All this is possible when one receives Śrī Caitanya Mahāprabhu's merciful glance.

In the *Caitanya-candrāmṛta* there are many more verses illustrating this same principle.

dhik kurvanti ca brahma-yoga-viduṣas taṁ gauracandraṁ numaḥ
(*Caitanya-candrāmṛta* 6)

tāvad brahma-kathā vimukta-padavī tāvan na tiktī-bhavet
tāvac cāpi viśṛṅkhalatvam ayate no loka-veda-sthitiḥ
tāvac chāstra-vidāṁ mithaḥ kala-kalo nānā-bahir-vartmasu
śrī-caitanya-padāmbuja-priya-jano yāvan na dig-gocaraḥ
(*Caitanya-candrāmṛta* 19)

gauraś cauraḥ sakalam aharat ko 'pi me tīvra-vīryaḥ
(*Caitanya-candrāmṛta* 60)

A discussion of the impersonal Brahman is not very palatable to a devotee. The so-called regulations of the *śāstras* also appear null and void to him. There are many people who argue over the *śāstras*, but for a devotee such discussions are but tumultuous roaring. By the influence of Śrī Caitanya Mahāprabhu, all these problems disappear.

TEXT 178

অদ্বৈতবীথীপথিকৈরুপাস্যাঃ, স্বানন্দসিংহাসন-লব্ধদীক্ষাঃ।
শঠেন কেনাপি বয়ং হঠেন, দাসীকৃতা গোপবধূবিটেন॥ ১৭৮॥

advaita-vīthī-pathikair upāsyāḥ
svānanda-siṁhāsana-labdha-dīkṣāḥ
śaṭhena kenāpi vayaṁ haṭhena
dāsī-kṛtā gopa-vadhū-viṭena

advaita-vīthī—of the path of monism; *pathikaiḥ*—by the wanderers; *upāsyāḥ*—worshipable; *sva-ānanda*—of self-realization; *siṁha-āsana*—on the throne; *labdha-dīkṣāḥ*—being initiated; *śaṭhena*—by a cheater; *kena-api*—some; *vayam*—I; *haṭhena*—by force; *dāsī-kṛtā*—made into a maidservant; *gopa-vadhū-viṭena*—by a boy engaged in joking with the *gopīs.*

TRANSLATION

Brahmānanda Bhāratī concluded, "'Although I was worshiped by those on the path of monism and initiated into self-realization through the yoga system, I have nonetheless been forcibly turned into a maidservant by some cunning boy who is always joking with the gopīs.'"

PURPORT

This is a verse written by Bilvamaṅgala Ṭhākura. It is quoted in the *Bhakti-rasāmṛta-sindhu* (3.1.44).

TEXT 179

প্রভু কহে,—কৃষ্ণে তোমার গাঢ় প্রেমা হয়।
যাহাঁ নেত্র পড়ে, তাহাঁ শ্রীকৃষ্ণ স্ফুরয়॥ ১৭৯॥

prabhu kahe, — kṛṣṇe tomāra gāḍha premā haya
yāhāṅ netra paḍe, tāhāṅ śrī-kṛṣṇa sphuraya

prabhu kahe — Lord Śrī Caitanya Mahāprabhu replied; *kṛṣṇe* — unto Kṛṣṇa; *tomāra* — your; *gāḍha* — deep; *premā* — love; *haya* — there is; *yāhāṅ* — wherever; *netra* — eyes; *paḍe* — fall; *tāhāṅ* — there; *śrī-kṛṣṇa* — Lord Śrī Kṛṣṇa; *sphuraya* — becomes manifest.

TRANSLATION

Lord Śrī Caitanya Mahāprabhu replied, "You have a deep ecstatic love for Kṛṣṇa; therefore wherever you turn your eyes, you simply heighten your Kṛṣṇa consciousness."

TEXT 180

ভট্টাচার্য কহে, — দোঁহার সুসত্য বচন ।
আগে যদি কৃষ্ণ দেন সাক্ষাৎ দরশন ॥ ১৮০ ॥

bhaṭṭācārya kahe, — doṅhāra susatya vacana
āge yadi kṛṣṇa dena sākṣāt daraśana

bhaṭṭācārya kahe — Sārvabhauma Bhaṭṭācārya said; *doṅhāra* — of both; *su-satya* — correct; *vacana* — statements; *āge* — first; *yadi* — if; *kṛṣṇa* — Lord Kṛṣṇa; *dena* — gives; *sākṣāt* — direct; *daraśana* — audience.

TRANSLATION

Sārvabhauma Bhaṭṭācārya said, "The statements of both of you are correct. Kṛṣṇa gives direct audience through His mercy.

TEXT 181

প্রেম বিনা কভু নহে তাঁর সাক্ষাৎকার ।
ইঁহার কৃপাতে হয় দরশন ইঁহার ॥ ১৮১ ॥

prema vinā kabhu nahe tāṅra sākṣātkāra
iṅhāra kṛpāte haya daraśana iṅhāra

prema vinā — without ecstatic love; *kabhu nahe* — there is never; *tāṅra* — His; *sākṣātkāra* — direct meeting; *iṅhāra kṛpāte* — by the mercy of Śrī Caitanya Mahāprabhu; *haya*—becomes possible; *daraśana*—visit; *iṅhāra*—of Brahmānanda Bhāratī.

TRANSLATION

"Without having ecstatic love for Kṛṣṇa, one cannot see Him directly. Therefore through the mercy of Śrī Caitanya Mahāprabhu, Brahmānanda Bhāratī has acquired direct vision of the Lord."

PURPORT

Śrī Caitanya Mahāprabhu said, "You are Brahmānanda Bhāratī, an advanced devotee who ecstatically loves the Supreme Lord. Therefore you see Kṛṣṇa everywhere, and there is no doubt about it." Sārvabhauma Bhaṭṭācārya was a mediator between Śrī Caitanya Mahāprabhu and Brahmānanda Bhāratī, and his judgment was that an advanced devotee like Brahmānanda Bhāratī was seeing Kṛṣṇa by Kṛṣṇa's mercy. Kṛṣṇa directly presents Himself before the vision of an advanced devotee. Since Brahmānanda Bhāratī was an advanced devotee, he saw Kṛṣṇa in the person of Śrī Caitanya Mahāprabhu. In the words of the *Brahma-saṁhitā* (5.38):

premāñjana-cchurita-bhakti-vilocanena
santaḥ sadaiva hṛdayeṣu vilokayanti
yaṁ śyāmasundaram acintya-guṇa-svarūpaṁ
govindam ādi-puruṣaṁ tam ahaṁ bhajāmi

"I worship the primeval Lord, Govinda, who is always seen by the devotee whose eyes are anointed with the pulp of love. He is seen in His eternal form of Śyāmasundara, situated within the heart of the devotee."

TEXT 182

প্রভু কহে,—'বিষ্ণু' 'বিষ্ণু', কি কহ সার্বভৌম।
'অতিস্তুতি' হয় এই নিন্দার লক্ষণ ॥ ১৮২ ॥

prabhu kahe,—'viṣṇu' 'viṣṇu', ki kaha sārvabhauma
'ati-stuti' haya ei nindāra lakṣaṇa

prabhu kahe—Śrī Caitanya Mahāprabhu said; *viṣṇu viṣṇu*—Lord Viṣṇu, Lord Viṣṇu; *ki kaha*—what are you speaking; *sārvabhauma*—

Sārvabhauma Bhaṭṭācārya; *ati-stuti*—overly glorifying; *haya*—is; *ei*—this; *nindāra lakṣaṇa*—symptom of blasphemy.

TRANSLATION

Śrī Caitanya Mahāprabhu said, "Sārvabhauma Bhaṭṭācārya, what are you saying? Lord Viṣṇu, save Me! Such glorification is simply another form of blasphemy."

PURPORT

Śrī Caitanya Mahāprabhu was a little embarrassed by the Bhaṭṭācārya's statement; therefore He uttered the name Viṣṇu to save Himself. The Lord herein confirms that if one is overestimated, glorification is just another form of blasphemy. In this way He protests this so-called offensive statement.

TEXT 183

এত বলি' ভারতীরে লঞা নিজ-বাসা আইলা ।
ভারতী-গোসাঞি প্রভুর নিকটে রহিলা ॥ ১৮৩ ॥

eta bali' bhāratīre lañā nija-vāsā āilā
bhāratī-gosāñi prabhura nikaṭe rahilā

eta bali'—saying this; *bhāratīre*—Brahmānanda Bhāratī; *lañā*—taking with Him; *nija-vāsā āilā*—returned to His own residence; *bhāratī-gosāñi*—Brahmānanda Bhāratī; *prabhura nikaṭe*—in the shelter of Śrī Caitanya Mahāprabhu; *rahilā*—remained.

TRANSLATION

After saying this, Śrī Caitanya Mahāprabhu took Brahmānanda Bhāratī with Him to His residence. From that time on, Brahmānanda Bhāratī remained with Śrī Caitanya Mahāprabhu.

TEXT 184

রামভদ্রাচার্য, আর ভগবান্ আচার্য ।
প্রভু-পদে রহিলা দুঁহে ছাড়ি' সর্ব কার্য ॥ ১৮৪ ॥

rāmabhadrācārya, āra bhagavān ācārya
prabhu-pade rahilā duṅhe chāḍi' sarva kārya

rāmabhadra-ācārya—Rāmabhadra Ācārya; *āra*—and; *bhagavān-ācārya*—Bhagavān Ācārya; *prabhu-pade*—under the shelter of Śrī Caitanya Mahāprabhu; *rahilā*—remained; *duṅhe*—both of them; *chāḍi'*—giving up; *sarva kārya*—all other responsibilities.

TRANSLATION

Later, Rāmabhadra Ācārya and Bhagavān Ācārya joined them and, giving up all other responsibilities, remained under Śrī Caitanya Mahāprabhu's shelter.

TEXT 185

কাশীশ্বর গোসাঞি আইলা আর দিনে ।
সম্মান করিয়া প্রভু রাখিলা নিজ স্থানে ॥ ১৮৫ ॥

kāśīśvara gosāñi āilā āra dine
sammāna kariyā prabhu rākhilā nija sthāne

kāśīśvara gosāñi—Kāśīśvara Gosāñi, another devotee; *āilā*—came; *āra dine*—the next day; *sammāna kariyā*—giving all respect; *prabhu*—Lord Śrī Caitanya Mahāprabhu; *rākhilā*—kept; *nija sthāne*—at His own place.

TRANSLATION

The next day, Kāśīśvara Gosāñi also came and remained with Śrī Caitanya Mahāprabhu, who received him with great respect.

TEXT 186

প্রভুকে লঞা করা'ন ঈশ্বর দরশন ।
আগে লোক-ভিড় সব করি' নিবারণ ॥ ১৮৬ ॥

prabhuke lañā karā'na īśvara daraśana
āge loka-bhiḍa saba kari' nivāraṇa

prabhuke—Śrī Caitanya Mahāprabhu; *lañā*—taking; *karā'na*—helps in; *īśvara daraśana*—visiting Lord Jagannātha; *āge*—in front of; *loka-bhiḍa*—crowds of people; *saba*—all; *kari' nivāraṇa*—restraining.

TRANSLATION

Kāśīśvara used to usher Śrī Caitanya Mahāprabhu into the Jagannātha temple. He would precede the Lord into the crowd and keep the people from touching Him.

TEXT 187

যত নদ নদী যৈছে সমুদ্রে মিলয়।
ঐছে মহাপ্রভুর ভক্ত যাহাঁ তাহাঁ হয়॥ ১৮৭॥

yata nada nadī yaiche samudre milaya
aiche mahāprabhura bhakta yāhāṅ tāhāṅ haya

yata—all; *nada nadī*—rivers; *yaiche*—as; *samudre*—in the sea; *milaya*—meet; *aiche*—similarly; *mahāprabhura*—of Śrī Caitanya Mahāprabhu; *bhakta*—devotees; *yāhāṅ tāhāṅ*—wherever; *haya*—they were.

TRANSLATION

As all the rivers flow into the sea, all the devotees throughout the country finally came to Śrī Caitanya Mahāprabhu's shelter.

TEXT 188

সবে আসি' মিলিলা প্রভুর শ্রীচরণে।
প্রভু কৃপা করি' সবায় রাখিল নিজ স্থানে॥ ১৮৮॥

sabe āsi' mililā prabhura śrī-caraṇe
prabhu kṛpā kari' sabāya rākhila nija sthāne

sabe—all; *āsi'*—coming; *mililā*—met; *prabhura*—of Śrī Caitanya Mahāprabhu; *śrī-caraṇe*—under the shelter; *prabhu*—Śrī Caitanya Mahāprabhu; *kṛpā kari'*—showing mercy; *sabāya*—every one of them; *rākhila*—kept; *nija sthāne*—under His protection.

TRANSLATION

Since all the devotees came to Him for shelter, Lord Śrī Caitanya Mahāprabhu showed them all mercy and kept them under His protection.

TEXT 189

এই ত' কহিল প্রভুর বৈষ্ণব-মিলন।
ইহা যেই শুনে, পায় চৈতন্য-চরণ ॥ ১৮৯ ॥

ei ta' kahila prabhura vaiṣṇava-milana
ihā yei śune, pāya caitanya-caraṇa

ei ta'—thus; *kahila*—I have described; *prabhura*—of Lord Caitanya Mahāprabhu; *vaiṣṇava-milana*—meeting with all the Vaiṣṇavas; *ihā*—this narration; *yei*—anyone who; *śune*—hears; *pāya*—gets; *caitanya-caraṇa*—the shelter of the lotus feet of Śrī Caitanya Mahāprabhu.

TRANSLATION

Thus I have described the meeting of all the Vaiṣṇavas with Śrī Caitanya Mahāprabhu. Whoever hears this description ultimately attains shelter at His lotus feet.

TEXT 190

শ্রীরূপ-রঘুনাথ-পদে যার আশ।
চৈতন্যচরিতামৃত কহে কৃষ্ণদাস ॥ ১৯০ ॥

śrī-rūpa-raghunātha-pade yāra āśa
caitanya-caritāmṛta kahe kṛṣṇadāsa

śrī-rūpa—Śrīla Rūpa Gosvāmī; *raghunātha*—Śrīla Raghunātha dāsa Gosvāmī; *pade*—at the lotus feet; *yāra*—whose; *āśa*—expectation; *caitanya-caritāmṛta*—the book named *Caitanya-caritāmṛta; kahe*—describes; *kṛṣṇadāsa*—Śrīla Kṛṣṇadāsa Kavirāja Gosvāmī.

TRANSLATION

Praying at the lotus feet of Śrī Rūpa and Śrī Raghunātha, always desiring their mercy, I, Kṛṣṇadāsa, narrate Śrī Caitanya-caritāmṛta, following in their footsteps.

Thus end the Bhaktivedanta purports to Śrī Caitanya-caritāmṛta, Madhya-līlā, *Tenth Chapter, describing the Lord's meeting the Vaiṣṇavas upon His return to Jagannātha Purī from South India.*

CHAPTER ELEVEN

The Beḍā-kīrtana Pastimes of Śrī Caitanya Mahāprabhu

Śrīla Bhaktivinoda Ṭhākura summarizes the Eleventh Chapter in his *Amṛta-pravāha-bhāṣya.* When Sārvabhauma Bhaṭṭācārya tried his best to arrange a meeting between Śrī Caitanya Mahāprabhu and King Pratāparudra, the Lord flatly denied his request. At this time Śrī Rāmānanda Rāya returned from his governmental post, and he praised King Pratāparudra highly in Lord Caitanya's presence. Because of this, the Lord became a little soft. The King also made promises to Sārvabhauma Bhaṭṭācārya, who hinted how the King might meet the Lord. During Anavasara, while Lord Jagannātha was resting for fifteen days, Śrī Caitanya Mahāprabhu, being unable to see Lord Jagannātha, went to Ālālanātha. Later, when the devotees from Bengal came to see Him, He returned to Jagannātha Purī. While Advaita Ācārya and the other devotees were coming to Jagannātha Purī, Svarūpa Dāmodara and Govinda, Śrī Caitanya Mahāprabhu's two personal assistants, went to receive all the devotees with garlands. From the roof of his palace, King Pratāparudra could see all the devotees arriving. Gopīnātha Ācārya stood on the roof with the King, and, following Sārvabhauma Bhaṭṭācārya's instructions, identified each and every devotee. The King discussed the devotees with Gopīnātha Ācārya, and he mentioned that the devotees were accepting *prasādam* without observing the regulative principles governing pilgrimages. They accepted *prasādam* without having shaved, and they neglected to fast in a holy place. After Sārvabhauma Bhaṭṭācārya had explained to the King why the devotees had apparently violated the scriptural injunctions for visiting a place of pilgrimage, the King arranged residential quarters for all the devotees and saw to their *prasādam.* Śrī Caitanya Mahāprabhu talked very happily with Vāsudeva Datta and other devotees. Haridāsa Ṭhākura also came, and due to his humble and submissive attitude, Śrī Caitanya Mahāprabhu gave him a nice solitary place near the temple. After this, the Lord began performing *saṅkīrtana,* dividing all the devotees into four groups. After *saṅkīrtana,* all the devotees left for their residential quarters.

TEXT 1

অত্যুদ্দণ্ডং তাণ্ডবং গৌরচন্দ্রঃ
কুর্বন্ ভক্তৈঃ শ্রীজগন্নাথগেহে।
নানাভাবালঙ্কৃতাঙ্গঃ স্বধাম্না
চক্রে বিশ্বং প্রেমবন্যা-নিমগ্নম্ ॥ ১ ॥

aty-uddaṇḍaṁ tāṇḍavaṁ gauracandraḥ
kurvan bhaktaiḥ śrī-jagannātha-gehe
nānā-bhāvālaṅkṛtāṅgaḥ sva-dhāmnā
cakre viśvaṁ prema-vanyā-nimagnam

ati—very much; *uddaṇḍam*—high jumping; *tāṇḍavam*—very graceful dancing; *gaura-candraḥ*—Lord Śrī Caitanya Mahāprabhu; *kurvan*—performing; *bhaktaiḥ*—with the devotees; *śrī-jagannātha-gehe*—in the temple of Lord Jagannātha; *nānā-bhāva-alaṅkṛta-aṅgaḥ*—having many ecstatic symptoms manifested in His transcendental body; *sva-dhāmnā*—by the influence of His ecstatic love; *cakre*—made; *viśvam*—the whole world; *prema-vanyā-nimagnam*—merged into the inundation of ecstatic love.

TRANSLATION

Śrī Caitanya Mahāprabhu merged the entire world into the ocean of ecstatic love by performing His beautiful dances within the temple of Jagannātha. He danced exquisitely and jumped high.

TEXT 2

জয় জয় শ্রীচৈতন্য জয় নিত্যানন্দ।
জয়াদ্বৈতচন্দ্র জয় গৌরভক্তবৃন্দ ॥ ২ ॥

jaya jaya śrī-caitanya jaya nityānanda
jayādvaita-candra jaya gaura-bhakta-vṛnda

jaya jaya—all glories; *śrī-caitanya*—to Lord Caitanya; *jaya*—all glories; *nityānanda*—to Nityānanda Prabhu; *jaya*—all glories; *advaita-candra*—to Advaita Prabhu; *jaya*—all glories; *gaura-bhakta-vṛnda*—to the devotees of Lord Śrī Caitanya Mahāprabhu.

TRANSLATION

All glories to Lord Śrī Caitanya Mahāprabhu! All glories to Lord Nityānanda Prabhu! All glories to Śrī Advaita Prabhu! And all glories to all the devotees of Śrī Caitanya Mahāprabhu!

TEXT 3

আর দিন সার্বভৌম কহে প্রভুস্থানে।
অভয়-দান দেহ' যদি, করি নিবেদনে ॥ ৩ ॥

āra dina sārvabhauma kahe prabhu-sthāne
abhaya-dāna deha' yadi, kari nivedane

āra dina—the next day; *sārvabhauma*—Sārvabhauma Bhaṭṭācārya; *kahe*—says; *prabhu-sthāne*—in the presence of Lord Caitanya Mahāprabhu; *abhaya-dāna*—the charity of fearlessness; *deha'*—You give; *yadi*—if; *kari*—I do; *nivedane*—submission.

TRANSLATION

The next day Sārvabhauma Bhaṭṭācārya requested Lord Śrī Caitanya Mahāprabhu to give him permission to submit a statement without fear.

TEXT 4

প্রভু কহে,—কহ তুমি, নাহি কিছু ভয়।
যোগ্য হৈলে করিব, অযোগ্য হৈলে নয় ॥ ৪ ॥

prabhu kahe,—kaha tumi, nāhi kichu bhaya
yogya haile kariba, ayogya haile naya

prabhu kahe—Lord Śrī Caitanya Mahāprabhu said; *kaha tumi*—yes, you can speak; *nāhi*—there is not; *kichu*—any; *bhaya*—fear; *yogya*—befitting; *haile*—if it is; *kariba*—I shall grant; *ayogya*—not befitting; *haile*—if it is; *naya*—then I shall not.

TRANSLATION

The Lord gave the Bhaṭṭācārya assurance that he could speak without fear, but added that if his statement were suitable He would accept it, and if it were not, He would reject it.

TEXT 5

সার্বভৌম কহে — এই প্রতাপরুদ্র রায় ।
উৎকণ্ঠা হঞাছে, তোমা মিলিবারে চায় ॥ ৫ ॥

sārvabhauma kahe—ei pratāparudra rāya
utkaṇṭhā hañāche, tomā milibāre cāya

sārvabhauma kahe—Sārvabhauma Bhaṭṭācārya said; *ei*—this; *pratāparudra rāya*—King Pratāparudra of Jagannātha Purī; *utkaṇṭhā hañāche*—has been very anxious; *tomā*—You; *milibāre*—to meet; *cāya*—he wants.

TRANSLATION

Sārvabhauma Bhaṭṭācārya said, "There is a king named Pratāparudra Rāya. He is very anxious to meet You, and he wants Your permission."

TEXT 6

কর্ণে হস্ত দিয়া প্রভু স্মরে 'নারায়ণ' ।
সার্বভৌম, কহ কেন অযোগ্য বচন ॥ ৬ ॥

karṇe hasta diyā prabhu smare 'nārāyaṇa'
sārvabhauma, kaha kena ayogya vacana

karṇe—on the ears; *hasta*—hands; *diyā*—placing; *prabhu*—Śrī Caitanya Mahāprabhu; *smare*—remembers; *nārāyaṇa*—the holy name of Lord Nārāyaṇa; *sārvabhauma*—My dear Sārvabhauma; *kaha*—you say; *kena*—why; *ayogya vacana*—a request that is not suitable.

TRANSLATION

As soon as Śrī Caitanya Mahāprabhu heard this proposal, He immediately covered His ears with His hands and said, "My dear Sārvabhauma, why are you requesting such an undesirable thing from Me?

TEXT 7

বিরক্ত সন্ন্যাসী আমার রাজ-দরশন ।
স্ত্রী-দরশন-সম বিষের ভক্ষণ ॥ ৭ ॥

virakta sannyāsī āmāra rāja-daraśana
strī-daraśana-sama viṣera bhakṣaṇa

virakta—unattached; *sannyāsī*—person in the renounced order; *āmāra*—My; *rāja-daraśana*—meeting a king; *strī-daraśana*—meeting a woman; *sama*—like; *viṣera*—of poison; *bhakṣaṇa*—drinking.

TRANSLATION

"Since I am in the renounced order, it is as dangerous for Me to meet a king as to meet a woman. To meet either would be just like drinking poison."

TEXT 8

নিষ্কিঞ্চনস্য ভগবদ্ভজনোন্মুখস্য
পারং পরং জিগমিষোর্ভবসাগরস্য ।
সন্দর্শনং বিষয়িণামথ যোষিতাঞ্চ
হা হন্ত হন্ত বিষভক্ষণতোঽপ্যসাধু ॥ ৮ ॥

niṣkiñcanasya bhagavad-bhajanonmukhasya
pāraṁ paraṁ jigamiṣor bhava-sāgarasya
sandarśanaṁ viṣayiṇām atha yoṣitāṁ ca
hā hanta hanta viṣa-bhakṣaṇato 'py asādhu

niṣkiñcanasya—of a person who has completely detached himself from material enjoyment; *bhagavat*—the Supreme Personality of Godhead; *bhajana*—in serving; *unmukhasya*—who is eager to be engaged; *pāram*—to the other side; *param*—distant; *jigamiṣoḥ*—who is desiring to go; *bhava-sāgarasya*—of the ocean of material existence; *sandarśanam*—the seeing (for some material purpose); *viṣayiṇām*—of persons engaged in material activities; *atha*—as well as; *yoṣitām*—of women; *ca*—also; *hā*—alas; *hanta hanta*—expression of great lamentation; *viṣa-bhakṣaṇataḥ*—than the act of drinking poison; *api*—even; *asādhu*—more abominable.

TRANSLATION

Greatly lamenting, the Lord then informed Sārvabhauma Bhaṭṭācārya, "'Alas, for a person who is seriously desiring to cross the material ocean and engage in the transcendental loving service of the Lord without material motives, seeing a materialist engaged in sense gratification or seeing a woman who is similarly interested is more abominable than drinking poison willingly.'"

PURPORT

This is a quotation from *Śrī Caitanya-candrodaya-nāṭaka* (8.23). Thus Śrī Caitanya Mahāprabhu enunciates the principles for a *sannyāsī* renouncing the material world for spiritual advancement. Spiritual advancement is not meant for magic shows and jugglery but for crossing the material world and being transferred to the spiritual world. *Pāraṁ paraṁ jigamiṣoḥ* means desiring to go to the other side of the material world. There is a river called Vaitaraṇī, and on one side of this river is the material world, and on the other side is the spiritual world. Since the Vaitaraṇī River is compared to a great ocean, it is named *bhava-sāgara,* the ocean of repeated birth and death. Spiritual life aims at stopping this repetition of birth and death and entering into the spiritual world, where one can live eternally cognizant and blissful.

Unfortunately, the general populace does not know anything about spiritual life or the spiritual world. The spiritual world is mentioned in the *Bhagavad-gītā* (8.20):

paras tasmāt tu bhāvo 'nyo 'vyakto 'vyaktāt sanātanaḥ
yaḥ sa sarveṣu bhūteṣu naśyatsu na vinaśyati

"Yet there is another unmanifested nature, which is eternal and is transcendental to this manifested and unmanifested matter. It is supreme and is never annihilated. When all in this world is annihilated, that part remains as it is."

Thus there is a spiritual nature beyond this material world, and that spiritual nature exists eternally. Spiritual advancement means stopping material activities and entering into spiritual activities. This is the process of *bhakti-yoga.* In the material world, the via media for sense gratification is mainly a woman. One who is seriously interested in spiritual life should strictly avoid women. A *sannyāsī* should never see a man or a woman for material benefit. In addition, talks with materialistic men and women are also dangerous, and they are compared to drinking poison. Śrī Caitanya Mahāprabhu was very strict on this point. He therefore refused to see King Pratāparudra, who was naturally always engaged in political and economic affairs. The Lord even refused to see the King despite the request of a personality like Sārvabhauma Bhaṭṭācārya, who was the Lord's intimate friend and devotee.

TEXT 9

সার্বভৌম কহে, — সত্য তোমার বচন ।
জগন্নাথ-সেবক রাজা কিন্তু ভক্তোত্তম ॥ ৯ ॥

sārvabhauma kahe, — satya tomāra vacana
jagannātha-sevaka rājā kintu bhaktottama

sārvabhauma kahe — Sārvabhauma Bhaṭṭācārya replied; *satya* — true; *tomāra* — Your; *vacana* — statement; *jagannātha-sevaka* — servant of Lord Jagannātha; *rājā* — the King; *kintu* — but; *bhakta-uttama* — a great devotee.

TRANSLATION

Sārvabhauma Bhaṭṭācārya replied, "My dear Lord, what You have said is correct, but this King is not an ordinary king. He is a great devotee and servant of Lord Jagannātha."

TEXT 10

প্রভু কহে, — তথাপি রাজা কালসর্পাকার ।
কাষ্ঠনারী-স্পর্শে যৈছে উপজে বিকার ॥ ১০ ॥

prabhu kahe,—tathāpi rājā kāla-sarpākāra
kāṣṭha-nārī-sparśe yaiche upaje vikāra

prabhu kahe—Lord Śrī Caitanya Mahāprabhu replied; *tathāpi*—still; *rājā*—the King; *kāla-sarpa-ākāra*—just like a venomous snake; *kāṣṭha-nārī*—a woman made of wood; *sparśe*—by touching; *yaiche*—as; *upaje*—arises; *vikāra*—agitation.

TRANSLATION

Śrī Caitanya Mahāprabhu said, "Although it is correct that the King is a great devotee, he is still to be considered a venomous snake. Similarly, even though a woman be made of wood, one becomes agitated simply by touching her form.

PURPORT

Śrī Cāṇakya Paṇḍita has stated in his moral instructions: *tyaja durjana-saṁsargaṁ bhaja sādhu-samāgamam.* This means that one has to abandon the association of materialistic people and associate with spiritually advanced people. However qualified a materialist may be, he is no better than a venomous serpent. Everyone knows that a snake is dangerous and poisonous, and when its hood is decorated with jewels, it is no less poisonous or dangerous. However qualified a materialist may be, he is no better than a snake decorated with jewels. One should therefore be careful in dealing with such materialists, just as one would be careful in dealing with a bejeweled serpent.

Even though a woman be made of wood or stone, she becomes attractive when decorated. One becomes sexually agitated even by touching the form. Therefore one should not trust his mind, which is so fickle that it can give way to enemies at any moment. The mind is always accompanied by six enemies—namely, *kāma, krodha, mada, moha, mātsarya* and *bhaya*—that is, lust, anger, intoxication, illusion, envy and fear. Although the mind may be merged in spiritual consciousness, one should always be very careful in dealing with it, just as one is careful in dealing with a snake. One should never think that his mind is trained and that he can do whatever he likes. One interested in spiritual life should always engage his mind in the service of the Lord so that the enemies of the mind, who always accompany the mind, will be subdued. If the mind is not engaged in Kṛṣṇa consciousness at every moment, there is a chance that it will give way to its enemies. In this way we become victims of the mind.

Chanting the Hare Kṛṣṇa *mantra* engages the mind at the lotus feet of Kṛṣṇa constantly; thus the mind's enemies do not have a chance to strike. Following Śrī Caitanya Mahāprabhu's example in these verses, we should be very careful in dealing with the mind, which should not be indulged in any circumstance. Once we indulge the mind, it can create havoc in this life, even though we may be spiritually advanced. The mind is specifically agitated through the association of materialistic men and women. Therefore Śrī Caitanya Mahāprabhu, through His personal behavior, warns everyone to avoid meeting a materialistic person or a woman.

TEXT 11

আকারাদপি ভেতব্যং স্ত্রীণাং বিষয়িণামপি ।
যথাহের্মনসঃ ক্ষোভস্তথা তস্যাকৃতেরপি ॥ ১১ ॥

ākārād api bhetavyaṁ
strīṇāṁ viṣayiṇām api
yathāher manasaḥ kṣobhas
tathā tasyākṛter api

ākārāt—from bodily features; *api*—even; *bhetavyam*—to be feared; *strīṇām*—of women; *viṣayiṇām*—of materialistic persons; *api*—even; *yathā*—as; *aheḥ*—from a serpent; *manasaḥ*—of the mind; *kṣobhaḥ*—agitation; *tathā*—so; *tasya*—of it; *ākṛteḥ*—from the appearance; *api*—even.

TRANSLATION

"'Just as one is immediately frightened upon seeing a live serpent or even the form of a serpent, one endeavoring for self-realization should similarly fear a materialistic person and a woman. Indeed, he should not even glance at their bodily features.'

PURPORT

This is a quotation from *Śrī Caitanya-candrodaya-nāṭaka* (8.24).

TEXT 12

ঐছে বাত পুনরপি মুখে না আনিবে।
কহ যদি, তবে আমায় এথা না দেখিবে ॥ ১২ ॥

aiche bāta punarapi mukhe nā ānibe
kaha yadi, tabe āmāya ethā nā dekhibe

aiche bāta—such a request; *punarapi*—again; *mukhe*—in the mouth; *nā*—do not; *ānibe*—bring; *kaha yadi*—if you speak; *tabe*—then; *āmāya*—Me; *ethā*—here; *nā*—not; *dekhibe*—you will see.

TRANSLATION

"Bhaṭṭācārya, if you continue to speak like this, you will never see Me here again. Therefore you should never let such a request come from your mouth."

TEXT 13

ভয় পাঞা সার্বভৌম নিজ ঘরে গেলা।
বাসায় গিয়া ভট্টাচার্য চিন্তিত হইলা ॥ ১৩ ॥

bhaya pāñā sārvabhauma nija ghare gelā
vāsāya giyā bhaṭṭācārya cintita ha-ilā

bhaya pāñā—being afraid; *sārvabhauma*—Sārvabhauma; *nija*—own; *ghare*—to home; *gelā*—returned; *vāsāya giyā*—reaching his residential place; *bhaṭṭācārya*—the Bhaṭṭācārya; *cintita ha-ilā*—became meditative.

TRANSLATION

Being afraid, Sārvabhauma returned home and began to meditate on the matter.

TEXT 14

হেন কালে প্রতাপরুদ্র পুরুষোত্তমে আইলা ।
পাত্র-মিত্র-সঙ্গে রাজা দরশনে চলিলা ॥ ১৪ ॥

hena kāle pratāparudra puruṣottame āilā
pātra-mitra-saṅge rājā daraśane calilā

hena kāle—at this time; *pratāparudra*—King Pratāparudra; *puruṣottame*—at Jagannātha Purī; *āilā*—arrived; *pātra-mitra-saṅge*—accompanied by his secretaries, ministers, military officers and so on; *rājā*—the King; *daraśane*—to visit Lord Jagannātha; *calilā*—departed.

TRANSLATION

At this time, Mahārāja Pratāparudra arrived at Jagannātha Purī, Puruṣottama, and, accompanied by his secretaries, ministers and military officers, went to visit the temple of Lord Jagannātha.

PURPORT

It appears that Mahārāja Pratāparudra used to live at Kaṭaka, his capital. Later he shifted his capital to Khurdā, a few miles from Jagannātha Purī. Presently there is a railway station there called Khurdā Road.

TEXT 15

রামানন্দ রায় আইলা গজপতি-সঙ্গে ।
প্রথমেই প্রভুরে আসি' মিলিলা বহুরঙ্গে ॥ ১৫ ॥

rāmānanda rāya āilā gajapati-saṅge
prathamei prabhure āsi' mililā bahu-raṅge

rāmānanda rāya—Rāmānanda Rāya; *āilā*—came; *gajapati-saṅge*—with the King; *prathamei*—in the first instance; *prabhure*—unto Lord Caitanya Mahāprabhu; *āsi'*—coming; *mililā*—met; *bahu-raṅge*—with great pleasure.

TRANSLATION

When King Pratāparudra returned to Jagannātha Purī, Rāmānanda Rāya came with him. Rāmānanda Rāya immediately went to meet Śrī Caitanya Mahāprabhu with great pleasure.

PURPORT

All Indian kings are given titles. Sometimes they are known as Chatrapati, sometimes as Narapati, sometimes as Aśvapati, and so on. The King of Orissa is addressed as Gajapati.

TEXT 16

রায় প্রণতি কৈল, প্রভু কৈল আলিঙ্গন।
দুই জনে প্রেমাবেশে করেন ক্রন্দন ॥ ১৬ ॥

rāya praṇati kaila, prabhu kaila āliṅgana
dui jane premāveśe karena krandana

rāya praṇati kaila—Rāmānanda Rāya offered his obeisances; *prabhu*—the Lord; *kaila*—did; *āliṅgana*—embracing; *dui jane*—both of them; *prema-āveśe*—in ecstatic love; *karena*—did; *krandana*—crying.

TRANSLATION

Upon meeting Śrī Caitanya Mahāprabhu, Rāmānanda Rāya offered his obeisances. The Lord embraced him, and both of them began to cry in the great ecstasy of love.

TEXT 17

রায়-সঙ্গে প্রভুর দেখি' স্নেহ-ব্যবহার।
সর্ব ভক্তগণের মনে হৈল চমৎকার ॥ ১৭ ॥

rāya-saṅge prabhura dekhi' sneha-vyavahāra
sarva bhakta-gaṇera mane haila camatkāra

rāya-saṅge—with Rāmānanda Rāya; *prabhura*—of Śrī Caitanya Mahāprabhu; *dekhi'*—seeing; *sneha-vyavahāra*—very intimate behavior; *sarva*—all; *bhakta-gaṇera*—of all the devotees; *mane*—in the mind; *haila*—there was; *camatkāra*—astonishment.

TRANSLATION

Seeing Lord Śrī Caitanya Mahāprabhu's intimate dealings with Śrī Rāmānanda Rāya, all the devotees there were astonished.

TEXT 18

রায় কহে,—তোমার আজ্ঞা রাজাকে কহিল ।
তোমার ইচ্ছায় রাজা মোর বিষয় ছাড়াইল ॥ ১৮ ॥

rāya kahe,—tomāra ājñā rājāke kahila
tomāra icchāya rājā mora viṣaya chāḍāila

rāya kahe—Rāmānanda Rāya said; *tomāra ājñā*—Your order; *rājāke kahila*—I informed the King; *tomāra icchāya*—by Your grace; *rājā*—the King; *mora*—my; *viṣaya*—material activities; *chāḍāila*—gave me relief from.

TRANSLATION

Rāmānanda Rāya said, "I duly informed King Pratāparudra of Your order for me to retire from service. By Your grace, the King was pleased to relieve me of these material activities.

PURPORT

Śrī Caitanya Mahāprabhu requested Rāmānanda Rāya to retire from his governorship, and according to the Lord's desire, Rāmānanda Rāya petitioned the King. The King was very pleased to give him relief, and thus Rāmānanda Rāya retired from service and received a pension from the government.

TEXT 19

আমি কহি,—আমা হৈতে না হয় 'বিষয়' ।
চৈতন্যচরণে রহোঁ, যদি আজ্ঞা হয় ॥ ১৯ ॥

āmi kahi,—āmā haite nā haya 'viṣaya'
caitanya-caraṇe rahoṅ, yadi ājñā haya

āmi kahi—I said; *āmā haite*—by me; *nā*—not; *haya*—is possible; *viṣaya*—government service; *caitanya-caraṇe*—at the lotus feet of Śrī Caitanya Mahāprabhu; *rahoṅ*—I may stay; *yadi ājñā haya*—if you kindly give me permission.

TRANSLATION

"I said, 'Your Majesty, I am now not willing to engage in political activities. I desire only to stay at the lotus feet of Śrī Caitanya Mahāprabhu. Kindly give me permission.'

TEXT 20

তোমার নাম শুনি' রাজা আনন্দিত হৈল।
আসন হৈতে উঠি' মোরে আলিঙ্গন কৈল ॥ ২০ ॥

tomāra nāma śuni' rājā ānandita haila
āsana haite uṭhi' more āliṅgana kaila

tomāra—Your; *nāma*—name; *śuni'*—hearing; *rājā*—the King; *ānandita*—very pleased; *haila*—became; *āsana haite*—from his throne; *uṭhi'*—standing; *more*—me; *āliṅgana kaila*—embraced.

TRANSLATION

"When I submitted this proposal, the King immediately became very pleased upon hearing Your name. Indeed, he instantly rose from his throne and embraced me.

TEXT 21

তোমার নাম শুনি' হৈল মহা-প্রেমাবেশ।
মোর হাতে ধরি' করে পিরীতি বিশেষ ॥ ২১ ॥

tomāra nāma śuni' haila mahā-premāveśa
mora hāte dhari' kare pirīti viśeṣa

tomāra—Your; *nāma*—name; *śuni'*—hearing; *haila*—became; *mahā*—great; *prema-āveśa*—ecstasy of love; *mora hāte*—my hand; *dhari'*—catching; *kare*—does; *pirīti*—loving symptoms; *viśeṣa*—specific.

TRANSLATION

"My dear Lord, as soon as the King heard Your holy name, he was immediately overwhelmed by great ecstatic love. Catching my hand, he displayed all the symptoms of love.

TEXT 22

তোমার যে বর্তন, তুমি খাও সেই বর্তন।
নিশ্চিন্ত হঞা ভজ চৈতন্যের চরণ ॥ ২২ ॥

tomāra ye vartana, tumi khāo sei vartana
niścinta hañā bhaja caitanyera caraṇa

tomāra—Your; *ye*—whatever; *vartana*—remuneration; *tumi*—you; *khāo*—take; *sei*—that; *vartana*—pension; *niścinta hañā*—without anxiety; *bhaja*—just worship; *caitanyera*—of Lord Śrī Caitanya Mahāprabhu; *caraṇa*—the lotus feet.

TRANSLATION

"As soon as he heard my petition, he immediately granted me a pension without reductions. Thus the King granted me a full salary as a pension and requested me to engage without anxiety in the service of Your lotus feet.

TEXT 23

আমি—ছার, যোগ্য নহি তাঁর দরশনে।
তাঁরে যেই ভজে তাঁর সফল জীবনে ॥ ২৩ ॥

āmi—chāra, yogya nahi tāṅra daraśane
tāṅre yei bhaje tāṅra saphala jīvane

āmi—I; *chāra*—very much fallen; *yogya*—fit; *nahi*—not; *tāṅra*—His; *daraśane*—for interviewing; *tāṅre*—Him; *yei*—anyone who; *bhaje*—worships; *tāṅra*—his; *saphala*—successful; *jīvane*—life.

TRANSLATION

"Then Mahārāja Pratāparudra very humbly said, 'I am most fallen and abominable, and I am unfit to receive an interview with the Lord. One's life is successful if one engages in His service.'

TEXT 24

পরম কৃপালু তেঁহ ব্রজেন্দ্রনন্দন।
কোন-জন্মে মোরে অবশ্য দিবেন দরশন ॥ ২৪ ॥

parama kṛpālu teṅha vrajendra-nandana
kona-janme more avaśya dibena daraśana

parama—very; *kṛpālu*—merciful; *teṅha*—Lord Caitanya Mahāprabhu; *vrajendra-nandana*—the son of Mahārāja Nanda; *kona-janme*—in some future birth; *more*—unto me; *avaśya*—certainly; *dibena*—will give; *daraśana*—interview.

TRANSLATION

"The King then said, 'Śrī Caitanya Mahāprabhu is Kṛṣṇa, the son of Mahārāja Nanda. He is very merciful, and I hope that in a future birth He will allow me an interview.'

TEXT 25

যে তাঁহার প্রেম-আর্তি দেখিলুঁ তোমাতে।
তার এক প্রেম-লেশ নাহিক আমাতে ॥ ২৫ ॥

ye tāṅhāra prema-ārti dekhiluṅ tomāte
tāra eka prema-leśa nāhika āmāte

ye—whatever; *tāṅhāra*—his; *prema-ārti*—painful feelings of love of Godhead; *dekhiluṅ*—I saw; *tomāte*—unto You; *tāra*—of that; *eka*—one; *prema-leśa*—fraction of love; *nāhika*—there is not; *āmāte*—in me.

TRANSLATION

"My Lord, I don't think that there is even a fraction of Mahārāja Pratāparudra's loving ecstasy in me."

TEXT 26

প্রভু কহে, — তুমি কৃষ্ণ-ভকতপ্রধান ।
তোমাকে যে প্রীতি করে, সেই ভাগ্যবান্ ॥ ২৬ ॥

prabhu kahe, — tumi kṛṣṇa-bhakata-pradhāna
tomāke ye prīti kare, sei bhāgyavān

prabhu kahe — Lord Śrī Caitanya Mahāprabhu said; *tumi* — you; *kṛṣṇa-bhakata-pradhāna* — the chief of the devotees of Lord Kṛṣṇa; *tomāke* — unto you; *ye* — anyone who; *prīti kare* — shows love; *sei* — such a person; *bhāgyavān* — most fortunate.

TRANSLATION

Śrī Caitanya Mahāprabhu then said, "My dear Rāmānanda Rāya, you are the foremost of all the devotees of Kṛṣṇa; therefore whoever loves you is certainly a very fortunate person.

TEXT 27

তোমাতে যে এত প্রীতি হইল রাজার ।
এই গুণে কৃষ্ণ তাঁরে করিবে অঙ্গীকার ॥ ২৭ ॥

tomāte ye eta prīti ha-ila rājāra
ei guṇe kṛṣṇa tāṅre karibe aṅgīkāra

tomāte — unto you; *ye* — that; *eta* — so much; *prīti* — love; *ha-ila* — was; *rājāra* — of the King; *ei guṇe* — for this reason; *kṛṣṇa* — Lord Kṛṣṇa; *tāṅre* — him; *karibe aṅgīkāra* — will accept.

TRANSLATION

"Because the King has shown so much love for you, Lord Kṛṣṇa will certainly accept him.

PURPORT

King Pratāparudra requested an interview with Śrī Caitanya Mahāprabhu through the Bhaṭṭācārya, who duly submitted the request. The Lord, however, immediately refused this interview. Now when Rāmānanda Rāya informed the Lord how eager the King was to see Him, the Lord was immediately pleased. Śrī Caitanya Mahāprabhu requested Rāmānanda Rāya to retire from his government post and come to Śrī Puruṣottama-kṣetra (Jagannātha Purī) to live with Him. When this proposal was submitted to King Pratāparudra, he immediately accepted it and also encouraged Rāmānanda Rāya by allowing him a full pension. This was very much appreciated by the Lord, and this confirms the fact that the Lord is more pleased when one serves the servant of the Lord. In ordinary parlance it is said, "If you love me, love my dog." To approach the Supreme Personality of Godhead, one has to go through His confidential servant. This is the method. Śrī Caitanya Mahāprabhu clearly says, "Because the King loves you, Rāmānanda Rāya, he is very fortunate. Kṛṣṇa will certainly accept him due to his love for you."

TEXT 28

যে মে ভক্তজনাঃ পার্থ ন মে ভক্তাশ্চ তে জনাঃ ।
মদ্ভক্তানাঞ্চ যে ভক্তাস্তে মে ভক্ততমা মতাঃ ॥ ২৮ ॥

ye me bhakta-janāḥ pārtha
na me bhaktāś ca te janāḥ
mad-bhaktānāṁ ca ye bhaktās
te me bhakta-tamā matāḥ

ye—those who; *me*—My; *bhakta-janāḥ*—devotees; *pārtha*—O Pārtha; *na*—not; *me*—My; *bhaktāḥ*—devotees; *ca*—and; *te*—those; *janāḥ*—persons; *mat-bhaktānām*—of My devotees; *ca*—certainly; *ye*—those who; *bhaktāḥ*—devotees; *te*—such persons; *me*—My; *bhakta-tamāḥ*—most advanced devotees; *matāḥ*—that is My opinion.

TRANSLATION

"[Lord Kṛṣṇa told Arjuna:] 'Those who are My direct devotees are actually not My devotees, but those who are the devotees of My servant are factually My devotees.'

PURPORT

Śrī Caitanya Mahāprabhu quotes this verse from the *Ādi Purāṇa.* The verse is also included in the *Laghu-bhāgavatāmṛta* (2.6).

TEXTS 29–30

আদরঃ পরিচর্যায়াং সর্বাঙ্গৈরভিবন্দনম্ ।
মদ্ভক্তপূজাভ্যধিকা সর্বভূতেষু মন্মতিঃ ॥ ২৯ ॥
মদর্থেষ্বঙ্গচেষ্টা চ বচসা মদ্গুণেরণম্ ।
ময্যর্পণঞ্চ মনসঃ সর্বকামবিবর্জনম্ ॥ ৩০ ॥

ādaraḥ paricaryāyāṁ
sarvāṅgair abhivandanam
mad-bhakta-pūjābhyadhikā
sarva-bhūteṣu man-matiḥ

mad-artheṣv aṅga-ceṣṭā ca
vacasā mad-guṇeraṇam
mayy arpaṇaṁ ca manasaḥ
sarva-kāma-vivarjanam

ādaraḥ—respect, care; *paricaryāyām*—in service; *sarva-aṅgaiḥ*—by all the parts of the body; *abhivandanam*—offering obeisances; *mat-bhakta*—of My devotees; *pūjā*—worshiping; *abhyadhikā*—very high; *sarva-bhūteṣu*—in all living entities; *mat-matiḥ*—realization of having a relationship with Me; *mat-artheṣu*—for the sake of My service; *aṅga-ceṣṭāḥ*—engaging the bodily energy; *ca*—and; *vacasā*—by words; *mat-guṇa-īraṇam*—describing My glories; *mayi*—unto Me; *arpaṇam*—dedicating; *ca*—and; *manasaḥ*—of the mind; *sarva-kāma*—all material desires; *vivarjanam*—giving up.

TRANSLATION

"'My devotees take great care and respect in rendering Me service. They offer obeisances to Me with all their bodily limbs. They worship other devotees and find all living entities related to Me. For Me they engage the entire energy of their bodies. They engage the power of speech in the glorification of My qualities and form. They also dedicate

their minds unto Me and try to give up all kinds of material desires. Thus My devotees are characterized.'

PURPORT

These two verses are quoted from *Śrīmad-Bhāgavatam* (11.19.21–22). They were spoken by the Supreme Personality of Godhead, Lord Kṛṣṇa, who was answering Uddhava's inquiry about devotional service.

TEXT 31

আরাধনানাং সর্বেষাং বিষ্ণোরারাধনং পরম্ ।
তস্মাৎ পরতরং দেবি তদীয়ানাং সমর্চনম্ ॥ ৩১ ॥

ārādhanānāṁ sarveṣāṁ
viṣṇor ārādhanaṁ param
tasmāt paratараṁ devi
tadīyānāṁ samarcanam

ārādhanānām—of varieties of worship; *sarveṣām*—all; *viṣṇoh*—of Lord Viṣṇu; *ārādhanam*—worship; *param*—the most exalted; *tasmāt*—and above such worship of Lord Viṣṇu; *parataram*—of greater value; *devi*—O goddess; *tadīyānām*—of persons in relationship with Lord Viṣṇu; *samarcanam*—rigid and firm worship.

TRANSLATION

"[Lord Śiva told the goddess Durgā:] 'My dear Devī, although the Vedas recommend worship of demigods, the worship of Lord Viṣṇu is topmost. However, above the worship of Lord Viṣṇu is the rendering of service to Vaiṣṇavas, who are related to Lord Viṣṇu.'

PURPORT

The *Vedas* are divided into three divisions—*karma-kāṇḍa, jñāna-kāṇḍa* and *upāsanā-kāṇḍa.* These are activities dealing with fruitive work, empiric philosophical speculation and worship. There are recommendations in the *Vedas* for the worship of various demigods as well as Lord Viṣṇu. In this quotation from the *Padma Purāṇa,* Lord Śiva answers a question posed to him by goddess Durgā. This verse is also included in the *Laghu-bhāgavatāmṛta* (2.4), by Śrīla Rūpa Gosvāmī. The words *viṣṇor ārādhanam* refer to the worship of Lord Viṣṇu, or Kṛṣṇa. Thus the supreme form of worship is the satisfaction of the Supreme Personality of Godhead, Śrī Kṛṣṇa. It is further concluded that the worshiper of Lord Viṣṇu renders better service by worshiping the devotee of Lord Kṛṣṇa. There are different types of devotees—those in *śānta-rasa, dāsya-rasa, sakhya-rasa, vātsalya-rasa* and *mādhurya-rasa.* Although all the *rasas* are on the transcendental platform, *mādhurya-rasa* is the supreme transcendental mellow. Consequently it is concluded that the worship of devotees engaged in the Lord's service in *mādhurya-rasa* is the supreme spiritual activity. Śrī Caitanya Mahāprabhu and His followers mainly worship Lord Kṛṣṇa in *mādhurya-rasa.* Other Vaiṣṇava *ācāryas* recommended worship up to *vātsalya-rasa.* Therefore Śrīla Rūpa Gosvāmī in his *Vidagdha-mādhava* (1.2) describes Śrī Caitanya Mahāprabhu's cult as supreme:

anarpita-carīṁ cirāt karuṇayāvatīrṇaḥ kalau
samarpayitum unnatojjvala-rasāṁ sva-bhakti-śriyam

Śrī Caitanya Mahāprabhu appeared in this Age of Kali to exhibit the superexcellence of *mādhurya-rasa,* a gift never previously bestowed by any *ācārya* or incarnation. Consequently Śrī Caitanya Mahāprabhu is accepted as the most magnanimous incarnation. It is He only who distributed love of Kṛṣṇa while exhibiting the superexcellence of loving Kṛṣṇa in the conjugal *rasa.*

TEXT 32

দুরাপা হ্যল্পতপসঃ সেবা বৈকুণ্ঠবর্ত্মসু।
যত্রোপগীয়তে নিত্যং দেবদেবো জনার্দনঃ ॥ ৩২ ॥

durāpā hy alpa-tapasaḥ
sevā vaikuṇṭha-vartmasu
yatropagīyate nityaṁ
deva-devo janārdanaḥ

durāpā—very difficult to achieve; *hi*—certainly; *alpa-tapasaḥ*—by a person not advanced in spiritual life; *sevā*—service; *vaikuṇṭha-vartmasu*—unto persons on the path back home, back to Godhead;

yatra—wherein; *upagīyate*—is worshiped and glorified; *nityam*—regularly; *deva-devaḥ*—the Supreme Personality of Godhead; *janārdanaḥ*—Lord Kṛṣṇa.

TRANSLATION

"'Those whose austerity is meager can hardly obtain the service of the pure devotees progressing on the path back to the kingdom of Godhead, the Vaikuṇṭhas. Pure devotees engage one hundred percent in glorifying the Supreme Lord, who is the Lord of the demigods and the controller of all living entities.'"

PURPORT

This verse is a quotation from *Śrīmad-Bhāgavatam* (3.7.20). It was spoken by Vidura in his conversation with Maitreya Ṛṣi, a great devotee of the Lord.

TEXT 33

পুরী, ভারতী-গোসাঞি, স্বরূপ, নিত্যানন্দ।
জগদানন্দ, মুকুন্দাদি যত ভক্তবৃন্দ ॥ ৩৩ ॥

purī, bhāratī-gosāñi, svarūpa, nityānanda
jagadānanda, mukundādi yata bhakta-vṛnda

purī—Paramānanda Purī; *bhāratī*—Brahmānanda Bhāratī; *gosāñi*—on the level of the spiritual master; *svarūpa*—Svarūpa Dāmodara Gosvāmī; *nityānanda*—Lord Nityānanda Prabhu; *jagadānanda*—Jagadānanda; *mukunda*—Mukunda; *ādi*—and others; *yata*—all; *bhakta-vṛnda*—devotees of Śrī Caitanya Mahāprabhu.

TRANSLATION

Paramānanda Purī, Brahmānanda Bhāratī Gosāñi, Svarūpa Dāmodara Gosāñi, Lord Nityānanda, Jagadānanda, Mukunda and others were present before the Lord at that time.

TEXT 34

চারি গোসাঞির কৈল রায় চরণ বন্দন ।
যথাযোগ্য সব ভক্তের করিল মিলন ॥ ৩৪ ॥

cāri gosāñira kaila rāya caraṇa vandana
yathā-yogya saba bhaktera karila milana

cāri gosāñira—of the four *gosāñis,* or spiritual masters; *kaila*—did; *rāya*—Rāmānanda Rāya; *caraṇa vandana*—worshiping the lotus feet; *yathā-yogya*—as it is befitting; *saba*—all; *bhaktera*—of the devotees; *karila*—did; *milana*—meeting.

TRANSLATION

Śrī Rāmānanda Rāya therefore offered his obeisances to all the Lord's devotees, in particular to the four spiritual masters. Thus Rāmānanda Rāya suitably met all the devotees.

PURPORT

The four spiritual masters referred to in this verse are Paramānanda Purī, Brahmānanda Bhāratī, Svarūpa Dāmodara and Lord Nityānanda.

TEXT 35

প্রভু কহে,—রায়, দেখিলে কমলনয়ন ?
রায় কহে—এবে যাই পাব দরশন ॥ ৩৫ ॥

prabhu kahe,—rāya, dekhile kamala-nayana?
rāya kahe,—ebe yāi pāba daraśana

prabhu kahe—the Lord said; *rāya*—My dear Rāmānanda Rāya; *dekhile*—have you seen; *kamala-nayana*—the lotus-eyed Lord Jagannātha; *rāya kahe*—Rāmānanda Rāya replied; *ebe yāi*—now I shall go; *pāba daraśana*—I shall visit the temple.

TRANSLATION

Śrī Caitanya Mahāprabhu next asked Rāmānanda Rāya, "Have you already visited the temple of the lotus-eyed Lord Jagannātha?"

Rāmānanda Rāya replied, "I shall now go visit the temple."

TEXT 36

প্রভু কহে,—রায়, তুমি কি কার্য করিলে ?
ঈশ্বরে না দেখি' কেনে আগে এথা আইলে ? ৩৬ ॥

prabhu kahe,—rāya, tumi ki kārya karile?
īśvare nā dekhi' kene āge ethā āile?

prabhu kahe—Śrī Caitanya Mahāprabhu said; *rāya*—My dear Rāmānanda Rāya; *tumi*—you; *ki kārya*—what; *karile*—have done; *īśvare*—the Supreme Personality of Godhead; *nā dekhi'*—without seeing; *kene*—why; *āge*—first; *ethā*—here; *āile*—you came.

TRANSLATION

Śrī Caitanya Mahāprabhu replied, "What have you done, My dear Rāya? Why did you not first see Lord Jagannātha and then come here? Why have you come here first?"

TEXT 37

রায় কহে, চরণ—রথ, হৃদয়—সারথি।
যাহাঁ লঞা যায়, তাহাঁ যায় জীব-রথী ॥ ৩৭ ॥

rāya kahe, caraṇa—ratha, hṛdaya—sārathi
yāhāṅ lañā yāya, tāhāṅ yāya jīva-rathī

rāya kahe—Rāmānanda Rāya replied; *caraṇa*—the legs; *ratha*—chariot; *hṛdaya*—the heart; *sārathi*—chariot driver; *yāhāṅ*—wherever; *lañā*—taking; *yāya*—goes; *tāhāṅ*—there; *yāya*—goes; *jīva-rathī*—the living entity on the chariot.

TRANSLATION

Rāmānanda Rāya said, "The legs are like the chariot, and the heart is like the charioteer. Wherever the heart takes the living entity, the living entity is obliged to go."

PURPORT

In the *Bhagavad-gītā* (18.61) Lord Kṛṣṇa explains:

īśvaraḥ sarva-bhūtānāṁ hṛd-deśe 'rjuna tiṣṭhati
bhrāmayan sarva-bhūtāni yantrārūḍhāni māyayā

"The Supreme Lord is situated in everyone's heart, O Arjuna, and is directing the wanderings of all living entities, who are seated as on a machine made of material energy."

Thus the living entity wanders within this universe riding upon a chariot (the body) bestowed by material nature. A similar explanation is given in the *Kaṭha Upaniṣad* (1.3.3–4):

ātmānaṁ rathinaṁ viddhi śarīraṁ ratham eva tu
buddhiṁ tu sārathiṁ viddhi manaḥ pragraham eva ca
indriyāṇi hayān āhur viṣayāṁs teṣu gocarān
ātmendriya-mano-yuktaṁ bhoktety āhur manīṣiṇaḥ

Here it is said that the living entity is the passenger riding in the chariot of the body, which is offered by material nature. The intelligence is the charioteer, the mind constitutes the reins controlling the horses, and the senses are the horses. Thus the living entity is the false enjoyer of the material world.

One who is advanced in Kṛṣṇa consciousness can control the mind and intelligence and in this way rein in the horses, the senses, even though they are very powerful. One who can control the senses by his mind and intelligence can very easily approach the Supreme Personality of Godhead, or Viṣṇu, who is the ultimate goal of life. *Tad viṣṇoḥ paramaṁ padaṁ sadā paśyanti sūrayaḥ.* Those who are actually advanced approach Lord Viṣṇu, their ultimate goal. Such people are never captivated by Lord Viṣṇu's external energy, the material world.

TEXT 38

আমি কি করিব, মন ইহাঁ লঞা আইল ।
জগন্নাথ-দরশনে বিচার না কৈল ॥ ৩৮ ॥

āmi ki kariba, mana ihāṅ lañā āila
jagannātha-daraśane vicāra nā kaila

āmi—I; *ki*—what; *kariba*—shall do; *mana*—my mind; *ihāṅ*—here; *lañā*—taking; *āila*—arrived; *jagannātha-daraśane*—to see Lord Jagannātha; *vicāra*—consideration; *nā*—did not; *kaila*—make.

TRANSLATION

Śrī Rāmānanda Rāya continued, "What shall I do? My mind has brought me here. I could not consider going first to Lord Jagannātha's temple."

TEXT 39

প্রভু কহে, —শীঘ্র গিয়া কর দরশন।
ঐছে ঘর যাই' কর কুটুম্ব মিলন ॥ ৩৯ ॥

prabhu kahe,—śīghra giyā kara daraśana
aiche ghara yāi' kara kuṭumba milana

prabhu kahe—Lord Śrī Caitanya Mahāprabhu said; *śīghra giyā*—going hastily; *kara daraśana*—see Lord Jagannātha; *aiche*—similarly; *ghara yāi'*—going home; *kara*—just do; *kuṭumba*—family; *milana*—meeting.

TRANSLATION

Śrī Caitanya Mahāprabhu advised, "Immediately go to Lord Jagannātha's temple to see the Lord. Then go home and meet your family members."

TEXT 40

প্রভু আজ্ঞা পাঞা রায় চলিলা দরশনে।
রায়ের প্রেমভক্তি-রীতি বুঝে কোন্ জনে ॥ ৪০ ॥

prabhu ājñā pāñā rāya calilā daraśane
rāyera prema-bhakti-rīti bujhe kon jane

prabhu ājñā—the Lord's permission; *pāñā*—getting; *rāya*—Rāmānanda Rāya; *calilā*—departed; *daraśane*—to see Lord Jagannātha; *rāyera*—of Rāmānanda Rāya; *prema-bhakti*—of ecstatic love for Kṛṣṇa; *rīti*—process; *bujhe*—understands; *kon jane*—what person.

TRANSLATION

Having received Śrī Caitanya Mahāprabhu's permission, Rāmānanda Rāya hastily went to the temple of Lord Jagannātha. Who can understand the devotional service of Rāya Rāmānanda?

TEXT 41

ক্ষেত্রে আসি' রাজা সার্বভৌমে বোলাইলা।
সার্বভৌমে নমস্করি' তাঁহারে পুছিলা ॥ ৪১ ॥

kṣetre āsi' rājā sārvabhaume bolāilā
sārvabhaume namaskari' tāṅhāre puchilā

kṣetre—to Jagannātha Purī; *āsi'*—coming; *rājā*—the King; *sārvabhaume*—for Sārvabhauma Bhaṭṭācārya; *bolāilā*—called; *sārvabhaume*—unto Sārvabhauma Bhaṭṭācārya; *namaskari'*—offering obeisances; *tāṅhāre puchilā*—he asked him.

TRANSLATION

When King Pratāparudra returned to Jagannātha Purī, he called for Sārvabhauma Bhaṭṭācārya. When the Bhaṭṭācārya went to see the King, the King offered him respects and made the following inquiries.

TEXT 42

মোর লাগি' প্রভুপদে কৈলে নিবেদন ?
সার্বভৌম কহে,—কৈনু অনেক যতন ॥ ৪২ ॥

mora lāgi' prabhu-pade kaile nivedana?
sārvabhauma kahe,—kainu aneka yatana

mora lāgi'—on my behalf; *prabhu-pade*—at the lotus feet of the Lord; *kaile nivedana*—did you submit my petition; *sārvabhauma kahe*—Sārvabhauma replied; *kainu*—I did; *aneka yatana*—much endeavor.

TRANSLATION

The King asked, "Have you submitted my petition to the Lord?"

Sārvabhauma replied, "Yes, with much endeavor I have tried my best.

TEXT 43

তথাপি না করে তেঁহ রাজ-দরশন।
ক্ষেত্র ছাড়ি' যাবেন পুনঃ যদি করি নিবেদন ॥ ৪৩ ॥

tathāpi nā kare teṅha rāja-daraśana
kṣetra chāḍi' yābena punaḥ yadi kari nivedana

tathāpi—yet; *nā kare*—does not do; *teṅha*—He; *rāja-daraśana*—visiting a king; *kṣetra chāḍi'*—leaving Jagannātha-kṣetra; *yābena*—He will go away; *punaḥ*—again; *yadi*—if; *kari nivedana*—I request.

TRANSLATION

"Yet despite my great endeavor, the Lord would not agree to see a king. Indeed, He said that if He were asked again, He would quit Jagannātha Purī and go elsewhere."

TEXT 44

শুনিয়া রাজার মনে দুঃখ উপজিল ।
বিষাদ করিয়া কিছু কহিতে লাগিল ॥ ৪৪ ॥

śuniyā rājāra mane duḥkha upajila
viṣāda kariyā kichu kahite lāgila

śuniyā—hearing; *rājāra*—of the King; *mane*—in the mind; *duḥkha*—unhappiness; *upajila*—arose; *viṣāda*—lamentation; *kariyā*—doing; *kichu*—something; *kahite*—to speak; *lāgila*—began.

TRANSLATION

Hearing this, the King became very unhappy and, greatly lamenting, began to speak as follows.

TEXT 45

পাপী নীচ উদ্ধারিতে তাঁর অবতার ।
জগাই মাধাই তেঁহ করিলা উদ্ধার ॥ ৪৫ ॥

pāpī nīca uddhārite tāṅra avatāra
jagāi mādhāi teṅha karilā uddhāra

pāpī—sinful; *nīca*—lowborn; *uddhārite*—to deliver; *tāṅra*—His; *avatāra*—incarnation; *jagāi*—Jagāi; *mādhāi*—Mādhāi; *teṅha*—He; *karilā uddhāra*—delivered.

TRANSLATION

The King said, "Śrī Caitanya Mahāprabhu has descended just to deliver all kinds of sinful, lowborn persons. Consequently He has delivered sinners like Jagāi and Mādhāi.

TEXT 46

প্রতাপরুদ্র ছাড়ি' করিবে জগৎ নিস্তার।
এই প্রতিজ্ঞা করি' করিয়াছেন অবতার ? ৪৬॥

pratāparudra chāḍi' karibe jagat nistāra
ei pratijñā kari' kariyāchena avatāra?

pratāparudra chāḍi'—except for Pratāparudra; *karibe*—He will do; *jagat*—of the whole universe; *nistāra*—deliverance; *ei pratijñā*—this promise; *kari'*—making; *kariyāchena*—has made; *avatāra*—incarnation.

TRANSLATION

"Alas, has Śrī Caitanya Mahāprabhu incarnated to deliver all kinds of sinners with the exception of a king named Mahārāja Pratāparudra?

PURPORT

Śrī Caitanya Mahāprabhu's mission is thus described by Narottama dāsa Ṭhākura: *patita-pāvana-hetu tava avatāra/ mo-sama patita prabhu nā pāibe āra.* If Śrī Caitanya Mahāprabhu descended to reclaim sinners, then one who is the most sinful and lowborn is the first candidate for the Lord's consideration. Mahārāja Pratāparudra considered himself a most fallen soul because he had to deal with material things constantly and enjoy material profits. Śrī Caitanya Mahāprabhu's business was the deliverance of the most fallen. How, then, could He reject the King? The more fallen a person is, the more he has the right to be delivered by the Lord—provided, of course, he surrenders unto the Lord. Mahārāja Pratāparudra was a fully surrendered soul; therefore the Lord could not refuse him on the grounds that he was a worldly pounds-shillings man.

TEXT 47

অদর্শনীয়ানপি নীচজাতীন্
সংবীক্ষতে হন্ত তথাপি নো মাম্।
মদেকবর্জ্জং কৃপয়িষ্যতীতি
নির্ণীয় কিং সোঽবততার দেবঃ ॥ ৪৭ ॥

adarśanīyān api nīca-jātīn
saṁvīkṣate hanta tathāpi no mām
mad-eka-varjaṁ kṛpayiṣyatīti
nirṇīya kiṁ so 'vatatāra devaḥ

adarśanīyān—upon those who are unfit to be seen; *api*—although; *nīca-jātīn*—the lower class of men; *saṁvīkṣate*—puts His merciful glance; *hanta*—alas; *tathā api*—still; *na u*—not; *mām*—upon me; *mat*—myself; *eka*—alone; *varjam*—rejecting; *kṛpayiṣyati*—He will bestow His mercy; *iti*—thus; *nirṇīya*—deciding; *kim*—whether; *saḥ*—Lord Śrī Caitanya Mahāprabhu; *avatatāra*—has descended; *devaḥ*—the Supreme Personality of Godhead.

TRANSLATION

"'Alas, has Śrī Caitanya Mahāprabhu made His advent deciding that He will deliver all others with the exception of me? He bestows His merciful glance upon many lower-class men who are usually not even to be seen.'"

PURPORT

This verse is found in the *Śrī Caitanya-candrodaya-nāṭaka* (8.28).

TEXT 48

তাঁর প্রতিজ্ঞা — মোরে না করিবে দরশন।
মোর প্রতিজ্ঞা — তাঁহা বিনা ছাড়িব জীবন ॥ ৪৮ ॥

tāṅra pratijñā — more nā karibe daraśana
mora pratijñā — tāṅhā vinā chāḍiba jīvana

tāṅra pratijñā—His determination; *more*—unto me; *nā*—not; *karibe*—will do; *daraśana*—seeing; *mora pratijñā*—my promise; *tāṅhā vinā*—without Him; *chāḍiba*—I will give up; *jīvana*—life.

TRANSLATION

Mahārāja Pratāparudra continued, "If Śrī Caitanya Mahāprabhu is determined not to see me, then I am determined to give up my life if I do not see Him.

PURPORT

A devotee with Mahārāja Pratāparudra's determination will certainly be victorious in advancing in Kṛṣṇa consciousness. Śrī Kṛṣṇa confirms this in the *Bhagavad-gītā* (9.14):

satataṁ kīrtayanto māṁ yatantaś ca dṛḍha-vratāḥ
namasyantaś ca māṁ bhaktyā nitya-yuktā upāsate

"Always chanting My glories, endeavoring with great determination, bowing down before Me, these great souls perpetually worship Me with devotion."

These are the symptoms of a *mahātmā* engaged in the Lord's service in full Kṛṣṇa consciousness. Thus Mahārāja Pratāparudra's determination is very much exalted and is called *dṛḍha-vrata.* Because of this determination, he was finally able to receive Lord Caitanya's direct mercy.

TEXT 49

যদি সেই মহাপ্রভুর না পাই কৃপা-ধন ।
কিবা রাজ্য, কিবা দেহ, —সব অকারণ ॥ ৪৯ ॥

yadi sei mahāprabhura nā pāi kṛpā-dhana
kibā rājya, kibā deha,—saba akāraṇa

yadi—if; *sei*—that; *mahāprabhura*—of Lord Śrī Caitanya Mahāprabhu; *nā*—not; *pāi*—I get; *kṛpā-dhana*—the treasure of mercy; *kibā rājya*—what is the value of my kingdom; *kibā deha*—what is the value of this body; *saba akāraṇa*—everything useless.

TRANSLATION

"If I do not receive Śrī Caitanya Mahāprabhu's mercy, my body and my kingdom are certainly useless."

PURPORT

This is an excellent example of *dṛḍha-vrata,* determination. If one does not receive the Supreme Personality of Godhead's mercy, one's life is defeated. In *Śrīmad-Bhāgavatam* (5.5.5) it is said: *parābhavas tāvad abodha-jāto yāvan na jijñāsata ātma-tattvam.* Unless one inquires into spiritual life, everything is useless. Without spiritual inquiry, our labor and the object of our labor are simply a waste of time.

TEXT 50

এত শুনি' সার্বভৌম হইলা চিন্তিত ।
রাজার অনুরাগ দেখি' হইলা বিস্মিত ॥ ৫০ ॥

eta śuni' sārvabhauma ha-ilā cintita
rājāra anurāga dekhi' ha-ilā vismita

eta śuni'—hearing this; *sārvabhauma*—Sārvabhauma; *ha-ilā*—became; *cintita*—very thoughtful; *rājāra*—of the King; *anurāga*—attachment; *dekhi'*—seeing; *ha-ilā*—became; *vismita*—astonished.

TRANSLATION

Hearing King Pratāparudra's determination, Sārvabhauma Bhaṭṭācārya became thoughtful. Indeed, he was very much astonished to see the King's determination.

PURPORT

Sārvabhauma Bhaṭṭācārya was astonished because such determination is not possible for a worldly man attached to material enjoyment. The King certainly had ample opportunity for material enjoyment, but he was thinking that his kingdom and everything else was useless if he could not see Śrī Caitanya Mahāprabhu. This is certainly sufficient cause for astonishment. In *Śrīmad-Bhāgavatam* it is stated that *bhakti,* devotional service, must be unconditional. No material impediments can actually check the advancement of devotional service, be it executed by a common man or a king. In any case, devotional service rendered to the Lord is always complete, despite the devotee's material position. Devotional service is so exalted that it can be executed by anyone in any position. One must simply be *dṛḍha-vrata,* firmly determined.

TEXT 51

ভট্টাচার্য কহে — দেব না কর বিষাদ ।
তোমারে প্রভুর অবশ্য হইবে প্রসাদ ॥ ৫১ ॥

bhaṭṭācārya kahe — deva nā kara viṣāda
tomāre prabhura avaśya ha-ibe prasāda

bhaṭṭācārya kahe — the Bhaṭṭācārya said; *deva* — O King; *nā kara viṣāda* — do not be worried; *tomāre* — unto you; *prabhura* — of Lord Śrī Caitanya Mahāprabhu; *avaśya* — certainly; *ha-ibe* — there must be; *prasāda* — mercy.

TRANSLATION

Finally Sārvabhauma Bhaṭṭācārya said, "My dear King, do not worry. Because of your firm determination, I am sure that Śrī Caitanya Mahāprabhu's mercy will definitely be bestowed upon you."

PURPORT

Due to King Pratāparudra's firm determination, the Bhaṭṭācārya predicted that the King would receive Śrī Caitanya Mahāprabhu's mercy without fail. As confirmed elsewhere in *Caitanya-caritāmṛta* (*Madhya* 19.151), *guru-kṛṣṇa-prasāde pāya bhakti-latā-bīja:* "By the mercy of the spiritual master and Kṛṣṇa, one gets the seed of devotional service." The Bhaṭṭācārya was the spiritual master of King Pratāparudra, and he gave his blessings to the effect that the Lord would be merciful upon the King. The mercy of the spiritual master and Kṛṣṇa combine to grant success to a devotee engaged in Kṛṣṇa consciousness. This is confirmed by the *Vedas:*

yasya deve parā bhaktir yathā deve tathā gurau
tasyaite kathitā hy arthāḥ prakāśante mahātmanaḥ

"Only unto those great souls who have implicit faith in both the Lord and the spiritual master are all the imports of Vedic knowledge automatically revealed." (*Śvetāśvatara Upaniṣad* 6.23)

Mahārāja Pratāparudra had firm faith in the Bhaṭṭācārya, who declared Śrī Caitanya Mahāprabhu to be the Supreme Personality of Godhead. Having firm faith in the Bhaṭṭācārya as his spiritual master, King Pratāparudra immediately accepted Śrī Caitanya Mahāprabhu as the Supreme Lord. Thus he began worshiping Śrī Caitanya Mahāprabhu in his mind. This is the process of devotional service. According to Lord Kṛṣṇa in the *Bhagavad-gītā* (9.34):

man-manā bhava mad-bhakto mad-yājī māṁ namaskuru
mām evaiṣyasi yuktvaivam ātmānaṁ mat-parāyaṇaḥ

"Engage your mind always in thinking of Me, become My devotee, offer obeisances to Me and worship Me. Being completely absorbed in Me, surely you will come to Me."

This process is very simple. One need only be firmly convinced by the spiritual master that Kṛṣṇa is the Supreme Personality of Godhead. If one decides this, he can make further progress by thinking of Kṛṣṇa, chanting of Kṛṣṇa and glorifying Him. There is then no doubt that such a fully surrendered devotee will receive the blessings of Lord Kṛṣṇa. Śrīla Sārvabhauma Bhaṭṭācārya explains this further.

TEXT 52

তেঁহ — প্রেমাধীন, তোমার প্রেম — গাঢ়তর।
অবশ্য করিবেন কৃপা তোমার উপর ॥ ৫২ ॥

teṅha — premādhīna, tomāra prema — gāḍhatara
avaśya karibena kṛpā tomāra upara

teṅha — He (Śrī Caitanya Mahāprabhu); *prema-adhīna* — under the control of love; *tomāra prema* — your love; *gāḍha-tara* — very deep; *avaśya* — certainly; *karibena kṛpā* — He will bestow mercy; *tomāra upara* — upon you.

TRANSLATION

As soon as the Bhaṭṭācārya saw the King's firm determination, he declared, "The Supreme Lord is approached only by pure love.

Your love for Śrī Caitanya Mahāprabhu is very, very deep; therefore without a doubt He will be merciful upon you."

PURPORT

Such determination is the first qualification. As confirmed by Rūpa Gosvāmī (*Upadeśāmṛta* 3): *utsāhān niścayād dhairyāt.* One must first have firm determination, firm faith. When one engages in devotional service, he must maintain this firm determination. Then Kṛṣṇa will be pleased with his service. The spiritual master can show the path of devotional service. If the disciple follows the principles rigidly and undeviatingly, he will certainly receive the mercy of Kṛṣṇa. This is confirmed by the *śāstras.*

TEXT 53

তথাপি কহিয়ে আমি এক উপায়।
এই উপায় কর' প্রভু দেখিবে যাহায় ॥ ৫৩ ॥

tathāpi kahiye āmi eka upāya
ei upāya kara' prabhu dekhibe yāhāya

tathāpi—still; *kahiye*—say; *āmi*—I; *eka upāya*—one means; *ei upāya*—this means; *kara'*—try to adopt; *prabhu*—Lord Śrī Caitanya Mahāprabhu; *dekhibe*—will see you; *yāhāya*—by that.

TRANSLATION

Sārvabhauma Bhaṭṭācārya then suggested, "There is one means by which you can directly see Him.

TEXT 54

রথযাত্রা-দিনে প্রভু সব ভক্ত লঞা।
রথ-আগে নৃত্য করিবেন প্রেমাবিষ্ট হঞা ॥ ৫৪ ॥

ratha-yātrā-dine prabhu saba bhakta lañā
ratha-āge nṛtya karibena premāviṣṭa hañā

ratha-yātrā-dine—on the day of the car festival ceremony; *prabhu*—Śrī Caitanya Mahāprabhu; *saba*—all; *bhakta*—devotees; *lañā*—taking with Him; *ratha*—the car; *āge*—in front of; *nṛtya karibena*—will dance; *prema-āviṣṭa hañā*—in great ecstatic love.

TRANSLATION

"On the day of the car festival, Śrī Caitanya Mahāprabhu will dance before the Deity in great ecstatic love.

TEXT 55

প্রেমাবেশে পুষ্পোদ্যানে করিবেন প্রবেশ।
সেইকালে একলে তুমি ছাড়ি' রাজবেশ ॥ ৫৫ ॥

premāveśe puṣpodyāne karibena praveśa
sei-kāle ekale tumi chāḍi' rāja-veśa

prema-āveśe—in ecstatic love; *puṣpa-udyāne*—into the garden at Guṇḍicā where the Lord stays; *karibena praveśa*—will enter; *sei-kāle*—at that time; *ekale*—alone; *tumi*—you; *chāḍi'*—giving up; *rāja-veśa*—the royal dress.

TRANSLATION

"On that Ratha-yātrā festival day, after dancing before the Lord, Śrī Caitanya Mahāprabhu will enter the Guṇḍicā garden. At that time you should go there alone, without your royal dress.

TEXT 56

'কৃষ্ণ-রাসপঞ্চাধ্যায়' করিতে পঠন।
একলে যাই' মহাপ্রভুর ধরিবে চরণ ॥ ৫৬ ॥

'kṛṣṇa-rāsa-pañcādhyāya' karite paṭhana
ekale yāi' mahāprabhura dharibe caraṇa

kṛṣṇa-rāsa-pañca-adhyāya—the five chapters in the Tenth Canto of *Śrīmad-Bhāgavatam* in which Lord Kṛṣṇa's pastimes of the *rāsa* dance are described; *karite paṭhana*—to recite; *ekale yāi'*—going alone; *mahāprabhura*—of Lord Śrī Caitanya Mahāprabhu; *dharibe caraṇa*—catch hold of the lotus feet.

TRANSLATION

"When Śrī Caitanya Mahāprabhu enters the Guṇḍicā garden, you should also go there and read the five chapters of Śrīmad-Bhāgavatam about Lord Kṛṣṇa's dancing with the gopīs. In this way you can catch hold of the Lord's lotus feet.

TEXT 57

বাহ্যজ্ঞান নাহি, সে-কালে কৃষ্ণনাম শুনি' ।
আলিঙ্গন করিবেন তোমায় 'বৈষ্ণব' জানি' ॥ ৫৭ ॥

bāhya-jñāna nāhi, se-kāle kṛṣṇa-nāma śuni,
āliṅgana karibena tomāya 'vaiṣṇava' 'jāni'

bāhya-jñāna nāhi—without external consciousness; *se-kāle*—at that time; *kṛṣṇa-nāma śuni'*—by hearing the holy name of Lord Kṛṣṇa; *āliṅgana karibena*—He will embrace; *tomāya*—you; *vaiṣṇava jāni'*—taking you to be a Vaiṣṇava.

TRANSLATION

"Lord Śrī Caitanya Mahāprabhu will be in a mood of ecstatic love, without external consciousness. At that time, as you recite those chapters from Śrīmad-Bhāgavatam, He will embrace you, knowing you to be a pure Vaiṣṇava.

PURPORT

A Vaiṣṇava is always ready to help another Vaiṣṇava progress toward realization of the Absolute Truth. Sārvabhauma Bhaṭṭācārya could understand the King's position as a pure Vaiṣṇava. The King was always thinking of Śrī Caitanya Mahāprabhu, and the Bhaṭṭācārya wanted to help him approach the Lord. A Vaiṣṇava is always compassionate, especially when he sees a prospective devotee very determined (*dṛḍha-vrata*). Consequently the Bhaṭṭācārya was ready to help the King.

TEXT 58

রামানন্দ রায়, আজি তোমার প্রেম-গুণ ।
প্রভু-আগে কহিতে প্রভুর ফিরি' গেল মন ॥ ৫৮ ॥

rāmānanda rāya, āji tomāra prema-guṇa
prabhu-āge kahite prabhura phiri' gela mana

rāmānanda rāya—Rāmānanda Rāya; *āji*—today; *tomāra*—your; *prema-guṇa*—quality of love; *prabhu-āge*—in front of the Lord; *kahite*—when he described; *prabhura*—of Lord Śrī Caitanya Mahāprabhu; *phiri' gela*—became changed; *mana*—the mind.

TRANSLATION

"The Lord has already changed His mind due to Rāmānanda Rāya's description of your pure love for Him."

PURPORT

At first the Lord did not want to see the King, but due to the Bhaṭṭācārya's and Rāmānanda Rāya's earnest endeavors, the Lord's mind was changed. The Lord already declared that Kṛṣṇa would be merciful upon the King due to the King's service to the devotees. This is the process by which one can advance in Kṛṣṇa consciousness. First there must be the devotee's mercy; then Kṛṣṇa's mercy will descend. *Yasya prasādād bhagavat-prasādo/ yasyāprasādān na gatiḥ kuto 'pi.* Our first duty, therefore, is to satisfy the spiritual master, who can arrange for the Lord's mercy. A common man must first begin to serve the spiritual master, or the devotee. Then, through the mercy of the devotee, the Lord will be satisfied. Unless one receives the dust of a devotee's lotus feet on one's head, there is no possibility of advancement. This is also confirmed by a statement of Prahlāda Mahārāja's in *Śrīmad-Bhāgavatam* (7.5.32):

naiṣāṁ matis tāvad urukramāṅghriṁ
spṛśaty anarthāpagamo yad-arthaḥ
mahīyasāṁ pāda-rajo-'bhiṣekaṁ
niṣkiñcanānāṁ na vṛṇīta yāvat

Unless one approaches a pure devotee, he cannot understand the Supreme Personality of Godhead. Mahārāja Pratāparudra worshiped both Rāmānanda Rāya and Sārvabhauma Bhaṭṭācārya. Thus he touched the lotus feet of pure devotees and was able thereby to approach Śrī Caitanya Mahāprabhu.

TEXT 59

শুনি' গজপতির মনে সুখ উপজিল ।
প্রভুরে মিলিতে এই মন্ত্রণা দৃঢ় কৈল ॥ ৫৯ ॥

śuni' gajapatira mane sukha upajila
prabhure milite ei mantraṇā dṛḍha kaila

śuni'—hearing; *gajapatira*—of King Pratāparudra; *mane*—in the mind; *sukha*—happiness; *upajila*—awakened; *prabhure*—Śrī Caitanya Mahāprabhu; *milite*—to meet; *ei*—this; *mantraṇā*—instruction; *dṛḍha kaila*—decided to accept rigidly.

TRANSLATION

Mahārāja Pratāparudra took the Bhaṭṭācārya's advice and firmly decided to follow his instructions. Thus he felt transcendental happiness.

TEXT 60

স্নানযাত্রা কবে হবে পুছিল ভট্টেরে ।
ভট্ট কহে,—তিন দিন আছয়ে যাত্রারে ॥ ৬০ ॥

snāna-yātrā kabe habe puchila bhaṭṭere
bhaṭṭa kahe,—tina dina āchaye yātrāre

snāna-yātrā—the bathing ceremony of Lord Jagannātha; *kabe*—when; *habe*—will be; *puchila*—he inquired; *bhaṭṭere*—from the Bhaṭṭācārya; *bhaṭṭa kahe*—the Bhaṭṭācārya said; *tina dina*—three days; *āchaye*—there are still; *yātrāre*—until the festival.

TRANSLATION

When the King asked the Bhaṭṭācārya when the bathing ceremony [Snāna-yātrā] of Lord Jagannātha would take place, the Bhaṭṭācārya replied that there were only three days left before the ceremony.

TEXT 61

রাজারে প্রবোধিয়া ভট্ট গেলা নিজালয় ।
স্নানযাত্রা-দিনে প্রভুর আনন্দ হৃদয় ॥ ৬১ ॥

rājāre prabodhiyā bhaṭṭa gelā nijālaya
snāna-yātrā-dine prabhura ānanda hṛdaya

rājāre—the King; *prabodhiyā*—encouraging; *bhaṭṭa*—Sārvabhauma Bhaṭṭācārya; *gelā*—departed; *nija-ālaya*—to his own home; *snāna-yātrā-dine*—on the day of the bathing ceremony of Lord Jagannātha; *prabhura*—of Śrī Caitanya Mahāprabhu; *ānanda*—full of happiness; *hṛdaya*—heart.

TRANSLATION

After thus encouraging the King, Sārvabhauma Bhaṭṭācārya returned home. On the day of Lord Jagannātha's bathing ceremony, Śrī Caitanya Mahāprabhu was very happy at heart.

TEXT 62

স্নানযাত্রা দেখি' প্রভুর হৈল বড় সুখ।
ঈশ্বরের 'অনবসরে' পাইল বড় দুঃখ ॥ ৬২ ॥

snāna-yātrā dekhi' prabhura haila baḍa sukha
īśvarera 'anavasare' pāila baḍa duḥkha

snāna-yātrā—the bathing ceremony of Lord Jagannātha; *dekhi'*—seeing; *prabhura*—of Lord Śrī Caitanya Mahāprabhu; *haila*—became; *baḍa*—very much; *sukha*—happiness; *īśvarera*—of the Lord; *anavasare*—during the pastime of retirement; *pāila*—got; *baḍa*—very much; *duḥkha*—unhappiness.

TRANSLATION

Upon seeing the bathing ceremony of Lord Jagannātha, Śrī Caitanya Mahāprabhu became very happy. But when Lord Jagannātha retired after the ceremony, Lord Caitanya became very unhappy because He could not see Him.

PURPORT

After the bathing ceremony of Śrī Jagannātha, which takes place just a fortnight before the Ratha-yātrā ceremony, the body of the Lord Jagannātha Deity is repainted, and this takes just about a fortnight to complete. This period is called Anavasara. There are many who visit the temple to see Lord Jagannātha regularly every day, and for them His retirement after the bathing ceremony is unbearable. Śrī Caitanya Mahāprabhu felt Lord Jagannātha's absence from the temple very much.

TEXT 63

গোপীভাবে বিরহে প্রভু ব্যাকুল হঞা।
আলালনাথে গেলা প্রভু সবারে ছাড়িয়া ॥ ৬৩ ॥

gopī-bhāve virahe prabhu vyākula hañā
ālālanāthe gelā prabhu sabāre chāḍiyā

gopī-bhāve—in the mood of the *gopīs; virahe*—in separation; *prabhu*—Lord Śrī Caitanya Mahāprabhu; *vyākula*—agitated; *hañā*—being; *ālālanāthe*—to Ālālanātha; *gelā*—went; *prabhu*—Lord Śrī Caitanya Mahāprabhu; *sabāre*—all; *chāḍiyā*—having given up.

TRANSLATION

Due to separation from Lord Jagannātha, Śrī Caitanya Mahāprabhu felt the same great anxiety the gopīs feel in separation from Kṛṣṇa. In this condition He gave up all association and went to Ālālanātha.

TEXT 64

পাছে প্রভুর নিকট আইলা ভক্তগণ।
গৌড় হৈতে ভক্ত আইসে, —কৈল নিবেদন ॥ ৬৪ ॥

pāche prabhura nikaṭa āilā bhakta-gaṇa
gauḍa haite bhakta āise,—kaila nivedana

pāche—behind; *prabhura*—of Śrī Caitanya Mahāprabhu; *nikaṭa*—in the presence; *āilā*—came; *bhakta-gaṇa*—the devotees; *gauḍa haite*—from Bengal; *bhakta*—devotees; *āise*—come; *kaila nivedana*—submitted.

TRANSLATION

The devotees who had followed the Lord came into His presence and requested Him to return to Purī. They submitted that the devotees from Bengal were coming to Puruṣottama-kṣetra.

TEXT 65

সার্বভৌম নীলাচলে আইলা প্রভু লঞা।
প্রভু আইলা, — রাজা-ঠাঞি কহিলেন গিয়া ॥ ৬৫ ॥

sārvabhauma nīlācale āilā prabhu lañā
prabhu āilā, — rājā-ṭhāñi kahilena giyā

sārvabhauma — Sārvabhauma Bhaṭṭācārya; *nīlācale* — to Jagannātha Purī; *āilā* — came; *prabhu* — Śrī Caitanya Mahāprabhu; *lañā* — taking; *prabhu* — Śrī Caitanya Mahāprabhu; *āilā* — arrived; *rājā-ṭhāñi* — to the King; *kahilena* — said; *giyā* — after going.

TRANSLATION

In this way Sārvabhauma Bhaṭṭācārya brought Lord Caitanya back to Jagannātha Purī. He then went to King Pratāparudra and informed him of the Lord's arrival.

TEXT 66

হেনকালে আইলা তথা গোপীনাথাচার্য।
রাজাকে আশীর্বাদ করি' কহে, — শুন ভট্টাচার্য ॥ ৬৬ ॥

hena-kāle āilā tathā gopīnāthācārya
rājāke āśīrvāda kari' kahe, — śuna bhaṭṭācārya

hena-kāle — during this time; *āilā* — came; *tathā* — there; *gopīnātha-ācārya* — Gopīnātha Ācārya; *rājāke* — unto the King; *āśīrvāda kari'* — offering a benediction; *kahe* — said; *śuna bhaṭṭācārya* — my dear Bhaṭṭācārya, kindly listen.

TRANSLATION

At this time, Gopīnātha Ācārya came there while Sārvabhauma Bhaṭṭācārya was with King Pratāparudra. Being a brāhmaṇa, he offered his benediction to the King and addressed Sārvabhauma Bhaṭṭācārya as follows.

TEXT 67

গৌড় হৈতে বৈষ্ণব আসিতেছেন দুইশত।
মহাপ্রভুর ভক্ত সব — মহাভাগবত ॥ ৬৭ ॥

gauḍa haite vaiṣṇava āsitechena dui-śata
mahāprabhura bhakta saba — mahā-bhāgavata

gauḍa haite — from Bengal; *vaiṣṇava* — devotees; *āsitechena* — are coming; *dui-śata* — numbering about two hundred; *mahāprabhura* — of Lord Śrī Caitanya Mahāprabhu; *bhakta* — the devotees; *saba* — all; *mahā-bhāgavata* — greatly advanced devotees.

TRANSLATION

"About two hundred devotees are coming from Bengal. All of them are greatly advanced and specifically devoted to Śrī Caitanya Mahāprabhu.

TEXT 68

নরেন্দ্রে আসিয়া সবে হৈল বিদ্যমান।
তাঁ-সবারে চাহি বাসা প্রসাদ-সমাধান ॥ ৬৮ ॥

narendre āsiyā sabe haila vidyamāna
tāṅ-sabāre cāhi vāsā prasāda-samādhāna

narendre — on the bank of Lake Narendra; *āsiyā* — coming; *sabe* — all of them; *haila vidyamāna* — staying; *tāṅ-sabāre* — for all of them; *cāhi* — I want; *vāsā* — residential quarters; *prasāda* — for distributing *prasādam; samādhāna* — arrangement.

TRANSLATION

"All of them have already arrived on the bank of Lake Narendra and are waiting there. I desire residential quarters and prasādam arrangements for them."

PURPORT

Narendra is a small lake still existing in Jagannātha Purī, where the Candana-yātrā festival takes place. Up to the present date, all the

Bengali devotees who visit the Jagannātha temple first take their bath in this lake. There they wash their hands and feet before entering the temple.

TEXT 69

রাজা কহে, — পড়িছাকে আমি আজ্ঞা দিব ।
বাসা আদি যে চাহিয়ে, — পড়িছা সব দিব ॥ ৬৯ ॥

rājā kahe, — paḍichāke āmi ājñā diba
vāsā ādi ye cāhiye, — paḍichā saba diba

rājā kahe — the King said; *paḍichāke* — unto the attendant; *āmi* — I; *ājñā diba* — shall give orders; *vāsā* — residential quarters; *ādi* — and other arrangements; *ye cāhiye* — whatever you want; *paḍichā* — the attendant; *saba* — everything; *diba* — will supply.

TRANSLATION

The King replied, "I shall give orders to the attendant in the temple. He will arrange for everyone's residential quarters and prasādam, as you desire.

TEXT 70

মহাপ্রভুর গণ যত আইলা গৌড় হৈতে ।
ভট্টাচার্য, একে একে দেখাহ আমাতে ॥ ৭০ ॥

mahāprabhura gaṇa yata āila gauḍa haite
bhaṭṭācārya, eke eke dekhāha āmāte

mahāprabhura — of Śrī Caitanya Mahāprabhu; *gaṇa* — associates; *yata* — all; *āila* — who have come; *gauḍa haite* — from Bengal; *bhaṭṭācārya* — Sārvabhauma Bhaṭṭācārya; *eke eke* — one after another; *dekhāha* — please show; *āmāte* — to me.

TRANSLATION

"Sārvabhauma Bhaṭṭācārya, please show me, one after another, all of Śrī Caitanya Mahāprabhu's devotees who are coming from Bengal."

TEXT 71

ভট্ট কহে, — অট্টালিকায় কর আরোহণ।
গোপীনাথ চিনে সবারে, করাবে দরশন ॥ ৭১ ॥

bhaṭṭa kahe, — aṭṭālikāya kara ārohaṇa
gopīnātha cine sabāre, karābe daraśana

bhaṭṭa kahe — the Bhaṭṭācārya said; *aṭṭālikāya* — on the roof of the palace; *kara ārohaṇa* — just go up; *gopīnātha* — Gopīnātha Ācārya; *cine* — knows; *sabāre* — everyone; *karābe daraśana* — he will show.

TRANSLATION

Sārvabhauma Bhaṭṭācārya requested the King, "Go up on the roof of the palace. Gopīnātha Ācārya knows every one of the devotees. He will identify them for you.

TEXT 72

আমি কাহো নাহি চিনি, চিনিতে মন হয়।
গোপীনাথাচার্য সবারে করা'বে পরিচয় ॥ ৭২ ॥

āmi kāho nāhi cini, cinite mana haya
gopīnāthācārya sabāre karā'be paricaya

āmi — I; *kāho* — anyone; *nāhi* — do not; *cini* — know; *cinite mana haya* — I desire to know; *gopīnātha-ācārya* — Gopīnātha Ācārya; *sabāre* — all of them; *karā'be paricaya* — will identify.

TRANSLATION

"Actually I do not know any of them, although I have a desire to know them. Since Gopīnātha Ācārya knows them all, he will give you their names."

TEXT 73

এত বলি' তিন জন অট্টালিকায় চড়িল।
হেনকালে বৈষ্ণব সব নিকটে আইল ॥ ৭৩ ॥

eta bali' tina jana aṭṭālikāya caḍila
hena-kāle vaiṣṇava saba nikaṭe āila

eta bali'—saying this; *tina jana*—the three persons (namely, the King, Gopīnātha Ācārya and Sārvabhauma Bhaṭṭācārya); *aṭṭālikāya*—on the roof of the palace; *caḍila*—went up; *hena-kāle*—at this time; *vaiṣṇava*—the Vaiṣṇava devotees; *saba*—all; *nikaṭe*—nearby; *āila*—came.

TRANSLATION

After Sārvabhauma said this, he went up to the top of the palace with the King and Gopīnātha Ācārya. At this time all the Vaiṣṇava devotees from Bengal drew closer to the palace.

TEXT 74

দামোদর-স্বরূপ, গোবিন্দ, —দুই জন।
মালা-প্রসাদ লঞা যায়, যাহাঁ বৈষ্ণবগণ ॥ ৭৪ ॥

dāmodara-svarūpa, govinda,—dui jana
mālā-prasāda lañā yāya, yāhāṅ vaiṣṇava-gaṇa

dāmodara-svarūpa—Svarūpa Dāmodara; *govinda*—Govinda; *dui jana*—two persons; *mālā-prasāda*—flower garlands and remnants of Lord Jagannātha's food; *lañā*—taking; *yāya*—went; *yāhāṅ*—where; *vaiṣṇava-gaṇa*—the Vaiṣṇavas.

TRANSLATION

Svarūpa Dāmodara and Govinda, taking the flower garlands and prasādam of Lord Jagannātha, proceeded to where all the Vaiṣṇavas were standing.

TEXT 75

প্রথমেতে মহাপ্রভু পাঠাইলা দুঁহারে।
রাজা কহে, এই দুই কোন্ চিনাহ আমারে ॥ ৭৫ ॥

prathamete mahāprabhu pāṭhāilā duṅhāre
rājā kahe, ei dui kon cināha āmāre

prathamete—at first; *mahāprabhu*—Śrī Caitanya Mahāprabhu; *pāṭhāilā*—sent; *duṅhāre*—two persons; *rājā kahe*—the King said; *ei dui*—these two; *kon*—who are they; *cināha*—kindly identify; *āmāre*—to me.

TRANSLATION

Lord Śrī Caitanya Mahāprabhu first sent those two persons in advance. The King inquired, "Who are these two? Please let me know their identities."

TEXT 76

ভট্টাচার্য কহে, — এই স্বরূপ-দামোদর ।
মহাপ্রভুর হয় ইঁহ দ্বিতীয় কলেবর ॥ ৭৬ ॥

bhaṭṭācārya kahe,—ei svarūpa-dāmodara
mahāprabhura haya iṅha dvitīya kalevara

bhaṭṭācārya kahe—the Bhaṭṭācārya said; *ei*—this gentleman; *svarūpa-dāmodara*—his name is Svarūpa Dāmodara; *mahāprabhura*—of Śrī Caitanya Mahāprabhu; *haya*—is; *iṅha*—he; *dvitīya*—the second; *kalevara*—expansion of the body.

TRANSLATION

Śrī Sārvabhauma Bhaṭṭācārya replied, "Here is Svarūpa Dāmodara, who is practically the second expansion of the body of Śrī Caitanya Mahāprabhu.

TEXT 77

দ্বিতীয়, গোবিন্দ — ভৃত্য, ইহাঁ দোঁহা দিয়া ।
মালা পাঠাঞাছেন প্রভু গৌরব করিয়া ॥ ৭৭ ॥

dvitīya, govinda—bhṛtya, ihāṅ doṅhā diyā
mālā pāṭhāñāchena prabhu gaurava kariyā

dvitīya—the second; *govinda*—Govinda; *bhṛtya*—personal servant; *ihāṅ*—here; *doṅhā diyā*—through these two persons; *mālā*—flower garlands; *pāṭhāñāchena*—has sent; *prabhu*—Śrī Caitanya Mahāprabhu; *gaurava kariyā*—giving much honor.

TRANSLATION

"The second person is Govinda, Lord Caitanya's personal servant. The Lord has sent garlands and remnants of Lord Jagannātha's food with these two persons simply to honor the devotees from Bengal."

TEXT 78

আদৌ মালা অদ্বৈতেরে স্বরূপ পরাইল ।
পাছে গোবিন্দ দ্বিতীয় মালা আনি' তাঁরে দিল ॥ ৭৮ ॥

ādau mālā advaitere svarūpa parāila
pāche govinda dvitīya mālā āni' tāṅre dila

ādau—in the beginning; *mālā*—a garland; *advaitere*—unto Advaita Ācārya; *svarūpa*—Svarūpa Dāmodara; *parāila*—offered; *pāche*—after that; *govinda*—Govinda, the Lord's personal servant; *dvitīya*—a second; *mālā*—garland; *āni'*—bringing; *tāṅre dila*—delivered to Him.

TRANSLATION

At the beginning, Svarūpa Dāmodara came forward and garlanded Advaita Ācārya. Govinda next came and offered a second garland to Advaita Ācārya.

TEXT 79

তবে গোবিন্দ দণ্ডবৎ কৈল আচার্যেরে ।
তাঁরে নাহি চিনে আচার্য, পুছিল দামোদরে ॥ ৭৯ ॥

tabe govinda daṇḍavat kaila ācāryere
tāṅre nāhi cine ācārya, puchila dāmodare

tabe—at that time; *govinda*—Govinda; *daṇḍavat*—falling flat to offer obeisances; *kaila*—did; *ācāryere*—unto Advaita Ācārya; *tāṅre*—him; *nāhi*—not; *cine*—recognized; *ācārya*—Advaita Ācārya; *puchila*—inquired; *dāmodare*—to Svarūpa Dāmodara.

TRANSLATION

When Govinda offered his obeisances by falling down flat before Advaita Ācārya, Advaita Ācārya asked Svarūpa Dāmodara about his identity, for He did not know Govinda at that time.

TEXT 80

দামোদর কহে, —ইহার 'গোবিন্দ' নাম।
ঈশ্বর-পুরীর সেবক অতি গুণবান্ ॥ ৮০ ॥

dāmodara kahe,—ihāra 'govinda' nāma
īśvara-purīra sevaka ati guṇavān

dāmodara kahe—Dāmodara said; *ihāra*—of him; *govinda*—Govinda; *nāma*—the name; *īśvara-purīra sevaka*—servant of Īśvara Purī; *ati guṇavān*—very much qualified.

TRANSLATION

Svarūpa Dāmodara informed Him, "Govinda was the servant of Īśvara Purī. He is very highly qualified.

TEXT 81

প্রভুর সেবা করিতে পুরী আজ্ঞা দিল।
অতএব প্রভু ইঁহাকে নিকটে রাখিল ॥ ৮১ ॥

prabhura sevā karite purī ājñā dila
ataeva prabhu iṅhāke nikaṭe rākhila

prabhura—of Śrī Caitanya Mahāprabhu; *sevā*—the service; *karite*—to perform; *purī*—Īśvara Purī; *ājñā dila*—ordered; *ataeva*—therefore; *prabhu*—Śrī Caitanya Mahāprabhu; *iṅhāke*—him; *nikaṭe*—by His side; *rākhila*—kept.

TRANSLATION

"Īśvara Purī ordered Govinda to serve Śrī Caitanya Mahāprabhu. Thus the Lord keeps him by His side."

TEXT 82

রাজা কহে, —যাঁরে মালা দিল দুইজন।
আশ্চর্য তেজ, বড় মহান্ত, —কহ কোন্ জন ? ৮২ ॥

rājā kahe, —yāṅre mālā dila dui-jana
āścarya teja, baḍa mahānta, —kaha kon jana?

rājā kahe—the King inquired; *yāṅre*—unto which person; *mālā*—garlands; *dila*—offered; *dui-jana*—Svarūpa Dāmodara and Govinda; *āścarya teja*—wonderfully effulgent; *baḍa mahānta*—a very great devotee; *kaha kon jana*—kindly let me know who He is.

TRANSLATION

The King inquired, "To whom did Svarūpa Dāmodara and Govinda offer the two garlands? His bodily effulgence is so great that He must be a very great devotee. Please let me know who He is."

TEXT 83

আচার্য কহে, —ইঁহার নাম অদ্বৈত আচার্য।
মহাপ্রভুর মান্যপাত্র, সর্ব-শিরোধার্য ॥ ৮৩ ॥

ācārya kahe, —iṅhāra nāma advaita ācārya
mahāprabhura mānya-pātra, sarva-śirodhārya

ācārya kahe—Gopīnātha Ācārya said; *iṅhāra nāma*—His name; *advaita ācārya*—Advaita Ācārya; *mahāprabhura*—of Śrī Caitanya Mahāprabhu; *mānya-pātra*—honorable; *sarva-śirodhārya*—the topmost devotee.

TRANSLATION

Gopīnātha Ācārya replied, "His name is Advaita Ācārya. He is honored even by Śrī Caitanya Mahāprabhu, and He is therefore the topmost devotee.

TEXT 84

শ্রীবাস-পণ্ডিত ইঁহ, পণ্ডিত-বক্রেশ্বর।
বিদ্যানিধি-আচার্য, ইঁহ পণ্ডিত-গদাধর ॥ ৮৪ ॥

śrīvāsa-paṇḍita iṅha, paṇḍita-vakreśvara
vidyānidhi-ācārya, iṅha paṇḍita-gadādhara

śrīvāsa-paṇḍita—Śrīvāsa Paṇḍita; *iṅha*—here; *paṇḍita-vakreśvara*—Vakreśvara Paṇḍita; *vidyānidhi-ācārya*—Vidyānidhi Ācārya; *iṅha*—here; *paṇḍita-gadādhara*—Gadādhara Paṇḍita.

TRANSLATION

"Here are Śrīvāsa Paṇḍita, Vakreśvara Paṇḍita, Vidyānidhi Ācārya and Gadādhara Paṇḍita.

TEXT 85

আচার্যরত্ন ইঁহ, পণ্ডিত-পুরন্দর।
গঙ্গাদাস পণ্ডিত ইঁহ, পণ্ডিত-শঙ্কর ॥ ৮৫ ॥

ācāryaratna iṅha, paṇḍita-purandara
gaṅgādāsa paṇḍita iṅha, paṇḍita-śaṅkara

ācāryaratna—Candraśekhara; *iṅha*—here; *paṇḍita-purandara*—Purandara Paṇḍita; *gaṅgādāsa paṇḍita*—Gaṅgādāsa Paṇḍita; *iṅha*—here; *paṇḍita-śaṅkara*—Śaṅkara Paṇḍita.

TRANSLATION

"Here are Ācāryaratna, Purandara Paṇḍita, Gaṅgādāsa Paṇḍita and Śaṅkara Paṇḍita.

TEXT 86

এই মুরারি গুপ্ত, ইঁহ পণ্ডিত নারায়ণ।
হরিদাস ঠাকুর ইঁহ ভুবনপাবন ॥ ৮৬ ॥

ei murāri gupta, iṅha paṇḍita nārāyaṇa
haridāsa ṭhākura iṅha bhuvana-pāvana

ei—this; *murāri gupta*—Murāri Gupta; *iṅha*—here; *paṇḍita nārāyaṇa*—Nārāyaṇa Paṇḍita; *haridāsa ṭhākura*—Haridāsa Ṭhākura; *iṅha*—here; *bhuvana-pāvana*—deliverer of the whole universe.

TRANSLATION

"Here are Murāri Gupta, Paṇḍita Nārāyaṇa and Haridāsa Ṭhākura, the deliverer of the whole universe.

TEXT 87

এই হরি-ভট্ট, এই শ্রীনৃসিংহানন্দ।
এই বাসুদেব দত্ত, এই শিবানন্দ ॥ ৮৭ ॥

ei hari-bhaṭṭa, ei śrī-nṛsiṁhānanda
ei vāsudeva datta, ei śivānanda

ei—this; *hari-bhaṭṭa*—Hari Bhaṭṭa; *ei*—this; *śrī-nṛsiṁhānanda*—Śrī Nṛsiṁhānanda; *ei*—this; *vāsudeva datta*—Vāsudeva Datta; *ei*—this; *śivānanda*—Śivānanda.

TRANSLATION

"Here is Hari Bhaṭṭa, and there is Nṛsiṁhānanda. Here are Vāsudeva Datta and Śivānanda Sena.

TEXT 88

গোবিন্দ, মাধব ঘোষ, এই বাসুঘোষ।
তিন ভাইর কীর্তনে প্রভু পায়েন সন্তোষ ॥ ৮৮ ॥

govinda, mādhava ghoṣa, ei vāsu-ghoṣa
tina bhāira kīrtane prabhu pāyena santoṣa

govinda—Govinda Ghoṣa; *mādhava ghoṣa*—Mādhava Ghoṣa; *ei*—this; *vāsu-ghoṣa*—Vāsudeva Ghoṣa; *tina bhāira*—of the three brothers; *kīrtane*—in the *saṅkīrtana; prabhu*—the Lord; *pāyena santoṣa*—gets very much pleasure.

TRANSLATION

"Here also are Govinda Ghoṣa, Mādhava Ghoṣa and Vāsudeva Ghoṣa. They are three brothers, and their saṅkīrtana, congregational chanting, pleases the Lord very much.

PURPORT

Govinda Ghoṣa belonged to the *kāyastha* dynasty of the Uttara-rāḍhīya section, and he was known as Ghoṣa Ṭhākura. Even to the present day there is a place named Agradvīpa, near Katwa, where a fair takes place and is named after Ghoṣa Ṭhākura. As far as Vāsudeva Ghoṣa is concerned, he composed many nice songs about Lord Śrī Caitanya Mahāprabhu, and these are all authorized Vaiṣṇava songs, like the songs of Narottama dāsa Ṭhākura, Bhaktivinoda Ṭhākura, Locana dāsa Ṭhākura, Govinda dāsa Ṭhākura and other great Vaiṣṇavas.

TEXT 89

রাঘব পণ্ডিত, ইঁহ আচার্য নন্দন ।
শ্রীমান্ পণ্ডিত এই, শ্রীকান্ত, নারায়ণ ॥ ৮৯ ॥

rāghava paṇḍita, iṅha ācārya nandana
śrīmān paṇḍita ei, śrīkānta, nārāyaṇa

rāghava paṇḍita—Rāghava Paṇḍita; *iṅha*—here; *ācārya nandana*—Ācārya Nandana; *śrīmān paṇḍita*—Śrīmān Paṇḍita; *ei*—this; *śrīkānta*—Śrīkānta; *nārāyaṇa*—and also Nārāyaṇa.

TRANSLATION

"Here is Rāghava Paṇḍita, here is Ācārya Nandana, there is Śrīmān Paṇḍita, and here are Śrīkānta and Nārāyaṇa."

PURPORT

Narottama dāsa Ṭhākura, honoring the personal associates of Lord Śrī Caitanya Mahāprabhu, has sung as follows (*Prārthanā* 13):

gaurāṅgera saṅgi-gaṇe nitya-siddha kari' māne
se yāya vrajendra-suta-pāśa

One who is intelligent understands that all the personal associates and devotees of Lord Śrī Caitanya Mahāprabhu are ever liberated. This means that because they are always engaged in the devotional service of the Lord, they do not belong to this material world. One who is engaged in the Lord's devotional service twenty-four hours daily and never forgets the Lord is called *nitya-siddha.* Śrīla Rūpa Gosvāmī confirms this statement:

īhā yasya harer dāsye karmaṇā manasā girā
nikhilāsv apy avasthāsu jīvan-muktaḥ sa ucyate

"A person acting in the service of Kṛṣṇa with body, mind, intelligence and words is a liberated person even within the material world, although he may be engaged in many so-called material activities." (*Bhakti-rasāmṛta-sindhu,* 1.2.187)

A devotee is always thinking of how better to serve Lord Kṛṣṇa, the Supreme Personality of Godhead, and how to broadcast His name, fame and qualities throughout the world. One who is *nitya-siddha* has no business other than broadcasting the glories of the Lord all over the world according to his ability. Such people are already associates of Lord Caitanya Mahāprabhu. Therefore Narottama dāsa Ṭhākura says, *nitya-siddha kari' māne.* One should not think that because Śrī Caitanya Mahāprabhu was personally present five hundred years ago, only His associates were liberated. Rather, Śrīla Narottama dāsa Ṭhākura says that anyone is a *nitya-siddha* if he acts on behalf of Śrī Caitanya Mahāprabhu by spreading the glories of the holy name of the Lord. We should respect those devotees preaching the glories of the Lord as *nitya-siddha* and should not consider them conditioned.

māṁ ca yo 'vyabhicāreṇa bhakti-yogena sevate
sa guṇān samatītyaitān brahma-bhūyāya kalpate

(Bg. 14.26)

One who has transcended the material modes of nature is said to be on the Brahman platform. That is also the platform of *nitya-siddha.* The *nitya-siddha* not only stays on the Brahman platform but also works on that platform. Simply by accepting the associates of Lord Caitanya Mahāprabhu as *nitya-siddha,* one can very easily go back home, back to Godhead.

TEXT 90

শুক্লাম্বর দেখ, এই শ্রীধর, বিজয়।
বল্লভ-সেন, এই পুরুষোত্তম, সঞ্জয় ॥ ৯০ ॥

śuklāmbara dekha, ei śrīdhara, vijaya
vallabha-sena, ei puruṣottama, sañjaya

śuklāmbara—Śuklāmbara; *dekha*—see; *ei*—this; *śrīdhara*—Śrīdhara; *vijaya*—Vijaya; *vallabha-sena*—Vallabha Sena; *ei*—this; *puruṣottama*—Puruṣottama; *sañjaya*—Sañjaya.

TRANSLATION

Gopīnātha Ācārya continued to point out the devotees: "Here is Śuklāmbara. See, there is Śrīdhara. Here is Vijaya, and there is Vallabha Sena. Here is Puruṣottama, and there is Sañjaya.

TEXT 91

কুলীন-গ্রামবাসী এই সত্যরাজ-খান ।
রামানন্দ-আদি সবে দেখ বিদ্যমান ॥ ৯১ ॥

kulīna-grāma-vāsī ei satyarāja-khāna
rāmānanda-ādi sabe dekha vidyamāna

kulīna-grāma-vāsī—residents of the village known as Kulīna-grāma; *ei*—these; *satyarāja-khāna*—Satyarāja Khān; *rāmānanda-ādi*—headed by Rāmānanda; *sabe*—everyone; *dekha*—you see; *vidyamāna*—present.

TRANSLATION

"And here are all the residents of Kulīna-grāma, such as Satyarāja Khān and Rāmānanda. Indeed, all of them are present here. Please see.

TEXT 92

মুকুন্দদাস, নরহরি, শ্রীরঘুনন্দন ।
খণ্ডবাসী চিরঞ্জীব, আর সুলোচন ॥ ৯২ ॥

mukunda-dāsa, narahari, śrī-raghunandana
khaṇḍa-vāsī cirañjīva, āra sulocana

mukunda-dāsa—Mukunda dāsa; *narahari*—Narahari; *śrī-raghunandana*—Śrī Raghunandana; *khaṇḍa-vāsī*—residents of Khaṇḍa; *cirañjīva*—Cirañjīva; *āra*—and; *sulocana*—Sulocana.

TRANSLATION

"Here are Mukunda dāsa, Narahari, Śrī Raghunandana, Cirañjīva and Sulocana, all residents of Khaṇḍa.

TEXT 93

কতেক কহিব, এই দেখ যত জন।
চৈতন্যের গণ, সব — চৈতন্যজীবন ॥ ৯৩ ॥

kateka kahiba, ei dekha yata jana
caitanyera gaṇa, saba — caitanya-jīvana

kateka kahiba — how many shall I speak; *ei* — these; *dekha* — see; *yata jana* — all the persons; *caitanyera gaṇa* — associates of Śrī Caitanya Mahāprabhu; *saba* — all of them; *caitanya-jīvana* — consider Śrī Caitanya Mahāprabhu their life and soul.

TRANSLATION

"How many names shall I speak to you? All the devotees you see here are associates of Śrī Caitanya Mahāprabhu, who is their life and soul."

TEXT 94

রাজা কহে — দেখি' মোর হৈল চমৎকার।
বৈষ্ণবের ঐছে তেজ দেখি নাহি আর ॥ ৯৪ ॥

rājā kahe — dekhi' mora haila camatkāra
vaiṣṇavera aiche teja dekhi nāhi āra

rājā kahe — the King said; *dekhi'* — after seeing; *mora* — my; *haila* — there is; *camatkāra* — astonishment; *vaiṣṇavera* — of the devotees of the Lord; *aiche* — such; *teja* — effulgence; *dekhi* — I see; *nāhi* — not; *āra* — anyone else.

TRANSLATION

The King said, "Upon seeing all these devotees, I am very much astonished, for I have never seen such an effulgence.

TEXT 95

কোটিসূর্য-সম সব — উজ্জ্বল-বরণ ।
কভু নাহি শুনি এই মধুর কীর্তন ॥ ৯৫ ॥

koṭi-sūrya-sama saba — ujjvala-varaṇa
kabhu nāhi śuni ei madhura kīrtana

koṭi-sūrya-sama — equal to the shining of millions of suns; *saba* — all of them; *ujjvala-varaṇa* — very bright luster; *kabhu nāhi śuni* — I have never heard; *ei* — this; *madhura kīrtana* — such melodious performance of congregational chanting.

TRANSLATION

"Indeed, their effulgence is like the brilliance of a million suns. Nor have I ever heard the Lord's names chanted so melodiously.

PURPORT

Such are the symptoms of pure devotees when they are chanting. All the pure devotees are as bright as sunshine, and their bodily luster is very effulgent. In addition, their performance of *saṅkīrtana* is unparalleled. There are many professional chanters who can perform congregational chanting with various musical instruments in an artistic and musical way, but their chanting cannot be as attractive as the congregational chanting of pure devotees. If a devotee sticks strictly to the principles governing Vaiṣṇava behavior, his bodily luster will naturally be attractive, and his singing and chanting of the holy names of the Lord will be effective. People will appreciate such *kīrtana* without hesitation. Even dramas about the pastimes of Lord Caitanya or Śrī Kṛṣṇa should be played by devotees. Such dramas will immediately interest an audience and be full of potency. The students of the International Society for Krishna Consciousness should note these two points and try to apply these principles in their spreading of the Lord's glories.

TEXT 96

ঐছে প্রেম, ঐছে নৃত্য, ঐছে হরিধ্বনি ।
কাহাঁ নাহি দেখি, ঐছে কাহাঁ নাহি শুনি ॥ ৯৬ ॥

aiche prema, aiche nṛtya, aiche hari-dhvani
kāhāṅ nāhi dekhi, aiche kāhāṅ nāhi śuni

aiche—such; *prema*—ecstatic love; *aiche nṛtya*—such dancing; *aiche hari-dhvani*—such vibration of the chanting of the holy name; *kāhāṅ*—anywhere; *nāhi dekhi*—I have never seen; *aiche*—such; *kāhāṅ*—anywhere; *nāhi śuni*—I never heard.

TRANSLATION

"I have never before seen such ecstatic love, nor heard the vibration of the holy name of the Lord chanted in such a way, nor seen such dancing during saṅkīrtana."

PURPORT

Because the temple of Lord Jagannātha is situated at Jagannātha Purī, many devotees from all parts of the world came to perform *saṅkīrtana* in glorification of the Lord. All these devotees were certainly seen and heard by Mahārāja Pratāparudra, but he herein admits that the *kīrtana* performed by the associates of the Lord was unique. He had never before heard such *saṅkīrtana* nor seen such attractive features manifest by the devotees. The members of the International Society for Krishna Consciousness should go to India during the birthday ceremony of Lord Caitanya Mahāprabhu at Māyāpura and perform *saṅkīrtana* congregationally. This will attract the attention of all the important personalities in India, just as the beauty, bodily luster and *saṅkīrtana* performance by the associates of Śrī Caitanya Mahāprabhu attracted the attention of Mahārāja Pratāparudra. The associates of Śrī Caitanya Mahāprabhu were unlimited during the Lord's presence on this planet, but anyone who is pure in life and devoted to the mission of Śrī Caitanya Mahāprabhu is to be understood as a *nitya-siddha* associate of the Lord.

TEXT 97

ভট্টাচার্য কহে এই মধুর বচন।
চৈতন্যের সৃষ্টি — এই প্রেম-সংকীর্তন ॥ ৯৭ ॥

bhaṭṭācārya kahe ei madhura vacana
caitanyera sṛṣṭi — ei prema-saṅkīrtana

bhaṭṭācārya — Sārvabhauma Bhaṭṭācārya; *kahe* — replied; *ei* — this; *madhura vacana* — transcendental sweetness of the voice; *caitanyera sṛṣṭi* — the creation of Lord Śrī Caitanya Mahāprabhu; *ei* — this; *prema-saṅkīrtana* — chanting in the ecstasy of love of Godhead.

TRANSLATION

Sārvabhauma Bhaṭṭācārya replied, "This sweet transcendental sound is a special creation of the Lord known as prema-saṅkīrtana, congregational chanting in love of Godhead.

TEXT 98

অবতরি' চৈতন্য কৈল ধর্মপ্রচারণ।
কলিকালে ধর্ম — কৃষ্ণনাম-সংকীর্তন ॥ ৯৮ ॥

avatari' caitanya kaila dharma-pracāraṇa
kali-kāle dharma — kṛṣṇa-nāma-saṅkīrtana

avatari' — descending; *caitanya* — Śrī Caitanya Mahāprabhu; *kaila* — did; *dharma-pracāraṇa* — preaching of real religion; *kali-kāle* — in this Age of Kali; *dharma* — religious principle; *kṛṣṇa-nāma* — of the holy name of Lord Kṛṣṇa; *saṅkīrtana* — chanting.

TRANSLATION

"In this Age of Kali, Śrī Caitanya Mahāprabhu has descended to preach the religion of Kṛṣṇa consciousness. Therefore the chanting of the holy names of Lord Kṛṣṇa is the religious principle for this age.

TEXT 99

সংকীর্তন-যজ্ঞে তাঁরে করে আরাধন।
সেই ত' সুমেধা, আর — কলিহতজন ॥ ৯৯ ॥

saṅkīrtana-yajñe tāṅre kare ārādhana
sei ta' sumedhā, āra — kali-hata-jana

saṅkīrtana-yajñe—in the performance of congregational chanting; *tāṅre*—unto Śrī Caitanya Mahāprabhu; *kare*—does; *ārādhana*—worship; *sei ta'*—such a person; *su-medhā*—sharply intelligent; *āra*—others; *kali-hata-jana*—victims of this Age of Kali.

TRANSLATION

"Anyone who worships Lord Caitanya Mahāprabhu by congregational chanting should be understood to be very intelligent. One who does not do so must be considered a victim of this age and bereft of all intelligence.

PURPORT

Rascals propose that anyone can invent his own religious process, and this proposition is condemned herein. If one actually wants to become religious, he must take up the chanting of the Hare Kṛṣṇa *mahā-mantra.* The real meaning of religion is stated in *Śrīmad-Bhāgavatam* (6.3.19–22):

dharmaṁ tu sākṣād-bhagavat-praṇītaṁ
na vai vidur ṛṣayo nāpi devāḥ
na siddha-mukhyā asurā manuṣyāh
kutaś ca vidyādhara-cāraṇādayaḥ

svayambhūr nāradaḥ śambhuḥ kumāraḥ kapilo manuḥ
prahlādo janako bhīṣmo balir vaiyāsakir vayam

dvādaśaite vijānīmo dharmaṁ bhāgavataṁ bhaṭāḥ
guhyaṁ viśuddhaṁ durbodhaṁ yaṁ jñātvāmṛtam aśnute

etāvān eva loke 'smin puṁsāṁ dharmaḥ paraḥ smṛtaḥ
bhakti-yogo bhagavati tan-nāma-grahaṇādibhiḥ

The purport of these verses is that *dharma,* or religion, cannot be manufactured by a human being. Religion is the law or code of the Lord. Consequently religion cannot be manufactured even by great saintly persons, demigods or *siddha-mukhyas,* and what to speak of *asuras,* human beings, Vidyādharas, Cāraṇas, and so on. The principles of *dharma,* religion, come down in the *paramparā* system beginning with twelve personalities—namely, Lord Brahmā; the great saint Nārada; Lord Śiva; the four Kumāras; Kapila, the son of Devahūti; Svāyambhuva Manu; Prahlāda Mahārāja; King Janaka; grandfather Bhīṣma; Bali

Mahārāja; Śukadeva Gosvāmī; and Yamarāja. The principles of religion are known to these twelve personalities. *Dharma* refers to the religious principles by which one can understand the Supreme Personality of Godhead. *Dharma* is very confidential, uncontaminated by any material influence, and very difficult for ordinary men to understand. However, if one actually understands *dharma,* he immediately becomes liberated and is transferred to the kingdom of God. *Bhāgavata-dharma,* or the principle of religion enunciated by the *paramparā* system, is the supreme principle of religion. In other words, *dharma* refers to the science of *bhakti-yoga,* which begins by the novice's chanting the holy name of the Lord (*tan-nāma-grahaṇādibhiḥ*).

Therefore in this Age of Kali, as recommended here in the *Caitanya-caritāmṛta* (text 98), *kali-kāle dharma—kṛṣṇa-nāma-saṅkīrtana:* the chanting of the holy name of the Lord is the method of religion approved by all Vedic scriptures. In the next text of the *Caitanya-caritāmṛta,* quoted from *Śrīmad-Bhāgavatam* (11.5.32), this principle is further stressed.

TEXT 100

কৃষ্ণবর্ণং ত্বিষাঽকৃষ্ণং সাঙ্গোপাঙ্গাস্ত্রপার্ষদম্ ।
যজ্ঞৈঃ সংকীর্তনপ্রায়ৈর্যজন্তি হি সুমেধসঃ ॥ ১০০ ॥

kṛṣṇa-varṇaṁ tviṣākṛṣṇaṁ
sāṅgopāṅgāstra-pārṣadam
yajñaiḥ saṅkīrtana-prāyair
yajanti hi su-medhasaḥ

kṛṣṇa-varṇam—repeating the syllables *kṛṣ-ṇa; tviṣā*—with a luster; *akṛṣṇam*—not black (golden); *sa-aṅga*—along with associates; *upāṅga*—servitors; *astra*—weapons; *pārṣadam*—confidential companions; *yajñaiḥ*—by sacrifice; *saṅkīrtana-prāyaiḥ*—consisting chiefly of congregational chanting; *yajanti*—they worship; *hi*—certainly; *su-medhasaḥ*—intelligent persons.

TRANSLATION

"'In the Age of Kali, intelligent persons perform congregational chanting to worship the incarnation of Godhead who constantly

sings the name of Kṛṣṇa. Although His complexion is not blackish, He is Kṛṣṇa Himself. He is accompanied by His associates, servants, weapons and confidential companions.'"

PURPORT

For an explanation of this verse, refer to *Ādi-līlā,* Chapter Three, verse 52.

TEXT 101

রাজা কহে, —শাস্ত্রপ্রমাণে চৈতন্য হন কৃষ্ণ ।
তবে কেনে পণ্ডিত সব তাঁহাতে বিতৃষ্ণ ? ১০১ ॥

rājā kahe, —śāstra-pramāṇe caitanya hana kṛṣṇa
tabe kene paṇḍita saba tāṅhāte vitṛṣṇa?

rājā kahe—the King said; *śāstra-pramāṇe*—by the evidence of revealed scripture; *caitanya*—Śrī Caitanya Mahāprabhu; *hana*—is; *kṛṣṇa*—the Supreme Personality of Godhead, Lord Kṛṣṇa; *tabe*—therefore; *kene*—why; *paṇḍita*—so-called learned scholars; *saba*—all; *tāṅhāte*—unto Him; *vitṛṣṇa*—indifferent.

TRANSLATION

The King said, "According to evidence given in the revealed scriptures, it is concluded that Lord Śrī Caitanya Mahāprabhu is Lord Kṛṣṇa Himself. Why, then, are learned scholars sometimes indifferent to Him?"

TEXT 102

ভট্ট কহে, —তাঁর কৃপা-লেশ হয় যাঁরে ।
সেই সে তাঁহারে 'কৃষ্ণ' করি' লইতে পারে ॥ ১০২ ॥

bhaṭṭa kahe, —tāṅra kṛpā-leśa haya yāṅre
sei se tāṅhāre 'kṛṣṇa' kari' la-ite pāre

bhaṭṭa kahe—Sārvabhauma Bhaṭṭācārya said; *tāṅra kṛpā*—of Lord Caitanya's mercy; *leśa*—even a fraction; *haya*—there is;

yāṅre—unto whom; *sei se*—that person only; *tāṅhāre*—Lord Śrī Caitanya Mahāprabhu; *kṛṣṇa kari'*—accepting as Kṛṣṇa; *la-ite pāre*—can take up.

TRANSLATION

The Bhaṭṭācārya replied, "A person who has received but a small fraction of mercy from Śrī Caitanya Mahāprabhu can understand that He is Lord Kṛṣṇa. No one else can.

PURPORT

The *saṅkīrtana* movement can be spread by a person who is especially favored by Lord Kṛṣṇa (*kṛṣṇa-śakti vinā nahe tāra pravartana*). Without first obtaining the mercy of the Lord, one cannot spread the holy name of the Lord. One who can spread the Lord's name is called *labdha-caitanya* in the words of Bhaktisiddhānta Sarasvatī. The *labdha-caitanya* is one who has actually awakened his original consciousness, Kṛṣṇa consciousness. The influence of the pure devotees in Kṛṣṇa consciousness is such that it can awaken others to become immediately Kṛṣṇa conscious and engage themselves in the transcendental loving service of Kṛṣṇa. In this way the descendants of pure devotees increase, and Lord Caitanya Mahāprabhu takes much pleasure in seeing the increase of His devotees. The word *su-medhasaḥ* means "sharply intelligent." When one's intelligence is sharp, he can increase the interests of common men in loving Caitanya Mahāprabhu and through Him in loving Rādhā-Kṛṣṇa. Those not interested in understanding Śrī Caitanya Mahāprabhu are simply material in their attempts at professional chanting and dancing for money, despite their supposed artistry. If one does not have full faith in Śrī Caitanya Mahāprabhu, he cannot properly chant and dance in the *saṅkīrtana* movement. Artificial chanting and dancing may be due to sentiments or sentimental agitation, but this cannot help one advance in Kṛṣṇa consciousness.

TEXT 103

তাঁর কৃপা নহে যারে, পণ্ডিত নহে কেনে ।
দেখিলে শুনিলেহ তাঁরে 'ঈশ্বর' না মানে ॥ ১০৩ ॥

tāṅra kṛpā nahe yāre, paṇḍita nahe kene
dekhile śunileha tāṅre 'īśvara' nā māne

tāṅra kṛpā—His mercy; *nahe*—there is not; *yāre*—unto whom; *paṇḍita*—learned scholar; *nahe*—even though; *kene*—nevertheless; *dekhile*—even by seeing; *śunileha*—even by listening; *tāṅre*—Him; *īśvara*—as the Supreme Personality of Godhead; *nā māne*—does not accept.

TRANSLATION

"If the mercy of Śrī Caitanya Mahāprabhu is not bestowed upon a person—regardless of how learned a scholar that person may be and regardless of his seeing or listening—he cannot accept Lord Caitanya as the Supreme Personality of Godhead.

PURPORT

The same principles can be applied to demoniac persons, even though they be in the *sampradāya* of Lord Śrī Caitanya Mahāprabhu. Without receiving the Lord's special power, one cannot preach His glories all over the world. Even though one may celebrate himself as a learned follower of Śrī Caitanya Mahāprabhu, and even though one may attempt to preach the holy name of the Lord all over the world, if he is not favored by Śrī Caitanya Mahāprabhu he will find fault with the pure devotee and will not be able to understand how a preacher is empowered by Lord Caitanya. One must be considered bereft of the mercy of Śrī Caitanya Mahāprabhu when he criticizes the Kṛṣṇa consciousness movement now spreading all over the world or finds fault with this movement or the leader of the movement.

TEXT 104

অথাপি তে দেব পদাম্বুজদ্বয়-
প্রসাদলেশানুগৃহীত এব হি।
জানাতি তত্ত্বং ভগবন্মহিম্নো
ন চান্য একোঽপি চিরং বিচিন্বন্ ॥ ১০৪ ॥

athāpi te deva padāmbuja-dvaya-
prasāda-leśānugṛhīta eva hi
jānāti tattvaṁ bhagavan-mahimno
na cānya eko 'pi ciraṁ vicinvan

atha—therefore; *api*—indeed; *te*—Your; *deva*—my Lord; *pada-ambuja-dvaya*—of the two lotus feet; *prasāda*—of the mercy; *leśa*—by only a trace; *anugṛhītaḥ*—favored; *eva*—certainly; *hi*—indeed; *jānāti*—one knows; *tattvam*—the truth; *bhagavat*—of the Supreme Personality of Godhead; *mahimnaḥ*—of the greatness; *na*—never; *ca*—and; *anyaḥ*—another; *ekaḥ*—one; *api*—although; *ciram*—for a long period; *vicinvan*—speculating.

TRANSLATION

"[Lord Brahmā said:] 'My Lord, if one is favored by even a slight trace of the mercy of Your lotus feet, he can understand the greatness of Your personality. But those who speculate to understand the Supreme Personality of Godhead are unable to know You, even though they continue to study the Vedas for many years.'"

PURPORT

This verse is a quotation from *Śrīmad-Bhāgavatam* (10.14.29). It is explained in the *Madhya-līlā,* in the Sixth Chapter, text 84.

TEXT 105

রাজা কহে, —সবে জগন্নাথ না দেখিয়া ।
চৈতন্যের বাসা-গৃহে চলিলা ধাঞা ॥ ১০৫ ॥

rājā kahe,—sabe jagannātha nā dekhiyā
caitanyera vāsā-gṛhe calilā dhāñā

rājā kahe—the King said; *sabe*—all of them; *jagannātha*—Lord Jagannātha; *nā dekhiyā*—without visiting; *caitanyera*—of Lord Śrī Caitanya Mahāprabhu; *vāsā-gṛhe*—to the residential place; *calilā*—they went; *dhāñā*—running.

TRANSLATION

The King said, "Instead of visiting the temple of Lord Jagannātha, all the devotees are running toward the residence of Śrī Caitanya Mahāprabhu."

TEXT 106

ভট্ট কহে, — এই ত' স্বাভাবিক প্রেম-রীত।
মহাপ্রভু মিলিবারে উৎকণ্ঠিত চিত ॥ ১০৬ ॥

bhaṭṭa kahe,—ei ta' svābhāvika prema-rīta
mahāprabhu milibāre utkaṇṭhita cita

bhaṭṭa kahe—the Bhaṭṭācārya replied; *ei ta'*—this is; *svābhāvika*—spontaneous; *prema-rīta*—attraction of love; *mahāprabhu*—Śrī Caitanya Mahāprabhu; *milibāre*—for meeting; *utkaṇṭhita*—anxious; *cita*—mind.

TRANSLATION

Sārvabhauma Bhaṭṭācārya replied, "This is spontaneous love. All the devotees are very anxious to meet Śrī Caitanya Mahāprabhu.

TEXT 107

আগে তাঁরে মিলি' সবে তাঁরে সঙ্গে লঞা।
তাঁর সঙ্গে জগন্নাথ দেখিবেন গিয়া ॥ ১০৭ ॥

āge tāṅre mili' sabe tāṅre saṅge lañā
tāṅra saṅge jagannātha dekhibena giyā

āge—first; *tāṅre*—Śrī Caitanya Mahāprabhu; *mili'*—meeting; *sabe*—all the devotees; *tāṅre*—Him; *saṅge*—with them; *lañā*—taking; *tāṅra saṅge*—with Him; *jagannātha*—Lord Jagannātha; *dekhibena*—they will see; *giyā*—going.

TRANSLATION

"First the devotees will meet Śrī Caitanya Mahāprabhu and then take Him with them to the temple to see Lord Jagannātha."

TEXT 108

রাজা কহে, — ভবানন্দের পুত্র বাণীনাথ।
প্রসাদ লঞা সঙ্গে চলে পাঁচ-সাত ॥ ১০৮ ॥

rājā kahe, — bhavānandera putra vāṇīnātha
prasāda lañā saṅge cale pāṅca-sāta

rājā kahe — the King said; *bhavānandera putra* — the son of Bhavānanda; *vāṇīnātha* — Vāṇīnātha; *prasāda lañā* — taking *mahā-prasāda*; *saṅge* — along; *cale* — goes; *pāṅca-sāta* — five or seven men.

TRANSLATION

The King said, "The son of Bhavānanda Rāya named Vāṇīnātha, along with five or seven other men, went there to obtain the remnants of Lord Jagannātha's food.

TEXT 109

মহাপ্রভুর আলয়ে করিল গমন।
এত মহাপ্রসাদ চাহি' — কহ কি কারণ ॥ ১০৯ ॥

mahāprabhura ālaye karila gamana
eta mahā-prasāda cāhi' — kaha ki kāraṇa

mahāprabhura — of Śrī Caitanya Mahāprabhu; *ālaye* — the residential place; *karila gamana* — he has already gone; *eta* — so much; *mahā-prasāda-maha-prasādam; cāhi'* — requiring; *kaha* — please tell; *ki kāraṇa* — what is the reason.

TRANSLATION

"Indeed, Vāṇīnātha has already gone to the residence of Lord Śrī Caitanya Mahāprabhu and has taken a huge quantity of mahā-prasādam. Please let me know the reason for this."

TEXT 110

ভট্ট কহে, — ভক্তগণ আইল জানিঞা।
প্রভুর ইঙ্গিতে প্রসাদ যায় তাঁরা লঞা ॥ ১১০ ॥

bhaṭṭa kahe,—bhakta-gaṇa āila jāniñā
prabhura iṅgite prasāda yāya tāṅrā lañā

bhaṭṭa kahe—Sārvabhauma Bhaṭṭācārya said; *bhakta-gaṇa*—all the devotees; *āila*—have come; *jāniñā*—knowing; *prabhura*—of Lord Śrī Caitanya Mahāprabhu; *iṅgite*—by the indication; *prasāda*—remnants of the food offered to Jagannātha; *yāya*—go; *tāṅrā*—all of them; *lañā*—taking.

TRANSLATION

Sārvabhauma Bhaṭṭācārya said, "Understanding that all the devotees have come, Lord Caitanya gave the sign, and therefore Vāṇīnātha and the others have brought such great quantities of mahā-prasādam."

TEXT 111

রাজা কহে,—উপবাস, ক্ষৌর—তীর্থের বিধান।
তাহা না করিয়া কেনে খাইব অন্ন-পান॥ ১১১॥

rājā kahe,—upavāsa, kṣaura—tīrthera vidhāna
tāhā nā kariyā kene khāiba anna-pāna

rājā kahe—the King said; *upavāsa*—fasting; *kṣaura*—shaving; *tīrthera vidhāna*—this is the regulation for visiting a holy place; *tāhā*—that; *nā kariyā*—without performing; *kene*—why; *khāiba*—they shall eat; *anna-pāna*—solid and liquid food.

TRANSLATION

The King then asked the Bhaṭṭācārya, "Why have the devotees not observed the regulations for visiting the pilgrimage place, such as fasting, shaving and so on? Why have they first eaten prasādam?"

TEXT 112

ভট্ট কহে,—তুমি যেই কহ, সেই বিধি-ধর্ম।
এই রাগমার্গে আছে সূক্ষ্মধর্ম-মর্ম॥ ১১২॥

bhaṭṭa kahe,—tumi yei kaha, sei vidhi-dharma
ei rāga-mārge āche sūkṣma-dharma-marma

bhaṭṭa kahe—the Bhaṭṭācārya said; *tumi yei kaha*—whatever you say; *sei vidhi-dharma*—that is a regulative principle; *ei rāga-mārge*—in this spontaneous love; *āche*—there are; *sūkṣma-dharma-marma*—subtle intricacies of the religious system.

TRANSLATION

The Bhaṭṭācārya told the King, "What you have said is right according to the regulative principles governing the visiting of holy places, but there is another path, which is the path of spontaneous love. According to those principles, there are subtle intricacies involved in the execution of religious principles.

PURPORT

According to the Vedic regulative principles, one has to be celibate before entering a holy place of pilgrimage. Generally people are very much addicted to sense gratification, and unless they have sex at night, they cannot sleep. The regulative principles therefore enjoin that before a common man goes to a holy place of pilgrimage, he should observe complete celibacy. As soon as one enters a holy place, he must observe fasting for the day, and after shaving his head clean, he must take a bath in a river or ocean near the holy place. These methods are adopted to neutralize the effects of sinful activities. Visiting a holy place of pilgrimage means neutralizing the reactions of a sinful life. Those who go to holy places of pilgrimage actually unload the reactions of their sinful lives, and consequently holy places are overloaded with sinful activities left there by visitors.

When a saintly person or pure devotee visits such a holy place, he absorbs the sinful effects left by the common men and again purifies the holy place. *Tīrthī-kurvanti tīrthāni* (*Bhāg.* 1.13.10). Therefore a common man's visit to a holy place and an exalted saintly person's visit there are different. The common man leaves his sins in the holy place, and a saintly person or devotee cleanses these sins simply by his presence. The devotees of Lord Caitanya Mahāprabhu were not common men, and they could not be subjected to the rules and regulations governing the visiting of holy places. Rather, they exhibited their spontaneous love for Śrī Caitanya Mahāprabhu. Immediately upon arrival at the holy place, they went to see Lord Caitanya, and by His order they took *mahā-prasādam* without following the regulations governing holy places.

TEXT 113

ঈশ্বরের পরোক্ষ আজ্ঞা — ক্ষৌর, উপোষণ ।
প্রভুর সাক্ষাৎ আজ্ঞা — প্রসাদ-ভোজন ॥ ১১৩ ॥

īśvarera parokṣa ājñā — kṣaura, upoṣaṇa
prabhura sākṣāt ājñā — prasāda-bhojana

īśvarera — of the Supreme Personality of Godhead; *parokṣa* — indirect; *ājñā* — order; *kṣaura* — shaving; *upoṣaṇa* — fasting; *prabhura* — of the Lord; *sākṣāt* — direct; *ājñā* — order; *prasāda-bhojana* — to take the *prasādam.*

TRANSLATION

"The scriptural injunctions for shaving and fasting are indirect orders of the Supreme Personality of Godhead. However, when there is a direct order from the Lord to take prasādam, naturally the devotees take prasādam as their first duty.

TEXT 114

তাহাঁ উপবাস, যাহাঁ নাহি মহাপ্রসাদ ।
প্রভু-আজ্ঞা-প্রসাদ-ত্যাগে হয় অপরাধ ॥ ১১৪ ॥

tāhāṅ upavāsa, yāhāṅ nāhi mahā-prasāda
prabhu-ājñā-prasāda-tyāge haya aparādha

tāhāṅ — there; *upavāsa* — fasting; *yāhāṅ* — where; *nāhi* — there is not; *mahā-prasāda* — remnants of food of the Lord; *prabhu-ājñā* — direct order of Śrī Caitanya Mahāprabhu; *prasāda* — remnants of food; *tyāge* — giving up; *haya* — there is; *aparādha* — offense.

TRANSLATION

"When mahā-prasādam is not available, there must be fasting, but when the Supreme Personality of Godhead directly orders one to take prasādam, neglecting such an opportunity is offensive.

TEXT 115

বিশেষে শ্রীহস্তে প্রভু করে পরিবেশন।
এত লাভ ছাড়ি' কোন্ করে উপোষণ ॥ ১১৫ ॥

viśeṣe śrī-haste prabhu kare pariveśana
eta lābha chāḍi' kon kare upoṣaṇa

viśeṣe—especially; *śrī-haste*—with His transcendental hands; *prabhu*—Śrī Caitanya Mahāprabhu; *kare*—does; *pariveśana*—distribution; *eta*—so much; *lābha*—profit; *chāḍi'*—giving up; *kon*—who; *kare*—does; *upoṣaṇa*—fasting.

TRANSLATION

"When Śrī Caitanya Mahāprabhu is distributing prasādam with His transcendental hand, who will neglect such an opportunity and accept the regulative principle of fasting?

TEXT 116

পূর্বে প্রভু মোরে প্রসাদ-অন্ন আনি' দিল।
প্রাতে শয্যায় বসি' আমি সে অন্ন খাইল ॥ ১১৬ ॥

pūrve prabhu more prasāda-anna āni' dila
prāte śayyāya vasi' āmi se anna khāila

pūrve—before this; *prabhu*—Śrī Caitanya Mahāprabhu; *more*—unto me; *prasāda-anna*—rice *mahā-prasādam; āni'*—bringing; *dila*—delivered; *prāte*—early in the morning; *śayyāya*—on my bed; *vasi'*—sitting; *āmi*—I; *se*—that; *anna*—rice; *khāila*—ate.

TRANSLATION

"Previously the Lord gave me mahā-prasādam rice one morning, and I ate it just sitting on my bed, without having even washed my mouth.

TEXT 117

যাঁরে কৃপা করি' করেন হৃদয়ে প্রেরণ।
কৃষ্ণাশ্রয় হয়, ছাড়ে বেদ-লোক-ধর্ম ॥ ১১৭ ॥

yāṅre kṛpā kari' karena hṛdaye preraṇa
kṛṣṇāśraya haya, chāḍe veda-loka-dharma

yāṅre—in whomever; *kṛpā*—mercy; *kari'*—bestowing; *karena*—does; *hṛdaye*—in the heart; *preraṇa*—inspiration; *kṛṣṇa-āśraya*—shelter of Lord Kṛṣṇa; *haya*—there is; *chāḍe*—he gives up; *veda*—Vedic principles; *loka-dharma*—social etiquette.

TRANSLATION

"The man to whom the Lord shows His mercy by inspiring him within the heart takes shelter only of Lord Kṛṣṇa and abandons all Vedic and social customs.

PURPORT

This is also the teaching of Lord Kṛṣṇa in the *Bhagavad-gītā* (18.66):

sarva-dharmān parityajya mām ekaṁ śaraṇaṁ vraja
ahaṁ tvāṁ sarva-pāpebhyo mokṣayiṣyāmi mā śucaḥ

"Abandon all varieties of religion and just surrender unto Me. I shall deliver you from all sinful reactions. Do not fear." Such firm faith in the Supreme Personality of Godhead is possible only by the mercy of the Lord. The Lord is sitting within everyone's heart, and when He personally inspires His devotee, the devotee does not stick to the Vedic principles or social customs but rather devotes himself to the transcendental loving service of the Lord. This is confirmed in the following verse from *Śrīmad-Bhāgavatam* (4.29.46).

TEXT 118

যদা যমনুগৃহ্ণাতি ভগবানাত্মভাবিতঃ ।
স জহাতি মতিং লোকে বেদে চ পরিনিষ্ঠিতাম্ ॥ ১১৮ ॥

yadā yam anugṛhṇāti
bhagavān ātma-bhāvitaḥ
sa jahāti matiṁ loke
vede ca pariniṣṭhitām

yadā—when; *yam*—to whom; *anugṛhṇāti*—shows special favor; *bhagavān*—the Supreme Personality of Godhead; *ātma-*

bhāvitaḥ—who is seated in everyone's heart; *saḥ*—that person; *jahāti*—gives up; *matim*—attention; *loke*—to social behavior; *vede*—to Vedic injunctions; *ca*—also; *pariniṣṭhitām*—attached.

TRANSLATION

"'When one is inspired by the Lord, who is sitting in everyone's heart, he does not care for social custom or Vedic regulative principles.'"

PURPORT

This instruction (*Bhāg.* 4.29.46) was given by Nārada Gosvāmī to King Prācīnabarhi in connection with the story of Purañjana. Here Nārada implies that without the mercy of the Supreme Personality of Godhead one cannot extricate himself from the fruitive activities that are under the jurisdiction of the *Vedas.* In previous verses (*Bhāg.* 4.29.42–44) Nārada admits that even personalities like Lord Brahmā, Lord Śiva, Manu, the Prajāpatis (headed by Dakṣa), the four Kumāras, Marīci, Atri, Aṅgirā, Pulastya, Pulaha, Kratu, Bhṛgu, Vasiṣṭha and even Nārada himself could not properly receive the causeless mercy of the Lord.

TEXT 119

তবে রাজা অট্টালিকা হৈতে তলেতে আইলা।
কাশীমিশ্র, পড়িছা-পাত্র, দুঁহে আনাইলা ॥ ১১৯ ॥

tabe rājā aṭṭālikā haite talete āilā
kāśī-miśra, paḍichā-pātra, duṅhe ānāilā

tabe—thereafter; *rājā*—the King; *aṭṭālikā haite*—from the top of the palace; *talete*—to the ground; *āilā*—came down; *kāśī-miśra*—Kāśī Miśra; *paḍichā-pātra*—the inspector of the temple; *duṅhe*—both of them; *ānāilā*—called for.

TRANSLATION

After this, King Pratāparudra came down from the top of his palace to the ground and called for Kāśī Miśra and the inspector of the temple.

TEXTS 120–121

প্রতাপরুদ্র আজ্ঞা দিল সেই দুই জনে।
প্রভু-স্থানে আসিয়াছেন যত প্রভুর গণে ॥ ১২০ ॥
সবারে স্বচ্ছন্দ বাসা, স্বচ্ছন্দ প্রসাদ।
স্বচ্ছন্দ দর্শন করাইহ, নহে যেন বাধ ॥ ১২১ ॥

pratāparudra ājñā dila sei dui jane
prabhu-sthāne āsiyāchena yata prabhura gaṇe

sabāre svacchanda vāsā, svacchanda prasāda
svacchanda darśana karāiha, nahe yena bādha

pratāparudra—King Pratāparudra; *ājñā dila*—ordered; *sei dui jane*—to those two persons; *prabhu-sthāne*—at the place of Śrī Caitanya Mahāprabhu; *āsiyāchena*—have arrived; *yata*—all the devotees who; *prabhura gaṇe*—associates of the Lord; *sabāre*—to all of them; *svacchanda*—convenient; *vāsā*—residential places; *svacchanda*—convenient; *prasāda*—remnants of the food offered to Jagannātha; *svacchanda darśana*—convenient visit; *karāiha*—arrange for; *nahe yena bādha*—so that there will not be any difficulties.

TRANSLATION

Mahārāja Pratāparudra then told both Kāśī Miśra and the temple inspector, "Provide all the devotees and associates of Śrī Caitanya Mahāprabhu with comfortable residences, convenient eating facilities for prasādam and convenient visiting arrangements at the temple so that there will not be any difficulty.

TEXT 122

প্রভুর আজ্ঞা পালিহ দুঁহে সাবধান হঞা।
আজ্ঞা নহে, তবু করিহ, ইঙ্গিত বুঝিয়া ॥ ১২২ ॥

prabhura ājñā pāliha duṅhe sāvadhāna hañā
ājñā nahe, tabu kariha, iṅgita bujhiyā

prabhura—of Lord Śrī Caitanya Mahāprabhu; *ājñā*—the order; *pāliha*—carry out; *duṅhe*—both of you; *sāvadhāna*—careful;

hañā—becoming; *ājñā nahe*—although there is no direct order; *tabu*—still; *kariha*—do; *iṅgita*—indication; *bujhiyā*—understanding.

TRANSLATION

"The orders of Śrī Caitanya Mahāprabhu must be carefully carried out. Although the Lord may not give direct orders, you are still to carry out His desires simply by understanding His indications."

TEXT 123

এত বলি' বিদায় দিল সেই দুই-জনে।
সার্বভৌম দেখিতে আইল বৈষ্ণব-মিলনে ॥ ১২৩ ॥

eta bali' vidāya dila sei dui-jane
sārvabhauma dekhite āila vaiṣṇava-milane

eta bali'—saying this; *vidāya dila*—granted permission to go; *sei dui-jane*—to those two persons; *sārvabhauma*—Sārvabhauma Bhaṭṭācārya; *dekhite*—to see; *āila*—came; *vaiṣṇava-milane*—in the meeting of all the Vaiṣṇavas.

TRANSLATION

Saying this, the King gave them permission to leave. Sārvabhauma Bhaṭṭācārya also went to see the assembly of all the Vaiṣṇavas.

TEXT 124

গোপীনাথাচার্য ভট্টাচার্য সার্বভৌম।
দূরে রহি' দেখে প্রভুর বৈষ্ণব-মিলন ॥ ১২৪ ॥

gopīnāthācārya bhaṭṭācārya sārvabhauma
dūre rahi' dekhe prabhura vaiṣṇava-milana

gopīnātha-ācārya—Gopīnātha Ācārya; *bhaṭṭācārya sārvabhauma*—Sārvabhauma Bhaṭṭācārya; *dūre rahi'*—standing a little off; *dekhe*—see; *prabhura*—of Śrī Caitanya Mahāprabhu; *vaiṣṇava-milana*—meeting with the Vaiṣṇavas.

TRANSLATION

From a distant place, Gopīnātha Ācārya and Sārvabhauma Bhaṭṭācārya watched the meeting of all the Vaiṣṇavas with Śrī Caitanya Mahāprabhu.

TEXT 125

সিংহদ্বার ডাহিনে ছাড়ি' সব বৈষ্ণবগণ।
কাশীমিশ্র-গৃহ-পথে করিলা গমন॥ ১২৫॥

siṁha-dvāra ḍāhine chāḍi' saba vaiṣṇava-gaṇa
kāśī-miśra-gṛha-pathe karilā gamana

siṁha-dvāra ḍāhine—on the right side of the lion gate; *chāḍi'*—leaving aside; *saba*—all; *vaiṣṇava-gaṇa*—devotees of Lord Śrī Caitanya Mahāprabhu; *kāśī-miśra-gṛha*—to the house of Kāśī Miśra; *pathe*—on the way; *karilā gamana*—began to proceed.

TRANSLATION

Beginning from the right side of the lion gate, or the main gate of the temple, all the Vaiṣṇavas began to proceed toward the house of Kāśī Miśra.

TEXT 126

হেনকালে মহাপ্রভু নিজগণ-সঙ্গে।
বৈষ্ণবে মিলিলা আসি' পথে বহুরঙ্গে॥ ১২৬॥

hena-kāle mahāprabhu nija-gaṇa-saṅge
vaiṣṇave mililā āsi' pathe bahu-raṅge

hena-kāle—at this time; *mahāprabhu*—Śrī Caitanya Mahāprabhu; *nija-gaṇa-saṅge*—in the association of His personal assistants; *vaiṣṇave*—all the Vaiṣṇavas; *mililā*—met; *āsi'*—coming; *pathe*—on the road; *bahu-raṅge*—in great jubilation.

TRANSLATION

In the meantime, Śrī Caitanya Mahāprabhu, accompanied by His personal associates, met all the Vaiṣṇavas on the road with great jubilation.

TEXT 127

অদ্বৈত করিল প্রভুর চরণ বন্দন।
আচার্য্যেরে কৈল প্রভু প্রেম-আলিঙ্গন ॥ ১২৭ ॥

advaita karila prabhura caraṇa vandana
ācāryere kaila prabhu prema-āliṅgana

advaita—Advaita Ācārya; *karila*—did; *prabhura*—of Lord Śrī Caitanya Mahāprabhu; *caraṇa*—of the lotus feet; *vandana*—worship; *ācāryere*—unto Advaita Ācārya; *kaila*—did; *prabhu*—Śrī Caitanya Mahāprabhu; *prema-āliṅgana*—embracing in ecstatic love.

TRANSLATION

First Advaita Ācārya offered prayers to the lotus feet of the Lord, and the Lord immediately embraced Him in ecstatic love.

TEXT 128

প্রেমানন্দে হৈলা দুঁহে পরম অস্থির।
সময় দেখিয়া প্রভু হৈলা কিছু ধীর ॥ ১২৮ ॥

premānande hailā duṅhe parama asthira
samaya dekhiyā prabhu hailā kichu dhīra

prema-ānande—in ecstatic love; *hailā*—became; *duṅhe*—both of them; *parama asthira*—greatly agitated; *samaya*—the time; *dekhiyā*—seeing; *prabhu*—the Lord; *hailā*—became; *kichu*—a little; *dhīra*—patient.

TRANSLATION

Indeed, Śrī Caitanya Mahāprabhu and Advaita Ācārya displayed agitation due to ecstatic love. Seeing the time and circumstance, however, Lord Caitanya Mahāprabhu remained patient.

TEXT 129

শ্রীবাসাদি করিল প্রভুর চরণ বন্দন।
প্রত্যেকে করিল প্রভু প্রেম-আলিঙ্গন ॥ ১২৯ ॥

śrīvāsādi karila prabhura caraṇa vandana
pratyeke karila prabhu prema-āliṅgana

śrīvāsa-ādi—devotees headed by Śrīvāsa Ṭhākura; *karila*—did; *prabhura*—of Śrī Caitanya Mahāprabhu; *caraṇa vandana*—worshiping the lotus feet; *pratyeke*—to everyone; *karila*—did; *prabhu*—Śrī Caitanya Mahāprabhu; *prema-āliṅgana*—embracing in love.

TRANSLATION

After this, all the devotees, headed by Śrīvāsa Ṭhākura, offered prayers to the lotus feet of the Lord, and the Lord embraced each and every one of them in great love and ecstasy.

TEXT 130

একে একে সর্বভক্তে কৈল সম্ভাষণ।
সবা লঞা অভ্যন্তরে করিলা গমন ॥ ১৩০ ॥

eke eke sarva-bhakte kaila sambhāṣaṇa
sabā lañā abhyantare karilā gamana

eke eke—one after another; *sarva-bhakte*—to every devotee; *kaila*—did; *sambhāṣaṇa*—address; *sabā lañā*—taking all of them; *abhyantare*—inside; *karilā gamana*—entered.

TRANSLATION

The Lord addressed all the devotees one after another and took all of them with Him into the house.

TEXT 131

মিশ্রের আবাস সেই হয় অল্প স্থান।
অসংখ্য বৈষ্ণব তাহাঁ হৈল পরিমাণ ॥ ১৩১ ॥

miśrera āvāsa sei haya alpa sthāna
asaṅkhya vaiṣṇava tāhāṅ haila parimāṇa

miśrera āvāsa—the residence of Kāśī Miśra; *sei*—that; *haya*—is; *alpa sthāna*—insufficient place; *asaṅkhya*—unlimited; *vaiṣṇava*—devotees; *tāhāṅ*—there; *haila*—were; *parimāṇa*—overcrowded.

TRANSLATION

Since the residence of Kāśī Miśra was insufficient, all the assembled devotees were very much overcrowded.

TEXT 132

আপন-নিকটে প্রভু সবা বসাইলা।
আপনি শ্রীহস্তে সবারে মাল্য-গন্ধ দিলা ॥ ১৩২ ॥

āpana-nikaṭe prabhu sabā vasāilā
āpani śrī-haste sabāre mālya-gandha dilā

āpana-nikaṭe—by His own side; *prabhu*—Śrī Caitanya Mahāprabhu; *sabā*—all of them; *vasāilā*—made sit; *āpani*—personally Himself; *śrī-haste*—with His hand; *sabāre*—unto everyone; *mālya*—garland; *gandha*—sandalwood pulp; *dilā*—offered.

TRANSLATION

Śrī Caitanya Mahāprabhu made all the devotees sit at His side, and with His own hand He offered them garlands and sandalwood pulp.

TEXT 133

ভট্টাচার্য, আচার্য তবে মহাপ্রভুর স্থানে।
যথাযোগ্য মিলিলা সবাকার সনে ॥ ১৩৩ ॥

bhaṭṭācārya, ācārya tabe mahāprabhura sthāne
yathā-yogya mililā sabākāra sane

bhaṭṭācārya—Sārvabhauma Bhaṭṭācārya; *ācārya*—Gopīnātha Ācārya; *tabe*—thereafter; *mahāprabhura sthāne*—at the place of Śrī Caitanya Mahāprabhu; *yathā-yogya*—as it is befitting; *mililā*—met; *sabākāra sane*—with all the Vaiṣṇavas assembled there.

TRANSLATION

After this, Gopīnātha Ācārya and Sārvabhauma Bhaṭṭācārya met all the Vaiṣṇavas at the place of Śrī Caitanya Mahāprabhu in a befitting manner.

TEXT 134

অদ্বৈতেরে কহেন প্রভু মধুর বচনে।
আজি আমি পূর্ণ হইলাঙ তোমার আগমনে॥ ১৩৪॥

advaitere kahena prabhu madhura vacane
āji āmi pūrṇa ha-ilāṅa tomāra āgamane

advaitere—unto Advaita Ācārya Prabhu; *kahena*—says; *prabhu*—Śrī Caitanya Mahāprabhu; *madhura vacane*—in sweet language; *āji*—today; *āmi*—I; *pūrṇa*—perfect; *ha-ilāṅa*—became; *tomāra*—Your; *āgamane*—on arrival.

TRANSLATION

Śrī Caitanya Mahāprabhu addressed Advaita Ācārya Prabhu, saying sweetly, "My dear Sir, today I have become perfect because of Your arrival."

TEXTS 135–136

অদ্বৈত কহে,—ঈশ্বরের এই স্বভাব হয়।
যদ্যপি আপনে পূর্ণ, সর্বৈশ্বর্যময়॥ ১৩৫॥
তথাপি ভক্তসঙ্গে হয় সুখোল্লাস।
ভক্ত-সঙ্গে করে নিত্য বিবিধ বিলাস॥ ১৩৬॥

advaita kahe,—īśvarera ei svabhāva haya
yadyapi āpane pūrṇa, sarvaiśvarya-maya

tathāpi bhakta-saṅge haya sukhollāsa
bhakta-saṅge kare nitya vividha vilāsa

advaita kahe—Advaita Ācārya Prabhu said; *īśvarera*—of the Lord; *ei*—this; *svabhāva*—feature; *haya*—becomes; *yadyapi*—although; *āpane*—Himself; *pūrṇa*—all-perfect; *sarva-aiśvarya-maya*—full of all opulences; *tathāpi*—still; *bhakta-saṅge*—in the association of devotees; *haya*—there is; *sukha-ullāsa*—great jubilation; *bhakta-saṅge*—with devotees; *kare*—does; *nitya*—eternally; *vividha*—various; *vilāsa*—pastimes.

TRANSLATION

Advaita Ācārya Prabhu replied, "This is a natural characteristic of the Supreme Personality of Godhead. Although He is personally complete and full in all opulences, He takes transcendental pleasure in the association of His devotees, with whom He has a variety of eternal pastimes."

TEXT 137

বাসুদেব দেখি' প্রভু আনন্দিত হঞা।
তাঁরে কিছু কহে তাঁর অঙ্গে হস্ত দিয়া ॥ ১৩৭ ॥

vāsudeva dekhi' prabhu ānandita hañā
tāṅre kichu kahe tāṅra aṅge hasta diyā

vāsudeva—Vāsudeva; *dekhi'*—seeing; *prabhu*—Lord Śrī Caitanya Mahāprabhu; *ānandita hañā*—becoming very pleased; *tāṅre*—unto him; *kichu kahe*—says something; *tāṅra aṅge*—on his body; *hasta diyā*—placing His hand.

TRANSLATION

As soon as Śrī Caitanya Mahāprabhu saw Vāsudeva Datta, the older brother of Mukunda Datta, He immediately became very happy and, placing His hand on his body, began to speak.

TEXT 138

যদ্যপি মুকুন্দ — আমা-সঙ্গে শিশু হৈতে।
তাঁহা হৈতে অধিক সুখ তোমারে দেখিতে ॥ ১৩৮ ॥

yadyapi mukunda—āmā-saṅge śiśu haite
tāṅhā haite adhika sukha tomāre dekhite

yadyapi—although; *mukunda*—Mukunda; *āmā-saṅge*—with Me; *śiśu haite*—from childhood; *tāṅhā haite*—than him; *adhika*—still more; *sukha*—happiness; *tomāre dekhite*—to see you.

TRANSLATION

Śrī Caitanya Mahāprabhu said, "Although Mukunda is My friend from childhood, I nonetheless take greater pleasure in seeing you than in seeing him."

PURPORT

Vāsudeva Datta was the older brother of Mukunda Datta, who was the childhood friend of Śrī Caitanya Mahāprabhu. It is naturally a great pleasure to see a friend, but Śrī Caitanya Mahāprabhu informed Vāsudeva Datta that although it was His pleasure to see His friend, His pleasure was increased by seeing the older brother.

TEXT 139

বাসু কহে, — মুকুন্দ আদৌ পাইল তোমার সঙ্গ ।
তোমার চরণ পাইল সেই পুনর্জন্ম ॥ ১৩৯ ॥

vāsu kahe, — mukunda ādau pāila tomāra saṅga
tomāra caraṇa pāila sei punar-janma

vāsu kahe — Vāsudeva Datta said; *mukunda* — Mukunda; *ādau* — in the beginning; *pāila* — got; *tomāra saṅga* — Your association; *tomāra caraṇa* — Your lotus feet; *pāila* — got; *sei* — that; *punaḥ-janma* — transcendental rebirth.

TRANSLATION

Vāsudeva replied, "Mukunda got Your association in the beginning. As such, he has taken shelter at Your lotus feet. That is his transcendental rebirth."

TEXT 140

ছোট হঞা মুকুন্দ এবে হৈল আমার জ্যেষ্ঠ ।
তোমার কৃপাপাত্র তাতে সর্বগুণে শ্রেষ্ঠ ॥ ১৪০ ॥

choṭa hañā mukunda ebe haila āmāra jyeṣṭha
tomāra kṛpā-pātra tāte sarva-guṇe śreṣṭha

choṭa hañā—being junior; *mukunda*—Mukunda; *ebe*—now; *haila*—has become; *āmāra*—my; *jyeṣṭha*—senior; *tomāra*—Your; *kṛpā-pātra*—favorite; *tāte*—therefore; *sarva-guṇe*—in all good qualities; *śreṣṭha*—superior.

TRANSLATION

Thus Vāsudeva Datta admitted his inferiority to Mukunda, his younger brother. "Although Mukunda is my junior," he said, "he first received Your favor. Consequently he became transcendentally senior to me. Besides that, You very much favored Mukunda. Thus he is superior in all good qualities."

TEXT 141

পুনঃ প্রভু কহে—আমি তোমার নিমিত্তে।
দুই পুস্তক আনিয়াছি 'দক্ষিণ' হইতে ॥ ১৪১ ॥

punaḥ prabhu kahe—āmi tomāra nimitte
dui pustaka āniyāchi 'dakṣiṇa' ha-ite

punaḥ—again; *prabhu kahe*—the Lord said; *āmi*—I; *tomāra nimitte*—for your sake; *dui*—two; *pustaka*—books; *āniyāchi*—have brought; *dakṣiṇa ha-ite*—from South India.

TRANSLATION

The Lord said, "For your sake only, I have brought two books from South India.

TEXT 142

স্বরূপের ঠাঁই আছে, লহ তা লিখিয়া।
বাসুদেব আনন্দিত পুস্তক পাঞা ॥ ১৪২ ॥

svarūpera ṭhāñi āche, laha tā likhiyā
vāsudeva ānandita pustaka pāñā

svarūpera ṭhāñi—in the possession of Svarūpa Dāmodara; *āche*—they are; *laha*—you take; *tā*—them; *likhiyā*—copying;

vāsudeva—Vāsudeva; *ānandita*—very glad; *pustaka*—the books; *pāñā*—getting.

TRANSLATION

"The books are being kept with Svarūpa Dāmodara, and you can get them copied." Hearing this, Vāsudeva became very glad.

TEXT 143

প্রত্যেক বৈষ্ণব সবে লিখিয়া লইল।
ক্রমে ক্রমে দুই গ্রন্থ সর্বত্র ব্যাপিল ॥ ১৪৩ ॥

pratyeka vaiṣṇava sabe likhiyā la-ila
krame krame dui grantha sarvatra vyāpila

pratyeka—each and every; *vaiṣṇava*—devotee; *sabe*—all; *likhiyā*—copying; *la-ila*—took; *krame krame*—by and by; *dui grantha*—the two books; *sarvatra*—everywhere; *vyāpila*—become broadcast.

TRANSLATION

Indeed, each and every Vaiṣṇava copied the two books. By and by, the two books [the Brahma-saṁhitā and Śrī Kṛṣṇa-karṇāmṛta] were broadcast all over India.

TEXT 144

শ্রীবাসাদ্যে কহে প্রভু করি' মহাপ্রীত।
তোমার চারি-ভাইর আমি হইনু বিক্রীত ॥ ১৪৪ ॥

śrīvāsādye kahe prabhu kari' mahā-prīta
tomāra cāri-bhāira āmi ha-inu vikrīta

śrīvāsa-ādye—unto Śrīvāsa and his three brothers; *kahe*—says; *prabhu*—the Lord; *kari'*—giving; *mahā-prīta*—great love; *tomāra*—of you; *cāri-bhāira*—of four brothers; *āmi*—I; *ha-inu*—became; *vikrīta*—purchased.

TRANSLATION

The Lord addressed Śrīvāsa and his brothers with great love and affection, saying, "I am so obliged that I am purchased by you four brothers."

TEXT 145

শ্রীবাস কহেন, — কেনে কহ বিপরীত।
কৃপা-মূল্যে চারি ভাই হই তোমার ক্রীত ॥ ১৪৫ ॥

śrīvāsa kahena, — kene kaha viparīta
kṛpā-mūlye cāri bhāi ha-i tomāra krīta

śrīvāsa kahena — Śrīvāsa Ṭhākura replied; *kene* — why; *kaha viparīta* — do You speak just the opposite; *kṛpā-mūlye* — by the price of Your mercy; *cāri bhāi* — we four brothers; *ha-i* — become; *tomāra* — of You; *krīta* — purchased.

TRANSLATION

Śrīvāsa then replied to the Lord, "Why are You speaking in a contradictory way? Rather, we four brothers have been purchased by Your mercy."

TEXT 146

শঙ্করে দেখিয়া প্রভু কহে দামোদরে।
সগৌরব-প্রীতি আমার তোমার উপরে ॥ ১৪৬ ॥

śaṅkare dekhiyā prabhu kahe dāmodare
sagaurava-prīti āmāra tomāra upare

śaṅkare dekhiyā — seeing Śaṅkara; *prabhu* — the Lord; *kahe* — says; *dāmodare* — unto Dāmodara; *sa-gaurava-prīti* — affection with awe and reverence; *āmāra* — My; *tomāra upare* — upon you.

TRANSLATION

After seeing Śaṅkara, Lord Śrī Caitanya Mahāprabhu told Dāmodara, "My affection for you is on the platform of awe and reverence.

PURPORT

Here the Lord is addressing Dāmodara Paṇḍita, who is different from Svarūpa Dāmodara. Dāmodara Paṇḍita is the elder brother of Śaṅkara. Thus the Lord informed Dāmodara that His affection toward him was on the platform of awe and reverence. However, the Lord's affection toward his younger brother, Śaṅkara, was on the platform of pure love.

TEXT 147

শুদ্ধ কেবল-প্রেম শঙ্কর-উপরে ।
অতএব তোমার সঙ্গে রাখহ শঙ্করে ॥ ১৪৭ ॥

śuddha kevala-prema śaṅkara-upare
ataeva tomāra saṅge rākhaha śaṅkare

śuddha kevala-prema—pure unalloyed affection; *śaṅkara-upare*—upon Śaṅkara; *ataeva*—therefore; *tomāra saṅge*—along with you; *rākhaha*—keep; *śaṅkare*—Śaṅkara.

TRANSLATION

"Therefore keep your younger brother Śaṅkara with you because he is connected to Me by pure unalloyed love."

TEXT 148

দামোদর কহে, —শঙ্কর ছোট আমা হৈতে ।
এবে আমার বড় ভাই তোমার কৃপাতে ॥ ১৪৮ ॥

dāmodara kahe,—śaṅkara choṭa āmā haite
ebe āmāra baḍa bhāi tomāra kṛpāte

dāmodara kahe—Dāmodara Paṇḍita replied; *śaṅkara*—Śaṅkara; *choṭa*—younger; *āmā haite*—than me; *ebe*—now; *āmāra*—my; *baḍa bhāi*—elder brother; *tomāra*—of You; *kṛpāte*—by the mercy.

TRANSLATION

Dāmodara Paṇḍita replied, "Śaṅkara is my younger brother, but from today he becomes my elder brother because of Your special mercy upon him."

TEXT 149

শিবানন্দে কহে প্রভু, — তোমার আমাতে।
গাঢ় অনুরাগ হয়, জানি আগে হৈতে॥ ১৪৯॥

śivānande kahe prabhu, — tomāra āmāte
gāḍha anurāga haya, jāni āge haite

śivānande — unto Śivānanda Sena; *kahe* — says; *prabhu* — the Lord; *tomāra* — your; *āmāte* — upon Me; *gāḍha anurāga* — deep affection; *haya* — there is; *jāni* — I know; *āge haite* — from the very beginning.

TRANSLATION

Then turning toward Śivānanda Sena, the Lord said, "I know that from the very beginning your affection for Me has been very great."

TEXT 150

শুনি' শিবানন্দ-সেন প্রেমাবিষ্ট হঞা।
দণ্ডবৎ হঞা পড়ে শ্লোক পড়িয়া॥ ১৫০॥

śuni' śivānanda-sena premāviṣṭa hañā
daṇḍavat hañā paḍe śloka paḍiyā

śuni' — hearing; *śivānanda-sena* — Śivānanda Sena; *prema-āviṣṭa hañā* — becoming absorbed in pure love; *daṇḍavat hañā* — offering obeisances; *paḍe* — falls down; *śloka* — a verse; *paḍiyā* — reciting.

TRANSLATION

Immediately upon hearing this, Śivānanda Sena became absorbed in ecstatic love and fell down on the ground, offering obeisances to the Lord. He then began to recite the following verse.

TEXT 151

নিমজ্জতোঽনন্ত ভবার্ণবান্তশ্চিরায় মে কূলমিবাসি লব্ধঃ।
ত্বয়াপি লব্ধং ভগবন্নিদানীমনুত্তমং পাত্রমিদং দয়ায়াঃ॥ ১৫১॥

nimajjato 'nanta bhavārṇavāntaś
cirāya me kūlam ivāsi labdhaḥ

tvayāpi labdhaṁ bhagavann idānīm
anuttamaṁ pātram idaṁ dayāyāḥ

nimajjataḥ—being immersed; *ananta*—O unlimited one; *bhava-arṇava-antaḥ*—within the ocean of nescience; *cirāya*—after a long time; *me*—of me; *kūlam*—the shore; *iva*—like; *asi*—You are; *labdhaḥ*—obtained; *tvayā*—by You; *api*—also; *labdham*—has been gained; *bhagavan*—O my Lord; *idānīm*—now; *anuttamam*—the best; *pātram*—candidate; *idam*—this; *dayāyāḥ*—for showing Your mercy.

TRANSLATION

"'O my Lord! O unlimited one! Although I was merged in the ocean of nescience, I have now, after a long time, attained You, just as one may attain the seashore. My dear Lord, by getting me, You have obtained the right person upon whom to bestow Your causeless mercy.'"

PURPORT

This is verse 21 from the *Stotra-ratna,* composed by Ālabandāru Yāmunācārya. One's relationship with the Supreme Personality of Godhead may be reestablished even after one has fallen into the ocean of nescience, which is the ocean of material existence involving the repetition of birth, death, old age and disease, all arising out of the acceptance of the material body. There are 8,400,000 species of material life, but in the human body one attains a chance to get release from the repetition of birth and death. When one becomes the Lord's devotee, he is rescued from this dangerous ocean of birth and death. The Lord is always prepared to shower His mercy upon fallen souls struggling against miserable material conditions. As Lord Kṛṣṇa states in the *Bhagavad-gītā* (15.7):

mamaivāṁśo jīva-loke jīva-bhūtaḥ sanātanaḥ
manaḥ-ṣaṣṭhānīndriyāṇi prakṛti-sthāni karṣati

"The living entities in this conditioned world are My eternal fragmental parts. Due to conditioned life, they are struggling very hard with the six senses, which include the mind."

Thus every living being is struggling hard in this material nature. Actually the living entity is part and parcel of the Supreme Lord, and when he surrenders unto the Supreme Personality of Godhead, he attains release from the ocean of birth and death. The Lord, being very kind to fallen souls, is always anxious to get the living entity out of the ocean of nescience. If the living entity understands his position and surrenders to the Lord, his life becomes successful.

TEXT 152

প্রথমে মুরারি-গুপ্ত প্রভুরে না মিলিয়া ।
বাহিরেতে পড়ি' আছে দণ্ডবৎ হঞা ॥ ১৫২ ॥

prathame murāri-gupta prabhure nā miliyā
bāhirete paḍi' āche daṇḍavat hañā

prathame—at first; *murāri-gupta*—Murāri Gupta; *prabhure*—to Śrī Caitanya Mahāprabhu; *nā*—without; *miliyā*—meeting; *bāhirete*—outside; *paḍi'*—falling down; *āche*—was there; *daṇḍavat*—falling flat like a stick; *hañā*—becoming so.

TRANSLATION

Murāri Gupta at first did not meet the Lord but rather remained outside the door, falling down like a stick to offer obeisances.

TEXT 153

মুরারি না দেখিয়া প্রভু করে অন্বেষণ ।
মুরারি লইতে ধাঞা আইলা বহুজন ॥ ১৫৩ ॥

murāri nā dekhiyā prabhu kare anveṣaṇa
murāri la-ite dhāñā āilā bahu-jana

murāri—Murāri; *nā*—without; *dekhiyā*—seeing; *prabhu*—the Lord; *kare*—does; *anveṣaṇa*—inquiry; *murāri*—Murāri Gupta; *la-ite*—to take; *dhāñā*—running; *āilā*—came; *bahu-jana*—many persons.

TRANSLATION

When Lord Śrī Caitanya Mahāprabhu could not see Murāri amongst the devotees, He inquired about him. Thereupon many people immediately went to Murāri, running to take him to the Lord.

TEXT 154

তৃণ দুইগুচ্ছ মুরারি দশনে ধরিয়া।
মহাপ্রভু আগে গেলা দৈন্যাধীন হঞা ॥ ১৫৪ ॥

tṛṇa dui-guccha murāri daśane dhariyā
mahāprabhu āge gelā dainyādhīna hañā

tṛṇa—of straw; *dui*—two; *guccha*—bunches; *murāri*—Murāri; *daśane*—in his teeth; *dhariyā*—catching; *mahāprabhu*—of Śrī Caitanya Mahāprabhu; *āge*—in front; *gelā*—went; *dainya-adhīna*—under obligation of meekness; *hañā*—becoming.

TRANSLATION

Thus Murāri Gupta, catching two bunches of straw in his teeth, went before Śrī Caitanya Mahāprabhu with humility and meekness.

TEXT 155

মুরারি দেখিয়া প্রভু আইলা মিলিতে।
পাছে ভাগে মুরারি, লাগিলা কহিতে ॥ ১৫৫ ॥

murāri dekhiyā prabhu āilā milite
pāche bhāge murāri, lāgilā kahite

murāri—Murāri; *dekhiyā*—seeing; *prabhu*—Lord Caitanya Mahāprabhu; *āilā*—came out; *milite*—to meet; *pāche*—thereafter; *bhāge*—runs away; *murāri*—Murāri; *lāgilā*—began; *kahite*—to speak.

TRANSLATION

Upon seeing Murāri come to meet Him, Lord Śrī Caitanya Mahāprabhu went up to him, but Murāri began to run away and speak as follows.

TEXT 156

মোরে না ছুঁইহ, প্রভু, মুঞি ত' পামর।
তোমার স্পর্শযোগ্য নহে পাপ কলেবর ॥ ১৫৬ ॥

more nā chuṅiha, prabhu, muñi ta' pāmara
tomāra sparśa-yogya nahe pāpa kalevara

more—me; *nā chuṅiha*—do not touch; *prabhu*—my Lord; *muñi*—I; *ta'*—certainly; *pāmara*—most abominable; *tomāra*—of You; *sparśa-yogya*—fit to be touched; *nahe*—not; *pāpa*—sinful; *kalevara*—body.

TRANSLATION

"My Lord, please do not touch me. I am most abominable and am not fit for You to touch because my body is sinful."

TEXT 157

প্রভু কহে,—মুরারি, কর দৈন্য সম্বরণ।
তোমার দৈন্য দেখি' মোর বিদীর্ণ হয় মন ॥ ১৫৭ ॥

prabhu kahe,—murāri, kara dainya saṁvaraṇa
tomāra dainya dekhi' mora vidīrṇa haya mana

prabhu kahe—the Lord said; *murāri*—My dear Murāri; *kara dainya saṁvaraṇa*—please restrain your great humility; *tomāra*—your; *dainya*—humility; *dekhi'*—seeing; *mora*—My; *vidīrṇa haya mana*—mind becomes disturbed.

TRANSLATION

The Lord said, "My dear Murāri, please restrain your unnecessary humility. My mind is disturbed to see your meekness."

TEXT 158

এত বলি' প্রভু তাঁরে কৈল আলিঙ্গন।
নিকটে বসাঞা করে অঙ্গ সম্মার্জন ॥ ১৫৮ ॥

eta bali' prabhu tāṅre kaila āliṅgana
nikaṭe vasāñā kare aṅga sammārjana

eta bali'—saying this; *prabhu*—the Lord; *tāṅre*—him; *kaila*—did; *āliṅgana*—embrace; *nikaṭe*—nearby; *vasāñā*—making sit down; *kare*—does; *aṅga*—of his body; *sammārjana*—cleansing.

TRANSLATION

Saying this, the Lord embraced Murāri and had him sit down by His side. The Lord then began to cleanse his body with His own hands.

TEXTS 159–160

আচার্যরত্ন, বিদ্যানিধি, পণ্ডিত গদাধর।
গঙ্গাদাস, হরিভট্ট, আচার্য পুরন্দর ॥ ১৫৯ ॥
প্রত্যেকে সবার প্রভু করি' গুণ গান।
পুনঃ পুনঃ আলিঙ্গিয়া করিল সম্মান ॥ ১৬০ ॥

ācāryaratna, vidyānidhi, paṇḍita gadādhara
gaṅgādāsa, hari-bhaṭṭa, ācārya purandara

pratyeke sabāra prabhu kari' guṇa gāna
punaḥ punaḥ āliṅgiyā karila sammāna

ācāryaratna—Ācāryaratna; *vidyānidhi*—Vidyānidhi; *paṇḍita gadādhara*—Paṇḍita Gadādhara; *gaṅgādāsa*—Gaṅgādāsa; *hari-bhaṭṭa*—Hari Bhaṭṭa; *ācārya purandara*—Ācārya Purandara; *pratyeke*—each and every one of them; *sabāra*—of all of them; *prabhu*—the Lord; *kari' guṇa gāna*—glorifying the qualities; *punaḥ punaḥ*—again and again; *āliṅgiyā*—embracing; *karila*—did; *sammāna*—honor.

TRANSLATION

Lord Śrī Caitanya Mahāprabhu then again and again embraced all the devotees, including Ācāryaratna, Vidyānidhi, Paṇḍita Gadādhara, Gaṅgādāsa, Hari Bhaṭṭa and Ācārya Purandara. The Lord described their good qualities and glorified them again and again.

TEXT 161

সবারে সম্মানি' প্রভুর হইল উল্লাস।
হরিদাসে না দেখিয়া কহে, —কাহাঁ হরিদাস॥ ১৬১॥

sabāre sammāni' prabhura ha-ila ullāsa
haridāse nā dekhiyā kahe, — kāhāṅ haridāsa

sabāre sammāni' — respecting everyone; *prabhura* — of the Lord; *ha-ila* — there was; *ullāsa* — jubilation; *haridāse* — Haridāsa Ṭhākura; *nā dekhiyā* — without seeing; *kahe* — says; *kāhāṅ haridāsa* — where is Haridāsa.

TRANSLATION

After thus offering respect to each and every devotee, Lord Śrī Caitanya Mahāprabhu became very jubilant. However, not seeing Haridāsa Ṭhākura, He inquired, "Where is Haridāsa?"

TEXT 162

দূর হৈতে হরিদাস গোসাঞে দেখিয়া।
রাজপথ-প্রান্তে পড়ি' আছে দণ্ডবৎ হঞা॥ ১৬২॥

dūra haite haridāsa gosāñe dekhiyā
rājapatha-prānte paḍi' āche daṇḍavat hañā

dūra haite — from a distance; *haridāsa gosāñe* — Haridāsa Ṭhākura; *dekhiyā* — seeing; *rājapatha-prānte* — at the side of the common road; *paḍi'* — falling down; *āche* — he was; *daṇḍavat hañā* — offering obeisances.

TRANSLATION

Śrī Caitanya Mahāprabhu then saw in the distance that Haridāsa Ṭhākura was lying down flat on the road offering obeisances.

TEXT 163

মিলন-স্থানে আসি' প্রভুরে না মিলিলা।
রাজপথ-প্রান্তে দূরে পড়িয়া রহিলা॥ ১৬৩॥

milana-sthāne āsi' prabhure nā mililā
rājapatha-prānte dūre paḍiyā rahilā

milana-sthāne—in the meeting place; *āsi'*—coming; *prabhure*—unto Lord Śrī Caitanya Mahāprabhu; *nā*—not; *mililā*—did meet; *rājapatha-prānte*—on the side of the common road; *dūre*—at a distant place; *paḍiyā*—falling flat; *rahilā*—remained.

TRANSLATION

Haridāsa Ṭhākura did not come to the Lord's meeting place but remained fallen flat on the common road at a distance.

TEXT 164

ভক্ত সব ধাঞা আইল হরিদাসে নিতে।
প্রভু তোমায় মিলিতে চাহে, চলহ ত্বরিতে ॥ ১৬৪ ॥

bhakta saba dhāñā āila haridāse nite
prabhu tomāya milite cāhe, calaha tvarite

bhakta—devotees; *saba*—all; *dhāñā*—running; *āila*—came; *haridāse*—Haridāsa; *nite*—to take; *prabhu*—Lord Śrī Caitanya Mahāprabhu; *tomāya*—you; *milite*—to meet; *cāhe*—wants; *calaha*—just come; *tvarite*—very soon.

TRANSLATION

All the devotees then went to Haridāsa Ṭhākura, saying, "The Lord wants to meet you. Please come immediately."

TEXT 165

হরিদাস কহে, —মুঞি নীচ-জাতি ছার।
মন্দির-নিকটে যাইতে মোর নাহি অধিকার ॥ ১৬৫ ॥

haridāsa kahe,—muñi nīca-jāti chāra
mandira-nikaṭe yāite mora nāhi ādhikāra

haridāsa kahe—Haridāsa Ṭhākura said; *muñi*—I; *nīca-jāti*—low caste; *chāra*—abominable; *mandira-nikaṭe*—near the temple; *yāite*—to go; *mora*—my; *nāhi*—there is not; *ādhikāra*—authority.

TRANSLATION

Haridāsa Ṭhākura replied, "I cannot go near the temple because I am a low-caste, abominable person. I have no authority to go there."

PURPORT

Although Haridāsa Ṭhākura was such a highly exalted Vaiṣṇava that he was addressed as Haridāsa Gosvāmī, he still did not like to disturb the common sense of the general populace. Haridāsa Ṭhākura was so exalted that he was addressed as *ṭhākura* and *gosāñi,* and these titles are offered to the most advanced Vaiṣṇavas. The spiritual master is generally called *gosāñi,* and *ṭhākura* is used to address the *paramahaṁsas,* those in the topmost rank of spirituality. Nonetheless, Haridāsa Ṭhākura did not want to go near the temple, although he was called there by Śrī Caitanya Mahāprabhu Himself. The Jagannātha temple still accepts only those Hindus who are in the *varṇāśrama* order. Other castes, especially those who are not Hindu, are not allowed to enter the temple. This is a long-standing regulation, and thus Haridāsa Ṭhākura, although certainly competent and qualified to enter the temple, did not want even to go near it. This is called Vaiṣṇava humility.

TEXT 166

নিভৃতে টোটা-মধ্যে স্থান যদি পাঙ ।
তাহাঁ পড়ি' রহো, একলে কাল গোঙাঙ ॥ ১৬৬ ॥

nibhṛte ṭoṭā-madhye sthāna yadi pāṅa
tāhāṅ paḍi' raho, ekale kāla goṅāṅa

nibhṛte—in a solitary place; *ṭoṭā-madhye*—within the gardens; *sthāna*—place; *yadi*—if; *pāṅa*—I get; *tāhāṅ*—there; *paḍi' raho*—I shall stay; *ekale*—alone; *kāla*—time; *goṅāṅa*—I shall pass.

TRANSLATION

Haridāsa Ṭhākura then expressed his desire: "If I could just get a solitary place near the temple, I could stay there alone and pass my time.

TEXT 167

জগন্নাথ-সেবকের মোর স্পর্শ নাহি হয়।
তাহাঁ পড়ি' রহোঁ, — মোর এই বাঞ্ছা হয় ॥ ১৬৭ ॥

jagannātha-sevakera mora sparśa nāhi haya
tāhāṅ paḍi' rahoṅ, — mora ei vāñchā haya

jagannātha-sevakera — of the servants of Lord Jagannātha; *mora* — my; *sparśa* — touching; *nāhi* — not; *haya* — takes place; *tāhāṅ* — there; *paḍi' rahoṅ* — I stay; *mora* — my; *ei* — this; *vāñchā* — desire; *haya* — is.

TRANSLATION

"I do not wish the servants of Lord Jagannātha to touch me. I would remain there in the garden alone. That is my desire."

TEXT 168

এই কথা লোক গিয়া প্রভুরে কহিল।
শুনিয়া প্রভুর মনে বড় সুখ হইল ॥ ১৬৮ ॥

ei kathā loka giyā prabhure kahila
śuniyā prabhura mane baḍa sukha ha-ila

ei kathā — this message; *loka* — people; *giyā* — going; *prabhure* — unto Lord Śrī Caitanya Mahāprabhu; *kahila* — informed; *śuniyā* — hearing; *prabhura mane* — in the mind of the Lord; *baḍa* — very much; *sukha* — happiness; *ha-ila* — became.

TRANSLATION

When this message was relayed to Śrī Caitanya Mahāprabhu by the people, the Lord became very happy to hear it.

TEXT 169

হেনকালে কাশীমিশ্র, পড়িছা, — দুই জন।
আসিয়া করিল প্রভুর চরণ বন্দন ॥ ১৬৯ ॥

hena-kāle kāśī-miśra, paḍichā, — dui jana
āsiyā karila prabhura caraṇa vandana

hena-kāle—at this time; *kāśī-miśra*—Kāśī Miśra; *paḍichā*—the superintendent; *dui jana*—two persons; *āsiyā*—coming; *karila*—did; *prabhura*—of Lord Śrī Caitanya Mahāprabhu; *caraṇa vandana*—worshiping the lotus feet.

TRANSLATION

At this time, Kāśī Miśra, along with the superintendent of the temple, came and offered his respects unto the lotus feet of Lord Śrī Caitanya Mahāprabhu.

TEXT 170

সর্ব বৈষ্ণব দেখি' সুখ বড় পাইলা ।
যথাযোগ্য সবা-সনে আনন্দে মিলিলা ॥ ১৭০ ॥

sarva vaiṣṇava dekhi' sukha baḍa pāilā
yathā-yogya sabā-sane ānande mililā

sarva vaiṣṇava—all the Vaiṣṇavas; *dekhi'*—seeing; *sukha*—happiness; *baḍa*—very much; *pāilā*—got; *yathā-yogya*—as is befitting; *sabā-sane*—along with everyone; *ānande*—in happiness; *mililā*—met.

TRANSLATION

Upon seeing all the Vaiṣṇavas together, Kāśī Miśra and the superintendent became very happy. With great happiness they met with the devotees in a befitting manner.

TEXT 171

প্রভুপদে দুই জনে কৈল নিবেদনে ।
আজ্ঞা দেহ', —বৈষ্ণবের করি সমাধানে ॥ ১৭১ ॥

prabhu-pade dui jane kaila nivedane
ājñā deha',—vaiṣṇavera kari samādhāne

prabhu-pade—unto the lotus feet of Śrī Caitanya Mahāprabhu; *dui jane*—both of them; *kaila*—did; *nivedane*—submission; *ājñā deha'*—please order; *vaiṣṇavera*—of all the Vaiṣṇavas; *kari*—let us do; *samādhāne*—accommodation.

TRANSLATION

Both submitted to Lord Śrī Caitanya Mahāprabhu, "Please give us orders so that we may make proper arrangements to accommodate all the Vaiṣṇavas.

TEXT 172

সবার করিয়াছি বাসা-গৃহ-স্থান ।
মহাপ্রসাদ সবাকারে করি সমাধান ॥ ১৭২ ॥

sabāra kariyāchi vāsā-gṛha-sthāna
mahā-prasāda sabākāre kari samādhāna

sabāra—for all of them; *kariyāchi*—we have arranged; *vāsā-gṛha-sthāna*—residential places for staying; *mahā-prasāda*—remnants of food offered to Jagannātha; *sabākāre*—to all of them; *kari*—let us do; *samādhāna*—distribution.

TRANSLATION

"Accommodations have been arranged for all the Vaiṣṇavas. Now let us distribute mahā-prasādam to all of them."

TEXT 173

প্রভু কহে, — গোপীনাথ, যাহ' বৈষ্ণব লঞা ।
যাহাঁ যাহাঁ কহে বাসা, তাহাঁ দেহ' লঞা ॥ ১৭৩ ॥

prabhu kahe,—gopīnātha, yāha' vaiṣṇava lañā
yāhāṅ yāhāṅ kahe vāsā, tāhāṅ deha' lañā

prabhu kahe—the Lord Caitanya Mahāprabhu said; *gopīnātha*—My dear Gopīnātha; *yāha'*—please go; *vaiṣṇava lañā*—taking all the Vaiṣṇavas; *yāhāṅ yāhāṅ*—wherever; *kahe*—they say; *vāsā*—staying place; *tāhāṅ*—there; *deha'*—give; *lañā*—accepting.

TRANSLATION

Śrī Caitanya Mahāprabhu immediately told Gopīnātha Ācārya, "Please go with the Vaiṣṇavas and accommodate them in whatever residences Kāśī Miśra and the temple superintendent offer."

TEXT 174

মহাপ্রসাদান্ন দেহ বাণীনাথ-স্থানে।
সর্ব বৈষ্ণবের ইঁহো করিবে সমাধানে ॥ ১৭৪ ॥

mahā-prasādānna deha vāṇīnātha-sthāne
sarva-vaiṣṇavera iṅho karibe samādhāne

mahā-prasāda-anna—the remnants of food; *deha*—deliver; *vāṇīnātha-sthāne*—unto Vāṇīnātha; *sarva-vaiṣṇavera*—unto all the Vaiṣṇavas; *iṅho*—he; *karibe*—will do; *samādhāne*—distribution.

TRANSLATION

Then the Lord told Kāśī Miśra and the temple superintendent, "As for the remnants of food left by Jagannātha, let them be delivered to Vāṇīnātha Rāya's charge, for he can take care of all the Vaiṣṇavas and distribute mahā-prasādam to them."

TEXT 175

আমার নিকটে এই পুষ্পের উদ্যানে।
একখানি ঘর আছে পরম-নির্জনে ॥ ১৭৫ ॥

āmāra nikaṭe ei puṣpera udyāne
eka-khāni ghara āche parama-nirjane

āmāra nikaṭe—nearby My place; *ei*—this; *puṣpera udyāne*—in a garden of flowers; *eka-khāni*—one; *ghara*—room; *āche*—there is; *parama-nirjane*—in a very solitary place.

TRANSLATION

Śrī Caitanya Mahāprabhu then said, "Nearby My place, in this garden of flowers, is a single room that is very solitary.

TEXT 176

সেই ঘর আমাকে দেহ' — আছে প্রয়োজন।
নিভৃতে বসিয়া তাহাঁ করিব স্মরণ ॥ ১৭৬ ॥

sei ghara āmāke deha'—āche prayojana
nibhṛte vasiyā tāhāṅ kariba smaraṇa

sei ghara—that room; *āmāke deha'*—please give to Me; *āche prayojana*—there is necessity; *nibhṛte*—in the solitary place; *vasiyā*—sitting; *tāhāṅ*—there; *kariba smaraṇa*—I shall remember the lotus feet of the Lord.

TRANSLATION

"Please give that room to Me, for I have a need for it. Indeed, I shall remember the lotus feet of the Lord sitting in that solitary place."

PURPORT

This statement of Śrī Caitanya Mahāprabhu is significant. *Nibhṛte vasiyā tāhāṅ kariba smaraṇa:* "I shall sit down there in that solitary place and remember the lotus feet of the Lord." Neophyte students are not to imitate sitting in a solitary place and remembering the lotus feet of the Lord by chanting the Hare Kṛṣṇa *mahā-mantra.* We should always remember that it was Śrī Caitanya Mahāprabhu Himself who wanted such a place, either for Himself or Haridāsa Ṭhākura. No one can suddenly attain the level of Haridāsa Ṭhākura and sit down in a solitary place to chant the Hare Kṛṣṇa *mahā-mantra* and remember the lotus feet of the Lord. Only an exalted person like Haridāsa Ṭhākura or Śrī Caitanya Mahāprabhu, who is personally exhibiting the proper behavior for an *ācārya,* can engage in such a practice.

At the present moment we see that some of the members of the International Society for Krishna Consciousness are tending to leave their preaching activities in order to sit in a solitary place. This is not a very good sign. It is a fact that Śrīla Bhaktisiddhānta Sarasvatī Ṭhākura has condemned this process for neophytes. He has even stated in a song, *pratiṣṭhāra tare, nirjanera ghare, tava hari-nāma kevala kaitava:* "Sitting in a solitary place intending to chant the Hare Kṛṣṇa *mahā-mantra* is considered a cheating process." This practice is not possible for neophytes at all. The neophyte devotee must act and work very laboriously under the direction of the spiritual master, and he must thus preach the cult of Śrī Caitanya Mahāprabhu. Only after maturing in devotion can he sit down in a solitary place to chant the Hare Kṛṣṇa *mahā-mantra* as Śrī Caitanya Mahāprabhu Himself did. Although Śrī Caitanya Mahāprabhu is the Supreme Personality of Godhead, to teach us a lesson He traveled all over India continuously for six years and only then retired at Jagannātha Purī. Even at Jagannātha Purī the Lord chanted the Hare Kṛṣṇa *mahā-mantra* in great meetings at the Jagannātha temple. The point is that one should not try to imitate Haridāsa Ṭhākura at the beginning of one's transcendental life. One must first become very mature in devotion and thus receive the approval of Śrī Caitanya Mahāprabhu. Only at such a time may one actually sit down peacefully in a solitary place to chant the Hare Kṛṣṇa *mahā-mantra* and remember the lotus feet of the Lord. The senses are very strong, and if a neophyte devotee imitates Haridāsa Ṭhākura, his enemies (*kāma, krodha, lobha, moha, mada* and *mātsarya*) will disturb and fatigue him. Instead of chanting the Hare Kṛṣṇa *mahā-mantra,* the neophyte will simply sleep soundly. Preaching work is meant for advanced devotees, and when an advanced devotee is further elevated on the devotional scale, he may retire to chant the Hare Kṛṣṇa *mantra* in a solitary place. However, if one simply imitates advanced spiritual life, he will fall down, just like the *sahajiyās* in Vṛndāvana.

TEXT 177

মিশ্র কহে,—সব তোমার, চাহ কি কারণে ?
আপন-ইচ্ছায় লহ, যেই তোমার মনে ॥ ১৭৭ ॥

miśra kahe,—saba tomāra, cāha ki kāraṇe?
āpana-icchāya laha, yei tomāra mane

miśra kahe—Kāśī Miśra said; *saba*—everything; *tomāra*—Yours; *cāha ki kāraṇe*—why do You beg; *āpana-icchāya*—by Your own will; *laha*—You take; *yei*—whatever; *tomāra mane*—is in Your mind.

TRANSLATION

Kāśī Miśra then told Śrī Caitanya Mahāprabhu: "Everything belongs to You. What is the use of Your begging? By Your own will You can take whatever You like.

TEXT 178

আমি-দুই হই তোমার দাস আজ্ঞাকারী।
যে চাহ, সেই আজ্ঞা দেহ' কৃপা করি' ॥ ১৭৮ ॥

āmi-dui ha-i tomāra dāsa ājñākārī
ye cāha, sei ājñā deha' kṛpā kari'

āmi—we; *dui*—two; *ha-i*—are; *tomāra*—Your; *dāsa*—servants; *ājñā-kārī*—order-carriers; *ye cāha*—whatever You want; *sei ājñā*—that order; *deha'*—give; *kṛpā kari'*—being merciful.

TRANSLATION

"My Lord, we are Your two servants and are here just to carry out Your orders. By Your mercy, please tell us to do whatever You want."

TEXT 179

এত কহি' দুই জনে বিদায় লইল।
গোপীনাথ, বাণীনাথ — দুঁহে সঙ্গে নিল ॥ ১৭৯ ॥

eta kahi' dui jane vidāya la-ila
gopīnātha, vāṇīnātha—duṅhe saṅge nila

eta kahi'—saying this; *dui jane*—both of them; *vidāya la-ila*—took leave; *gopīnātha*—Gopīnātha Ācārya; *vāṇīnātha*—Vāṇīnātha Rāya; *duṅhe saṅge nila*—took both of them with them.

TRANSLATION

Saying this, Kāśī Miśra and the temple inspector took their leave, and Gopīnātha and Vāṇīnātha went with them.

TEXT 180

গোপীনাথে দেখাইল সব বাসা-ঘর।
বাণীনাথ-ঠাঞি দিল প্রসাদ বিস্তর ॥ ১৮০ ॥

gopīnāthe dekhāila saba vāsā-ghara
vāṇīnātha-ṭhāñi dila prasāda vistara

gopīnāthe—unto Gopīnātha Ācārya; *dekhāila*—showed; *saba*—all; *vāsā-ghara*—residential places; *vāṇīnātha-ṭhāñi*—unto Vāṇīnātha Rāya; *dila*—delivered; *prasāda vistara*—remnants of food in large quantities.

TRANSLATION

Gopīnātha was then shown all the residential places, and Vāṇīnātha was given large quantities of food [mahā-prasādam] left by Lord Jagannātha.

TEXT 181

বাণীনাথ আইলা বহু প্রসাদ পিঠা লঞা।
গোপীনাথ আইলা বাসা সংস্কার করিয়া ॥ ১৮১ ॥

vāṇīnātha āilā bahu prasāda piṭhā lañā
gopīnātha āilā vāsā saṁskāra kariyā

vāṇīnātha—Vāṇīnātha; *āilā*—returned; *bahu*—a very large quantity of; *prasāda*—remnants of food; *piṭhā lañā*—also taking cakes with them; *gopīnātha*—Gopīnātha Ācārya; *āilā*—returned; *vāsā*—residential places; *saṁskāra kariyā*—cleansing.

TRANSLATION

Thus Vāṇīnātha Rāya returned with large quantities of Lord Jagannātha's food remnants, including cakes and other good eatables. Gopīnātha Ācārya also returned after cleansing all the residential quarters.

TEXT 182

মহাপ্রভু কহে,—শুন, সর্ব বৈষ্ণবগণ।
নিজ-নিজ-বাসা সবে করহ গমন ॥ ১৮২ ॥

mahāprabhu kahe,—śuna, sarva vaiṣṇava-gaṇa
nija-nija-vāsā sabe karaha gamana

mahāprabhu kahe—Lord Śrī Caitanya Mahāprabhu said; *śuna*—kindly listen; *sarva vaiṣṇava-gaṇa*—all Vaiṣṇavas; *nija-nija-vāsā*—to the respective residential quarters; *sabe*—all of you; *karaha*—make; *gamana*—departure.

TRANSLATION

Śrī Caitanya Mahāprabhu then addressed all the Vaiṣṇavas and requested that they listen to Him. He said, "Now you can go to your respective residential quarters.

TEXT 183

সমুদ্রস্নান করি' কর চূড়া দরশন ।
তবে আজি ইহঁ আসি' করিবে ভোজন ॥ ১৮৩ ॥

samudra-snāna kari' kara cūḍā daraśana
tabe āji ihaṅ āsi' karibe bhojana

samudra-snāna—bathing in the sea; *kari'*—finishing; *kara*—just do; *cūḍā daraśana*—observing the top of the temple; *tabe*—thereafter; *āji*—today; *ihaṅ*—here; *āsi'*—coming back; *karibe bhojana*—take your lunch.

TRANSLATION

"Go to the sea and bathe and look at the top of the temple. After so doing, please come back here and take your lunch."

TEXT 184

প্রভু নমস্করি' সবে বাসাতে চলিলা ।
গোপীনাথাচার্য সবে বাসা-স্থান দিলা ॥ ১৮৪ ॥

prabhu namaskari' sabe vāsāte calilā
gopīnāthācārya sabe vāsā-sthāna dilā

prabhu namaskari'—after offering obeisances to Lord Śrī Caitanya Mahāprabhu; *sabe*—all the devotees; *vāsāte calilā*—departed for their residential quarters; *gopīnātha-ācārya*—Gopīnātha Ācārya; *sabe*—to everyone; *vāsā*—residential quarters; *sthāna*—place; *dilā*—delivered.

TRANSLATION

After offering obeisances to Śrī Caitanya Mahāprabhu, all the devotees departed for their residences, and Gopīnātha Ācārya showed them their respective quarters.

TEXT 185

মহাপ্রভু আইলা তবে হরিদাস-মিলনে।
হরিদাস করে প্রেমে নাম-সংকীর্তনে ॥ ১৮৫ ॥

mahāprabhu āilā tabe haridāsa-milane
haridāsa kare preme nāma-saṅkīrtane

mahāprabhu—Śrī Caitanya Mahāprabhu; *āilā*—came; *tabe*—thereafter; *haridāsa-milane*—to meet Ṭhākura Haridāsa; *haridāsa*—Ṭhākura Haridāsa; *kare*—does; *preme*—in ecstatic love; *nāma-saṅkīrtane*—chanting of the holy name.

TRANSLATION

After this, Śrī Caitanya Mahāprabhu went to meet Haridāsa Ṭhākura, and He saw him engaged in chanting the mahā-mantra with ecstatic love. Haridāsa chanted, "Hare Kṛṣṇa, Hare Kṛṣṇa, Kṛṣṇa Kṛṣṇa, Hare Hare/ Hare Rāma, Hare Rāma, Rāma Rāma, Hare Hare."

TEXT 186

প্রভু দেখি' পড়ে আগে দণ্ডবৎ হঞা।
প্রভু আলিঙ্গন কৈল তাঁরে উঠাঞা ॥ ১৮৬ ॥

prabhu dekhi' paḍe āge daṇḍavat hañā
prabhu āliṅgana kaila tāṅre uṭhāñā

prabhu dekhi'—after seeing the Lord; *paḍe*—fell down; *āge*—in front of Him; *daṇḍavat*—flat like a stick; *hañā*—becoming; *prabhu*—Lord Śrī Caitanya Mahāprabhu; *āliṅgana kaila*—embraced; *tāṅre*—him; *uṭhāñā*—raising him up.

TRANSLATION

As soon as Haridāsa Ṭhākura saw Śrī Caitanya Mahāprabhu, he immediately fell down like a stick to offer Him obeisances, and Lord Śrī Caitanya Mahāprabhu raised him up and embraced him.

TEXT 187

দুইজনে প্রেমাবেশে করেন ক্রন্দনে ।
প্রভু-গুণে ভৃত্য বিকল, প্রভু ভৃত্য-গুণে ॥ ১৮৭ ॥

dui-jane premāveśe karena krandane
prabhu-guṇe bhṛtya vikala, prabhu bhṛtya-guṇe

dui-jane—both of them; *prema-āveśe*—in loving ecstasy; *karena krandane*—were crying; *prabhu-guṇe*—by the qualities of the Lord; *bhṛtya*—servant; *vikala*—transformed; *prabhu*—the Lord; *bhṛtya-guṇe*—by the qualities of the servant.

TRANSLATION

Then both the Lord and His servant began to cry in ecstatic love. Indeed, the Lord was transformed by the qualities of His servant, and the servant was transformed by the qualities of his master.

PURPORT

The Māyāvādī philosophers say that the living entity and the Supreme Lord are nondifferent, and therefore they equate the transformation of the living entity with the transformation of the Lord. In other words, Māyāvādīs say that if the living entity is pleased, the Lord is also pleased, and if the living entity is displeased, the Lord is also displeased. By juggling words in this way, Māyāvādīs try to prove that there is no difference between the living entity and the Lord. This, however, is not a fact. In this verse Kṛṣṇadāsa Kavirāja Gosvāmī explains: *prabhu-guṇe bhṛtya vikala, prabhu bhṛtya-guṇe.* The Lord and the living entity are not equal, for the Lord is always the master, and the living entity is always the servant. Transformation takes place due to transcendental qualities, and it is thus said that the servant of the Lord is the heart of the Lord, and the Lord is the heart of the servant. This is also explained by Lord Kṛṣṇa in the *Bhagavad-gītā* (4.11):

ye yathā māṁ prapadyante tāṁs tathaiva bhajāmy aham
mama vartmānuvartante manuṣyāḥ pārtha sarvaśaḥ

"As all surrender unto Me, I reward them accordingly. Everyone follows My path in all respects, O son of Pṛthā."

The Lord is always eager to congratulate the servant because of the servant's transcendental qualities. The servant pleasingly renders service unto the Lord, and the Lord also very pleasingly reciprocates, rendering even more service unto the servant

TEXT 188

হরিদাস কহে, — প্রভু, না ছুঁইও মোরে ।
মুঞি — নীচ, অস্পৃশ্য, পরম পামরে ॥ ১৮৮ ॥

haridāsa kahe, — prabhu, nā chuṅio more
muñi — nīca, aspṛśya, parama pāmare

haridāsa kahe — Haridāsa Ṭhākura said; *prabhu* — my dear Lord; *nā chuṅio more* — please do not touch me; *muñi* — I; *nīca* — most fallen; *aspṛśya* — untouchable; *parama pāmare* — the lowest of mankind.

TRANSLATION

Haridāsa Ṭhākura said, "My dear Lord, please do not touch me, for I am most fallen and untouchable and am the lowest among men."

TEXT 189

প্রভু কহে, — তোমা স্পর্শি পবিত্র হইতে ।
তোমার পবিত্র ধর্ম নাহিক আমাতে ॥ ১৮৯ ॥

prabhu kahe, — tomā sparśi pavitra ha-ite
tomāra pavitra dharma nāhika āmāte

prabhu kahe — the Lord said; *tomā sparśi* — I touch you; *pavitra ha-ite* — just to become purified; *tomāra* — your; *pavitra* — purified; *dharma* — occupation; *nāhika* — is not; *āmāte* — in Me.

TRANSLATION

The Lord said, "I wish to touch you just to be purified, for your purified activities do not exist in Me."

PURPORT

This is an example of the reciprocation of feelings between master and servant. The servant thinks that he is most impure and that the master should not touch him, and the master thinks that because He has become impure by associating with so many impure living entities, He should touch a pure devotee like Haridāsa Ṭhākura just to purify Himself. Actually both the servant and the master are already purified because neither of them is in touch with the impurities of material existence. They are already equal in quality because both of them are the purest. There is a difference in quantity, however, because the master is unlimited and the servant is limited. Consequently the servant always remains subordinate to the master, and this relationship is eternal and undisturbed. As soon as the servant feels like becoming the master, he falls into *māyā.* Thus it is by misuse of free will that one falls under the influence of *māyā.*

The Māyāvādī philosophers try to explain the equality of master and servant in terms of quantity, but they fail to explain why, if the master and servant are equal, the servant falls victim to *māyā.* They try to explain that when the servant, the living entity, is out of the clutches of *māyā,* he immediately becomes the so-called master again. Such an explanation is never satisfactory. Being unlimited, the master cannot become a victim of *māyā,* for in such a case His unlimitedness would be crippled or limited. Thus the Māyāvāda explanation is not correct. The fact is that the master is always master and unlimited, and the servant, being limited, is sometimes curtailed by the influence of *māyā. Māyā* is also the master's energy and is also unlimited; therefore the limited servant or limited living entity is forced to remain under the master or the master's potency, *māyā.* Being freed from *māyā's* influence, one can again become a pure servant and equal qualitatively to the Lord. The relationship between master and servant continues due to their being unlimited and limited respectively.

TEXT 190

ক্ষণে ক্ষণে কর তুমি সর্বতীর্থে স্নান।
ক্ষণে ক্ষণে কর তুমি যজ্ঞ-তপো-দান ॥ ১৯০ ॥

kṣaṇe kṣaṇe kara tumi sarva-tīrthe snāna
kṣaṇe kṣaṇe kara tumi yajña-tapo-dāna

kṣaṇe kṣaṇe—at every moment; *kara*—do; *tumi*—you; *sarva-tīrthe snāna*—bathing in all the holy places of pilgrimage; *kṣaṇe kṣaṇe*—at every moment; *kara*—perform; *tumi*—you; *yajña*—sacrifices; *tapaḥ*—austerities; *dāna*—charity.

TRANSLATION

Śrī Caitanya Mahāprabhu exalted Haridāsa Ṭhākura, stating, "At every moment you take your bath in all the holy places of pilgrimage, and at every moment you perform great sacrifices, austerity and charity.

TEXT 191

নিরন্তর কর চারি বেদ অধ্যয়ন।
দ্বিজ-ন্যাসী হৈতে তুমি পরম-পাবন ॥ ১৯১ ॥

nirantara kara cāri veda adhyayana
dvija-nyāsī haite tumi parama-pāvana

nirantara—constantly; *kara*—you do; *cāri*—four; *veda*—of the *Vedas*; *adhyayana*—study; *dvija*—*brāhmaṇa*; *nyāsī*—*sannyāsī*; *haite*—than; *tumi*—you; *parama-pāvana*—supremely pure.

TRANSLATION

"You are constantly studying the four Vedas, and you are far better than any brāhmaṇa or sannyāsī."

TEXT 192

অহো বত শ্বপচোঽতো গরীয়ান্
যজ্জিহ্বাগ্রে বর্ততে নাম তুভ্যম্।

তেপুস্তপস্তে জুহুবুঃ সস্নুরার্যা
ব্রহ্মানূচুর্নাম গৃণন্তি যে তে ॥ ১৯২ ॥

aho bata śva-paco 'to garīyān
yaj-jihvāgre vartate nāma tubhyam
tepus tapas te juhuvuḥ sasnur āryā
brahmānūcur nāma gṛṇanti ye te

aho bata—how wonderful it is; *śva-pacaḥ*—dog-eaters; *ataḥ*—than the initiated *brāhmaṇa; garīyān*—more glorious; *yat*—of whom; *jihvā-agre*—on the tongue; *vartate*—remains; *nāma*—holy name; *tubhyam*—of You, my Lord; *tepuḥ*—have performed; *tapaḥ*—austerity; *te*—they; *juhuvuḥ*—have performed sacrifices; *sasnuḥ*—have bathed in all holy places; *āryāḥ*—really belonging to the Āryan race; *brahma*—all the *Vedas; anūcuḥ*—have studied; *nāma*—holy name; *gṛṇanti*—chant; *ye*—who; *te*—they.

TRANSLATION

Śrī Caitanya Mahāprabhu then recited the following verse: "'My dear Lord, one who always keeps Your holy name on his tongue becomes greater than an initiated brāhmaṇa. Although he may be born in a family of dog-eaters and therefore by material calculation may be the lowest among men, he is still glorious. This is the wonderful effect of chanting the holy name of the Lord. It is therefore concluded that one who chants the holy name of the Lord should be understood to have performed all kinds of austerities and great sacrifices mentioned in the Vedas. He has already taken his bath in all the holy places of pilgrimage. He has studied all the Vedas, and he is actually an Āryan.'"

PURPORT

The word Āryan means advanced. Unless one is spiritually advanced, he cannot be called an Āryan, and this is the difference between Āryan and non-Āryan. Non-Āryans are those who are not spiritually advanced. By following the Vedic culture, by performing great sacrifices and by becoming a strict follower of the Vedic instructions, one may become a *brāhmaṇa*, a *sannyāsī* or an Āryan. It is not possible to become a *brāhmaṇa, sannyāsī* or Āryan without being properly qualified. *Bhāgavata-dharma* never allows one to become a cheap *brāhmaṇa, sannyāsī* or Āryan. The qualities or qualifications described herein are quoted from *Śrīmad-Bhāgavatam* (3.33.7) and were spoken by Devahūti, the mother of Kapiladeva, when she understood the influence of devotional service (*bhakti-yoga*). In this way Devahūti praised the devotee, pointing out his greatness in all respects.

TEXT 193

এত বলি তাঁরে লঞা গেলা পুষ্পোদ্যানে ।
অতি নিভৃতে তাঁরে দিলা বাসা-স্থানে ॥ ১৯৩ ॥

eta bali tāṅre lañā gelā puṣpodyāne
ati nibhṛte tāṅre dilā vāsā-sthāne

eta bali—saying this; *tāṅre lañā*—taking him; *gelā*—went; *puṣpa-udyāne*—in the flower garden; *ati nibhṛte*—in a very secluded place; *tāṅre*—unto him; *dilā*—delivered; *vāsā-sthāne*—a place to remain.

TRANSLATION

Saying this, Śrī Caitanya Mahāprabhu took Haridāsa Ṭhākura within the flower garden, and there, in a very secluded place, He showed him his residence.

TEXT 194

এইস্থানে রহি' কর নাম-সংকীর্তন ।
প্রতিদিন আসি' আমি করিব মিলন ॥ ১৯৪ ॥

ei-sthāne rahi' kara nāma saṅkīrtana
prati-dina āsi' āmi kariba milana

ei-sthāne—in this place; *rahi'*—remaining; *kara*—perform; *nāma saṅkīrtana*—chanting of the holy name; *prati-dina*—every day; *āsi'*—coming; *āmi*—I; *kariba*—shall do; *milana*—meeting.

TRANSLATION

Śrī Caitanya Mahāprabhu requested Haridāsa Ṭhākura, "Remain here and chant the Hare Kṛṣṇa mahā-mantra. I shall personally come here to meet you daily.

TEXT 195

মন্দিরের চক্র দেখি' করিহ প্রণাম ।
এই ঠাঞি তোমার আসিবে প্রসাদান্ন ॥ ১৯৫ ॥

mandirera cakra dekhi' kariha praṇāma
ei ṭhāñi tomāra āsibe prasādānna

mandirera—of the temple of Jagannātha; *cakra*—the wheel on the top; *dekhi'*—seeing; *kariha praṇāma*—offer your obeisances; *ei ṭhāñi*—in this place; *tomāra*—your; *āsibe*—will come; *prasāda-anna*—remnants of food offered to Jagannātha.

TRANSLATION

"Remain here peacefully and look at the cakra on the top of the temple and offer obeisances. As far as your prasādam is concerned, I shall arrange to have that sent here."

PURPORT

Since he was born in a Muslim family, Śrīla Haridāsa Ṭhākura could not enter the temple of Jagannātha due to temple restrictions. Nonetheless, he was recognized by Śrī Caitanya Mahāprabhu as Nāmācārya Haridāsa Ṭhākura. Haridāsa Ṭhākura, however, considered himself unfit to enter the Jagannātha temple. Śrī Caitanya Mahāprabhu could have personally taken Haridāsa Ṭhākura into the Jagannātha temple if He wished, but the Lord did not like to disturb a popular custom. Consequently the Lord asked His servant simply to look at the Viṣṇu wheel on top of the temple and offer obeisances (*namaskāra*). This means that if one is not allowed to enter the temple, or if he thinks himself unfit to enter the temple, he can look at the wheel from outside the temple, and that is as good as seeing the Deity within.

Śrī Caitanya Mahāprabhu promised to come daily to see Śrīla Haridāsa Ṭhākura, and this indicates that Śrīla Haridāsa Ṭhākura was so advanced in spiritual life that, although considered unfit to enter the temple, he was being personally visited by the Lord every day. Nor was there any need for his going outside his residence to collect food. Śrī Caitanya Mahāprabhu assured Haridāsa Ṭhākura that the remnants of

His food would be sent there. As the Lord states in the *Bhagavad-gītā* (9.22), *yoga-kṣemaṁ vahāmy aham:* "I arrange all life's necessities for My devotees."

A reference is made here for those who are very anxious to imitate the behavior of Ṭhākura Haridāsa in an unnatural way. One must receive the order of Śrī Caitanya Mahāprabhu or His representative before adopting such a way of life. The duty of a pure devotee or a servant of the Lord is to carry out the order of the Lord. Śrī Caitanya Mahāprabhu asked Nityānanda Prabhu to go to Bengal and preach, and He asked the Gosvāmīs, Rūpa and Sanātana, to go to Vṛndāvana and excavate the lost places of pilgrimage. In this case the Lord asked Haridāsa Ṭhākura to remain there at Jagannātha Purī and constantly chant the holy names of the Lord. Thus Śrī Caitanya Mahāprabhu gave different persons different orders, and consequently one should not try to imitate the behavior of Haridāsa Ṭhākura without being ordered by Śrī Caitanya Mahāprabhu or His representative. Śrīla Bhaktisiddhānta Sarasvatī Ṭhākura condemns such imitations in this way:

duṣṭa mana! tumi kisera vaiṣṇava?
pratiṣṭhāra tare, nirjanera ghare,
tava hari-nāma kevala kaitava

"My dear mind, you are trying to imitate Haridāsa Ṭhākura and chant the Hare Kṛṣṇa *mantra* in a secluded place, but you are not worth being called a Vaiṣṇava because what you want is cheap popularity and not the actual qualifications of Haridāsa Ṭhākura. If you try to imitate him you will fall down, for your neophyte position will cause you to think of women and money. Thus you will fall into the clutches of *māyā,* and your so-called chanting in a secluded place will bring about your downfall."

TEXT 196

নিত্যানন্দ, জগদানন্দ, দামোদর, মুকুন্দ।
হরিদাসে মিলি' সবে পাইল আনন্দ ॥ ১৯৬ ॥

nityānanda, jagadānanda, dāmodara, mukunda
haridāse mili' sabe pāila ānanda

nityānanda—Nityānanda; *jagadānanda*—Jagadānanda; *dāmodara*—Dāmodara; *mukunda*—Mukunda; *haridāse*—Haridāsa; *mili'*—meeting; *sabe*—all of them; *pāila*—got; *ānanda*—great pleasure.

TRANSLATION

When Nityānanda Prabhu, Jagadānanda Prabhu, Dāmodara Prabhu and Mukunda Prabhu met Haridāsa Ṭhākura, they all became very pleased.

TEXT 197

সমুদ্রস্নান করি' প্রভু আইলা নিজ স্থানে।
অদ্বৈতাদি গেলা সিন্ধু করিবারে স্নানে ॥ ১৯৭ ॥

samudra-snāna kari' prabhu āilā nija sthāne
advaitādi gelā sindhu karibāre snāne

samudra-snāna kari'—after bathing in the sea; *prabhu*—Śrī Caitanya Mahāprabhu; *āilā*—came; *nija sthāne*—to His own place; *advaita-ādi*—devotees, headed by Advaita Prabhu; *gelā*—went; *sindhu*—to the ocean; *karibāre*—just to take; *snāne*—bath.

TRANSLATION

When Śrī Caitanya Mahāprabhu returned to His residence after taking a bath in the sea, all the devotees, headed by Advaita Prabhu, went to bathe in the sea.

TEXT 198

আসি' জগন্নাথের কৈল চূড়া দরশন।
প্রভুর আবাসে আইলা করিতে ভোজন ॥ ১৯৮ ॥

āsi' jagannāthera kaila cūḍā daraśana
prabhura āvāse āilā karite bhojana

āsi'—coming back; *jagannāthera*—of Lord Jagannātha; *kaila*—did; *cūḍā daraśana*—looking at the top of the temple; *prabhura*—of Lord Caitanya Mahāprabhu; *āvāse*—at the residence; *āilā*—came; *karite bhojana*—to take their luncheon.

TRANSLATION

After bathing in the sea, Advaita Prabhu and all the other devotees returned, and on their return they saw the top of the Jagannātha temple. They then went to the residence of Śrī Caitanya Mahāprabhu to take their luncheon.

TEXT 199

সবারে বসাইলা প্রভু যোগ্য ক্রম করি' ।
শ্রীহস্তে পরিবেশন কৈল গৌরহরি ॥ ১৯৯ ॥

sabāre vasāilā prabhu yogya krama kari'
śrī-haste pariveśana kaila gaurahari

sabāre—all the devotees; *vasāilā*—made to sit; *prabhu*—Śrī Caitanya Mahāprabhu; *yogya*—befitting; *krama*—in order, one after another; *kari'*—setting; *śrī-haste*—by His own transcendental hand; *pariveśana*—distribution; *kaila*—did; *gaurahari*—Lord Śrī Caitanya Mahāprabhu.

TRANSLATION

One after the other, Śrī Caitanya Mahāprabhu made all the devotees sit in their proper places. He then began to distribute prasādam with His own transcendental hand.

TEXT 200

অল্প অন্ন নাহি আইসে দিতে প্রভুর হাতে ।
দুই-তিনের অন্ন দেন এক এক পাতে ॥ ২০০ ॥

alpa anna nāhi āise dite prabhura hāte
dui-tinera anna dena eka eka pāte

alpa anna—a small quantity of *prasādam; nāhi*—does not; *āise*—come; *dite*—to give; *prabhura*—of Śrī Caitanya Mahāprabhu; *hāte*—in the hand; *dui*—two; *tinera*—or of three; *anna*—food; *dena*—He delivers; *eka eka pāte*—on each and every plantain leaf.

TRANSLATION

All the devotees were served prasādam on plantain leaves, and Śrī Caitanya Mahāprabhu distributed on each leaf a quantity suitable for two or three men to eat, for His hand could not distribute less than that.

TEXT 201

প্রভু না খাইলে কেহ না করে ভোজন ।
ঊর্ধ্ব-হস্তে বসি' রহে সর্ব ভক্তগণ ॥ ২০১ ॥

prabhu nā khāile keha nā kare bhojana
ūrdhva-haste vasi' rahe sarva bhakta-gaṇa

prabhu—Śrī Caitanya Mahāprabhu; *nā khāile*—without eating; *keha*—anyone; *nā*—not; *kare*—does; *bhojana*—eating; *ūrdhva-haste*—raising the hand; *vasi'*—sitting; *rahe*—remain; *sarva*—all; *bhakta-gaṇa*—devotees.

TRANSLATION

All the devotees kept their hands raised over the prasādam distributed to them, for they did not want to eat without seeing the Lord eat first.

TEXT 202

স্বরূপ-গোসাঞি প্রভুকে কৈল নিবেদন ।
তুমি না বসিলে কেহ না করে ভোজন ॥ ২০২ ॥

svarūpa-gosāñi prabhuke kaila nivedana
tumi nā vasile keha nā kare bhojana

svarūpa-gosāñi—Svarūpa Dāmodara Gosāñi; *prabhuke*—unto Śrī Caitanya Mahāprabhu; *kaila*—did; *nivedana*—submission; *tumi*—You; *nā vasile*—if not sitting; *keha*—anyone; *nā*—not; *kare*—does; *bhojana*—eating.

TRANSLATION

Svarūpa Dāmodara Gosvāmī then informed Śrī Caitanya Mahāprabhu, "Unless You sit and take prasādam, no one will accept it.

TEXT 203

তোমা-সঙ্গে রহে যত সন্ন্যাসীর গণ ।
গোপীনাথাচার্য তাঁরে করিয়াছে নিমন্ত্রণ ॥ ২০৩ ॥

tomā-saṅge rahe yata sannyāsīra gaṇa
gopīnāthācārya tāṅre kariyāche nimantraṇa

tomā-saṅge—along with You; *rahe*—remain; *yata*—as many as; *sannyāsīra gaṇa*—rank of sannyāsīs; *gopīnātha-ācārya*—Gopīnātha Ācārya; *tāṅre*—all of them; *kariyāche*—has done; *nimantraṇa*—invitation.

TRANSLATION

"Gopīnātha Ācārya has invited all the sannyāsīs who remain with You to come and take prasādam.

TEXT 204

আচার্য আসিয়াছেন ভিক্ষার প্রসাদান্ন লঞা ।
পুরী, ভারতী আছেন তোমার অপেক্ষা করিয়া ॥ ২০৪ ॥

ācārya āsiyāchena bhikṣāra prasādānna lañā
purī, bhāratī āchena tomāra apekṣā kariyā

ācārya—Gopīnātha Ācārya; *āsiyāchena*—has come; *bhikṣāra*—for eating; *prasāda-anna lañā*—taking the remnants of all kinds of food; *purī*—Paramānanda Purī; *bhāratī*—Brahmānanda Bhāratī; *āchena*—are; *tomāra*—for You; *apekṣā kariyā*—waiting.

TRANSLATION

"Gopīnātha Ācārya has already come, bringing sufficient remnants of food to distribute to all the sannyāsīs, and sannyāsīs like Paramānanda Purī and Brahmānanda Bhāratī are waiting for You.

TEXT 205

নিত্যানন্দ লঞা ভিক্ষা করিতে বৈস তুমি ।
বৈষ্ণবের পরিবেশন করিতেছি আমি ॥ ২০৫ ॥

nityānanda lañā bhikṣā karite vaisa tumi
vaiṣṇavera pariveśana karitechi āmi

nityānanda lañā—taking along Śrī Nityānanda Prabhu; *bhikṣā*—luncheon; *karite*—to take; *vaisa*—sit down; *tumi*—You; *vaiṣṇavera*—to all the devotees; *pariveśana*—distribution of *prasādam; karitechi*—am doing; *āmi*—I.

TRANSLATION

"You may sit down and accept the luncheon with Nityānanda Prabhu, and I shall distribute the prasādam to all the Vaiṣṇavas."

TEXT 206

তবে প্রভু প্রসাদান্ন গোবিন্দ-হাতে দিলা।
যত্ন করি' হরিদাস-ঠাকুরে পাঠাইলা ॥ ২০৬ ॥

tabe prabhu prasādānna govinda-hāte dilā
yatna kari' haridāsa-ṭhākure pāṭhāilā

tabe—thereafter; *prabhu*—Śrī Caitanya Mahāprabhu; *prasāda-anna*—remnants of Jagannātha's food; *govinda-hāte*—in the hand of Govinda; *dilā*—delivered; *yatna kari'*—with great attention; *haridāsa-ṭhākure*—unto Haridāsa Ṭhākura; *pāṭhāilā*—sent.

TRANSLATION

After this, Śrī Caitanya Mahāprabhu carefully delivered some prasādam into the hands of Govinda to be given to Haridāsa Ṭhākura.

TEXT 207

আপনে বসিলা সব সন্ন্যাসীরে লঞা।
পরিবেশন করে আচার্য হরষিত হঞা ॥ ২০৭ ॥

āpane vasilā saba sannyāsīre lañā
pariveśana kare ācārya haraṣita hañā

āpane—personally; *vasilā*—sat down; *saba*—all; *sannyāsīre lañā*—taking with Him the *sannyāsīs; pariveśana kare*—distributes; *ācārya*—Gopīnātha Ācārya; *haraṣita hañā*—with great pleasure.

TRANSLATION

Then Śrī Caitanya Mahāprabhu personally sat down to accept lunch with the other sannyāsīs, and Gopīnātha Ācārya began to distribute the prasādam with great pleasure.

TEXT 208

স্বরূপ গোসাঞি, দামোদর, জগদানন্দ।
বৈষ্ণবেরে পরিবেশে তিন জনে — আনন্দ ॥ ২০৮ ॥

svarūpa gosāñi, dāmodara, jagadānanda
vaiṣṇavere pariveśe tina jane — ānanda

svarūpa gosāñi — Svarūpa Gosāñi; *dāmodara* — Dāmodara; *jagadānanda* — Jagadānanda; *vaiṣṇavere pariveśe* — distributed to the Vaiṣṇavas; *tina jane* — the three persons; *ānanda* — very jubilant.

TRANSLATION

Then Svarūpa Dāmodara Gosvāmī, Dāmodara Paṇḍita and Jagadānanda all began to distribute prasādam to the devotees with great pleasure.

TEXT 209

নানা পিঠাপানা খায় আকণ্ঠ পূরিয়া।
মধ্যে মধ্যে 'হরি' কহে আনন্দিত হঞা ॥ ২০৯ ॥

nānā piṭhā-pānā khāya ākaṇṭha pūriyā
madhye madhye 'hari' kahe ānandita hañā

nānā — various; *piṭhā-pānā* — cakes and sweet rice; *khāya* — eat; *ā-kaṇṭha pūriyā* — filling up to the throat; *madhye madhye* — occasionally; *hari* — the holy name of Kṛṣṇa; *kahe* — they speak; *ānandita hañā* — in great jubilation.

TRANSLATION

They ate all kinds of cakes and sweet rice, filling themselves up to their throats, and at intervals they vibrated the holy name of the Lord in great jubilation.

PURPORT

It is the practice of Vaiṣṇavas while taking *prasādam* to chant the holy name of Lord Hari at intervals and also sing various songs, such as *śarīra avidyā-jāla.* Those who are honoring *prasādam,* accepting the remnants of food offered to the Deity, must always remember that *prasādam* is not ordinary food. *Prasādam* is transcendental. We are therefore reminded:

mahā-prasāde govinde nāma-brahmaṇi vaiṣṇave
sv-alpa-puṇya-vatāṁ rājan viśvāso naiva jāyate

Those who are not pious cannot understand the value of *mahā-prasādam* or the holy name of the Lord. Both *prasādam* and the Lord's name are on the Brahman platform, or spiritual platform. One should never consider *prasādam* to be like ordinary hotel cooking. Nor should one touch any kind of food not offered to the Deity. Every Vaiṣṇava strictly follows this principle and does not accept any food that is not *prasādam.* One should take *prasādam* with great faith and should chant the holy name of the Lord and worship the Deity in the temple, always remembering that the Deity, *mahā-prasādam* and the holy name do not belong to the mundane platform. By worshiping the Deity, eating *prasādam* and chanting the Hare Kṛṣṇa *mahā-mantra,* one can always remain on the spiritual platform (*brahma-bhūyāya kalpate*).

TEXT 210

ভোজন সমাপ্ত হৈল, কৈল আচমন।
সবারে পরাইল প্রভু মাল্য-চন্দন ॥ ২১০ ॥

bhojana samāpta haila, kaila ācamana
sabāre parāila prabhu mālya-candana

bhojana—lunch; *samāpta*—ending; *haila*—there was; *kaila*—did; *ācamana*—washing the mouth; *sabāre*—on everyone; *parāila*—put; *prabhu*—Śrī Caitanya Mahāprabhu; *mālya-candana*—a garland and sandalwood pulp.

TRANSLATION

After everyone had finished his lunch and washed his mouth and hands, Śrī Caitanya Mahāprabhu personally decorated everyone with flower garlands and sandalwood pulp.

TEXT 211

বিশ্রাম করিতে সবে নিজ বাসা গেলা।
সন্ধ্যাকালে আসি' পুনঃ প্রভুকে মিলিলা ॥ ২১১ ॥

viśrāma karite sabe nija vāsā gelā
sandhyā-kāle āsi' punaḥ prabhuke mililā

viśrāma karite—going to take rest; *sabe*—all the Vaiṣṇavas; *nija*—to their own; *vāsā*—residential quarters; *gelā*—went; *sandhyā-kāle*—in the evening; *āsi'*—coming; *punaḥ*—again; *prabhuke mililā*—met Śrī Caitanya Mahāprabhu.

TRANSLATION

After thus accepting prasādam, they all went to take rest at their respective residences, and in the evening they again came to meet Śrī Caitanya Mahāprabhu.

TEXT 212

হেনকালে রামানন্দ আইলা প্রভু-স্থানে।
প্রভু মিলাইল তাঁরে সব বৈষ্ণবগণে ॥ ২১২ ॥

hena-kāle rāmānanda āilā prabhu-sthāne
prabhu milāila tāṅre saba vaiṣṇava-gaṇe

hena-kāle—at this time; *rāmānanda*—Rāmānanda; *āilā*—came; *prabhu-sthāne*—at the place of Śrī Caitanya Mahāprabhu; *prabhu*—Śrī Caitanya Mahāprabhu; *milāila*—caused to meet; *tāṅre*—him (Śrī Rāmānanda Rāya); *saba*—all; *vaiṣṇava-gaṇe*—the devotees of the Lord.

TRANSLATION

At this time Rāmānanda Rāya also came to meet Śrī Caitanya Mahāprabhu, and the Lord took the opportunity to introduce him to all the Vaiṣṇavas.

TEXT 213

সবা লঞা গেলা প্রভু জগন্নাথালয়।
কীর্তন আরম্ভ তথা কৈল মহাশয় ॥ ২১৩ ॥

sabā lañā gelā prabhu jagannāthālaya
kīrtana ārambha tathā kaila mahāśaya

sabā lañā—taking all of them; *gelā*—went; *prabhu*—Śrī Caitanya Mahāprabhu; *jagannātha-ālaya*—to the temple of Lord Jagannātha; *kīrtana*—congregational chanting; *ārambha*—beginning; *tathā*—there; *kaila*—did; *mahāśaya*—the great personality.

TRANSLATION

The great Personality of Godhead, Śrī Caitanya Mahāprabhu, then took all of them to the temple of Jagannātha and began the congregational chanting of the holy name there.

TEXT 214

সন্ধ্যা-ধূপ দেখি' আরম্ভিলা সংকীর্তন ।
পড়িছা আসি' সবারে দিল মাল্য-চন্দন ॥ ২১৪ ॥

sandhyā-dhūpa dekhi' ārambhilā saṅkīrtana
paḍichā āsi' sabāre dila mālya-candana

sandhyā-dhūpa—*dhūpa-ārati* just in the beginning of the evening; *dekhi'*—they all saw; *ārambhilā*—began; *saṅkīrtana*—congregational chanting; *paḍichā*—the inspector of the temple; *āsi'*—coming; *sabāre*—unto everyone; *dila*—offered; *mālya-candana*—flower garlands and sandalwood pulp.

TRANSLATION

After seeing the dhūpa-ārati of the Lord, they all began congregational chanting. Then the paḍichā, the superintendent of the temple, came and offered flower garlands and sandalwood pulp to everyone.

TEXT 215

চারিদিকে চারি সম্প্রদায় করেন কীর্তন ।
মধ্যে নৃত্য করে প্রভু শচীর নন্দন ॥ ২১৫ ॥

cāri-dike cāri sampradāya karena kīrtana
madhye nṛtya kare prabhu śacīra nandana

cāri-dike—in the four directions; *cāri*—four; *sampradāya*—groups; *karena*—performed; *kīrtana*—congregational chanting; *madhye*—in the middle; *nṛtya kare*—dances; *prabhu*—Śrī Caitanya Mahāprabhu; *śacīra nandana*—the son of mother Śacī.

TRANSLATION

Four parties were then distributed in four directions to perform saṅkīrtana, and in the middle of them the Lord Himself, known as the son of mother Śacī, began to dance.

TEXT 216

অষ্ট মৃদঙ্গ বাজে, বত্রিশ করতাল ।
হরিধ্বনি করে সবে, বলে — ভাল, ভাল ॥ ২১৬ ॥

aṣṭa mṛdaṅga bāje, batriśa karatāla
hari-dhvani kare sabe, bale — bhāla, bhāla

aṣṭa mṛdaṅga—eight *mṛdaṅgas; bāje*—sounded; *batriśa*—thirty-two; *karatāla*—cymbals; *hari-dhvani*—vibrating the transcendental sound; *kare*—does; *sabe*—every one of them; *bale*—says; *bhāla bhāla*—very good, very good.

TRANSLATION

In the four groups there were eight mṛdaṅgas and thirty-two cymbals. All together they began to vibrate the transcendental sound, and everyone said, "Very good! Very good!"

TEXT 217

কীর্তনের ধ্বনি মহামঙ্গল উঠিল ।
চতুর্দশ লোক ভরি' ব্রহ্মাণ্ড ভেদিল ॥ ২১৭ ॥

kīrtanera dhvani mahā-maṅgala uṭhila
caturdaśa loka bhari' brahmāṇḍa bhedila

kīrtanera dhvani—the vibration of the *saṅkīrtana; mahā-maṅgala uṭhila*—all good fortune awakened; *catur-daśa*—fourteen; *loka*—

planetary systems; *bhari'*—filling up; *brahmāṇḍa*—the whole universe; *bhedila*—penetrated.

TRANSLATION

When the tumultuous vibration of saṅkīrtana resounded, all good fortune immediately awakened, and the sound penetrated the whole universe through the fourteen planetary systems.

TEXT 218

কীর্তন-আরম্ভে প্রেম উথলি' চলিল।
নীলাচলবাসী লোক ধাঞা আইল ॥ ২১৮ ॥

kīrtana-ārambhe prema uthali' calila
nīlācala-vāsī loka dhāñā āila

kīrtana-ārambhe—in the beginning of the *saṅkīrtana; prema*—ecstasy of love; *uthali'*—overpowering; *calila*—began to proceed; *nīlācala-vāsī*—all the residents of Jagannātha Purī; *loka*—people; *dhāñā*—running; *āila*—came.

TRANSLATION

When the congregational chanting began, ecstatic love immediately overflooded everything, and all the residents of Jagannātha Purī came running.

TEXT 219

কীর্তন দেখি' সবার মনে হৈল চমৎকার।
কভু নাহি দেখি ঐছে প্রেমের বিকার ॥ ২১৯ ॥

kīrtana dekhi' sabāra mane haila camatkāra
kabhu nāhi dekhi aiche premera vikāra

kīrtana dekhi'—seeing the performance of *saṅkīrtana; sabāra*—of all of them; *mane*—in the mind; *haila*—there was; *camatkāra*—astonishment; *kabhu*—at any time; *nāhi*—never; *dekhi*—see; *aiche*—such; *premera*—of ecstatic love; *vikāra*—transformation.

TRANSLATION

Everyone was astonished to see such a performance of saṅkīrtana, and they all agreed that never before had kīrtana been so performed and ecstatic love of God so exhibited.

TEXT 220

তবে প্রভু জগন্নাথের মন্দির বেড়িয়া ।
প্রদক্ষিণ করি' বুলেন নর্তন করিয়া ॥ ২২০ ॥

tabe prabhu jagannāthera mandira beḍiyā
pradakṣiṇa kari' bulena nartana kariyā

tabe—thereafter; *prabhu*—Śrī Caitanya Mahāprabhu; *jagannāthera*—of Lord Jagannātha; *mandira*—temple; *beḍiyā*—walking all around; *pradakṣiṇa*—circumambulation; *kari'*—doing; *bulena*—walks; *nartana kariyā*—dancing.

TRANSLATION

At this time Śrī Caitanya Mahāprabhu circumambulated the temple of Jagannātha and continuously danced about the whole area.

TEXT 221

আগে-পাছে গান করে চারি সম্প্রদায় ।
আছাড়ের কালে ধরে নিত্যানন্দ রায় ॥ ২২১ ॥

āge-pāche gāna kare cāri sampradāya
āchāḍera kāle dhare nityānanda rāya

āge-pāche—in front and in the rear; *gāna*—singing; *kare*—do; *cāri*—four; *sampradāya*—groups; *āchāḍera*—of falling down; *kāle*—at the time; *dhare*—captures; *nityānanda rāya*—Lord Śrī Nityānanda Prabhu.

TRANSLATION

As the circumambulation was performed, the four kīrtana parties sang in front and in the rear. When Śrī Caitanya Mahāprabhu fell down to the ground, Śrī Nityānanda Rāya Prabhu lifted Him up.

TEXT 222

অশ্রু, পুলক, কম্প, স্বেদ, গম্ভীর হুঙ্কার।
প্রেমের বিকার দেখি' লোকে চমৎকার ॥ ২২২ ॥

aśru, pulaka, kampa, sveda, gambhīra huṅkāra
premera vikāra dekhi' loke camatkāra

aśru—tears; *pulaka*—jubilation; *kampa*—trembling; *sveda*—perspiration; *gambhīra huṅkāra*—deep resounding; *premera*—of ecstatic love; *vikāra*—transformation; *dekhi'*—seeing; *loke*—all the people; *camatkāra*—were astonished.

TRANSLATION

While kīrtana was going on, there was a transformation of ecstatic love and much tears, jubilation, trembling, perspiration and deep resounding in the body of Śrī Caitanya Mahāprabhu. Upon seeing this transformation, all the people present became very much astonished.

TEXT 223

পিচ্‌কারি-ধারা জিনি' অশ্রু নয়নে।
চারিদিকের লোক সব করয়ে সিনানে ॥ ২২৩ ॥

pickāri-dhārā jini' aśru nayane
cāri-dikera loka saba karaye sināne

pickāri-dhārā—like water coming in force from a syringe; *jini'*—conquering; *aśru*—tears; *nayane*—in the eyes; *cāri-dikera*—in all four directions; *loka*—people; *saba*—all; *karaye sināne*—moistened.

TRANSLATION

The tears from the eyes of the Lord came out with great force, like water from a syringe. Indeed, all the people who surrounded Him were moistened by His tears.

TEXT 224

'বেড়ানৃত্য' মহাপ্রভু করি' কতক্ষণ।
মন্দিরের পাছে রহি' করয়ে কীর্তন ॥ ২২৪ ॥

'beḍā-nṛtya' mahāprabhu kari' kata-kṣaṇa
mandirera pāche rahi' karaye kīrtana

beḍā-nṛtya—the dancing surrounding the temple; *mahāprabhu*—Śrī Caitanya Mahāprabhu; *kari'*—performing; *kata-kṣaṇa*—for some time; *mandirera pāche*—at the rear of the temple; *rahi'*—staying; *karaye*—performed; *kīrtana*—congregational chanting.

TRANSLATION

After circumambulating the temple, Śrī Caitanya Mahāprabhu for some time remained at the rear of the temple and continued His saṅkīrtana.

TEXT 225

চারিদিকে চারি সম্প্রদায় উচ্চৈঃস্বরে গায় ।
মধ্যে তাণ্ডব-নৃত্য করে গৌররায় ॥ ২২৫ ॥

cāri-dike cāri sampradāya uccaiḥsvare gāya
madhye tāṇḍava-nṛtya kare gaurarāya

cāri-dike—on four sides; *cāri sampradāya*—the four groups; *uccaiḥ-svare*—very loudly; *gāya*—chant; *madhye*—in the middle; *tāṇḍava-nṛtya*—jumping and dancing; *kare*—performs; *gaurarāya*—Śrī Caitanya Mahāprabhu.

TRANSLATION

On all four sides the four saṅkīrtana groups chanted very loudly, and in the middle Śrī Caitanya Mahāprabhu danced, jumping high.

TEXT 226

বহুক্ষণ নৃত্য করি' প্রভু স্থির হৈলা ।
চারি মহান্তেরে তবে নাচিতে আজ্ঞা দিলা ॥ ২২৬ ॥

bahu-kṣaṇa nṛtya kari' prabhu sthira hailā
cāri mahāntere tabe nācite ājñā dilā

bahu-kṣaṇa—for a long period; *nṛtya kari'*—dancing; *prabhu*—Śrī Caitanya Mahāprabhu; *sthira hailā*—became still; *cāri mahāntere*—

to four great personalities; *tabe*—then; *nācite*—to dance; *ājñā dilā*—ordered.

TRANSLATION

After dancing for a long time, Śrī Caitanya Mahāprabhu became still and ordered four great personalities to begin to dance.

TEXT 227

এক সম্প্রদায়ে নাচে নিত্যানন্দ-রায়ে ।
অদ্বৈত-আচার্য নাচে আর সম্প্রদায়ে ॥ ২২৭ ॥

eka sampradāye nāce nityānanda-rāye
advaita-ācārya nāce āra sampradāye

eka sampradāye—in one group; *nāce*—dances; *nityānanda-rāye*—Lord Nityānanda; *advaita-ācārya*—Advaita Ācārya Prabhu; *nāce*—dances; *āra*—another; *sampradāye*—in a group.

TRANSLATION

In one group Nityānanda Prabhu began to dance, and in another group Advaita Ācārya began to dance.

TEXT 228

আর সম্প্রদায়ে নাচে পণ্ডিত-বক্রেশ্বর ।
শ্রীবাস নাচে আর সম্প্রদায়-ভিতর ॥ ২২৮ ॥

āra sampradāye nāce paṇḍita-vakreśvara
śrīvāsa nāce āra sampradāya-bhitara

āra sampradāye—in another *sampradāya,* or group; *nāce*—dances; *paṇḍita-vakreśvara*—Vakreśvara Paṇḍita; *śrīvāsa*—Śrīvāsa Ṭhākura; *nāce*—dances; *āra*—another; *sampradāya-bhitara*—in the middle of a group.

TRANSLATION

Vakreśvara Paṇḍita began to dance in another group, and in yet another group Śrīvāsa Ṭhākura began to dance.

TEXT 229

মধ্যে রহি' মহাপ্রভু করেন দরশন ।
তাহাঁ এক ঐশ্বর্য তাঁর হইল প্রকটন ॥ ২২৯ ॥

madhye rahi' mahāprabhu karena daraśana
tāhāṅ eka aiśvarya tāṅra ha-ila prakaṭana

madhye rahi'—keeping in the middle; *mahāprabhu*—Śrī Caitanya Mahāprabhu; *karena daraśana*—looks over; *tāhāṅ*—there; *eka*—one; *aiśvarya*—miracle; *tāṅra*—of Him; *ha-ila*—became; *prakaṭana*—exhibited.

TRANSLATION

While this dancing was going on, Śrī Caitanya Mahāprabhu watched them and performed a miracle.

TEXT 230

চারিদিকে নৃত্যগীত করে যত জন ।
সবে দেখে,—প্রভু করে আমারে দরশন ॥ ২৩০ ॥

cāri-dike nṛtya-gīta kare yata jana
sabe dekhe,—prabhu kare āmāre daraśana

cāri-dike—on four sides; *nṛtya-gīta*—chanting and dancing; *kare*—does; *yata jana*—all people; *sabe dekhe*—everyone sees; *prabhu*—Śrī Caitanya Mahāprabhu; *kare*—does; *āmāre daraśana*—looking at me.

TRANSLATION

Śrī Caitanya Mahāprabhu stood in the middle of the dancers, and all the dancers in all directions perceived that Śrī Caitanya Mahāprabhu was looking at them.

TEXT 231

চারি জনের নৃত্য দেখিতে প্রভুর অভিলাষ ।
সেই অভিলাষে করে ঐশ্বর্য প্রকাশ ॥ ২৩১ ॥

cāri janera nṛtya dekhite prabhura abhilāṣa
sei abhilāṣe kare aiśvarya prakāśa

cāri janera—of the four persons; *nṛtya*—dancing; *dekhite*—to see; *prabhura*—of Śrī Caitanya Mahāprabhu; *abhilāṣa*—desire; *sei abhilāṣe*—for that purpose; *kare*—does; *aiśvarya prakāśa*—exhibition of a miracle.

TRANSLATION

Wanting to see the dancing of the four great personalities, Śrī Caitanya Mahāprabhu exhibited this miracle of seeing everyone.

TEXT 232

দর্শনে আবেশ তাঁর দেখি' মাত্র জানে।
কেমনে চৌদিকে দেখে, —ইহা নাহি জানে ॥ ২৩২ ॥

darśane āveśa tāṅra dekhi' mātra jāne
kemane caudike dekhe,—ihā nāhi jāne

darśane—while looking over; *āveśa*—emotional ecstasy; *tāṅra*—His; *dekhi'*—seeing; *mātra jāne*—only knows; *kemane*—how; *caudike*—on four sides; *dekhe*—He sees; *ihā nāhi jāne*—one does not know.

TRANSLATION

Everyone who saw Śrī Caitanya Mahāprabhu could understand that He was performing a miracle, but they did not know how it was that He could see on all four sides.

TEXT 233

পুলিন-ভোজনে যেন কৃষ্ণ মধ্য-স্থানে।
চৌদিকের সখা কহে, —আমারে নেহানে ॥ ২৩৩ ॥

pulina-bhojane yena kṛṣṇa madhya-sthāne
caudikera sakhā kahe,—āmāre nehāne

pulina-bhojane—eating on the bank of Yamunā; *yena*—as; *kṛṣṇa*—Lord Kṛṣṇa; *madhya-sthāne*—sitting in the middle; *cau-*

dikera—on four sides; *sakhā*—cowherd boyfriends; *kahe*—say; *āmāre nehāne*—just seeing me.

TRANSLATION

In His own pastimes in Vṛndāvana, when Kṛṣṇa used to eat on the bank of the Yamunā and sit in the center of His friends, every one of the cowherd boys would perceive that Kṛṣṇa was looking at him. In the same way, when Caitanya Mahāprabhu observed the dancing, everyone saw that Caitanya Mahāprabhu was facing him.

TEXT 234

নৃত্য করিতে যেই আইসে সন্নিধানে।
মহাপ্রভু করে তাঁরে দৃঢ় আলিঙ্গনে ॥ ২৩৪ ॥

nṛtya karite yei āise sannidhāne
mahāprabhu kare tāṅre dṛḍha āliṅgane

nṛtya karite—dancing; *yei*—anyone who; *āise*—comes; *sannidhāne*—nearby; *mahāprabhu*—Śrī Caitanya Mahāprabhu; *kare*—does; *tāṅre*—unto him; *dṛḍha*—tight; *āliṅgane*—embracing.

TRANSLATION

When someone came nearby while dancing, Śrī Caitanya Mahāprabhu would tightly embrace him.

TEXT 235

মহানৃত্য, মহাপ্রেম, মহাসংকীর্তন।
দেখি' প্রেমাবেশে ভাসে নীলাচল-জন ॥ ২৩৫ ॥

mahā-nṛtya, mahā-prema, mahā-saṅkīrtana
dekhi' premāveśe bhāse nīlācala-jana

mahā-nṛtya—great dancing; *mahā-prema*—great love; *mahā-saṅkīrtana*—great congregational chanting; *dekhi'*—seeing; *prema-āveśe*—in ecstatic love; *bhāse*—float; *nīlācala-jana*—all the residents of Jagannātha Purī.

TRANSLATION

Upon seeing the great dancing, great love and great saṅkīrtana, all the people of Jagannātha Purī floated in an ecstatic ocean of love.

TEXT 236

গজপতি রাজা শুনি' কীর্তন-মহত্ত্ব।
অট্টালিকা চড়ি' দেখে স্বগণ-সহিত ॥ ২৩৬ ॥

gajapati rājā śuni' kīrtana-mahattva
aṭṭālikā caḍi' dekhe svagaṇa-sahita

gajapati rājā—the King of Orissa; *śuni'*—hearing; *kīrtana-mahattva*—the greatness of *saṅkīrtana; aṭṭālikā caḍi'*—ascending to the top of the palace; *dekhe*—sees; *svagaṇa-sahita*—along with his personal associates.

TRANSLATION

Hearing the greatness of the saṅkīrtana, King Pratāparudra went up to the top of his palace and watched the performance with his personal associates.

TEXT 237

কীর্তন দেখিয়া রাজার হৈল চমৎকার।
প্রভুকে মিলিতে উৎকণ্ঠা বাড়িল অপার ॥ ২৩৭ ॥

kīrtana dekhiyā rājāra haila camatkāra
prabhuke milite utkaṇṭhā bāḍila apāra

kīrtana dekhiyā—seeing the performance of *kīrtana; rājāra*—of the King; *haila*—there was; *camatkāra*—astonishment; *prabhuke*—Śrī Caitanya Mahāprabhu; *milite*—to meet; *utkaṇṭhā*—anxiety; *bāḍila*—increased; *apāra*—unlimitedly.

TRANSLATION

The King was very much astonished to see Śrī Caitanya Mahāprabhu's kīrtana, and the King's anxiety to meet Him increased unlimitedly.

TEXT 238

কীর্তন-সমাপ্ত্যে প্রভু দেখি' পুষ্পাঞ্জলি ।
সর্ব বৈষ্ণব লঞা প্রভু আইলা বাসা চলি' ॥ ২৩৮ ॥

kīrtana-samāptye prabhu dekhi' puṣpāñjali
sarva vaiṣṇava lañā prabhu āilā vāsā cali'

kīrtana-samāptye—at the end of the performance of *kīrtana; prabhu*—Śrī Caitanya Mahāprabhu; *dekhi'*—after seeing; *puṣpāñjali*—offering flowers to the Lord Jagannātha Deity; *sarva vaiṣṇava*—all the devotees; *lañā*—accompanying; *prabhu*—Śrī Caitanya Mahāprabhu; *āilā*—returned; *vāsā*—to His residence; *cali'*—going.

TRANSLATION

After the saṅkīrtana ended, Śrī Caitanya Mahāprabhu watched the offering of flowers to the Lord Jagannātha Deity. Then He and all the Vaiṣṇavas returned to His residence.

TEXT 239

পড়িছা আনিয়া দিল প্রসাদ বিস্তর ।
সবারে বাঁটিয়া তাহা দিলেন ঈশ্বর ॥ ২৩৯ ॥

paḍichā āniyā dila prasāda vistara
sabāre bāṅṭiyā tāhā dilena īśvara

paḍichā—the superintendent of the temple; *āniyā*—bringing; *dila*—delivered; *prasāda*—of remnants of Jagannātha's food; *vistara*—a large quantity; *sabāre*—unto everyone; *bāṅṭiyā*—distributing; *tāhā*—that; *dilena*—gave; *īśvara*—the Lord.

TRANSLATION

The superintendent of the temple then brought large quantities of prasādam, which Śrī Caitanya Mahāprabhu personally distributed to all the devotees.

TEXT 240

সবারে বিদায় দিল করিতে শয়ন।
এইমত লীলা করে শচীর নন্দন ॥ ২৪০ ॥

sabāre vidāya dila karite śayana
ei-mata līlā kare śacīra nandana

sabāre—unto everyone; *vidāya*—bidding farewell; *dila*—gave; *karite śayana*—to take rest; *ei-mata*—in this way; *līlā*—pastimes; *kare*—performed; *śacīra nandana*—the son of Śacī.

TRANSLATION

Finally they all departed to rest in bed. In this way Śrī Caitanya Mahāprabhu, the son of Śacīmātā, performed His pastimes.

TEXT 241

যাবৎ আছিলা সবে মহাপ্রভু-সঙ্গে।
প্রতিদিন এইমত করে কীর্তন-রঙ্গে ॥ ২৪১ ॥

yāvat āchilā sabe mahāprabhu-saṅge
prati-dina ei-mata kare kīrtana-raṅge

yāvat—so long; *āchilā*—remained; *sabe*—all the devotees; *mahāprabhu-saṅge*—along with Śrī Caitanya Mahāprabhu; *prati-dina*—every day; *ei-mata*—in this way; *kare*—performed; *kīrtana-raṅge*—*saṅkīrtana* in great pleasure.

TRANSLATION

As long as the devotees remained at Jagannātha Purī with Śrī Caitanya Mahāprabhu, the pastime of saṅkīrtana was performed with great jubilation every day.

TEXT 242

এই ত' কহিলুঁ প্রভুর কীর্তন-বিলাস।
যেবা ইহা শুনে, হয় চৈতন্যের দাস ॥ ২৪২ ॥

ei ta' kahiluṅ prabhura kīrtana-vilāsa
yebā ihā śune, haya caitanyera dāsa

ei ta' kahiluṅ—thus I have explained; *prabhura*—of the Lord; *kīrtana-vilāsa*—pastimes in *saṅkīrtana; yebā*—anyone who; *ihā*—this; *śune*—listens to; *haya*—becomes; *caitanyera dāsa*—a servant of Śrī Caitanya Mahāprabhu.

TRANSLATION

In this way I have explained the Lord's pastime of saṅkīrtana, and I bless everyone with this benediction: By listening to this description, one will surely become a servant of Śrī Caitanya Mahāprabhu.

TEXT 243

শ্রীরূপ-রঘুনাথ-পদে যার আশ ।
চৈতন্যচরিতামৃত কহে কৃষ্ণদাস ॥ ২৪৩ ॥

śrī-rūpa-raghunātha-pade yāra āśa
caitanya-caritāmṛta kahe kṛṣṇadāsa

śrī-rūpa—Śrīla Rūpa Gosvāmī; *raghunātha*—Śrīla Raghunātha dāsa Gosvāmī; *pade*—at the lotus feet; *yāra*—whose; *āśa*—expectation; *caitanya-caritāmṛta*—the book named *Caitanya-caritāmṛta; kahe*—describes; *kṛṣṇadāsa*—Śrīla Kṛṣṇadāsa Kavirāja Gosvāmī.

TRANSLATION

Praying at the lotus feet of Śrī Rūpa and Śrī Raghunātha, always desiring their mercy, I, Kṛṣṇadāsa, narrate Śrī Caitanya-caritāmṛta, following in their footsteps.

Thus end the Bhaktivedanta purports to Śrī Caitanya-caritāmṛta, Madhya-līlā, *Eleventh Chapter, describing the* beḍā-kīrtana *pastimes of Śrī Caitanya Mahāprabhu.*

Appendixes

The Author

His Divine Grace A. C. Bhaktivedanta Swami Prabhupāda appeared in this world in 1896 in Calcutta, India. He first met his spiritual master, Śrīla Bhaktisiddhānta Sarasvatī Gosvāmī, in Calcutta in 1922. Bhaktisiddhānta Sarasvatī, a prominent religious scholar and the founder of sixty-four Gauḍīya Maṭhas (Vedic institutes), liked this educated young man and convinced him to dedicate his life to teaching Vedic knowledge. Śrīla Prabhupāda became his student and, in 1933, his formally initiated disciple.

At their first meeting, in 1922, Śrīla Bhaktisiddhānta Sarasvatī requested Śrīla Prabhupāda to broadcast Vedic knowledge in English. In the years that followed, Śrīla Prabhupāda wrote a commentary on the *Bhagavad-gītā,* assisted the Gauḍīya Maṭha in its work and, in 1944, started *Back to Godhead,* an English fortnightly magazine. Single-handedly, Śrīla Prabhupāda edited it, typed the manuscripts, checked the galley proofs and even distributed the individual copies. The magazine is now being continued by his disciples in the West.

In 1950 Śrīla Prabhupāda retired from married life, adopting the *vānaprastha* (retired) order to devote more time to his studies and writing. He traveled to the holy city of Vṛndāvana, where he lived in humble circumstances in the historic temple of Rādhā-Dāmodara. There he engaged for several years in deep study and writing. He accepted the renounced order of life (*sannyāsa*) in 1959. At Rādhā-Dāmodara, Śrīla Prabhupāda began work on his life's masterpiece: a multivolume commentated translation of the eighteen-thousand-verse *Śrīmad-Bhāgavatam* (*Bhāgavata Purāṇa*). He also wrote *Easy Journey to Other Planets.*

After publishing three volumes of the *Bhāgavatam,* Śrīla Prabhupāda came to the United States, in September 1965, to fulfill the mission of his spiritual master. Subsequently, His Divine Grace wrote more than fifty volumes of authoritative commentated translations and summary studies of the philosophical and religious classics of India.

When he first arrived by freighter in New York City, Śrīla Prabhupāda was practically penniless. Only after almost a year of great difficulty did he establish the International Society for Krishna Consciousness, in July of 1966. Before he passed away on November 14, 1977, he had guided the Society and seen it grow to a worldwide confederation of more than one hundred *āśramas,* schools, temples, institutes and farm communities.

In 1972 His Divine Grace introduced the Vedic system of primary and secondary education in the West by founding the *gurukula* school in Dallas, Texas. Since then his disciples have established similar schools throughout the United States and the rest of the world.

Śrīla Prabhupāda also inspired the construction of several large international cultural centers in India. The center at Śrīdhāma Māyāpur is the site for a planned spiritual city, an ambitions project for which construction will extend over many years to come. In Vṛndāvana are the magnificent Kṛṣṇa-Balarāma Temple and International Guesthouse, *gurukula* school, and Śrīla Prabhupāda Memorial and Museum. There is also a major cultural and educational center in Bombay. Other centers are planned in a dozen important locations on the Indian subcontinent.

Śrīla Prabhupāda's most significant contribution, however, is his books. Highly respected by scholars for their authority, depth and clarity, they are used as textbooks in numerous college courses. His writings have been translated into over fifty languages. The Bhaktivedanta Book Trust, established in 1972 to publish the works of His Divine Grace, has thus become the world's largest publisher of books in the field of Indian religion and philosophy.

In just twelve years, from his arrival in America in 1965 till his passing away in Vṛndāvana in 1977, despite his advanced age Śrīla Prabhupāda circled the globe fourteen times on lecture tours that took him to six continents. Notwithstanding such a vigorous schedule, Śrīla Prabhupāda continued to write prolifically. His writings constitute a veritable library of Vedic philosophy, religion, literature and culture.

References

The purports of *Śrī Caitanya-caritāmṛta* are all confirmed by standard Vedic authorities. The following scriptures are cited in this volume. For specific page references, consult the general index.

Adhyātma-rāmāyaṇa
Ādi Purāṇa
Amṛta-pravāha-bhāṣya
Anubhāṣya
Bhagavad-gītā
Bhakti-rasāmṛta-sindhu
Bhakti-ratnākara
Brahmāṇḍa Purāṇa
Brahma-saṁhitā
Bṛhad-bhāgavatāmṛta
Bṛhad-vāmana Purāṇa
Bṛhan-nāradīya Purāṇa
Caitanya-bhāgavata
Caitanya-candrāmṛta
Caitanya-candrodaya-nāṭaka
Garuḍa Purāṇa
Gīta-govinda
Govinda-līlāmṛta
Hari-bhakti-vilāsa
Itihāsa-samuccaya
Kaṭha Upaniṣad
Kūrma Purāṇa
Laghu-bhāgavatāmṛta
Lalita-mādhava-nāṭaka
Mahābhārata
Manaḥ-śikṣā
Manu-saṁhitā
Muṇḍaka Upaniṣad
Nārada-pañcarātra
Nārāyaṇa-vyūha-stava
Padma Purāṇa
Premāmbhoja-maranda
Prapannāmṛta
Prārthanā
Purāṇas
Rāmāyaṇa
Sapta-śatī
Śaraṇāgati
Śrīmad-Bhāgavatam
Stava-mālā
Stotra-ratna
Śvetāśvatara Upaniṣad
Ujjvala-nīlamaṇi
Upadeśāmṛta

Uttara-rāma-racita
Vaiṣṇava-tantra
Vedārtha-saṅgraha
Viṣṇu Purāṇa

Glossary

A

Abhiṣeka — the bathing ceremony of the Deity.

Ācārya — a spiritual master who teaches by his own example.

Acintya-bhedābheda-tattva — Lord Caitanya's "simultaneously one and different" doctrine.

Adhama — the lowest among men.

Ādi-līlā — the first twenty-four years of Lord Caitanya's pastimes.

Ahaṅgrahopāsanā — self-worship.

Ajita — the Supreme Lord who is unconquerable.

Amṛta — nectar.

Anna — food grains.

Antya-līlā — the last eighteen years of Lord Caitanya's pastimes.

Anubhāva — bodily symptoms manifested by a devotee in ecstatic love for Kṛṣṇa.

Arcā-mūrti — the form of the Lord appearing within material elements.

Arcana — Deity worship.

Arcā-vigraha — See: *Arcā-mūrti.*

Āśutoṣa — Lord Śiva, who is very easily satisfied when one worships him.

Ātma-nivedana — the devotional process of sacrificing everything for the Lord.

Ātmārāmas — those who are self-satisfied.

Avadhūta — one who is above all rules and regulations.

Avatāra — an incarnation of the Lord who descends from the spiritual sky.

Avidyā-śakti — material energy, or nescience.

B

Bahirmukha-jana — a person influenced by the external energy.

Bhagavān — Kṛṣṇa, who is full in six opulences.

Bhakti — purified service of the senses of the Lord by one's own senses.

Bhakti-rasa — the mellow derived from devotional service.

Bhakti-yoga — devotional service to the Lord.

Bhāva — manifestation of ecstatic symptoms in the body of a devotee.

Bhaya — fear.

Bhinna-rūpa-sandhi — the meeting of contradictory ecstasies.

Brahma-bhūta — the state of being freed from material contamination; characterized by transcendental happiness and engagement in the service of the Lord.

Brahmajyoti — the impersonal effulgence emanating from the body of Kṛṣṇa.

Brahman — the all-pervading impersonal aspect of Kṛṣṇa.

Brahmānanda — the bliss derived from realizing the impersonal Brahman.

Brāhmaṇa — a person wise in Vedic knowledge, fixed in goodness, and knowledgeable of Brahman, the Absolute Truth; a member of the first Vedic social order.

Brahmaṇya-deva — the Supreme Lord, who is the protector of brahminical culture.

C

Channa-avatāra — an incarnation in disguise.

D

Dadhi — yogurt.

Dāna — charity.

Daṇḍa-bhaṅga-līlā — the pastime of Lord Nityānanda breaking the staff of Lord Caitanya.

Daṇḍavats — offering obeisances by falling flat like a stick.

Dāsya — the devotional process of serving the Lord as a friend.

Dhūmāyitā — the stage exhibited by a devotee when only one or two transformations are slightly present and it is possible to conceal them.
Dīkṣā — initiating a disciple with transcendental knowledge.
Dīpta — the stage exhibited by a devotee when four of five ecstatic symptoms are manifest.
Dugdha — milk.
Durgā-śakti — the material energy.
Duṣkṛtī — a miscreant.
Dvija-bandhus — unworthy sons of the twice-born.

G

Gauḍa-maṇḍala-bhūmi — the places in Bengal where Lord Caitanya stayed.
Gaura — of fair complexion.
Ghṛta — ghee.
Govardhana-dhārī — Kṛṣṇa, the lifter of Govardhana Hill.
Gṛhamedhi — envious householder who lives only for sense gratification.
Gṛhastha — a God-conscious householder.
Guru-pūjā — worship of the spiritual master.

H

Hari-kīrtana — See: *Saṅkīrtana.*
Hlādinī śakti — the bliss portion of the Lord's spiritual potency.
Hṛṣīkeśa — a name of Kṛṣṇa meaning "the master of all senses."

I

Indra — the King of the heavenly planets.

J

Jāḍya — the ecstatic symptom of loss of memory.
Jīva-bhūta — the living force within matter.
Jñāna — knowledge.

Jñāna-kāṇḍa — the division of the *Vedas* dealing with speculation in pursuit of truth; also, such speculation itself.

Jñānī — one who is engaged in the cultivation of knowledge.

Jvalitā — the stage exhibited by a devotee when more than two or three transcendental transformations are manifest and it is possible to conceal them with difficulty.

K

Kali-yuga — the age of quarrel in which we are now living.

Kāma — lusty desire.

Karma — (1) material action performed according to scriptural regulations; (2) action pertaining to the development of the material body; (3) any material action which will incur a subsequent reaction; (4) the material reaction one incurs due to fruitive activities.

Karma-kāṇḍa — the division of the *Vedas* dealing with fruitive activities and their reactions; also, such activities themselves.

Karma-tyāga — the giving of the results of *karma* to the Supreme Lord.

Kīrtana — glorification of the Supreme Lord; the devotional process of chanting.

Krodha — anger.

Kṛṣṇa-kathā — topics spoken by or about Kṛṣṇa.

Kṛṣṇa-viraha — the feeling of spiritual separation from Kṛṣṇa.

Kṛṣṇe matir astu — greeting of Vaiṣṇava *sannyāsīs* meaning "Let your attention be on Kṛṣṇa."

Kṣīra-corā — Lord Gopīnātha, the thief who stole the sweet rice.

Kṣudhā-tṛṣṇā — hunger and thirst.

Kūrma — the tortoise incarnation of the Lord.

Ku-viṣaya — sense gratificatory activities performed under sinful conditions.

L

Līlā-avatāras — incarnations who descend to display spiritual pastimes in the material world.

Lobha — greed.

M

Madana-mohana — Kṛṣṇa, the enchanter of Cupid.

Madhya-līlā — the pastimes Lord Caitanya performed during the middle part of His manifest presence, while He was traveling throughout India; the portion of the *Caitanya-caritāmṛta* recounting those pastimes.

Mahā-bhāgavata — a great devotee of the Lord.

Mahābhāva — the highest stage of love of God.

Mahā-mahā-prasādam — the remnants of food left by a pure Vaiṣṇava.

Mahā-mantra — the great chanting for deliverance: Hare Kṛṣṇa, Hare Kṛṣṇa, Kṛṣṇa Kṛṣṇa, Hare Hare/ Hare Rāma, Hare Rāma, Rāma Rāma, Hare Hare.

Mahā-snāna — a vast bath with ghee and water used to bathe the Deity.

Mahā-vākya — transcendental sound vibration.

Mālā — chanting with beads.

Mantra — (*manas* — mind; *tṝ* — to deliver) a pure sound vibration that delivers the mind from its material inclinations.

Mātsarya — enviousness.

Matsya — the fish incarnation of the Lord.

Māyā — illusion; an energy of Kṛṣṇa's which causes the living being to forget Him.

Māyādhīśa — the Lord of all energy.

Māyāvādīs — impersonalists or voidists who believe that ultimately God is formless and without personality.

Māyā-vaśa — subjected to the influence of the illusory energy.

Mleccha — a meat-eater.

Moha — illusion.

Mūḍha — a fool or rascal.

Mukti — liberation.

Mukti-pāda — the Supreme Lord under whose feet exist all kinds of liberation.

Mukunda — the Lord who gives transcendental bliss by offering all kinds of *mukti*.

N

Namo nārāyaṇāya — greeting of Māyāvādī *sannyāsīs* meaning "I offer my obeisances to Nārāyaṇa."
Nirvāṇa — the cessation of all material activities.
Nitya-baddhas — eternally conditioned living beings.
Nitya-siddhas — the eternally liberated associates of the Lord.
Nṛsiṁhadeva — the half-man, half-lion incarnation of the Lord.

O

Oṁkāra — the transcendental syllable which represents Kṛṣṇa.

P

Pāda-sevana — the devotional process of serving at the Lord's feet.
Pañca-gavya — five kinds of products of the cow used to bathe the Deity.
Pañcāmṛta — five kinds of nectar used to bathe the Deity.
Paramahaṁsa — the highest stage of the renounced order of life.
Paramātmā — the Supersoul, the localized aspect of the Supreme Lord within the heart of all living beings.
Paramparā — the disciplic succession through which spiritual knowledge is transmitted.
Pariṇāma-vāda — the theory of transformation in the creation of the universe.
Paṭhana — a *brāhmaṇa's* duty to be conversant with the Vedic scriptures.
Prakṛti — energy or nature.
Praṇava — See: *Oṁkāra.*
Prasādam — spiritualized food offered to Kṛṣṇa.
Pratibimba-vāda — the worship of a form that is the reflection of a false material form.
Pratigraha — the duty of a *brāhmaṇa* to accept contributions from his followers.
Pūrṇa — complete.
Puruṣa — person or enjoyer.

Puruṣāvatāras — incarnations of the Lord who create, maintain and destroy the material universes.

R

Rāgānuga-bhakti — spontaneous love of Godhead.

Rāsa-līlā — the group dancing of Kṛṣṇa and His cowherd girlfriends in His Vṛndāvana pastimes.

S

Sac-cid-ānanda-vigraha — the transcendental form of the Lord which is eternal, full of knowledge and blissful.

Ṣaḍ-aiśvarya-pūrṇa — the Supreme Lord who is complete with six opulences.

Sahajiyās — pseudo devotees with a mundane conception of Kṛṣṇa's pastimes.

Śālagrāma-śilā — a Deity of Nārāyaṇa in the form of a small stone.

Sālokya — the liberation of being promoted to the planet where the Lord resides.

Sāmīpya — the liberation of becoming an associate of the Lord.

Sampradāya — disciplic succession through which spiritual knowledge is transmitted.

Saṁskāra — Vedic reformatory rituals.

Samvit-śakti — the knowledge portion of the Lord's spiritual potency.

Sandhinī-śakti — the eternity portion of the Lord's spiritual potency.

Saṅkīrtana — congregational chanting of the Lord's holy names.

Sannyāsa — renounced life; the fourth order of Vedic spiritual life.

Sannyāsa-daṇḍa — the staff carried by a *sannyāsī.*

Sannyāsī — one in the renounced order of life.

Śānta — the neutral stage of love of God.

Sārṣṭi — the liberation of attaining opulences like those of the Lord.

Sārūpya — the liberation of obtaining a body like the Lord's.

Sarvātma-nivedana — See: *Ātma-nivedana.*

Śāstra — revealed scripture.

Sāttvika — symptoms of ecstatic love coming from the transcendental platform.

Sāyujya-mukti — merging into the Brahman effulgence of the Lord.

Śeṣa-līlā — the last twenty-four years of Lord Caitanya's pastimes.

Sevā-pūjā — Deity worship.

Siddha — one who has realized the Brahman effulgence.

Śiva — the personality in charge of the mode of ignorance.

Śravaṇa — the devotional process of hearing.

Strī — woman.

Śuddha-sattva — the spiritual platform of pure goodness.

Sūddīpta — the manifestation in a devotee of all eight ecstatic symptoms multiplied a thousand times and all visible at once.

Śūdras — the laborer class of men.

Su-viṣaya — regulated sense gratification according to the *Vedas.*

Svādhyāya — personal study of Vedic literature.

Svāṁśa — Kṛṣṇa's plenary portions.

Svarūpa-sandhi — the meeting of similar ecstasies from separate causes.

T

Tamasaḥ — the coverings of the universe.

Tattva — truth.

Tilaka — sacred clay markings on the body of a devotee; the clay used for such markings.

Triyuga — a name of Viṣṇu meaning one who appears in only three *yugas.*

U

Uddīpta — the manifestation in a devotee of five, six or all eight ecstatic symptoms simultaneously.

V

Vaikāli-bhoga — food offered to the Deity at the end of the day.

Vaikuṇṭha-jagat — *See:* Vaikuṇṭhalokas.

Vaikuṇṭhalokas — variegated spiritual planets situated in the *brahmajyoti.*

Vairāgya — renunciation.

Vaiṣṇava — a devotee of the Supreme Lord Viṣṇu, or Kṛṣṇa.

Vaiśyas — people engaged in agriculture and commerce.

Vanas — forests.

Vandana — the devotional process of praying.

Varāha — the boar incarnation of the Lord.

Vedāśraya-nāstikya-vāda — agnosticism under the shelter of Vedic culture.

Vibhāva — the causes or bases for relishing transcendental mellows.

Vibhinnāṁśa — the minute living entities, who are part and parcel of the Supreme Lord.

Vijita-ṣaḍ-guṇa — one who has conquered the six material qualities.

Viṣaya — entanglement in the laws of nature by sense gratification.

Viṣṇoḥ smaraṇa — the devotional process of remembering.

Vrajendra-nandana — Kṛṣṇa, the son of Nanda Mahārāja.

Vṛndāvana — the site of Kṛṣṇa's pastimes exhibited when He was present on earth five thousand years ago.

Y

Yajana — the duty of a *brāhmaṇa* to perform Vedic rituals.

Yājana — the duty of a *brāhmaṇa* to assist others in performing ceremonies.

Yamarāja — the demigod who punishes sinful living beings after their deaths.

Yavana — one who has deviated from Vedic culture.

Yoga — linking one's consciousness with the Supreme Lord.

Yoga-māyā — the eternal creative potency of the Lord.

Yuga-avatāra—an incarnation of the Lord in each millennium who prescribes the process of self-realization for that age.

Bengali Pronunciation Guide

BENGALI DIACRITICAL EQUIVALENTS AND PRONUNCIATION

Vowels

অ a   আ ā   ই i   ঈ ī   উ u   ঊ ū   ঋ ṛ

ৠ ṝ   এ e   ঐ ai   ও o   ঔ au

ং ṁ (*anusvāra*)   ঁ ṅ (*candra-bindu*)   ঃ ḥ (*visarga*)

Consonants

Gutturals:	ক ka	খ kha	গ ga	ঘ gha	ঙ ṅa
Palatals:	চ ca	ছ cha	জ ja	ঝ jha	ঞ ña
Cerebrals:	ট ṭa	ঠ ṭha	ড ḍa	ঢ ḍha	ণ ṇa
Dentals:	ৎ, ত ta	থ tha	দ da	ধ dha	ন na
Labials:	প pa	ফ pha	ব ba	ভ bha	ম ma
Semivowels:	য়, য ya	র ra	ল la	ব va	ড় ḍa
Sibilants:	শ śa	ষ ṣa	স sa	হ ha	ঢ় ḍha

Vowel Symbols

The vowels are written as follows after a consonant:

া ā   ি i   ী ī   ু u   ূ ū   ৃ ṛ   ৄ ṝ   ে e   ৈ ai   ো o   ৌ au

For example: কা kā   কি ki   কী kī   কু ku   কূ kū   কৃ kṛ

কৄ kṝ   কে ke   কৈ kai   কো ko   কৌ kau

The letter **a** is implied after a consonant with no vowel symbol.

The symbol *virāma* (्) indicates that there is no final vowel. क् k

The letters on the previous page should be pronounced as follows:

a — like the **a** in **a**lone; sometimes like the **o** in g**o**; final **a** is usually silent.
ā — like the **a** in f**a**r.
i, ī — like the **ee** in m**ee**t.
u, ū — like the **u** in r**u**le.
ṛ — like the **ri** in **ri**m.
ṝ — like the **ree** in **ree**d.
e — like the **ai** in p**ai**n; rarely like the **e** in b**e**t.
ei — like the **ai** in p**ai**n.
ai — like the **oi** in b**oi**l.
o — like the **o** in g**o**.
au — like the **ow** in **ow**l
ṁ — (*anusvāra*) like the **ng** in so**ng**.
ḥ — (*visarga*) a final **h** sound like in **Ah**.
ṅ (ँ) — (*candra-bindu*) a nasal **n** sound like in the French word *bon;* almost silent.
ñ — like **n** above.
k — like the **k** in **k**ite.
kh — like the **kh** in Ec**kh**art.
g — like the **g** in **g**ot.
gh — like the **gh** in bi**g-h**ouse.
ṅ — like the **n** in ba**n**k.
c — like the **ch** in **ch**alk.
ch — like the **chh** in mu**ch-h**aste.
j — like the **j** in **j**oy.
jh — like the **geh** in colle**ge-h**all.
ṭ — like the **t** in **t**alk, but with the tip of the tongue against the roof of the mouth.
ṭh — like the **th** in ho**t-h**ouse, but with the tip of the tongue against the roof of the mouth.
ḍ — like the **d** in **d**awn, but with the tip of the tongue against the roof of the mouth.
ḍh — like the **dh** in goo**d-h**ouse, but with the tip of the tongue against the roof of the mouth.
ṇ — like the **n** in g**n**aw, but with the tip of the tongue against the roof of the mouth.
t — as in **t**alk, but with the tongue against the teeth.
th — as in ho**t-h**ouse, but with the tongue against the teeth.
d — as in **d**awn, but with the tongue against the teeth.
dh — as in goo**d-h**ouse, but with the tongue against the teeth.
n — as in **n**or, but with the tongue against the teeth.
p — like the **p** in **p**ine.
ph — like the **ph** in **ph**ilosopher.
b — like the **b** in **b**ird.
bh — like the **bh** in ru**b h**ard.
m — like the **m** in **m**other.
y (য) — like the **j** in **j**aw.
y (য়) — like the **y** in **y**ear.
r — like the **r** in **r**un.
l — like the **l** in **l**aw.
v — like the **b** in **b**ird or the **w** in d**w**arf.
ś, ṣ — like the **sh** in **sh**op.
s — like the **s** in **s**un.
h — like the **h** in **h**ome.

This is a general guide to Bengali pronunciation. The Bengali transliterations in this book accurately show the original Bengali spelling of the text. One should note, however, that in Bengali, as in English, spelling is not always a true indication of how a word is pronounced. Audiocassettes of His Divine Grace A. C. Bhaktivedanta Swami Prabhupāda chanting the original Bengali verses are available from the International Society for Krishna Consciousness.

Index of Bengali and Sanskrit Verses

This index constitutes a complete listing of the first and second lines of the two-line texts and the first and third lines of the four-line texts in this volume of *Śrī Caitanya-caritāmṛta*. The references are to chapter and verse.

E

H

I

J

K

L

M

N

P

R

S

T

U

V

Y

Index of Verses Quoted

This index lists the Sanskrit and Bengali verses and prose passages quoted in the purports of this volume of *Śrī Caitanya-caritāmṛta*. The references are to chapter and verse. Numbers in boldface type refer to the first or third line of four-line verses quoted in full or to the first or second line of two-line verses quoted in full; numbers in roman type refer to partially quoted verses; numbers in parentheses refer to the approximate page of long purports

General Index

The references are to chapter and verse. Numbers in boldface type refer to translations of the texts of *Śrī Caitanya-caritāmṛta.* Numbers in parentheses indicate the approximate page of long purports.

B

C

Caitanya, Lord (*continued*)
chronology of tour by, 9.14
cited on religious behavior, 8.38
cited on *varṇāśrama,* 8.60
compared to cloud, **10.1**
compared to lion, **7.95**
compared to ocean, **8.1, 10.187**
compared to puppet, **7.18**
compared to puppeteer, **8.132–33**
complexion of, **8.287**
conjugal *rasa* distributed by, 11.31
crowds assemble to see, **7.106–8, 9.40, 9.88–90, 9.326–27**
Dāmodara Paṇḍita &, **7.25–27**
dancing by, **11.1, 11.220, 11.225–26**
departure for South India by, **7.57–76, 7.91–94**
devotee role by, **10.13**
devotees sheltered by, **10.187–88**
disciplic succession &, 7.66
discrimination between *āśramas* &, 7.69
discussion of Kṛṣṇa & *gopīs* by, 8.56
distress dissipated by, **9.88**
dramas about, 11.95
empowerment by, **7.99–103, 7.110**
faith in, **7.111**
feelings of separation by, **11.62–63**
Ghoṣa brothers &, 11.88
glorification rejected by, **10.182**
Govinda &, **10.131–35, 10.141–48**
hearing about, **9.360,** 9.362, **9.364, 10.189, 11.242**

Caitanya, Lord (*continued*)
holy places visited by, **9.3–8, 10.11–13**
See also: names of specific holy places
humility by, **8.124–27**
illiterate *brāhmaṇa* &, **9.96–107**
initiation of, 8.128 (2)
instructions by, for householders, **7.127–29**
Jagadānanda &, **7.21–22**
Jagannātha Deity blesses, **7.55–58**
Jagannātha Purī residents desire to see, **10.24–28**
Jagannātha's bathing ceremony &, **11.61–62**
Kālā Kṛṣṇadāsa &, **9.226–34, 9.338, 10.62–66**
Kali-yuga &, **11.100**
Kāśī Miśra &, **9.349, 10.32–33, 11.174–79**
Kāśīśvara &, **10.185–86**
as Kṛṣṇa Himself, 8.23, **8.287–88, 11.100–2**
Kṛṣṇa-karṇāmṛta &, **9.306, 9.309, 9.323**
Kūrma *brāhmaṇa* &, **7.121–29, 7.130–33, 7.135**
Kūrma Purāṇa &, **9.200–14**
love for Lord distributed by, 11.31
Mahābhārata describes, **10.170–71**
mercy of
nondevotional philosophies &, **9.1**
power of, **8.38**
sinners &, **11.45–46**
Svarūpa Dāmodara's verse on, **10.119**
understanding Lord &, **11.103**

E

Ecstasy of Caitanya (*continued*)
at Raṅganātha temple, **9.87**
Rāmānanda Rāya &, **8.22–25, 8.193, 8.233, 9.321–22, 11.16**
reunion with associates &, **9.342**
saṅkīrtana performance &, **11.221–23**
Śrī Raṅga Purī &, **9.287–88, 9.290–92**
Svarūpa Dāmodara &, **10.120**
symptoms of, **7.79–80, 8.24**
at Uḍupī temple, **9.245**
Education, **8.245**
Ekādaśī, 7.113
Elements, material, 8.87, 8.88, 8.90 (4), 8.274
Empiric philosophers, 8.258–59
Energy (Energies) of Lord
Brahman effulgence as, 8.257
categories of, three, **8.151**
devotee's vision &, 8.274
illusory, **8.13–31,** 8.285, 10.65, 11.189
internal, 8.90 (4), **8.152–59, 8.163**
material, 8.90 (4), 8.130–31, **8.153, 8.257**
material world &, 8.64
personality indicated by, 9.49 (2)
spiritual world &, 8.64

F

Fame, **8.246**
Fruitive work / workers
demigod worship &, 8.90 (2)
destination of, **8.257**
devotional service &, 8.65, **9.266**
knowledge acquisition &, 7.66
love for Lord &, **9.263**
Fruitive work / workers (*continued*)
Tattvavādīs &, **9.276,** 9.277
impotence of, 9.360
spiritual realization &, 8.138 (2)
Vedas &, 11.31

G

Gadādhara Paṇḍita, **10.82, 11.84, 11.159–60**
Gajapatis, 9.11
Gajendra, 9.1
Gajendra-mokṣaṇa, **9.221**
Gambling, 7.128
Gandha-mādana, 9.11
Gaṇeśa, 8.90 (2), 9.239–40, 9.360 (2)
Gaṅgādāsa Paṇḍita, **11.85, 11.159–60**
Gāṅga Pradesh, 9.245 (2)
Ganges River, **9.170**
Gañjāma, 9.245 (2)
Gañjāma Manual, 7.113
Garbhodakaśāyī Viṣṇu, 9.239–40
Garuḍa Purāṇa, 8.246 (1, 2)
Gauḍīya-sampradāya, 9.11
Gautama Ṛṣi, 9.14, **9.42**
Gautamī-gaṅgā, **9.14**
Gāyatrī *mantra,* **8.138,** 8.138 (3, 4), 8.139 (3–4), 8.265, 9.239–40
Gīta-govinda, **8.106–7, 8.144, 10.115**
Go-samāja, **9.75**
Godādevī (Śrī Āṇḍāl), 9.79
Godāvarī River, **7.62, 8.10–13, 9.14,** 9.245 (2), 9.311, **9.317,** 9.318
Goddess of fortune
Nṛsiṁhadeva &, **8.5**
austerities by, **8.147, 9.113–14**
devotees &, 8.247

N

R

Crimea
BLACK SEA
CASPIAN SEA
Constantinople
Trebizond
Sivas
Erzerum
Smyrna
Mosul
Kazvin
Tigris R.
Euphrates R.
Bagdad
Ispahan
Damascus
Acre
Syria
Alexandria
Jerusalem
Basra
1529
Cairo
Suez
Egypt
Arabia
RED SEA
Kais I.
1507
Muscat
Medina
Jiddah
Mecca
Nubia
Dongola
Nile R.
Massowah
1520
Kamaran I.
Aden
Tigre
Amhara
Abyssinia
Zeila
Berbera
Ajana
Magadoxo
(Mukdishu)
Brava
Portuguese trade route
Malindi
Mombasa
1498
Quiloa
(Kilwa)